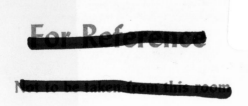

D0098904

WORD
BIBLICAL
COMMENTARY

General Editors
David A. Hubbard
Glenn W. Barker

Old Testament Editor
John D. W. Watts

New Testament Editor
Ralph P. Martin

WORD
BIBLICAL
COMMENTARY

VOLUME 21

Psalms 101-150

LESLIE C. ALLEN

WORD BOOKS, PUBLISHER • WACO, TEXAS

Word Biblical Commentary:
PSALMS 101–150
Copyright © 1983 by Word, Incorporated

Library of Congress Cataloging in Publication Data
Main entry under title:

Word biblical commentary.
  Includes bibliographies.
   1. Bible—Commentaries—Collected works.
BS491.2.W67   220.7'7   81–71768
ISBN 0–8499–0220–7 (v. 21) AACR2

Printed in the United States of America

To our daughter Miriam

Contents

Author's Preface

One of my students recently remarked that as the Psalter moves toward its close the treatment by commentators becomes correspondingly shorter. Whether they succumb to weariness or suffer from a sense of *dejà vu*, who can say? Certainly it has been good to come fairly fresh to those Psalms. Earlier encounter with them in the course of writing a short commentary on Pss 73–150 in *A Bible Commentary for Today*, edited by G. C. D. Howley, F. F. Bruce and H. L. Ellison (London: Pickering and Inglis, 1979) proved a useful apprenticeship. The study of Ps 139 published in *Vox Evangelica* 10 (1977) 5–23 provided experience in deeper analysis of a particular psalm and whetted the appetite for further work on the Psalter. I am grateful to the editors of the Word Biblical Commentary for giving me the opportunity of delving into the final third of the Psalter. I am especially thankful to Dr. J. D. W. Watts and to Dr. D. A. Hubbard for editorial involvement in my volume.

Many have given willing help; perhaps the Librarian of Northwood Hills Library may be singled out for his unstinting efforts in obtaining material otherwise inaccessible. Not least my wife Elizabeth is to be thanked for valiantly warding off interruption and for making what I wrote more intelligible.

London Bible College   Leslie C. Allen

Editorial Preface

The launching of the *Word Biblical Commentary* brings to fulfillment an enterprise of several years' planning. The publishers and the members of the editorial board met in 1977 to explore the possibility of a new commentary on the books of the Bible that would incorporate several distinctive features. Prospective readers of these volumes are entitled to know what such features were intended to be; whether the aims of the commentary have been fully achieved time alone will tell.

First, we have tried to cast a wide net to include as contributors a number of scholars from around the world who not only share our aims, but are in the main engaged in the ministry of teaching in university, college and seminary. They represent a rich diversity of denominational allegiance. The broad stance of our contributors can rightly be called evangelical, and this term is to be understood in its positive, historic sense of a commitment to scripture as divine revelation, and to the truth and power of the Christian gospel.

Then, the commentaries in our series are all commissioned and written for the purpose of inclusion in the *Word Biblical Commentary*. Unlike several of our distinguished counterparts in the field of commentary writing, there are no translated works, originally written in a non-English language. Also, our commentators were asked to prepare their own rendering of the original biblical text and to use those languages as the basis of their own comments and exegesis. What may be claimed as distinctive with this series is that it is based on the biblical languages, yet it seeks to make the technical and scholarly approach to a theological understanding of scripture understandable by—and useful to—the fledgling student, the working minister as well as to colleagues in the guild of professional scholars and teachers.

Finally, a word must be said about the format of the series. The layout in clearly defined sections has been consciously devised to assist readers at different levels. Those wishing to learn about the textual witnesses on which the translation is offered are invited to consult the section headed "Notes." This volume varies from the usual format of the series in uniting the "Notes" and "Comment" sections into one with the heading "Notes/Comments." If the readers' concern is with the state of modern scholarship on any given portion of scripture, then they should turn to the sections on "Bibliography" and "Form/Structure/Setting." For a clear exposition of the passage's meaning and its relevance to the ongoing biblical revelation, the "Comment" and concluding "Explanation" are designed expressly to meet that need. There is therefore something for everyone who may pick up and use these volumes.

If these aims come anywhere near realization, the intention of the editors will have been met, and the labor of our team of contributors rewarded.

General Editors: *David A. Hubbard*
Glenn W. Barker
Old Testament: *John D. W. Watts*
New Testament: *Ralph P. Martin*

Abbreviations

1. Periodicals, Reference Works, Serials, and Ancient Sources

α′   Aquila
Θ′   Theodotion
σ′   Symmachus
AB   Anchor Bible
AcOr   *Acta orientalia*
AER   *American Ecclesiastical Review*
AJSL   *American Journal of Semitic Languages and Literature*
AnBib   Analecta biblica
ANEP   J. B. Pritchard (ed.), *Ancient Near East in Pictures*
ANET   J. B. Pritchard (ed.), *Ancient Near Eastern Texts*
AOAT   Alter Orient und Altes Testament
ASTI   *Annual of the Swedish Theological Institute*
ATR   *Anglican Theological Review*
BA   *Biblical Archaeologist*
BASOR   *Bulletin of the American Schools of Oriental Research*
BBB   Bonner biblische Beiträge
BDB   F. Brown, S. R. Driver and C. A. Briggs, *Hebrew and English Lexicon of the Old Testament*
BHK   R. Kittel. *Biblia hebraica*
BHS   *Biblia hebraica stuttgartensia*
Bib   *Biblica*
BibB   Biblische Beiträge
BibLeb   *Bibel und Leben*
BibOr   Biblica et orientalia
BJRL   *Bulletin of the John Rylands University Library of Manchester*
BKAT   Biblischer Kommentar: Altes Testament
BSO(A)S   *Bulletin of the School of Oriental (and African) Studies*
BTB   *Biblical Theology Bulletin*
BWANT   Beiträge zur Wissenschaft vom Alten und Neuen Testament
BZ   *Biblische Zeitschrift*
BZAW   Beihefte zur ZAW

CAT   Commentaire de l'Ancien Testament
CBQ   *Catholic Biblical Quarterly*
CBQMS   Catholic Biblical Quarterly Mongraph
CJT   *Canadian Journal of Theology*
ConB   Coniectanea biblica
CQR   *Church Quarterly Review*
DJD   *Discoveries in the Judean Desert*
DOTT   D. W. Thomas (ed.), *Documents from Old Testament Times*
EstBib   *Estudios biblicos*
ETL   *Ephemerides theologicae lovanienses*
EvQ   *Evangelical Quarterly*
EvT   *Evangelische Theologie*
ExpTim   *Expository Times*
FRLANT   Forschungen zur Religion und Literatur des Alten und Neuen Testaments
FZTP   *Freiburger Zeitschrift für Theologie und Philosophie*
G Septuagint
G^* original Greek text
G^A Codex Alexandrinus
G^B Codex Vaticanus
G^L Lucian's recension
G^O Hexaplaric recension
G^S Codex Sinaiticus
GKC   *Gesenius' Hebrew Grammar*, ed. E. Kautsch, tr. A. E. Cowley
GNB   *Good News Bible*
Greg   *Gregorianum*
HALAT   W. Baumgartner et al., *Hebräisches und aramäisches Lexikon zum Alten Testament*
HAT   Handbuch zum Alten Testament
Hier   Jerome
HKAT   Handkommentar zum Alten Testament
HSM   Harvard Semitic Monographs
HTR   *Harvard Theological Review*
HUCA   *Hebrew Union College Annual*

ICC	International Critical Commentary	RSR	*Recherches de science religieuse*
		RSV	*Revised Standard Version*
IDB	G. A. Buttrick (ed.), *Interpreter's Dictionary of the Bible*	RV	*Revised Version*
		S	Peshitta
IEJ	*Israel Exploration Journal*	SANT	Studien zum Alten und Neuen Testament
Int	*Interpretation*		
ITQ	*Irish Theological Quarterly*	SBB	Stuttgarter biblische Monographien
JAOS	*Journal of the American Oriental Society*		
		SBLDS	SBL Dissertation Series
JB	A. Jones (ed.), *Jerusalem Bible*	SBLMS	SBL Monograph Series
JBL	*Journal of Biblical Literature*	SBM	Stuttgarter biblische Monographien
JETS	*Journal of the Evangelical Theological Society*		
		SBS	Stuttgarter Bibelstudien
JJS	*Journal of Jewish Studies*	SBT	Studies in Biblical Theology
JNES	*Journal of Near Eastern Studies*	SEÅ	Svensk exegetisk årsbok
JPOS	*Journal of the Palestine Oriental Society*	Sem	*Semitica*
		SJT	Scottish Journal of Theology
JQR	*Jewish Quarterly Review*	SNTSMS	Society for New Testament Studies Monograph Series
JSS	*Journal of Semitic Studies*		
JTS	*Journal of Theological Studies*	Syh	Syrohexaplaric text
K	Kethib	T	Targum
KAI	H. Donner and W. Rollig, *Kanaanäische und aramäische nschriften*	TBT	*The Bible Today*
		TDOT	*Theological Dictionary of the Old Testament*
KB	L. Koehler and W. Baumgartner, *Lexicon in Veteris Testament libros*	TGI	*Thelogie und Glaube*
		TLZ	*Theologische Literaturzeitung*
		TS	*Theological Studies*
KD	*Kerygma und Dogma*	TSK	*Theologische Studien und Kritiken*
KJV	*King James Version*	TTZ	*Trierer theologische Zeitschrift*
LD	*Lectio divina*	TZ	*Theologische Zeitschrift*
Leš	*Lešonenu*	UF	*Ugaritische Forschungen*
LXX	Septuagint	UT	C. H. Gordon, *Ugaritic Textbook*
Ms(s)	Manuscript(s)		
MT	Massoretic Text	UUÅ	Uppsala universitets årsskrift
NEB	*New English Bible*	V	Vulgate
NICNT	*New International Commentary on the New Testament*	VD	*Verbum domini*
		Vrs	ancient versions
NKZ	*Neue kirchliche Zeitschrift*	VT	*Vetus Testamentum*
NorTT	*Norsk Teologisk Tidsskrift*	VTSup	Vetus Testamentum, Supplements
NTS	*New Testament Studies*		
NTSMS	New Testament Studies Monograph Series	WMANT	Wissenschaftliche Monographien zum Alten und Neuen Testament
OLZ	*Orientalische Literaturzeitung*		
Or	*Orientalia* (Rome)	WO	*Die Welt des Orients*
OTS	*Oudtestamentische Studiën*	ZAW	*Zeitschrift für die alttestamentliche Wissenschaft*
PEQ	*Palestine Exploration Quarterly*		
Q	Qere	ZDMG	*Zeitschrift der deutschen morgenländischen Gesellschaft*
RB	*Revue biblique*		
RevQ	*Revue de Qumran*	ZTK	*Zeitschrift für Theologie und Kirche*
RHPR	*Revue d'histoire et de philosophie religieuses*		
RSPT	*Revue des sciences philosophiques et théologiques*		

2. Biblical and Apocryphal Books

Old Testament

Gen	Genesis	Eccl	Ecclesiastes
Exod	Exodus	Cant	Song of Solomon
Lev	Leviticus	Isa	Isaiah
Num	Numbers	Jer	Jeremiah
Deut	Deuteronomy	Lam	Lementations
Josh	Joshua	Ezek	Ezekiel
Judg	Judges	Dan	Daniel
Ruth	Ruth	Hos	Hosea
1 Sam	1 Samuel	Joel	Joel
2 Sam	2 Samuel	Amos	Amos
1 Kgs	1 Kings	Obad	Obadiah
2 Kgs	2 Kings	Jonah	Jonah
1 Chr	1 Chronicles	Mic	Micah
2 Chr	2 Chronicles	Nah	Nahum
Ezra	Ezra	Hab	Habakkuk
Neh	Nehemiah	Zeph	Zephaniah
Esth	Esther	Hag	Haggai
Job	Job	Zech	Zechariah
Ps	Psalms	Mal	Malachi
Prov	Proverbs		

New Testament

Matt	Matthew	1 Tim	1 Timothy
Mark	Mark	2 Tim	2 Timothy
Luke	Luke	Titus	Titus
John	John	Phlm	Philemon
Acts	Acts	Heb	Hebrews
Rom	Romans	Jas	James
1 Cor	1 Corinthians	1 Pet	1 Peter
2 Cor	2 Corinthians	2 Pet	2 Peter
Gal	Galatians	1 John	1 John
Eph	Ephesians	2 John	2 John
Phil	Philippians	3 John	3 John
Col	Colossians	Jude	Jude
1 Thess	1 Thessalonians	Rev	Revelation
2 Thess	2 Thessalonians		

Apocrypha

1 Kgdms	1 Kingdoms	Ep Jer	Epistle of Jeremy
2 Kgdms	2 Kingdoms	1 Macc	1 Maccabees
3 Kgdms	3 Kingdoms	2 Macc	2 Maccabees
4 Kgdms	4 Kingdoms	3 Macc	3 Maccabees
Add Esth	Additions to Esther	4 Macc	4 Maccabees
Bar	Baruch	Pr Azar	Prayer of Azariah
Bel	Bel and the Dragon	Pr Man	Prayer of Manasseh
1 Esdr	1 Esdras	Sir	Sirach
2 Esdr	2 Esdras	Sus	Susanna
4 Ezra	4 Ezra	Tob	Tobit
Jdt	Judith	Wis	Wisdom of Solomon

3. Rabbinic and Other Ancient References

Ber.	Berakot	*RS*	Ras Shamra
Bik.	Bikkurim	*Sop.*	Sopherim
C	Cairo Geniza	*Tg*	Targum
Ros. Has.	Rosh Hashanah		

4. Dead Sea Scrolls and Related Texts

CD	Cairo (Genizah text of the) Damascus (Document)
Hev	Nahal Hever texts
Mas	Masada texts
Mird	Khirbet Mird texts
Mur	Wadi Murabba at texts
p	Pesher (commentary)
Q	Qumran
1Q, 2Q, 3Q, etc.	Numbered caves of Qumran, yielding written material; followed by abbreviation of biblical or apocryphal book
QL	Qumran literature
1QapGen	*Genesis Apocryphon* of Qumran Cave 1
1QH	*Hôdāyôt* (*Thanksgiving Hymns*) from Qumran Cave 1
1QIsa*a,b*	First or second copy of Isaiah from Qumran Cave 1
1QpHab	*Pesher on Habakkuk* from Qumran Cave 1
1QM	*Milḥāmāh* (*War Scroll*)
1QS	*Serek hayyaḥad* (*Rule of the Community, Manual of Discipline*)
1QSa	Appendix A (*Rule of the Congregation*) to 1QS
1QSb	Appendix B (*Blessings*) to 1QS
3Q*15*	Copper Scroll from Qumran Cave 3
4QFlor	*Florilegium* (or *Eschatological Midrashim*) from Qumran Cave 4
4QMess ar	Aramaic "Messianic" text from Qumran Cave 4
4QPrNab	Prayer of Nabonidus from Qumran Cave 4
4QTestim	*Testimonia* text from Qumran Cave 4
4QTLevi	*Testament of Levi* from Qumran Cave 4
4QPhyl	Phylacteries from Qumran Cave 4
11QMelch	*Melchizedek* text from Qumran Cave 11
11QtgJob	*Targum of Job* from Qumran Cave 11

Main Bibliography

1. Commentaries (in chronological order)

Brande, W. G. *The Midrash on Psalms.* Yale Judaica Series 13. New Haven: Yale University Press, 1959. **Alexander, J. A.** *The Psalms.* Edinburgh: Andrew Elliott, 1864. **Delitzsch, F.** *Biblical Commentary on the Psalms.* Tr. D. Eaton. 3 vols. London: Hodder and Stoughton, 1887–89. **Duhm, B.** *Die Psalmen.* Kurzer HKAT. Leipzig, Tübingen: J. C. B. Mohr (Paul Siebeck), 1899; 2nd ed. 1922. **Kirkpatrick, A. F.** *The Book of Psalms.* Cambridge Bible for Schools and Colleges. Cambridge: Cambridge University Press, 1902. **Ehrlich, A. B.** *Die Psalmen neu übersetzt und erklärt.* Berlin: M. Poppelauer, 1905. **Briggs, C. A. and E. G.** *A Commentary on the Books of Psalms.* 2 vols. ICC. New York: Charles Scribners' Sons, 1907, 1909. **Gunkel, H.** *Die Psalmen.* HKAT 2.2. 4. Ausgabe. Göttingen: Vandenhoek und Ruprecht, 1926. **Schmidt, H.** *Die Psalmen.* HAT 1. 15. Tübingen: J. C. B. Mohr (Paul Siebeck), 1934. **Oesterley, W. O. E.** *The Psalms.* 2 vols. London: SPCK, 1939. **Cohen, A.** *The Psalms: Hebrew Text, English Translation and Commentary.* Hindhead, Surrey: Soncino Press, 1945. **Kissane, E. J.** *The Book of Psalms.* 2 vols. Dublin: Browne and Nolan, 1953, 1954. **Brockington, L. H.** *The Hebrew Text of the OT: The Readings Adopted by the Translators of the NEB.* Oxford: Oxford University Press; Cambridge: Cambridge University Press, 1973. **Budde, K.** "Zum Text der Psalmen." *ZAW* 35 (1915) 175–95. **Buhl, F.** "Psalmi." *Biblia Hebraica*, ed. R. Kittel. 3. Ausgabe. Stuttgart: Württembergische Bibelanstalt, 1937. **Driver, G. R.** "Textual and Linguistic Problems in the Book of Psalms." *HTR* 29 (1936) 171–95. ———. "Notes on the Psalms. 2. 73–150." *JTS* 44 (1943) 12–23. **Field, F.** *Origenis Hexaplorum quae supersunt.* Tomus 2. *Jobus-Malachias.* Oxonii: e Typographeo Clarendoniano, 1875. **Kennicott, B.** *Vetus Testamentum Hebraicum cum variis lectionibus.* Vol. 2. Oxford: Clarendon Press, 1780. **de Lagarde, P.** *Hagiographa chaldaice.* Leipzig: B. G. Teubner, 1873. **Rahlfs, A.** *Psalmi cum Odis. Septuaginta. Vetus Testamentum Graecum Auctoritate Academiae Litterarum Gottingensis editum.* Vol. 10. Göttingen: Vandenhoeck und Ruprecht, 1931. **Sanders, J. A.** *The Psalms Scroll of Qumran Cave 11 (11QPsª).* Discoveries in the Judaean Desert of Jordan 4. Oxford: Clarendon Press, 1965. **Thomas, D. W.** *The Text of the Revised Psalter.* London: SPCK, 1963. **Vogel, A.** "Studien zum Pešitta-Psalter." *Bib* 32 (1951) 32–56, 198–231, 336–63, 481–502. **Weiser, A.** *The Psalms: A Commentary.* Tr. H. Hartnell. OTL. Philadelphia: Westminster Press, 1962. **Deissler, A.** *Die Psalmen.* Die Welt der Bibel. Düsseldorf: Patmos-Verlag, 1963. **Dahood, M.** *Psalms I: 1–50, Psalms II: 51–100, Psalms III: 101–150.* AB 16, 17, 17A. Garden City, New York: Doubleday, 1966, 1968, 1970. **Eaton, J. H.** *Psalms: Introduction and Commentary.* Torch Bible Commentaries. London: SCM Press, 1967. **Anderson, A. A.** *The Book of Psalms.* 2 vols. New Century Bible. London: Oliphants, 1972. **Kidner, D.** *Psalms 73–150. A Commentary on Books 3–5 of the Psalms.* Tyndale OT Commentaries. London: Inter-Varsity Press, 1975. **Rogerson, J. W., and McKay, J. W.** *Psalms 101–150.* Cambridge Bible Commentary on the New English Bible. Cambridge: Cambridge University Press, 1977. **Kraus, H.-J.** *Psalmen.* BKAT 15: 2. 5. Ausgabe. Neukirchen-Vluyn: Neukirchener Verlag, 1978.

2. Texts, Versions, and Textual Studies

Bardtke, H. "Liber Psalmorum." *Biblia Hebraica Stuttgartensia*, ed. Karl Elliger et Wilhelm Rudolph. Stuttgart: Würtembergische Bibelanstalt, 1969. **Barnes, W. E.** *The*

Peshitta Psalter According to the West Syrian Text. Cambridge: Cambridge University Press, 1904.

3. Linguistic Tools

Brown, F., Driver, S. R., and **Briggs, C. A.** *A Hebrew and English Lexicon of the OT with an Appendix Containing the Biblical Aramaic.* Oxford: Clarendon Press, 1906. **Jastrow, M.** *A Dictionary of the Targumim, the Talmud Babli and Yerushalmi and the Midrashic Literature.* London, New York: Trübner, 1903. **Joüon, P.** *Grammaire de l'hébreu biblique.* 2nd ed. Rome: Institut Biblique Pontifical, 1947. **Koehler, L.** und Baumgartner, W. *Lexicon in Veteris Testamenti libros.* Leiden: E. J. Brill, 1958.

4. Major Monographs and Articles

Alden, R. L. "Chiastic Psalms (3): A Study in the Mechanics of Semitic Poetry in Psalms 101–150." *Journal of the Evangelical Theological Society* 21 (1978) 199–210. **Barth, C.** *Die Erretung vom Tode in den individuellen Klage-und Dankliedern des AT.* Zollikon: Evangelischer Verlag, 1947. **Baumann, E.** "Struktur-Untersuchungen im Psalter. 2." *ZAW* 62 (1949/50) 115–52. **Beaucamp, E.** "Structure strophique des Psaumes." *RSR* 56 (1968) 199–223. **Becker, J.** *Israel deutet seine Psalmen: Urform und Neuinterpretation in den Psalmen.* SBS 18. Stuttgart: Verlag Katholisches Bibelwerk, 1966. **Birkeland, H.** *The Evildoers in the Book of Psalms.* Oslo: Jacob Dybwad, 1955. **Clines, D. J. A.** "Psalm Research Since 1955: 1. The Psalms and the Cult." *Tyndale Bulletin* 17 (1966) 103–26. ———. "Psalm Research Since 1955: 2. The Literary Genres." *Tyndale Bulletin* 20 (1969) 105–25. **Crüsemann, F.** *Studien zur Formgeschichte von Hymnus und Danklied in Israel.* WMANT 32. Neukirchen-Vluyn: Neukirchener Verlag, 1969. **Eaton, J. H.** *Kingship and the Psalms.* SBT 2.32. London: SCM Press, 1976. **Eissfeldt, O.** *The OT: An Introduction.* Tr. P. R. Ackroyd. Oxford: Basil Blackwell, 1965. **Fohrer, G.** *Introduction to the OT.* Tr. D. Green. Nashville: Abingdon Press, 1968. **Gerstenberger, E.** "Psalms." *OT Form Criticism,* ed. J. H. Hayes. Trinity University Monograph Series in Religion 2. San Antonio: Trinity University Press, 1974. **Gunkel, H.** and **Begrich, J.** *Einleitung in die Psalmen.* Göttingen: Vandenhoeck und Ruprecht, 1933. **Johnson, A. R.** *The Cultic Prophet in Ancient Israel.* 2nd ed. Cardiff: University of Wales Press, 1962. ———. *The Cultic Prophet and Israel's Psalmody.* Cardiff: University of Wales Press, 1979. **Kraus, H.-J.** *Worship in Israel. A Cultic History of the OT.* Tr. G. Buswell. Oxford: Basil Blackwell, 1966. **Michel, D.** *Tempora und Satzstellung in den Psalmen.* Abhandlungen zur evangelischen Theologie 1. Bonn: H. Bouvier, 1960. **Mowinckel, S.** *Psalmenstudien.* Bd. 1–6. Oslo: Kristiana, 1921–24. ———. *The Psalms in Israel's Worship.* 2 vols. Tr. D. R. Ap-Thomas. Oxford: Basil Blackwell, 1962. **Robertson, D. A.** *Linguistic Evidence in Dating Early Hebrew Poetry.* SBLDS 3. Missoula, MT: Scholars Press, 1972. **Schildenberger, J.** "Bemerkungen zum Strophenbau der Psalmen." *Estudios Eclesiásticos* 34 (1960) 673–87. **Westermann, C.** *The Praise of God in the Psalms.* Tr. K. R. Crim. Richmond, VA: John Knox Press, 1965.

Introduction

Bibliography

Gese, H. "Die Entstehung der Büchereinteilung des Psalters." *Wort, Lied und Gottesspruch. Festschrift für J. Ziegler,* ed. J. Schreiner. Forschungen zur Bibel 2. Würzburg: Echter Verlag, 1972. **Westermann, C.** "Zur Sammlung des Psalters." *Theologia Viatorum* 8 (1972) 278–84.

The reader is referred to the comprehensive introduction to the Psalter in *Psalms 1–50* by P. C. Craigie. Here it remains to draw attention to the composition of the final third of the Psalter. By way of general comment, there is a preponderance of praising psalms in Pss 101–150. There are twenty-nine psalms in which praise of various kinds predominates; complaints are thirteen in number. The ratio contrasts with that found earlier in the Psalter. The leaning toward praise in the latter part of the book may help to explain why it is canonically called תהלים "praises."

The so-called Songs of Ascents (Pss 120–134) comprise the largest collection. An excursus placed after the commentary on Ps 134 investigates the nature and purpose of this collection. Psalms 140–143 exhibit a rare phenomenon in the Psalter: a group of psalms of identical genre, the *individual complaint.* In their headings they are all entitled Davidic. Psalms 138–139 and 144–145 also classified thus, clearly became associated with the group and were placed before and after it respectively. Similarly Pss 135–137 may have been added as a supplement to the Songs of Ascents. Psalms 146–150 are, like Pss 140–143, a relatively homogeneous collection in form-critical terms: they are hymns of various types, each supplied with a framework of *Hallelujahs.* The last, Ps 150, appears to serve as a doxology to the fifth book of the Psalter (Pss 107–150) and to the Psalter as a whole.

Substantially Pss 120–150 comprise three cultic collections. Psalms 101–119 are more complex in respect of identifying their earlier groupings. Psalm 119 is akin to Ps 1 in its content of Torah-related piety. Accordingly it has been suggested that the two psalms once marked the bounds of an earlier, shorter Psalter. Psalms 113–118 form the *Hallel* sung at the three annual festivals; it is feasible that they were a group similarly used before they were incorporated into the Psalter. Their redactional *Hallelujahs* at beginning and/or end are shared by Pss 111 and 112, which were thus associated with the following collection.

Psalms 108–110 are a small collection of Davidic psalms. Psalm 108 has occurred earlier in the Psalter as 60:7–14 (5–12); here it has been provided with a different introduction, 57:8–12 (7–11). The common introductions of Pss 105–107 (הודו ליהוה "Give thanks to Yahweh") explain their collocation. In view of the similarity of these three psalms, the doxology at 106:48 closing the fourth book of the Psalter appears to have been an insertion subsequent to the juxtaposing of Pss 105–107. The division of the Book of Psalms into five books probably occurred late in its development.

Psalms 103 and 104 have clearly been placed together because of their identical beginnings. Their hymnic character may have been the reason for putting them before the praising Pss 105–107. Psalm 101 is a *royal psalm*, placed seemingly at random like a number of other royal psalms. Psalm 102 may have been appended to Pss 95–100 in view of its common motif of Yahweh's universal rule. In the course of the commentary suggestions are made as to why particular psalms were juxtaposed.

The King's Duty Done (101:1-8)

Bibliography

Bauer, J. B. " 'Incedam in via immaculata, quando venias ad me?' (Ps. 100 [101]:2)," *VD* 30 (1952) 219–24. **Brueggemann, W.** "A Neglected Sapiential Word Pair." *ZAW* 89 (1977) 234–58. **Galling, K.** "Der Beichtspiegel. Eine gattungsgeschichtliche Studie." *ZAW* 6 (1929) 125–30. **Johnson, A. R.** *Sacral Kingship in Ancient Israel.* 2nd ed. Cardiff: University of Wales Press, 1967. **Kaiser, O.** "Erwägungen zu Psalm 101." *ZAW* 74 (1962) 195–205. **Kenik, H. A.** "Code of Conduct for a King: Psalm 101." *JBL* 95 (1976) 391–403.

Translation

[1] Davidic. A Psalm.

I sing of loyalty and justice,[a]	(3+2)
I celebrate you, Yahweh, with music,	
[2] I rhapsodize [a] about (your) perfect path—	(3+3)
when [b] will you come to me?	
I have behaved [c] with integrity of mind [d]	(3+2)
at my court.	
[3] I have set before my eyes	(3+2)
no wicked [a] purpose.	
I hate [b] devious actions,[c]	(3+2)
they have not clung to me.	
[4] A perverse mind [a]	(2+2+2)
has been far from me,	
I have not been involved in wrong.	
[5] Whoever secretly slandered [a] his associate,	(3+2)
him I have silenced.[b]	
If any had arrogant eyes	(2+2+2)
and big ideas,	
him I have not tolerated.[c]	
[6] I have had my eyes on faithful countrymen,	(3+2)
for them to live with me.	
The person who walks a path of integrity	(3+2)
has been my minister.	
[7] No one has lived at my court	(3+2)
who acts deceitfully.	
None who speaks lies [a] has stayed long	(3+2)
before my eyes.	
[8] In the mornings I have destroyed	(3+2)
all wicked countrymen,	
ridding Yahweh's city [a]	(3+2)
of all doers of evil.	

Notes/Comments

1.a. Whose attributes are in view, Yahweh's, the monarch's or both? The rest of the psalm could be regarded as an expansion of these attributes as royal ones, but it seems rather to represent a human response to Yahweh's own qualities. חסד "loyalty" is a key term used throughout the royal Ps 89 to describe the divine commitment to the Davidic covenant (cf. Isa 55:3), while in the royal Ps 72 (v 1) the king's justice is grounded in that of God. The pair is featured in the non-royal Ps 119 (v 149). The decisive factor is the hymnic nature of the context. J. A. Alexander (*The Psalms*, 406) observed that in the OT "To 'sing . . . to Jehovah' never means to praise someone else in an address to him." The two verbs of v 1 and the first of v 2 have a cohortative form, here expressing a determined statement of simultaneous announcement and fulfilment (cf. JB, NEB, and GNB).

2.a. M. Dahood (*Psalms III*, 3) so renders. Usually the Hiph'il of שכל has been taken in its standard senses of "consider" or "behave wisely." But A. R. Johnson (*Sacral Kingship*, 114) has related it to the noun משכיל, a type of poem, probably "a skilfull composition" (cf. H. -J. Kraus, *Psalmen*, 19–20, with reference to 2 Chr 30:22). In support Dahood has noted the juxtaposition of the nouns related to the three verbs of vv 1aβ–2aα in the heading to Ps 88. The common cohortative form of the three verbs suggests that the third relates to a poetic composition. Then the "perfect way" is Yahweh's as in 18:31(30). For אשכילה some Heb. mss have אשכילך "I rhapsodize concerning you" and Tg renders similarly, in accord with "you" of v 1. The variant is simply an explanatory change.

2.b. H. Gunkel (*Die Psalmen*, 432, 434) and Kraus (*Psalmen*, 858) and some others find a question out of place and emend מתי "when" to אמת "truth": "truth will come" or "may truth come." A succinct summary of other emendations is presented by J. B. Bauer (*VD* 30 [1952] 220–21). See *Form/Structure/Setting*. The question is an appeal to Yahweh from whom alone help can come (cf. 121:1, 2). The king prays for a manifestation of Yahweh in his saving attributes of loyalty and justice (cf. 36:6, 7 [5, 6]; 89:15 [14]). The external parallelism indicates that the celebration of Yahweh is intended to elicit a dynamic response from him.

2.c. The time-reference in Hebrew poetry is often equivocal. The prefix conjugation is used for this and all succeeding except שנאתי "I hate(d)" in v 3a. Does it represent a future, continuous present or past reference? LXX used past (imperfect) tenses. See *Form/Structure/Setting*.

2.d. This is contrasted with "a perverse mind" in v 4. H. A. Kenik (*JBL* 95 [1976] 401) and W. Brueggemann (*ZAW* 89 [1977] 245) both note that תם and עקש are a sapiential word pair.

3.a. Heb. בליעל has been variously analyzed; see the critical survey of N. J. Tromp (*Primitive Conceptions of Death and the Nether World*. [BibOr 21. Rome: Pontifical Biblical Institute, 1969] 125–28). Perhaps the best etymology is to relate it to בלע "swallow, devour" with D. W. Thomas ("בְּלִיַּעַל in the Old Testament," in *Biblical and Patristic Studies in Memory of Robert C. Casey*, ed. J. N. Birdsall and R. W. Thomson. [Freiburg: Herder, 1963] 11–19; cf. דברי בלע "devouring, destructive words" in 52:6 [4]). It is clearly a comprehensive negative emotive term (cf. 2 Sam 16:7). As Tromp paraphrases V. Maag's discussion in *TZ* 21 (1965) 287–99, "it comprises all that is contrary to God and the fundamental regulations concerning social life."

3.b. Heb. שנאתי "I hate(d)" is used in a formula of renunciation; cf. 26:5; 31:7 (6); 119:104. The stereotyped suffix conjugation (except in the question of 139:21) may account for its presence in a sea of prefix conjugations.

3.c. סטים is a *hapax legomenon*, generally related to שוט "fall away," cf. שטה. This meaning is supported by the external parallelism; עקש "perverse" is its counterpart. MT עשה is evidently a variant of the usual Qal infinitive construct form עשות (cf. GKC § 75n). LXX presupposes עשׂי "doers of" and S, Tg Hier. עשׂה "one doing." The impersonal object in v 3a favors MT.

4.a. Calvin judged long ago that it is rather forced to take the "perverse mind" as personal in the sense of perverse men and "wrong" as an evil man (Weiser, *Psalms*, 649; Johnson, *Sacral Kingship*, 115; Dahood, *Psalms III*, 5).

5.a. The vocalization of Qere reflects an alternative ms tradition which anomalously reduced the *holem* of the Po'el to a *qames hatuph* (cf. GKC § 55d). For the -*y* morpheme see GKC § 90m and D. A. Robertson, *Linguistic Evidence*, 72, 76 (where he judges it insignificant for dating the psalm), 144.

5.b. Heb. צמת like Ugaritic *ṣmt* means basically "be silent" and then "destroy." Its parallel terms in 73:27; 94:23; 143:12 attest its sinister development; cf. ארץ דומה "land of silence," of Sheol in 94:17 (*aliter* Tromp, *Primitive Conceptions,* 76) and Latin *loca tacentia* for the underworld and *silentes* for the dead. In v 8 it is used in the developed sense (cf. the different renderings in LXX).

5.c. The structure of the psalm (see *Form/Structure/Setting*) does not favor the interpretation of the consonantal text in LXX and *S* as אוֹכֵל . . . אִתוֹ "I will eat with him" followed by S. Mowinckel (*He That Cometh.* [Tr. G. W. Anderson. Nashville: Abingdon Press, 1954] 91) and NEB.

7.a. Heb. שקרים is taken by T. W. Overholt (*The Threat of Falsehood* [SBT 2:16; London: SCM Press, 1970] 89, note 8) in a legal sense as part of "a king's promise to maintain justice." Similarly M. A. Klopfenstein (*Die Lüge nach dem AT,* [Zürich, Gotthelf Verlag, 1964] 74) found reference to some kind of legal connotation. But the external parallelism suggests otherwise.

8.a. The parallelism between "land" and "Yahweh's city" is noteworthy. The link between the two was not merely political, Jerusalem being the capital, but also theological; cf. in general R. E. Clements, "Temple and Land. A Significant Aspect of Israel's Worship," *Transactions of the Glasgow Oriental Society* 19 (1961/62) 16–28.

Form/Structure/Setting

That this is a royal psalm is generally agreed. It may be deduced from the claim to judicial authority in "Yahweh's city" (v 8), i.e. Jerusalem, and the stress upon the household and its members. It was thus composed by or for a king in the pre-exilic period. This is most probably how לדוד in the heading is to be understood, referring to the Davidic king.

To determine its genre is more difficult. Most commentators regard the psalm as a vow of loyalty or the like whereby the king commits himself to the ideals of the Davidic covenant. Then the setting is the royal coronation (cf. Ps 2) and also any subsequent royal celebration. Gunkel (*Die Psalmen,* 433) compared the statements of future royal policy in 1 Kgs 12:14; 2 Kgs 10:18, while Kraus (*Psalmen,* 859) and Weiser (*Psalms,* 649) have suggested the influence of the Egyptian enthronement ceremony, following S. Herrmann. The psalm is difficult to analyze in standard form-critical terms. K. Galling (*ZAW* 6 [1929] 128) regarded its statements of innocence as a development of the entrance liturgy, which included conditions of admittance to the sanctuary (cf. Pss 15, 24). On the other hand, Kraus (*Psalmen,* 859) has been able to relate this element to a royal context. He compares the protestation of innocence in the royal Ps 18:21–25 (20–24), evidently viewing this psalm as a forward projection, a promise of innocence. The hymnic introduction of v 1 he compares with the *Gerichtsdoxologie,* or praise of God's judgment as just, which accompanies an oath of innocence in Ps 7. It is, however, more difficult to see the relevance of a *Gerichtsdoxologie* in this new context. Kenik (*JBL* 95 [1976] 397) has suggested that the profession of innocence in Ps 18 itself looks back to an ingredient in the enthronement ceremony, to which Ps 101 is an actual witness. She has also drawn attention to wisdom motifs that appear in the psalm, finding parallels with Prov 1–9, which she regards as originally addressed to the king. O. Keel (*Feinde und Gottesleugner. Studien zum Image der Widersacher in den Individualpsalmen.* [SBM 7; Stuttgart: Verlag Katholisches Bibelwerk, 1969] 118) too, noting that only here do "the wicked" feature in a royal psalm, has referred to passages in Proverbs that draw a specific antithesis between the wicked and the king, viz. 20:26; 25:5; 29:12. It is interesting to find wisdom parallels, but by no means surprising

in view of the close connection between the wisdom movement and the royal
court which gave it patronage.

Brueggemann (*ZAW* 89 [1977] 245), in the course of investigating a link
between the psalm and wisdom traditions, has suggested that behind its royal
oath of innocence lies the background of the "grant" type of ancient treaty
between king and servant, for which he refers to M. Weinfeld ("The Covenant
of Grant in the Old Testament and in the Ancient Near East," *JAOS* 90
[1970] 184–203). Certainly there are similarities of language ("perfection"
in the sense of perfect service) and in the theme of loyalty. However, the
time perspective of the grant should not be overlooked in the tracing of
parallels: it was a reward for past loyalty.

An entirely different basic genre for the whole psalm has been argued
by O. Kaiser (*ZAW* 74 [1962] 195–205): the individual complaint (or lament).
Focusing upon the temporal question in v 2, he observes that it is characteristic
of a complaint. The interrogative adverb מתי recurs in 42:3 (2) 119:82, 84
in complaint passages and the more common עד-מתי "how long?" in 6:4
(3); 74:10; 80:5 (4); 90:13 (12); 94:3. The dominant meter of the psalm,
3+2, is that often used for a complaint, the so-called *qinah* meter. As for
the hymnic introduction, Kaiser notes that two royal complaints, Pss 89 and
144, begin in a similar way. The body of the psalm is to be interpreted as
a confession of innocence, as in 17:3–5 and 26:3–6. He explains the setting
as a cult drama in which the king engages in ritual humiliation. Johnson
(*Sacral Kingship*, 144), followed in turn by J. H. Eaton (*Psalms*, 242; he is
less certain in some respects in *Kingship*, 122–24), has adopted Kaiser's interpretation of the psalm. Johnson himself had earlier developed the concept
of a dramatic background in which the king featured, as in the Babylonian
New Year festival. The imperfect verbs of the negative confession he takes
in a present sense. Dahood (*Psalms III*, 2, 4) also understands the psalm as
a complaint, but regards the verbs as past "according to the Canaanite-biblical
employment of the *yqtl* form in poetry to describe past activity." He finds
himself unable to reconstruct a cultic or historical setting.

The interpretation of Ps 101 as a complaint seems to do most justice to
its evidence overall. It can explain the hymnic introduction and takes seriously
the question of v 2, which otherwise is either emended away or virtually
ignored. The question sets the tone for what follows, and controls its understanding as a negative confession. The matter of the verbs is significant. D.
Michel (*Tempora und Satzstellung in den Psalmen*, 35–36) claims that a confession
would require perfect verbs. He finds some difficulty in explaining the perfect
שנאתי in v 3, suggesting that it makes a basic statement about the king's
character. Moreover, he is uneasy about the imperfects in the negative confession of Ps 26 (vv 4b, 5b; *Tempora*, 187), where it is noteworthy that שנאתי
also occurs (v 5a). Both Johnson's and Dahood's explanations of the verbs
seems feasible; they yield a similar meaning. Most probably the psalm is a
royal complaint, more precisely a psalm of innocence, containing a hymnic
passage and wisdom motifs. The hymnic introduction has the function of a
motivation for the interrogative prayer (cf. C. Westermann, *Praise*, 55–57).
A setting of a cult drama is rather speculative; it is safer to postulate a background of political distress, for which even Kaiser feels the need to find a

place, and to understand the psalm as a cultic complaint composed for use at such times. As to its eventual understanding in non-monarchical post-exilic Judaism, Westermann ("Zur Sammlung des Psalters," *Theologia Viatorum* 8 [1961/62] 284) is probably correct in deducing from the scattering of the royal psalms throughout the Psalter an understanding of them in eschatological and messianic terms.

For such a short psalm there has been a surprising variety of structural analyses. Most commonly two divisions are found, on the basis of content: vv 1–4 the king's personal standards and vv 5–8 those for his people. On the same principle Weiser (*Psalms*, 649) divides into vv 1–3 and 4–8, taking v 4 as the beginning of the king's directions for others. Similarly, but with greater sensitivity to the preliminary elements, Eaton (*Psalms*, 242) splits the psalm into vv 1αβ–2a, 2b–3, 4–8. Dahood (*Psalms III*, 4, 6) makes the form-critical diversity a primary consideration, dividing into vv 1αβ–2a and 2b–8. He also adduces the factor of a double poetical device: he finds inclusion in the repetition of בקרב ביתי "within my house," (vv 2, 7) and לנגד עיני "before my eyes," (vv 3, 7). However, L. J. Liebreich ("Psalms 34 and 145 in the Light of Their Key Words," *HUCA* 27 [1956] 183 note 7) has interpreted these phenomena in terms of general inclusion, marking the early and late parts of the whole psalm; he can also cite בדרך תמים "in a perfect way," (vv 2, 6) which Dahood did not take into account. Kenik's analysis is mainly exegetical. The psalm is framed by a hymnic passage in v 1αβ-b and another lyrical (*sic*) one in v 8, both of which use the divine name and feature justice. Within this framework are three sections: (a) vv 2–3αβ are a programmatic statement concerning the moral conduct appropriate for a king, which is expanded in vv 3αγ–7; (b) vv 3αγ–5 are a negative declaration of what the king must reject; and (c) vv 6, 7 are a more positive declaration concerning his people's attitude. The three pairs of repeated terms she regards as a sign of structural unity. They appear in three statements about the king's conduct and in three about his people's conduct (actually in her first and third sections).

Repetition is clearly the key to the structure. It seems to point to two largely symmetrical strophes, vv 1αβ–5, 6–8, a strophe being understood in the broad sense of a unit of poetic material bound together by both content and stylistic features. In fact the layout in both *BHK* and *BHS* follows this pattern. The divine name in vv 1, 8 gives overall inclusion (cf. too דבר "word, speaking" in vv 3, 7). The three sets of repeated terms feature in vv 2–3 and in the same order in vv 5–8. A fourth pair, involving אצמית "silence, destroy," appears in vv 5, 8. Moreover, the repeated אתו "him" in the two lines of v 5 is balanced by a repeated כל "all" in v 8, a factor which safeguards the second אתו against repointing. The second strophe is itself marked by inclusion, that of ארץ "land" in vv 6, 8. Other minor inclusions are the repetitions of (י)לבב "mind" in vv 2, 4 and of עיני "my eyes" in vv 6, 7; עיני/עינים in vv 5, 6 function as a strophic hinge. The strophes are of eight (= 2+6) and six lines respectively: in the former the two initial lines comprise the mainly hymnic preface. The psalm has clearly been structured most carefully into these component parts. A further feature is that the bicola are apparently grouped in pairs with external parallelism.

Explanation

The king stands in dire need, but he is conscious that he does not have to stand alone. He is committed to Yahweh and Yahweh to him in a binding covenant. He praises the God who in this relationship is loyal, just and perfectly committed. But help must come soon, and so the king turns to a direct and urgent plea, after the indirect appeal represented by his praise.

Alert to the two-sided nature of the Davidic covenant, he further urges his God to intervene by testifying how seriously he has taken his own side of the commitment. Far from being "intoxicated with the splendors of royalty," as Calvin put it, he has discharged his responsibility to his Patron honorably. Yahweh's integrity has found an echo in his own personal integrity (cf. 18:26 [25]), which has been demonstrated in both thought and action. Vv 2b–5 might be summed up in terms of 18:24 [23]: "I have been perfectly committed to him and kept myself from iniquity." The king's definition of his sense of moral commitment is expressed in wisdom terms. A twisted, warped attitude (cf. Prov 3:20; 11:20) he has eschewed, in particular refusing to listen to intrigue (cf. Prov 30:10) or to countenance pride. He has lived up to his ethical education.

Perhaps inevitably the statement of the king's personal ethics has come to include his attitude to others. It is this aspect which is developed in the second strophe, and once again it coincides with wisdom themes. His sense of social commitment comes to the fore. He bears before God a responsibility for his countrymen (vv 6, 8). Accordingly he has ensured that the members of his administration are men committed to Yahweh, whose trustworthiness is grounded in their religious faith. His ministers are men picked for their moral integrity and cleanness (cf. Prov 25:5, unlike the royal chamberlain Shebna according to Isa 22:18). The principle of truth, so prized in his own life, he has sought to find equally honored among his entourage (cf. Prov 29:12). Supremely, as upholder of justice (cf. Prov 20:8, 26) at his regular morning judicial sessions (cf. 2 Sam 15:2; Jer 21:12) he has endeavored to express nationally his commitment to high moral principles. It is only fitting that the God who has deigned to reveal his cultic presence in the capital should be served by a nation that is free from moral defilement, and to this end the king has devoted himself with enthusiasm ("all . . . all").

The psalm as a whole bears a close relationship to Ps 18, a royal thanksgiving. Psalm 18 looks back to God's intervention in response to the king's appeal and testimonial, and gives thanks that he was delivered from a situation of distress. Psalm 101 is set at an earlier stage in royal experience. In hope of deliverance an appeal is presented to Yahweh, claiming his covenant loyalty. The appeal is supported by a report that the king has not been negligent in his own endeavors to be true to his covenant partner.

The royal protestations may grate on Christian ears as self-righteous and far from the ideal that "they who fain would serve thee best are conscious most of wrong within." It must be appreciated that there is a difference of religious culture at this point. The tone is sincere; a sense of boasting is absent (cf. v 5). The psalm pleads not sinless perfection but a conscientious attitude toward royal duties; the covenant terms set by God for the king to observe have not been disregarded so as to warrant punishment (cf. 89:31–33 [30–32]). Underlying the psalm is the king's keen sense of obligation as God's representative in the theocracy of Israel. The psalm is also an expression of dependence upon his stronger partner.

The messianic interpretation of the royal psalms which seems to lie behind the arrangement of the Psalter in its final form became part of the heritage of the NT. No clear echo of Ps 101 occurs there, but ultimately the Christian will view the psalm in the light of Isa 11:1–5. It becomes a testimony to the One who did all things well (cf. Heb 4:15; 5:7), who, endued with the spirit of wisdom, has been appointed Judge of the world (Acts 17:31) and whose servants are called to be above reproach (cf. Titus 2:24).

Through Tears to Praise (102:1–29)

Bibliography

Airoldi, N. "Note critiche ai Salmi." *Augustinianum* 10 (1970) 174–80. **Asensio, F.** "El Salmo 102 y la antropología teológica." *Greg* 55 (1974) 541–53. **Becker, J.** *Israel deutet seine Psalmen: Urform und Neuinterpretation in den Psalmen.* SBS 18, 1966. **Driver, G. R.** "Birds in the OT. 1. Birds in Law." *PEQ* (1955) 5–20. **Jones, D.** "The Cessation of Sacrifice after the Destruction of the Temple in 586 B.C." *JTS* 14 (1963) 12–31. **Ludwig, T. M.** "The Traditions of the Establishing of the Earth in Deutero-Isaiah." *JBL* 92 (1973) 345–57. **Mansoor, M.** "The Thanksgiving Hymns and the Massoretic Text (Part 1)." *RevQ* 3 (1961) 259–66. **Martin-Achard, R.** *Approche des Psaumes.* Neuchatel: Delachaux et Niestlé, 1969. **Seybold, K.** *Das Gebet des Kranken im AT. Untersuchungen zur Bestimmung und Zuordnung der Krankheits- und Heilungspsalmen.* BWANT 5:19. Stuttgart: W. Kohlhammer Verlag, 1973. **Urban, A.** "Verrinnendes Leben und ausgeschüttete Klage. Meditation über Psalm 102 (101)." *BibLeb* 10 (1969) 137–45.

Translation

[1] A prayer [a] for a sufferer when he feels weak and pours out his
  worries [b] before Yahweh.

[2] *Yahweh, listen to my prayer,*   (3+3)
  let my cry for help reach you.

[3] *Do not hide your face away from me*   (3+2)
  now that I am in trouble.

  Turn your ear toward me,   (3+4)
  answer me quickly now that I call.

[4] *For my life is vanishing in smoke;*   (3+3)
  my bones burn like embers. [a]

[5] *My heart* [a] *has been seared like grass and is shriveled up.*   (4+3)
  I even forget [b] *to eat my food.*

[6] *Beacuse of my loud groans* [a]   (2+3)
  my bones [b] *stick to my skin.*

⁷ *I have become like a desert owl,*^a   (3+3)
     I am like the owl ^a *that lives in ruins.*

⁸ *I lie awake and am*   (2+3)
     like a solitary bird on a housetop.

⁹ *All day long* ^a *my enemies insult me,*   (3+3)
     they use my name as a curse, ridiculing me.^b

¹⁰ *Ashes I eat for my food,*   (3+3)
     with my drink I mingle tears

¹¹ *because of your anger and wrath:*   (3+3)
     you have picked me up and thrown me away.^a

¹² *My life is like a lengthening shadow.*   (3+3)
     I am shriveled up like grass.

¹³ *But* ^a *you, Yahweh, sit enthroned forever,*   (4+3)
     invocation ^b *of you continues generation after generation.*

¹⁴ *You will arise and treat Zion with compassion*   (4+4)
     because it is time to show her favor,^a *the right time has come.*

¹⁵ *For your servants value its stones*   (3+3)
     and its rubble they regard with favor.^a

¹⁶ *Then the nations will revere* ^a *Yahweh's name,*^b   (4+3)
     all the kings on earth your glory,

¹⁷ *when Yahweh has rebuilt* ^a *Zion,*   (3+2)
     revealing himself in his glory,

¹⁸ *having regard for the prayer* ^a *of the destitute*   (3+3)
     instead of despising their prayer.

¹⁹ *This* ^a *will be recorded for another generation*   (4+3)
     and the people yet to be created ^b *will praise Yah(weh),*

²⁰ *when* ^a *Yahweh* ^b *has looked down from his lofty sanctuary,*   (4+3)
     looked from heaven to earth

²¹ *to listen to prisoners' groans*   (3+3)
     and release men under sentence of death.

²² *And so Yahweh's name will be proclaimed in Zion*   (3+3)
     his praise in Jerusalem,

²³ *when peoples are met together,*   (3+3)
     kingdoms to worship Yahweh.

²⁴ *He has brought low my* ^a *strength part way through my course,*   (3+3)
     he has decreed a short life ^b *for me.*

²⁵ *My God, do not remove me halfway through my life—*   (4+3)
     your years continue generation after generation.

²⁶ *Once you laid earth's foundation*   (3+3)
     and the heavens were your handiwork.^a

²⁷ *They* ^a *may perish, but you will continue,*   (4+3)
     while they all wear out as clothes do.

     You can discard them like mere garments so that they disappear.   (3+4)

²⁸   *but you are the same,*^a *your years do not end.*

²⁹ *The sons of your servants will go on living here,*   (3+3)
     their posterity secure in your presence.^a

Notes/Comments

1.a. Heb תפלה "prayer" functions as a technical term for a complaint, whether individual or communal (K. Heinen, "Das Nomen *tᵉfillā* als Gattungsbezeichnung," *BZ* 17 [1973] 103–5; cf. H. -J. Kraus, *Psalmen*, 21).

1.b. See S. Mowinckel, "The Verb *śiᵃḥ* and the Nouns *śiᵃḥ, śiḥa,*" *ST* 15 (1961) 7. He seems to be correct in rejecting the common assumption of a developed meaning "complaint."

4.a. The reading קמו-כמו in the ms used by *BHS* is an individual quirk for the well-attested כמוקד "like embers."

5.a. Heb. לב "heart" is here used as the seat of morale (cf. H. W. Wolff, *Anthropology of the OT.* [Tr. M. Kohl; Philadelphia: Fortress Press, 1974] 45).

5.b. Heb. שכח is often related to a homonym "wither" found probably at 137:5 and evidently the counterpart of Ugar. *ṭkḥ;* cf. M. H. Pope, *JSS* 11 (1966) 240, with references to earlier literature; M. Dahood, *Psalms III*, 11–12. The proposal offers good parallelism with v 5a and it may be significant that שכח "forget" is nowhere else construed with מן. But what does מאכל mean? *The Revised Psalter* (1966) renders "I waste away because I cannot eat my bread," but the possibility of a negative causal construction is dubious. The syntactically possible "I am too wasted away (or "parched," Pope) to eat my food" is logically improbable. The parallelism of the line is more probably synthetic than synonymous. For lack of interest in food cf. Job 33:20–21. For the anomalous use of מן cf. the equally anomalous עוב מן in Jer 18:14.

6.a. It is often suggested that a verb has fallen out of the text and that the meter was originally 3+3, as predominantly in this psalm. It is difficult to envisage the two proposals listed in *BHS*, יגעתי or חלשתי, easily being dropped. Text-critically more feasible is the suggestion of G. R. Driver (*HTR* 29 [1936] 190), followed by NEB, that כי שכחתי, which seems to overload v 5, is not only a corruption of כחשתי "I am grown lean," as others suggested before him, but originally began v 6. But MT can stand; in v 5 the meter is 4+3 as elsewhere in the psalm, while in v 6 a 2+3 meter is a permissible variant of the 3+2 rhythm, which seems to recur in v 8.

6.b. The reason for the singular עצמי appears to be assonance. An -*î* sound runs poignantly through vv 6–12.

7.a. Heb. קאת and כוס are birds not yet identified with certainty. Plausibly G. R. Driver (*PEQ* [1955] 8, 20) has onomatopoeically equated the former with the small scops owl which cries "kiu-kiu" and the latter with the larger tawny owl whose cry is "cho-cho-cho." The point of the comparison appears to be loneliness rather than cries of distress or uncleanness (cf. Lev 11:17, 18; Deut 14:16, 17).

9.a. Dahood (*Psalms III*, 13, 14) links כל-היום with v 8b as an example of merismus: the psalmist suffers continually not only by night, as v 8a implies, but all day too. His suggestion has been followed by N. Airoldi (*Augustinianum* 10 [1970] 180) and by J. Krašovec, (*Der Merismus im Biblisch-Hebräischen und Nordwestsemitischen* [BibOr 33; Rome: Pontifical Biblical Institute, 1977] 155–56). In support of the present structuring may be cited the thematically similar 56:2, 6 (1, 5); Lam 3:14.

9.b. Heb. מהוללי is vocalized in MT as a Poʿal with loose use of a pronominal suffix, "those who are mad against me" (cf. GKC § 116i). LXX and S reflect מְהַלְלַי "those who (used to) praise me." It is perhaps best to point as a Poʿel מְהוֹלְלַי "those who make a fool of me" with *BHS.* M. Mansoor (*RevQ* 3 [1961] 263–64), noting that the Qumran *Hodayoth* associate הולל with falsehood, has urged a rendering here "those who deceive me."

11.a. Cf. Job 30:19, 22. The psalmist sees himself as the victim of Yahweh's stormy wrath. C. Westermann (*The Praise of God in the Psalms,* 64, 66) has drawn attention to the trilogy of "I—enemies—God" as subjects commonly found in a complaint description.

13.a. The adversative *waw* often marks a change of mood in a complaint, here in a confession of trust (Westermann, *Praise,* 70, 72).

13.b. Heb. זכר refers to the cultic invocation of Yahweh's name (B. S. Childs, *Memory and Tradition in Israel* [SBT 37; London: SCM Press, 1962] 71).

14.a. K. W. Neubauer (*Der Stamm CH N N im Sprachgebrauch des AT* [Berlin: Kirchlichen Hochschule dissertation, 1964] esp. 48, 98–99) has shown that the term לחננה refers to the favor expected from a master by his faithful servant and the duty which the master owes him within the master-servant relationship. Here the reference to עבדיך "your servants," v 15, is significant.

14.b. The repetition has aroused suspicion and one of the two terms for "time" is generally omitted as a gloss or textual variant (cf. *BHK, BHS*). D. Michel (*Tempora und Satzstellung in den Psalmen*, 123) interprets in non-repetitive fashion "for there is (still) time to show her compassion—yes, this time will come," but his rendering is not an obvious one. Probably the text can stand. The meter is 4+4, as v 16 could be, while the poetic style of the line is akin to v 11 in reverse.

15.a. Dahood (*Psalms III*, 17) appositely refers to Ezek 26:12. For אבן "stone" in relation to destruction cf. Mic 1:6; for עפר "dust" used of Jerusalem's debris cf. Neh 3:34; 4:4 (4:2, 10).

16.a. Structural parallelism with vv 19, 22 counters the proposal of H. Gunkel (*Die Psalmen*, 440) and J. Becker (*Gottesfurcht im AT*. [AnBib 25; Rome: Pontifical Biblical Institute, 1965] 27–28) to derive the verb from ראה "see" in accord with a ms variant ויראו (cf. *BHS*). A. Weiser (*Psalms*, 651, 654) interprets v 16 (and v 23) as a present event, but more naturally it is to be regarded as the expression of a future hope; cf. 138:4; Isa 62:2. Yahweh's glorious intervention on Zion's behalf would prompt universal reverence. That intervention is most naturally to be connected with the (re)building of Zion, v 17, where it is significant that כבוד "glory" recurs. For the pilgrimage of the nations to Zion which in the light of v 23 is implied in v 16 cf. F. Stolz, *Strukturen und Figuren im Kult von Jerusalem.* (BZAW 118; Berlin: A. Töpelmann, 1970) 94–95. He notes the centrality of the temple in the motif (Isa 2:2–4; Hag 2:7) and that its original setting was in the hymn of praise.

16.b. The mention of שם "name" expresses a major theme of this strophe (see *Form/Structure/Setting*). For the importance of the divine name in the individual complaint see J. W. Wevers, "A Study in the Form Criticism of Individual Complaint Psalms," *VT* 6 (1956) 80–96, and O. Grether, *Name und Wort Gottes im AT.* (BZAW 64; Giessen: A. Töpelmann, 1934). Apart from שם and the use of יהוה there is also a word play שם—שמים—שמע "name—heavens—hear" (cf. vv 20, 21), which interestingly also appears in 69:31–36 (with the addition of שם "there") in a Zion context. The same word play also occurs in Ps 103; both that and the combination of individual and communal references probably afforded the reason why Ps 102 was placed immediately before the group Pss 103–107. Other links are suggested by J. W. Rogerson and J. W. McKay (*Psalms 101–150*, 24).

17.a. The interpretation of כי, whether temporal or causal, and of the perfect state of בנה "build" and also of the following three perfect verbs is controversial. The translation takes כי as temporal, qualifying v 16, and the verbs as future perfect in sense (cf. GKC, § 106o) as in Isa 16:12; 1 Chr 17:11.

18.a. The variant תולעת "worm" in 11QpsᵃQpsᵃ is odd. Cf. *Midrash Tehillim* on 22:7: "Like the worm whose only resource is its mouth, so the children of Israel have no resource other than the prayer of their mouths." Seemingly a marginal exegetical comment of this nature displaced the similar looking תפלת. For this type of textual corruption cf. L. C. Allen, "Cuckoos in the Textual Nest at 2 Kings 20:13; Isa. 42:10; 49:24; Ps. 22:17; 2 Chr. 5:9," *JTS* 22 (1971) 143–50; "More Cuckoos in the Textual Nest: At 2 Kings 23:5; Jer. 17:3; Mic. 3:3 (LXX); 2 Chr. 20:25 (LXX)," *JTS* 24 (1973) 69–73.

19.a. That is, the divine intervention first mentioned in v 14 and subsequently developed. Vv 16, 19 appear to be parallel events within the twin passages of vv 16–18 and 19–21, eventually brought together in vv 22, 23.

19.b. Cf. P. Humbert, "Emploi et portée du verbe *bārā'* créer dans l'AT," *TZ* 3 (1947) 401–22; K. -H. Bernhardt, "ברא *bārā'* ," *TDOT* 2 (1977) 247. The soteriological usage evidently reflects that of Second Isaiah, e.g. Isa 43:7; 48:7.

20.a. The construction of conjunction and verb is interpreted as parallel to that in v 17.

20.b. *BHS* is probably correct in urging that the *athnach* be moved to יהוה; this yields a 4+3 meter.

24.a. Q כחי is to be read; cf. *BHS*.

24.b. Heb. אמר seems to be superfluous in v 25a. Job 10:2, which is sometimes compared, adds a qualifying addressee. LXX and S significantly take the verb with v 24, though they regard it as an imperative and attach אלי to it as אֵלַי "to me." Also they may well be correct in interpreting קצר as a noun (צֶר). A perfect verb אָמַר would secure a chiastic order, as in v 20; it was first proposed by J. Len ("Emendationen zu den Psalmen mit Helfe der Metrik," *TSK* 50 [1877] 509).

26.a. Appeal is made to cultic hymnic traditions concerning the divine creation of the world

(T. M. Ludwig, *JBL* 92 [1973] 345–57; cf. N. C. Habel "Yahweh, Maker of Heaven and Earth: A Study in Tradition Criticism," *JBL* 91 [1972] 321–37). Ludwig observes that the formula ארץ יסד "earth's foundation," is associated with Yahweh's kingship (24:1, 2, 7–10; 89:6–15 [5–14]; cf. Isa 40:21–23), while in 78:68, 69 it is linked with Zion in that the building of the temple is a repetition of creation. Accordingly the collocation of divine enthronement (v 13), the rebuilding of Zion and creation in this psalm is not accidental but represents an appeal to a composite tradition.

27.a. Weiser (*Psalms*, 655) relates to the enemies of v 9. Such a reference would be abrupt, though not impossibly so. But Isa 51:6 is so suggestively similar that its influence cannot be ignored.

28.a. Cf. especially Isa 48:12 in its context and the discussion of H. Ringgren, "הוא *hû*," *TDOT* 3 (1978) 344. For a criticism of N. Walker's claim in *ZAW* 74 (1962) 205 that הוא in the phrase אני הוא echoes the divine name see A. Schoors, *I am God Your Savior. A Form-Critical Study of the Main Genres in Isa, 40–55* (VT Sup 24; Leiden: E. J. Brill, 1973) 212.

29.a. 11QPsᵃ לדור and LXX εἰς τὸν αἰῶνα appear to be related exegetical and/or liturgical expansions (cf. 37:27, 29) which in both cases displaced לפניך.

Form/Structure/Setting

A bewildering multiplicity of interpretations have been offered for this complex psalm. Exegetical ambiguities have been exploited to the full and intertwined with a variety of views as to form and setting. Is the psalm an individual complaint? Is it cultic or non-cultic in origin? Does the psalmist speak as representative of the community and if so is he a king? Is the psalm a single unit? Has it been reinterpreted with supplementary material? Does the psalm assume the destruction of Zion (vv 15, 17)? What kind of divine intervention is envisaged in v 14?

All would be clear if the psalm consisted only of vv 2–12 and 24, 25a. They bear the stamp of an individual complaint, the prayer of a sick person, making an initial appeal to Yahweh, vv 2, 3, describing what is wrong, vv 4–12, 24, and offering a petition, v 25. But what of the psalm's two other parts, vv 13–23, 25b–29? They include obviously communal references, vv 14–23, 29, while the transition from v 23 to v 24 is remarkably abrupt. A counsel of despair to which some older commentators resorted in the light of this disparity was to find two separate psalms here. B. Duhm (*Psalmen*, 237–39) isolated vv 2–12, 24, 25a from vv 13–23, 25b. C. A. and E. G. Briggs (*Psalms*, vol. 2, 317, 318) envisaged two psalms, vv 2–12 and 13–23, 29, the rest being (typically) glosses. H. Schmidt *Die Psalmen*, 184) distinguished between vv 2–12, 24, 25 and a subsequent amplification, vv 13–23, 26–29. J. Becker has developed Schmidt's view more positively: (*Israel deutet seine Psalmen*, 43–45: vv 13–23, 25b–29 are additions made for the purpose of giving the psalm a collective sense. An old individual lament or part of one was made a vehicle of the prayer of the exiled people of God and of their hope of returning to Zion. Earlier S. Mowinckel (*Psalmen-studien*, vol. 1, 166) also regarded the psalm in its present form as a communal adaptation of an individual complaint.

J. H. Eaton (*Kingship*, 80–81) can offer an interpretation of the blend of individual and collective elements without recourse to re-use of the psalm: a leader of the community is speaking as its representative (similarly Mowinckel, *The Psalms in Israel's Worship*, vol. 1, 227). He laments in the style of an individual in vv 2–12, 24, 25, but reveals his representative colors plainly elsewhere. That the psalm was used in the penitential rites of the autumn festival Eaton deduces from references to God's kingship, v 13, creation, v 26, and the new era of salvation, vv 14, 16, 17. He leaves open whether the psalm was composed in the pre-exilic period and so whether the speaker was originally the king, but notes that similarities to the language of Second Isaiah may indicate merely common cultic vocabulary and need not entail a post-exilic date. Eaton insists that the psalm says nothing about the destruction of Jerusalem in 586 B.C.: he refers to A. Weiser's interpretation of vv 15 and 21 and compares a prayer for the repair of city and temple used in the Babylonian New Year festival. Dahood (*Psalms III*, 10) regards the speaker of the whole psalm as a king, but strangely does not relate this view to his exegesis of vv 15, 17 in terms of the rebuilding of the destroyed Jerusalem. A combination of the approaches of Becker and Eaton may be seen in the stance of C. Lindhagen (*The Servant Motif in the OT* [Uppsala: Lundequistka Bokhandeln, 1950] 167 note 3; 183 note 4) who, following H. Birkeland and A. Bentzen, interpreted the psalm in its present form as a "democratized" form of an originally royal psalm.

Weiser (*Psalms*, 652–55) interprets the entire psalm simply as an individual complaint; its cultic background is sufficient to explain the interweaving of individual and communal concerns. In accord with his distinctive approach to the Psalter, he understands vv 14–15 in terms of Yahweh's cultic revelation to the worshiping community. V 15 concerns their love for Zion and its holy ground; v 16 is given a present reference, while the perfect verb in v 17 is related to the past. So are those of vv 18, 20: v 18 is an assurance that Yahweh has heard the psalmist's own prayer (inexplicably the plural suffix is translated as if singular), while in v 20 his expected deliverance is associated with Yahweh's continual work of salvation, which in the future would be permanently commemorated as a sacred tradition (v 19). Weiser can see no reference to a destroyed Zion in vv 14, 15, 17 nor to exiles in Babylon at v 21.

K. Seybold (*Das Gebet des Kranken*, 138–41) follows Weiser to a large extent, but assesses the cultic situation differently. The sick psalmist associates himself with prisoners who could not take part in temple worship (v 21). He offers his prayer at the same time as temple services were being held (v 14). He intends to write down his prayer to be recited after his healing in the cultic context of communal praise (vv 19, 22). For H. -J. Kraus (*Psalmen*, 864–65) the psalm is a sick individual's complaint; its hymnic content, vv 13, 26–28, is nothing exceptional (cf. 77:12–21 [11–20]; 86:8–10) nor is its renewed description of lament in v 24. What is unusual is its "prophetic" promises, vv 14–23, 29. This unusual element is to be explained by its temporal setting in the period of exile. The experience of divine judgment ruled out reference to the normal hymnic themes of Yahweh's salvation of Israel. Instead, the psalmist derives his hope from prophetic promises of future salvation, perhaps those delivered by Second Isaiah or he may himself be functioning as a prophet.

From a form-critical standpoint C. Westermann (*Praise*, 66–75) finds no difficulty in explaining the entire psalm as an individual complaint. He interprets vv 13–23 as a confession of trust. The final passage he considers from two aspects: on the one hand he regards vv 26–29 as containing motifs designed to urge Yahweh to intervene; on the other, noting that the common vow of praise is missing from this complaint, he suggests that it has been replaced by "descriptive praise" in vv 25b–28 and adduces as parallels 10:16–18 and 12:6, while he suggests that v 29 may represent an assurance of being heard.

Overall there seems to be no compelling need to reject the organic unity of the psalm. The form of the individual complaint is elastic enough to contain elements of trust and praise. Kraus's post-587 B.C. setting, which represents in fact the judgment of the majority of commentators, provides sufficient warrant for the transition from praise to promise in vv 13–23 and 29. It is difficult to sustain the exegetical position of Weiser and others with regard to Zion (see *Notes/Comments*). Nor does a representative interpretation seem to be required. The terminological links with royal psalms given by Dahood (*Psalms III*, 10) are not compelling, and Eaton (*Kingship*, 80) admits that "there is little to identify a king." On balance, it appears better to take the references to individual suffering at their face value and to interpret the communal elements as Kraus does and also in terms of the traditional Israelite sense of communal solidarity. It is probable that vv 19 and 22 function as the counterpart to and adaptation of an individual vow of praise (cf. Seybold). The psalmist envisages a scene of worship in the restored, glorified Jerusalem. Whether the psalm is cultic in origin depends on its dating. D. Jones (*JTS* 14 [1963] 30) has assigned the psalm to the early post-exilic period. In support of this dating one might adduce the statement in v 13b, which seems to refer to the celebration of cultic worship and to imply that it was current when the psalm was composed.

Claims that the psalm employed earlier material are difficult to substantiate, as Weiser is (often rightly) never weary of stressing. But it is difficult to evade the impression that 79:11 is echoed in v 21 and Isa 51:6 in v 27 (and possibly Isa 48:12 in v 28a); if so, the implications for relative dating and exegesis are clear. The psalm appears also to have a certain relationship with Ps 69 (cf. v 3 with 69:18, v 17 with 69:36, v 18 [cf. v 21] with 69:33 and v 29 with 69:37). The significance of these parallels could not be clarified without a close study of Ps 69, but at least they seem to confirm the unity of vv 2–12 with vv 13–23 and, unless Ps 69 has made use of a supplemented Ps 102, of both with vv 25b–29.

As to structure, the psalm seems to fall into three strophes, of twelve, eleven and six lines respectively. Vv 4–12 are bound together by the repetition of ימי "my days," vv 4 and 12; by the resumption of כעשב ויבש, v 5a, in כעשב איבש, v 12b; and by the accumulation of similes; כ "like" occurs six times. The repeated motif of divine rejection in vv 3, 11 points to a larger unit vv 2–12 as the first strophe. The second consists of vv 13–23. It is dominated by the divine name: יהוה occurs six times (and יה once), and שם "name" at the middle and end (vv 16, 22) is balanced by זכר, its regular parallel term, at the beginning (v 13, cf., for example, 135:13). Another emphatic concern of the strophe is ציון, vv 14, 17, 22. Other terms which tie the strophe together by repetition are the stem עבד "serve," vv 15, 23; דור "generation," vv 13, 19; and עם, עמים "people(s)," vv 19, 23. Smaller portions are also evidenced by repetition: אתה "you" in vv 13, 14; the verb חנן "favor" in vv 14–15; כבוד "glory" in vv 16–17; תפלה "prayer" in vv 18a, 18b; while, as Dahood (*Psalms III*, 17) has observed, word plays occur in both vv 16–17 and 17–18.

In content vv 24–29 are a repetition of the earlier elements of complaint, praise and hope. Structurally they seem to comprise a final strophe. The swift transition within v 25 suggests that vv 24, 25a are to be taken closely with what follows. Internal bonds are the repetition of שנותיך "your years," vv 25, 28, and the echo of לפנים "before," v 26, in לפניך "before you," v 29. As might be expected, earlier motifs and wording are resumed. Vv 24, 25a take up those of vv 2–12: the double ימי of vv 4, 12 in vv 24, 25a; אל "not," v 3, in v 25; and ענה "he brought low," v 24, functions as a homonymous echo of עני "answer me," v 3. Likewise vv 25b–29 resume vv 13–23: עבדיך "your servants," vv 15, 29; a doubled אתה "you," vv 13, 14, 28; and שמים "heavens," vv 20, 26. For בדור דורים "generation after generation," v 25, cf. לדר ודר, v 13. Moreover, the double כ in v 27 is reminiscent of the first strophe. The psalm bears an abundance of evidence of skillful technical construction as a vehicle for its thought.

For the use of vv 25–27 in Heb 1:10–12 see F. F. Bruce, *The Epistle to the Hebrews* (NICNT; Grand Rapids: Eerdmans, 1964) 21–23. For the traditional Christian use of Ps 102 as one of the seven penitential psalms see N. H. Snaith, *The Seven Psalms*.

Explanation

A desperately sick man turns to Yahweh as his only hope. In vv 2–12, following the usual pattern of a complaint, he first invokes Yahweh and craves a hearing, yearning for the light of God's face in renewal and blessing (cf. Num 6:25). He backs his appeal with a poignant description of his plight, vividly saturated with negative similes. Fever wracks his body and has left him utterly demoralized. It has stolen his appetite and capacity for sleep, and now he is nothing but skin and bones. In a culture where ill health was regarded as divine punishment for sins, he has found himself ostracized and persecuted. Rivals have seized the opportunity to taunt him and cruelly misuse his name. But cruellest cut of all is the spiritual implication of his suffering. A strong sense of divine providence combined with monotheism compelled Israel to trace suffering directly back to Yahweh. The psalmist feels the victim of omnipotent violence. He leaves unexplained his reference to divine wrath, not linking it with personal wrongdoing but mentioning it virtually as an amoral force. But it has driven him to submissive rites of mourning—ashes are now as intimate a part of his life as formerly was his food—in the hope of averting the divine displeasure. Otherwise death is inevitable, for fast falls the eventide of his life's little day.

The psalmist's hope lies not merely in his own measures of ritual self-abasement. Hope is grounded in Yahweh himself. The assurance of God's permanence is the answer to his overwhelming sense of transience. So in praising trust he turns afresh to Yahweh, now as the eternal King, worshiped as such by countless generations of his people. But this kingship does more than impinge upon Israel's life at a cultic point: it is necessarily manifested in the time and space of their historical experience. Sight belies such faith, but faith can take the form of a hope centered in God's prophetic promises. The promises to whose fulfilment he lays claim are the logical corollary of Yahweh's kingship, which is only temporarily concealed from the world. He ventures to remind God of the ruined state of Jerusalem, to move him to compassion. He appeals to Yahweh's faithfulness, to his covenant relationship which still binds Yahweh to Israel and Zion ("favor," "servants"). Jerusalem is Yahweh's earthly agency. So its despicable state is a contradiction in terms and can by no means represent his last word. One day it would be the religious center of a world moved to reverence and would echo with that universal homage which alone can adequately reflect his worth as King of kings (cf. 86:9). Such adoration would be instigated by Yahweh's dynamic intervention to restore suffering people and ruined Zion, in response to their prayers.

Dominating vv 13–23 is the motif of the divine name. The psalmist rapturously explores its ramified associations, mainly in a triple word play. שם suggests שמים, Yahweh's seat of power and celestial sanctuary (v 20; cf. v 13 in the light of Isa 40:22; Pss 2:4; 103:19). Zion is the place where the name is proclaimed in praise (v 22) and also the earthly counterpart of the heavenly temple: thus the divine name involves the religious prominence of Zion, where universal homage must be paid to the King of the world. שם also suggests שמע, a positive hearing for (the psalmist as well as) fellow sufferers (v 21). That the psalmist is not completely altruistic in his mention of the name and meditation upon it is suggested by v 2; the psalm begins with invocation of the divine name and a request for a hearing (שמעה). The hearing of v 21 is a powerful echo of his own request to God. The central strophe enthusiastically celebrates the power of the divine name and so undergirds his trembling prayers with strong assurance. Since he is a member of the people of Zion (cf. "my God," v 25), he too can lay claim to an earthly manifestation of divine power, it is implied. His exultant faith rises above both personal and national circumstances and clings to the God of hope.

The underlying relevance of the second strophe to the psalmist's personal suffering is shown by his sudden return to it at the outset of the third. Just as Zion must be restored by God's power, so it is in God's power to restore him. The third strophe recapitulates the first and second. But while hitherto negative and positive themes have been accorded much the same amount of attention, there is now much greater emphasis upon the positive.

The psalmist still lives in a painful present. In renewed direct explanation and petition he sets side by side the mysterious twosidedness of God's power, demonstrable in present humiliation and potential deliverance, and also the poignant contrast of his own shortened "days" and Yahweh's unending years. Israel was able to face eventual death and Sheol with equanimity (cf. Gen 25:8), but they jibbed at premature death, eventide at noon (vv 12, 24). The psalmist craves a tiny share in the unending life of his God to whom he is linked by grace and faith. Reverting to the theme of Yahweh as King, he alludes to the third of a traditional triad of divine-royal motifs. He is not only enthroned forever over a realm which must be manifested in time and space with Zion as its capital: his kingship was established at creation (cf.

24:1, 2, 7–10; 93:1, 2), a fact which Zion itself was designed to mirror (78:68, 69). So the psalmist sets his hope upon Yahweh as King of creation. Returning to his earlier word play, he wonders at the heavens and earth as objects of God's creative power. Creator and creation are distinct: he is so much greater than they and must outlive them, as a man outlives his clothes! Unlike material things, Yahweh alone is immortal and immune from decay. Yet through the covenant he has linked himself with his chosen people and shares himself with them: because he lives, they may live also, safe in his caring presence. This assurance the psalmist hugs to his heart as an implicit hope that he in his suffering may personally find God's pledge of life fulfilled.

The psalm had a continuing role in the prayer life of members of the community. The heading indicates that it was put to general use as a set prayer for an individual sufferer. It became a vehicle to express his need and also, one is sure, to bring him comfort and renew his conviction of the positive implications of membership of the covenant people.

Theologically the psalm is resonant with themes which the NT takes up and transmutes. The contrasts of faith and sight, of present suffering and vindicating glory reappear. God's people are citizens of a heavenly Jerusalem where he is ever worshiped (Heb 12:22, 23; cf. Gal 4:26), and in hopeful trust they seek it through suffering (Heb 13:14). The Letter to the Hebrews uses the psalm (vv 26–28) explicitly at 1:10–12. A Christological understanding of the quotation was facilitated by use of the LXX in which God speaks directly from v 24 onwards, addressing one who is called κύριε "Lord" in v 26. The passage is regarded as a heritage to be claimed for Christ as the divine Creator (Heb 1:2). In similar vein the author at 13:8 can reassuringly hail Jesus as the eternal one who is "the same."

Traditionally in the Christian church Ps 102 has played an apparently quite different role as fifth in a chain of penitential psalms. But this understanding of the psalm not only pushes to the fore the psalmist's references to mourning and divine wrath, but is also intended to include a longing for the heavenly Jerusalem.

Grace That Forgives   (103:1–22)

Bibliography

Driver, G. R. "Studies in the Vocabulary of the OT 3." *JTS* 32 (1931) 361–66. **Jepsen, A.** "Gnade und Barmherzigkeit im AT," *KD* 7 (1961) 261–71. **McKeating, H.** "Divine Forgiveness in the Psalms." *SJT* 18 (1965) 69–83. **Parker, N. H.** "Psalm 103: God is Love. He will have Mercy and Abundantly Pardon." *CJT* 1 (1955) 191–96. **Sakenfeld, K. D.** *The Meaning of Hesed in the Hebrew Bible: A New Enquiry.* HSM 17. Missoula, MT: Scholars Press, 1978. **Scharbert, J.** "Formgeschichte und Exegese von Exod. 34:6f. und seiner Parallelen." *Bib* 38 (1957) 130–50. **Seybold, K.** *Das Gebet des Kranken im AT. Untersuchungen zur Bestimmung und Zuordnung der Krankheits- und Heilungspsalmen.* BWANT 5:19. Stuttgart: W. Kohlhammer Verlag, 1973.

Translation

¹ Davidic.

Bless Yahweh, I tell myself: ª	(3+3)
every part of me,ᵇ bless his transcendent name.	
² Bless Yahweh, I tell myself,	(3+3)
and do not forget any of his benefits.	
³ He is the one who has forgiven all your iniquity, ª	(3+3)
who has cured all your ailments, ᵇ	
⁴ the one who has redeemed your life from the Pit, ª	(3+3)
who has crowned you with loyal love and affection,	
⁵ the one who has filled your existence ª with good	(3+3)
so that your youth has come back, new ᵇ as an eagle's.	
⁶ Yahweh performs saving deeds, ª	(3+3)
winning justice ᵇ for all victims of oppression.	
⁷ He made his ways ª known to Moses,	(3+3)
to the Israelites his actions:	
⁸ "Yahweh is affectionate and dutiful, ª	(3+3)
patient and lavish in loyal love." ᵇ	
⁹ He does not perpetually rebuke	(3+3)
nor does he retain his anger ª forever.	
¹⁰ He has not treated us in proportion to our sins	(4+4)
nor has he dealt ª with us as our iniquities deserved.	
¹¹ But as high as heaven is above the earth,	(3+3)
has his loyal love towered ª over those who revere him.ᵇ	
¹² As far as east is from west	(3+3)
has he removed from us punishment for our rebel ways.	
¹³ As tender as a father's affection ª for his children	(3+3)
has been Yahweh's affection for those who revere him.	
¹⁴ For he knows our make-up,	(3+3)
he is mindful ª that we are dust. ᵇ	
¹⁵ Man is as shortlived as grass.	(3+3)
He blossoms as briefly as a wild flower ª	
¹⁶ which, when the wind passes over it, is gone,	(3+3)
known no more by its former place.	
¹⁷ But Yahweh's loyal love stays from age	(3+3+3?)
to age upon those who revere him, ª	
and his vindication is for children's children	
¹⁸ of those who keep his covenant ª	(2+3?)
and are mindful to perform his charges. ᵇ	
¹⁹ Yahweh has set his throne firmly in heaven	(4+3)
and his kingly power rules over all. ª	
²⁰ Bless Yahweh, you angels of his,	(3+3+3)
strong and mighty ones who perform his word,	
ready to obey his word. ª	
²¹ Bless Yahweh, all his forces,	(3+3)
you servants of his who perform his will.	

²² *Bless Yahweh, all his creatures,*   (3+3+3)
    in all places where he rules.
   Bless Yahweh, I tell myself.

Notes/Comments

1.a. Heb. נפש is literally "throat," perhaps as the organ of the voice, in which case קרבי in
v 1b may refer to the origin of the voice in the intestines and heart (T. Collins, "The Physiology
of Tears in the OT," *CBQ* 33 [1971] 37–38). But more probably a total emotional response is
elicited, from those parts of the body where the emotions were held to be seated. Cf. H. W.
Wolff, *Anthropology*, 15–25.

1.b. The fact that the plur. of קרב occurs only here has prompted some scholars, such as
H.-J. Kraus (*Psalmen*, 871; cf. *BHK, BHS*) to repoint as sing., קִרְבִּי. But post-biblical use of the
dual or plur. "intestines, entrails" (M. Jastrow, *Dictionary*, 1411) may serve to confirm MT.

3.a. Stylistically the כי- form of the suffix used here and in following verb and nouns in vv
3b–5 probably represents assonance with ברכי in vv 1, 2, which serves to bind together the
call to praise and its motivation. It appears to be an Aramaizing form (GKC, § 91e). Less likely
is M. Dahood's suggestion (*Psalms III*, 25) that it is a Canaanite archaism.

3.b. The obviously synonymous parallelism is striking: healing is a tangible result of divine
forgiveness (cf. 32:3–4; Mark 2:10–11): cf. H. McKeating, *SJT* 18 (1965) 69–74. For the direct
link between sin and sickness cf. 107:17 (and 1 Cor 11:30; Jas 5:15–16).

4.a. Heb. שחת "Pit" is a term for Sheol, as the parallelism in 16:10 makes clear. Cf. N. J.
Tromp, *Primitive Conceptions*, 69–71.

5.a. Heb. עדיך "your ornamentation" is dubious. LXX ἐπιθυμίαν "desire," which usually renders תאוה in the Psalter, most probably here represents simply a guess; it is not to be retranslated
as עֶדְיֵךְ (A. Weiser, *Psalms*, 656, cf. *BHS*). The standard emendation, עֹדֵכִי "your existence," is
a simple one and fits the context well both as to sense (cf. 104:33; 146:2) and form.

5.b. The imperfect implies consequence (GKC § 156d; D. Michel, *Tempora*, 128).

5.c. Heb. כנשר is hardly a reference to the phoenix, contra H. Gunkel (*Die Psalmen*, 445)
and Dahood (*Psalms III*, 27), but to the eagle as a symbol of vitality (cf. Isa 40:31).

6.a. Heb. צדקות is at Judg 5:11, 1 Sam 12:7, and Mic 6:5 a traditional term for the *Heilsgeschichte*,
Yahweh's vindicating, saving acts. Here the reference is not historical—the Exodus is not in
view as a prelude to v 7—but general, in the light of v 6b.

6.b. Heb. משפטים is literally "(favorable) verdicts"; cf. 36:6–7 (5–6), where the probably
plur. term occurs with חסד "loyal love" and צדקה "vindication" (cf. v 17).

7.a. Heb. דרכיו refers to Yahweh's "mode of action, moral administration" (B. Albrektson,
History and the Gods [ConB OT Series 1; Lund: C. W. K. Gleerup, 1967] 75–76 with reference
to BDB, 204a). The line functions as a preface to v 8 and obviously echoes Exod 33:13.

8.a. Heb. חנון "dutiful" is synonymously parallel to רב-חסד "lavish in loyal love" at the
end of the line and רחום "affectionate" has the notion of pardoning love which restores to
fellowship with God; cf. the parallelism of Isa 55:7 (K. W. Neubauer, *Der Stamm CH N N*, 127–
30). Similarly K. D. Sakenfeld (*The Meaning of Hesed*, 126, 227) has noted the psalmist's intention
to expound חסד in terms of forgiveness in vv 9–14.

8.b. For a study of this formula see J. Scharbert, *Bib* 38 (1957) 130–50; W. Beyerlin, *Origins
and History of the Oldest Sinaitic Traditions* (Tr. S. Rudman; Oxford: Basil Blackwell, 1961) 136–
38; R. C. Dentan, "The Literary Affinities of Exodus 34:6f," *VT* 13 (1963) 34–51; K. D. Sakenfeld,
The Meaning of Hesed, 112–22. Whether or not the formula is of cultic origin, here it appears
to function as a literary quotation of Exod 34:6. Not only does the echo of Exod 33:13 support
this conclusion, but there appear to be other allusions in the psalm to the Exodus passage.
Compare the three terms for sin in vv 10, 12 with Exod 34:7; v 3 with Exod 34:9; v 18 with
Exod 34:10–11; perhaps טוב "good" v 5, with Exod 33:19 (cf. Ps 86 which also appears to
echo Exodus rather than simply liturgical language). The psalmist meditates upon the formula
in the light of its present literary setting, which presupposes that a process of redaction had
already taken place (cf. B. S. Childs, *Exodus. A Commentary* [London: SCM Press, 1974] 608,
610, 613).

9.a. Heb. נטר was related by G. R. Driver (*JTS* 32 [1931] 361–63) to AKK. *nadāru* "be
angry," but he admitted the rarity of such a consonantal interchange (*d/ṭ*) in loanwords and

suggested that the verbs represented an independent development of one proto-Semitic root. The usual explanation is to assume an ellipse of אף "anger." Perhaps the English phrase, "keep on at someone," with a negative connotation, is relevant.

10.a. K. Seybold, "גמל *gāmal.*" *TDOT* 3 (1978) 29–33, has plausibly argued that גמל does not of itself refer to retribution.

11.a. The conjectural emendation גבה is frequently adopted in view of the repetition of verb in the same construction in vv 12, 13, but it is not necessary. MT is confirmed by 117:2 and by its stylistic echo in גברי at v 20. For the meaning cf. its use with reference to high flood waters in Gen 7:18–20, 24 and post-biblical Hithpaᶜel "rise, swell," of a river.

11.b. McKeating (*SJT* 18 [1965] 75) has emphasized the covenantal context of divine forgiveness in vv 11–13, 17, 18: "The sins are the sins of a believer . . . [whose] general desire is to please God, lapses from obedience by a man whose ultimate will is to maintain that covenant" (cf. Sakenfeld, *The Meaning of Hesed,* 126).

13.a. Heb. רחם refers to the natural love of a parent, here of a father as in Hos 2:6 (4); cf. A. Jepsen, *KD* 7 (1961) 261–71.

14.a. Heb. זכור has the form of a verbal adjective (GKC, § 50f). P. Joüon (*Grammaire* § 50e) suggested that it is an Aramaism, corresponding to Aram. דכיר.

14.b. Reference is made to Gen 2:7 (cf. 3:19).

15.a. Isa 40:6–8 appears to be the basis of the sentiments expressed in vv. 15–17. It is true that corresponding to חסד here is דבר "word," but the "word" is itself the loyal promise of God, as the contrast with human חסד in 40:6 makes clear.

17.a. Dahood (*Psalms III,* 29) has been followed in taking the verse as a tricolon, but the parallelism is suspiciously poor. A number of attempts have been made to reconstruct a shorter line by means of deleting elements, either על-יראיו (e.g. *BHK;* Weiser, *Psalms,* 656) or מעולם-עד-עולם (A. A. Anderson, *Psalms,* 716). A more complex solution is to abbreviate the time reference to עד-עולם and to transfer על-יראיו to the beginning of the short v 18 in the form of ליראיו and then to read ולשמרי (H. Schmidt, *Die Psalmen,* 186; H.-J. Kraus, *Psalmen,* 871; *BHS*).

18.a. The line is unusually short; see Note 17.a.

18.b. There appears to be an echo of Exod 20:6 (Deut 5:10) in vv 17–18 (Sakenfeld, *The Meaning of Hesed,* 227).

19.a. C. Westermann (*Praise,* 135–36) has observed that in Ps 103 the usual praise of God for both his grace and majesty is here developed onesidedly, but the theme of majesty does finally emerge at this point.

20.a. The presence of a tricolon and the value of the last colon have been doubted; it is often regarded as a gloss and its omission in S is noted as significant (cf. *BHS*). But why should the preceding colon require a gloss?

Form/Structure/Setting

The forms used in the various parts of the psalm are not difficult to recognize, but which one is determinative for the role of the entire psalm is an area of dispute. The psalm begins with an individual self-exhortation to praise which proceeds to give reasons for praise in a series of hymnic participles (vv 1–5). At v 6 the psalm develops into a communal hymn of praise, describing Yahweh's revelation of himself to Israel and using first plural pronominal suffixes at vv 10, 12, 14. Finally vv 19–22 represent an imperative hymn, a summons to all Yahweh's creatures and subjects to praise him as King and Lord. The psalm is rounded off by reiteration of its preliminary self-exhortation.

The psalm is most often summed up as an individual thanksgiving strongly marked by hymnic features. Its setting is then a cultic one, like Ps 22. Kraus (*Psalmen,* 871–72), Weiser (*Psalms,* 658) and Anderson (*Psalms,* 712) are representative of this conclusion. K. Seybold (*Das Gebet des Kranken,* 142–45) has sought to confirm this understanding of the psalm in a detailed study; vv 3–5 refer to sickness as the theme for thanksgiving. They relate to a single event variously described and do not look back also to earlier healings. He stresses that the evidently didactic aim of vv 6–18 and their appeal to wider, national experiences of salvation fit the pattern of an individual song of thanksgiving. Both the hymnic and didactic elements of the psalm correspond exactly to the situation of a service of thanksgiving, which not only provided an opportunity to give thanks but prompted praise and exhortation.

F. Crüsemann (*Studien zur Formgeschichte*, 298–304) regards the hymnic features of the psalm as decisive evidence that it is in fact an individual hymn. In this stance he follows Gunkel (*Die Psalmen*, 442). In particular the hymnic participles of vv 3–5 do not reflect a single event. The hymn is combined in didactic fashion with a meditation on Yahweh's grace, vv 9–18. The setting of the psalm is in a pious circle of "God-fearers," vv 11, 13, 17, where the old forms of hymnic proclamation lived on but were embued with a new spirit. J. Becker concurs in this type of non-cultic origin for the psalm (*Gottesfurcht im AT*, 149–150; *Israel deutet seine Psalmen*, 74–77). Its twenty-two verses are evidence of "alphabetizing," like Ps 33. It is an anthological composition, like Pss 33, 111, 119, which took over old cultic forms and put them to new use. Its has nomistic coloring: it is significant that פקודים "charges" recurs only in Pss 19, 111, 119; ברית "covenant," v 18, is a metonym for the Torah.

J. H. Eaton (*Psalms*, 246–47) has also regarded the psalm's hymnic form as the primary one, but he places it firmly in a cultic setting, the autumn festival. The personal references in vv 1–5, 22b he explains as a stylistic variation of the communal expressions in vv 10, 11: the congregation would naturally apply them to themselves, as they would the calls to praise in vv 20–22a. The participial construction does not suggest a specific individual experience. The "dynastic" heading to the psalm suggests a public setting.

These three basic positions are all possible reconstructions of the psalm's original purpose; they lay stress upon different formal and other aspects. In principle the communal and even universal references do not impede an origin at the thanksgiving service (cf. 22:23–29 [22–28] and note יראו at v 26 [25]) nor does the didactic element. A difficulty arises with regard to the balance of individual and collective features. Yet, as Crüsemann has observed, the self-exhortation of vv 1, 2, 22b does not only form a framework for the psalm but is developed and stressed in vv 3–5. Whether the participles are intended to refer to a single theme—recovery from sickness—is difficult to clarify. The suggestion of Kraus (*Psalmen*, 872) is worthy of consideration, that vv 6, 9, 10 reflect experiences in the psalmist's own life, personal oppression and accusation which led to a court case over certain misdemeanors. It is significant that the theological motif which dominates the psalm is Yahweh's חסד "loyal love," vv 4, 8, 11, 17, a motif which was celebrated at the cultic service of thanksgiving according to Jer 33:11. Was the psalm composed for use by a soloist singer in the thanksgiving liturgy, to stimulate every individual present to praise Yahweh, and accordingly so composed as to reflect a number of experiences of deliverance in vv 1–6? Both individual and collective elements may be explained in this way.

The "nomistic" features to which Becker has pointed do not all demand such an interpretation: e.g. Anderson (*Psalms*, 712) denies any "alphabetizing" intent. Remaining ones do not necessarily exclude a cultic situation, but may serve to push the dating of the psalm later into the post-exilic period. Already the presence of Aramaisms, including perhaps מלכות at v 20, and the evident reflection of Isa 40:6–8 in vv 15, 16 and possibly of Isa 57:16 in v 9 have led most commentators to exclude an early dating. The Davidic reference in the heading may indicate that the psalm became attached to a collection of earlier psalms.

Structurally the psalm falls into three strophes, the first and third of practically the same size (vv 1–5, 19–22), flanking the main central one (vv 6–18): these poetic divisions coincide with the form-critical ones. The whole poem is marked by inclusion: the self-exhortation of vv 1–2 is echoed in v 22b and the fourfold כל "all" in vv 1–5 recurs in vv 19–22. The throbbing assonance of the repeated כי- syllable in vv 1–5—eight times, including the emendation in v 5a—has already been noted. The first strophe obviously subdivides into two parts, vv 1–2 and 3–5. The final strophe has its own inclusion, the stem משל "rule" in vv 19, 22.

The main portion of the psalm has its own artistic marks of inclusion: עשה "doing" and צדקות "righteous acts," v 6, are balanced by צדקתו "his righteousness" at v 17 and לעשותם "to do them" at v 18, while לבני "to the sons," v 7, is repeated at v 17. It is strongly characterized by triadic groupings: חסד vv 8, 11, 17, along with the stem רחם, vv 8, 13a, 13b; על־דראיו vv 11, 13, 17; three terms for sin in vv 10, 12; the stem עשה, vv 6, 10, 18, which is matched by a corresponding threefold use in vv 20–22. These triads reveal the dominant themes. Another feature is the sevenfold occurrence of כ "like" in vv 10–15 along with a fourfold use of כי in vv 11, 14, 18.

The central section has been variously subdivided (e.g. *BHK* and *BHS* vv 6–14, 15–18; Dahood, *Psalms III*, 24; vv 6–10, 11–18; Weiser, *Psalms*, 658, vv 6–13, 14–18), but all these attempts are purely exegetical and receive no support from the stylistic evidence. Vv 9–10 belong together and so do vv 12–13, in view of their respective identical beginnings. The repetition of חסד may point to a division vv 6–8, 9–11, 12–18.

There are various interstrophic links. גמוליו "his benefits," v 2, is resumed by גמל "deal," v 10; עונכי "your iniquity," v 3, by עונותינו, v 10. כל throughout the first and third strophes is echoed once in the second, at v 6. In v 4 חסד ורחמים "loyal love and affection" anticipates the recurring terms of the central strophe, while the sound of גבר "towers," v 11, is echoed by גברי "mighty ones," v 20. The type of word play observed in Ps 102 recurs here throughout: שם "name," v 1, שמים "heavens," vv 11, 19, שמרי "keeping," v 18, לשמע "to hear," v 20. Accordingly the divine name יהוה also plays a dominant role, occurring no less then eleven times, twice in the first strophe, four times in the second and five in the third. In the third the final one echoes the instances in the first strophe, so that the remaining four balance the four in the second one. Much care has clearly been lavished upon this artistic composition.

Explanation

Ps 103 opens a group of psalms of praise, Pss 103–107. In this first one a cultic singer gives voice to the sentiments of the many gathered at the temple for a service of thanksgiving and thank offering in response to Yahweh's benefits to them as individuals. His self-exhortation is a message to each worshiper to lift up his own heart in earnest praise. Yahweh is worthy of a total response of grateful worship for the totality of his blessing. On the congregation's behalf the soloist enthusiastically counts their personal blessings. For some the crippling handicap of sin had earlier manifested itself in illness. Now, thank God, it had been removed by healing, which was the outward sign of his gracious forgiveness. He had proved their champion, rescuing them from Sheol's premature clutches. He had lavished upon the worshipers gifts fit for a king, blessings grounded in his loyal, pardoning love. He had enriched and revitalized their whole lives. Others were there at that time who had known oppression and harassment—until Yahweh had marvelously vindicated them.

Wonderful as these benefits were, by no means were they inconsistent with age-old divine revelation. They were a creed come true. Yahweh had ever been the answer to his people's needs. The content of his "transcendent name" (v 1) had once and for all been revealed in the propositional statement of Exod 34:6. Moses in response to his plea (Exod 33:13) had received as Israel's representative a definition of the divine name in terms of Yahweh's gracious attitude toward his covenant people. This loyal love, the focus of praise at every service of thanksgiving—what was it? The psalmist expounds its significance in the course of vv 9–18.

First, vv 9–11, it means that, judge of sins through Yahweh must be, yet his charitableness toward his own predominates and eventually bids him drop the charges he might have pressed (cf. Exod 34:9; Isa 54:7–8). By word play שֵׁם "name," v 1, suggests שָׁמַיִם "heavens." That loyal love which is an unfolding of the name could certainly be compared in its massive grandeur with the heavens above (cf. 36:6 [5]). Furthermore, vv 12–18, this divine חֶסֶד had aptly been defined in terms of pardoning love (v 8; cf. Exod 34:7a). It took the form of fatherly forgiveness. Moved by the children's woeful needs, it had banished beyond a far horizon the guilt of the sins which had caused those needs. It was the nature of the Father of the covenant people (Exod 4:22; Jer 31:20 [19]; Hos 11:1, 3, 4) to welcome back prodigal sons. Well did he know their feeble frame, and took it into considerate account. And so his loyal love could make up for inherent limitations. Like a wild flower, mortal man is soon gone with the wind. Generations come and generations go; but one factor which survives from age to age is this love which ever takes his people's side. It guarantees the survival of the people of the covenant, as from father to son the same constant relationship with God is handed on.

But take heed, warns the psalmist: this love is not to be wilfully abused. Its recipients must respond with respectful awe, vv 11, 13, 17. Yahweh lives up to his name (שֵׁם) on behalf of those who keep (שֹׁמְרֵי) the requirements of his covenant. The activity of God, v 6, must find an echo of obedient activity in their lives. His mindfulness, v 14, calls for a corresponding mindfulness from his people. חֶסֶד is essentially a two-way relationship of obligation.

Like Ps 22, another song of thanksgiving, this psalm opens out into ever-widening circles: the individual, the community of God's people, the world. The development is an attempt at total praise. How can Yahweh be praised enough? One way is to expand the area of praiseworthiness. Grace and majesty go together in Israel's hymns of praise. His very grace, which is so great, v 11, is a pointer to his universal greatness. Once more the divine name, which is the overall focus of the psalm, suggests שׁמים, this time in the sense of Yahweh's heavenly kingship. How can Yahweh be adequately praised? A further solution is to admit that his revelation is too much for the individual or even the congregation to respond to. The psalmist calls poetically upon the King's supernatural courtiers and executives of his purposes to join in the chorus of praise. In passing he takes an opportunity for exhortation by stressing *their* obedience. They actively comply with Yahweh's will (cf. v 18) and in the light of his name (שׁם) they are ready to obey (לשׁמע). Nothing less than the praises of angelic forces and of all the creatures of his vast realm can adequately reflect Yahweh's greatness. But will not the little voice of the individual bringer of thanks be lost in this universal chorale? By no means. "Ransomed, healed, restored, forgiven, who like thee his praise should sing?" (H. F. Lyte)

The NT both shares and develops the themes of this spiritually beautiful psalm, which itself takes the reader into the heart of OT theology. The Christian can echo its praise with even greater insight into the grace of God—and must likewise hedge his praise with moral commitment (cf. Eph 1:3–2:10; 4:1). In Christ a new dimension of life has been revealed, banishing fear of death's Pit and ensuring the survival not only of the covenant community but of every individual member. Bless the Lord, O my soul!

How Great Thou Art! (*104:1–35*)

Bibliography

Barucq, A. *L'expression de la louange divine et de la prière dans la Bible et en Égypte.* Bibliotheque d'Étude Tom. 33. Cairo: Institut Francais d'Archeologie Orientale, 1962. **Bernhardt, K.-H.** "Amenhophis IV and Psalm 104." *Mitteilungen des Instituts für Orientforschung* 15 (1969) 193–206. **Craigie, P. C.** "The Comparison of Hebrew Poetry: Psalm 104 in the Light of Egyptian and Ugaritic Poetry." *Semitics* 4 (1974) 10–21. **Driver, G. R.** "The Resurrection of Marine and Terrestrial Creatures." *JSS* 7 (1962) 12–22. **Eissfeldt, O.** "Gott und das Meer in der Bibel." *Studia orientalia Ioanni Pedersen.* Hauniae: Einar Munksgaard, 1953. **Fullerton, K.** "The Feeling for Form in Psalm 104." *JBL* 40 (1921) 43–56. **Grill, S.** "Textkritische Notizen: 1. Ps. 104:26." *BZ* 3 (1959) 102. **Habel, N. C.** *Yahweh Versus Baal: A Conflict of Religious Cultures.* New York: Bookman Associates, 1964. _____. "He Who Stretches Out the Heavens." *CBQ* 34 (1972) 417–30. **Humbert, P.** "La relation de Genèse 1 et du Psaume 104 avec la liturgie du Nouvel-An israélite." *RHPR* 15 (1935) 1–27. _____. "En marge du dictionnaire hébraïque." *ZAW* 62 (1949/50) 199–207. **Jeremias, J.** *Theophanie. Die Geschichte einer alttestamentlichen Gattung.* WMANT 10. 2. Ausgabe. Neukirchen-Vluyn: Neukirchener Verlag, 1965. **Köhler, L.** "פרא = equus Grevyi OUSTALET." *ZAW* 44 (1926) 55–62. **Kruse, H.** "Archetypus Psalmi 104 (103)." *VD* 29 (1951) 31–43. **Leonardi, G.** "Note su alcuni versetti del Salmo 104." *Bib* 49 (1968) 238–42. **Ludwig, T. M.** "The Traditions of the Establishing of the Earth in Deutero-Isaiah." *JBL* 92 (1973) 345–57. **Nagel,**

G. "À propos des rapports du Psaume 104 avec les textes égyptiens." *Festschrift A. Bertholet*, ed. W. Baumgartned *et al.* Tübingen: J. C. B. Mohr, 1950. **Rogerson, J. W.** "The OT View of Nature: Some Preliminary Questions." *OTS* 20 (1977) 67–84. **Sutcliffe, E. F.** "A Note on Psalm CIV 8." *VT* 2 (1952) 177–79. **Terrien, S.** "Creation, Cultus and Faith in the Psalter." *Theological Education* 2 (1966) 116–28. **Vawter, B.** "A Note on the Waters Beneath the Earth." *CBQ* 22 (1960) 71–73. **van der Voort, A.** "Genèse 1:1 à 2:4a et le Psaume 104." *RB* 58 (1951) 321–47. **Whybray, R. N.** *The Intellectual Tradition of the OT.* BZAW 135. Berlin: A. Töpelmann, 1974. **Williams, R. J.** "The Hymn to Aten." *DOTT* (1958) 142–50.

Translation

1 *Bless Yahweh, I tell myself.*[a]   (3+4)
  Yahweh, my God, you are so great.
  You are clothed with majesty and splendor,[b]   (3+3)
2   *clad* [a] *in a robe of light.*[b]
  You are the one who spread out [c] *the skies like a tent,*   (3+3)
3   *who laid on the water the beams of his high home,*
  who makes the clouds his chariot,   (3+3)
    who travels on the wings of the wind,
4 *who uses winds as his messengers,*   (3+3)
  flaming fires [a] *as his servants.*

5 *You are the one who founded* [a] *the earth on its bases*   (3+3)
    so that it cannot move for ever and ever.
6 *The deep covered* [a] *it like a robe,*   (3+3)
    water stood upon the mountains.
7 *At your shout it ran away*   (3+3)
    in anxious flight from your loud thunder.
8 *It went up mountain and down dale* [a]   (4+3)
    to the place you had established for it.
9 *You set a boundary it could not pass;*   (3+3)
    it could not cover the earth again.
10 *You are the one who releases springs into the wadis:*   (3+3)
    they flow between the mountains.
11 *The wild animals* [a] *all drink from them,*   (3+3)
    wild asses [b] *quench* [c] *their thirst.*
12 *Birds of the sky nest beside them,*   (3+3)
    singing among the foliage.
13 *You are the one who waters the mountains from his high home*   (3+4)
    so that the earth is filled with the fruit you make (?).

14 *You are the one who makes grass grow for the cattle*   (3+3)
    and crops for man to tend, [a]
  causing breadcorn to come from the earth   (3+4)
15   *and with wine gladdening man's heart,* [a]
  causing the face to glisten [b] *with oil*   (3+4)
    and with bread sustaining man's heart. [c]

16 Yahweh's trees receive plenty, (3+3)
    the cedars of Lebanon which he planted,
17 where birds nest, (3+3)
    storks whose homes are the firs.
18 The high mountains are for the wild goats, (3+3)
    the rocks are the conies' retreat.[a]
19 You are the one who made [a] the moon to show the seasons, (3+3)
    the sun which knows [b] when to set.
20 When you make darkness and night falls,[a] (3+3)
    through its hours all the forest animals prowl.
21 Lions roar for their prey, (3+3)
    asking God for their food.
22 At sunrise they move away (3+3)
    and lie down in their lairs.
23 Man goes out to his work, (3+3)
    to his labors till evening.

24 How many things there are which you have made, Yahweh! (3+3+3)
    You have made them all in wisdom.[a]
    The earth is filled with your creatures.
25 The sea over there is vast, stretching in all directions. (4+4+3)
    in it swim things innumerable,
    animate beings both small and large.
26 Boats [a] move there (3+4)
    (and) Leviathan [b] which you fashioned to play in it.[c]
27 In hope all of them look to you (3+3)
    to give their food as needed.
28 You give to them, they gather it up. (3+4)
    You open your hand, they receive good things in plenty.
29 You hide your face, they are overwhelmed. (3+3+3)
    You take away their breath,[a] they die
    and revert to their dust.
30 You send out your breath, creatures are made [a] (3+3)
    and you renew the surface of the ground.

31 May Yahweh's glory last for ever, (4+3)
    may Yahweh find joy in what he has made,
32 who looks at the earth and it quakes, (3+3)
    who touches the mountains and they smoke.[a]
33 I will sing to Yahweh all my life (3+3)
    and celebrate my God with music as long as I live.
34 May my reflections please him, (3+3)
    as I have rejoiced in Yahweh.
35 May sinners be destroyed from the earth (3+3)
    and wicked men exist no more.
    Bless Yahweh, I tell myself. (3)

Hallelujah

Notes/Comments

1.a. For the self-exhortation see 103:1a and *Comment.* Claims that both psalms were composed by the same author are unlikely. Certainly their common framework must have provided the reason for juxtaposition within the collection.

1.b. Heb. והדר הוד "majesty and splendor" have royal connotation: cf. 96:6; Job 40:10.

2.a. The participle עטה presents some difficulty in parallelism with לבשת. Vv 1b–2a appear to be a bicolon in view of their synonymous content, *contra* MT which paired vv 2a and 2b. The proposed emendation הֹעֶטָה, simply assuming haplography of ת, adopted by H. Gunkel (*Die Psalmen,* 454), H.-J. Kraus (*Psalmen,* 879) and F. Crüsemann (*Studien zur Formgeschichte,* 287, note 2), while not essential, would ease the problem.

2.b. Heb. אור "light" is not here regarded as a work of creation, as in Gen 1:3, but as an aura of Yahweh in his self-manifestation: cf. Hab 3:4 where it appears in a setting of theophany.

2.c. It is tempting to assume haplography and read הנוטה for נוטה with *BHK, BHS,* Kraus (*Psalmen,* 879), *et al.* MT's erroneous division may have facilitated an error. The phrase נטה שמים "spread out the skies" (cf. N. C. Habel, *CBQ* [1972] 417–30) refers to the cosmic tent prepared by Yahweh as his special place of self-revelation, from which he was to come in theophany to create the earth.

3.a. For the temple or palace built above the celestial waters cf. 29:10; Amos 9:6. The descriptions of theophany in v 3aβ–b are derived from Baal imagery and were doubtless used for polemical purposes originally (cf. Habel, *Yahweh Versus Baal,* 82; J. Jeremias, *Theophanie,* 70). Cf. 18:11 (10); 68:5 (4); Hab 3:8, 15. S. Terrien (*Theological Education* 2 [1966] 127, note 38) has compared such mythical allusions as this with allusions of medieval and Renaissance poets to the mythology of Greco-Roman antiquity, but notes their numinous rather that aesthetic associations for the OT poets.

4.a. The plur. predicate seems to require a plur. or multiple subject. M. Dahood (*Psalms III,* 35) takes אש להט as two coordinated nouns, "flame (and) fire." Heb. אש may have been regarded as collective (cf. GKC, § 145d). A common emendation (cf. *BHK, BHS*) is to read אש ולהט. 11QPsª (לוהטת) corrects the participle according to the normal gender of אש. Wind and fire feature in theophanic descriptions: cf. Ezek 1:4; Nah 1:3, 6. For Canaanite antecedents of fire in this role see F. M. Cross, *Canaanite Myth and Hebrew Epic,* 168, note 95. The quotation of v 4 in Heb 1:7 is basically from LXX and is understood in a disparaging sense by reversing predicate and object, an interpretation which is grammatically possible but contextually improbable. Cf. S. Kistemaker, *The Psalm Citations in the Epistle to the Hebrews* (Amsterdam: Van Soest, 1961) 23–24, 137–38; F. F. Bruce, *The Epistle to the Hebrews,* 17–18.

5.a. יָסַד is more probably to be pointed as a hymnic participle יֹסֵד with LXX ᴬᴸ, Tg and Hier (*BHK;* Kraus, *Psalmen,* 879; Dahood, *Psalms III,* 35; *et al.*). For ארץ יסד "found the earth" and its OT associations see T. M. Ludwig, *JBL* 92 (1973) 345–57. Cf. 24:2; Job 38:4–6.

6.a. A feminine suffix seems to be required, referring to the earth (cf. v 9b), and is reflected in α', θ', Hier, and Tg. The masculine suffix of MT, already supported by LXX, may be an adaptation of an original הָ regarded as an archaic הָ. V 9 further seems to suggest that the verbal form is not as in MT second masculine but third feminine with "the deep" as subject, כִּסָּתָה (Gunkel, *Die Psalmen,* 454; Kraus, *Psalmen,* 879; *et al.*) so that v 6a and 6b are synonymously parallel. In vv 6–9 is presented a version of the ancient Near Eastern myth of the *Chaoskampf* or divine war against chaos. In the OT it is generally reapplied to Yahweh's interventions in Israelite history such as the Exodus, but here it appears in what was probably its primary setting of creation, reflecting a Ugaritic model, for which cf. L. R. Fischer, "Creation at Ugarit and in the OT," *VT* 15 (1965) 313–24. But the hostility of the deep or the waters plays a minor role and serves to underline Yahweh's creative power (B. Vawter, *CBQ* 22 [1960] 72). Habel (*Yahweh Versus Baal,* 66) observes that there is no explicit description of a battle: the waters simply flee at his coming. In the light of v 3 the waters flee in reaction to the theophany of Yahweh (cf. v 32). Terrien (*Theological Education* 2 [1966] 122) maintains that here "the creative act begins not with a struggle aiming at defeating and constraining a preexistent chaos but as an architectural masterwork."

7.a. For גער in the sense of a war cry see A. Caquot, "גער *gāʿar,*" *TDOT* 3 (1978) 49–53; Jeremias, *Theophanie,* 33. A. A. Anderson (*Psalms,* 720) suggests that it corresponds to the less picturesque "and God said" of Gen 1:9.

8.a. Vv 7, 9 suggest that the primeval waters are the subject of both verbs and that הרים

and בקעות are accusatives of place after verbs of motion (cf. 107:26; GKC, § 118d-f. Cf. the discussion of E. F. Sutcliffe, *VT* 2 [1952] 177–79). However, his own explanation, favored by Kraus (*Psalmen*, 882) and Anderson (*Psalms*, 720), that in v. 8a the waters flow to mountain springs, ill accords with vv 8b, 9, which in the light of OT thinking generally (e.g. Gen 1:9) must be understood to refer to the ocean. His objection that the waters are already upon the mountains (v 6) is wooden. V 8 is to be understood in terms of disorganized movement helter-skelter, back and forth, as they leave the mountains (v 7).

10.a. The psalm moves abruptly from myth-based theophany to quiet praise of the order of nature, which is related to the *Listenwissenschaft* of ancient Near Eastern wisdom tradition (D. J. McCarthy, " 'Creation' Motifs in Ancient Hebrew Poetry," *CBQ* 29 [1967] 399).

11.a. Heb. חיתו occurs also in v 20 and Gen 1:24. The ending apparently emphasizes the construct state (GKC, § 90k, o; D. A. Robertson, *Linguistic Evidence*, 77).

11.b. Heb. פרא was interpreted as "zebra" by L. Köhler (*ZAW* 44 [1926] 59–62), but P. Humbert (*ZAW* 62 [1949/50] 202–6) impressively countered his arguments.

11.c. Heb. ישברו is literally "break." G. R. Driver (*JTS* 44 [1943] 19) referred to an Arabic parallel for "breaking" one's thirst.

13.a. For the background in Baal mythology see P. C. Craigie, *Semitics* 4 (1974) 17; *Deuteronomy* (Grand Rapids: Eerdmans, 1976) 337–38. Its use affirms that Yahweh is the true provider of rain.

13.b. A host of emendations have been suggested to secure obvious reference to rain (cf. *BHK*, *BHS*). Structurally retention of (ו)מעשי seems to be demanded (see *Form/Structure/Setting*). The use of the same verb in v 16 would support a reference to rain, but it is difficult to take פרי "fruit" figuratively in this context of natural phenomena. Perhaps it is to be taken literally and points forward to vv 14, 15 (A. F. Kirkpatrick, *Psalms*, 609), in which case v 13 does not exhibit synonymous parallelism. A further difficulty is caused by the second person suffix after a hymnic participle (cf. Crüsemann, *Studien zur Formgeschichte*, 287 note 2) but perhaps it can stand as a loose construction.

14.a. Heb. עבדת has been variously interpreted; its meaning in v 23 does not necessarily determine it here. Is האדם a subjective or objective genitive? The phrase may mean "for the service of man" i.e. for man to make use of or "for man to cultivate," which interestingly accords with Gen 2:5 where עשב and עבד occur together. Another suggestion is to repoint עֲבָדַת "servants," here "work animals" (A. B. Ehrlich, *Psalmen*, 249).

15.a. The grammatical construction of vv 14b–15 has been variously explained. The lines are best taken in a pattern of external parallelism with Yahweh as subject throughout. Circumstantial infinitives are twice continued with imperfects (cf. GKC § 114r); יין "wine" and לחם "bread" function as accusatives of means (G. Leonardi, *Bib* 49 [1968] 241–42). Man's לבב "heart" is the seat of his morale and vitality: see 102:4 and *Comment*.

15.b. The *hapax legomenon* צהל seems to be a variant of צהר "shine."

15.c. Grain, wine and oil feature as the three staple products of Palestine: cf. Deut 7:13.

18.a. For the comprehensive survey of subhuman animate creation in vv 17–18 cf. Job 38:39–39:30.

19.a. The perfect עָשָׂה is best repointed as a participle עֹשֶׂה (cf. v 5), especially in view of the direct address in v 20.

19.b. The context suggests a short relative clause, as in 95:5 "The sea belongs to him . . . , so does the dry land which his hands shaped" (cf. *JB*). Terrien (*Theological Education* 2 [1966] 122–23), finds intentional condemnation of Egyptian religion in "the reduction of the sun to the role of an obedient slave who knows exactly the moment when he must get off the stage."

20.a. For the construction see P. Joüon, *Grammaire* § 167a and note 4; the apodosis begins at v 20b, not at v 20αβ, which would be tautologous.

24.a. For the significance of חכמה here see R. N. Whybray, *Intellectual Tradition*, 78, 95–97.

26.a. An emendation to אמות "terrors, monsters" (Gunkel, *Die Psalmen*, 456; *et al.*) or תנינים "sea monsters" (e.g. A. Weiser, *Psalms*, 665), in the interests of parallelism, is upheld by S. Grill (*BZ* 3 [1959] 102). But it rightly receives no mention in the apparatus of *BHS*. MT strikingly accords with the Egyptian hymn to Aten (see *Form/Structure/Setting*).

26.b. Leviathan functions here not as the Canaanite chaos monster, not even as a captive prisoner, but simply in a demythologized capacity as a created being, a marine creature (O. Eissfeldt, "Gott und das Meer," 81), perhaps a whale. Such is the measure of the distance traveled from its primary mythological meaning. Cf. its use in Job 40:25–41:2 (41:1–10) to refer, probably, to a crocodile. Terrien (*Theological Education* 2 [1966] 122–23) finds here "ironical polemic against the dualism of the Semitic cultus."

26.c.   Heb. בו probably functions as a chiastic counterpart to שם "there" in v 26a. For animals "playing" cf. Job 40:20. Alternatively Weiser (*Psalms*, 665), Dahood (*Psalms III*, 45), *et al.* have explained as "for him [= Yahweh] to play with it": cf. Job 40:29 (41:5).

29.a.   For רוח "breath" in vv 29, 30 see H. W. Wolff, *Anthropology*, 33–34.

30.a.   G. R. Driver (*JSS* 7 [1962] 12–22) related the verb ברא to the homonym "be healthy" (cf. NEB "they recover"), rendered יגועון "they gasp (for breath), collapse" and restricted the reference to marine life. His claim that the Egyptian hymn contains no allusion to death is contradicted by lines 99–100 ("When thou hast risen, they live; when thou dost set, they die") with reference to mankind. The frequent OT association of ברא "create" with חדש "renew" (Isa 48:7; 65:17; Jer 31:22; Ps 51:12 [10]) is significant.

32.a.   Another theophanic motif is employed, concerning nature's reaction to the divine appearing, here evidently in terms of a volcanic eruption; cf. Jeremias, *Theophanie*, 21, 106, 161.

35.a.   This general summons to praise falls outside the poetic structure of the psalm. It functions either as a liturgical phrase or as a liturgical direction. In LXX it introduces Ps 105.

Form/Structure/Setting

Ps 104 takes the form of an individual hymn. Its individual nature is clear not only from the initial and final self-exhortation but also from the personal references in vv 33–34. A striking feature of this hymn is its combination of a hymnic participial style with direct address to Yahweh (cf. Crüsemann, *Studien zur Formgeschichte*, 286, 305). Apart from the cluster of participles in vv 2–5 (for repointing of MT at v 5 and elsewhere see *Notes/Comments*), they serve mainly to initiate themes, while direct address is used for their development, vv 7, 9, 13b, 20: significant exceptions to the latter usage occur at vv 1aβ–b and vv 24–34, where direct address has a prominent role.

The hymn moves into a positive wish at v 31 and a negative one at v 35, between which are set a vow of praise, v 33, and a votive formula, v 34. Elements belonging originally to the complaint are put to new use in the hymn as direct or indirect vehicles of praise. The psalm is generally assigned a role in the corporate worship of Israel: the self-exhortation to praise, as in Ps 103, and the setting out of its reasons were presumably intended to inspire communal praise. More specifically the fact that creation, a key theme of the psalm, was theologically associated in the OT, especially in the psalms, with Yahweh's kingship has directed many scholars to the autumn festival as the particular cultic setting (cf. Zech. 14:16). Humbert (*RHPR* 15 [1935] 22–27) attempted to link the psalm with motifs of the Babylonian New Year festival and even regarded 103:19–22 as the original beginning of the hymn. A. van der Voort (*RB* 58 [1951] 343–45) has argued against Humbert's position.

P. C. Craigie (*Semitics* 4 [1974] 19–21) has ventured to suggest a yet more specific setting, the dedication of Solomon's temple. He has appealed to the poem preserved in its fuller form in the LXX text of 1 Kgs 8:12, 13 (3 Kgdms 8:53). He has suggested first that the psalm, similar as its content is to Egyptian sun hymns and a Mesopotamian one, had an apologetic role of stressing Yahweh's transcendence, especially in respect of the sun (cf. 1 Kgs 8:12); and secondly that the psalm adapts Ugaritic material concerning the palace or temple of Baal in order to express the cosmic meaning of the temple built by Solomon (cf. 1 Kgs 8:13). Whether or not this hypothesis is acceptable, he urges that anyway "the psalm has to do with the relationship between God and his temple." It might be argued that Craigie with his stress upon material relating to the Baal myth has thrown out of proportion one element within the psalm. Yet, coming as it does very near the beginning of the psalm, it might be held to be intended to establish from the outset the temple setting of the psalm, and the *Comments* on 102:26 (*q.v.*) lend support to his general hypothesis.

Mention should be made of Crüsemann's setting of Ps 104 (*Studien zur Formgeschichte*, 301–2): in view of the mixed nature of its form of the hymn and the transformation of the plural summons of an imperatival hymn to a self-exhortation, he assigns the psalm to a late date and to the same non-cultic, corporate setting as Ps 103 where the formula of self-exhortation recurs. On the other hand, as to dating Kraus (*Psalmen*, 881) expresses the more cautious position of many in holding that the period of the psalm's origin cannot be determined and a pre-exilic date cannot be excluded. Note should be taken of D. A. Robertson's claim that the preterite use of the "imperfect" verbs in vv 6–8 may point to an early date for the psalm; moreover, the use of חיתו in vv 11, 20 he considers may have similar significance. But he observes that the use of זו as a relative pronoun in vv 8, 26 must be archaistic in view of אשר in vv 16, 17 (*Linguistic Evidence*, 42–43, 54, 63, 77). The presence of an apparent Aramaism, עפאים "foliage," v 12, may point to a late date, but of itself is slender evidence. Scholars of an earlier generation tended to urge that the psalm is post-exilic on the grounds of its dependence on Gen 1.

Thereby the whole issue of the literary Gattung of Ps 104 is raised. In general there is a parallel with the Egyptian *Onomastica* or cosmological lists (see G. von Rad, "Job 38 and Egyptian Wisdom," *The Problem of the Hexateuch and Other Essays*, 281–91). But in particular its relation to at least two literary parallels, Gen 1 and the Egyptian hymn of Amenhotep IV (Akhenaten, early fourteenth century B.C.) warrants consideration. This latter text, which may be found in translation in *ANET*, 370–71 and *DOTT*, 145–48, is a hymn to Aten the sun disc. It reflects an espousal of a type of monotheism which was novel and shortlived but whose ideas nevertheless were echoed in later Egyptian religious texts (cf. *DOTT*, 149). There are a number of parallels with Ps 104. Lines 70–73 speak of the Nile in the sky descending and making waves on the mountains to water the fields (cf. vv 10, 13 and perhaps 6). Lines 31–34 mention beasts satisfied with their pasture, trees, plants and birds which fly from their nests (cf. vv 11, 12, 14aα). Lines 11, 12 ("When thou dost set . . . , the earth is in darkness") and line 17 ("every lion has come forth from his den") are akin to vv 20–21. The rising of the sun in lines 21–24 is similar to v 21, and line 30 ("the whole land performs its labor") to v 23. Lines 52 ("How manifold is that which thou has made") and 54 ("Thou didst create the earth according to thy will, being alone") are close to v 24. Lines 37 and 39 couple "ships on the Nile" with "fish" which "leap in the river before thee": cf. vv 25, 26. Line 60 ("each man has his food") is comparable with v 27. Finally lines 99–100 ("when thou hast risen, they live; when thou dost set they die") are similar to vv 29–30.

In the light of these detailed parallels a correspondence of some kind between the hymn to Aten and Ps 104 cannot be denied. Crüsemann (*Studien zur Formgeschichte*, 287) has combined the stylistic variety of Ps 104 with apparent dependence upon the Egyptian hymn to produce a source theory. He notes that the important and specific similarities occur in vv 20–30, which employ direct address to Yahweh, and deduces that this stylistically distinct portion of the psalm has been influenced by an old Egyptian model. But the correspondences in the earlier part of the psalm can hardly be differentiated from the later ones in this way. G. Nagel ("À propos des rapports," 402) has underlined that the differences between the two texts are more important than the similarities, and direct influence upon Ps 104 must be ruled out. K.-H. Bernhardt (*Mitteilungen des Instituts für Orientforschung* 15 [1969] 205–6) has contrasted the evil associations of night in the Aten hymn with its positive value in the psalm, the role of the sun as subject of creation in the Egyptian text and object in the Hebrew one, and the differences caused by the Nile-centered setting and culture. A. Barucq (*L'expression de la louange divine*, 319) has stressed two other types of difference, the material in the Aten hymn which is missing, such as Aten's care for the embryos of the baby in the womb and of the chick in the egg, and the different order in which comparable material is found in the two texts.

Bernhardt has deduced from this mixture of similarity and dissimilarity a quite general relationship. The same motifs appear simply because of a similar literary Gattung characteristic of ancient Egypt and it is not necessary to posit specific knowledge of an Egyptian model, with or without Canaanite mediation. Craigie (*Semitics* 4 [1974] 13–15) adopts a comparable position, but posits a possibly broader background with which the psalm should be compared. Observing a general similarity between the psalm, the Aten hymn, other Egyptian sun hymns and a Mesopotamian hymn to Shamash, he suggests that this similarity is the result of certain common themes, principally of creation from a cosmological, rather than cosmogonic, aspect. The fact that the psalm is closest to the Aten hymn must take into account basic theological similarity: "Given a common subject matter, those traditions with more basic theological similarities have produced the most similar hymns."

A chronological and cultural bridge between the texts has been built by the widespread hypothesis that the Aten hymn was known to Israel via Canaanite, specifically Phoenician, translations and adaptations (cf. Kraus, *Psalmen*, 880; Dahood, *Psalms III*, 33), although Barucq, for one, finds this unnecessary and prefers to think in terms of direct use of a later Egyptian model (*L'expression de la louange divine*, 320–21; cf. H. Kruse, *VD* 29 [1951] 42–43). The links with the Ugaritic Baal myth at vv 1–7, 13, 16 and 26, carefully set out by Craigie (*Semitics* 4 [1974] 16–17), may serve to lend some weight to this hypothesis, although Craigie stresses that the parallels indicate a close association of ideas rather than a direct relationship. The combination of motifs reminiscent of both Egyptian and Ugaritic religious poetry within one and the same psalm may furnish a clue as to the means whereby a knowledge of Egyptian cosmological motifs became known to Israel.

But the literary association of the psalm is even more complex: its immersion in a distinctively Hebrew cosmology is revealed by its relationship to Gen 1. The links have been explored especially by Humbert (*RHPR* 15 [1935]

19–21) and van der Voort (*RB* 58 [1951] 321–47). The correspondences are striking. The sequence of material is largely the same: light, the concept of the heavenly waters, the draining of the waters from the earth, vegetation, the sun and moon as timekeepers, sea creatures and the provision of food. Moreover, the overlap of vocabulary is remarkable, especially למועדים (v 19 = Gen 1:14), חיתו (vv 11, 20 = Gen 1:24), עוף השמים (v 12 = Gen 1:26, 28, 30), עשב (v. 14 = Gen 1:11–12, 29–30) and מקום (v 8 = Gen 1:9). Yet there is a basic difference of style between the two Hebrew texts. Genesis 1 is logical and schematic in its approach, while the psalm is exuberant and free, and employs a rich, varied vocabulary. There is a difference of order: mention of animals and men appears at an earlier point in the psalm than in the scheme of Gen 1. Humbert followed Gunkel (*Die Psalmen,* 453) and others in his view that the psalmist directly used Gen 1 as his model (*RHPR* 15 [1935] 21). Van der Voort, on the other hand, points to these and other differences between the two texts, such as the anthropomorphisms of the psalm and its use of myth. He argues that they are best explained by assuming that not only does the Genesis narrative mark a later stage of theological development, but it reflects the use of Ps 104 (*RB* 58 [1951] 341–42, 346).

But is the issue so simple as to be explained by a direct relationship? Anderson (*Psalms,* 717) and others tread what is perhaps a wiser path in preferring to think in terms of a common cultic origin for both texts. Craigie similarly suggests that "the two texts may be relatively independent expressions of the same part of Israelite theology" (*Semitics* 4 [1974] 18). He emphasizes that the significance of links with Gen 1 and other Hebrew literature is that "external influences on the psalm have undergone thorough adaptation and have been brought into harmony with the general tenor of Hebrew religious thought" (ibid.).

A careful investigation into that thought, where the world of nature is concerned, has been broached by J. W. Rogerson (*OTS* 20 [1977] 67–84; cf. too G. J. Blidstein, "Nature in Psalms," *Judaism* 13 [1964] 29–36). He defines the religious interpretation of the natural world, such as Ps 104 offers, as by no means a statement of what was self-evident but "a courageous act of faith, persisted in when there was often much in personal experience and competing religions and outlooks that suggested that such a conviction was false" (*OTS* 20 [1977] 84).

Little specific work has been done on the structure of the psalm apart from that of K. Fullerton (*JBL* 40 [1921] 43–56), in whose era it was more permissible to rewrite and reorder the text in the interests of a novel theory. He thought mainly in terms of a five-line strophe. A similar division of the text into short, though generally irregular, portions tends to be made by commentators who make exegesis rather than stylistics their guide. This is the basis of division, too, in E. Beaucamp's discussion of the strophical structure of the psalm (*RSR* 56 [1968] 206–8). But there is no general agreement. For example *BHS* divides into vv 1–9, 10–12, 13–18, 19–23, 24–26, 27–32, 33–35, while Kraus (*Psalmen,* 879, 880) offers vv 1–4, 5–9, 10–12, 13–18, 19–24, 25–26, 27–30, 31–35. Most commonly a break is made at the end of v 9 (either after vv 1–9 or 1–4, 5–9) and v 18 (either after vv 10–18 or 10–12, 13–18). Then vv 19–23, 24–26, 27–30, 31–35 are divisions often preferred.

Dahood (*Psalms III*, 33), who rather unusually provides no analysis of the psalm's structure, does refer to the inclusion of the self-exhortation in vv 1, 35. Further echoes of the beginning at or near the end are אלהי "my God," parallel to יהוה, vv 1, 33, כבוד "glory" as a synonym of הוד והדר "majesty and splendor," vv 1, 31, theophanic language in vv 3, 4, 32, the repetition of (ל)עולם "forever," vv 5, 31, and a repeated double use of רוח "wind, spirit, breath," vv 3–4, 29–30. This multiple evidence of inclusion points the reader to the author's shrewd sense of structure and encourages him to investigate further.

The stem עשה "make" has an interesting distribution, at vv 4, 13, 19, 24 (twice), 31. Does the repetition of this key term reveal a concentric structure? Certainly vv 1–4 are well matched by vv. 31–35: in addition to parallels already noted, both passages stress the divine name יהוה (used twice and four times respectively). Is there a central strophe, vv 14–23? If so, the repetition of אדם "man" together with עבדה "work" in vv 14, 23 would yield a remarkable strophic inclusion. That a break comes after v 13 (instead of v 12, where it is generally found) is suggested by the presence of שמים "sky" and עליותיו "upper chambers" in vv 12, 13, echoing their juxtaposition in the line vv 2b–3a. That the hymnic participle does not herald a new beginning is indicated by the fact that in this case it merely repeats the verb of v 11. Then the strophic inclusion of ארץ "earth," vv 5, 13, together with a central instance at v 9, yields a strophic emphasis which is enhanced by a fourfold repetition of the related הרים "mountains," vv 6, 8, 10, 13. In confirmation of a middle strophe, vv 14–23, is the fact that the exclamation at v. 24 obviously begins a new thought. So does the wish of v 31 after the preceding descriptive material. In fact a strophe of vv 24–30 is marked by a stress upon Yahweh as creator and sustainer (=re-creator) and its direct address. Apart from a double use of the overall key term עשה at v 24, four terms relating to creation occur, at vv 24, 26 and 30. Significant too is the repetition of כלם "all of them" at vv 24, 27: Yahweh is the sole creator. In vv 31–35 notable intra-strophic repetitions are יהוה, four times, ארץ, vv 32, 35, and שמח "rejoice," vv 31, 34.

The distribution of עשה may now be seen to be most striking: at the end and beginning respectively of the two short strophes, vv 1–4 and 31–35, at the end and beginning of the two adjacent strophes, vv 5–13 and 24–30, and in the middle of the central strophe, vv 14–23. Thus the psalm emerges as a concentric composition, the first and last of its five strophes being half the size of the central one. In the body of the psalm the first and third strophes consist of approximately the same number of cola, eighteen and seventeen, while the central one has its major role underlined by greater length, twenty-two cola. This is the main framework of the psalm; each of the middle strophes subdivides into two smaller units, vv 5–9 + 10–13, vv 14–18 + 19–23 and vv 24–26 + 27–30. The common exegetical divisions are thus vindicated by and large, but their role within the overall structure has hitherto been missed.

Explanation

This psalm is a solo hymn of praise, doubtless offered in the course of temple worship. It comprises "reflections," v 32, upon Yahweh's mighty power and loving care, to which the poet sees the world around him bearing witness.

In the introductory strophe he exclaims in wonder at the greatness of the God he worships. He uses a description of divine theophany to convey a sense of the power of Yahweh, to whom the elemental forces of nature render homage as minions and adjuncts in his royal service. He paints a picture with colors borrowed from the palette of Canaanite lore, to the greater glory of the true God. It is a picture of Yahweh majestically manifesting himself from his celestial tent or palace. He appears royally clad in radiant light, traveling on cloud and wind, and attended by an impressive retinue. He comes down to create the earth and to impose upon it his benevolent order, and thus to extend from heaven to earth his achievement of dominion.

The first main strophe, vv 5–13, is concerned with the earth in relation to water, from both negative and positive aspects. The modern scientific view of the world is different from that of the ancient Near East, which thought in quaint (to us) terms of an oil-rig structure miraculously fixed in the subterranean ocean. Yet modern man, to whom this psalm is ultimately given, is also meant to share in the psalmist's awe and trust as his response to the God who from his own viewpoint has fixed the planet earth in its orbit and made it capable of supporting life. Such was Yahweh's power that, as it were, "he spoke and it was done" (33:9). His thunderous shout was sufficient to expel the primeval waters to their appointed station (cf. Gen 1:9). The Hebrews ever found a source of praise and assurance in *terra firma* and in the keeping at bay of the cruel sea so that the world was a safe place to live in.

The psalmist's concern in this strophe, as in each of the three main ones, is to portray Yahweh not only as creator but as sustainer of his world. Accordingly he proceeds to describe how water, the potential enemy of terrestrial life, has been harnessed to become its means of sustenance, serving God by serving his creatures. Springs, supplying water from the subterranean ocean and forming rivers, are supplemented by rain from his palace in the area of the celestial ocean (cf. v 3). Yahweh's providential care and control are thus made evident. He is by no means remote from the world he has created.

The second strophe in the body of the psalm, vv 14–23, stands at the center of the poet's masterpiece of praise. It is significant that it begins and ends with man at work, and concern with man occupies a third of the strophe. Here is creation's central focus. Yet man does not stand alone. He shares the world not only with domestic animals but also with wild beasts, for some of whom Yahweh has provided mountainous terrain unfit for human habitation to be their home. Man shares his world, too, with birds, whose God-given homes are the majestic trees. The psalmist is not indifferent to areas of the created world beyond man's immediate concern nor has he a selfish view of nature as being merely man's to exploit (cf. Job 38, 39). From his widened perspective he can lose a purely human fear of ferocious beasts and hear the lion's roar as a prayer (cf. Job 38:41; Joel 1:20). Animals prowling at night form a counterpart to man at work by day, all sharing in a divinely programmed cycle of activity. Human work belongs to a God-ordained pattern (cf. Gen 2:15; 3:23). Even the sun and moon are subordinate to this pattern, as Yahweh's clock and calendar for his animate creation (cf. Gen 1:14). The psalmist marvels at the order he can discern in the natural world—and at God's sustaining provision of food for man and beast.

He cannot resist exclaiming in wonder at the earth's prolific evidence of Yahweh's activity and planning skill behind it. He is the sole creator, and also the sole sustainer, vv 24, 27. The poet weaves into his praise even the sea, traditional object of dread to the Israelite landlubber. He sketches its vastness and teeming life, its population of foreign boats and marine giants. His fear of the latter is transmuted by his portrayal of them as frisky, puppylike beings, as much a product of Yahweh's creative work as anything else.

All creatures, great and small, depend upon Yahweh. The psalmist develops most fully in vv 27–30 the theme of divine sustenance. God is their father-figure and they are members of his extended family. They are at the mercy of his outstretched hand or averted face. The power of life and death is his: Yahweh's own breath is the secret of physical life (cf. Gen 2:7; 6:17). Whenever this life-force is withdrawn, the animate reverts to dust (cf. Gen 3:19). Each new generation is evidence of a renewal of Yahweh's creative activity, replenishing human and animal stock.

In his closing strophe the poet reverts to his initial motif of Yahweh's power. He expresses a hope that his glorious power will never cease to be revealed in the natural world. He prays that his creatures may continue to receive his smile of favor, as once he took delight in his creation (cf. Gen 1:31). How wary man should be: one look from Yahweh and the earth quakes, one touch and the mountains erupt! The psalmist is again using the material of theophany to portray Yahweh's awesome power (cf. 97:4–5). For himself he takes a vow of lifelong praise. He offers his meditations as a sacrifice acceptable, he trusts, to God (and also implicitly as an aid to congregational worship, which the appended Hallelujah in v 35 makes explicit). His final prayer is that man-made flaws in Yahweh's beautiful handiwork may be removed. Those who by flouting his moral order deliberately spoil the harmony of creation forfeit their God-given privilege of sharing in it. But the psalmist cannot end on such a somber note: direct praise is man's due response to so great a God.

The psalm speaks from within its own culture, but its basic view of the world as evoking awe, appreciation and fear transcends cultural barriers. Uncanny fear is recognized and overcome in principle via the concept of chaos put to flight. Awe and appreciation are set in a religious context: the world and its phenomena are regarded as windows through which divine activity of love and power may be glimpsed. One cannot accuse the psalmist of blindness. That he was aware of "nature red in tooth and claw" may be gleaned from v 21. He knew, too, of natural disasters such as earthquake (v 32), but it became grist for his mill, in this case for the mills of divine judgment (cf. v 35). He is deliberately selective in his citation of material and subordinates nature to his basic belief in an unchanging God. The world's stability is divine stability writ large (cf. divine/human joy, vv 15, 31, 34). He does not so much deduce theological truth from the world of nature as portray that world in a way consistent with his theology (cf. "my God," vv 1, 33). His philosophy is a response to God, just as a sacrifice is (v 34). Its expression in the psalm is an act of religious commitment. He is able to combine divine transcendence and separateness from the natural world with a strong sense of God's direct involvement in its processes. He produces a sketch rather than an analysis, but he does lay down guidelines to stimulate his fellow believers to devotion and doubtless to further enquiry. As such, it is a key part of the OT heritage which underlies Paul's statement in Rom 1:20 concerning the relation between God and the natural world, and also Peter's exhortation to his readers to "entrust their souls to a faithful creator" (1 Pet 4:19).

God's Faithfulness *(105:1–45)*

Bibliography

Brinktrine, J. "Zur Übersetzung von Ps. 105 (104):18: בַּרְזֶל בָּאָה נַפְשׁוֹ." *ZAW* 64 (1952) 251–58. **Ceresco, A. R.** "The Chiastic Word Pattern in Hebrew." *CBQ* 38 (1976) 303–11. ———. "The Function of Chiasmus in Hebrew Poetry." *CBQ* 40 (1978) 1–10. **Holm-Nielsen, S.** "The Exodus Traditions in Psalm 105." *ASTI* 11 (1978) 22–30. **Lauha, A.** *Die Geschichtsmotive in den alttestamentlichen Psalmen.* Annales academiae scientiarum, fennicae 16:1. Helsinki: Suomalainen Tiedeakatemia, 1945. **Loewenstamm, S. E.** "The Number of Plagues in Psalm 105." *Bib* 52 (1971) 34–38. **Margulis, B.** "The Plagues Tradition in Psalm 105." *Bib* 50 (1969) 491–96. **Thomas, D. W.** "Hebrew עֱנִי 'Captivity'." *JTS* 16 (1965) 444–45. **Wolverton, W. I.** "Sermons in the Psalms." *CJT* 10 (1964) 166–76.

Translation

[1] *Give thanks to Yahweh, proclaim his name,* [a]	(4+3)
make known his actions among the peoples.	
[2] *Sing to him songs, celebrate him with music,*	(3+3)
make all his wonders your theme.	
[3] *Praise with pride his sacred name.*	(3+3)
Let those who seek Yahweh rejoice in heart.	
[4] *Come to Yahweh and his might,* [a]	(3+3)
Seek his presence always.	
[5] *Remember* [a] *the wonders he has performed,*	(3+3)
his portents and the judgments from his mouth,	
[6] *you descendants of his servant* [a] *Abraham,*	(3+3)
his chosen [b] *sons of Jacob.*	
[7] *He is Yahweh our God:*	(3+3)
his judgments are pronounced throughout the world.	
[8] *He always remembers his covenant,* [a]	(3+3)
for a thousand generations his commanded word,	
[9] *the covenant he made with Abraham,* [a]	(3+3)
and the promise he swore to Isaac.	
[10] *He confirmed it to Jacob as a permanent ruling,*	(3+3)
to Israel [a] *as an everlasting covenant,*	
[11] *saying,* [a]	
"I will give you [b] *Canaan,* [c]	(4+3)
allocating it to you to possess."	

¹² *When they were few in number,* (3+3)
   a tiny group and temporary residents in it,
¹³ *moving from nation to nation,* (3+3)
   from one realm to another people,
¹⁴ *He did not let anyone oppress them,* (3+3)
   but he warned kings [a] *about them:*
¹⁵ *"Do not touch my anointed ones,* [a] (3+3)
   to my prophets [b] *do no harm."*
¹⁶ *Then he called for a famine to befall the country,* (3+3)
   he broke every bread stick. [a]
¹⁷ *But he had sent a man ahead of them,* (3+3)
   Joseph who was sold [a] *as a slave.*
¹⁸ *His feet were forced* [a] *into fetters,* (3+3)
   his neck was put in irons, [b]
¹⁹ *until his prediction came true* (3+3)
   and Yahweh's words proved him right. [a]
²⁰ *The king sent* [a] *and set him free,* (3+3)
   the ruler of peoples released him.
²¹ *He put him in charge of his palace,* (3+3)
   to rule all his possessions,
²² *free to instruct* [a] *his officials as he wished* [b] (3+2)
   and to teach his elders wisdom.
²³ *Then Israel came to Egypt,* (3+3)
   Jacob took up temporary residence in Ham's country. [a]

²⁴ *He made his people abundantly fruitful* (3+3)
   and too numerous for [a] *their foes.*
²⁵ *He turned their hearts to hate his people* (4+3)
   and to trick his servants. [a]
²⁶ *He sent his servant Moses* (3+3)
   and Aaron whom he had chosen. [a]
²⁷ *They announced among them his signs* [a] (3+3)
   and marvels [b] *in Ham's country.*
²⁸ *He sent darkness and made it dark,* (3+3)
   and they did not defy [a] *his commands.*
²⁹ *He turned their water blood red* (3+2)
   and caused their fish to die.
³⁰ *Their country teemed with frogs,* (3+2)
   even in the royal [a] *apartments.*
³¹ *He spoke the word, and there came flies* (3+3)
   and gnats [a] *throughout their territory.*
³² *He gave them hail for rain* (3+3)
   and flashes of lightning across their country.
³³ *He attacked their vines and figtrees* [a] (3+3)
   and broke down the trees in their territory.
³⁴ *He spoke the word, and there came swarming locusts,* (3+3)
   too many locusts to count. [a]
³⁵ *They devoured all the plants in their country,* (3+3)

they devoured [a] *the produce of their ground.*
³⁶ *He killed all the firstborn in their country,*   (3+3)
   all the firstfruits of their masculinity.

³⁷ *Then he brought them out* [a] *with silver and gold,*   (3+3)
   among his tribes there was no one who stumbled. [b]
³⁸ *Egypt was glad when they left* [a]   (3+3)
   because dread of them had fallen upon them.
³⁹ *He spread a cloud to cover them* [a]   (3+3)
   and fire by night to give them light.
⁴⁰ *They asked,* [a] *and there came quails*   (3+3)
   and with food from heaven [b] *he filled them.* [c]
⁴¹ *He opened up the rock and water gushed out;*   (3+3)
   it flowed as a river through arid places. [a]
⁴² *For he remembered his sacred word*   (3+3)
   spoken with [a] *his servant Abraham.*
⁴³ *He brought out his people with rejoicing,*   (3+3)
   his chosen ones singing. [a]
⁴⁴ *He gave them the lands* [a] *of the nations*   (4+3)
   and they enjoyed the fruit of the peoples' toil,
⁴⁵ *to the end that they might observe his rulings*   (3+3)
   and obey his laws. [a]

Hallelujah

Notes/Comments

1.a. Heb. קרא בשם here refers not to the invoking of Yahweh, as in a complaint, but to the proclamation of him by name, as in 116:13, 17: cf. A. R. Johnson, *The Cultic Prophet in Ancient Israel,* 54–55; H. A. Brongers, "Die Wendung *bešem jhwh* im AT, " *ZAW* 77 (1965) 12–13.

4.a. Heb. עזו "his might" may at an earlier stage in cultic usage of the phrase have been a reference to the ark (cf. 78:61), but here it seems simply to characterize Yahweh as powerful, an attribute well illustrated in this psalm.

5.a. For the cultic significance of remembering see B. S. Childs, *Memory and Tradition,* 51.

6.a. The singular is confirmed by v 42. 11QPsᵃ and LXX represent a plural עבדיו.

6.b. Two mss and also 11QPsᵃ read a singular בחירו, referring to Jacob, which has been adopted by H. Gunkel (*Die Psalmen,* 459), A. Weiser (*Psalms,* 671) and H.-J. Kraus (*Psalmen,* 890) to secure parallelism. Verse 43, set in a passage which deliberately repeats the wording of these verses, supports MT. For Israel's election, which is a theme of this psalm (vv 6, 43; cf. v 6) and its suggested patriarchial roots and association with the land see B. E. Shafer, "The Root *bḥr* and Pre-Exilic Concepts of Chosenness in the Bible," *ZAW* 89 (1977) 35–37, 42.

8.a. The historical narrative which follows in vv 12–41 with its focus on the acts of God is understood as his remembering the promissory covenant: cf. v 42 (F. Crüsemann, *Studien zur Formgeschichte,* 76).

9.a. For this covenant see R. E. Clements, *Abraham and David: Genesis 15 and Its Meaning for Israelite Tradition.* (SBT 2:5; London: SCM Press, 1967) 15–34.

10.a. S. Holm-Nielsen (*ASTI* 11 [1978] 23) interprets Jacob and Israel as the people rather than the patriarch, but note the change after v 23 to עמו "his people" for the rest of the psalm.

11.a. Heb. לאמר appears to be in anacrusis.

11.b. The singular form (plural in v 11b) is supported by 1 Chr 16:18, against 11QPsᵃ לכם. a clearly secondary reading. The oscillation in number (cf. v 6) is in line with the theme of the psalm, the people's receiving the patriarchal promises.

11.c. The psalmist's selectiveness appears in his limiting the content of the covenant to the promise of the land. The promise of descendants, another important element in Genesis, is only glanced at, in v 24. For the biblical concept of the land see W. D. Davies, *The Gospel and the Land. Early Christianity and Jewish Territorial Doctrine.* (Berkeley: University of California Press, 1974); W. Brueggemann, *The Land: Place as Gift, Promise and Challenge in Biblical Faith.* (Philadelphia: Fortress Press, 1977).

14.a. The main clause begins here (D. Michel, *Tempora,* 71).

14.b. The kings were Pharaoh (Gen 12:17) and Abimelech (Gen 20:3; 26:11). S. Holm-Nielsen (*ASTI* 11 [1978] 24) has suggested that the psalmist's freedom in using the verb עשק "oppress" may be explained by its associations with Israel's experience at the hands of foreign nations: cf. Isa 52:4; Jer 50:33.

15.a. Heb. משיחי "my anointed ones" is used in a secondary sense (cf. Isa 45:1); it carries the thought of inviolability (cf. 2 Sam 1:14, 15). The psalmist is transferring to the patriarchal period a term especially associated with the Davidic monarchy: cf. T. N. D. Mettinger, *King and Messiah,* 229.

15.b. Cf. Gen 20:7.

16.a. Does מטה לחם "staff of bread" refer concretely to a stick upon which ring-shaped loaves were hung or figuratively to bread as the staff of life?

17.a. S. Holm-Nielsen (*ASTI* 11 [1978] 24–25) has noted the applicability of the verb מכר "sell" to the exilic situation (cf. Isa 50:1; 52:3 [in the niph'al as here]), apart from echoing Gen 37:28, while the stress upon Joseph's sufferings in prison in v 18 he has compared with Isa 42:22, as intentionally evoking Israel's experience in exile.

18.a. D. Winton Thomas (*JTS* 16 [1965] 444–45) suggested a meaning "imprisoned" in accord with Arab. ʿaniya "became a captive" (also 107:10; Job 36:8), but the usage in Judg 16:5 seems to support the normal etymology.

18.b. Is ברזל subject or object? See the discussion of J. Brinktrine (*ZAW* 64 [1952] 251–58), who renders "iron [= a sword] pierced his soul [till . . .]." But more naturally the cola of the line are synonymously parallel and reference is made to an iron collar. For נפש with the sense of "neck" cf. H. W. Wolff, *Anthropology,* 14. A reading בברזל (Gunkel *Die Psalmen,* 460; Kraus, *Psalmen,* 890) is not necessary: cf. 100:4, etc. for an accusative after בוא (Thomas, *JTS* 16 [1965] 444–45). M. Dahood (*Psalms III,* 57) has aptly compared Jer 27:12 for the sense.

19.a. The second colon could be a main clause (". . . tested him, put him on his mettle"), but "the surrounding lines point to a direct parallelism" (Holm-Nielsen, *ASTI* 11 [1978] 29 note 12). The explicit יהוה differentiates from the suffix ו (דבר) in v 19a and indicates that it refers to Joseph. The reference in v 19a is to Joseph's prophetic dreams (Gen 37:5–11) and/ or his interpretations of his fellow prisoners' dreams (Gen 40:5–23); v 19b refers to Joseph's interpretations of Pharaoh's dreams (Gen 41:1–32, esp. 25, 28).

20.a. Is Yahweh the subject of שלח "send" and מלך "king" the object (Kraus, *Psalmen,* 890; Dahood, *Psalms III,* 58)? The suggestion is attractive in view of v 17 (cf. vv 26, 28) and the overall stress on divine providence, but Gen 41:14 points otherwise, and the king is clearly the subject of v 21.

22.a. LXX, S, Hier seem to imply ליסר "to instruct"; MT לאסר normally means "to bind." Dahood (*Psalms III,* 58) interestingly points לְאַסֵּר an aph'el infinitive construct, which labors under the difficulty that the hiph'il of יסר occurs only in Hos 7:12, where the pointing has been doubted. G. R. Driver (*JTS* 44 [1943] 20) harmonized MT with the versions in a plausible manner by interpreting as לְאַסֵּר, a byform of יסר; he compared Syr. ʾsr/ysr "bind."

22.b. Ezek 16:27 supports MT. Two Heb. mss. read and the Versions may imply וכנפש, adopted by *BHK* and Kraus, (*Psalmen,* 890).

23.a. For this designation of Egypt cf. 78:51; 106:22; Gen 10:6.

24.a. Dahood (*Psalms III,* 59) is probably correct in interpreting the preposition thus with Gunkel and Ehrlich. The meaning "be numerous" seems to be determined by Exod 1:7, 20.

25.a. The second colon presumably refers to Exod 1:10.

26.a. The "choice" of Aaron is an instance of the psalmist's poetic freedom.

27.a. The colon is a textual crux. MT שמו takes Moses and Aaron as subject, while LXX S imply שם with Yahweh as subject, which suits the contextual stress on his providential actions. Commentators usually follow LXX S, but cf. perhaps v 18 (after v 17). For דברי אתותיו A. F. Kirkpatrick (*Psalms,* 621) compared 145:5, but the text is not certain there. The omission of דברי in S most probably reflects the translator's difficulty. Perhaps the sense is "set among them the words" i.e. "announced": cf. Exod 19:7. *NEB* ("They were his mouthpiece to announce," reading a singular verb) plausibly sees a reference to Exod 4:15. For בם דברי E. J. Kissane

(*Psalms II*, 162) and Kraus (*Psalmen*, 890) read במצרים, a good parallel to v 27b but palaeographically not convincing. Closer to MT is the emendation במדבר "in the wilderness" (M. Scott, *Textual Discoveries in Proverbs, Psalms and Isaiah* [London: SPCK, 1927] 152, with reference to Exod 4:8; cf. Dahood, *Psalms III*, 59).

27.b. The reading מפתיו "his marvels" (cf. *BHS*) is hardly necessary: the force of the pronominal suffix earlier (אתותיו) easily carries over (Dahood, *Psalms III*, 60). The verse echoes a traditional formula, for which see Childs, "Deuteronomic Formulae of the Exodus Tradition," in *Hebräische Wortforschung* (VTSup 16; Leiden: E. J. Brill, 1967) 30–39.

28.a. LXX and *S* omit the negative, seeing a reference to Pharaoh's hardness of heart. Implausibly H. Schmidt (*Die Psalmen*, 191, following E. König) reached the same end by taking v 28b as a question. Heb. מרו is often viewed as a corruption of שמרו "they did (not) keep" (Gunkel, *Die Psalmen*, 461, following F. Hitzig; Kraus, *Psalmen*, 890; *et al.*), but Holm-Nielsen (*ASTI* 12 [1978] 30 note 18) pertinently asks why the Egyptians should be expected to keep Yahweh's words. Kirkpatrick (*Psalms*, 621) may be right in seeing a reference to Exod 11:2–3. Worth consideration is his suggestion that this plague appears first because it resulted in the submission of the Egyptians to the fact of Yahweh's power. In view of the general closeness of the passage to the Exodus plague sequence and the poetic freedom with which the psalmist has evidently treated the Genesis material it is hardly justified to invoke here a separate tradition with J. W. Rogerson and J. W. McKay (*Psalms 101–150*, 39). As to the absence of the fifth and sixth plagues, B. Margulis (*Bib* 50 [1969] 493–96) has attempted to restore the fifth via evidence of a longer text in 11QPs^a than in MT. He has also explained the omission of the sixth as an exegetical device to harmonize with the apparent destruction of its victims already in the fifth plague (Exod 9:6), finding it significant that vv 32–33 restrict the effect of the hail to trees and plants and exclude animals (cf. Exod 9:25). S. E. Loewenstamm (*Bib* 52 [1971] 34–38) has plausibly objected that Margulis's restoration of the fifth plague of Exodus would insert it between the first and second, unlike the traditions of both Exodus and Ps 78.

30.a. The plural מלכיהם in BMS is best explained as a double plural in a genitival phrase (cf. GKC § 124q), although Dahood's suggestion of a plural of majesty (*Psalms III*, 61) is also a possibility.

31.a. The identification of the insects is uncertain: cf. Childs, *Exodus*, 129.

33.a. Holm-Nielsen (*ASTI* 12 [1978] 30 note 16) interprets the free reference as a "Palestinization" of the tradition.

34.a. In v 34a ארבה is apparently derived from the root רבה "be many" and refers to the gregarious habit of the insect. In v 34b probably ילק (not used in Exod 10:1–21, but necessary here for poetic parallelism) properly refers to the first larval form of the young locust as a wingless, jumping insect (P. Haupt, "The Book of Nahum," *JBL* 26 [1907] 34).

35.a. The proposal to read ויכל for ויאכל (cf. *BHK*, *BHS*) or for the verb in v 35a (G. R. Driver, *JTS* 44 [1943] 20) is unnecessary (cf. Kraus, *Psalmen*, 890). The stylistic structure of vv 33–36 supports MT (see *Form/Structure/Setting*).

37.a. For the formula here echoed see Childs, "Deuteronomic Formulae," 30–39.

37.b. Exodus says nothing about stumbling, but Isa 63:13 provides a parallel.

38.a. Or "at, over their leaving" (W. Gross, "Die Herausführungsformel—zum Verhältnis von Formel und Syntax," *ZAW* 86 [1974] 438 note 73).

39.a. The conception of the cloud as a protection differs from its representation as a guide in Exod 13:21; Ps 78:14, but it does accord with Exod 14:19, 20.

40.a. MT שאל "he asked" is simply explained as due to haplography and mechanical harmonization to adjacent singular verbs. The Versions preserve a plural (שאלו).

40.b. Heb. לחם שמים is a paraphrase of Exod 16:4. Contrast the looser paraphrase of 78:25. The psalmist is deliberately selective in that no reference is made to the people's complaining.

40.c. D. A. Robertson (*Linguistic Evidence*, 47, 51) regards the isolated preterite as an archaism.

41.a. Holm-Nielsen (*ASTI* 11 [1978] 26) has related the heightened description to Isa 41:18, set in a divine promise concerning a second Exodus, the return from exile.

42.a. Heb. את is the preposition, echoing v 9 (Dahood, *Psalms III*, 62), rather than the object sign: cf. דבר את "spoke with," Gen 17:3, 22, 23; 21:2 (P).

44.a. The plural—contrast the singular in v 11—suggests a post-exilic provenance for the psalm: cf. Ezra 3:3; 9:1–2 (cf. Exod 15:15); Neh 10:29, 31–32 (28, 30–31).

45.a. For the didactic note cf. 78:7; 95:7b.

45.b. See the comment on 104:35.

Form/Structure/Setting

In form Ps 105 is an expanded hymn of the imperatival type (C. Westermann, 122–24, 140; F. Crüsemann, *Studien zur Formgeschichte*, 76). It begins
with a summons to praise, vv 1–6, naming its addressees in v 6, and continues
with the ground for praise, vv 7–11. The long historical section, vv 12–44,
represents an expansion of vv 7–11, as the resumptive v 42 makes clear.
The psalm concludes with an implicit exhortation, v 45.

The literary Gattung of the psalm is that of Ps 78 and 106: a selective
review of Israel's history, here with the accent on Yahweh's work on his
people's behalf and his faithfulness to his ancient promise. The psalm was
placed next to the creation-oriented Ps 104 in the collection doubtless because
the themes of Yahweh's lordship of creation and history are frequently juxtaposed within psalms.

As to the original setting of the psalm, S. Mowinckel ("Psalms and Wisdom,"
in *Wisdom in Israel and the Ancient Near East*, ed. M. Noth and D. W. Thomas
[VTSup 3; Leiden: E. J. Brill, 1955] 213–14) regarded these historical psalms
as noncultic: Ps 105 is a product of learned psalmography and merely adopts
the style of a hymn. R. E. Murphy ("A Consideration of the Classification
'Wisdom Psalms,'" in *Congress Volume Bonn 1962* [VTSup 9; Leiden: E. J.
Brill, 1963] 164) has rightly countered this conclusion as too extreme: a
didactic purpose does not turn the historical psalms into wisdom psalms.
W. I. Wolverton (*CJT* 10 [1964] 166–76) assigned the psalm to a cultic setting
of rejoicing: it is an adaptation of what was originally a sermon, vv 1–6 being
a hymnic replacement of earlier appeals. F. Baumgärtel (*ZAW* 65 [1953] 263–
65), followed by Weiser (*Psalms*, 674), has traced the original setting to a
covenant renewal ceremony, finding a parallel with the covenant renewal
liturgy of the Qumran sect described in the Community Rule, 1QS 1:16–
2:1. The psalm would then accord with the priests and Levites praising "the
God of salvation and all his faithfulness" (1QS 1:19). The link is a slender
one, and the reconstruction of setting depends very much on connecting
the psalm closely with Ps 106.

A pointer toward cultic use is afforded by the citation of vv 1–15 in 1
Chr 16 (vv 8–22) in association with David's installation of the ark in Jerusalem.
D. Kidner (*Psalms 73–150*, 347 note 1) pertinently observes that 1 Chr 16:7
leaves the exact relation of the psalm(s) to the narrative undefined. It is
not likely that the psalm goes back to the Davidic period. Nor is it necessarily
to be concluded from its citation that it is pre-exilic, *pace* Dahood (*Psalms
III*, 51). Rather, the Chronicler was evidently supplying from cultic material
used in his own day words suitable for the occasion, linking it with the promise
of the land given to the patriarchs. The use of the psalm probably points
to a cultic origin, though it could theoretically have been re-used in a cultic
setting.

Upon what historical traditions does the psalm rely? The question has
been investigated fully by A. Lauha (*Die Geschichtsmotive*, 39–50). He has concluded that in the patriarchal material the psalm is little different from Genesis
in its completed redactional form. The psalmist by his use of the plural in
vv 14–15 betrays an awareness of repeated references to the endangering

of patriarchal lives. But his treatment was a free one. The oath of v 9 harks back loosely to Gen 26:3, though it was not sworn to Isaac himself. The promise of v 11 is not found in this exact wording: it is the psalmist's own free reformulation. The references to "anointed ones" and "prophets" in v 15 are heightened descriptions of the patriarchs' relation to Yahweh. The rigors of Joseph's imprisonment in v 18 seem to be due to poetic license. But overall it appears that the psalmist used the source material combined in its present form in Genesis and that he did not have at his disposal separate traditions. Likewise, in the plagues material Lauha finds the composite form of Exodus behind the psalm in its representation of Yahweh, Moses and Aaron as executors of the plagues and in its enumeration of the plagues. Despite the omission of the fifth and sixth, the inversion of the third and fourth and the priority given to the ninth, the account is so similar that it can reflect only a free handling of the source material arranged as in the book of Exodus. B. Margulis (*Bib* 50 [1969] 492) and Holm-Nielsen (*ASTI* 11 [1978] 25) have concurred in this judgment. On the other hand S. E. Loewenstamm (*Bib* 52 [1971] 38) has concluded that the plagues account represents a tradition prior to the Pentateuch, whether the psalm itself is later or earlier. He finds it significant that both Pss 78 and 105 have a total of seven (different) plagues, seven being a traditional number of completeness. He achieves this total for Ps 105—instead of eight—by taking v 31 to refer to one plague. But the fact that some plagues are covered in one line and others in two makes it feasible to conclude that two plagues may be included in a single line. Moreover, he appears to underestimate the much greater closeness of Ps 105 to the Exodus narratives and to overlook the significance of the use of the Genesis material. Kraus (*Psalmen*, 892) is surely right to follow Gunkel (*Die Psalmen*, 458) in concluding that a knowledge of the Pentateuch in its canonical final form must be presupposed; accordingly a post-exilic date is implied (cf. the note on v 44). Kraus allows too for the use of separate traditions, but whether it is necessary to invoke these is doubtful. The work of Holm-Nielsen has done much to clarify apparent deviations.

As to structure, commentators have been content to let form and subject matter dictate their outlines. That of Kraus is typical: vv 1–6, 7–11, 12–15, 16–23, 24–38, 39–41, 42–45. Dahood has pointed to the device of inclusion in the double reference to Abraham and the covenant "with" him, vv 9, 42; he also notes the stylistic use of chiasmus at vv 15, 22, 43–45 (*Psalms III*, 51, 62). A. R. Ceresco (*CBQ* 38 [1976] 305) has seen a more complex chiastic word pattern in vv 2–5, נפלאותיו : בקשו : יהוה :: יהוה : מבקשי : נפלאותיו (repeating "his wonders," "seek" and "Yahweh"; in *CBQ* 40 [1978] 2 Ceresco widens the extent of the chiasmus unconvincingly). Similar patterns emerge at vv 5–8, זכר : משפטי :: משפטיו : זכרו (repeating "remember" and "judgments") and at vv 7–11, ארץ : עולם : ברית :: ברית : עולם : הארץ (repeating "land," "[for]ever" and "covenant." This latter case in vv 7–11 has been noted by Ceresco (*CBQ* 40 [1978] 2–3). Thus vv 1–11 are tightly inter-locked with these three chiastic structures. The call to praise and its content belong together as an opening strophe. The second is vv 12–23, which is marked by the inclusion of (גר(ים "sojourn" at vv 12, 23 and the triple occur-rence within it of the stem מלך "reign" at vv 13, 14, 20. It too has extended chiasmus, in vv 18–22, נפשו : משל :: ומשל : בנפשו (repeating "his soul" and "rule"). The verb שלח "sent" is repeated, though probably with different subjects, at vv 17, 20. A reference to "Israel . . . Jacob" ends the strophe, relating chiastically to the ending of the first (v 10). Vv 24–36 comprise the third strophe. It echoes and develops בארץ חם of v 23 in vv 27, 30, 32, 35, 36. It has two instances of chiastic grouping, vv 25–29, שלח : הפך :: הפך : שלח (repeating "sent" and "turned") and vv 33–36, ויך : ויאכל :: ויאכל : ויך (repeating "devoured" and "struck"). The repetition of אמר "spoke" in vv 31, 34 is also to be noted. The fourth strophe, vv 37–45, is dominated by the triple use of the stem יצא "go out" in vv 37–38, 43. By way of overall inclusion it echoes the first strophe at a number of points: זכר "remembered," vv 8, 42; דבר "word," vv 8, 42 again; קדשו "his holiness," vv 3, 42; את-אברהם "with Abraham," vv 9, 42; אברהם עבדו, vv 6, 42; בחיריו "his chosen ones," vv 6, 43; ויתן "and he gave," v 44, echoes אתן, v 11; חקיו "his rulings," v 45, echoes חק, v 10. Moreover, עמו "his people," v 43, supplies the second part of a standard covenant formula, of which the first has been given in v 7a.

There are then four strophes, of eleven, twelve, thirteen and nine lines. The first incorporates the introductory call to praise and the last the conclusion after the historical narrative. The last three fall into a tripartite narrative scheme. The historical movement of the psalm exhibits balance: it moves from Canaan to Egypt (second strophe), lingers in Egypt (third strophe) and eventually moves back from Egypt to Canaan in the fourth.

Explanation

Psalm 105 has the triple aim of inciting the people of God to praise, encouraging them in their faith in his continuing purpose and exhorting them to live in accordance with his revealed will. Its overall theme is Yahweh's faithfulness to his eternally valid promises concerning the land.

The post-exilic congregation is invited to give grateful voice to Yahweh as they look back to the historical origins of their religion. Surrounded as they were by pagan peoples, they were an enclave dedicated to him and bearing witness to the revelation of his activity on their behalf. They are called to meet with him, to appreciate afresh his power and presence, and to bring home to their hearts the ancient proofs of Yahweh's marvelous intervention. Time could not deaden these proofs, for they had a once-and-for-all significance. The present generation of Israel were contemporary bearers of a heritage which stretched back to Abraham. It was their privilege to look back with gratitude to the laying of their religious foundations as God's chosen people.

Yahweh is Israel's covenant God. To establish the covenant he made use of his universal authority for the benefit of Israel. His relationship with his people and the land of Canaan constituted an eternal triangle. It was grounded in a promise made to each patriarch in turn (cf. Gen 17:8; 26:3; 28:13). In a recital of historical traditions the rest of the psalm relates how that promise was kept or remembered (cf. Exod 2:24).

After the call to praise and statement of the theme of praise in the first strophe, the second (vv 12–23) presents the providential intervention of God by word and deed within a framework of the patriarchs' movements. To the little group of patriarchal clans the hope must have seemed an unattainable dream, surrounded as they were by alien peoples. The psalmist is surely speaking implicitly to the hearts of the post-exilic community at this point, and seeking to encourage them as he goes on to represent the few as standing under Yahweh's protection. For even then he was at work. When kings would endanger the succession, he intervened on behalf of those who enjoyed with him a special relationship of inviolability. Even a famine was the tool of his providence (cf. Hag 1:11).

In the bitter fortunes of Joseph he was preparing the way for eventual blessing not only for him but for his kin. Joseph's experience was that of Israel in miniature. The path to glory lay through suffering—and had not Israel suffered in the exile? The prophetic word came true in the end—take heart!—and made all the trial and testing worthwhile. The strophe ends at the climatic point of Jacob's arrival in Egypt. The promise was seemingly as far off as ever: the homelessness of v 12 is forcefully repeated.

The third strophe, vv 24–36, is centered in Egypt and majors in Yahweh's control of events. Even the enmity and wily schemes of the Egyptians—and did not post-exilic Israel know such treatment all too well?—were Yahweh's intended means of proving his power on his people's behalf. In the throes and wake of victimization the key terms of v 6 flash out in vv 25–26, giving the assurance of election and divine patronage. Yahweh did and would work out his purposes for and through his own. As Joseph was God's man for an earlier need, so Moses and Aaron were raised up for this hour of need. In v 27 the formula of signs and marvels, around which the strophe is clustered, serves as an introduction to the detailed plague account and also echoes v 5. His power was at work to execute his covenant promise. Plague after plague came at his command to force the submission of the Egyptians to the universal Overlord (v 28, cf. v 7). The strophe ends impressively with the triple use of כל "all" to express the totality of the effect of Yahweh's might.

If the second strophe ended with Jacob's coming to Egypt and the third was pervaded with the people's stay in Egypt, the fourth (vv 37–45) opens with their departure, the Exodus event, taking up another traditional formula and later echoing it in v 43. Both the third and fourth strophes open with mention of God's physical/material blessing as the pledge of his love (cf. Ezra 7:15; Hag 2:7, 8). But now in reaction Egyptian hatred has given way to dread of Israel, who are recognized as being under the championship of this powerful God.

He went on protecting, guiding and supplying their daily needs by dynamic means. Such then was the outworking of Yahweh's faithfulness to his covenant promise. They were liberated from Egypt with a song on their lips. Their joy was to be echoed down the ages till the present generation took up the strain (v. 3), who indeed had fresh cause for exultation as they could look back to their second Exodus, the return from exile. The promise of the land had finally come true as a package of divine gifts (cf. Deut 6:10–11). By implication Yahweh's present people could also look forward to a fresh fulfillment of the promise, the land actually theirs. Redeemed by divine initiative and recipients of divine grace, what was left for Israel to do? Simply to comply with Yahweh's revealed will, constrained by his faithfulness to be faithful in turn. His revelation consisted of precepts as well as promise (vv 10, 45). So praise and obedience were to be their twin response, as they waited upon Yahweh to continue his work of remembering the covenant.

The psalm takes up a constant OT complex in celebrating the interrelatedness of Yahweh, the people and the land. Here it is set in a context of promise and power, of hope and realization. The NT argues for a continuance of the covenant relationship and the fresh fulfilment of God's promise to Abraham (Luke 1:72, 73). The Church in turn is the seed of Abraham via Jesus Christ (Gal 3:16–29) and the recipient of a new covenant (1 Cor 11:25). In him too it receives its own election (Eph 1:4). Unlike Judaism, Christianity turns its back upon a geographically and politically localized promise. The motif of the land is generally superseded in the NT, apart perhaps from Luke 21:24. Christ is the inheritance: kinship in the land is replaced by fellowship in Christ (cf. Gal 3:18). The Letter to the Hebrews seeks to justify this Christian shift in theological emphasis since it transcends the older hope with a new dimension. The promise to Abraham was not exhausted by Israel's temporal occupation of the land. Canaan was a shadow of the reality, which is a heavenly country destined to be the final home of God's people of the covenants old and new (Heb 3:7–4:1; 11:13–16, 39, 40).

Penitential Prayer   (106:1–48)

Bibliography

Baumgärtel, F. "Zur Liturgie in der 'Sektenrolle' vom Toten Meer." *ZAW* 65 (1953) 263–65. **Beyerlin, W.** "Der nervus rerum in Psalm 106." *ZAW* 86 (1974) 50–64. **Carroll, R. P.** "Rebellion and Dissent in Ancient Israelite Society." *ZAW* 89 (1977) 176–204. **Coats, G. W.** *Rebellion in the Wilderness.* Nashville: Abingdon Press, 1968. **Hooker, M. D.** "A Further Note on Romans 1." *NTS* 13 (1966/67) 181–83. **Lauha, A.** *Die Geschichtsmotive in den alttestamentlichen Psalmen.* Annales academiae scientarum, fennicae 16:1. Helsinki: Soumalainen Tiedeakatemia, 1945. **von Rad, G.** "Faith Reckoned as Righteousness." *The Problem of the Hexateuch and Other Essays.* Tr. E. W. T. Dicken. Edinburgh: Oliver & Boyd, 1966, 125–30. **Speiser, E. A.** "The stem *PLL* in Hebrew." *JBL* 82 (1963) 301–6. **Tunyogi, A. C.** "The Rebellions of Israel." *JBL* 81 (1962) 385–90. **Wolverton, W. I.** "Sermons in the Psalms." *CJT* 10 (1964) 166–76. **Zimmerli, W.** "Zwillungspsalmen." *Wort, Lied und Gottesspruch.* Festschrift für J. Ziegler, ed. J. Schreiner. Forschungen zur Bibel 2. Würzburg: Echter Verlag, 1972, 105–13.

Translation

1 *Hallelujah* [a]
Give Yahweh thanks for [b] *his goodness,*   (3+3)
   for the everlastingness of his loyal love. [c]
2 *Who can tell of Yahweh's great deeds*   (3+3)
   or declare all his praiseworthiness? [a]

3 *How fortunate* [a] *are those who maintain justice,* (3+3)
   who do [b] *what is right* [c] *all the time.*

4 *Remember me,* [a] *Yahweh, when you show your people favor,* (4+3)
   notice me when you save them

5 *so that I may witness the good enjoyed by your chosen ones,* [a] (3+3+3)
   join in your nation's [b] *joy*
   and proudly praise together with your own people. [c]

6 *We have sinned along with our forefathers,* (3+2)
   we have done wrong, we are guilty. [a]

7 *Our forefathers in Egypt* (2+3)
   failed to appreciate your wonders. [a]
   They did not remember your many acts of loyal love, (3+3)
   but rebelled against the Most High [b] *by the Reed Sea.*

8 *Yet he saved them for the sake of his name,* (3+3)
   to reveal his greatness.

9 *He shouted* [a] *at the Reed Sea and it dried up,* (3+3)
   he led them through its depths as through a desert. [b]

10 *From the power of the adversary he saved them,* (3+3)
   from the enemy's power he redeemed them.

11 *Water covered their foes,* (3+3)
   not one of them survived. [a]

12 *They believed his promises* (3+3)
   and sang [a] *his praise.* [b]

13 *They soon forgot what he had done,* (3+3)
   they did not wait to learn his intention. [a]

14 *They got a craving in the wilderness* (3+3)
   and put God to the test in the desert. [a]

15 *He gave them what they asked for,* (3+3)
   then let loose a wasting disease [a] *upon them.*

16 *In the camp they grew jealous of Moses* (3+3)
   and of Yahweh's holy one, Aaron.

17 *The earth opened up and swallowed Dathan* (4+3)
   and covered Abiram's group.

18 *Fire broke out against their group,* (3+3)
   flames burned up those wicked people.

19 *At Horeb they constructed a calf* (3+3)
   and worshipped it, cast metal. [a]

20 *They exchanged their glorious One* [a] (3+3)
   for a copy of a grass-eating ox!

21 *They forgot the God who had saved them,* (3+3)
   who had done great deeds in Egypt,

22 *wonders in Ham's country,* (3+3)
   awesome exploits by the Reed Sea.

23 *So he threatened to destroy them—* (3+3)
   only his chosen one Moses
   stood in the breach before him (3+3)
   to stop his anger doing away with them. [a]

24 *Then they refused the land, desirable though it was,*   (3+3)
      and put no faith in his promise. [a]
25 *They grumbled inside their tents*   (3+3)
      and would not obey Yahweh.
26 *So he lifted up his hand,*   (3+3)
      swearing he would overthrow them in the wilderness, [a]
27 *scatter* [a] *their posterity among the nations*   (3+3)
      and disperse them throughout the world. [b]
28 *They took the yoke of Baal of Peor*   (3+3)
      and ate sacrifices offered to dead things! [a]
29 *They provoked anger* [a] *by their deeds*   (3+3)
      and a plague broke out against them.
30 *Phineas stood up in mediation,*   (3+3)
      and the plague was stopped.
31 *It has been regarded by God as a virtuous act* [a]   (3+3)
      throughout all generations forever. [b]
32 *At Quarrel Waters they provoked wrath*   (3+3)
      and Moses suffered on their account:
33 *they had made him so bitter* [a]   (3+3)
      that he spoke with temerity. [b]

34 *They failed to destroy the peoples,*   (3+3)
      as Yahweh had told them to, [a]
35 *but entered into partnership with the nations*   (3+3)
      and learned to do as they did.
36 *They worshiped their idols,*   (3+3)
      and these proved their snare:
37 *they sacrificed their own sons*   (3+3)
      and daughters to demons! [a]
38 *They shed innocent blood,*   (3+3)
      the blood of their own sons and daughters, [a]
      whom they sacrificed to Canaanite idols, [b]   (3+3)
      and the country was defiled by the bloodshed.
39 *They became unclean through what they did*   (3+3)
      and unfaithful by such behavior.

40 *So Yahweh's anger flared up against his people*   (3+3)
      and he showed how he loathed his own.
41 *He handed them over to the nations*   (3+3)
      so that their adversaries ruled them. [a]
42 *Their enemies oppressed them*   (3+3)
      and they were brought into subjection [a] *under their control.*
43 *Many times he would rescue* [a] *them,*   (3+3+3)
      although they persisted [a] *in a policy of rebellion*
      and sank deeper into their wrongdoing. [b]

44 *Yet he paid regard to their distress*   (3+2)
      on hearing their cry. [a]

45 *He recalled his covenant with* ᵃ *them*   (3+3)
    and relented ᵇ *in accord with the abundance of his*
    loyal love. ᶜ

46 *He made all their captors*   (3+3)
    treat them with kindness.

47 *Save us, Yahweh our God,*   (3+3)
    gather ᵃ *us from among the nations*
    so that we may give thanks to your holy name   (3+3)
    and tell proudly of your praiseworthiness.

48 Blessed be Israel's God Yahweh   (4+3+3)
    from everlasting to everlasting,
    and let all the people say "Amen." ᵃ
        Hallelujah

Notes/Comments

1.a. See the comment on 104:35. The addition at the beginning and end of the psalm echoes its strong element of praise, which was reinforced by the doxology of v 48.

1.b. Heb. כי is generally taken as causal, giving reasons for thanksgiving. But H. Grimme ("Der Bergriff von hebräischem הודה und תודה," *ZAW* 58 [1940/41] 236) construed it as "that" and F. Crüsemann (*Studien zur Formgeschichte*, 32–35) as a deictic particle, "ja," initiating the reply of those who are summoned to praise Yahweh.

1.c. K. Koch (". . . denn seine Güte währet ewiglich," *EvT* 21 [1961] 531–44) has traced the history and range of the liturgical formula of v 1aβ–b, which functioned as an introduction to the thank offering and also to the history psalms, Pss 106, 107. Cf. also K. D. Sakenfeld, *The Meaning of Hesed*, 165–68.

2.a. A question of this kind is normally rhetorical and expresses the inadequacy of praise to match God's praiseworthiness. In the light of vv 3, 6 it seems also to take on a further meaning. "The guilty conscience of the community already casts . . . a shadow which lies on the whole psalm" (A. Weiser, *Psalms*, 680; cf. W. Beyerlin, *ZAW* 86 [1974] 59).

3.a. The beatitude formula has been investigated especially by W. Janzen ("ʾAšrê in the OT," *HTR* 58 [1965] 215–26); cf. E. Lipinski, *RB* 75 (1968) 321–67. It describes a state to be emulated and here it functions not simply as an exhortation to obey (A. A. Anderson, *Psalms*, 737) but also as an answer to the question of v 2.

3.b. Heb. עשה can be regarded as a collective singular harking back to v 2; the well-attested plural עשי (cf. *BHS*) represents an easier reading.

3.c. For משפט and צדקה see the discussion of Th. C. Vriezen (*An Outline of OT Theology* [Tr. S. Neuijen; 2nd ed.; Newton, MA: C. T. Branford, 1970] 388–89) and his definition of them as consequences of Israel's relationship with Yahweh, "that true relations [within the community] are not disturbed and that the integrity of each man in the community is maintained fully."

4.a. The readings זכרנו "remember us" and פקדנו "notice us" despite wide attestation (see *BHS*) are to be rejected as cases of assimilation to the first plural suffixes of vv 6, 7. The representative of the religious community who has issued to them the summons to praise now prays on his own account.

5.a. See the comment on 105:6.

5.b. Heb. גוי "nation" here functions merely as a parallel for "people" (A. Cody, "When Is the Chosen People Called a *gôy*?" *VT* 14 [1964] 2).

5.c. For the suggested deletion of vv 4, 5 as secondary and the attachment of vv 1–3 to Ps 105 see *Form/Structure/Setting*.

6.a. For this formula of confession cf. 1 Kgs 8:47. The line is significantly in the (*qinah*) meter of complaint.

7.a. This is the first of a series of negative archetypes presented in the psalm: see A. C. Tunyogi, *JBL* 81 (1962) 388–90. Weiser (*Psalms*, 681) compares Exod 14:10–12, but sees here a variation from the Pentateuch and evidence of use of an independent tradition. Similarly but more explicitly G. W. Coats (*Rebellion*, 225) is surprised that the Exodus generation are accused of forgetting Yahweh's mighty acts while in Egypt and envisages a broadening of the wilderness rebellion tradition. But the latter bicolon of the verse is to be distinguished from the first as a separate stage. The first bicolon is adequately explained by his references to Exod 4:1, 8; 5:20, 21; 6:9.

7.b. MT עַל־יָם "by the sea" is generally conjecturally emended to עֶלְיוֹן (cf. 78:17, 56). G. R. Driver (*JTS* 44 [1943] 20) suggested an original בָּךְ עַל־יַם־סוּף "against you by the Reed Sea," comparing v 22 and the second person suffix of v 7a, but a third person reference is acceptable as a transition to v 8. Probably a marginal reading עַל־יָם, relating to יָם either as a ms. variant or as a gloss comparing v 22, displaced the similar-looking עֶלְיוֹן. For this type of error see the note on 102:18.

8.a. The vindication of Yahweh's "name" is here the motivation for deliverance: cf. Exod 14:18.

9.a. See the comment on 104:7. Here the *Chaoskampf* is echoed in a historicized form relating to the Exodus. The poetic term expands rather than replaces the prose narrative of Exod 14:21, 22: cf. F. M. Cross, *Canaanite Myth and Hebrew Epic*, 134–35.

9.b. Coats (*Rebellion*, 226–27; cf. NEB) interprets כַמִּדְבָּר as "as (he led them) through the wilderness," seeing a relation between the Reed Sea tradition and that of Yahweh's help in the wilderness. But GKC § 126o adequately explains the use of the definite article, and the expanded comparison in the parallel Isa 63:13 which interpreted in terms of surefooted progress cannot be ignored.

11.a. Cf. Exod 14:28.

12.a. D. A. Robertson (*Linguistic Evidence*, 47, 51) regards the preterite verbs here and in vv 17–19 as archaisms.

12.b. Cf. Exod 14:31; 15:1.

13.a. Heb. עֵצָה "plan" refers to Yahweh's intention to supply their material needs.

14.a. For vv 14–15 cf. Num 11:4, 31–33. The desolate desert functions as a foil for God's grace (R. P. Carroll, *ZAW* 89 [1977] 188). Carroll has observed that the rebellion motif serves to heighten the graciousness of Yahweh and to introduce the motif of judgment in reaction to Israel's negative archetypal behavior (cf. Jer 7:25–26); the judgment functions as a model for divine judgment throughout Israel's history (*ZAW* 89 [1977] 189, 197).

15.a. Underlying LXX S is evidently a misreading הוֹנָם* "abundance" (cf. E. J. Kissane, *Psalms II*, 171), with allusion to Num 11:20.

20.a. MT כְּבוֹדָם "their glory" is traditionally listed as one of the *Tiqqune sopherim* or "scribal corrections" for כְּבוֹדוֹ "his glory" or כְּבוֹדִי "my glory," changed out of reverence for God. O. Eissfeldt ("Die Psalmen als Geschichtsquelle," in *Near Eastern Studies in Honor of William F. Albright*, ed. H. Goedicke [Baltimore: Johns Hopkins Press, 1971] 106) has related כְּבוֹדָם to the ark, as in 1 Sam 4:21–22, and viewed the golden calf as a threat to the ark as a symbol of Yahweh. More commonly it is regarded as a metonym for Yahweh, as in Jer 2:11, on which the psalm may well depend here. K. H. Fahlgren (*Ṣ^e daka, nahestehende und entgegengesetzte Begriffe im AT*. [Uppsala: Almquist & Wiksell, 1932] 148 note 3) finds an implicit contrast with בֹּשֶׁת "shame" used of idols (cf. Hos 9:10 and H. W. Wolff, Tr. G. Stansell; Philadelphia: Fortress Press, *Hosea* [1974] 165). J. W. Rogerson and J. W. McKay (*Psalms 101–150*. 44) draw attention to the explicit contrast between a created object dependent on created things and the Lord of nature of v 21.

21.a. The perfect שָׁכְחוּ does not function as a summary of vv 7b–20, as D. Michel (*Tempora*, 37) claims. The break reflects emotional shock.

23.a. For vv 19–23 cf. Deut 9:8–21.

24.a. For vv 24–27 cf. Deut 1:21–33 (and also Num 13:25–14:45).

26.a. The oath of Num 14:28 is vividly introduced by a reference to a gesture of oath-taking (cf. Deut 32:40).

27.a. MT וּלְהַפִּיל "and to cause to fall" is generally corrected to וּלְהָפִיץ with the support of S Tg. in the light of the parallel Ezek 20:23. MT has suffered assimilation to the preceding verb.

27.b. Cf. Ezek 20:23 and the doubtless underlying covenant curses of Lev 26:33; Deut 28:64–65 (cf. Deut 4:26–27). Coats (*Rebellion*, 229) has observed that an explanation is here provided for the theological problems caused by the exile: the current generation are held responsible for the sins of their forefathers (cf. v 6).

28.a. For vv 28–31 cf. Num 25:1–3, 11–13. In v 28b Weiser (*Psalms,* 677) renders "sacrifices for the dead" (cf. Deut 26:14), but מתים seems to be a comment on אלהיהן "their gods" in Num 25:2, characterizing them as lifeless (cf. Lev 26:30).

29.a. For the absolute use of the verb cf. J. A. Montgomery and H. S. Gehman (*A Critical and Exegetical Commentary on the Books of Kings* [ICC; Edinburgh: T. & T. Clark, 1951] 522, 541) with reference to 2 Kgs 21:6; 23:19.

31.a. This originally cultic and subsequently spiritualized formula has been analyzed by G. von Rad in *The Problem of the Hexateuch and Other Essays,* 125–30.

31.b. The special honor bestowed on Phineas is to be associated with the later preeminence of the Zadokite priests (cf. 1 Chr 24:4 and N. H. Snaith, *Leviticus and Numbers* [London: Nelson, 1967] 13, 304). For a study of the verb פלל see E. A. Speiser, *JBL* 82 (1963) 301–6.

33.a. MT הָמְרוּ "defied" is better pointed הַמְרוּ with two Heb mss. LXX S Hier: cf. Job 27:2.

33.b. For vv 32–33 cf. Num 20:8–13. The episode historically belongs earlier but is placed here because Moses's failure prevented his entering the promised land. For suggested explanations of the precise fault of Moses see Snaith, *Leviticus and Numbers,* 276. Here the psalmist expresses his sympathy for Moses by stressing his provocation.

34.a. For vv 34–39 cf. Judg 1:21; 2:3, 17; 3:6.

37.a. Cf. Deut 32:17 and F. Stolz, *Strukturen,* 206.

38.a. The repetition expresses emotional shock: cf. 2 Kgs 18:4–5. For the association of child sacrifice with innocent blood cf. Jer. 19:4–5.

38.b. The two cola are often deleted as a gloss (cf. *BHK, BHS*). H. -J. Kraus (*Psalmen,* 899, 905) regards it as a misinterpretation of "innocent blood," but vv. 38–39 may be compared with Ezek 20:30–31. The text is vindicated by its stylistic role in the context (see *Form/Structure/Setting*). Moreover, M. Dahood (*Psalms III,* 75) has observed the break up of a composite phrase ארץ כנען "land of Canaan" in v 38aγ–b, and a word play ויכנעו/כנען in vv 38, 42.

41.a. cf. Judg 2:14; 3:1.

42.a. The word play with כנען "Canaan," v 38, ironically makes the punishment fit the crime.

43.a. In the context the verbs are probably frequentative (Robertson, *Linguistic Evidence,* 49) rather than preterite (Dahood, *Psalms III,* 75).

43.b. The final colon is frequently deleted as a gloss on the preceding one (cf. *BHK, BHS*). The emendation וימק "and pined away" for וימכו (cf. Lev 26:39; Ezek 4:17; 24:23; 33:10) is interesting but unnecessary.

44.a. Cf. Judg 3:9; 6:7.

45.a. The preposition ל qualifies ברית: cf. כרת ברית ל "make a covenant with" (Dahood, *Psalms III,* 76).

45.b. Dahood (*Psalms III,* 76) follows S in pointing וַכְנֶחָם "and led." But the psalmist is surely echoing the phrase רב-חסד ונחם על-הרעה "abundant in loyal love and relenting over punishment" (Joel 2:13; Jonah 4:2). Accordingly K חַסְדּוֹ is to be followed: Q has been influenced by the plural in v 7.

45.c. Allusion is made in vv 45–46 to the liturgical formula of Joel 2:13. For Yahweh's remembering see the note on 105:8, 42. With v 45 cf. Judg 2:18; with v 46 cf. 2 Kgs 8:50. The "covenant" is not elucidated, but is presumably that with Abraham (cf. Exod 2:24; Ps 105:8).

47.a. The addition in 1 Chr 16:35 (and thence in mss. of Psalms) והצילנו "and rescue us" represents a conflated text in MT. LXX in Chronicles omits וקבצנו, which in MT seems to be an intrusion from the text of Psalms. The two verbs are recensional variants (see L. C. Allen, *The Greek Chronicles* [VTSup 25; Leiden: E. J. Brill, 1974] 217).

48.a. For congregational response to a doxological benediction cf. 41:14 (13).

Form/Structure/Setting

The limitations of the form-critical method are evident from the fact that Ps 106 has been regarded both as a hymn (Kraus, *Psalmen,* 900) and as a communal complaint (C. Westermann, *Praise,* 57, 141; cf. H. Gunkel, *Die Psalmen,* 464–65). An assessment depends on the relative weight given to elements of praise and complaint. There is of course a close and fluid relationship between the two in the Psalter. It is quite possible to fit the psalm into the flexible pattern of the complaint, although this classification does not necessarily determine its function. V 1 is a hymnic call to praise, underlined by the question of v 2. It looks back to Yahweh's ancient work on his people's behalf, as the development in vv 8–12 shows (cf. 89:1–18). In between is what corresponds to the normal introductory petition, vv 4–5, here dislodged from first place by the element of praise and spoken in the name of the representative of the community. This personal factor explains the imperatival nature of the praise of v 1, as the representative addresses his fellow worshipers. The imperative "remember" addressed to God in v 4 is characteristic of the complaint (cf. B. S. Childs, *Memory and Tradition*, 33, 44). The development of praise in vv 8–12, together with vv 43–46, also has the role of a confession of trust, a normal constituent of the complaint, and functions too as an appeal for God's intervention (Westermann, *Praise*, 55, 57). Interwoven with the praise of vv 8–12 (cf. too vv 21b, 22) is a confession of guilt in vv 6, 7, 13–21a, 24–39, which serves to enhance Yahweh's praiseworthiness (cf. the summary in v 43) and also to preface the complaint proper of vv 40–42, which has both Yahweh and the nations as subject and so contains two of the three standard constituents of this element (cf. Westermann, *Praise*, 53). A final petition follows in v 47a, which develops into a vow of praise in v 47b. (V 48 is unrelated to the psalm: it forms a closing doxology to the fourth book of the Psalter.) Formally then the psalm can be defined as a communal complaint strongly marked by hymnic features. Direct address of God occurs in vv 4–7, 47 and first plural suffixes in vv 6, 7, 47. The beatitude of v 3 reveals a didactic, moralizing function comparable with 105:45; so too does the historical account of vv 8–46 with references to Yahweh in the third person.

What was the function of such a psalm with its checkered mixture of elements? Crüsemann (*Studien zur Formgeschichte*, 77), following Gunkel, ibid., has characterized the psalm as a general confession, noting that Israel's acts rather than Yahweh's are the central feature. F. Baumgärtel (*ZAW* 65 [1953] 263–65) has compared the annual renewal of the covenant described in the Qumran Community Rule (1QS 1:16–2:18). The first four of the seven elements of this liturgy were as follows: 1. The priests and Levites praise God; 2. The priests proclaim his righteousness displayed in his mighty deeds; 3. The Levites recite Israel's sins; and 4. Those entering upon the covenant confess their sins and those of their forefathers, and praise him for his mercy. Baumgärtel saw a reflection of these four elements in vv 1, 8–12, 13–43 and 6, 7 respectively, and deduced an older cultic use behind the Qumran liturgy. Weiser (*Psalms*, 679–80) gladly seized upon these parallels as evidence for his covenant festival and placed the psalm within the covenantal liturgy, along with Ps 105.

An apparent difficulty in stressing the notes of confession of sin and complaint arises from the interpretation of the psalm in terms of praise revealed by the secondary framework of Hallelujahs with which the psalm has been supplied in vv 1, 48. W. Beyerlin (*ZAW* 86 [1974] 56–64) has been able to interpret Ps 106 in a manner consistent with the framework. He finds the introductory call to praise of v 1aβ–b decisive for the understanding of the psalm. It takes up the promise of Jer 33:10–11, which associates the praise formula with the promise of return to the land. But first the (exilic) community must endure the exile and recognize that it is suffering due punishment for its sins. V 2 reflects present inadequacy to praise, because of the sins of v 6 and the unattained standards of v 3. Vv 6–46 function not only as a confession of sin and an interpretation of the exile as divine punishment; they also stress God's grace and past help, which prompted praise, and so they give confidence that present deportation and dispersal would also end in praise. The focal point of the psalm is not the narrative but vv 1, 47b, the renewal of praise which only Yahweh's reversal of the people's present circumstances can bring about. There is a tension between guilt and praise which only divine forgiveness can resolve. Kraus (*Psalmen*, 900) also makes praise the center of the psalm, with the motif of Israel's guilt set in a context of penitence and prayer playing a less important role. He accordingly has classified the form of the psalm as a hymn. As to the setting of the psalm, with its accent on thanksgiving and praise it served as introduction to a post-exilic liturgy of confession (cf. Zech 7:1–4; 8:19).

One must still ask whether even the place given to praise does not fit better into an overall complaint. V 1 calls for praise for what Yahweh did in the past (vv 8–12; cf. Isa 63:7), which constitutes hope for his intervention in the future. Beyerlin (*ZAW* 86 [1974] 61) has noted that טוב "good" in v 1 is taken up in טובה "goodness" in v 5. The vow of praise in v 47 looks to the future. These two types of praise, here organically linked, are well attested elements of the complaint (cf. Westermann, *Praise*, 55–57, 59, 60). In this complaint the community praises Yahweh for what he has done in the past and looks forward to praising him again in the future when he has provided fresh grounds for praise. The perspective of the psalm was subsequently altered from complaint to praise by subsequent additions, the doxology and the Hallelujahs (cf. Ps 115).

As to its literary Gattung Ps 106 is a historical psalm like Ps 78 and 105. (See *Form/Structure/Setting* of Ps 105 for this categorization and also for suggested classifications of both as wisdom psalms.) The treatment of history in vv 7–46 is different from that of Ps 105: it is an expansion of the confession of sin in v 6 set in a framework of Yahweh's salvation and grace (vv 8–12, 44–46). W. I. Wolverton (*CJT* 10 [1964] 166–76) explained the psalm like Ps 105 as originally a sermon. The speaker identified himself with his audience and his task was to induce lament rather than to lament. To achieve this end Wolverton had to prune the psalm of vv 1–5 and view v 47 as a congregational response. It is doubtful whether the psalm ever existed in this truncated form.

Can the relation of the treatment of Israel's history to the canonical historical books be established? The Deuteronomistic structure underlying the psalm is evident, especially in vv 40–46, and Coats (*Rebellion*, 225–30) has noted Deuteronomistic influence elsewhere in the psalm. Evidence pointing to a period when Pentateuchal material had received its final redaction comes from vv 16–18, where older material in Num 16 is supplemented with reference to (Aaron's) holiness and to judgment by fire, as in the priestly sections of 16:3, 5, 7, 35, and from vv 28–31, where similarly different traditions have already been combined, as in Num 25 (A. Lauha, *Die Geschichtsmotive*, 88–

90; Coats, *Rebellion,* 227–29). Coats (*Rebellion,* 227–29) also observes that in contrast to Ps 78 this psalm betrays no trace of conflict between the Northern and Southern Kingdoms. He concludes that the psalm presupposes the exile, without necessarily being post-exilic. Probably the origin of the psalm is in fact to be set in the exilic period with Beyerlin and Coats (cf. Dahood, *Psalms III,* 76; Rogerson and McKay, *Psalms 101–150,* 41). The two Aramaisms, מלל and שבח (vv 2, 43; מכך, v 47, need not be an Aramaism: cf. Robertson, *Linguistic Evidence,* 127, 128) are thus easily accommodated. The psalm was doubtless used in a service of penitence. It lent itself naturally to re-use in the Post-exilic period, in hope of the return of the Diaspora Jews. Weiser's contention (*Psalms,* 682) that v 47 need refer only to the deportation of the people of the Northern Kingdom becomes unlikely in the light of the total evidence.

Other factors which deserve consideration are the use of vv 47–48 in 1 Chr 16:35–36, the close affinity of the psalm with Isa 61:7–14, the link between v 45 and Joel 2:13 and the parallel with Ezek 20:23 in v 27. The last factor again suggests at least an exilic date for the psalm. The implications of the links with Isa 61 are not at all clear, and deserve close investigation. The link with the post-exilic Joel does not necessarily indicate a post-exilic provenance since the form of the confessional formula evidently employed cultically in Joel's time is itself rooted in the Jeremian and the related Deuteronomic traditions (H. W. Wolff, *Joel and Amos* [Tr. W. Janzen, S. D. McBride, and C. A. Muenchow; Philadelphia: Fortress Press, 1977] 49) and it need not be post-exilic in origin. For the use of the psalm in 1 Chr 16 see the comments in *Form/Structure/Setting* of Ps 105. Remarkably the doxology and call for congregational response, v 48, are included, although the usual corollary that a division in the Psalter is presupposed by the use in Chronicles has been vigorously disputed (see H. Gese, "Die Entstehung der Büchereinteilung des Psalters," in *Wort, Lied, und Gottespruch,* ed. J. Schreiner [Forschungen zur Bibel 2; Würzburg, Stuttgart: Echter Verlag, 1972] 61–62; Weiser, *Psalms,* 682–83).

The structure of Ps 106 seems hardly to have been studied hitherto beyond divisions based on formal and exegetical considerations. Dahood (*Psalms III,* 76) does note that in v 47 להדות "to give thanks" and תהלתך "your praise" form an inclusion with vv 1, 2, הודו and תהלתו. In fact there is evidence of extended inclusion, to some of which R. L. Alden (*Journal of the Evangelical Society* 21 [1978] 202) has pointed: חסד "loyal love," vv 1, 7, 45; עם "people," vv 4, 40; נחלה "property," vv 5, 40; the stems זכר "remember," vv 4, 7, 45, and ישע "save," vv 4, 47; ראה ב "look upon," vv 5, 44; (ים)גוי "nation(s)," vv 5, 47; (ו)ימרו "they rebelled," vv 7, 43; שם "name," vv 8, 47. Moreover the threefold occurrence of the divine name in vv 1, 2, 4 is matched in vv 34, 40, 47. Direct address to Yahweh occurs in vv 4–7, 47; and the first person plural pronominal references of vv 6, 7 recur in v 47.

All these parallels point to a complementary pair of passages, vv 1–12, 34–47. They comprise two strophes of thirteen and fifteen lines respectively. The first is marked by a repetition of the sequences חסד-גבורה-תהלה in vv 1/7, 2/8, 2/12 and also by a threefold occurrence of the stem ישע "save" in vv 4, 8, 10. The final strophe, which coincides with the division in *BHS,* is tied together by a threefold use of גוים "nations" at vv 35, 41, 47. As already noted, Dahood has pointed out the word play כנע/כנע at vv 38, 42. In addition vv 34–40 are interwoven by an extended chiastic pattern of the type noted in Ps 105:

:: יהוה : מעשיהם : עצביהם : את-בניהם ואת-בנותיהם : דם ::
דם : בניהם ובנותיהם : לעצבי : במעשיהם : יהוה

(repeating "Yahweh," "their deeds," "idols," "their sons and daughters" and "blood"). And what of vv 13–33? A triadic division for the psalm is indicated by the three cases of the stem שמע "hear" at vv 4, 25, 43 and by the positioning of the stem ישע "save": after the cluster in vv 4–10 it recurs at vv 21, 47. Accordingly a long central strophe of twenty-two lines is to be envisaged. An obvious break in the flow of the narrative does take place at v 13 (Michel, *Tempora*, 36, 37). The strophe is marked by a double play on the stem מרה "rebel" used in vv 7, 43: מהרו "hastened" and המרו "embittered" occur at beginning and end, vv 13, 33. Moses features three times, in vv 16, 23, 32. Repeated terms are במדבר "in the wilderness," vv 14, 26, עמד "stood," vv 23, 30, יהוה, vv 16, 25, and אל "God," vv 14, 21.

Psalm 106 has obviously been placed next to Ps 105 as an intended double statement (W. Zimmerli, *Zwillingspsalmen*, 109–11). Both psalms review Israel's history, but this one presents a reverse side of the coin. Israel, bound to a faithful God and yet herself unfaithful, is called to a deepened self-understanding, to praise and to trembling hope.

For the use of the psalm in Rom 1:23–28 via the LXX see L. C. Allen, "The OT in Romans 1–8," *Vox Evangelica* 3 (1964) 28–29; M. D. Hooker, *NTS* 13 (1966/69) 181–83. Paul not only quoted v 20 in Rom 1:23 but echoed v 14 at 1:24, v 39 in 1:26, 27, and v 48 in 1:26 (cf. vv 23, 32, 40 with 1:18). Moreover, he used v 41 as the basis for a threefold refrain in 1:24, 26, 28. The apostle described sin and its consequences in terms of Israel's experience, which was mirrored and magnified in the Gentile world.

Explanation

The worship leader calls upon the exiled religious community to praise, using time-honored words which carry their own message of reassurance. Yahweh's loyal love is everlasting: this is the ground of their hope that he will save. Who can praise? His praiseworthiness is too great for any mortal lips to capture. The question is asked with a sigh. Right living must ever be the preface to worship (cf. Ps 15). At present a barrier lies across the way of fullness of praise, a barrier to be mentioned in v 6. But the leader looks forward to a new manifestation of Yahweh's goodness in the form of national restoration, when full praise too will be restored. He prays that he personally may be privileged to see that day. Thereby he expresses his own assurance that eventually it will dawn.

The present experience of exile is described deuteronomistically as punishment for a backlog of sins. It has piled up over the centuries and been added to by each generation in turn, not excluding the contemporary one. They form no island but are joined to the continent of history by national solidarity. They are victims of their own and their predecessors' sins, they confess.

The psalmist looks back to the great archetype of salvation, the complex of the Egyptian plagues and the Exodus, and finds even that to be sin-stained. It inaugurated a pattern of heedlessness and rebellion. But, thank God, where sin abounded, grace much more abounded. He still proceeded to save. From this viewpoint the Exodus was a key positive factor for the future: it revealed Yahweh as Savior of his sinning people. It provided hope for the penitent. Just as the people of old trusted and praised Yahweh, this generation may implicitly look forward to the creation of a new context for the exercise of faith and praise.

In the first strophe, vv 1–12, Yahweh is praised for his loyal love, power and salvation, active attributes which are duly enhanced by the failures of their recipients. The second, vv 13–33, is concerned with Yahweh, Moses and Israel in the wilderness. From the wilderness narratives the psalmist extracts six episodes of sin and punishment. These further negative archetypes constitute an expansion of the confession of v 6 and an implied affirmation that they are justly under sentence of condemnation since they are receiving the due reward of their deeds. The forgotten Savior ever turns judge, and they have borne the rod of his judgment. Thus, when the wilderness generation challenged his will and ability to provide for their hunger, they received a two-edged settlement of their complaints. When mutiny broke out against Moses and Aaron, Yahweh's appointed leaders, the instigators had to be exterminated. At Horeb, of all places, Israel's career of ingratitude reached an all-time low, in the golden calf incident. The psalmist pauses to reflect: the themes of Yahweh's wonders in Egypt and of election which clustered around the confession at the heart of the first strophe (vv 5, 7) now reappear at the center of the second, but in reverse order (vv 22, 23). The sin against Yahweh is seen to be all the more heinous in that it was a deliberate loss of memory, a willful rejection of salvation history and of the meaning it ought to have had. The people behaved as if they had never been chosen—Moses was the only exception and through this narrow door of intercession Israel's survival had to pass. The covenant mediator threw himself into the breach, like a courageous soldier defending a gap in the defenses of a beleaguered city. And so they were reprieved.

But they had not yet learned their lesson. They actually refused the promised land. In cowardly disbelief and discontent they stayed stubbornly inside their tents. They fully deserved Yahweh's curse barring them from the land, a curse whose long-range effect Israel had recently experienced. Just as this middle strophe looked back to the first, it now looks forward to the next (v 41). The present generation are caught up in the outworking of the divine word.

Again the wilderness generation defected from Yahweh's service and got involved in Moabite rites. Provoking divine wrath, they were spared once more only by one man's intervention. A living memorial to Phineas existed thereafter among the people, the special priestly work of his descendants, which was Yahweh's accolade of appreciation. Meribah was the scene of further trouble, with tragic repercussions. The people's provocation of Moses led to his own fall from grace and debarring from the promised land.

The theme of the third strophe, vv 34–47, is a triangular one: Yahweh, Israel and the nations. But it also takes up the positive themes of the first strophe. First it continues the tragic story of Israel's defection, once they had reached Canaan, and divine punishment. The people's sin is considered in vv 34–39, separately from the reaction of Yahweh, in vv 40–42, which leads on to an account of Yahweh's positive dealings, in vv 43–46. Involvement with the nations of Canaan led to exile among nations outside Canaan, from which the community prays to be delivered in v 47.

Entry into the promised land proved a disaster: it exposed the people to fresh temptation to religious syncretism, as the narrative of Judg 1–3 disclosed. Here again ancient history held up a mirror to more recent events. The psalmist deliberately paints the Judges period in colors borrowed from the fateful last pre-exilic centuries (cf. 2 Kgs 17:17; 21:16; Jer 3:1–3). Yahweh had to punish his own people. As nations featured in their sin, he fittingly used nations as agents of his punishment. As they had become Canaanized, they fell into a canyon of disaster, declares the psalmist with a word play (more effective on the ancient Hebrew ear than upon the modern Western one). Israel suffered national humiliation, which was no stranger to recent generations, including the psalmist's own.

But that was not the end of the story: Israel's history had had happier turns. Yahweh's "many acts of loyal love" (v 7) were not exhausted in ancient Egypt. They kept on appearing in the form of deliverance down the ages, despite Israel's rebellion. The traditional formula of Yahweh's character kept coming true in their experience: "Yahweh is kindly, lavish in loyal love and ready to relent over punishment" (cf. Joel 2:13). Forgetful though his people had been, he remembered and implemented his covenant promises.

And, humanly speaking, it was the people's penitent cry that inaugurated a turn for the better. The present generation dare to take these past deliverances as precedents for their own future and to bring their own cries to the God of the covenant. They plead for deliverance and restoration to their own land. They vow thanksgiving if their prayer is answered, promising to make Yahweh's praise their pride. The psalm has come round full circle to the theme of praise (cf. vv 1, 5, 12). The community waits upon Yahweh, all too aware of their own sin and its wages, but conscious too of their waiting Savior.

The psalmist speaks as heir of the deuteronomic history and weaves its themes into the fabric of the penitential history of the exilic community. He stands too in the interim period foretold by the pre-exilic prophets, between God's judgment and salvation of his people. He is able to recreate a cultic representation of the past to fit contemporary needs, to be the vehicle of both deep repentance and assured hope.

The use of the Egyptian experience to provide a negative archetype together with its echoes in the wilderness period finds partial parallels elsewhere in the OT, notably in Pss 81 and 95, and thence in the NT, in 1 Cor 10:1–11; Heb 3:7–4:11. Paul uses the saga of human failure and divine wrath and abandonment found in this psalm as a pattern for sin worldwide (Rom 1:18–28). The Exodus complex of events had not only a once-and-for-all significance for salvation and election but also a shadow side. Likewise there is for Christians a looking back to the cross as a signpost both to God's saving love and to human sin (Rom 5:6–8).

Manifold Mercies   (107:1–43)

Bibliography

Becker, J. *Israel deutet seine Psalmen.* **Beyerlin, W.** *Werden und Wesen in 107. Psalms.* BZAW 153. Berlin: Walter de Gruyter, 1979. **Borger, R.** "Weitere ugaritologische Kleinigkeiten. III. Hebräisch MḤWZ (Psalm 107:30)." *UF* 1 (1969) 1–4. **Mejía, J.** "Some Observations on Psalm 107." *BTB* 5 (1975) 56–66. **Snaith, N. H.** *Five Psalms (1; 27; 51; 107; 134). A New Translation with Commentary and Questionary.* London: Epworth Press, 1938.

Translation

1 *Give Yahweh thanks for his goodness,*   (3+3)
   for the everlastingness of his loyal love. [a]

2 *Let Yahweh's redeemed ones say so,* [a]   (3+3)
   whom he has redeemed from the enemy's power,

3 *gathering them from other countries,*   (2+2+2)
   from east and west,
   from north [a] *and overseas.* [b]

4 *They wandered* [a] *in the wild wastelands,*   (3+3)
   unable to find their way to an inhabited town.

5 *They were hungry and thirsty,*   (3+3)
   their inner vitality [a] *was sapped.*

6 *In their distress they cried to Yahweh:*   (4+3)
   he rescued them from their predicament,

7 *leading them on their way*   (3+3)
   straight to an inhabited town.

8 *Let them give Yahweh thanks for his loyal love,* [a]   (3+3)
   for his wonders on behalf of men, [b]

9 *for the way he satisfied ravenous thirst*   (3+3)
   and filled hungry stomachs with good things.

10 *Those who lived* [a] *in darkness grim as death,* [b]   (3+3)
   fettered to misfortune's [c] *iron chains*

11 *because they had defied God's commands*   (3+3)
   and despised the will of the Most High—

12 *he wore down their spirit with hard labor,*   (3+3)
   they stumbled about helplessly.

13 *In their distress they cried to Yahweh:*   (4+3)
   he saved them from their predicament,

¹⁴ *releasing them from darkness grim as death*   (3+3)
    and snapping their fetters—
¹⁵ *let them give Yahweh thanks for his loyal love,*   (3+3)
    for his wonders on behalf of men,
¹⁶ *for the way he broke down bronze doors*   (3+3)
    and hacked away iron bars. [a]

¹⁷ *Those fools* [a] *who had indulged in rebellious ways,*   (3+3)
    who were suffering for their misdemeanors [b]*—*
¹⁸ *all food their stomachs rejected with loathing*   (3+3)
    until they reached the gates of death. [a]
¹⁹ *In their distress they cried to Yahweh:*   (4+3)
    he saved them from their predicament,
²⁰ *sending his message* [a] *of healing*   (3+3)
    to rescue them [b] *from their Pit* [c]*—*
²¹ *let them give Yahweh thanks for his loyal love,*   (3+3)
    for his wonders on behalf of men. [a]
²² *Let them offer thanksgiving sacrifices*   (3+3)
    and recount in loud song what he has done. [a]

²³ *Those who embarked* [a] *on ships to go to sea*   (3+4)
    whose business took them onto the ocean—
²⁴ *they too saw what Yahweh could do,*   (4+3)
    his wonders in the deep.
²⁵ *He gave the word, and roused*   (2+2+2)
    a storm wind,
    and it raised its waves. [a]
²⁶ *Up to the sky, down into the depths they went,*   (4+3)
    their hearts melting in anguish.
²⁷ *They reeled* [a] *and staggered like drunks,*   (3+3)
    all their expertise wrecked.
²⁸ *In their distress they cried to Yahweh*   (4+3)
    and he brought them out of their predicament,
²⁹ *He made the storm fall silent*   (3+3)
    and their waves [a] *grew still.*
³⁰ *They were glad to be at peace*   (3+3)
    and he brought them to the port [a] *they wanted—*
³¹ *let them give Yahweh thanks for his loyal love,*   (3+3)
    for his wonders on behalf of men.
³² *Let them extol him in the congregation of the people,*   (3+3)
    at the session of the elders [a] *give him praise.*

³³ *He can turn* [a] *rivers into desert,*   (3+3)
    springs of water into parched ground, [b]
³⁴ *fertile land into a salt marsh,*   (3+3)
    so wicked are the people who live there. [a]
³⁵ *He can turn desert into pools of water,*   (3+4)
    dry land into springs of water, [a]

³⁶ *where he settles the hungry*   (3+3)
    and they build a town to live in.

³⁷ *They sow fields and plant vineyards*   (4+3)
    and get a fruitful harvest.

³⁸ *he blesses them so that they grow very numerous*   (3+3)
    and does not let their cattle diminish.

³⁹ *They diminish and suffer* ᵃ   (2+3)
    from oppression, trouble and sorrow. ᵇ

⁴⁰ *He pours contempt upon leaders*   (3 + 3)
    and makes them wander in a trackless waste. ᵃ

⁴¹ *But he raises the needy high above affliction*   (3+3)
    and makes their families prolific as flocks.

⁴² *The upright rejoice to see it,* ᵃ   (3+3)
    while all wickedness keeps its mouth shut.

⁴³ *Let whoever is wise take this to heart,*   (3+3)
    let them reflect ᵃ *on Yahweh's acts of loyal love.* ᵇ

Notes/Comments

1.a. For the formula of summons to thanksgiving see the note on 106:1. The fact that both psalms have the same opening must have encouraged their juxtaposition in the collection. Another contributory factor was that in the light of v 3, Ps 107 may be viewed as a testimony to the fulfilment of the prayer of 106:47. Here the formula functions in the cultic setting of a thanksgiving service, as in Jer 33:11.

2.a. The addition to v 1 (see *Form/Structure/Setting*) is slightly awkward. The "redeemed" are obviously not urged to issue the call to thanksgiving of v 1. The lack of flow contrasts with 124:1; 129:1. Here the "redeemed" are to respond either with thanksgiving or with the congregational response of v 1b (cf. 118:2–4). For גאולי with reference to returned exiles cf. Isa 62:12. Heb. צר here means "enemy" (so LXX). In the refrain of vv 6, 13, 19, 28 it means "distress," but it cannot do so here because it is never used with יד "hand" in the OT (W. Beyerlin, *Werden und Wesen*, 69). The different meaning is an indication of a fresh stratum. Presumably צר in the rest of the psalm was re-interpreted as distress caused by the enemy, forced expatriation.

2.b. M. Dahood (*Psalms III*, 81) and Beyerlin (*Werden und Wesen*, 9, 73) take אשר as "that."

3.a. In *BHS* "ut 28" in the apparatus at note 3 ᵇ is misplaced from note 6 ᵃ.

3.b. Heb. ומים depends upon Isa 49:12 and looks forward to v 23 (cf. Beyerlin, *Werden und Wesen*, 68, 101). There is no need for the common emendation to the suspiciously easier ומימין (cf. *BHS*) "and from the south." *Tg.* "southern sea" is simply explanatory.

4.a. Heb. תעו is usually emended to a participle תעי on the analogy of vv 10, 23. Probably this did stand in the text at an earlier stage, but MT reflects the interpretation caused by the insertion of vv 2–3 (cf. A. A. Anderson, *Psalms*, 750; see *Form/Structure/Setting*). In the re-interpretation the passage evokes Second Isaiah's description (in terms of a second Exodus) of a journey across the wilderness to the homeland (cf. Isa 40:3, 4). The "inhabited town," vv 4, 7, then becomes "a city to live in" (NEB).

5.a. Heb. נפשם (also vv 18, 26; cf. לבם, v 12) may refer to the throat as the organ of eating (H. W. Wolff, *Anthropology*, 11), as it does in the resumptive v 9, but in the light of the parallels it appears to have overtones of morale (cf. JB and NEB; cf. the comment on לב in 102:5; and cf. Wolff, *Anthropology*, 17–18).

8.a. Heb. חסד has associations of deliverance in this and the parallel refrains (K. D. Sakenfeld, *The Meaning of Hesed*, 218).

8.b. Dahood *Psalms III*, 83) regards the double ל as parallel, referring to persons to whom confession or avowal is to be made; likewise J. H. Eaton (*Psalms*, 25), who compares v 32; LXX could be cited in support. But 31:22 (21); 36:8 (7) confirm the usual interpretation, the latter passage showing that the reference to "men" is in order to stress divine grace.

9.a. The etymology of שׁקֵקָה "ravenous" is uncertain: contrast BDB, 1055; KB, 957 and Dahood, *Psalms III*, 83.

10.a. The participle is a *casus pendens*, taken up in v 15 (likewise in vv 17, 23).

10.b. For reviews of צלמות "deathly shadow" see D. Winton Thomas, "צלמות in the Old Testament," *JSS* 7 [1977] 191–200; N. J. Tromp, *Primitive Conceptions*, 140–42. Probably the מות- ("death") element has a superlative negative force.

10.c. D. Winton Thomas (*JTS* 16 [1965] 444–45) rendered עני "captivity" (see the comment on 105:18), but Dahood (*Psalms III*, 83) is probably right in rejecting it.

12.a. The repointing as a passive יְדֻכָּֽנּוּ implied by LXX (cf. *BHS*, RSV) is not compelling. Cf. the implicit reference to divine punishment in v 17.

16.a. Is a common expression cited both here and Isa 45:2 (H.-J. Kraus, *Psalmen*, 913) or is Isa 45:2 quoted in an adapted sense? If the latter is true, the original psalm must have been post-exilic.

17.a. Generally אולים is conjecturally emended to חולים "sick" or אמללים "languishing" (cf. *BHS*). Dahood (*Psalms III*, 85) renders MT "weak" by recourse to a different root. JB and NEB retain MT in the sense of "fools," and so does J. Mejía (*BTB* 5 [1975] 62). *Contra BHS* LXX, followed by S, reflects not עורם but simply אולם (its Heb. *Vorlage* lacked a vowel letter), relating the word to the three singular verbs of v 16; cf. its equivalents in 21(22):20; 87(88):4.

17.b. For the association between wrongdoing and sickness see the note on 103:3.

18.a. For Sheol as a city in the OT see Tromp, *Primitive Conceptions*, 152–54.

20.a. *Contra* Beyerlin (*Werden und Wesen* 19) דבר need not depend upon Isa 55:11. Nor is there need to see incipient hypostatization here, as does W. H. Schmidt ("דבר *dābhar*," *TDOT* 3 [1978] 120–21). Cf. Judg 11:28; Ps 20:3 (2); Prov 26:6. The primary reference seems to be to a priestly oracle of healing (cf. Kraus, *Psalmen*, 913) brought from the holy place to the enquirer or his proxy waiting in the temple court.

20.b. Heb. וימלט probably shares the pronominal suffix in v 20a (cf. Dahood, *Psalms III*, 85).

20.c. MT משחיתותם is commonly emended to משחת חיתם "their life from the Pit." Kraus (*Psalmen*, 909) prefers משחת תמים "unharmed from the Pit" as closer to MT. But MT is apparently confirmed by the same form in Lam 4:20, on which D. Hillers (*Lamentations: Introduction, Translation and Notes* [AB 7A; Garden City, NY: Doubleday, 1972] 85) comments that the meaning (there "traps") is not seriously in question, though the form is slightly suspect. Possibly the term is an intensive plural of שחת "Pit" (cf. 103:4) or a slightly variant form of it (cf. BDB, 1005a; GKC § 95q). "Their Pit" is the place of death to which they would otherwise have gone (cf. v 18). Dahood (*Psalms III*, 86) relates to שחין "boil" and assumes assimilation of the third radical.

21.a. For the inverted *nun* in MT at vv 21–26 (in another tradition 23–28), 40 see GKC §§ 5n, 17e; E. Würthwein, *The Text of the OT* (Tr. P. R. Ackroyd; Oxford: Basil Blackwell, 1957) 13. It is usually explained as a reference to misplacement, which would apply to v 40 but hardly to the earlier verses.

22.a. The sacrifice of thanksgiving was accompanied by an oral testimony: cf. D. Bach, "Rite et parole dans l'AT. Nouveaux éléments apportés par l'étude de Torah," *VT* 28 (1978) 10–19.

23.a. The parallelism suggests that יורדי here means "embark" as in Jonah 1:3. For Hebrew seafaring cf. 1 Kgs 10:22.

25.a. Heb. גליו appears to lack an antecedent. Dahood (*Psalms III*, 87) renders "his waves." Probably the suffix refers back to הים "the sea" in v 23, via מצולה "deep" in v 24; S (cf. *BHS*) merely makes this fact explicit.

27.a. Probably a primary meaning of the stem חגג is reflected in יחוגו "they reeled" (KB, 3rd ed., 278).

29.a. I.e. the waves which had been attacking them. S "waves of the sea" (cf. *BHS*) is a targumic type of rendering (cf. v 25).

30.a. This meaning (=LXX S Hier) has been confirmed by an Ugaritic multilingual text: see R. Borger, *UF* 1 (1969) 1–4.

32.a. "Elders" may be mentioned as the most characteristic part of the congregation (cf. F. S. Frick, *The City in Ancient Israel* [SBLDS 36; Missoula, MT: Scholars Press, 1977] 160 note 232). For Beyerlin's interpretation see *Form/Structure/Setting*. He has contrasted the lameness of this refrain with the climactic v. 22 (*Werden und Wesen*, 81), but note must be taken of the stylistic feature of chiasmus, which accords well with the psalm as a whole.

33.a. D. Michel (*Tempora*, 239) rightly follows H. Gunkel (*Die Psalmen*, 473) in regarding the verbs in vv 33–41 as expressing timeless statements; more precisely the verbs in vv 33, 35 are modal imperfects, "he can . . . ," followed by consecutive imperfects with a similar sense.

33.b. Isa 50:2 is evidently echoed.

34.a. There is probably an allusion to the overthrow of Sodom: cf. Deut 29:22–23.

35.a. Isa 41:18 is echoed (cf. 43:19).

39.a. The brevity of v 39a has led to attempts to supply an extra beat. S. Mowinckel ("Notes on the Psalms," *ST* 13 [1959] 160) supplied רשעים "the wicked"; NEB עריצים (cf. *BHK*) "tyrants," assuming pseudo-haplography before מעצר.

39.b. Vv 39 and 40 are commonly reversed (cf. the inverted *nun*) to suit the context and avoid a Job-like satire. M. Scott (*Discoveries*, 155–56) suggested that the double occurrence of the stem מעט in vv 38–39 caused the mistake: a copyist assumed that they should be placed together. Scott noted that the transposition would yield two lines concerning the doom of oppressors and two concerning God's vindication of the pious poor (vv 40, 39//41, 42). NEB (see above) is able to keep MT's order, but the sequence reads a little strangely with the change of subject so late in the line: it would have been wiser to transpose, as Mowinckel does. Dahood (*Psalms III*, 90) attempts to keep the order by taking the nouns as subject and re-dividing as ישחום עצר. He regards the suffix as datival: "oppression . . . declined from them." He refers to the same re-division made by H. D. Hummel ("Enclitic *Mem* in Early Northwest Semitic, Especially Hebrew," *JBL* 76 [1957] 104), who took the *mem* as enclitic: "while oppression diminished and declined." Robertson (*Linguistic Evidence*, 96–97) rejects this latter solution. Beyerlin (*Werden und Wesen*, 65) considers that a moral change for the worse can be presupposed in the light of v 34b. But the abruptness is difficult: if v 35 had preceded vv 33, 34, Beyerlin's argument would have been more impressive. Anderson (*Psalms*, 757) has suggested that v 39 is a protasis to v 40 (cf. RSV, GNB). Scott's text-critical explanation and indication of the merits of transposition make it appealing. For the repetition of terms (מעט-מעט) in a contrary sense in alternate pairs cf. vv 33, 35. But the pairing of lines fails to work out in detail in vv 33–42 or 43. Rather the structure appears to be that three groups of three lines are followed by a pair of lines (vv 42–43). In the first two groups of three lines the initial and final lines each contain verbs with a divine subject (vv 33, 35, 36, 38), which suggests a parallel order, vv 40, 39, 41.

40.a. Job 12:21a is evidently quoted in v 40a and Job 12:24b in v 40b.

42.a. Job 22:19a is quoted except that ישרים "upright" replaces צדיקים "righteous."

43.a. The plural verb can stand *ad sensum* contra *BHK*, which read a singular with S.

43.b. R. N. Whybray (*Intellectual Tradition*, 97) aptly compares the wisdom reference which concludes a hymn at 110:10.

Form/Structure/Setting

Academic treatment of Ps 107 has been marked by such a bewildering array of permutations of questions of form, content and unity that here it is possible to give only a representative selection of reconstructions. In form the psalm falls into two Gattungen: vv 1–32 are a type of song of thanksgiving, while vv 33–43 are a hymn or more precisely a passage marked by both hymnic and sapiential features. C. Westermann (*Praise*, 104–5, 117, 121, 124) has related the former part to the individual thanksgiving in view of its account of need and deliverance and vow of praise, and described the psalm as a liturgical combination of four such songs, in which the individual no longer speaks, but individuals are called to praise God for the deliverance they have experienced. All four accounts are concerned with everyday occurrences, with reality in its manifold fulness. Thanksgiving can pass into final hymnic praise of God (cf. 18:26–28 [25–27]), and such praise can be expressed in terms of God exalting and bringing low (cf. 147:6; 1 Sam 2:4–8) and also in a double description of the wicked and the righteous, as in v 42 (cf. 34:16, 17 [15, 16]). The exhortation of v 43 can be compared with the reflection of 92:1–3.

Kraus (*Psalmen*, 909) has related the question of form to matters of content and setting. He speaks for many commentators in concluding that the psalm falls into three diverse elements. The oldest, vv 1, 4–32, is a priest's summons of individuals to thanksgiving, recalling the obligations of their vows to praise and to sacrifice thank offerings, and describing situations which entail such a response. It served as a cultic inauguration of a thanksgiving service in which many individuals brought their offerings of praise and sacrifice. Kraus rejects the setting of Crüsemann (*Studien zur Formgeschichte*, 73) who, following Gunkel, envisages a mass thanksgiving service held at festival times. Vv 2–3 are a post-exilic addition, which imports an extra element, reflecting the situation of those who have returned from exile and the Diaspora. As to vv 33–43, Kraus follows Duhm and Gunkel in regarding them too as supplementary: they adapt the earlier composition to communal use by celebrating Yahweh's control over nature and men.

Mention should be made of the contribution of J. Becker (*Israel deutet seine Psalmen*, 53–55). In a sense he has little to add to Kraus's interpretation of the psalm, but his concern is to give a positive evaluation of the subsequent re-interpretation: "secondary" additions are not to be dismissed but are authoritative for the biblical understanding of the composition.

Crüsemann (*Studien zur Formgeschichte*, 73–74) assigns vv 33–43 to a noncultic setting: the earlier cultic poem was re-used in the late post-exilic context of the wisdom school. But Weiser (*Psalms*, 685–86), like Kraus, holds to a cultic setting throughout. However, he is concerned to stress its unity. The psalm is a communal thanksgiving probably recited before the thank offering. Pilgrims from every part of the world are gathered, v 3. Their experiences are woven into a recollection of the Israelites' wilderness wanderings till finally they reached the city of God, vv 4–9. Then in vv 10–32 the experiences of particular groups are related, while vv 33–42 are a general testimony to God's blessing of his people. The psalm is not necessarily late: apparent echoes of Second Isaiah may well reflect ancient cultic traditions also used by the prophet.

N. H. Snaith (*Five Psalms*, 17–21) associated the psalm with communal praise. It looks back over the history of God's people. He found them in the wilderness and brought them to Canaan, vv 4–9. He freed them both from bondage in Egypt and exile in Babylon and brought them to the land, vv 10–16. When they were well-nigh perished as a nation (in exile), he brought virtually dead bones to life, vv 17–22. The storm of vv 23–30 is like the allegory of Israel's exile in the book of Jonah: the "great waters" of v 23 are symbolic of the nations, as in Isa 17:12, 13. The concluding section sums up the whole section of God's mighty deeds of salvation.

Somewhat similar is Dahood's historical interpretation (*Psalms III*, 80–91). Pilgrims from all parts have assembled to sing this hymn of national thanksgiving. They praise God for the Exodus, v 2. He saved them from the wilderness, from its threat of death, the prison of Sheol, and from its sickness (cf. Num 11:33). Vv 23–30 he is evidently unable to fit into this historical framework. Vv 33–43 contain historical allusions to the destruction of wicked Canaanites (v 34) and to Israelite settlement in Canaan. References in this section to some of the earlier verses prove that the entire psalm is a unity composed by a single psalmist. Following Weiser, he urges that references to seafaring do not demand a post-exilic date, although he contradicts himself by seeing a reference to the Babylonian exile and widespread dispersion in v 3.

A historical interpretation is also given by E. J. Kissane (*Psalms II*, 174–80) and also A. F. Kirkpatrick (*Psalms*, 637, 638) who find in the (post-exilic) psalm metaphors of the exile. Israel in the dungeon of exile, sick on account of its own sin, all but swallowed up in the sea of the nations, had been redeemed, and returned. The last section offers consolation and encouragement to the post-exilic community. Kirkpatrick assigns to the psalm a double intention, to praise God for both personal and national deliverances.

Beyerlin has written a whole book on the psalm (*Werden und Wesen*), which would warrant an extended review for an adequate critique. He reconstructs four stages in the growth of the psalm: vv 1, 4–22 were amplified first by vv 23–32, then by vv 2–3, and finally by vv 33–43. Vv 4–22 present varied metaphors for the sphere of death from which Yahweh delivers. The wilderness is the result of straying morally along the wrong path, the way that leads to death. Suffering as the result of rebelling against God, vv 10, 11, brings to the prison of death. A particular crisis which threatens life and brings its victim to the Pit of death is sickness caused by taking the path of rebellion, vv 17–18, 20. Beyerlin finds use of material from Second Isaiah and especially from Job to support his metaphorical interpretation. This earliest element of the psalm is a post-exilic introduction for a cultic service of individual thanksgiving and thank offering. It has been amplified by vv 23–32, which is separated from the earlier strophes by its greater length, its metrical variation and its untypicalness in that there is no reference to sin; moreover, it uses only wisdom material and no prophetic. It is concerned with Yahweh's sovereignty over the sea as a further illustration of his deliverance from the sphere of death. Its deliberate omission of the thank offering and mention of wisdom teachers (cf. Sir 6:32–37) in v 32 indicate a double setting, both the temple and the wisdom school. The addition of vv 2–3 incorporates a further group, those restored from the Diaspora, into the cultic introduction to the thanksgiving of individuals. Finally, the appendix in vv 33–43 develops vv 23–32 by adding that other areas of nature too are subordinate to Yahweh's power, besides the sea, and that history as well as nature is under his control. Its author was a wisdom teacher versed in the scriptures and associated with the Levitical school attached to the temple (cf. 1 Chr 25:1–8).

Beyerlin's intensive analysis represents a stimulating tour de force. But in his treatment of the earlier parts of the psalm his citation of biblical material which he claims to underlie vv 10–22 betrays a certain selectiveness and a perhaps overhasty conclusion that parallelism of motifs implies dependence. His isolation of vv 23–32 is not compelling: on stylistic grounds one could claim that vv 17–22 are the least artistic of the four strophes and smack of later imitation, in comparison with the poetic artistry of vv 4–16, 23–32!

It is hardly possible to resist an impression of the composite nature of the psalm. The (pre-exilic?) summons to a service of individual thanksgiving appears to have undergone radical re-interpretation by the addition of vv 2–3, which transformed it into a post-exilic communal thanksgiving for immigrants from the Diaspora. Vv 33–43, which take up earlier vocabulary in new senses, represent a didactic meditation which is not necessarily inconsistent with thanksgiving (cf. Westermann, *Praise*, 104–5, 117, 121, 124): wisdom elements were freely incorporated into psalms of thanksgiving (cf. R. E. Murphy, "Wisdom Psalms," 160–61, 167).

The structure of the psalm is self-evident. After the call to thanksgiving in v 1, vv 4–9, 10–16, 17–22, 23–32 present a repeated pattern. Groups are called to give thanks. The naming of each group broadens into a description of their particular distress, prayer and subsequent deliverance. The references to prayer and jussive calls to praise form a double refrain with variations. In the latter case the variation is that vv 9, 16 supply summarizing reasons for thanksgiving, while instead vv 22, 32 amplify the summons. Most of the strophes are bound together internally by repetition: דרך "way" and עיר מושב "inhabited city," vv 4, 7 רעבים and רעבה "hungry," vv 5, 9, חשך וצלמות "darkness and deadly darkness," vv 10, 14, אסירי "bound" and מוסרות "bonds," vv 10, 14, ברזל "iron," vv 10, 16, the stem ירד "go down," vv 23, 26, and the polel רומם "make high," vv 25, 32, גליו and גליהם "its/ their waves," vv 25, 29. Vv 17–22 are a striking exception to this intrastrophic repetition; moreover, chiasmus, which Dahood (*Psalms III*, 81) has discovered in vv 4, 9, 11, 14, 16, 19 (and so also in vv 6, 13, 28), 32, features here only once. Vv 33–43 are marked by a resumption of earlier vocabulary, six times from vv 4–9, five from vv 23–32 (apart from כל, vv 27, 42) and only once from vv 10–16 and once from vv 17–22 (apart from כל, vv 18, 42). In addition it summarizes the four instances of חסדו "his loyal love" at the end of each strophe and the initial חסדו of v 1 with a comprehensive plural in v 43. It falls into three groups of three verses with a concluding couplet (cf. the note on v 39). The addition of vv 2–3 and the consequent alteration of a probably original תעי to תעו points to a long initial strophe of vv 1–9.

Mejía (*BTB* 5 [1975] 57–58) has noted the chiastic structure of vv 4–32; traveling features in both vv 4–9 and 23–32, while sin is specified in the two central divisions, at vv 11, 17. He interprets desert and sea as symbols of chaos, forces opposed to God, so that two acts of salvation from sin are framed by two of salvation from chaos.

Explanation

The Christian reader of the OT has to learn to regard certain psalms from a double perspective. Pss 8 and 22 have their own validity within their OT context, but the NT invites re-interpretation in terms of Christ. This process of re-interpretation can be detected in the OT itself: Ps 51 is a probable example. In Ps 107, too, an older poem appears to have been taken over and re-used for a new situation. The original was evidently vv 1, 4–32 and the setting in which it was employed was the service of thanksgiving at the temple, in which individuals had the opportunity, and duty, of paying vows with a thank offering. The composition is a priestly exhortation to give thanks, which doubtless inaugurated the service. Four different experiences are cited as examples of Yahweh's deliverance and testimonies to his love and power. They probably represent types rather than standard cases: peril on the high seas must have been a rare phenomenon for the land-loving

Hebrew. In the first example, vv 4–9, travelers were out in the wilds, hopelessly lost, far from civilization. Their supplies of food and drink had run out, and they were at the end of their tether. But they could pray. Then they set off again and were led, they believed, to safety. Yahweh can work wonders in such providential ways; he is well able to meet the material needs of all those who trust in him.

The second case features release from prison, vv 10–16. Prisoners who had committed crimes—and so sins against the God of law and order—were languishing in their dark dungeon, dispirited and, humanly speaking, helpless in a culture where prisoners were liable to be forgotten, serving indefinite sentences (cf. Gen 40:23). But they, too, could pray, and in due course found themselves free men. They could explain it only as a divine answer to their praying. Yahweh can break even prison bars.

A third group had recovered from serious sickness, vv 17–22. Behind their illnesses lay an unwise way of life and they had no one to blame but themselves. Yet in response to prayer they were given priestly assurance of healing. Soon they knew the joy of God-given health. Yahweh can heal the sick.

The fourth type of deliverance is the most thrilling of all (vv 23–32). Like the first it features travel, but now on the perilous sea. Mariners were able to experience at first hand the forces of nature in their awe-inspiring rage. But to the Israelite monotheist it was Yahweh's wonders at work. The sailors found their nautical expertise of no avail, and could trust only to prayer. Miraculously, to their eyes, the storm subsided. Yahweh can still the stormy waves.

Imposed upon this original psalm is a fresh interpretation related to the community. They owe their entire existence to Yahweh's goodness. The exile was past, and from all over the ancient world Jews were being repatriated—by Yahweh!—to their homeland. He had claimed them back as his own people, and of that truth their presence in the temple was a proof. They had an obligation to render communal thanksgiving for his covenant grace. From land and sea they had come. Homeward bound, they had endured the dangers of desert and ocean. They were so glad to be home in their own land, in Jerusalem and in their settlements (vv 7, 36). Now they are urged to turn their relief and joy into thanksgiving and praise.

But a deeper spiritual note also needed to be struck. Rebellion against Yahweh had sent them into exile (cf. Ps 106). It had been a prison where they had had to serve their sentence (Isa 42:7; 49:9; cf. Mic 7:8). It had been a sickbed to which their own moral perversity had sent them (cf. 147:2–3; 2 Chr 36:16; Isa 53:4; Jer 33:6, 7). But Yahweh's liberating and healing word had come to them with assurance of forgiveness (cf. Isa 40:1–2). How gladly the restored community could add to the priest's report its own Amen in the form of offering and song.

The final parts of the psalm take up terms from the strophes which spoke of traveling home and weaves them into a meditation of praise concerning the activity of Yahweh. It is spoken from the perspective of the community as pious and poor (v 41), out of a deep sense of the moral providence of their God. The God of the storm can cause similar disruption on land. Sodom is a warning to believers concerning the havoc to which wickedness can lead. But Yahweh's reversal of nature can happily work another way, as Second

Isaiah had once proclaimed to the exiled people. In the second sub-unit of the strophe, vv 36–38, reference is made in tones of praise and trust to the blessings with which Yahweh endows his people. The third, vv 40, 39, 41, like the first, caps two negative statements with a positive, but now puts men to the fore. For those who were underdogs in the world, as post-exilic Judah felt itself to be, there was consolation in dwelling upon a theme borrowed from the book of Job, that those in high estate are liable to be toppled (cf. 1 Cor 1:26–29). Yahweh can demote and drive into the social wilderness; in a sense Judah in its restoration had known the reverse (v 7). When such happens, it is a proof to those with eyes to see that a moral God rules the world. It is part of his manifold "acts of loyal love" to his own that their persecutors fall.

Psalm 107 in its final form is an impressive example of how the written word can come alive for a later generation of God's people and speak to them in a new way corresponding to their new situation. It is a mark of the living word that it is not exhausted in an ancient situation nor does it require repetition of history to become valid again, but runs freely, challenging a new generation of believers to see a fresh correspondence between word and experience.

The psalm celebrates the deliverance of God both in the lives of individuals and in the life of the religious community. It celebrates, too, divine forgiveness which brings liberation and renewal of life to sinful men. As it praises, it intends also to teach concerning the way of folly and the way of wisdom. Divine providence concerning both the overthrown of tyrants and the blessing of the faithful must teach a moral lesson. The message spoken from faith to faith is that God rules in the lives of men and works wonders of love and power.

In the NT divine deliverance is focused upon the agency of Jesus Christ. He announced an era of liberation and performed wondrous works of healing and stilling of the storm. These proclaim their perpetrator to be Lord of nature, bringer of wholeness and forgiveness and ruler of the lives of men, who in response are summoned to praise and thanksgiving (Luke 4:18–19; 8:22–25; 17:11–19; cf. Acts 12:1–17).

Old, Yet Ever New   (108:1–14)

Bibliography

Becker, J. *Israel deutet seine Psalmen.* **North, C. R.** "אֶעְלֹזָה אֲחַלְּקָה שְׁכֶם (Ps. 60:8//Ps. 108:8)." *VT* 17 (1967) 242–43. **Weisman, Z.** " 'אעלזה' של לפישרה." *Bet Miqra* 34 (1968) 49–52. **Yaron, R.** "The Meaning of *zanaḥ.*" *VT* 13 (1963) 237–39.

Translation

¹ A Song. A Psalm. Davidic.[a]
² *My heart is steadfast,*[a] *O God;*[b]   (3+3)
   I will sing and celebrate with music from my heart.[c]

³ *Wake up, harp and lyre.*   (3+2)
   I will wake up the dawn.
⁴ *I will give you thanks among the peoples, Yahweh,* ᵃ   (3+2)
   celebrate you ᵇ *with music among the nations,* ᶜ
⁵ *because your loyal love towers above the heavens,*   (3+3)
   your faithfulness reaches the skies.

⁶ *Be exalted above the heavens, O God,*   (3+3)
   and let your glory cover all the earth.
⁷ *In reply to me help with your right hand*   (3+3)
   so that those you love may be rescued.
⁸ *God himself spoke in his sanctuary:* ᵃ   (3+3+3)
   "I will exult, ᵇ *I will divide out Shechem*
   and measure out Succoth Valley into parts.
⁹ *Gilead is mine, Manasseh is mine,*   (4+3+3)
   Ephraim is my headguard,
   Judah is my baton.
¹⁰ *Moab is my wash basin,*   (3+3+3)
   I throw my sandal onto Edom
   and shout in triumph over Philistia."

¹¹ *Who can take me to the fortified city?*   (3+3)
   Who can lead ᵃ *me to Edom?*
¹² *Have you not rejected* ᵃ *us, O God?*   (3+3)
   Will you not march out, O God, with our forces? ᵇ
¹³ *Give us aid against* ᵃ *the enemy,*   (3+3)
   because human help is useless.
¹⁴ *With God we shall prevail:*   (3+3)
   he is the one who will trample down our enemies.

Notes/Comments

1.a. Here begins a group of three diverse Davidic psalms. That both Pss 57 and 60 are so labelled is the obvious warrant for this ascription. The present psalm may have existed too in a supplement to a pre-exilic collection. Its position after Ps 107 reflects not only the shared divine attribute of חסד "loyal love" (v 5), but also its historical and theological setting: after return to the land, the hope of total repossession and of vindication of God's sovereignty by means of Edom's conquest remains as the goal of his people.

2.a. It is possible that the nonrepetition of לבי נכון (contrast 57:8 [7]) represents haplography. But most probably the witnesses to a different text (see BHS), as elsewhere in this psalm, exhibit simply assimilation to the other psalm rather than independent testimony. M. Dahood (*Psalms III*, 93) wisely counsels against standardization. The shorter text of MT in v 2 (including the omission of עורה) exhibits a feasible metrical bicolon which is to be respected as a recensional variant. Heb. נכון לבי may have referred originally to the psalmist's act of will, his firm resolve to promise his thanksgiving ("my mind is made up"), but in this new context it refers to confidence.

2.b. H.-J. Kraus (*Psalmen*, 916) alters to יהוה here and in vv 6, 8, 12, although he grants (917) that אלהים has been taken over from an "elohistically" edited part of the Psalter. It is most doubtful that a version of Ps 108 ever existed which used יהוה.

2.c. Heb. כבודי functions as an elaboration of the personal subject of the verb: see GKC § 144l, m and cf. v 7. Should the form be revocalized as כְּבֵדִי "my liver" (cf. Lam 2:11)? In the Psalter the suggestion is sometimes made in places where the term functions as seat of the emotions (cf. H. W. Wolff, *Anthropology*, 64). A. R. Johnson (*The Vitality of the Individual in the Thought of Ancient Israel* [2nd ed.; Cardiff: University of Wales Press, 1964] 75 note 5) urges that each case must be examined on its merits. He has suggested that it denoted "the person of man in all its dignity and worth." J. W. Rogerson and J. W. McKay (*Psalms 51–100*, 44) define it as "the God-given faculty of praise."

4.a. For this less common type of thanksgiving formula in which God is directly addressed rather than speaking of him in the third person see F. Crüsemann, *Studien zur Formgeschichte*, 274–76.

4.b. The variant text in S (see *BHS*) is to be explained as an instance of contamination from other passages, a frequent phenomenon in S, here from 18:50 (A. Vogel, *Bib* 32 [1951] 51–52).

4.c. For the *maqqeph* in MT see *BHS*.

5.a. Heb. מֵעַל has replaced עַד "as far as" in 57:11 (10), probably to stress the link with v 6a. In this new composition עַל־שָׁמַיִם(מ) functions as a strophic hinge (see *Form/Structure/Setting*).

7.a. See note 2.c. above.

8.a. An ancient oracle concerning God's hegemony over Palestine and Transjordan is cited as the basis of the request of vv 6–7. E. Lipinski (*La liturgie penitentielle*, 101–5) has urged that this was already its significance in Ps 60.

8.b. C. R. North (*VT* 17 [1967] 242–43), comparing Num 13:17, has restructured אֶעְלֹזָה as אֶעֱל־זֹה "I will go up now" (=NEB), with an enclitic זֹה. He noted that עלז is not used elsewhere with a divine subject. Dahood (*Psalms III*, 94) parries this argument by reference to Ugaritic text where verbs of joy are so used in a military context. The apparent function of the verb as inclusive counterpart to אֶתְרוֹעָע "shout in trumph" at the end of the oracle (v. 10) favors MT. Z. Weisman (*Bet Miqra* 34 [1968] 49–52) proposed אֶעַל לוֹזָה "I will go up to Luz," thus securing a triple reference to place names.

11.a. MT is generally emended to an imperfect יַנְחֵנִי "lead," assuming haplography of *yod*. The verbal parallelism so suggests and the ancient versions so imply.

12.a. R. Yaron (*VT* 13 [1963] 237–39) has argued that זְנַחְתָּנוּ be rendered "be angry with us" in the light of the Accadian cognate verb *zenû* "be angry."

12.b. The construction of the second colon is ambiguous. (a) It could be consecutive, "so that you do not. . . ." But the repetition of אֱלֹהִים "God" suggests rather synonymous parallelism. (b) The force of the interrogative could carry over. But when the clause is taken as a further question, its implication is positive while that of the first colon is negative. (c) A third possibility would be as (b) but to render at the end "against our forces" (for "against" with verbs of fighting cf. BDB, 89a). This would perfect the parallelism. But probably (b) is to be preferred. From the despair of vv 11, 12a there is a movement within the interrogative line to a plea in v 12b, which develops into the explicit prayer of v 13. The change from perfect verb to imperfect within v 12 enhances this preference.

13.a. For מִן after the stem עֹזר "aid" cf. Deut 33:7; Ezra 8:22. The construction is probably to be explained by analogy with verbs of salvation.

Form/Structure/Setting

Psalm 108 consists of the latter halves of two other psalms, 57:8–12 (7–11) and 60:7–14 (5–12). The formal ingredients are largely those of the earlier contexts. But whereas 57:8–12 functioned within an individual complaint, the verses now have a role to play within a communal complaint spoken by a representative of the community (cf. 108:7, 11–14). In fact the section taken from Ps 60 is the determinative one, which has here been provided with a new introduction, from Ps 57. It is not necessary here or elsewhere in the discussion of Ps 108 to retrace ground already covered by the commentary on the two earlier psalms; the present task is to concentrate upon the re-use of the older material. A vow of praise (vv 2–4) is grounded in divine love (v 5). Then prayers for God's saving intervention (vv 6, 7) are followed by citation of a divine oracle (vv 8–10). Finally, questions representing implicit appeal to God (vv 11, 12) move first to a direct prayer and then to a declaration of trust (vv 13, 14).

It is to be noted that three times praise or prayer is substantiated by an assertion with a divine reference. This exegetical parallelism points to a triadic structure of vv 2-5, 6-10, 11-14, four, five and four lines respectively (cf. *BHK* and *BHS* which indent at v 6). The structure suggested by J. Schildenberger (*Estudios Eclesiásticos* 34 [1960] 684), whereby the psalm consists of two strophes each with two sub-strophes of three lines, vv 2-4 + 5-7, 8-10 + 11-13, and a final line, has little to commend it. The strophic hinge שמים-על(מ) already noted in vv 5-6 is matched by another, אדום "Edom" in vv 10-11. In each strophe the divine noun or name occurs at two places, in vv 2, 4, then vv 6, 8, and finally vv 12 (twice), 14. The first and second strophes both begin with references to כבוד "glory," albeit in different senses (vv 2, 6). The first and second at or near their close contain a reference to nations, specified in the latter case (vv 4, 10). At the beginning of the first strophe is a chiastic pattern of verbs, in vv 2b-4, ואומרך : אעירה :: עורה : ואזמרה, repeating "celebrate with music" and "awake." This pattern is balanced by chiastic parallelism at the end of the third strophe: v 14b corresponds to v 13a, repeating צר "enemy," while v 14a functions as a contrast to v 13b. The poetic reshaping of the material from Pss 57 and 60 is to be noted. The end of the former material now functions as the head of a new strophe, dovetailing into the latter's source material but sacrificing the crucial role of the repeated stem ישע "save" which brought two strophes to a close (60:7, 13 [5, 11] = 108:7, 13). The shorter introduction to the whole composition, compared with 57:8-10 (7-9), provides a more fitting counterpart to its new ending. The result is by no means a misshapen gluing together of two ends but a new creation of three beautifully balanced strophes. Its stylistic unity warns against disregarding its new unity and suggests that the psalm be taken seriously as a composition in its own right.

J. Becker (*Israel deutet seine Psalmen*, 65-67) has stressed that the whole is more than a sum of its parts. He has suggested that vv 4, 6 invest the Ps 60 material with a new universal dimension. Its mention of different tribes and nationalities becomes an illustration of the eschatological relationship between Israel and the nations. He dates the new composition to the exilic or post-exilic period and sees a reflection of the כבוד proclaimed by Second Isaiah (Isa 40:5; 59:19; 60:2, etc.) in the new association of divine glory with the deliverance of the people. He suggests severance from the cultic roots of the original material, such as thanksgiving; the "sanctuary" of v 8 would be for the redactor a heavenly one.

Over against Becker's chronological setting may be placed the pre-exilic one suggested by O. Eissfeldt ("Die Psalmen als Geschichtsquelle," 105) on the grounds of the psalm's particular combination of nationalistic and religious attitudes. More particularly S. Mowinckel (*Psalmenstudien*, vol. 3, 72-73) related the psalm to the period of Jehoram, king of Judah in the ninth century B.C. (cf. 2 Kgs 8:20-22). Rogerson and McKay (*Psalms 101-150*, 56) offer a less rarified interpretation than Becker. The new psalm, like Ps 60, was intended for use in a time of military crisis. Psalm 57:8-12 (7-11) was originally a prayer associated with a night vigil, and such a setting is possibly still presupposed. "The king or commander of the army could then be imagined dedicating his cause to God . . . just before first light on the day of a military expedition or of battle." The enemy is not specified: the reference to Edom in v 11 is judged to be a symbol of any aggressor.

One factor relevant to chronology is the replacement מֵעַל in v 5 which appears to be so tied to the structure of the psalm as to be due to the redactor. BDB (759a) observe that its use with the sense of עַל "upon" is a feature of late Hebrew. Dahood's reference to Phoenician heaped-up prepositions (*Psalms III,* 94), if intended as a chronological pointer, cannot convincingly offset the impact of the actual Hebrew examples set out in BDB. The universalism of vv 4, 6 does not necessarily dilute the sequel. The focus upon Edom in v 11 would have special meaning for the Jewish community after 587 B.C., as the book of Obadiah eloquently testifies. The same book attests the organic link between conquest of Edom and possession of the whole land, the first being viewed as a signal for the second and also for the vindication of Yahweh and Israel against "all the nations" (Obad 15–21). Accordingly there appears to be good reason for taking the reference to Edom as literal. Whether the new composition was used first for an actual campaign against Edomites cannot be clarified. It may simply reflect confidence expressed by a leader of the community in Yahweh's ultimate victory on their behalf.

Explanation

A new situation prompted the re-use of the second half of Ps 60, a prayer anchored in God's promise. The post-exilic religious community looked back hungrily to the old boundaries of the promised land and therefore prized highly an ancient oracle. Shechem and Succoth, v 8, immediately west and east of the Jordan, represented God's claim to the whole land. He was a warrior who used his people as instruments of war. Neighboring nations were claimed as vassals subject to his authority. The leader of the community took this oracle as warrant for his plea on their behalf for vindication.

The older poem itself pinpointed Edom as the most relevant ingredient claimed from the promise. The specification received fresh warrant after Edom's treachery when Jerusalem fell in 587 B.C. (cf. Obad 11–14). Edom became the focus of the community's appeal for divine justice. In their eyes the corollary of Edomite ascendancy was Judean humiliation, which spelled God's own dishonor. But God could and would, it is confidently affirmed, give the victory in the inaugural struggle for repossession of the whole land. Human aid is solemnly renounced, to stress total dependence upon him.

So Ps 60 came alive with a new relevance. But the grim beginning of that psalm was judged less auspicious. The post-exilic community knew all too well the theme of divine judgment (cf. v 12), and encouragement was what was needed on the occasion(s) when the new psalm would be sung. Accordingly it was replaced with the confident assurance of the second half of Ps 57. Its vow of praise breathed certainty, uncowed by the pagan environment. It grounded its hope in the reality of God's overwhelming loyalty to his own. It looked for manifestation of his glory so that all men might know Yahweh to be the true God.

So the psalm became the vehicle of believing prayer. It came to speak for the religious community at their contemporary level of revelation and experience. They prayed as best they knew, taking seriously the ancient revelation of national election and the covenant tradition concerning God, Israel and the land. By using this psalm, they sought to be faithful to that revelation and to enhance God's glory. The combination of earlier psalms illustrates the vitality of older scriptures as they were appropriated and applied to new situations in the experience of God's people. Evidently Ps 60 had harked back to a promise already old: over and over again God's word speaks to the hearts of his people.

Not Guilty (109:1-31)

Bibliography

Creager, H. L. "Note on Psalm 109." *JNES* 6 (1947) 121–23. Guillaume, A. "A Note on Ps. 109:10." *JTS* 14 (1963) 92–93. Hugger, P. " 'Das sei meiner Ankläger Lohn . . .'? Zur Deutung von Ps. 109:20." *BibLeb* 14 (1973) 105–12. Kaddary, M. Z. "חלל = 'Bore,' 'Pierce'? Note on Ps. 109:22." *VT* 13 (1963) 486–89. McKenzie, J. L. "The Imprecations of the Psalter." *AER* 111 (1944) 81–96. Schmidt, H. *Das Gebet der Angeklagten im AT.* BZAW 49. Giessen: A. Töpelmann, 1928.

Translation

¹ Director's. Davidic.[a] A Psalm.
 God whom I praise, do not be silent,[b]   (3+2)
² *for wicked [a] mouths,*
 deceitful [b] mouths [c] have they opened [d] against me,   (4+4)
  they have spoken to me [e] with lying tongues,
³ *and surrounded me with hateful talk*   (3+3)
  and attacked me without reason.
⁴ *In return for my love [a] they accuse me,*   (3+2)
  while my whole attitude has been one of prayer.[b]
⁵ *They have accorded me evil in return for good,*   (4+3)
  with hatred in return for my love:

⁶ *"Get a wicked person [a] to testify against him,*   (3+3)
  let an accuser stand on his right.[b]
⁷ *When he is tried, he will end up guilty*   (3+3)
  and his plea will be [a] counted as sin.
⁸ *May his life be a short one*   (3+3)
  and someone else take his office.[a]
⁹ *May his children become fatherless*   (3+2)
  and his wife a widow.
¹⁰ *May his children leave their ruined homes to beg [a]*   (4+3)
  and wander about asking for money.

¹¹ *May the creditor* ª *exact* ᵇ *all he has,*   (4+3)
  may strangers plunder his earnings.

¹² *May he have no one to extend him loyal help,*   (3+3)
  no one to care for his fatherless ones.

¹³ *May his offspring be destroyed,*   (3+3)
  their name ª *blotted out in the next generation.*

¹⁴ *May his forefathers' wrongs be remembered in Yahweh's presence* ª   (4+3)
  and his mother's sins not be blotted out.

¹⁵ *Let them ever confront Yahweh,*   (3+3)
  and may he destroy memory of the family ª *from the earth.*

¹⁶ *For he did not remember to show loyal help,* ª   (3+3+3)
  but persecuted the poor and needy
  and the disheartened to their death. ᵇ

¹⁷ *He loved cursing—may he experience it.* ª   (3+3+2)
  He did not like to bless—
  may it keep ª *its distance from him.*

¹⁸ *He made cursing his habit:*   (3+3+3)
  may it seep into him like water,
  into his bones like oil. ª

¹⁹ *May it be like the clothing he wears,*   (3+3)
  as tight as the belt he always has around him."

²⁰ *May this be the way Yahweh punishes* ª *my accusers,*   (4+3)
  those who speak such evil against me.

²¹ *But may you, Yahweh my Lord,*   (3+4)
  act on my behalf, in accord with your name.
  Rescue me because your loyal love ª *is so good.* ᵇ   (3+3+3)

²²   *For I am poor and needy*
  and my heart within beats wildly with distress. ª

²³ *I am fading like a lengthening shadow,*   (3+2)
  shaken off like a locust.

²⁴ *Through fasting my knees cannot support me,*   (3+3)
  my body is thin through losing weight.

²⁵ *I have become the butt of their insults,*   (4+3)
  when they see me they toss their heads.

²⁶ *Help me, Yahweh my God,*   (3+2)
  save me in accord with your loyal love,

²⁷ *so that they may know that this is your handiwork,*   (3+3)
  that you yourself have done it, Yahweh. ª

²⁸ *They are cursing, but may you bless,* ª   (4+4)
  may my assailants be confounded, ᵇ *but your servant* ᶜ *be gladdened.*

²⁹ *May my accusers be covered with disgrace*   (3+3)
  and clothed with confusion. ª

³⁰ *I will offer Yahweh many thanks with my mouth,*   (4+3)
  I will praise him among the assembly ª

³¹ *for standing on the right of the needy person,*   (3+3)
  ready to save him from those who put him on trial. ª

Notes/Comments

1.a. The psalm evidently reached the Psalter via two earlier collections, a Davidic one and that of the director of cultic music. J. H. Eaton (*Kingship*, 81), partly in view of the Davidic reference, regards the psalm as royal, taking the reference to fighting in v 3 in a military sense and noting royal features such as עֶבֶד "servant," v 28; but the evidence he cites is not compelling. Why the psalm should be placed at this point is unclear, except that it shares with Ps 108 membership of a Davidic collection and a concern for Yahweh's חֶסֶד "loyal love" (vv 21, 26).

1.b. The psalmist hopes for a priestly oracle of salvation (H. -J. Kraus, *Psalmen*, 922), which in the judicial context of the psalm would take the form of a favorable verdict.

2.a. MT רָשָׁע is better pointed רֶשַׁע "wickedness" in the light of the abstract nouns after terms relating to speech in vv 2–3 (H. Gunkel, *Die Psalmen*, 478; *et al.*). The pointing has been influenced by רָשָׁע in vv 6–7.

2.b. Heb. שֶׁקֶר "lying" probably has a legal connotation of giving false evidence (T. W. Overholt, *The Threat of Falsehood*, 88). This conclusion supports A. F. Kirkpatrick's forensic interpretation of דִּבְּרוּ אִתִּי, as in 127:5 (*Psalms*, 655; cf. Jer 12:1).

2.c. It is not necessary to delete וּפִי מִרְמָה as an interpolation with Gunkel (*Die Psalmen*, 478); Kraus (*Psalmen*, 919); *et al.* The first three words of v 2 may be taken with v 1b by enjambement.

2.d. The psalmist plunges *in medias res*, describing his enemies. The passive verb of LXX S Hier (cf. *BHS*) avoids this abruptness. Probably the Heb. verb was regarded as indefinite; it is unlikely that a different *Vorlage* underlies their rendering.

2.e. M. Dahood (*Psalms III*, 100) repoints to אֹתִי, assigning the verb to a different root. But structurally there seems to be correspondence with אוֹתִי in v 21 (see *Form/Structure/Setting*).

4.a. The deletion of תַּחַת אַהֲבָתִי "in return for my love" (*BHS et al.*) runs counter to the psalm's repetition of terms in adjacent verses, e.g. vv 9, 10, 13, 14, 17, 18.

4.b. The Heb. expression (lit. "and I prayer") is compressed but not without parallel: cf. 110:3; 120:7 (cf. GKC, § 141c). For the thought cf. 35:13. The addition "for them" in S seems to be exegetical. On its basis Kraus, *Psalmen*, 919; *et al.* add לָהֶם, but it is difficult to explain how it could have fallen out of the text, and it smacks of an easier reading. The prayer may have been cultic by proxy for those who were sick and excluded from public worship (Kraus, *Psalmen*, 922). E. A. Speiser (*JBL* 82 [1963] 306) tentatively suggested that in vv 4, 7 תְּפִלָּה means not "prayer" but "plea or right to be heard," here "whereas I am yet to be heard." With reference to v 7 it is sometimes objected that תְּפִלָּה in the sense of prayer can hardly be used with a human judge as the object, but if a religious court is postulated, there appears to be little difficulty.

6.a. Are vv 6–19 the psalmist's maledictions on his accusers or his citation of their maledictions against him? In favor of the latter is the change to a singular throughout (for vv 13, 15 see below), in differentiation from the psalmist's plural references in vv 1–5, 20–31. The singular might be explained as individualizing or collective, but the duration and consistency of the practice suggests otherwise.

H. Schmidt (*Das Gebet*, 41 note 1) mentions a view that the singular belonged to a traditional formula of execration employed here, but of that there is no evidence. More feasible is A. F. Kirkpatrick's supposition (*Psalms*, 654–55) that the ringleader is singled out. But his argument that in v 1b (MT) this ringleader is already mentioned is less impressive than it appears at first sight: "they have opened a wicked man's mouth" is most stilted. Dahood (*Psalms III*, 99, 102) finds reference to the knavish judge (in a secular court) who considered that the charges warranted a hearing. Appeal is often made to 55:14–15, 21–22 (13–14, 20–21) as a parallel for the change to a singular. But the texts are not exactly parallel: there the singling out (of a friend who turned traitor) is adequately explained in the psalm, and the psalmist's concern with this individual is expressed in a double reference rather than in a single block which ends as abruptly as it begins.

A good argument against vv 6–19 being a quotation is that עָנִי וְאֶבְיוֹן "needy and poor," v 16, is exactly repeated in v 22, which suggests that someone other than the psalmist is the subject of v 16 and hence of vv 6–19. It is possible to parry this argument by supposing that the quotation extends only to v 15 and that in vv 16–20 the psalmist indignantly retorts and reminds his adversaries that curses have a habit of coming home to roost (M. Scott, *Discoveries*, 156–57; JB), but the text gives no signal of a change of speaker at v 16.

In v 6 the only signal would be the change of number. Would it not have been introduced more obviously as a quotation, if it were that? P. Hugger (*BibLeb* 14 [1973] 110; cf. Schmidt, *Das Gebet,* 41) has claimed that both in the Psalter and in prophetic sayings quotations need not have a special introduction (e.g. 52:9 [7]; 95:8; 132:14; 137:3; Isa 28:9–10) and that adequate notice is given in vv 2–5. NEB exploits this practice by making simply v 6 the quotation: "They say, 'Put up some rascal to denounce him, an accuser to stand at his right side.' But when judgment is given, that rascal will be exposed. . . ." Thus the singulars of the following verses may be explained as harking back to "some rascal." It seems rather unreasonable that he rather than the enemies should bear the brunt of the psalmist's wrath, although J. W. Rogerson and J. W. McKay (*Psalms 101–150,* 59–60, 62) in tentative support argue from the Israelite law of evidence that "those found guilty of giving false evidence should suffer the same penalty that the accused would have suffered had he been found guilty (Deut 19:16–21)." But why then are not the whole group attacked in view of v 2?

The quotation theory is often dismissed as moralistic evasion of the imprecatory content: e.g. ". . . , however it may jar one's pious senses" (Eaton, *Kingship,* 81). Then one may go on triumphantly to deliver a coup de grâce: "in any case, in v 20 the psalmist hopes that God will do to his enemies what has previously been wished" (Rogerson and McKay, *Psalms 101–150,* 62). It is to be hoped that the aim of all serious scholars, whichever view they hold, is that theology should grow out of exegesis and not vice versa. With this subjective slur disposed of, it may be asked: can a good case be made for the view of vv 6–19 as a quotation? V 31a seems to stand as a climactic reprisal to v 6b (Kraus, *Psalmen,* 921). The claim that Yahweh was to stand at the psalmist's right would be an impressive retort to a maneuver to set an accuser there. If this interpretation is correct, it follows that the term "poor" (with overtones of piety) used of the psalmist in v 31 (cf. v 22) similarly serves to counter the claim that "the poor and needy man" was the object of his persecution (v 16). The uncontested contrast of the enemies' mouths and the psalmist's (vv 2, 30) adds weight to interpreting the two other cases at the end of the psalm as deliberate contrasts.

A second argument is that vv 6–19 appear to be set in a framework of repeated terms. H. L. Creager (*JNES* 6 [1947] 122) referred to (רעה) "evil," vv 5, 20. One might also cite the terms from the stem דבר "speak," vv 3, 20 and the repeated verb שטן "accuse," vv 4, 20. Is not this repetition the psalmist's own signal that first he is about to quote the words of accusation and then has finished quoting them? Thirdly, the psalm picks up a surprising number of earlier terms in apparently resumptive fashion. In the culminating v 31 שפטי נפשו "those who put him on trial" seems to echo בהשפטו "when he is put on trial," v 7. The "prayer" of v 4 seems to be taken up by "his prayer," v 7, while עלי "against me," v 5, is resumed by עליו "against him," v 7. In v 18 the curse associated with a triple comparison (כ) and directed against the psalmist's body (בקרבו) seems to be working itself out in vv 22–23 with its triple comparison and בקרבי. In the light of these clues, is it really "the natural, direct meaning" (Eaton, *Kingship,* 81) to interpret vv 6–19 as the psalmist's own maledictions?

Furthermore Hugger (*BibLeb* 14 [1973] 111) has argued that in individual complaints the psalmist's own wishes and prayers for retribution are always couched in direct address to Yahweh, as in 69:23–29 (22–28), whereas oblique divine references are a feature of a psalmist's quotation of his enemies' standpoint, as in 3:3 (2); 22:9 (8) 71:11 (cf. Jer 11:18–21). He has also cited 71:8–14 as a miniature counterpart to Ps 108 (*BibLeb* 14 [1973] 109). A. A. Anderson (*Psalms,* 758) has objected that it is questionable whether the psalmist would dare to repeat such curses originally directed against himself in view of current belief in the inherent power of the spoken word. But for a critique of this supposed belief see A. C. Thistleton, "The Supposed Power of Words in the Biblical Writings," *JTS* 25 (1974) 283–99.

6.b. In a trial the right hand side of the accused appears to have been the customary position of both the accuser and of the witness for the defense (cf. v. 31: Zech 3:1; cf. R. de Vaux, *Ancient Israel: Its Life and Institutions* [Tr. J. McHugh; London: Darton, Longman and Todd, 1965] 156).

7.a. The imperfect form suggests that the verse is a double statement of the anticipated result of the plot announced in v 6.

8.a. Heb. פקדה could mean "property," but since that is the subject of v 11 the alternative "position of authority" is preferable. V 8 is applied to Judas in Acts 1:20 as warrant for posthumous forfeiture of his apostleship to a successor. For this and other echoes of the psalm in Acts 2:37 and Mark 15:29 see B. Lindars, *NT Apologetic* (London: SCM Press, 1961) 109–10.

10.a. MT דרשו is commonly emended to יגרשו "be driven out" with the apparent support of LXX (see *BHS*). But A. Guillaume (*JTS* 14 [1963] 92) rightly complains that the line then represents a *hysteron proteron*. LXX may be due to a misreading of the text which misunderstood the pregnant construction of the preposition מן (cf. GKC § 119ff). The line has a chiastic order like v 23.

11.a. Cf. 2 Kgs 4:1 for the extreme powers of a creditor.

11.b. LXX "seek out" does not necessarily presuppose a different Heb. text *contra BHS:* cf. ἐκζητεῖν in Deut 12:30. Some such meaning as "seize" would suit the context better than "strike at" (BDB, 669b). Dahood (*Psalms III*, 103) regards נקש as a byform of יקש "seize with a snare," but comparison with Arab. *naḳaša* "exact money," which would involve repointing to ינקש, may well be relevant (Anderson, *Psalms*, 762; cf. NEB).

13.a. Heb. שממ and זכרם, v 15, have been cited as evidence that the singulars in the context have a collective force (e.g. D. A. Robertson, *Linguistic Evidence*, 86). H. D. Hummel (*JBL* 76 [1957] 99–100; cf. Dahood, *Psalms III*, 104–5) has argued in favor of a singular suffix and an enclitic *mem.* More probably the plurals refer to the family. For destruction of the name or memory see B. S. Childs, *Memory and Tradition*, 71.

14.a. For reminder to Yahweh to punish rather than overlook sins cf. 1 Kgs 17:18.

15.a. Lit. "their memory."

16.a. For חסד as a human phenomenon here and in v 16 see K. D. Sakenfeld, *The Meaning of Hesed*, 217, who compares Zech 7:9–10.

16.b. Lit. "so as to kill." Note should be taken of Dahood's construing as emphatic *lamed* and conative polel: "he seeks even to slay" (*Psalms III*, 105, 106). The proposal of Gunkel (*Die Psalmen*, 479) *et al.* to read לְמָוֶת with S in a superlative sense, as in Jonah 4:9, is hindered by the evidently chiastic order, observed by Dahood (*Psalms III*, 99).

17.a. Heb. יהי in v 19 suggests a repointing with weak *waw* (cf. *BHS*) here and in the case of ותבא, v 18, with the support of LXX.

18.a. There is no need to see a reference to the waters of ordeal of Num 5:22 or to assume that oil was similarly used ritually. Soaking is probably metaphorical for being completely under the curse's power. T. N. D. Mettinger (*King and Messiah*, 223) has compared the use of oil in connection with a vassal's oath and cited a parallel from the vassal treaties of Esarhaddon. The principle of *talio* is applied in vv 17–19.

20.a. "Retribution" or "punishment" is a possible meaning for פעלת (cf. Isa 65:7) and a jussive sense can easily be understood from v 19. Heb. זאת "this" has a structural counterpart in v 27: it relates to the two-sided intervention of Yahweh, there to vindicate the psalmist and here to punish his enemies. In v 21 ואתה "but you" accentuates the turning point in the psalm (cf. C. Westermann, *Praise*, 70–73), but it cannot be concluded that v 20 does not refer to a request for divine activity: cf. 59:5b–6 (4b–5). In the overall structure of the psalm a break comes at the end of v 19 (see *Form/Structure/Setting*) *contra* Kraus (*Psalmen*, 920, 921), *BHK* and *BHS*. Here ואתה highlights the contrast between the words of the accusers, now sent into reverse, and the work of Yahweh (cf. אתי "with me," vv 2, 21). Heb. מאת יהוה is often deleted on metrical grounds, e.g. by Gunkel, (*Die Psalmen*, 480). Kraus (*Psalmen*, 919–21) also requires deletion because he renders פעלת "work" rather than "recompense" and understands the sentence as a statement. Creager (*JNES* 6 [1947] 123) argued that S *dskryn lmry* "those who regard the Lord with malignity" represents a superior text שטני יהוה "those who accuse Yahweh," but it is the psalmist who is the object of accusation elsewhere in the psalm. Hugger (*BibLeb* 14 [1973] 108) has correctly seen that S corresponds simply to שנים את-יהוה (likewise A. Vogel, *Bib* 32 [1951] 209). This is to be explained simply as a case of wrong word division. But, insisting on the reading of S as significant, Hugger assumes an original שטני את-יהוה "my accusers before Yahweh" (i.e. at a religious trial), distorted in S by palaeographical pseudo-dittography of מ/ני. He aligns with S the minority LXX reading παρὰ κυρίῳ, but it is in fact secondary, attempting to get some sense out of the standard ἔργον . . . παρὰ κυρίου "work . . . from the Lord" (cf. *BibLeb* 14 [1973] 107).

21.a. Heb. חסד here and in v 26 has the nuance of divine ability to deliver; it also implies disaster for those who are outside the relationship (Sakenfeld, *The Meaning of Hesed*, 220–21).

21.b. There is no need to emend כי-טוב to כטוב (*BHS*): cf. 69:17 (16).

22.a. Heb. חלל is evidently intended as an indefinite third singular, "one has pierced." Dahood (*Psalms III*, 107) points as a passive qal, "has been pierced," which is syntactically easier (cf. the puʿal in Ezek 32:26). But the verb occurs only here with לב; 77:11 (10), the nearest parallel, is set in a different conceptual context. Perhaps MT has been wrongly influenced by 37:14–15. In the context of v 24 a reference is expected to throbbing or palpitation of the heart as a symptom of ill health and distress: cf. H. W. Wolff, *Anthropology*, 42, and especially his reference to 38:11 (10). Accordingly a form of חיל "writhe" and so "throb" is expected, and the similarly phrased 55:5 (4) לבי יחיל בקרבי so suggests. LXX associated the passages by using the same verb ταράσσειν. M. Z. Kaddary (*VT* 13 [1963] 486–89) assumes a byform of חיל, but there is hardly need to cling so closely to the present pointing. More commonly a polal חלל is read (*BHS*): the passive form accords with those of v 23.

27.a. *BHS*'s sign "b" has been wrongly attached to יהוה instead of עשׂיתה. The interpretation that Yahweh caused the death of which the psalmist is accused (v 16) must be rejected: cf. the use of עשׂה to express Yahweh's dynamic, saving intervention in v 21, as in 22:32 (31); 37:5; 52:11 (9). For זאת "this" cf. v 20.

28.a. A curse could be annulled by the more powerful word of divine blessing: see S. H. Blank, "The Curse, Blasphemy, the Spell, and the Oath," *HUCA* 23 (1950/51) 94, and cf. Deut 23:6 (5); Neh 13:2.

28.b. The text is commonly emended slightly to קָמַי יֵבשׁוּ in view of the parallelism, with the support of LXX (cf. *BHS*, where קּ is an error for קָמַי; cf. Isa 65:13).

28.c. C. Lindhagen (*The Servant Motif*, 266–70) has analyzed the contextual associations of עבד, a term characteristic of the individual complaint. The correlate within the relationship is אלהי "my God," v 26, as in 86:2, cf. 31:15–16 (14–15); 143:10, 12. The basis of appeal is the divine name, as in 143:11: Yahweh bears responsibility for his servant. One might also mention the divine חסד, vv 21, 26, as in 31:16 (15); 69:14, 17 (13, 16) and the correlation between "servant" and "Lord," vv 21, 28.

29.a. For the moral problem raised for the Christian reader see J. L. McKenzie, *AER* 111 (1944) 81–96. Rogerson and McKay's observation that according to OT law false witnesses were liable to the same penalty as their accused would have suffered if found guilty (*Psalms 101–150*, 59) renders intelligible the psalmist's flinging back his accusers' maledictions in v 20. McKenzie has observed that the theoretical Christian ideal of hatred of sin but love of the sinner is hardly reflected in Acts 23:1–6; 1 Tim 1:19–20; 2 Tim 4:14; James 5:1–6; Rev 6:9–10 and in such dominical sayings as Matt 23:32–35. In fact "the love of God hates all that is opposed to God; and sinners—not merely sin—are opposed to God" (*AER* 111 [1944] 92). He pertinently asks whether "the imprecatory psalms are not a model, not because of their lower degree of perfection, but because they are too lofty for most of us to imitate without danger" (AER 111 [1944] 96).

30.a. For רבים cf. קהל רב "great congregation" in the context of a thanksgiving service, 22:26 (25).

31.a. Heb. שׁפט is apparently used in a sense more commonly attached to ריב; but cf. the niph'al and po'el. LXX (see *BHS*) may represent a paraphrase considered necessary because of the unusual meaning.

Form/Structure/Setting

Psalm 109 has the form of an individual complaint. Its introductory petition (v 1b), description of distress occasioned by his enemies (vv 2–5, cf. v 25), main petition (v 26), double wish (vv 28–29) and vow of praise (vv 30–31) clearly delineate the psalm as such. C. Westermann ("Struktur und Geschichte der Klage im AT," *ZAW* 66 [1954] 56) has categorized vv 22–25 as a description of personal distress; it is worth adding that it includes a reference to voluntary fasting (v 24) by way of appeal to Yahweh's sympathy. More exactly the psalm may be analyzed as the prayer of an accused man who professes his innocence (Schmidt, *Das Gebet*, 40–45; Kraus, *Psalmen*, 920–22; *et al.*). The setting is then to be reconstructed as a religious court where the psalmist claimed his innocence before priestly judges as representatives of Yahweh (cf. Exod 22:7–8 [8, 9]; Deut. 17:8–13; 1 Kgs 8:31–32; cf. W. Beyerlin, *Die*

Rettung, 1970). The combination of forensic vocabulary and direct prayer lends strong support to such a role and setting for the psalm.

As to structure Dahood (*Psalms III*, 100) has observed the inclusive roles of the stem הלל "praise" and פי "mouth" in vv 1b, 2, 30. The psalm appears to fall into two halves, vv 1–19, 20–31, which further subdivide into two strophes each, vv 1–5, 6–19, 20–25, 26–31, in an ABA'B' pattern. Strophes A and A' have much in common: the stems דבר "speak," vv 3, 20, and שטן "accuse," vv 4, 20, רע(ה) "evil," vv 5, 20, כי "for," vv 2, 22, ואני "and I," vv 4, 25, and אתי "with me," vv 2, 21. So do strophes B and B': the stems שפט "put on trial," vv 7, 31, שטן "accuse," vv 6, 20, לבש "clothe," vv 18, 29, עטה "clothe," vv 19, 29, קלל "curse," vv 17, 18, 28, ברך "bless," vv 17, 28, and עשה "do," vv 16, 27, עמד "stand" with ימין "right hand," vv 6, 31, אביון "poor," vv 16, 31 and חסד "loyal love," vv 12, 16, 26.

The overall section vv 20–31 has its own inclusion in נפש/י vv 20, 31. Further links between strophes A' and B' are חסדך "your loyal love," vv 21, 26, שטני "my accusers," vv 20, 29, אביון "poor," vv 22, 31, the stem עשה "do," vv 21, 27, זאת "this," vv 20, 27, and the relationship between "Lord" and "servant" in vv 21, 28. Strophe B is marked by a host of minor repeated, self-interlocking elements, notably חסד, vv 12, 16, the verbs זכר "remember," vv 14–16, and הכרית "destroy," vv 13, 15, and יתומים/יו "orphans," vv 9, 12.

This stylistic analysis cannot solve the exegetical relation of strophes B and B'. Strophes A and A' obviously correspond as initial prayer grounded (כי "for") in description. Strophe B either continues strophe A as an amplification of the description of the slandering of enemies, as strophe B' by amplifying the element of prayer, or expresses the psalmist's own negative wishes as an introductory counterpart to his negative and positive wishes/prayers in strophe B'.

There are no clues to solve the issue of the age of the psalm; nothing precludes a pre-exilic origin (Kraus, *Psalmen*, 922). To judge it post-exilic on the grounds that the imprecatory vv 6–20 are reminiscent of Jer 18:19–23 (Anderson, *Psalms*, 759) is to ignore the factor of traditional language.

Explanation

The psalmist evidently stands on trial at a religious court. Before the priestly judges representing Yahweh he testifies that the accusations laid against him are unwarranted and false. He appeals to the God who hitherto has given him cause for praise by coming to his aid (cf. 27:9; Jer 17:14). How shabbily his love, intercession and concern for those who now accuse him have been rewarded, with malevolence and pure lies!

The accused proceeds to quote their evil scheming and hostile attitude. The very trial was an outworking of their plot, vv 6–7. They had planned to bring trumped-up charges against him and to attack him by means of judicial persecution (cf. 1 Kgs 21:8–14; Mark 14:55–64). Thus they hoped that his very plea of innocence would incriminate him. Next, in vv 8–11 are cited a string of imprecations against his life, family and property. For him they wished a premature death; for his children a beggar's lot after losing their inheritance to their father's creditors and to usurpers. Their imprecations turn into curses in the course of vv 12–16. In a close-knit society where bonds of kinship and caring were keenly felt, they urged that the accused had forfeited such social rights. They wanted the extinction of the family name, the ultimate of maledictions in a culture where its being handed down through the generations was prized as a surrogate for personal survival (cf. Gen 3:19, 20; Jer 11:19). In explicit curses mentioning Yahweh they invoked the concept of family solidarity which bound the past to the present (cf. Exod 20:5). They desired that Yahweh should do his worst and exact the punishment for every regulation in the book infringed by former generations. Thus they desired that the whole family line be wiped out.

Finally in vv 17–19 are reported their wishes that the accused should suffer the effects of his own alleged "habit" of cursing and instead feel it holding him in its tight grip.

In reprisal the psalmist himself invokes Yahweh. Their sentiments are such an affront to the truth that their proponents deserve to suffer them. He appeals to his divine judge to live up to the name he has for justice and protection of the oppressed. Yahweh's honor is at stake. It will be satisfied only by his taking the side of the psalmist to whom he is bound in a relationship of "loyal love." As in vv 2–5, his appeal is grounded in a description of his suffering. His worry has made him a shadow of his former self. He feels at his accusers' mercy: they can flick him off like an insect and dispose of him. He has been fasting in preparation for this religious trial (cf. 69: 11–12 [10, 11] and so is physically weak. He has to bear their taunts as they mock him now that he is down.

He renews his appeal in a plea for vindication and so for the failure of his accusers and for their humiliation. Their curses can be rendered ineffective by the superior power of God's blessing. The psalmist ventures to remind Yahweh of the close relationship between them, like that between a dutiful vassal and his sovereign lord and master. His cause is God's cause. If his appeal is answered, he promises to testify to Yahweh's saving help before the religious community at the thanksgiving service, and so to renew his former praise (cf. v 1). He trusts that his judge will also be his defense witness so that he may be vindicated (cf. Isa 50:8, 9; Rom 8:33–34).

The Christian reader of this psalm is acutely aware of the conspicuous absence of NT ideals of loving one's enemies and blessing persecutors (Matt 5:44; Rom 12:14). However, it should be stressed that the psalmist was motivated not simply by personal animosity, although it is evident from vv 4–5 that he felt sorely provoked. His supreme concern is for divine justice and honor. It is worth remembering also the OT concentration upon the temporal. The Christian is influenced by the eternal dimension of his religion and can wait for an eschatological Day of Judgment. But for the Israelite believer God's justice had virtually to be condensed into his short life if it was to be meaningful. In his own way the psalmist is leaving vengeance to the wrath of God (Rom 12:19), but he expected this vengeance to be manifested in the here and now rather than in the hereafter of Rom 2:5, 8. He lived in a theocratic society and duly expected that God's standards of right and wrong should be seen to be in operation (cf. Prov 17:13). Moreover, the psalmist saw the situation in black and white terms. His accusers had pitted themselves implacably not only against his own good nature and all he stood for morally, but against God himself. They had put themselves in the position of God's enemies for whom there could be no future. There is a place for a solemn curse (cf. 1 Cor 16:22; 1 Tim 1:20). The Christian may feel himself most hesitant to judge its expediency. But at least he should seek to understand the psalmist and respect the validity of his position within the framework of OT religion.

The psalm was presumably put to prolonged use in the context of the religious court and as a prayer to be recited by victims of legal persecution generally. But eventually it received a new role. As if to make up for its detractors, Ps 109 received the supreme accolade of being interpreted as a mirror of Christ's sufferings. Behind its use in Acts 1:20 lies an understanding of the psalm, as in the case of so many psalms of innocent suffering, whereby it found its loudest echo in the experience of Jesus. From this perspective Judas became the fitting heir of its curse, as history's archetype of wanton infidelity.

God's King and Priest (110:1-7)

Bibliography

Bernhardt, K. -H. *Das Problem der altorientalischen Königsideologie im AT unter besonderer Berücksichtigung der Geschichte der Psalmenexegese dargestellt und kritisch gewürdigt.* VTSup 8. Leiden: E. J. Brill, 1961. **Bowker, J. W.** "Psalm 110," *VT* 17 (1967) 31–42. **Caquot, A.** "Remarques sur le Psaume 110." *Sem* 6 (1956) 33–52. **Del Medico, H. E.** "Melchisedech." *ZAW* 69 (1957) 160–70. **Driver, G. R.** "Psalm 110: Its Form, Meaning and Purpose." *Studies in the Bible Presented to M. H. Segal,* ed. J. M. Grintz and J. Liver. Publications of the Israel Society for Biblical Research, vol. 17. Jerusalem: Kiryat Sepher, 1964. **Gaster, T. H.** "Psalm 110." *Journal of the Manchester University Egyptian and Oriental Society* 21 (1937) 37–44. **Hardy, E. R.** "The Date of Psalm 110." *JBL* 64 (1945) 385–90. **Hay, D. M.** *Glory at the Right Hand: Psalm 110 in Early Christianity.* SBLMS 18. Nashville: Abingdon Press, 1973. **Horton, F. L.** *The Melchizedek Tradition. A Critical Examination of the Sources to the Fifth Century A.D. and in the Epistle to the Hebrews.* SNTSMS 30. Cambridge: Cambridge University Press, 1976. **Ishida, T.** *The Royal Dynasties in Ancient Israel. A Study on the Formation and Development of Royal-Dynastic Ideology.* BZAW 142. Berlin: Walter de Gruyter, 1977. **Jefferson, H. G.** "Is Psalm 110 Canaanite?" *JBL* 73 (1954) 152–56. **Kissane, E. J.** "The Interpretation of Psalm 110." *ITQ* 21 (1954) 103–14. **Krinetzki, L.** "Psalm 110 (109). Eine Untersuchung seines dichterischen Stils." *TGl* 51 (1961) 110–21. **Mettinger, T. N. D.** *King and Messiah. The Civil and Sacral Legitimation of the Israelite Kings.* ConB OT Series 8. Lund: C. W. K. Gleerup, 1976. **Nober, P.** "De torrente in via bibet." *VD* 26 (1948) 351–53. **Podechard, E.** "Psaume 110." *Études de critique et d'histoire religieuse. Volume offert à L. Vaganay.* Lyons: Facultés Catholiques, 1948. **Rehm, M.** *Der königliche Messias im Licht der Immanuel-Weissagungen des Buches Jesaja.* Eichstatter Studien neue Folge, Band 1. Kevelaer: Butzon und Bercker, 1968. **Rowley, H. H.** "Melchizedek and Zadok." *Festschrift für A. Bertholet,* ed. W. Baumgartner, et al. Tübingen: J. C. B. Mohr, 1950. **Schedl, C.** " 'Aus dem Bache am Wege': Textkritische Bemerkungen zu Ps. 110 (109):7." *ZAW* 73 (1961)

290–97. **Schmidt, W. H.** "Kritik am Königtum." *Probleme biblischer Theologie. G. von Rad zum 70. Geburtstag,* ed. H. W. Wolff. München: C. Kaiser, 1971. **Schreiner, J.** *Sion-Jerusalem Jahwehs Königssitz. Theologie der heiligen Stadt im AT.* SANT 7. München: Kösel-Verlag, 1963. **Schreiner, S.** "Psalm 110 und die Investitur des Hohenpriesters." *VT* 27 (1977) 216–22. **Stoebe, H. J.** "Erwägungen zu Ps. 110 auf dem Hintergrund von 1 Sam. 21." *Festschrift F. Baumgärtel zum 70. Geburtstag.* Erlanger Forschungen 1:10. Erlangen: Universitätsbund, 1959. **Tournay, R.** "Le Psaume 110." *RB* 67 (1960) 5–41. **Treves, M.** "Two Acrostic Psalms." *VT* 15 (1965) 81–90. **Widengren, G.** *Sakrales Königtum im AT und im Judentum.* Stuttgart: W. Kohlhammer Verlag, 1955. **Wolff, H. W.** "Psalm 110:1–4." *Herr, tue meine Lippen auf,* ed. G. Eichholz. vol. 5. 2nd ed. Wuppertal-Barmen: Emil Müller Verlag, 1961, 310–23.

Translation

[1] Davidic.[a] A Psalm.

Yahweh's oracle [b] *to my master:*	(3+2)
"*Sit enthroned on my right,* [c]	
until [d] *I make your enemies*	(2+2)
a stool [d] *for your feet.*" [e]	

[2] *Your strong sceptre* (2+3+3)
will Yahweh extend [a] *from Zion*
so that you rule [b] *over your enemies around you.*

[3] *Your people will* [a] *volunteer* [b] (2+2)
on your day of power. [c]
On the holy mountains [d] (2+2+3)
from the womb of dawn [e]
you will have the dew [f] *of your youth.* [g]

[4] *Yahweh has sworn* (2+2)
an irrevocable oath: [a]
"*You are a perpetual* [b] *priest* (3+3)
on the pattern of Melchizedek." [c]
[5] *The Lord* [a] *on your right* [b] *shatters* [c] (3+3)
kings on his day of anger. [d]
[6] *He executes judgment among the nations,* (2+2)
heaping up corpses, [a]
shattering heads (2+2)
the wide world over.
[7] *He* [a] *drinks from the stream beside the road:* [b] (3+3)
therefore he holds his head high.

Notes/Comments

1.a. Unless the heading points simply to the royal nature of the psalm, it may refer to its origin in David's reign. The first line of the psalm indicates that the king is addressed (cf. 1 Sam 22:12; 26:18; 1 Kgs 1:13). Mark 12:35–37, which reflects the contemporary Jewish understanding of the psalm as messianic and of the heading in terms of authorship, may represent an *argumentum ad hominem.* The insertion of the psalm into the Psalter, either beside a pair of Davidic psalms, Pss 108, 109, or subsequently attracting them to it as a cluster, already reflects a messianic understanding (C. Westermann, *Theologia Viatorum* 8 [1961/62] 284; cf. the note on 101:1).

1.b. This introductory formula of prophetic revelation occurs only here in the Psalter apart from the ironic 36:2 (1). It here stands before the actual oracle, as in Num 24:3, 15, etc.; 2 Sam 23:1.

1.c. For sitting on the right as a place of honor cf. 1 Kgs 2:19. For an Egyptian parallel see illustration 353 in O. Keel, *The Symbolism of the Biblical World: Ancient Eastern Iconography and the Book of Psalms* (Tr. T. J. Hallett; New York: Seabury Press, [1978] 263). Does the invitation relate to a corresponding ritual position at the cultic enthronement? H. W. Wolff ("Psalm 110," 314) has suggested that the ark may have been brought to the Gihon spring and the throne placed beside it. Those who envisage a temple setting think of the throne to one side of the holy of holies wherein lay the ark (H. -J. Kraus, *Psalmen*, 931) or beside the pillar of 2 Kgs 11:14; 23:3 (A. Weiser, *Psalms*, 694 note 1). According to Kirkpatrick (*Psalms*, 666) the reference is to the palace on the south side of the temple. But more probably the reference is simply metaphorical (J. Schreiner, *Sion-Jerusalem*, 113).

1.d. Heb. עד can mark a relative limit beyond which the activity of the main clause still continues: cf. 112:8 (GKC § 164f).

1.e. For the comparison cf. Josh 10:24; Isa 51:23. Again reflection of an ancient Near Eastern cultural pattern is evident: in the El Amarna letters vassals refer to themselves as the footstool of Pharaoh, while a similar promise features in an oracle from Marduk to the Assyrian king Esarhaddon (see Kraus, *Psalmen*, 932, and illustrations 341, 342 in Keel, *Symbolism*, 254–55). Victory over enemies is regularly promised in royal psalms: cf. 2:9; 21:10 (9); 45:6 (5). Wolff regards the parallelism as polemical ("Ps. 110," 315): only Yahweh and no other god can give victory.

2.a. M. Dahood (*Psalms III*, 115) takes the *yqtl* form to represent past time, but the usual understanding of v 1b, from which Dahood dissents, suggests that its amplification in v 2a relates to the future. W. H. Schmidt ("Kritik am Königtum," 455–56) has drawn attention to the stress upon Yahweh's conducting the war alone here and in vv 5–6.

2.b. The imperative here expresses a certain consequence (GKC § 110c, cf. 110i).

3.a. This verse has been called the most obscure verse in the whole Psalter (R. Tournay, *RB* 67 [1960] 11). Its two nominal clauses give no indication of time, which must be inferred from the context.

3.b. LXX interpreted the first pair of words as עִמְּךָ נְדָבֹת "in your possession is princely rank," adopted by scholars such as H. Gunkel *Die Psalmen*, 486), who find in v 3 a reference to the king's personal relationship to Yahweh. MT has the merit of continuing the military vein of v 2. נדבת functions as predicative and intensive plural, "willingness itself" (GKC, 141c). Cf. Judg 5:2 for the association of the terms with the theme of holy war.

3.c. A repointing חֵילְךָ, qal infinitive construct (E. J. Kissane, *ITQ* 21 [1954] 108; A. R. Johnson, *Sacral Kingship* 131) or a reading חֹלֶלְךָ, polal infinitive (Gunkel, Die Psalmen, 486, *et al.*) with the sense "your birth" is generally allied with a repointing of ילדתיך later in the verse.

3.d. MT בהדרי קדש may mean "in holy adornment." The plural of הדר is never found elsewhere; the form could conceivably be pointed הֲדָרְךָ, a singular with an -y ending like דברתי in v 4 (A. Caquot, *Sem* 6 [1957] 40). It is often related to בהדרת קדש (29:2; 96:9) which may mean "in holy manifestation" (cf. Dahood, *Psalms III*, 116; J. H. Eaton, *Kingship*, 147, 209 note 25). An alternative ms. reading, also represented in O'Hier is בהרֵרי קדש "on the holy mountains" (cf. הר קדשי "my holy mountain," 2:6. The following reference to "dew" suits הררי: cf. 133:3). Even more ancient support for this reading may be forthcoming from Joel 2:2, set in a passage redolent with echoes of other biblical material, including Ps 97 (see Wolff, *Joel and Amos*, 43–47). There the juxtaposition of שחר "dawn," הרים "mountains" and עם "people" in connection with the Day of Yahweh (cf. 110:5) may be intended as a prophetic reversal of 110:3 (cf. the reversal of Isa 2:4 in Joel 4 [3]:10); the victorious army backed by Yahweh is not Israel but a force directed against Israel.

3.e. Heb. משחר is a hapax legomenon, though by no means an impossible form. It may be a corruption of the normal שחר by dittography (*BHS*), as Joel 2:2 perhaps suggests. H. D. Hummel (*JBL* 76 [1957] 98) explained the *mem* as enclitic. A mythological reference to a Canaanite deity Shahar is excluded since he was evidently male. T. N. D. Mettinger (*King and Messiah*, 264 note 35a) judges J. W. McKay's attempts to demonstrate a reference to a goddess here ("Helel and the Dawn Goddess," *VT* 20 [1970] 458) to be "very doubtful" (cf. P. C. Craigie, "Helel, Athtar and Phaeton (Jes 14:12–15)," *ZAW* 85 [1973] 224).

3.f. The omission of טל לך in LXX is most probably due simply to the translator's inability to understand the words in their context, which was aggravated by his construing ילדתיך as a verbal form. The military context suggests that the basically abstract ילדות is used concretely and collectively with the sense "young men." In its only other occurrence, Eccl 11:9–10, it means "youth, boyhood." For the development in meaning cf. Syr. talyû(tâ) "youth, young men." The significance of טל is uncertain. Wolff ("Ps 110," 317) plausibly interprets in terms of mysterious origin: the army is the wonderful gift of Yahweh to his vice-regent. In support of this interpretation might be cited the traditional reference to the morning (cf. משחר[מ] earlier) as the time when Yahweh comes to his people's aid (cf. 46:6 [5] and Ch. Barth, "בקר bōqer," *TDOT* 2 [1975] 226–28). It could be a reference to multiplicity and so to an innumerable host (Weiser, *Psalms*, 695), but vast numbers were not a desideratum in the theology of the holy war. In 2 Sam 17:12 it is used in a military context in the sense of an irresistible force.

3.g. LXX S understood as יְלָדְתִּיךָ, a pointing found in many Heb. mss., "I have begotten you." This reading is preferred by many, including Kraus (*Psalmen*, 927). It recurs in 2:7 with reference to the divine legitimation of the Davidic king. There are many parallels between Pss 2 and 110. Is this a further one or has the overall similarity encouraged this variant? The structure of the psalm suggests the latter: the divine oracles in which Yahweh speaks seem to be clearly marked out by their introductions in vv 1, 4. After the third person reference to Yahweh in v 2 the difficulty of postulating a divine "I" at this point has been noted by E. Podechard ("Psaume 110," 10; cf. Caquot, *Sem* 6 [1956] 43; Tournay, *RB* 67 [1960] 12; Wolff, "Ps. 110," 316). For the meaning of ילדתיך see note 3.f. above. The form is irregular. The *yod* could theoretically indicate a plural (cf. GKC § 95u), but a plural is not expected here. It could be abnormal *scriptio plena*, though if the psalm is early this is unlikely. The form may represent a mixed reading, combining textual variants יְלַדְתָּ and יְלָדְתִּיךָ.

4.a. Such an oath is especially associated with the Davidic covenant (89:4, 35–36 [3, 34–35]; 132:11; cf. 2 Sam 3:9).

4.b. Cf. the permanence of the Davidic dynasty attested in 89:29–30 (28–29); 2 Sam 7:13, 15–16.

4.c. For the ending of דברתי within a genitival phrase see D. A. Robertson, *Linguistic Evidence*, 69–76. S. Schreiner (*VT* 27 [1977] 217) construes as a pronominal suffix: "(a) Melchizedek according to my promise." Heb. על דבר can mean "because of" (BDB, 184a). Caquot (*Sem* 6 [1956] 44) noted that in the Elephantine papyri על דבר is used after verbs of swearing and accordingly rendered ". . . sworn concerning Melchizedek," but the order of words suggests otherwise. Here the usage appears to be not causal but modal (Podechard, "Psaume 110," 11; Tournay, *RB* 67 [1960] 19): "according to the case of, on the model of," here implying succession of some kind. There is an evident allusion to the tradition preserved in Gen 14:17–24. Attempts to evade this reference such as those of T. H. Gaster (*Journal of the Manchester University Egyptian and Oriental Society* 21 [1937] 41: "a king rightfully appointed") or H. E. Del Medico (*ZAW* 69 [1957] 167: an imperative "reign in justice" or "make justice reign," an expedient favored by K.-H. Bernhardt, *Königsideologie*, 235 note 3) are not convincing. In Gen 14 according to a more natural understanding of the text Abraham pays tithes to Melchizedek, king of Salem as priest of "El Elyon" who is equated with Yahweh in the form of an epithet, "God Most High." The same identification is presupposed here evidently with the purpose of legitimating both Jerusalem in the Yahwistic tradition of Israel and the priestly prerogative of the Davidic monarchy (T. Ishida, *Royal Dynasties*, 137–40). Appeal is made to the mysterious figure of Melchizedek as the ancient priest of Yahweh rather than of a pagan Canaanite god. Similarly in Gen 14 Abraham's submission to Melchizedek was probably intended aetiologically to encourage Israel's submission to a new Melchizedek ruling from Jerusalem in the person of David. J. W. Bowker (*VT* 17 [1967] 39) has found deliberate stress in the contrast between Abraham's accepting bread and wine from Melchizedek and rejecting gifts from the king of Sodom. It implies that "David's action is not to be extended into a general principle of syncretism, nor is his action to be criticized on that ground."

The unique reference to the king's role as "priest" raises the controversial issue of Israelite sacral or sacerdotal kingship. The attempt of F. L. Horton (*Melchizedek Tradition*, 45–48, 50–52) to interpret כהן here (and the plural in 2 Sam 8:17) as primarily referring to a secular office of chieftain or administrative official is not convincing. For a positive evaluation of a priestly role for David and his sons see C. E. Armerding, "Were David's Sons Really Priests?"

in *Current Issues in Biblical and Patristic Interpretation,* ed. G. F. Hawthorne (Grand Rapids: Eerdmans, (1975) 75–86. R. de Vaux (*Ancient Israel,* 113–14) carefully evaluated the evidence for the sacerdotal activity of the Judean kings. Bowker has urged that 110:3 agrees with that evidence that the king seems to have acted as priest only on special occasions or in exceptional circumstances: it emphasizes that the king's priesthood is not the normal one but of a strange and different sort (*VT* 17 [1967] 35–36). The episode of 2 Chr 26 may reflect a dispute over the interpretation and application of the special royal priesthood rather than constitute an utter denial: Uzziah trespasses upon the territory of the *Aaronic* priesthood (2 Chr 26:18, "the sons of Aaron").

5.a. MT points as a divine title. Four syntactical constructions are possible: to take אֲדֹנִי (1) as the divine subject or (2) as a divine vocative or, repointing אֲדֹנִי "my lord," (3) as a human subject or (4) as a human vocative. The first possibility is supported by v 2 where Yahweh is subject, by אַפּוֹ "his anger" with divine reference in 2:5, 12 (and probably 21:10 [9]) and by יוֹם אַפּוֹ with reference to Yahweh in Job 20:28 (cf. Isa 13:13; Lam 1:12; 2:1). Despite the difficulty that the king is clearly the subject of v 7, it is to be preferred. The second option is urged by Caquot (*Sem* 6 [1956] 45) and followed by Tournay (*RB* 67 [1960] 30: "at your right hand, Lord"). Its advantages are that יְמִי exactly echoes v 1, and vv 5–7 can have a consistent subject, the human king. Tournay has noted the consequent symmetry: after the first oracle the king is addressed concerning Yahweh, vv 2–3, while after the second Yahweh is addressed concerning the king. Apart from consistency of subject the third possibility also achieves verbal consistency with אֲדֹנִי, v 1 and with the fact that elsewhere in the psalm יהוה is used for divine reference. It has been favored by C. A. and E. G. Briggs (*Psalms,* Vol. 2, 378–80) and Kissane (*ITQ* 21 [1954] 110). Dahood (*Psalms III,* 118) has suggested the fourth way: he regards the second oracle as running from v 4b to v 5a and then assigns vv 5b–7 to a divine subject. But his assumption of indirect citation of the oracle via a prophet, in which a third person reference to Yahweh in v 4b and address of the king as אֲדֹנִי feature, is unnatural after v 4aα, which suggests a divine speaker. Mettinger (*King and Messiah,* 264) has observed that the psalm stresses the closeness between Yahweh and the king by using אֲדֹן of both in vv 1, 5.

5.b. The right side here signifies divine protection (cf. 16:8; 121:5). As Weiser (*Psalms,* 698) has observed, the sense is metaphorical and is not necessarily at variance with v 1. For an Assyrian parallel see *ANET* (450a): "The god Sin is at your right, the god Shamash at your left."

5.c. Metrically it is better to take מָחַץ with v 5a in a 3+3 line (Tournay, *RB* 67 [1960] 31; L. Krinetzki, *TGI* 51 [1961] 112–13 note 13). The amplification of the first oracle in terms of future victory might suggest that the perspective is also future in vv 5–6 and that the perfect forms relate to the future (cf. GKC § 106n). But it is also possible that they refer to the past (Dahood, *Psalms III,* 118, 119) and that the *yqtl* forms in vv 6–7 are preterites. Then past conquest of Jerusalem (and of the Philistines, 2 Sam 5:17–25?) may be in view, understood as an earnest of world dominion. To convey this double perspective a translation with present tenses is appropriate.

5.d. A. A. Anderson (*Psalms,* 772) has suggested that this may be the prototype of the later concept of the Day of Yahweh (cf. Isa 13:9; Zeph 2:3 and G. von Rad, *OT Theology,* vol. 2 [Tr. D. M. Stalker; Edinburgh: Oliver and Boyd, 1965] 119–25). Ps. 2:5 presents a close parallel.

6.a. In *BHS* note 6ª מ' ג' is an error for מ' ג' בַּג (cf. Gunkel, *Die Psalmen,* 487). The emendation מְלֹא גָאוּת (or the like) "full of majesty," with the support of the Samaritan Psalter (Podechard, "Psaume 110," 12; Kissane, *ITQ* 21 [1954] 112; G. R. Driver, "Psalm 110," 25) is generally associated with deletion of מָחַץ. In support of MT cf. Ezek 32:5; 35:8, whence probably has come the variant גֵּאָיוֹת "valleys" attested by α′ σ′ Hier.

7.a. The psalm reverts to the third person reference of v 1. It is not likely that Yahweh is represented as "pausing to slake his thirst" (Johnson, *Sacral Kingship,* 132).

7.b. Since the following עַל-כֵּן places great import on v 7a as the secret of strength, a mere drink before resuming battle is inappropriate. Reference is frequently seen to a rite of drinking from the Gihon spring as part of the enthronement ceremony (cf. 1 Kgs 1:38). H.-J. Stoebe ("Erwägungen zu Psalm 110," 191), following B. Eerdmans, plausibly found allusion to the important part the spring played in the capture of Jerusalem (cf. 2 Sam 5:8). Mention should be made of P. Nober's revocalization as יַשְׁתֵהוּ "מַנְחֵל בְּדֶרֶךְ" "he (Yahweh) will make him heir of dominion," taking דרך in the sense of Ugar. *drkt* (*VD* 26 [1948] 351–53; cf. Ps 2:8). J. Schreiner (*Sion-Jerusalem,* 120–21) concurs, though preferring a hoph'al participle.

Form/Structure/Setting

In form Ps 110 is a royal song. On the basis of the two divine oracles of vv 1, 4 it is commonly held that it was uttered by a court prophet who addresses the king according to royal etiquette as his "master." The most popular setting of the psalm is a royal coronation at the temple in Jerusalem. The psalm has been made the basis of elaborate reconstructions of the enthronement ritual, e.g. by Gaster (*Journal of The Manchester University Egyptian and Oriental Society* 21 [1937] 37–44) and G. Widengren (*Sakrales Königtum*, 49). But Kraus (*Psalmen*, 930) has rightly warned that the psalm represents only one of the many traditions associated with the enthronement. Wolff ("Psalm 110," 312) has attempted to locate the recitation of the psalm before the royal investiture by means of the reference to the scepter in v 2. Eaton (*Kingship*, 124) relates it to the concluding phase of the enthronement ceremony, looking back in vv 5–6 to a dramatic enactment of the defeat of the king's enemies.

Some scholars have associated the psalm with an annual New Year festival, notably A. Bentzen (*King and Messiah* [London: Lutterworth Press, 1955] 23–25) and Johnson (*Sacral Kingship*, 130–32). The psalm is considered to relate to a ritual combat.

The military language has encouraged at least three scholars to link the psalm with a real battle. Del Medico (*ZAW* 69 [1957] 169) associated the psalm with a pre-battle ritual as a promise of victory. Dahood (*Psalms III*, 112) and Horton (*Melchizedek Tradition*, 34) judge that it celebrates a victory already won. The ambivalent time perspective of Psalm 110 is clearly a factor which complicates its evaluation.

A sizeable group of scholars have refused to associate the psalm with any activity of the human Davidic king and regard it as eschatological and messianic from the outset. Representatives of this position are Kissane (*ITQ* 21 [1954] 106), M. Rehm (*Der königliche Messias*, 329–31), and D. Kidner (*Psalms 75–150*, 392).

Closely linked with the issue of setting is the question of the psalm's age. Efforts to date it have ranged from the Davidic period right down to the Maccabean. The attempts to relate it to Simon Maccabeus (142–134 B.C.) as an acrostic, either שמען, confined to vv. 1–4 (B. Duhm, *Psalmen*, 254–55) or שמען איש "Simon is terrible," extending over the whole psalm (M. Treves, *VT* 15 [1965] 86), have received condign criticism from Gunkel (*Die Psalmen*, 485) and Bowker (*VT* 17 [1967] 31–34). In the light of v 4 a group of scholars refer the psalm to a high priest of the post-exilic period: Tournay (*RB* 67 [1960] 38), in the period of Chronicles and Qoheleth, and S. Schreiner (*VT* 27 [1977] 216–22), in the time of the revised text of Zech 6:9–15, the psalm itself being regarded as a revision of an earlier royal song (cf. Bernhardt, *Königsideologie*, 95). Rehm (*Der königliche Messias*, 330–31), who adopts an eschatological interpretation, assigns it to the period of Zech 3:8. His preference for a post-exilic origin is based on content and language: the attack of the nations and divine judgment executed upon them, which he considers late themes, and the terms ילדות and דברתי.

Most scholars opt for the period of the monarchy, generally in its early stages. Two who prefer a later placing are C. Schedl (*ZAW* 73 [1961] 295–

97), who, following B. Bonkamp, has connected the psalm with Josiah and the upsurge of nationalism between 630 and 609 B.C. and envisages as a setting some such highlight as celebrating the finding of the lawbook or the Passover (2 Kgs 22–23), and D. S. Shapiro ("Psalm 110," *Bet Miqra* 57 [1974] 286–89), who locates the origin of the psalm in the early part of the reign of Azariah (Uzziah). Robertson (*Linguistic Evidence*, 76) tentatively concluded that the morpheme *-y* in v 4 was evidence for an early date. E. R. Hardy (*JBL* 64 [1945] 385–90) argued for an origin early in the monarchical period, principally because of the textual difficulties (similarly Anderson, *Psalms*, 767) and the reference to the Jebusite Melchizedek. Wolff ("Psalm 110," 312) has insisted that the psalm was composed before the enthronement of Jehoash on the basis of v 7, from which he deduces that the area of the Gihon spring was the place of enthronement rather than the temple, as in 2 Kgs 11:9. H. G. Jefferson (*JBL* 73 [1954] 152–56) stressed the strong Canaanite coloring of the psalm's vocabulary, for 71 percent of which she claimed Ugaritic parallels. Gaster ("Psalm 110," 43 note 1) regarded the psalm as a "Yahwized" form of an earlier Canaanite model.

Mettinger (*King and Messiah*, 259) is inclined to regard the Solomonic era as the time of origin. S. Mowinckel (*The Psalms in Israel's Worship*, 153) judged a setting of Solomon's enthronement not impossible, while Caquot (*Sem* 6 [1956] 51) opted for David's enthronement. H. H. Rowley ("Melchizedek and Zadok," 461–72) reconstructed the psalm's setting as a cultic ceremony of recognition after the capture of Jerusalem, in which Zadok whom he held to be the pre-Israelite priest of the Jebusite sanctuary addressed David in vv 1–3, while David confirmed Zadok in his priesthood in v 4 and Zadok blessed David in vv 5–7. Podechard ("Psaume 110," 17–23) connected the psalm with the ceremony of transfer of the ark to Jerusalem (2 Sam 6) or a little later in the period immediately following the conquest of Jerusalem. Horton (*Melchizedek Tradition*, 34) considers the psalm a song of victory sung on David's return to Jerusalem after defeating Ammon. He understands ארץ רבה in v 7 as "the land of Rabbah" and relates the singular ראש to the Ammonite king Hanun and the plural מלכים of v 5 to the various kings of the Syro-Ammonite coalition fighting David.

A thorough evaluation of all these different efforts to classify the primary purpose of the psalm is obviously not possible here, and any attempt must appear subjective and selective. Every Christian scholar would agree concerning the canonical value of the psalm as a messianic promise. One respects the worthy motives of those who seek to restrict the psalm to a messianic intent from the beginning. But it hardly accords with the pattern of historical and theological development discernible in the royal psalms in general and with the ancient cultural and historical royal references within Ps 110. The issue of the priesthood in v 4 is a strong factor which predisposes the choice of a post-exilic date and also probably that of a purely eschatological interpretation. If v 4 can be harmonized with the Davidic monarchy, the way is mainly open toward a pre-exilic setting. Association of the psalm with enthronement may be forcing the evidence of its content. The divine oracles of vv 1, 4 certainly appear to belong to such a context, but the psalm as a whole may simply echo them (cf. 2 Sam 3:18; 5:2). The military amplification of the oracles in vv 2, (3), 5, 6 is strangely uniform—strangely because v 4 has no obviously military reference. The link between v 4 and vv 5–6 may well be the capture of Jerusalem. The psalm may have been composed to celebrate David's earlier conquest of Jerusalem and succession to Jebusite kingship (cf. 2 Sam 8:30), bringing out their implication as pledges of universal dominion. Subsequently the psalm could well have been used by succeeding kings in a context of national enthronement and also in any other cultic settings in which the king's relation to Yahweh was celebrated.

The structure of the psalm appears to be determined by the oracular introductions of vv 1, 4, which are evidently both followed by amplifications. Stylistic considerations support a division into two strophes, each of twelve cola. The double occurrence of the divine name in vv 1–2 is matched by the presence of יהוה and אדני in vv 4–5. The second strophe is marked by the fourfold repetition of the preposition על in vv 4–7. The first is characterized by the eightfold repetition of the pronominal suffix ‑ך "your" in vv 1–3, which is echoed in the second strophe by a single occurrence in v 5. Apart from this and the divine name, interstrophic links are the repetition of ימין "right," vv 1, 5, and ביום "on the day," vv 3, 5. Within the strophes word repetition is a marked feature: איביך "your enemies," vv 1–2, מחץ "strike," vv 5–6 and ראש "head," vv 6–7. The first and last verses are bound together by a double inclusion, the enemies beneath the king's "feet" corresponding to his triumphant "head" and the third person reference to the king (Dahood, *Psalms III*, 119, 120). Krinetzki (*TGI* 51 [1961] 110–21) had drawn attention to a number of stylistic features of the psalm, principally the use of alliteration.

A tripartite structure has been championed, notably by Kraus, who interprets v 3 as a second of three oracles despite its lack of introduction (*Psalmen*, 928–29). Podechard ("Psaume 110," 13) urged that in content v 3 seems to pave the way for the oracle of v 4. Accordingly he divided the psalm into three strophes, vv 1–2, 3–4, 5–7, of which the first begins and the second ends with an oracle. Somewhat similarly W. Schlisske (*Gottessöhne und Gottessohn im AT. Phasen der Entmythisierung im AT* [Stuttgart: W. Kohlhammer Verlag, 1973] 99 note 17) divides into vv 1–3aα, the king's mandate to rule, vv 3aβ–4, his personal relation to Yahweh, and vv 5–6, conquest of his enemies. He regards v 7 as a liturgical note together with Wolff ("Psalm 110," 310). S. Schreiner (*VT* 27 [1977] 218) also detached v 7 from the earlier material. He noted the parallelism of vv 1–6 (an introductory formula, quotation of divine speech, vv 1, 4, explanation, vv 2, 5, and reason or amplification, vv 3, 6) and claimed that v 7 is the conclusion to the whole. The vagueness of his description of the parallelism between vv 3 and 6, the quantitative balance of a division into two strophes and the stylistic repetition of על throughout vv 4–7 are factors which suggest that v 7 be closely related to vv 5–6.

For the Hasmonean application of v 4 (1 Macc 14:41), the rabbinic understanding of the psalm and the use throughout the NT of v 1 as a basic witness to the heavenly exaltation of the ascended and risen Christ and of v 4 in Hebrews as a testimony to his eternal priesthood see especially D. M. Hay, *Glory at the Right Hand*, and Horton, *Melchizedek Tradition*. Hay judges that a prime reason for the popularity of v 1 was that the session image affirmed supreme exaltation without calling into question the glory of God the Father. It permitted Christians to confess faith in the absoluteness of Jesus before they had resolved such problems as ditheism or subordinationism. "Over against expressions like 'Jesus is Lord' this image intrinsically affirmed a continuing relationship between the exalted Christ and God, precluding any possibility of conceiving Christ as a new deity dethroning an older one" (*Glory at the Right Hand*, 159–60).

Explanation

The composer of Ps 110 was evidently a court poet whose tongue, like that of the author of Ps 45, was as fluent as the pen of an expert scribe. Unfortunately, for the exegete so many centuries later his song poses many problems requiring sensitive decisions, and a reconstruction of its setting and original meaning can be only tentative. The poet appears to celebrate the capture of Jerusalem and David's accession to the Jebusite throne. His composition is based on two divine oracles, which are cited in vv 1, 4. The first oracle is an invitation from Yahweh for the king to take up a seat of honor beside him. The metaphor underlines the fact that God is the real king. David rules not in his own right but as co-regent and representative, deriving his authority from his divine counterpart. This assurance of prestige and power expresses a typically Israelite ideal of kingship as derivative and responsible rather than autocratic. It seems that the basis of the invitation is that Yahweh himself is the age-old divine king of Jerusalem as the Most High God of Melchizedek (cf. v 4; Gen 14:18–23). The human king is picturesquely promised dominion over his national foes. Yahweh would fight on his behalf, while the king sat, as it were, serene and secure.

The poet enlarges upon the prophetic revelation. He accentuates that the work will be Yahweh's. The royal scepter (or mace) is strong and its martial authority (cf. 2:9; Jer. 48:17) will be extended only because of the military presence of David's God. It will be Yahweh who does the fighting and gains the victory, so that by implication all the glory must go to him. Stress upon divine warfare is characteristic of the Hebrew concept of holy war (cf. Exod 14:13; 2 Chr 20:17; Isa 7:4–9). The sole agency of Yahweh did not in fact preclude the involvement of the Israelite army according to the holy war theme (cf. Deut 20:4; 2 Sam 5:24), as v 3 too appears to assume. The corollary of the divine promise of v 1 is that the king's people will freely volunteer, yet they themselves will be God's blessing to the king, materializing like the mysterious, God-given dew upon the mountains at daybreak. They will be the instruments of Yahweh's timely aid and power, ready to defend his sacrosanct land and fight on its behalf.

The second oracle quoted is a solemn pledge of the king's sacred role in Yahweh's purposes. There was now a divinely appointed successor to the dynastic line of Jebusite priest-kings, but his rule was destined not to be superseded as theirs had been. From his Jebusite predecessors he inherited the title of priest to Yahweh the Most High God, as sacred mediator between

God and his people. In practice comparatively little use seems to have been made of this honor in a cultic capacity, and it may be for this reason that the poet does not proceed to give a direct exposition of this oracle. It reminds him rather of the capture of Jerusalem which made historically possible the endowment of Jebusite kingship. The poet resumes his military theme and sees in the victory an assurance of Yahweh's continuing aid.

The right hand as a token of divine honor in v 1 is matched by its function as divine protection in v 5. Again the sole agency of Yahweh comes to the fore. God whose authority bestowed Jebusite kingship on David is the power behind his throne in military matters. As the narrator of David's military campaigns made clear, the secret of his success was that Yahweh was with him (2 Sam 5:10; 8:6, 14). In furious theophany he intervenes to conquer on the king's behalf his rival peers (cf. 2:5; 68:22 [21]; Hab 3:13). With the royal mace of v 2 he shatters their power. As the universal God, he wrests their territory from them, quelling all willful resistance to his rule and endowing his liegeman with worldwide dominion (cf. 2:8–9; 72:8–11). The king's realm must logically cover the earth, since he represents in his rule the Lord of the world. The secret of his triumph is enigmatically described as his drinking from the stream, possibly a reference to a ritual drinking from the Gihon spring as a sacramental means of receiving divine resources for his task.

The psalm broaches themes which powerfully overshadow the Israelite king and enfold him in their massive embrace. They express much of the high theology of Judean kingship. But, like Saul's armor, they give an impression of being too big for the recipient, especially as the Davidic monarchy wore on and wore out. Doubtless each king received them by faith and bequeathed them to his successor with the hope that the divine "until" of v 1 would eventually dawn. With the eclipse of the Davidic dynasty the psalm lived on as an expression of faith in God's ultimate fulfilment of his king-centered purposes for his people.

The great assurances of the psalm fell deep into the well of time till they finally plunged into the waters of NT revelation. According to Mark 12:35–37 Jesus echoed the messianic understanding of the psalm when he challenged his contemporaries and showed that on their own premises the Messiah had a higher standing than they were prepared to admit. It is implied that his kingdom transcends the military and political one of David. Following the lead of their Lord (cf. Mark 14:62, where v 1 is combined with the Son of Man vision of Dan 7:13), the apostles freely applied v 1 to his post-resurrection exaltation in heaven and his victory over cosmic foes (e.g. Acts 2:34, 35; 1 Cor 15:25; Eph 1:20; Col 3:1; Heb1:3; 1 Pet 3:22). It holds the record for being the OT text most frequently cited or alluded to in the NT. The NT makes no use of the amplifications of the oracles. Generally only the first oracle is taken up, but the writer to the Hebrews also expounds the second, v 4, in terms of Jesus' exercise of a heavenly non-Aaronic priesthood after the sacrifice of the cross. In the light of the ascension of Jesus Ps 110 took on a new perspective of meaning as witness to God's new Christ-centered order for the world.

God at Work (111:1–10)

Bibliography

Becker, J. *Gottesfurcht im AT.* AnBib 25. Rome: Pontifical Biblical Institute, 1965. **Holm-Nielsen, S.** "The Importance of Late Jewish Psalmody for the Understanding of OT Psalmodic Tradition," *ST* 14 (1960) 1–53. **Lauha, A.** *Die Geschichtsmotive in den alttestamentlichen Psalmen.* Annales academiae scientarum, fennicae 16:1. Helsinki: Suomalainen Tiedeakatemia, 1945. **Munch, P. A.** "Die alphabetische Akrostie in der judischen Psalmendichtung." *ZDMG* 90 (1936) 703–10. **Schildenberger, J.** "Bemerkungen zum Strophenbau der Psalmen." *Estudios Eclesiásticos* 34 (1960) 673–87. **Wolff, H. W.** "Psalm III." *Herr, tue meine Lippen auf,* ed. G. Eichholz. vol. 5. 2nd ed. Wuppertal-Barmen: Emil Müller Verlag, 1961, 229–42.

Translation

¹ Hallelujah [a]

א   *I will give Yahweh wholehearted thanks*   (4+3)
ב   *in the assembled congregation of the upright.*

² ג   *Yahweh's deeds are so great,*   (3+3)
ד   *worth studying [a] by all who revel in them.* [b]

³ ה   *His activity is marked by majesty and splendor,* [a]   (3+3+3)
ו   *and his loyalty [b] continues for ever.*

⁴ ז   *He has caused his wonders to be proclaimed.* [a]
ח   *Yahweh is dutiful and affectionate.* [b]   3+3+3)

⁵ ט   *He gave food [a] to those who revered him;*
י   *he is mindful of his covenant for ever.*

⁶ כ *He declared his mighty deeds to his people,*   (4+4+4)
ל   *that he would give [a] them the possessions of the nations.*

⁷ מ   *The deeds of his hands are marked by faithfulness and justice.*

נ   *All his charges are faithful,*   (3+3+3)
⁸ ס   *maintained for ever and ever,*
ע   *to be performed [a] with faithfulness and uprightness.* [b]

⁹ פ *He sent redemption [a] to his people,*   (3+3)
צ   *he has commanded his covenant be kept forever.*

ק   *Holy and reverend [b] is his name:*   (3+4)
¹⁰ ר *reverence [a] of Yahweh is the beginning of wisdom.* [b]
ש   *All who do them [c] have good success.* [d]   (4+3)
ת   *His praise will continue forever.*

Notes/Comments

1.a. This stands outside the acrostic psalm and is an added heading or liturgical instruction (cf. 112:1; 113:1): see the comment on 104:35.

2.a. Heb. דרושים "worth studying" has a gerundive force (P. Joüon, *Grammaire* § 121e, i).

2.b. MT חֶפְצֵיהֶם appears to be an alternative form for חֲפָצֵיהֶם. Usually the construct plural of a verbal adjective קָטֵל is קְטֵלֵי, but cf. יִרְאֵי from יָרֵא. The present form follows the latter development, the guttural inducing a *seghol* (cf. GKC §§ 22i, 93ii).

3.a. For this formulaic description of royal attributes cf. 45:4 (3); 104:1; 145:5.

3.b. Heb. צדקה "righteousness" here has the connotation of faithfulness to the covenant relationship whereby he comes to Israel's help.

4.a. Cultic celebration of the Exodus event seems especially to be in view (cf. 78:1–4, 11–12). A. Lauha (*Die Geschichtsmotive*, 59) found here an echo of Exod 12:14. B. S. Childs (*Memory and Tradition*, 72) has judged the primary meaning of זכר to be proclamation rather than remembrance; similarly W. Schottroff (*Gedenken*, 292), who, comparing 145:7, describes it as hymnic praise.

4.b. For this credal formula see the comment on 103:8. The reference is here evidently a literary one to Exod 34:6 (see *Form/Structure/Setting*).

5.a. Heb. טרף "prey" is here used with the later meaning of food (cf. Job 24:5; Prov 31:15; Mal 3:10). Lauha (*Die Geschichtsmotive*, 83) observed that this cannot be a general statement in the light of the contextual references to the Exodus, the occupation of Canaan (v 6) and the Sinai event (v 5b), but must refer to the provision of manna and quails in the wilderness (Exod 16; Num 11). The psalm is itself a study of Yahweh's deeds (v 2).

6.a. Heb. לתת is generally taken as "by giving them" or "when he gave," but it is difficult to connect that with the previous verb of saying. More probably it expresses the content of the declaration as the divine purpose. The reference is to Exod 34:10b, 11; v 5b has echoed Exod 34:10a.

8.a. The participle has a gerundive force (cf. note 2.a.; cf. RSV; A. Weiser, *Psalms*, 698; H.-J. Kraus, *Psalmen*, 939, 941). Wolff ("Psalm 111," 237) insists that the context of hymnic confession requires reference to Yahweh, but he has failed to appreciate the turn the psalm makes toward Israelite obligation in the second strophe.

8.b. MT ישָׁר is anomalous as an adjectival form: ישָׁר is to be read with a few mss. LXX S Tg. Hier render with a noun.

9.a. Is Exod 8:19 specifically in the poet's mind? The general reference is to the Exodus (cf. Deut 7:8; Ps 78:42).

9.b. Wolff ("Psalm 111," 237) has helpfully related to the description of the theophany in terms of thunder and lightning associated with the Sinai tradition (Exod 19), as well as to the theme of greatness and majesty of vv 2–3.

10.a. Heb. יראת has the connotation of obedience to the law, here associated with a numinous content, v 9b (J. Becker, *Gottesfurcht im AT*, 270).

10.b. Cf. Prov 9:10 for this basic motto of OT wisdom literature. Heb. ראשית may mean "chief part" (H. Gunkel, *Die Psalmen*, 489). Heb. חכמה is the ordering of life in accord with Yahweh's moral will as interpreted by the Israelite tradition of wisdom teaching.

10.c. MT עשיהם is commonly emended to עשׂיה "those who do it (= wisdom)" with LXX S Vg. Contra BHK and BHS Hier (*ea*) supports MT: cf. J. Schildenberger, *Estudios Eclesiásticos* 34 (1960) 683. The plural suffix could refer only to פקודי "his charges," v 7, which seems rather far away. But לכל־עשיהם does provide an inclusive counterpart to לכל־חפציהם, v 2. Moreover, Schildenberger (*Estudios Eclesiásticos* 34 [1960] 683) has argued for the structural importance of v 7b as the initial colon of the first of a new strophe, vv 7b–10. Accordingly פקודי is dominant in the psalmist's thought and can be resumed in v 10 (cf. Becker, *Gottesfurcht im AT*, 271).

10.d. Cf. Prov 3:4. For שכל cf. W. McKane, *Proverbs* [London: SCM Press, 1970] 292.

10.e. Wolff ("Psalm 111," 239) takes the suffix not as objective, referring to Yahweh, but as subjective: the (song of) praise of the one who practices the fear of Yahweh. But תהלתו appears to balance אודה יהוה, v 1, as an inclusion. Becker (*Gottesfurcht im AT*, 272) has urged that the parallel v 3b points to a yahwistic reference here.

Form/Structure/Setting

The most obvious characteristic of Ps 111 is its literary form as an acrostic. Here, as in Ps 112, the initial letter of each colon is a successive letter of the alphabet. The acrostic is used in conjunction with a number of form-critical genres (cf. F. Crüsemann, *Studien zur Formgeschichte*, 296), in this case a hymn, as in Ps 145. Wolff ("Psalm 111," 231) has analyzed the psalm as a summons to praise, v 1, and the reason for praise, vv 2–10, which might be better expressed as an announcement of praise and its substance. The latter part contains a wisdom saying, v 10a. The combination of hymn and wisdom saying Wolff ("Psalm 111," 232) sees as a development of such passages as Ps 95, where the pilgrim's praise is paired with prophetic or priestly warning, except that here there is only one speaker. Strictly v 1 uses the language of thanksgiving, the testimony of an individual among the cultic community. It is here linked not with deliverance from personal distress, but with the history of the nation's salvation. Kraus (*Psalmen*, 941) notes that the didactic element of the psalm was itself a feature of the individual thanksgiving.

A recurring problem in the study of the Psalter is how far form needs to be distinguished from the purpose and setting of a particular psalm. In this case is a cultic situation envisaged or have cultic forms and language been re-used in a non-cultic context? Kraus posits a cultic setting, any of the great national festivals and not necessarily the Passover, as others have urged from concentrating upon the detail of v 4. Precisely v 1 envisages the singer gathering a crowd around him in the temple court. Weiser (*Psalms*, 698), J. H. Eaton (*Psalms*, 773), Dahood (*Psalms III*, 122) and A. A. Anderson concur in a cultic context for the psalm. On the other hand, P. A. Munch (*ZDMG* 90 [1936] 703–10) ascribed to it a pedagogic purpose in the late post-exilic schools of the scribes. As an acrostic it was a sample passage compiled for instruction in the schools in which the writing of the alphabet and good composition were learned (cf. S. Mowinckel, "Psalms and Wisdom," 212–13). S. Holm-Nielsen (*ST* 14 [1960] 37–38) also sets the psalm against the background of a school or circle of instruction. Wolff ("Psalm 111," 231–32) likewise speaks in terms of a group of pious men who, anticipating the later meeting of instruction in the synagogue, gathered for religious edification in the face of pagan cultural pressure (cf. Crüsemann, *Studien zur Formgeschichte*, 296–98). Becker (*Gottesfurcht im AT*, 151–52, 270; *Israel deutet seine Psalmen*, 77) describes the psalm as a late expression of nomistic piety used at gatherings of the pious. Its content reflects not merely wisdom but nomistic wisdom in that the covenant and Israel's salvation history feature, unlike pre-nomistic wisdom. The cultic form of the hymn has been taken over and re-employed in this anthological composition. R. E. Murphy is more cautious and prefers to speak of wisdom influence upon the psalm ("Wisdom Psalms," 164).

The reader of this commentary may well have a sense of *déjà vu* at this point: a number of these issues have already come to the fore in the study of Ps 103. In fact comparison with that psalm yields two further interesting parallels. First, there are at least six vocabulary links between 103:17–18 and Ps 111, including ברית "covenant" in the sense of covenant terms. Secondly, just as Ps 103 was seen to be a meditation upon Exod 34:6 in the light of its literary context, so here not only does v 4b cite the formula of Exod 34:6 (but in the order חנון ורחום instead of רחום וחנון, undoubtedly to satisfy the acrostic), but there are no less than five links of vocabulary between the psalm and Exod 34:10, one with Exod 34:5 and one with Exod 34:11. Accordingly, if Ps 103 was rightly assigned to a cultic setting, there appears to be justification for so assigning this one; in this case the more general content points to any one of the religious festivals. Crüsemann's assertion

(*Studien zur Formgeschichte*, 297) that the acrostic form was intended to be read not heard is not necessarily true.

There is fairly general agreement that the psalm is post-exilic; Weiser (*Psalms*, 698) and Dahood (*Psalms III*, 125) protest characteristically that this is not necessarily so. The use of nomistic wisdom and probably the use of טרף "prey" in the late sense of "food" points to the post-exilic period, probably later rather than earlier.

Can one speak in terms of a structure for the psalm apart from the acrostic scheme? Even the pattern of lines is a matter of dispute. Mowinckel (*ZAW* 68 [1956] 101), following Gunkel (*Die Psalmen*, 488), judged the psalm to consist of single cola (cf. the layout of *BHS*), but he did note (synthetic) parallelism of thought and form in the two cola respectively of vv 1, 2, 3, 6, 8, 9 (aα and aβ). Holm-Nielsen (*ST* 14 [1960] 35) saw in the psalm an arrangement of bicola, except for single cola at vv 9b, 10b. Wolff ("Psalm 111," 231) regards vv 1–8 as bicola, mostly synthetically parallel, with tricola in vv 9, 10, just in fact as the verses are apportioned in MT. Schildenberger (*Estudios Eclesiásticos* 34 [1960] 682–83) has offered a more ambitious metrical and even strophical scheme. After the introductory v 1, the psalm falls into two strophes of four lines. The first, vv 2–6a, deals with Yahweh's saving deeds and falls into a bicolon, v 2, and three bicola, vv 3–4a, 4b–5, 6–7a. The second, vv 7b–10, is concerned with Yahweh's covenant ordinances and falls into a tricolon, vv 7b–8, and three bicola, vv 9aα-β, 9b–10aα, 10aβ-b. Schildenberger's scheme was a refinement of that of E. J. Kissane (*Psalms II*, 196), who isolated an initial bicolon and concluding tricolon, vv 1, 10, and divided the rest into three strophes of two lines—tricola except for one bicolon, v 2—relating in turn to the wonders of the Exodus, to the wilderness period and conquest, and to the law. There is much to be said for Schildenberger's structure. The separation of v 1 conforms with Wolff's analysis. Over against Kissane's division of vv 9–10, Schildenberger's is confirmed by Becker's discovery of a chiastic structure in vv 9b, 10aα, 10aβ, 10b (*Gottesfurcht im AT*, 273). There is a close relation between שם "name" and תהלה "praise": cf. 106:47; Isa 48:9. Moreover, the chiasmus is reflected even in the meter (3+4, 4+3). Schildenberger noted the extended parallelism whereby the stem זכר occurs in the last colon of adjacent tricola, vv 4a, 5b. He could have made the same observation about the stem נתן in the middle colon of adjoining tricola, vv 5a, 6b. He explained the second strophe as a development of the theme of the covenant commandments. The second line justifies their reliable and eternal nature (vv 7b, 8a; in v 9 ברית refers to the covenant ordinances, as in Deut 4:13), and by implication urges gratitude, while the third line adds the motivation of reverence for a holy God.

In confirmation of Schildenberger's strophical division it may be noted that both strophes begin with plural adjectival or participial forms and with ישר(ים) "upright(ness)," vv 2, 7b–8. The first strophe begins and ends with reference to Yahweh's מעשי "deeds," vv 2, 7. The term אמת functions as a hinge between the two strophes (vv 7a, 8b; cf. נאמנים, v 8a). Heavy climactic four-beat cola occur in vv 6–7, 10, as well as in the introductory v 1.

Besides the acrostic and strophical schemes there is also an intricate concentric pattern in operation in vv 2b–10, which more or less accord with what

constitutes the body of the psalm in respect of both content and poetic structure, לכל . . . עמדת לעז : יהוה : ליראיו : לעולם בריתו : לעמו : אמת :: לעד
לעולם :: אמת : לעמו : לעולם בריתו : נורא/יראת : יהוה : לכל . . . עמדת לעד
Mention has already been made of the double indicators of inclusion, in
the notes on vv 2, 9. It only remains to refer to the stem עשה which runs
through the psalm, referring four times to Yahweh's deeds in the first strophe
and twice in the second, seemingly to Israel's practical response.

It is clear that the poet was well able to overcome the limitations the
acrostic form might have imposed upon him. Wolff ("Psalm 111," 238) has
called attention to the orderly references to the Exodus, wilderness events
and the occupation of the land in vv 4–6. Gunkel's disparaging reference
to the psalm as "modest art" (*Die Psalmen*, 489) requires drastic correction.
Weiser's comparison with "a string of unmatched pearls" (*Psalms*, 698) is
doubtful. H. Schmidt is fully vindicated in his reference to the psalm's careful
composition (*Die Psalmen*, 205). The poet displays remarkable versatility, jug-
gling successfully with scheme upon scheme.

Explanation

Psalm 111 is a skillfully composed acrostic, intended for solo recitation
at the annual festivals of Judah in the post-exilic period. Although it begins
in a manner characteristic of cultic thanksgiving, its testimony will be to no
purely personal deliverance but to Yahweh's saving deeds for Israel. The
psalmist intends to speak for the assembled people as he worships in spirit
and truth (contrast Isa 29:13). He hints in passing at the moral qualifications
of those who would worship Yahweh: they come as "upright" (cf. Pss 15,
24; Matt 5:23–24).

After announcing his praise, the psalmist proceeds to its substance in the
first of two strophes. His theme is declared at the outset: the great salvation
history of ancient Israel to which Israel owed its creation and meaning. The
singer, taking his own advice, proceeds to study it with joy. It reveals Yahweh
as King, both in his lordship of all human history and in his continuing
care and concern for his people. The psalmist expresses his gratitude that
Yahweh has instituted the festivals at which the tradition of saving history
may be reaffirmed: specifically he has the Exodus in mind (cf. Exod 3:20;
12:14). He moves on to the credal statement of Exod 34:6, which is associated
with the renewal of the covenant and enshrines Yahweh's loving patronage,
and then to his provision of quails and manna in the wilderness. From both
he deduces the strong saving and keeping reality assured by the covenant
of the law made at Sinai. Yahweh committed himself to his people in a permanent relationship. Associated with the renewal of the covenant was the divine
promise of Canaan (Exod 34:10–11). This then is the sacred history which
was Israel's foundation stone: the Exodus, protection during the wilderness
trek and the gifts of the law and the promised land. This is the cluster of
events to be celebrated as the touchstone of Yahweh's power and purposes
for his chosen people. They mark him out as faithful to his own and their
just defender from all who would oppress them.

In the second strophe the gift of the law is given prominence. The laws given at Sinai are prized as Israel's national and religious constitution. They provide permanent guidelines given for the welfare of the people, as an expression of Yahweh's benevolent will. But they are intended also to evoke faithfulness as a response to their faithful God, and to provide a standard of uprightness which his people are to attain (cf. v 1). How powerful are the incentives to obedience: the redemption from Egypt (cf. Exod 20:2) and the very command of a holy God (cf. Deut 4:10–13)! True reverence, which is demonstrated in awesome obedience of God's laws, is the only door to an ability to cope with life's meaning and problems. Such secrets are opened only to the willing practitioner of his precepts (cf. Matt 7:24–27). Doing and praising, these are ever to be the dual response to the revelation of what Yahweh has done, celebrated afresh at each of Israel's festivals.

Psalm 111 glories in the present and permanent relevance of the ancient events of salvation: it is the OT counterpart of Rom 5:1–11. Those events have a once-and-for-all value which the NT in turn attaches to their christological counterparts (cf. Rom 6:10; Heb 10:10; 1 Pet 3:18). They are a window through which God's purposes for each generation of his people can be clearly discerned. They are a signpost pointing to his enduring care and claim. The psalm contains a fine balance of praising exuberance (v 2) and sober sense of duty, of privilege for the recipients of the covenant and obligation for the recipients of its laws.

Godliness at Work (112:1–10)

Bibliography

Holm-Nielsen, S. "The Importance of Late Jewish Psalmody for the Understanding of OT Psalmodic Tradition." *ST* 14 (1960) 1–53. **Kuntz, J. K.** "The Canonical Wisdom Psalms of Ancient Israel—Their Rhetorical, Thematic and Formal Dimensions." *Rhetorical Criticism. Essays in Honor of J. Muilenburg.* Ed. J. J. Jackson and M. Kessler. Pittsburgh: Pickwick Press, 1974. ———. "The Retribution Motif in Psalmic Wisdom." *ZAW* 89 (1977) 223–33. **Lipiński, E.** "Macarismes et psaumes de congratulation." *RB* 75 (1968) 321–67. **Mowinckel, S.** "Marginalien zur hebräischen Metrik." *ZAW* 68 (1956) 97–123. **Perdue, L. G.** *Wisdom and Cult: A Critical Analysis of the Views of Cult in the Wisdom Literatures of Israel and of the Ancient Near East.* SBLDS 30. Missoula, MT: Scholars Press, 1977. **Zimmerli, W.** "Zwillingspsalmen." *Wort, Lied und Gottesspruche. Festschrift für J. Ziegler.* Ed. J. Schreiner. Forschungen zur Bibel 2. Wurzburg: Echter Verlag, 1972.

Translation

¹ Hallelujah [a]
א *How fortunate* [b] *is the person who reveres Yahweh,*   (3+3)
ב *who takes great delight in his commands.*

² ג   *His descendants will be powerful in the land;*   (4+3)
ד   *the circle* ᵃ *of the upright receive blessing.*
³ ה   *Wealth and riches are in his home*   (3+3)
ו   *and his righteousness* ᵃ *continues for ever.*
⁴ ז   *Light rises in the dark for the upright.* ᵃ   (4+3)
ח   *The righteous person* ᵇ *is dutiful and affectionate.* ᶜ
⁵ ט   *It is good* ᵃ *for a man to lend dutifully,*   (3+3)
י   *to order his affairs justly.* ᵇ
⁶ כ   *Never* ᵃ *will he be shaken.*   (3+4)
ל   *The righteous person will ever be remembered.*

⁷ מ   *He is not afraid of bad news:*   (4+4)
נ   *his mind is firm, trusting in Yahweh,*
⁸ ס   *his mind is steady,* ᵃ *he will not be afraid*   (3+3)
ע   *as he awaits looking at his foes with gratification.*
⁹ פ   *He gives generously to the poor,*   (3+3)
צ   *his righteousness continues for ever.*
ק   *His horn* ᵃ *is raised in honor.*   (3+3)
¹⁰ ר   *The wicked person sees it with anger,*
ש   *he gnashes his teeth and fades away.*   (3+3)
ת   *The desires of the wicked come to nothing.*

Notes/Comments

1.a. See the comment on 111:1.

1.b. The beatitude is used in wisdom literature to refer to an ideal to emulate: it is an implicit exhortation (cf. W. Janzen, "ʾAŠRÊ in the Old Testament," *HTR* 58 [1965] 215–26; E. Lipiński, *RB* 75 [1968] 321–67; L. G. Perdue, *Wisdom and Cult*, 328 note 23).

2.a. Or "class, group": cf. 24:6.

3.a. Heb. צדקה here refers to behavior consistent with the covenant (H.-J. Kraus, *Psalmen*, 947–48, citing K. H. Fahlgren and K. Koch).

4.a. The colon echoes Isa 58:10. J. K. Kuntz (*ZAW* 89 [1977] 223–33) has classified the retribution motif in wisdom psalms into three types—traditional, realistic and futuristic. This psalm he assigns to the realistic group along with Pss 34; 37:39–40; 94:8–15. It frankly admits that the righteous person suffers. Disaster, bad news (v 7) and unprincipled adversaries (v 8) may threaten his present life, yet his prospects are bright. Heb. אור "light" is not a reference to the help given by the person of vv 1, 2a, 3a (A. Weiser, *Psalms*, 702: "he is like a light"; JB): he must be the recipient of help, being identical with the ישרים "upright," vv 2b, 4a.

4.b. In MT וצדיק "and righteous" is attached to the other adjectives in a combination not found elsewhere, probably by assimilation to 116:5. In six cases the psalm transfers to the righteous person terms predicated of Yahweh in Ps 111. Heb. צדיק functions structurally as one of the two words used for the ideal figure of the psalm. These facts suggest that here 111:4b is applied to a human plane and that the *waw* is rightly omitted in some Heb. mss (H. Gunkel, *Die Psalmen*, 490; cf. Kraus, *Psalmen*, 945). Under the influence of 111:4 LXX mss added ὁ κύριος "the Lord" (cf. RSV) and one Heb. ms. substituted יהוה for וצדיק (cf. *BHS*).

4.c. For this partial formula see 103:8; 111:4 and notes.

5.a. Sc. כי "that": cf. Ruth 2:22; Lam 3:26–27. RSV "it is well with" would demand ל.

5.b. ERV "maintain his cause in judgment" is less likely.

6.a. Heb. כי is emphatic (Kraus, *Psalmen*, 948).

8.a. For vv 7b–8a cf. Isa 26:3.

8.b. Lit. "until": cf. the note on 110:1.

9.a. For this OT metaphor for power and success in face of opposition cf. 92:11 (10); 1 Sam 2:1.

Form/Structure/Setting

There is no doubt that Ps 112 is a wisdom psalm. It exhibits all four of the thematic criteria suggested by Kuntz for wisdom poetry (fear of Yahweh and veneration of the Torah, contrast between the righteous and the wicked, the reality and inevitability of retribution and counsels concerning everyday conduct); of his seven rhetorical criteria it exhibits one, the אשרי formula of v 1, and also has an acrostic structure like Pss 34 and 37, while it contains six terms belonging to wisdom vocabulary ("Canonical Wisdom Psalms," 208–15). The psalm is a specimen of Torah-centered piety (cf. Ps 119), and in this and other respects it resembles Ps 1. But it lays more stress upon virtue and its blessings and devotes only the three final cola to the wicked. S. Holm-Nielsen (*ST* 14 [1960] 39) has emphasized that Ps 1, which praises the man who spends his time studying the Torah, idealizes a different person from the busy extrovert of Ps 112, but he may have overdrawn the contrast.

There are few who would defend a primary cultic setting. H. Schmidt (*Die Psalmen,* 206) regarded the psalm as a priestly response at the thanksgiving liturgy. As Kraus (*Psalmen,* 946) has observed, his setting is a conclusion drawn from linking the psalm closely with Ps 111, for which Schmidt found the same situation. E. Lipiński (*RB* 74 [1968] 346–47) associates the psalm with the entrance liturgies, Pss 15 and 24, used at the ceremony of solemn welcome for pilgrims to the temple, in view of its emphasis upon reverence, trust and obedience. Weiser (*Psalms,* 703) tentatively attached the psalm to the cultic bestowal of blessing. But it is more likely that its background lies in a sapiential milieu, although a precise setting cannot be discerned (R. E. Murphy, "Wisdom Psalms," 160–61, 167; cf. Kuntz, "Canonical Wisdom Psalms," 221).

The psalm's most obvious feature is its close relationship to Ps 111 (cf. W. Zimmerli, "Zwillungspsalmen," 107–9). Accordingly a number of scholars have suggested the same author for both or at least the same circle. All that can be said with certainty is that the composer of Ps 112 made use of Ps 111 (cf. Holm-Nielsen, *ST* 14 [1960] 38). Eleven terms or phrases have been taken over from Ps 111, often with a different sense. Four relate to the righteous in both psalms: ירא, v 1 (cf. 111:5, 10), חפץ, v 1 (cf. 111:2), ישרים, vv 2, 4 (cf. 111:1), טוב, v 5 (cf. 111:10). No less than seven transfer to the righteous terms related to Yahweh or his law in Ps 111:vv 3b, 9b (cf. 111:3), חנון ורחום, v 4 (cf. 111:4), משפט, v 5 (cf. 111:7), זכר, v 6 (cf. 111:4), סמוך, v 8 (cf. 111:8), נתן, v 9 (cf. 111:5). The remaining one is לעולם, v 6 (cf. 111:5, 8, 9). It is clear that the psalm is closely modelled upon Ps 111, in view not only of its vocabulary but also its particular acrostic structure which uses a fresh letter for each colon. Accordingly the date of the psalm must be the later post-exilic period, a verdict with which most concur, apart from Lipiński (*RB* 75 [1968] 347), who tentatively suggests the later pre-exilic era, and Weiser (*Psalms,* 703), who finds it impossible to assign a definite date in view of the general nature of the content.

Generally the cola are regarded as separate metrical units. S. Mowinckel (*ZAW* 68 [1956] 101) has noted parallelism between the cola of vv 1, 2, 3 (wealth being a fruit of צדקה), 5, 6, 7, 8, 10aβ-b. In the face of so much parallelism (of a sort) it is difficult to resist the conclusion that the author intended a series of bicola and provided what parallelism he could in conjunction with his acrostic scheme. He would then have been following his model in that Ps 111 appears to exhibit more than detached cola. Attempts to impose upon the psalm a strophical structure include that of E. J. Kissane (*Psalms II*, 199–200) who suggested an introductory bicolon, v 1, and four strophes of two lines, vv 2–3, 4–6a, 6b–8, 9–10, including tricola. J. Schildenberger (*Estudios Eclesiásticos* 34 [1960] 683) offered a scheme of five strophes of two bicola, except for two tricola in the last. Neither of these carries conviction on close examination. Perdue (*Wisdom and Cult*, 292–93) finds, after the introductory v 1, a chiastic structure of four strophes of three, five, five and three cola. After each strophe is a refrain, vv 3b, 6b, 9b, and an antithesis to the refrain, v 10b. The refrains and their antithesis together make up an antithetical proverb around which the poem is structured. The proverb is a tricolon consisting of vv 6b, 3b and 10b. It does not spring naturally to the reader's view. The scheme appears rather forced. His four subjects of blessings, behavior, faith and the wicked do not correspond exactly with the strophes.

Since the psalm was evidently intended to be a counterpart to Ps 111, the question naturally arises whether the poetic techniques previously discerned in that composition reappear here. The acrostic clearly does. Evidence is not lacking of an overall chiastic structure to balance the concentric one of Ps 111, וצדקתו עמדת לעד : לעולם :: עולם : צדקתו עמדת לעד. There are two thematic pairs which seem to supplement this word scheme: הון ועשר, v 3a, is complemented by כבוד, v 9b (cf. Prov 3:16), and טוב, v 5a, contrasts with רעה, v 7a. Even so this chiastic structure is not so developed as the corresponding one of Ps 111. It appears that Perdue has confused two different types of scheme and mistaken two pieces of chiastic evidence for strophical guidelines.

Strophically Ps 111 was seen to divide into two parts after the initial bicolon. It is interesting to apply the same test here. Both Kissane and Perdue isolated v 1, a feasible procedure which corresponds to an analysis of content. Are there intended to be two strophes, each of ten cola or five bicola, vv 2–6, 7–10? Word repetition suggests that such a second strophe is bound together by the word play יירא "fear" and יראה "see," vv 7a, 8a, 8b, 10a (cf. Zimmerli, "Zwillungspsalmen," 112 note 31; M. Dahood, *Psalms III*, 129). The first is bound by ישרים, vv 2b, 4a, and the synonymous צדיק, vv 4b, 6b, in addition to the inclusive יהיה, vv 2a, 6b. How would such a structure accord with the pattern of thought, if any? The psalm seems to alternate blessing and behavior. Blessing features in vv 2–3a, 4a, 6, 8b, 9b–10 (reinforced by a contrast). Behavior occupies vv 3b, 4b–5, 7–8a, 9a. It is noticeable that the psalm lacks the careful development of thought of Ps 111 and also the relation of meter to strophical features. Yet the poet appears to have modelled himself upon the earlier psalm in his attempt to juggle with three basic schemes, acrostic, chiastic and strophical. There was a chiastic order in the last four cola of Ps 111, and the same is probably true of vv 9b–10. Another might be seen in the four cola of vv. 7–8, but A. R. Ceresco (*CBQ* 38 [1976] 305) is probably wiser in restricting it to three, לא יירא : לבו :: לבו : לא יירא (cf. the parallelism of 111:7b–8). Perdue (*Wisdom and Cult*, 294) has drawn attention to the poet's penchant for pairing words: vv 3a, 4b, 5a, 7b, 9a, 10aα, 10aβ. Even this takes up a feature of Ps 111 (vv 1b, 3a, 4b, 7a, 8a, 8b, 9b).

Explanation

This acrostic psalm takes up where the previous one left off. It is the intentional counterpart of Ps 111, elaborating 111:10 and urging that Yahweh's own characteristics detailed in the former psalm should be reflected in the life of the believer.

The opening beatitude creates the perspective of the whole psalm. What follows is a kaleidoscopic definition of the incentives and life style of the type of person here praised. Willing obedience of Yahweh's will revealed in the Torah is set forth as a virtue to emulate. But what in practice does it mean to obey and in what ways is such a person fortunate? Obedience wins the fulfillment of the covenant promise of material benefits; the posterity of the "upright" are destined to share their blessing by achieving social prominence (cf. Exod 20:6). In line with normative wisdom teaching the psalm expresses a conviction that virtue brings tangible results into the lives of the virtuous and their families. Virtue leads to prosperity (cf. Prov 3:16; 22:4). But there is the price to pay, consistent conformity to Yahweh's covenant claims, conformity which itself follows the divine example (cf. 111:3).

The psalm realistically affirms that the good believer is not immune from the natural shocks "to which flesh is heir." But it can promise a happy issue out of such afflictions. There is further stress upon godlike behavior, here a remarkable one: the credal statement of 111:4, so prized especially in post-exilic times, must find a moral echo in the life of the Yahwist. The lesson of obligation is hammered home in v 5a in a specific area, that of lending money to help others over disaster (cf. 37:21, 26). Another pertinent moral requirement is equity in dealings with one's fellows. To the one who lives like this can be given the promise of enjoying fundamental security in life (cf. Prov 12:3)—despite temporary setbacks—and a measure of immortality in that his good example will never be forgotten (cf. Prov 10:7). One of the setbacks may be unwelcome news (cf. Prov 3:25–26; 31:21), but the firm trust he puts in Yahweh will enable him to cope: "he overcomes his fears" (JB). In the light of v 1 the message of the psalm at this point is "Fear him, ye saints, and you will then have nothing else to fear" (N. Tate and N. Brady). The believer waits confidently for the tide of misfortune to turn, and for vindication whereby his malignant rivals get their just deserts.

Again the drumbeat of obligation is sounded: general conformity to the standards of the covenant and in particular generosity as the corollary of God's gift of wealth (v 3). The God who gives (111:5) expects the recipient to be godlike in his giving. As a consequence he will know success in his life and command the respect of others. The picture of prosperity as the reward of virtue is enhanced by the final reference to the frustrated chagrin of the "wicked" who see none of their ambitions come true.

The psalm is a fine example of post-exilic piety and morality, which it seeks to advertise. Three especially attractive features are its pervading motif of the divine as a model for human ethics (cf. Matt 5:45; Eph 4:32–5:2), its large measure of realism in portraying life's experiences, and the consequent role it gives to the virtue of a strong faith as a catalyst to overcome misfortune. The NT lays less emphasis on earthly reward (see Matt 6:33; 2 Cor 9:11), being set in a broader framework which includes the hereafter. The basic principles of the psalm still apply. In particular material prosperity, though not always or necessarily the reward of virtue, when it is given does create an obligation for the Christian too (cf. 1 Tim 6:17–19). Paul quoted v 9 in 2 Cor 9:9 as an illustration of a "cheerful giver" whom "God loves."

Glory and Grace   (113:1-9)

Bibliography

Becker, J. "Einige Hyperbata im AT." *BZ* 17 (1973) 257–63. Crüsemann, F. *Studien zur Formgeschichte.* Labuschagne, C. J. *The Incomparability of Yahweh in the OT.* Pretoria Oriental Series 5. Leiden: E. J. Brill, 1966. Willis, J. T. "The Song of Hannah and Ps 113." *CBQ* 35 (1973) 139–54.

Translation

1 Hallelujah [a]
    Praise, Yahweh's servants, [b]   (3+3)
    praise Yahweh's name.
2 *Let Yahweh's name be blessed*   (3+3)
    from now on and for evermore.
3 *From the sun's rising to its setting*   (3+2)
    let Yahweh's name be praised.

4 *Exalted is Yahweh above all nations,*   (3+2)
    his glory above the heavens.
5 *Who is like Yahweh our God* [a]—   (3+2)
    enthroned so high, [b]
6 *looking down so low—*   (2+2)
    in heaven or on earth? [a]

7 *He who raises the needy from the dust,*   (3+3)
    exalts the poor from the rubbish heap,
8 *giving a seat* [a] *among nobles,*   (3+2)
    among the nobles of his people;
9 *he who settles* [a] *the sterile woman of the family*   (3+3)
    as a happy mother of children. [b]
                      Hallelujah

Notes/Comments

1.a. Cf. 106:1, 48 and the comment on 104:35.
1.b. LXX, α', σ', θ', Hier treat "Yahweh" as the object of the verb and עבדי as vocative, as

if עבדים. Probably at some stage abbreviation (עבדי = עבדים) has been assumed: cf. G. R. Driver, "Abbreviations in the Massoretic Text," *Textus* 1 (1960) 114–18; "Once Again Abbreviations," *Textus* 4 (1964) 78–79; L. C. Allen, *The Greek Chronicles*, VTSup 27 (1974) 87–88. Does the term refer to priestly (or Levitical) singers or to the whole cultic assembly? Most probably to the latter in view of the amplification of the similar 135:1 in 135:19–20 (C. Lindhagen, *The Servant Motif*, 100–103; I. Riesener, *Der Stamm* עבד *im AT. Eine Wortuntersuchung unter Berücksichtigung neuer sprachwissenschaftlicher Methoden* [BZAW 149; Berlin: de Gruyter, 1979] 228).

5.a. For a study of the rhetorical question expressing Yahweh's uniqueness see C. J. Labuschagne, *Incomparability*, 22, 99, 102.

5.b. For the morpheme -*y* used with an appositional participle here and in vv 6–7, 9 see D. A. Robertson, *Linguistic Evidence*, 69–76. M. Dahood (*Psalms III*, 130) regards it as a genitive ending, the participles depending upon כ, but Robertson rejects this explanation. GKC § 90m judges the ending to be purely ornamental. For the subordination of verbs in vv 5b, 6a see GKC § 114n.

6.a. If v 6b is taken closely with v 6a ("looks down upon . . ."), Yahweh is regarded as higher than the heavens: cf. 57:6, 12 (5, 11); 148:13. V 4 could justify this interpretation. The issue has an exegetical importance for vv 4–6, implying that the passage deals exclusively with the majesty of Yahweh, while his grace is the theme of vv. 7–9 (A. Weiser, *Psalms*, 706–7; JB). Another expedient is to distribute v 6b between vv 5b, 6a ("is enthroned high in heaven and looks down on earth") as an example of hyperbaton (B. Duhm, *Psalmen*, 258; A. F. Kirkpatrick, *Psalms*, 678; cf. J. Becker, *BZ* 17 [1973] 262–63). But the conventional formula of divine incomparability strongly suggests that v 6b goes closely with v. 5a: see Deut. 3:24; 1 Kgs 8:23 (cf. Exod 15:11; Ps 73:25). Accordingly a highly favored solution is to transpose v 6b after v 5a (e.g. H. Gunkel, *Die Psalmen*, 492–93; H.-J. Kraus, *Psalmen*, 950; Labuschagne, *Incomparability*, 77 note 1). More probably this required effect is to be achieved by assuming that the psalmist had a chiastic order in mind, suspending the continuation of v 5a with two parenthetical cola (J. A. Alexander, *Psalms*, 466; see *Form/Structure/Setting*). V 6a indicates not divine omniscience (cf. 33:13–15) but deliverance (cf. 106:44; 138:6).

8.a. The ending of MT להושיבי is grammatically incomprehensible unless Dahood's explanation as a third masculine suffix -*y* is accepted (*Psalms III*, 132). Generally false assimilation to the adjacent endings is assumed, and להושיבו is read with the support of LXX S Hier (e.g. Gunkel, *Die Psalmen*, 493; Kraus, *Psalmen*, 950), but the original may have been להושיב, as in 1 Sam 2:8.

9.a. Cf. the use of הושיב for marriage in Ezra 10:2, 14; Neh 13:23 in the sense "give a home to." Here the meaning appears to be that "he gives her a secure and happy position in her home" (Kirkpatrick, *Psalms*, 679). Tg., inspired by Isa 54:1; 66:8, explicitly relates v 9 to Yahweh's blessing of Israel. This national interpretation must underlie the use of the psalm in the Hallel (see *Form/Structure/Setting*); v 7 was doubtless understood similarly (cf. Isa 52:2).

9.b. For the definite article cf. GKC § 127e. It was used to secure assonance with the first colon (הבית, הבנים).

Form/Structure/Setting

Psalm 113 is a hymn which praises Yahweh in the third person. It integrates two forms, the imperatival hymn and hymnic participles, into a harmonious unit (F. Crüsemann, *Studien zur Formgeschichte*, 134–35). A summons to praise, v 1, developed in vv 2–3, is followed by the content of praise in vv 4–9. The hymnic participles of vv 6–7, 9 reflect a typical motif and are attached to a rhetorical question mainly found in hymns or hymnic passages (cf. Labuschagne, *Incomparability*, 22, 65 note 2).

The setting was clearly cultic. In v 1 the congregation appears to be addressed by a temple choir or soloist. Kraus (*Psalmen*, 950) regards the psalm as antiphonal, vv 1–4 and 5–9 being sung by two choirs. In traditional Jewish worship the psalm together with Pss 114–118 formed "the (Egyptian) Hallel,"

which was sung at the three main annual festivals together with those of
the new moon and the dedication of the temple. At the family celebration
of the Passover Pss 113 and 114 were sung at the beginning of the meal
and Pss 115–118 at the end (Matt 26:30; Mark 14:26. Cf. I. Elbogen, *Die
jüdische Gottesdienst in seine geschichtlichen Entwirklung* [Leipzig: Buchhandlung
Gustav Fock, 1913] 125, 130, 136–38; J. Jeremias, *The Eucharistic Words of
Jesus* [Tr. A. Ehrhardt; Oxford: Basil Blackwell, 1955] 55 note 15, 255–
61).

J. T. Willis (*CBQ* 35 [1973] 139–54) has argued that the psalm is a song
of victory and traces parallels of language and thought with such early songs.
On the basis of similarities with 1 Sam 2:5, 8 he has suggested that both
come from the same milieu, the sanctuary of Shiloh, and thus that the psalm
may have originated in North Israel and been taken over and used in the
worship of the Jerusalem temple. Over against this hypothesis must be set
Crüsemann's conclusion that the psalm is the end product of a long, complicated Formgeschichte (*Studien zur Formgeschichte*, 135). He himself was opposing C. Westermann's view of the psalm as the basic form of the Israelite
hymn (*Praise*, 118–20). It is impossible to determine whether the psalm is
pre-exilic or post-exilic. Traditional expressions are used, yet in an independent manner (Kraus, *Psalmen*, 951). A question which affects dating to some
degree is whether vv 7–9 reflect literary usage of 1 Sam 1, 2. Certainly the
identity of vv 7–8a with 1 Sam 2:8aα–γ (apart from the endings of the two
verbs) is remarkable. V 9 is generally compared with עקרה ילדה שבעה "the
barren woman has borne seven," 1 Sam 2:5, but also שמחה "joyful" may
relate to שמחתי, 1 Sam 2:1, so that Hannah is regarded as the reciter of
the song; and בנים "sons" may relate to 1 Sam 1:8; 2:21.

From the perspective of content the psalm might be divided into two, vv
1–4, 5–9 (Gunkel, *Die Psalmen*, 491, 492; Kraus, *Psalmen*, 950). Gunkel regards
the question of v 5 as marking a new beginning. But in form the psalm
divides into vv 1–3 and 4–9, summons to praise and its substance. Accordingly
many have divided it into three parts, vv 1–3, 4–6, 7–9 (e.g. Weiser, *Psalms*,
705) and indeed into three strophes of three lines (J. A. Montgomery, "Stanza
Formation in Hebrew Poetry," *JBL* 64 [1945] 382; E. J. Kissane, *Psalms II*,
202; J. Schildenberger, *Estudios Eclesiásticos* 34 [1960] 675; E. Beaucamp, *RSR*
56 [1968] 211; Dahood, *Psalms III*, 130). Stylistically there is much to commend this division. Vv 1–3 are bound together by the threefold שם יהוה and
by the inclusion of the stem הלל in vv 1, 3. There are also inclusive elements
in vv 4 and 6: השמים . . . כל-גוים correspond to בשמים ובארץ. In vv 7, 9
the participles מקימי and משיבי are an obvious inclusive pair. The third strophe
takes up the qal verbal forms of the second in the hiph'il conjugation, placing
them at the same points of the first and second lines: רם, ירים, vv 4, 7 and
לשבת, (י)להושיב, vv 5, 8. Yahweh's heavenly status is echoed in his bestowal
of human status. Two remarkable symmetrical features of the psalm are (1)
that prepositions are repeated in every line except the first, last and middle
ones, vv 1, 5, 9, and (2) that the chiastic order of cola in vv 2, 3 (Dahood,
Psalms III, 131) is matched by a similar one in vv 5–6 (see *Notes/Comments*)
and by a partial one in vv 8–9 (מושיבי ; עם נדיבי :: עם נדיבים : [(י)להושיב].

Explanation

This artistically structured hymn celebrating Yahweh's majesty and grace must often have been selected for use in festival services. The first strophe is an extended summons to praise, addressed to the worshiping community. Three times they are urged to bless Yahweh's name, the revelation of his being and will. How can he be praised enough? To worship adequately would take the rest of time and the concerted tongues of all creatures on earth (cf. 48:11 [10]). No less response in space or time is worthy of him. The congregation is not being excused from praise, but assured of their obligation to play their own part there and then.

The second and third strophes give the substance of praise. Israel may proudly affirm that their covenant God is greater than all else which stands for power. Imperial nations, imposing and often menacing to little Israel, are nothing compared with the great Lord of history (cf. Isa 40:15). Their gods cannot match his omnipotence. He is unique in his royal glory (cf. 102:13 [12]; Isa 6:1)—and also in his grace (cf. 138:6; Isa. 57:15). The third strophe uses 1 Sam 1–2 to illustrate this grace in terms of the providential reversal Yahweh brings about, raising the socially underprivileged to positions of respect. From the song of Hannah the psalmist takes the theme of rescue (1 Sam 2:8).

Yahweh cares for the poverty-stricken wretch scavenging in the rubbish dump outside the city and for the suffering outcast for whom the community had no room (cf. Job 2:8). From the experience of Hannah the psalmist teaches that Yahweh can miraculously remove the stigma of childlessness (cf. 1 Sam 1:5–8) by granting the blessing of motherhood and with it full acceptance within the family.

These cases function as illustrations of Yahweh's providential intervention in the lives of individuals (cf. 107:41; Job 5:11). Israel celebrated Yahweh as a God who focused his power upon the individual as well as upon the world. Here his intervention represents part of his care for the chosen nation. Individual and nation belonged together in solidarity. Yahweh was ever working out his will not only for a society whose members were integrated but also for the nucleus of the community, the family. His desire was for it to be united and fulfilling its purposes in harmony. To that end he redressed the balance in a God-ward direction: the exaltation of v 7 corresponds to his own in v 4 and the seating and settling of vv 8–9 to his kingly session in v 5. This is one aspect of the ideal that Yahweh's own characteristics be reflected among his chosen people. Divine grace is the impartation of divine glory; it bestows a measure of divine power and honor.

Later generations of worshipers broadened the scope of vv 7–9 as typifying the chosen nation itself as recipient of God's blessing: probably the placing of the psalm before Ps 114 already implies this interpretation. The NT treated the grace of God in similar vein: he "chose what is weak, . . . low and despised in the world" (1 Cor 1:26–29). Likewise the theme of vv 4–9 finds a remarkable correspondence in God's raising and seating the church in a manner parallel to his mighty acts with his Son (Eph 1:19–2:7). Both Paul and

James discuss the theme of divinely intended honor within the Christian community, in 1 Cor 12:14–26 (cf. Rom 12:10) and Jas 2:1–9.

The Relevance of Sacred History (114:1–8)

Bibliography

Jeremias, J. *Theophanie. Die Geschichte einer alttestamentlichen Gattung.* WMANT 10. 2nd ed. Neukirchen-Vluyn: Neukirchener Verlag, 1965. **Lauha, A.** *Die Geschichtsmotive in den alttestamentlichen Psalmen.* Annales academiae scientarum, fennicae 16:1. Helsinki: Suomalainen Tiedeakatemia, 1945. **Lubsczyk, H.** "Einheit und heilsgeschichtliche Bedeutung von Ps. 114/115 (113)." *BZ* 11 (1967) 161–73. **Macintosh, A. A.** "Christian Exodus. An Analysis of Psalm 114." *Theology* 72 (1969) 317–19.

Translation

¹ When ª Israel came out of Egypt,ᵇ   (3+3)
    the community of Jacob from a people of incoherent speech,
² Judah became his sanctuary,   (3+3)
    Israel ª his royal dominion.ᵇ

³ The sea ª looked ᵇ and ran away,   (3+3)
    the Jordan turned back.ᶜ
⁴ The mountains jumped ª like rams,   (3+3)
    the hills like lambs.

⁵ What is the matter with you, sea, that you run away,ª   (3+3
    and Jordan, that you turn back,
⁶ mountains, that you jump like rams,   (3+3)
    hills, like lambs?

⁷ At the coming of the Lord tremble,ª O land,ᵇ   (4+3)
    at the coming of the God ᶜ of Jacob,
⁸ who turned ª the rock into a pool of water,   (4+3)
    flintstone into a spring ᵇ of water.

Notes/Comments

1.a. LXX connects the הללו־יה closing Ps 113 with Ps 114, which would then create a sequence of four psalms beginning thus. According to J. W. Rogerson and J. W. McKay (*Psalms 101–150*, 75) it would provide an antecedent for the pronominal suffixes in v 2 (cf. A. F. Kirkpatrick, *Psalms*, 681), but most probably it would serve as a heading or the like rather than as an integral part of the psalm.

1.b. For the use of this formula in the OT see W. Gross, *ZAW* 86 (1974) 438; he notes that it can include the time of wandering up to entry into Canaan (cf. Deut 4:46; Josh 5:4, 5). It has been speculated that the form of the theophany, the absence of an antecedent for the suffixes of v 2 and different uses of ישראל "Israel" in vv 1–2 presuppose an original beginning in which Yahweh was the explicit subject, as in 68:8 (7); Judg 5:4 (C. Westermann, *Praise*, 96 note 47; E. Lipiński, *La royauté de Yahwé*, 201–2; J. Jeremias, *Theophanie*, 173). However, formal development is more likely than textual adaptation.

2.a. The significance of ישראל constitutes an exegetical crux. Does it refer to the Northern. Kingdom, while "Judah" is the Southern (H. Gunkel, 494; Jeremias, *Theophanie*, 128 note 5; *et al.*)? Kirkpatrick (*Psalms*, 681), A. Weiser (*Psalms*, 710) and M. Dahood (*Psalms III*, 134) treat the verse as composite in its parallelism: the whole of Palestine, north and south, became Yahweh's sanctuary and realm. Or does the term stand for the total community, as in v 1, from which in v 2a Judah is singled out as specially honored (G. A. Danell, *Studies in the Name Israel in the OT* [Uppsala: Appelbergs Boktryckeri, 1946] 104. H.-J. Kraus, *Psalmen*, 957, leaves the two possibilities open)? Identity of meaning in vv 1, 2b would impart a natural flow, but v 2a constitutes an obstacle. So a third possibility is the most probable, that the fall of the Northern Kingdom is presupposed and Judah is the sole heir of the cultic designation "Israel." The two names of v 2 are then synonymous, while ישראל in v 2 functions as the contemporary historical counterpart of that in v 1.

2.b. For the combination of the stem משל with קדש and מקדש cf. Isa 63:18–19. It is often suggested that the two terms allude to ממלכת כהנים וגוי קדוש, Exod 19:6 (cf. בית יעקב v 1 and Exod 19:3, and the Exodus formula of Exod 19:1). There may be a double perspective, the covenant promise of Exod 19:6 and its historical fulfillment in Palestine. For the designation in Exod 19:6 see W. J. Moran, "A Kingdom of Priests," in *The Bible in Current Catholic Thought*, ed. J. L. McKenzie (New York: Herder and Herder, 1962) 7–20; B. S. Childs, *Exodus*, 342, 367. The plural ממשלותיו is strange. It has been explained as a plural of local extension (cf. GKC § 124b). Stylistically a singular ממשלתו is expected (see *Form/Structure/Setting*). LXX S Hier use singular terms, though a singular in their Hebrew *Vorlagen* is not thereby proved. The force of the preposition in v 2a extends to this noun. *Pace BHS* the Versions do not imply ל(ממשלתו). The plural of MT is probably to be explained as a true plural and an attempt to elucidate ישראל as bipartite.

3.a. This is a reference to the Reed Sea: for the combination of the two miraculous crossings cf. 66:6; Josh 4:23. Dahood (*Psalms III*, 135) relates to the Dead Sea, comparing Josh 3:16, in consequence of his view that the psalm celebrates Yahweh's choice of Palestine.

3.b. The object of seeing is left mysteriously inexplicit, as in 48:6 (5); it is not the act of election of v 2, as A. Lauha interprets (*Die Geschichtsmotive*, 69). For the literary pattern of suspense in vv 3–7, consisting of a sequence of reaction, question and final explanatory statement cf. Dan 3:24–25.

3.c. The personalized description in vv 3–4 is associated with theophany and specifically the divine battle with chaos, borrowed from the mythology of the Canaanite storm god and here used metaphorically and historicized (cf. Jeremias, *Theophanie*, 128, 161; F. M. Cross, *Canaanite Myth and Hebrew Epic*, 147–58). Here, as in 77:17 (16); 104:7, there is no fighting as such, only the flight of Yahweh's enemies, so formidable is he. Lauha (*Die Geschichtsmotive*, 104) rightly judged that the heightening of the Jordan miracle whereby the river is not only dammed but turned back preserves no separate tradition but rather exhibits the product of a lively imagination. The verb יסב is a preterite (Dahood, *Psalms III*, 136; D. A. Robertson, *Linguistic Evidence*, 54).

4.a. Cf. 29:6 where the same verbal stem is used. There may be a double reference to Sinai and to the mountains of Canaan (cf. Exod 19:8; and Ps 29:8 as explained by Weiser, *Psalms*, 264), especially if the tradition of Exod 19 is used in v 2.

5.a. For this dramatic personified actualization cf. 68:16–17 (15–16). Dahood (*Psalms III*, 136) renders the prefix verbs of vv 5–6 as past, as in v 4b, but the imperative of v 7, which he retains, suggests a present sense.

7.a. Should חולי אדון be emended to כל אדון "Lord of all (the earth/land)," a phrase found in 97:5; Josh 3:11, 13; Mic 4:13; Zech 4:14; 6:5 (H. L. Ginsberg, "Some Emendations in the Psalms," *HUCA* 23 [1950/51] 102–3; Cross, *Canaanite Myth and Hebrew Epic*, 138 note 91; Kraus, *Psalmen*, 953)? Ginsberg found a command very weak after the questions and was uneasy about the anarthrous אדון "lord." Kraus is influenced by the view that the psalm has special links with Josh 3–5. He also claims the support of parallelism, comparing the form of v 1, and urges that a restored 3+3 meter would conform with the rest of the psalm. His metrical argument is won or lost by v 8: both vv 7 and 8 may have a climactic 4+3 rhythm. As to parallelism, the resultant line would stylistically align better with the more simple vv 1–2, 8: vv 1–2 are the structural counterpart of vv 7–8. The conjecture is attractive but not compelling. H. Lubsczyk (*BZ* 11 [1967] 166–67) has urged that the address to אֶרֶץ "land" is quite feasible after the apostrophizing of vv 5–6; he cited 96:9; 97:4; Jer 51:29 in support of MT. Gunkel (*Die Psalmen*, 496) compared Sir 32:22 for אֲדוֹן, but this appears to be a secondary reading.

7.b. Heb. אֶרֶץ here has the force of land, referring to Palestine (Dahood, *Psalms III*, 136; Kraus, *Psalmen*, 953), rather than earth.

7.c. The normal phrase is אֱלֹהֵי (יַעֲקֹב), to which many would emend אֱלוֹהַּ, with the support of a few Heb. mss., MT then having suffered haplography. But אֱלוֹהַּ is of a piece with the archaisms of the psalm.

8.a. For the -*y* morpheme attached to an appositional participle see Robertson, *Linguistic Evidence*, 69–76.

8.b. For the -*w* morpheme see Robertson, *Linguistic Evidence*, 76–79.

Form/Structure/Setting

Psalm 114 is a hymn of a special kind. Its theme, like that of Ps 29, is the divine theophany (cf. Westermann, *Praise*, 81–83, 93–98; Jeremias, *Theophanie, passim*). The only characteristic hymnic language is the hymnic participle of v 8. Its treatment of Israel's history makes it comparable as a hymn with Pss 105 and 135, but its crisp and dramatic style sets it apart.

Its concern with Israel's election and salvation history (Dahood, *Psalms III*, 133, unduly limits the range of the psalm by categorizing its theme as Yahweh's choice of Palestine) would make its use suitable at any of the annual festivals. Some scholars, such as Gunkel (*Die Psalmen*, 494) and Lauha (*Die Geschichtsmotive*, 69), regard it as a Passover hymn; this accords with the later Jewish tradition of singing it on the eighth day of the Passover. It is also of course the second of the Hallel psalms in Jewish worship (see *Form/Structure/Setting* of Ps 113). Others have claimed it according to their cultic predilections, H. Schmidt (*Die Psalmen*, 207) and S. Mowinckel (*The Psalms in Israel's Worship*, vol. 1, 114–15) for the feast of Yahweh's enthronement and Weiser (*Psalms*, 709) for his covenant festival. Weiser associates the theme of theophany with cultic epiphany. Certainly it appears to represent cultic actualization, which brought the Heilsgeschichte home to the worshipers as a present reality.

Kraus (*Psalmen*, 955) rightly observes that the Judean perspective of v 2 and the implicit reference to Jerusalem as the central sanctuary does not demand a post-deuteronomic date. He himself uses its archaic features and references to crossing the Jordan as support for the inference that the psalm's traditions derive from the sanctuary of Gilgal. He links it with Josh 3–5, which is widely believed to be associated with the worship of Gilgal (cf. Kraus *Worship in Israel*, 154–59; J. A. Soggin, *Joshua* [Philadelphia: Westminster Press, 1972] 51–53). The date of the present composition does not appear to be early, though it need not be post-exilic. V 2 probably points to a period after 721 B.C. (see *Notes/Comments*). Robertson (*Linguistic Evidence*, 145) rules out an early date on the basis of the psalm's three early poetic forms in view of the accompanying forms of standard poetry. Westermann (*Praise*, 96) describes the psalm as giving a late variation of the literary genre of theophany in view of the non-divine subject in v 1.

Structurally there is widespread agreement that the psalm falls into four strophes of two bicola each (Gunkel, *Die Psalmen*, 494–95; J. A. Montgomery, *JBL* 64 [1945] 382; E. Beaucamp, *RSR* 56 [1968] 210). Kraus (*Psalmen*, 954) dissents in view of his emendation of v 7. He runs vv 5–8 into a single unit. Structural study of the past few psalms have indicated that a psalmist can employ more than one scheme, whether mutually compatible or not. Here an overall chiastic pattern is noticeable. Vv 3–4 and 5–6 form obvious inner parallels. They are surrounded by vv 1–2 and 7–8: in both of the latter units יעקב and repetition of the preposition מ(לפני) occur in the first line. In the second lines the preposition ל occurs once. The rhyming ends of the cola of v 8 would be finely balanced with v 2 if a singular noun with suffix, ממשלתו, were restored to match לקדשו.

Explanation

Psalm 114 looks back to the basics of Israel's faith and self-understanding. It begins by recalling the theologically significant time when the burden of foreign oppression rolled away and they became free, not merely to develop their own nationalism but to enter Yahweh's service. By the Exodus they became a holy people who worshiped him as their God, and a vassal people who owned him as their King (cf. 59:14 [13]). Judah, guardian of Yahweh's sanctuary and now sole heir of the covenant nation of old, rejoices in the fulfillment of his covenant promise of Exod 19:6. The strange absence of direct mention of Yahweh in v 2 may be the start of a process of building up suspense, which is very evident in vv 3–6.

Vv 3–4 celebrate a demonstration of power in vivid and dramatic terms. Something dynamic happened long ago. It was so tremendous that it routed the sea, made the Jordan turn tail and caused solid mountains to leap into the air like startled lambs! How formidable must have been the foe that they reacted to his advance in such demoralized terror? With gleeful triumph the psalmist re-enacts the ancient scenario for the contemporary generation of God's people.

What could it have been? What was the matter? The poet pauses over the scene in vv 5–6, savoring it and deliberately delaying his eventual disclosure. He revels in these past events, pretending not to know, so that its wonder may shine out afresh. In line with the cultic practice of actualizing religious history, the psalmist puts himself into the past and makes the worshipers feel themselves there, as if it had all just happened. He addresses the participants rhetorically in mock astonishment to discover the secret of their consternation.

His question is a device to pave the way for the grand dénouement of v 7. The curtains are swept back, as it were, to reveal Yahweh as the divine hero, the victorious warrior whose impact has been measured obliquely by his enemies' reactions. Vv 3–4 in retrospect are seen to be the description of a theophany in traditional terms of nature's reaction to Yahweh's coming (cf. 18:8[7]). This majestic whimsicality is applied to Israel's archetypal history (cf. 77:17–20 [16–19]; Judg 5:4, 5; Hab 3:3–15). The crossing of the Reed Sea and Jordan (Exod 14:21–22; 15:4–12; Josh 3:14–17), the earthquake of Sinai and, imaginatively, that of Canaan's hill country (Exod 15:14–16; 19:18) are all encompassed in the sweep of vv 3–4. Now the psalmist discards the objective role of observer and interviewer, and excitedly plunges into Israel's situation on the eve of the conquest of Canaan. He orders the land to respond with terror to the coming of its new master, who is none other than Israel's God (cf. 97:4, 5). He comes as one who on his people's behalf has already demonstrated his power over nature, in the wonders of the wilderness (cf. Exod 17:1–16; Num 20:1–11; Deut 8:15). He is a God who both saves and keeps his people (cf. 77:16, 21 [15, 20]), and Canaan must submit to his sovereign will concerning them.

With its staccato momentum and evocative imagery the psalm is as exciting as the music of drum or cymbals. It is alive with radiant assurance: Israel shares in the victory of her God and moves in his protective wake. His saving and keeping acts of the past are real and relevant for today. Yahweh's covenant promise, in the good of which Judah now lives (v 2), is ever undergirded by his power (cf. Col 1:11–14).

A Help and Shield (115:1–18)

Bibliography

Becker, J. *Gottesfurcht im AT.* AnBib 25. Rome: Pontifical Biblical Institute, 1965. **Habel, N. C.** " 'Yahweh, Maker of Heaven and Earth': A Study in Tradition Criticism." *JBL* 91 (1972) 321–37. **Luke, K.** "The Setting of Psalm 115." *ITQ* 34 (1967) 347–57. **Preuss, H. D.** *Die Verspottung fremder Religionen im AT.* BWANT 5:12. Stuttgart: W. Kohlhammer Verlag, 1971.

Translation

1a Not to us, Yahweh, not to us,   (3+3+3)
  but to your name give glory,[b]
  for the sake of your loyal love,[c] your faithfulness.
2 Why should the nations ask   (3+2)
  "Where, pray, is their God?"
3 In fact our God is in heaven:[a]   (2+3)
  he does[b] anything he pleases.
4 Their idols[a] are silver and gold,   (3+3)
  made by human hands.

5 They have mouths but cannot speak,[a]   (4+4)
  they have eyes but cannot see.
6 They have ears but cannot hear,   (4+4)
  they have noses but cannot smell.
7 Their hands—they cannot feel with them,   (3+3+3)
  their feet—they cannot walk with them.[a]
  They cannot produce any sounds in their throats.[b]
8 Like them may their makers become,[a]   (3+3)
  anyone who trusts in them.

9 *"Israel,*[a] *trust*[b] *in Yahweh."*   (3+3)
  "He is their help, their shield."[c]
10 *"House of Aaron, trust in Yahweh."*   (3+3)
   "He is their help, their shield."
11 *"You who revere Yahweh,*[a] *trust in Yahweh."*   (3+3)
   "He is their help, their shield."

12 *"Yahweh has remembered us: he will bless.*[a]   (3+3+3)
   He will bless the house of Israel,
   he will bless the house of Aaron,
13 *he will bless those who revere Yahweh,*   (3+3)
   young and old alike."[a]

14 *"May Yahweh add to you,*   (3+3)
   to you and to your children.[a]
15 *May you be blessed by Yahweh,*   (3+3)
   maker of heaven and earth."[a]
16 *Heaven is Yahweh's heaven,*   (3+4)
   but the earth he has entrusted[a] *to mankind.*
17 *The dead cannot praise Yah(weh)*[a]   (3+3)
   nor any who go down to Silence.[b]
18 *But we*[a] *will bless Yah(weh)*   (3+3)
   from now on and for evermore.
                    Hallelujah[b]

Notes/Comments

1.a. Many Heb. mss. and LXX, θ', S, Hier combine Ps 115 with Ps 114, and so H. Lubsczyk (*BZ* 11 [1967] 161–73) has urged. But the psalms are distinct in tone, structure and style (A. F. Kirkpatrick, *Psalms*, 683); in particular "the terse vitality of Ps 114 is all its own: the refrains and catchwords of 115 are a different form of writing" (D. Kidner, *Psalms 73–150*, 404). The seemingly abrupt ending of Ps 114 (but cf. Ps 77) may have encouraged the union.

1.b. Cf. 79:9; 138:2aβ (and v 2 with 79:10). It is often held that a colon has been omitted after v la (cf. *BHS*; H.-J. Kraus, *Psalmen*, 960).

1.c. Heb. חסד "loyal love" is here hailed as the basis of deliverance: cf. 107:8; 109:26 and K. D. Sakenfeld, *The Meaning of Hesed*, 218–21.

3.a. LXX adds ἄνω "above," whence H. Gunkel (*Die Psalmen*, 499), JB and NEB restore מִמַּעַל. But it is more likely to be simply a Greek dittograph (after οὐρανῷ), encouraged by liturgical phraseology (J. S. Sibinga, *The OT Text of Justin Martyr*, vol. 1 [Leiden: E. J. Brill, 1963] 90). The error is found frequently in LXX. LXX also adds ἐν τοῖς οὐρανοῖς καὶ ἐν τῇ γῇ "in the heavens and in the earth," which JB incorporates. The addition is due to assimilation to the parallel 135:6. Since LXX there renders slightly differently, the contamination must have already occurred in LXX's Heb. *Vorlage*.

3.b. A. Weiser (*Psalms*, 713) renders "he created" (cf. v 15), but the stress here seems rather to be on Yahweh's activity over against the idols' inactivity.

4.a. LXX, S and Hier render עצבי הגוים "idols of the nations," 135:15, which probably at least LXX's Heb. text read. For the biblical attack upon idolatry see Y. Kaufmann, *The Religion of Israel from Its Beginnings to the Babylonian Exile* (Tr. M. Greenberg; London: Allen and Unwin, 1960) 7–20; G. von Rad, *Wisdom in Israel* (Tr. J. D. Martin; London: SCM Press, 1972) 177–85; and for this passage in particular H. D. Preuss, *Verspottung*, 251–53. Worship of images was regarded as purely superstitious fetishism and there was no evident awareness that the image was representational. Such ridiculing tirades as these (cf. Isa 40:18–20; 44:9–20; Jer 10:1–16), which simply identified image and deity were intended not as serious debate with pagan religion but as Israel's propaganda for Israelite ears, as a corollary of their own exclusive and aniconic faith.

5.a. The imperfects in vv 5–7 and also 17 are modal (D. Michel, *Tempora*, 146, 149). Gunkel (*Die Psalmen*, 497) gave a specifically divine application of the defects of vv 5–6 in terms of speaking oracles, seeing men's deeds (cf. 33:13), hearing prayer and smelling sacrifices (cf. Gen 9:21).

7.a. So render Gunkel (*Die Psalmen*, 499) and Weiser (*Psalms*, 713; cf. NEB). Others see datival suffixes here (cf. GKC §§ 117z, 147e).

7.b. D. N. Freedman's explanation, cited by M. Dahood (*Psalms III*, 140, 141), is probably correct, that v 5a refers to articulate sounds of the mouth and v 7b to rudimentary sounds made in the throat to express elemental emotions.

8.a. Probably a wish is intended, as LXX interprets the ambivalent Hebrew (Gunkel, *Die Psalmen*, 497; Michel, *Tempora*, 163).

9.a. Probably the laity is meant (Gunkel, *Die Psalmen*, 497, with reference to Ezra 9:1; 10:25). The insertion of בֵּית "house" by many Heb. mss. and LXX S in line with vv 12 and 135:19 may be simply a case of assimilation. MT is to be retained as the harder reading.

9.b. LXX implies a vocalization as perfects, בָּטַח, vv 9–10, and בְּטָחוּ, v 11, which NEB adopts. Gunkel (*Die Psalmen*, 499) rightly refers to 118:2–4; 135:19, 20, where similar groups are associated with an imperatival summons. The third person suffixes led LXX astray. Probably the first and second cola of each line were sung antiphonally.

9.c. Cf. 33:20b, 21b.

11.a. Kraus (*Psalmen*, 965–66) *et al.* consider that proselytes are in view and so that the community as a whole is referred to as "Israel" rather than by this phrase. It is much more likely that the whole community is described comprehensively in this final phrase: see J. Becker's full discussion in *Gottesfurcht im AT*, 155–60. A. A. Anderson (*Psalms*, 788) observes that v 13 so suggests and compares 22:24 (23).

12.a. Michel (*Tempora*, 166) finds jussive wishes in vv 12–14, but the preceding perfect indicates rather an assured future sense.

13.a. Cf. 2 Chr 31:15 and Weiser, *Psalms*, 714; Becker, *Gottesfurcht im AT*, 157. V 14 suggests an age differential.

14.a. For blessing in terms of life see J. Pedersen, *Israel: Its Life and Culture 1–2* (London: Oxford University Press, 1926) 204–12.

15.a. For this cultic formula see N. C. Habel, *JBL* 91 (1972) 321–37. He judges Gen 14:19 to be the prototype of this formula of blessing (cf. 134:3).

16.a. Dahood (*Psalms III*, 142) so renders, with reference to Gen 30:35; Deut 10:14.

17.a. Cf. 88:10–12; Isa 38:18–19 and C. Westermann, *Praise*, 155, 158–61, for the impossibility of praising God in Sheol and the converse that "nowhere [in the OT] is there the possibility of abiding, true life that does not praise God." For יָהּ see the second note on 118:5.

17.b. See the note on 101:5. Dahood (*Psalms III*, 143) translates "the Fortress," but the usual rendering is strikingly relevant here.

18.a. LXX adds οἱ ζῶντες "the living," adopted by JB and NEB. It is the result of contamination from Isa 38:19, most probably at the Greek level: the identical Greek verbs (unlike the Hebrew) encouraged the assimilation.

18.b. This stands outside the psalm proper: see the note on 104:35. LXX places at the head of Ps. 116.

Form/Structure/Setting

This complex psalm appears to be basically a communal complaint. This is evident from the opening invocation and petition, v 1, the complaint concerning foes in the form of a sneering question, v 2, as in 79:10, the confession of trust formulated in terms both positive (cf. 74:12) and negative, vv 3–7, the negative wish, v 8 (cf. 79:12; 80:17 [16]), and what looks like a final vow of praise, vv 16–18, as in 79:13 (cf. Westermann, *Praise*, 52–60). But it is clear that different voices feature in the psalm, which is consequently a liturgy. Vv 9–11 are best understood as a priest's encouragement (cf. 27:14) and an antiphonal response (cf. Gunkel, *Die Psalmen*, 498; Weiser, *Psalms*, 716–17) involving another singer or choir. Vv 12–13 originally presuppose a prophetic voice (cf. 85:9–14 [8–13]) or perhaps a priestly one. Taking up the formal language of vv 9–11 and identifying himself sympathetically with the congregation in v 12, the speaker reports Yahweh's positive hearing of the complaint and can declare the certainty of blessing (cf. Gunkel, *Die Psalmen*, 498; Kraus, *Psalmen*, 966; Westermann, *Praise*, 61–64. For v 12aα K. Luke (*ITQ* 34 [1967] 355) suggests an implicit underlying petition like 137:7. In vv 14, 15 a priestly voice delivers an invocation of blessing formulated in the jussive mood (cf. 1 Sam 1:17; 2:20): the different tone suggests a new speaker. In vv 16–18 the original voice representing the community returns with a confession of trust and praise of Yahweh in consequence of the assurance of having been heard (cf. this feature in individual complaints, such as 22:23–25 [22–24]; 28:6, 7, and Westermann, *Praise*, 79–81). As a whole the psalm is a liturgical complaint with a strong note of assurance. When it was incorporated into its present grouping of psalms, its emphasis was changed to praise (Anderson, *Psalms*, 786; cf. Ps 106).

The background of this cultic liturgy is a situation of national demoralization, probably longstanding in view of v 14 (Gunkel, *Die Psalmen*, 498). A precise cultic setting cannot be determined. Luke (*ITQ* 34 [1967] 347–57) suggested that it was the renewal of the covenant at the Feast of Tabernacles. He stressed—probably too much—the renunciation of false gods in vv 4–7, comparing Josh 24:14–15, 20. As to date the psalm may be pre-exilic (S. Mowinckel, *Psalmenstudien 5*, 45, who posited either the early post-exilic or the late pre-exilic period; Weiser, *Psalms*, 715 [even if proselytes are indicated in vv 11, 13]). But more probably v 14 reflects the small population of post-exilic Judah (cf. Ezra 9:8, 15). Kraus (*Psalmen*, 964) and Preuss (*Verspottung*, 252) regard the rationalistic, matter-of-fact way in which idols are lampooned in vv 4–8 as evidence of the psalm being later than the heated controversy of Second Isaiah.

As to structure, Gunkel's content-based divisions are largely followed: vv 1–2, 3–8, 9–11, 12–15, 16–18 (*Die Psalmen*, 497–98). A noticeable stylistic feature of the psalm is the cluster of identical terms at its beginning and end: כל "all," vv 3, 17, ולא "and not," vv 1, 17, the stem עשה "do, make," vv 3, 4, 15, אדם "man," vv 4, 16 and שמים "heaven," vv 3, 15, 16. If these inclusive elements coincide with strophical sections, which need not be so, they suggest strophes of vv 1–4, 14–18. In the latter case the repeated עליכם, v 14, nicely balances and answers the repeated לנו, v 1; the strophe is bound together by the inclusive elements ברוכים אתם, v 15, and ואנחנו נברך, v 18. As to vv 1–4, at first sight v 5 is not an obvious place to begin a fresh strophe, but vv 3–4 do seem to exhibit a chiastic order, heavenly location being pitted against human origin, and intelligent activity against inanimate metals. This pattern matches the chiasmus of vv 16–18, which features superlatives of space and time and human obligations. In content the petition, complaint and positive and negative confessions of vv 1–4 correspond to the blessing, confession and negatively and positively formulated praise of vv 14–18.

Vv 5–8 develop the negative confession of trust with inclusion of oral sounds at vv 5b, 7b. The new element of v 8 accords with that of v 4. Vv

9–11 are closely echoed by vv 12–13 in that the same three groups are involved, new voices speak and the repetition of verbs, בטח and ברך, correspond. The structure of the psalm appears to follow an ABCC′A′ pattern. The voice of the community's representative stands out remarkably from the other voices by the threefold repetition of a multiple לא and כל (vv 1–3, 5–8, 17).

Explanation

God's people in post-exilic Judah are in a state of distress and weakness. They bring their trusting petition to him in the temple. They appeal to his honor in vv 1–2, referring obliquely to their needs by citing the mocking taunt of surrounding pagan states. Yahweh's reputation is at stake, and this is the community's concern rather than any self-seeking, as they crave his intervention. They take their stand upon the promises of God and his covenant relationship with them as grounds for hope of deliverance. Taking the sarcastic question of v 2 literally, they affirm that their covenant God occupies the supreme place of supernatural power. At this point the psalm corresponds to the Christological passage Eph 1:20–23. They continue their praise indirectly by dismissing the gods of other nations as earthly and man-made idols.

There follows a satire of divine images as dumb, blind, deaf and devoid of any powers their personal form might indicate. Yahwism was unique in the ancient Near East as an aniconic religion: the community's faith is bolstered by exploiting the basic difference here. It is an implicit testimony to the power of the true God and to the potential of those who trust in him (for v 8 cf. 2 Kgs 17:15; Jer 2:5).

A priestly voice intervenes, taking up the theme of trust and applying it to the troubled congregation. He calls upon laity and fellow priests alike, upon the whole religious community, to exercise faith. He is backed by an assurance from (an)other voice(s) that Yahweh is able and willing to defend them. Fuel for faith materializes in vv 12–13: another temple minister, probably a prophet, declares that he has received an assurance that Yahweh will honor his covenant promises. He can affirm that the community which has heeded the call to trust may confidently expect divine blessing. He seeks to bring comfort to their hearts by repeating the verb "bless" (cf. 121:7, 8). A priest, perhaps the figure of vv 9a, 10a, 11a, now imparts this blessing (cf. Num 6:23–27), specifying its content as a gift of abundant life to the numerically diminished community and focusing upon the Giver, the traditional source of blessing and power. The renewal of an ancient promise of increase in population (cf. Gen 22:17; Deut 1:11) meets them at the point of their present need.

As the priest took up the congregation's word in v 9, now they smoothly take up his words in praise. Yahweh claims for himself the divine sphere of the heavens and so he possesses transcendent power, they reaffirm (cf. v 3). He it is who has entrusted the earth to mankind as his stewards. The uncompromising implication, which they can boldly pit against foreign political dominance, is that he is the sole God and has a unique claim to man's vocal gratitude. This, rather than making idols (v 4), should be man's concern! True, the privilege is temporary according to the general tenor of OT faith.

But that only accentuates the obligation of the present generation of God's people to use every opportunity for praise. They respond to priestly blessing by "blessing" Yahweh in turn (cf. Eph 1:3). In faith their praise begins now, anticipating the promised blessing, and becomes a new song of salvation which will last them the rest of their lives.

Psalm 115 is a stirring lesson to the people of God in every age concerning survival in an alien, hostile environment. It teaches the necessity of rising above life's questions and paradoxes on God-given wings of prayer and faith. The reality of a relationship with God imparts strong resistance to rival human ideologies and creates a hope so certain to believing hearts that its prospect can already induce praise (cf. Rom 5:2; 8:38–39; 1 Pet 1:3–9).

He Saved Me (116:1–19)

Bibliography

Beyerlin, W. "Kontinuität beim 'berichtenden' Lobpreis des Einzelnen," *Wort und Geschichte. Festschrift für K. Elliger,* H. Gese *et al.* AOAT 18. Neukirchen-Vluyn: Neukirchener Verlag, 1973. **Crüsemann, F.** *Studien zur Formgeschichte.* **Daiches, S.** "Interpretation of Psalm 116." *Occident and Orient. Gaster Anniversary Volume.* London: Taylor's Foreign Press, 1936. **Fensham, F. C.** "The Son of a Handmaid in Northwest Semitic." *VT* 19 (1969) 312–21.

Translation

1 *I love* [a] *because Yahweh has heard* [b] 　*my imploring cry,* [c]	(3+2)
2 *because he leaned his ear to me,* 　*and all my life I will proclaim:* [a]	(3+2)
3 *"Death's cords were all around me,* 　*Sheol's nooses had seized me,* [a] 　*I encountered distress and anguish.*	(3+3+3)
4 *Then I invoked the name of Yahweh:* [a] 　*'Oh, Yahweh,* 　*deliver me.'*	(3+2+2)
5 *Yahweh is dutiful* [a] *and true,* 　*our God shows affection.*	(3+2)
6 *Yahweh takes care of simple folk:* 　*when I was down, he saved me."*	(3+3)
7 *Return to your rest,* [a] *my heart,* [b] 　*for Yahweh has treated you* [a] *well.*	(3+3)
8 *Yes,* [a] *you rescued* [b] *me from death,* 　*my eye* [c] *from tears* 　*and my foot from stumbling.*	(3+2+2)

⁹ *I can walk* ᵃ *in Yahweh's presence*   (3+2)
   through the regions of the living. ᵇ
¹⁰ᵃ *I had faith, even when* ᵇ *I declared,*   (3+3)
   "I am suffering acutely."
¹¹ *I said in my alarm,*   (3+2)
   "All men are unreliable." ᵃ
¹² *How can I repay Yahweh*   (3+3)
   for all his benefits ᵃ *to me?*
¹³ *I am taking salvation's cup* ᵃ   (3+3)
   and proclaiming the name of Yahweh.
¹⁴ *My vows I am paying to Yahweh*   (3+3)
   in front ᵃ *of all his people.* ᵇ

¹⁵ *Yahweh counts too costly*   (3+2)
   the death ᵃ *of his lieges.* ᵇ
¹⁶ *Oh, Yahweh,*   (2+2)
   I am indeed your servant, ᵃ
   I am your servant, your houseborn slave: ᵇ   (3+2)
   you have loosed my fetters. ᶜ
¹⁷ *I am sacrificing to you a thank offering*   (3+3)
   and proclaiming the name of Yahweh.
¹⁸ *My vows I am paying to Yahweh*   (3+3)
   in front of all his people,
¹⁹ *in the courts of Yahweh's temple*   (3+2)
   at the center ᵃ *of Jerusalem.*
                              Hallelujah ᵇ

Notes/Comments

1.a. "Yahweh" is the implied object: cf. האמנתי "I had faith (in Yahweh)," v 10. Many bring
יהוה forward (e.g. *BHS*, RSV), but A. A. Anderson (*Psalms*, 791) rightly judges MT not impossible.
For the sentiment cf. 18:2 (1); 31:24 (25).

1.b. MT ישׁמע may be a preterite (cf. v 6) but it looks suspiciously like the result of dittography
from an original שׁמע (cf. *BHS*), in accord with הטה "he leaned," v 2.

1.c. Elsewhere in this pair of nouns קול is always construct, which suggests that the ending
is the -y morpheme associated with the construct state (BDB, 337b), misunderstood in MT as
a pronominal suffix, as the accent indicates. S. Daiches ("Psalm 116," 65) suggested that the
purpose of the ending was to provide assonance with v la.

2.a. MT ובימי is commonly emended to ביום with *S* (e.g. H.-J. Kraus, *Psalmen*, 969): "on
the day I cried." But W. Beyerlin ("Kontinuität," 19) has justified MT as an expression of
continual thanksgiving (cf. 30:13 [12]; 34:2 [1]; then the following verses contain what he is to
proclaim.

3.a. Cf. 18:5–6 (4–5). For the imagery see N. J. Tromp, *Primitive Conceptions*, 172–75: death
is a hunter seeking to drag into Sheol.

3.b. Heb. אמצא, אקרא in v 4 and יהושׁיע in v 6 are preterites (M. Dahood, *Psalms III*, 145).

4.a. See 105:1 and note: the formula can stand for both prayer and (vv 13, 17) praise which
employed the divine name.

5.a. For this shortened traditional formula cf. 103:8 and note. Heb. חנון "dutiful" refers to
the relationship between master and servant: see K. W. Neubauer, *Der Stamm CH N N*, 126–30
(cf. 27:7, 9; 86:2–4; 102:14–15 [13–14]). In v 5b מרחם echoes the more customary רחום.

7.a. The suffixes are Aramaic forms (GKC § 911).

7.b. Cf. the self-exhortation in 103:1 and, in a complaint, 42:6(5).

8.a. Heb. כי is here and in v 16 emphatic (Kraus, *Psalmen*, 968, *et al.*).

8.b. LXX S^U render as if third person singular. MT is to be retained as *lectio difficilior* (F. Crüsemann, *Studien zur Formgeschichte*, 244 note 1).

8.c. The singular suffixes of עֵינִי and רַגְלִי accord in sound with נַפְשִׁי (Daiches, "Psalm 116," 65). LXX S Hier render with plural nouns.

9.a. The imperfect is modal (D. Michel, *Tempora*, 69).

9.b. For vv 8–9 cf. 56:14 (13).

10.a. LXX Hier begin a fresh psalm at this point (some Heb. mss. make a break after v 11), probably influenced by the ending of Ps 56.

10.b. LXX διό "therefore," is followed by 2 Cor 4:13. Was it corrupted from διότι "because"? The corruption occurs in LXX^{mss} occasionally, e.g. Isa 3:8; Jer 20:4. In the Greek Psalter διότι is never found and διό only here.

11.a. M. A. Klopfenstein (*Die Lüge*, 200) has observed that כֹּזֵב means here the failure to fulfill expectations: it indicates the opposite of what Yahweh does (vv 5–6) and accordingly MT's participial form is better than כָּזָב implied by α' Hier. He considers that it probably retains the notion of speaking: men gave promises of help which turned out to be empty lies (cf. 146:3). J. A. Alexander (*Psalms*, 473) rightly judges v 11b to be an (implicit) profession of faith.

12.a. The suffix is purely Aramaic in form (GKC § 91l).

13.a. In view of the parallel v 17a a libation is indicated (cf. Num 28:7), associated with the thank offering and celebrating divine deliverance. Cf. the fifth-century Yeḥawmilk stele on which the king offers to his goddess a bowl as a libation (*ANEP*, 305 [picture 477]).

14.a. Dahood (*Psalms III*, 149) has related the anomalous נגדה-נא here and in v 18 to the intensive form of certain Ugar. and Phoen. prepositions, reinforced with an -*n* ending, such as *bn*, *b'dn*.

14.b. The pre-hexaplaric text of LXX omits v 14 (cf. A. Rahlfs, *Psalmi cum Odis*, 284); two Heb. mss. also omit. The omission has by some been judged significant for the Heb. text (cf. *BHK*, following Duhm and Gunkel), but it is noteworthy that v 17b is also omitted in the earliest mss. of LXX. Both omissions may reflect deliberate abbreviation of repeated material at some stage in the history of the text.

15.a. Heb. הַמָּוְתָה is an anomalous feminine form. It may be justified as a form lengthened with a euphonic unaccented ending on the analogy of עֶזְרָתָה, etc. (cf. GKC § 90g). A pointing הַמֹּותָה (Dahood, *Psalms III*, 150) is not necessary in view of GKC § 90i.

15.b. For Heb. חֶסֶד see K. D. Sakenfeld, *The Meaning of Hesed*, 241–44.

16.a. H. Gunkel (*Die Psalmen*, 503; cf. NEB) moved v 16aα to v 4b, but the structure requires its presence here (see *Form/Structure/Setting*). But he was correct in associating the clause אֲנִי עַבְדֶּךָ "I am your servant" with the complaint (cf. 143:12). Generally it is understood in terms of commitment to Yahweh in consequence of deliverance, but v 16b must be the consequence of v 16a: the psalmist's vassal status, often the motivating claim in a complaint, has now been vindicated.

16.b. The pointing בֶּן אֲמִתְּךָ "your faithful son" suggested by Dahood (*Psalms III*, 150) has been criticized by F. C. Fensham (*VT* 19 [1969] 320). For the phrase in a religious context cf. 86:17 and for its sociological roots cf. Exod 21:4; 23:12. The children of slaves belonged to the master (cf. R. de Vaux, *Ancient Israel*, 82).

16.c. The clause develops v 3: restriction has been turned into release.

19.a. Heb. תוֹכֵכִי is confirmed by 135:9, but a direct address appears out of place. Is the ending not a second person suffix but the -*y* morpheme with the construct state? Is the noun a form of תָּוֶךְ with reduplication of the third radical? Cf. GKC (84 b, k–m) and post-biblical Heb. תָּוֶךְ (M. Jastrow, *Dictionary*, 1668).

19.b. Cf. the note on 104:35. LXX transfers to the beginning of Ps 117.

Form/Structure/Setting

In form Ps 116 is an individual thanksgiving. Proclamation and an introductory summary, vv 1–2a, looking back to the earlier complaint and its situation, vv 3, 10, 11, 16a, a report of deliverance, vv 4, 6b, 8, 9, 16b, generalization in hymnic terms, vv 5, 6a, 15 (cf. 18:31 [30]; 34:23 [22]), probably with didactic intent, and announcement of the thank offering as a discharge of vows, vv 12–14, 17–19, are all characteristic elements (cf. C. Westermann, *Praise*, 102–12). It consists mainly of testimony, but direct praise of Yahweh occurs in vv 8, 16, 17a. It was evidently composed for recitation at a service of thank offering in the temple courts during one of the great festivals (vv 14, 18, 19). It uses traditional language which may often be paralleled elsewhere in the Psalter, but it has a vivacity of its own. The actual situation of distress envisaged is not clearly described, except that it represented a threat to life, vv 3, 8, 15, and involved human infidelity, v 11. To a certain extent this vagueness is typical: "The psalmist does not intend to relate what happened to him, but to testify what God has done for him" (Westermann, *Praise*, 109). But this psalm is more indefinite than usual. Sickness which led to ostracization and persecution is a probable background. Persecution in the form of false accusation (Kraus, *Psalmen*, 970) is hardly implied by v 11. Perhaps the psalm was deliberately framed indefinitely to cover more than one occasion for thanksgiving.

Crüsemann (*Studien zur Formgeschichte*, 245–46) has observed that the non-cohortative verbs of vv 13–14, 17–18 were intended to accompany the libation and thank offering. He urges (cf. too D. Bach, *VT* 28 [1978] 10–19) that the specific mention of libation settles the old question whether the psalm refers to a spiritualizing re-interpretation of the thank offering as purely oral thanksgiving. Daiches ("Psalm 116," 67) so held, while H.-J. Hermission (*Sprache und Ritus*, 36–37) has left the issue open.

The psalm is generally assigned to the post-exilic period on account of the Aramaisms in vv 7, 12, 16 (ל indicating the object). If this dating is correct (contrast Dahood, *Psalms III*, 145), as it probably is, it rules out attempts to regard the psalm as royal. I. Engnell (*Studies in Divine Kingship in the Ancient Near East* [2nd ed.; Oxford: Basil Blackwell, 1967] 210 and note 2) described it as a royal passion liturgy, understanding v 15 as a reference to the king's vicarious ritual death. J. H. Eaton (*Kingship*, 81–82) argues, less bizarrely, that it is a royal thanksgiving.

The structure of the psalm is not at all obvious, apart from the refrains of vv 13b, 14, 17b, 18. Often a new section is seen to begin at v 12 (e.g. Gunkel, *Die Psalmen*, 498; Crüsemann, *Studien zur Formgeschichte*, 245); v 10 has also been suggested (A. F. Kirkpatrick, *Psalms*, 687). *BHS* divides the psalm into vv 1–4, 5–14, 15–19. Certainly a threefold partition is favored by the repeated (ה)מות "death," vv 3, 8, 15, formulae of vv 4, 13, 17 and complaint motifs, vv 3, 10, 11, 16a. In v 5 אלהינו "our God" is duly matched by עמו "his people," vv 14, 18. Accordingly a first strophe runs to at least v 5. The repeated stems גמל "benefit" and שוב "return," vv 7, 12 appear to be structurally important as closing, or bringing to a close, strophes. The related sentiments of vv 5, 6, 11 and the language of salvation in vv 6, 13 seem to be structurally parallel. So the three strophes appear to be vv 1–7, 8–14, 15–19. All three begin with a chiastic pattern, vv 1–2 (Beyerlin, "Kontinuität," 19), 8–9, 15–16, and the repeated אני "I" of vv 10, 11, 16 balances the double לי "to me" of vv 2, 6. These are both good reasons why v 16a should be retained in its present position. A small chiastic unit also occurs in vv 10–11. The first and third strophes both end with כי- and contain reflections on Yahweh's character, vv 5, 6a, 15 (cf. v 11), a repeated אנה יהוה, vv

4, 16, and a contrast of restraint and release, vv 3, 16. They also counter Yahweh's attributes as חנון וצדיק "dutiful and true," v 5, with the corresponding חסידיו "his lieges," v 15, and עבדך "your servant," v 16. The second and third strophes both end with the refrain, in the third amplified as a climax and echoing the sound of אשלם "I pay," v 18, with ירושלם; and they contain direct address of Yahweh, vv 8, 16, 17a.

Explanation

The people had gathered for a festival. Amidst the communal worship in the temple courts there were services in which individuals had opportunity to bring thank offerings and to accompany their sacrificial worship with words of testimony and praise for answered prayer. This psalm was composed for recitation in front of the congregation on such happy occasions. It expresses well the joy and gratitude of a person delivered from an overwhelming crisis which had threatened his life.

The psalmist declares his love and commitment to lifelong thanksgiving in return for Yahweh's positive hearing of his previous complaint. His praise rehearses how his life had been pervaded by an aura of death. He was being lured to his doom—until he used Yahweh's powerful name in appeal. He has learned a lesson he commends to others, that Yahweh fulfills his obligations to those in covenant relationship and shows himself true to his promises. This divine act of love is what prompts his own love of v 1 (cf. 1 John 4:19). The general truth that Yahweh looks after the helpless who cannot cope by themselves has been proved from his personal experience of grace. Yahweh has taken away his source of anxiety (cf. 42:6 [5], and now he may enjoy new peace of mind. He challenges himself to enter into this blessing. The human mind does not quickly lose its habit of worrying and needs urging to keep pace with reality instead of dwelling on the nightmares of the past.

It is all over now. In relief and fervent praise the psalmist turns from the congregation to address God directly, giving thanks for renewal of life and for the gifts of security and happiness. He can now enjoy fellowship with God in God's world, whereas before he felt already in Sheol and far away from Yahweh (cf. 22:2, 16 [1, 15]; 88:4–6 [3–5]). How right he was to keep his faith in his extremity! Dire circumstances forced him to admit human infidelity and to turn to the only one who was reliable (cf. 62:9–10 [8–9]; 118:8). His faith has been vindicated and implicitly he encourages others to hold onto their faith, come wind, come weather. Yahweh has certainly proved worthy of his trust. So indebted does he feel that he despairs of responding adequately to divine blessing. But the unpayable nature of the debt does not absolve him from making what contribution he can. He has come forward to offer a libation of wine as part of the ritual of the thank offering. It is a testimony to God's salvation for all to see, accompanying a vocal testimony to his great name for all to hear. He is thus publicly fulfilling the vows to bring a thank offering, which he made in his time of distress.

The psalmist has learned by experience how reluctant Yahweh is to allow the premature death of those who are united to him in covenant relationship, and how quickly he rushes to avert such a tragedy (cf. 72:14). His earlier

appeals to that relationship had borne fruit, thank God. True to his obligations
as Lord, Yahweh came to his aid and released him from Sheol's prison. So
he brings his thank offering and thanksgiving in humble gratitude to his
divine patron. He is glad to stand there in the temple precincts, testifying
to Yahweh's faithfulness.

Psalm 116 is a devout and radiant song of thanksgiving. Its negative reminis-
cences serve to enhance the greatness of the God who keeps faith and delivers.
Its positive assessment of everyday life is that it has rich potential for enjoying
God's grace and peace. God is here—in this world—and that to bless us, is
his grateful testimony, vv 5–6. A Christian thanksgiving cannot resist a reference to eternal life, and properly so (2 Tim 4:17–18), but the Israelite believer's lack of such a long-sighted perspective at least made him set maximum
value upon the God-given resources of this life, and so upon God himself.

A Thousand Tongues   (117:1–2)

Bibliography

Crüsemann, F. *Studien zur Formgeschichte.* **Martin-Achard, R.** *A Light to the Nations,*
Tr. J. P. Smith. London: Oliver and Boyd, 1962.

Translation

1 *Praise Yahweh, all nations,* [a]   (3+3)
   laud [b] *him, all you peoples,* [c]
2 *because his loyal love has towered* [a] *over us*   (3+3)
   and Yahweh's faithfulness is everlasting. [b]
                                    Hallelujah [c]

Notes/Comments

1.a. The primary rationale of the summons is not contemporary missionary intent or eschatological hope of conversion but the truth that Yahweh deserves the praise of the whole world.
For the world has witnessed the blessings which God has given his people, but derives no
direct benefit itself, although Israel's ultimate hope was that the nations would be convinced
of the greatness of her God (R. Martin-Achard, *A Light to the Nations,* 54–59; cf. Y. Kaufmann,
The Religion of Israel, 297–98).

1.b. Heb. שבח "laud" is probably an Aramaism: cf. M. Wagner, *Die lexikalischen und grammatikal-
ischen Aramaismen in alt Hebräisch* (BZAW 96; Berlin: A. Töpelmann, 1966) 111.

1.c. Heb. אמים "peoples" is an anomalous plural: אמות appears in Num 25:15. Accordingly
many scholars (e.g. H.-J. Kraus, *Psalmen,* 974) emend to לאמים. But H. Gunkel (*Die Psalmen,*
504) pointed out the masculine plural אמיא seven times in biblical Aramaic (six in Dan 3, 5, 7,
and also Ezra 4:10; similarly in later Jewish Aramaic according to M. Jastrow, *Dictionary,* 27b).
M. Dahood (*Psalms III,* 152) treats as אמ(י)ם "gods" (*sic*), comparing Jer 50:38 where it means
"terrible (idols)," but a synonym of גוים is expected.

2.a. Cf. 103:11 and note.

2.b. The affirmation is based upon Exod 34:6. See 103:8 and comment.

2.c. See 104:35 note. LXX attaches to Ps 118.

Form/Structure/Setting

Psalm 117 is a hymn of praise. Its single sentence encapsulates the basic form of the imperatival hymn with its summons to praise and complementary כי clause (F. Crüsemann, *Studien zur Formgeschichte*, 41). The setting of the psalm is evidently a cultic one of some kind. A. Weiser (*Psalms*, 721) considers that proselytes are addressed. He gives a precise placing to the psalm, as a priestly summons issued at the autumn festival "to introduce the festival hymn which follows the theophany" associated with Exod 34:6. Weiser's setting betrays the domination of his special interest; it is unlikely, moreover, that the psalm envisages the presence of proselytes. Rather, the summons is rhetorical, the imperative having lost its original direct purpose (Crüsemann, *Studien zur Formgeschichte*, 41; cf. Isa 44:23).

The brevity of the psalm has led to various theories concerning an ancillary role for it. Many Hebrew mss. attach it to Ps 116, and H. Schmidt (*Die Psalmen*, 210) understood it as the conclusion to Ps 116 in a thanksgiving liturgy (cf. I. Engnell; *Divine Kingship*, 210 note 2). Gunkel (*Die Psalmen*, 504) observed that theoretically this was quite possible in the light of 22:28–29 (27–28), etc. Advocates of a royal character for Ps 116 naturally view this attachment with favor: besides Engnell, cf. J. H. Eaton, *Kingship*, 82. Other Hebrew mss. join the psalm to Ps 118, but Weiser (*Psalms*, 721) notes that it would conflict with the liturgical introduction, 118:1–4. C. Westermann (*Theologia Viatorum* 8 [1961/62] 282) categorizes the psalm as a closing doxology to a collection of psalms of praise, Pss 111–116, to which Ps 118 was subsequently added. But if this is so, it may indicate a secondary rather than primary use for the psalm. The psalm may well have been a unit on its own used in the ritual of some of the festivals (A. A. Anderson, *Psalms*, 795–96). Indeed, v 2, as a summary of Israel's covenant-oriented theology, would admirably suit any festival.

As to dating, Kraus (*Psalmen*, 974), following B. Duhm, finds the influence of Second Isaiah in the psalm's sentiments. Crüsemann (*Studien zur Formgeschichte*, 50) judges the use of the כי clause purely as a reason for the summons rather than as an implementation of it to be a secondary, post-exilic development. Whether or not these hypotheses are justified, linguistically שבח and the masculine plural אמים are probably Aramaisms, indicating a post-exilic date for this cultic composition. Dahood (*Psalms III*, 152) unconvincingly urges a seventh or sixth century B.C. date.

Dahood, ibid., has noted the chiastic structure of the psalm, with יהוה in the first and fourth cola and pronominal suffixes in the second and third. One might add the double *lamed* at the beginning of the first and the end of the fourth. V 1 is marked by perfect synonymous parallelism, while v 2 has its own chiasmus, with חסדו and אמת adjoining. External parallelism is apparent in the assonance of גוים and גבר, and of אמים and אמת.

Explanation

This small, and indeed beautiful, hymn is in fact the shortest psalm in the Psalter. Its theme is based upon the favorite text of the post-exilic religious community, Exod 34:6, specifically upon Yahweh's attribute as רב חסד ואמת "abundant in loyal love and faithfulness." He had once and for all revealed himself to Israel as the covenant God who made promises of grace and kept them. Their history was a monument to the greatness of his loyal love, for it was full of instances of his loving, protecting, delivering, pardoning grace. And just as this grace spanned the past and present, so it could be relied upon to encompass the present and future. At the center of these two enormous arcs of theological time stood the contemporary generation of God's people, exulting in that love which "knows neither measure nor end" (J. Hart).

But how could they discharge adequately their responsibility of praising? Rhetorically they enlisted the aid of the rest of the nations in the world, wishing for "a thousand tongues," as it were, to help them to sing their "great Redeemer's praise" (Charles Wesley). Unwittingly they thus let loose in the world an invitation which later enabled Gentiles too to share in this covenant grace (Rom 15:8–12). Israel's would-be hired choristers were destined eventually to become their partners in faith in the international religion of the NT. In that new context the psalm was to take on a new breadth and depth of meaning. But its own insight into OT revelation concerning Israel must not be underestimated.

God-given Victory   (118:1–29)

Bibliography

Becker, O. "Psalm 118:12 דְּעֲכוּ כְּאֵשׁ קוֹצִים." *ZAW* 70 (1958) 174. **Driver, G. R.** "Ps. 118:27 אסורי חג." *Textus* 7 (1969) 130–31. **Frost, S. B.** "Asseveration by Thanksgiving." *VT* 8 (1958) 380–90. ———. "Psalm 118: An Exposition." *CJT* 7 (1961) 155–66. **Haupt, P.** "Schmücket das Fest mit Maien!" *ZAW* 35 (1915) 102–9. **May, H. S.** "Psalm 118: The Song of the Citadel." *Religions in Antiquity. Essays in Memory of E. R. Goodenough.* Supplements to Numen 14. Leiden: E. J. Brill, 1968, 97–106. **Meysing, J.** "A Text-Reconstruction of Ps. 117 (118):27." *VT* 10 (1960) 130–37. **Petuchowski, J. J.** " 'Hoshiᶜah na' in Psalm 118:25—A Prayer for Rain." *VT* 5 (1955) 266–71. **Robinson, W.** "Psalm 118. A Liturgy for the Admission of a Proselyte." *CQR* 144 (1947) 179–83. **Schmidt, H.** "Erklärung des 118. Psalms." *ZAW* 40 (1922) 1–14. **Wolff, H. W.** "Psalm 118:14–24." *Herr, tue meine Lippen auf,* ed. G. Eichholz, vol. 5. 2nd ed. Wuppertal-Barmen: Emil Müller Verlag, 1961, 251–57.

Translation

¹ *Give Yahweh thanks for his goodness,*   (3+3)
   for the everlastingness of his loyal love. [a]
² *Let Israel declare,*   (3+3)
   "His loyal love is everlasting."
³ *Let Aaron's house declare,*   (3+3)
   "His loyal love is everlasting."

⁴ *Let you who revere Yahweh* ᵃ *declare,* (3+3)
"His loyal love is everlasting."

⁵ *From my narrow straits* ᵃ *I called Yah(weh):* ᵇ (3+3)
Yah(weh) answered me with spacious freedom.
⁶ *Yahweh is on my side, I need not fear* (3+3)
what men can ᵃ *do to me.*
⁷ *Yahweh is on my side as my helper,* ᵃ (3+3)
and so I can look in triumph at my enemies.
⁸ *It is better to take refuge in Yahweh* (3+2)
than to trust in men.
⁹ *It is better to trust in Yahweh* (3+2)
than to trust in rulers. ᵃ
¹⁰ *All nations surrounded me,* (3+3)
with Yahweh's name ᵃ *I warded them off.* ᵇ
¹¹ *They surrounded me, yes, surrounded me,* (3+3)
with Yahweh's name I warded them off.
¹² *They surrounded me like bees,* ᵃ (3+3+3)
they were extinguished ᵇ *like a fire of thorns.* ᶜ
With Yahweh's name I warded them off.
¹³ *I was forcibly pushed* ᵃ *into falling,* (3+2)
but Yahweh helped me.

¹⁴ *Yah(weh) is my strength and protection,* ᵃ (3+2)
he has become my savior.
¹⁵ *Hark at the shouts of salvation* (3+2)
in the tents of the righteous: ᵃ
¹⁶ *"Yahweh's right hand acts mightily,* (3+3+3)
Yahweh's right hand exalts,
Yahweh's right hand acts mightily." ᵃ
¹⁷ *I did not die, but survived* ᵃ (3+3)
to recount Yah(weh)'s acts.
¹⁸ *Yah(weh) severely chastised* ᵃ *me,* (3+3)
but he did not give me over to death.
¹⁹ *Open the gates* ᵃ *of righteousness to me* (3+3)
so that I may enter through them and give Yah(weh) thanks.

²⁰ *"This is Yahweh's gateway:* (3+3)
the righteous may enter through it." ᵃ
²¹ *I give you thanks because you answered me* (3+2)
and became my savior. ᵃ
²² *"The stone the builders rejected* (3+3)
has become the main corner support. ᵃ
²³ *This has been brought about by Yahweh,* (3+3)
it impresses us as something wonderful.
²⁴ *This is the day Yahweh has made,* ᵃ (3+3)
let us exult and rejoice in it. ᵇ

25 *Please, Yahweh, save (us), please,*   (3+3)
please, Yahweh, prosper (us), please. " ᵃ
26 *"Blessed is the one who comes with Yahweh's name!*   (3+3)
We bless ᵇ *you (all) from Yahweh's temple."*
27 *"Yahweh is God,*   (2+2)
and he has given us light." ᵃ
"Bind the festival sacrifice with cords   (3+2)
onto the altar's horns." (?) ᵇ
28 *You are my God, and I give you thanks,*   (3+2)
my God, I exalt you. ᵃ

29 *Give Yahweh thanks for his goodness,*   (3+3)
for the everlastingness of his loyal love.

Notes/Comments

1.a. For this liturgical formula see 106:1 and note. Heb. חסד "loyal love" here has the nuance of deliverance (cf. K. D. Sakenfeld, *The Meaning of Hesed*, 218–22).

4.a. For the groups of vv 2–4 and the role of יהוה יראי "those who revere Yahweh" as a comprehensive designation for the religious community see 115:9–13 and notes.

5.a. H. Schmidt (*ZAW* 40 [1922] 9–10) interpreted מצר as "prison" here and in 116:3, but cf. Lam 1:3. H. S. May ("Psalm 118," 97–106) translated it "citadel" and envisaged the setting of the psalm to be a sanctuary in the border fortress of Arad in the Negeb; he took מרחב as "the wide open spaces" of the desert. For criticism see F. Crüsemann, *Studien zur Formgeschichte*, 218 note 1.

5.b. Heb. יה is generally regarded as a contracted form of יהוה. In this psalm it is inspired by the formula of Exod 15:2 (v 14).

5.c. For the pregnant construction see GKC § 119gg. The theological motif of spaciousness has been studied by J. F. A. Sawyer (*ASTI* 6 [1967/8] 20–34).

6.a. D. Michel (*Tempora*, 241) has observed that this verb and those in vv 7, 20 are modal.

7.a. For the *beth essentiae* and plural of majesty see GKC § 119i, 124g-i.

9.a. The sequence in vv 8–9 stresses the contrast between Yahweh and men by indicating that no men, not even rulers, are reliable (J. Krašovec, *Der Merismus*, 54).

10.a. Mention of the divine name is a reference both to its use in the prayer of complaint (H. W. Wolff, "Psalm 118," 252) and to its power as a weapon (H. A. Brongers, *ZAW* 77 [1965] 6–7; cf. 1 Sam 17:45).

10.b. Heb. כי is emphatic. Most understand אמילם as "ward off" with LXX αʹ Hier. D. Winton Thomas (*Text*, 28), following P. Joüon, compared Arab. *māla* "lean, incline to" (cf. KB, 502b). The parallelism indicates that the form is preterite. Moreover, "from vv 5 and 13 it is clear that the crisis was over" (M. Dahood, *Psalms III*, 157).

12.a. LXX κηρίον "honeycomb" corresponds to יער (S. T. Byington, "Hebrew Marginalia. 3," *JBL* 64 [1945] 747; L. H. Brockington, *Hebrew Text*, 151 [=NEB]), translated as in 1 Sam 14:27, and not to דונג (H. Gunkel, *Die Psalmen*, 508; *et al.*), which is always rendered κηρός. It probably originated in an exegetical gloss seeking to compare כאש קוצים with 83:15 (14) כאש תבער יער (cf. Jer 21:14). LXX misunderstood יער "forest" as its homonym "honeycomb."

12.b. In MT v 12aβ is in antithetic parallelism with v 12aα and refers to quick disappearance. LXX ἐξεκαύθησαν "they were burned" is often retroverted as בערו "they burned" (if so, it may be linked with the gloss mentioned in note 12.a.) and, as a synthetic parallel, preferred to MT (cf. *BHS*), which has been explained as a relic of בערו דונג (Gunkel, *Die Psalmen*, 508). LXX may imply "they were burned up." Cf. καίω "burn and destroy (in war)" in Xenophon, *Hist. Graec.*, 4. 2. 15; 6. 5. 27.

12.c. O. Becker (*ZAW* 70 [1958] 174), followed by Crüsemann (*Studien zur Formgeschichte*, 218), has rendered "cut off wick ends" as better suiting the verb; he compared G. R. Driver ("Mistranslations," *WO* 1 [1947] 30) and KB (834a).

13.a. MT דְחִיתַנִי "you pushed me" is hardly possible. It cannot refer to Yahweh, who essentially is not addressed in the second person till v 21 (see Form/Structure/Setting) nor is an apostrophizing of a defeated enemy likely. LXX S Hier imply a passive נִדְחֵיתִי "I was pushed," which is preferable. In MT the nun was probably transposed under the influence of עֲזָרַנִי "he helped me."

14.a. For the stereotyped formula of a song of victory in v 14 cf. Exod 15:2; Isa 12:2. S. E. Loewenstamm ("The Lord Is My Strength and My Glory," VT 19 [1969] 464–70) has defended the traditional rendering of זִמְרָת as "song," but more probably it is to be related to Ugar. dmr, as in RS 24. 252, reverse line 9 ʿzk.dmrk "your strength, your protection" (P. C. Craigie, "Psalm 29 in the Hebrew Poetic Tradition," VT 22 [1972] 145–46, prefers "your protection, your guard" with J. C. De Moore, UF 1 [1969] 176, 179). It is also attested in names of Hebrew (זמרי) and on the Samarian Ostraca בעלזמר and זמריה), S. Arabian and Amorite origin (cf. F. M. Cross and D. N. Freedman, JNES 14 [1955] 243). Cf. LXX σκεπαστής "shelterer" at Exod 15:2. The suffix on עֻזִּי is probably a double duty one (cf. Dahood, Psalms III, 158): זמרת occurs in all three texts and it is methodologically unsound to emend to זמרתי (BHS et al.).

15.a. Heb. צַדִּיקִים is apparently a reference to the victorious army, either in general terms as representing the people in covenant relation with God or, more probably, particularly as those vindicated by Yahweh and recipients of Yahweh's covenanted aid in the battle (cf. 103:6 and note). "Victors" (B. Ehrlich, Psalmen, 299; Dahood, Psalms III, 158; NEB) gives the sense at the expense of the theological content, which in view of vv 19–20 is not insignificant.

16.a. The deletion of v 16b with one Heb ms. and LXXˢ (BHS) breaks the correspondence with the threefold repetition in vv 10–12 (Dahood, Psalms III, 158). MT's full text is confirmed by 11QPsª whose reading גבורה "acts mightily" is a stylistic variant.

17.a. For vv 17–18 cf. 66:9–10. The external parallelism with v 18 indicates that the verbs in v 17a are preterites (Dahood, Psalms III, 158).

18.a. For a brief analysis of יסר as divine chastisement in the OT see H. W. Wolff, Hosea, 99.

19.a. J. Morgenstern (HUCA 6 [1929] 19 note 42) explained the plural as a reference to the eastern gate of the temple, which was traditionally represented as a double gate with two sections (cf. 24:7–10).

20.a. This is probably not a general condition of entry ("only the righteous," S. B. Frost, VT 8 [1958] 381), but permission for the צדיקים of v 15 to enter (cf. Crüsemann, Studien zur Formgeschichte, 221). Here the emphasis is not moral, as in Isa 26:2 (cf. Pss 15, 24); the victory attests the covenant status and consequent right to enter the temple which is associated with the maintenance of the covenant relationship (v 19).

21.a. Frost (VT 8 [1958] 380–90) urged that the thanksgiving was a way of affirming the speaker's righteousness: the deliverance vouched for the fact that he was in good favor with Yahweh. But he underestimated the role of v 21 (see Form/Structure/Setting) and also misunderstood v 20.

22.a. This was either a foundation stone stabilizing the two adjacent walls or a keystone.

24.a. Or "on which Yahweh has acted" (A. R. Johnson, Sacral Kingship, 118; Dahood, Psalms III, 159; NEB), but the rendering suits Johnson's overall exegetical position much better than Dahood's. A. Berlin ("Psalm 118:24," JBL 96 [1977] 567–68) interprets as "This (thing) today is what the Lord has done," regarding זה as a parallel and equivalent term to זאת in v 23, but the seemingly parallel structuring of v 20 does not favor this interpretation.

24.b. Dahood (Psalms III, 159) renders "in him," but again the similarly structured v 20 suggests otherwise. Berlin (JBL 96 [1977] 567–68) relates to זה as "in it" i.e. what God has done.

25.a. The petition is unexpected in a thanksgiving, but cf. 138:8b. Judg 18:5, 6; Pss 3:9 (8); 28:9 may support the suggestion of S. Mowinckel (VT 5 [1955] 28) that v 25 represents a standard formula of prayer for the cultic blessing of v 26. J. J. Petuchowski (VT 5 [1955] 266–71) deduced from Talmudic tradition that it is a prayer for rain at the Feast of Tabernacles, but it is doubtful whether the tradition reflects the original sense.

26.a. MT's accentuation links בשם יהוה with ברוך (so O. Grether, Name und Wort, 47; S. H. Blank, HUCA 32 [1961] 75–79; A. A. Anderson, Psalms, 803; NEB). But Brongers (ZAW 77 [1965] 6–7) is more probably correct in understanding in terms of v 19b: the main speaker comes with a song of praise on his lips. Accordingly הבא is not a generic singular, as Mowinckel (VI 5 [1955] 28 Anderson (Psalms, 803); et al. have interpreted.

26.b. The perfect is declarative (Michel, Tempora, 93, 242).

27.a. For the response to the impartation of blessing cf. Num 6:25a.
27.b. Or "begin the procession with branches as far as the altar's horns." The line is an exegetical crux. Heb. עבת normally means "rope," but can mean "branch." Proponents of this latter meaning (e.g. Schmidt, ZAW 40 [1922] 14; Petuchowski, VT 5 [1955] 268–70) link the psalm with the use of the *lulab* branches at the Feast of Tabernacles (Lev 23:40). Heb. חג apparently means "festal offering" in Exod 23:18 (B. S. Childs, *Exodus*, 446). But a practice of tying a sacrifice to the horns of the altar is not attested elsewhere. Alternatively חג can mean a festal procession or dance, but the verb אסר is then employed in an unusual sense. P. Haupt (ZAW 35 [1915] 102–9) compared its use with מלחמה as "join battle" and claimed the support of LXX Hier. H. Gunkel (*Die Psalmen*, 510), followed by H.-J. Kraus (*Psalmen*, 985), envisaged dancers roped together and to the altar. J. Meysing (VT 10 [1960] 130–37) urged that אשׁה "fire offering," as the object of יאר, underlay MT's corrupt אסרו: "May El Yahweh light for us the feast-offering among the twigs . . ." G. R. Driver (*Textus* 7 [1969] 130–31) and NEB read אֲסֻרֵי (cf. 11QPs ᵃ אסורו or אסורי) "(us pilgrims) lined up (beside the horns of the altar)."
28.a. Cf. Exod 15:2b.

Form/Structure/Setting

The bulk of the psalm exhibits the form of an individual thanksgiving (vv 5–19, 21, 28; cf. C. Westermann, *Praise*, 102–11). V 5 is an introductory summary, reporting the speaker's former adversity and complaint, and Yahweh's hearing and deliverance. Vv 6–9 are a general avowal in praise of Yahweh: cf. 18:29–31 (28–30); 34:8, 23 (7, 22). Vv 8–9, clearly didactic in intent, are a double wisdom saying: cf. 2:11b; 32:1–2; 144:15; Prov 21:19. Vv 10–13 develop v 5, reporting adversity (cf. the use of סבב "surrounded" in individual complaints, 17:11; 22:13 [12], etc.), prayer and deliverance. V 14 seems to be another introductory summary, a short avowal and report of deliverance, which vv 15–18 develop. Vv 15–16 are a further avowal in the form of a song of victory, while vv 17–18 report deliverance and echo a vow of praise associated with an earlier prayer of complaint. V 19 is a request reflecting the religious setting, while v 21 is direct thanksgiving to Yahweh for his hearing prayer and delivering; v 28 is renewed thanksgiving.

As framework for this thanksgiving stand vv 1–4, 29, a summons to praise issued to sections of the religious community, and antiphonal response. The summons has associations with the thank offering service (cf. Jer 33:11; Ps 22:24 [23]). Vv 22–25, 27 are communal praise for the main speaker's thanksgiving, vv 22–24, and for blessing received, v 27, in response to their prayer, v 25. V 20 is the gatekeepers' response to the request of v 19: both verses are reminiscent of the entrance liturgy (cf. Pss 15, 24). V 26 is a priestly blessing, while v 27 is a priestly cultic direction. It is noteworthy that the Targum recognized the participation of different voices in vv 23–29.

Accordingly Ps 118 is a thanksgiving liturgy. H. Schmidt (ZAW 40 [1922] 1–14) was inspired by Ps 107 to divide vv 5–19 into the voices of solo representatives of three groups, those falsely accused, vv 5–7, travelers, vv 10–14, and the sick, vv 17–19, but his findings must be judged no more than eisegetical. What is evident is that the psalm's liturgy was processional in nature. Vv 1–19 took place outside the temple gate, and vv 20–29 inside, in the temple court (cf. 116:19). The locations are differentiated by the form of vv 5–18, a report testifying to Yahweh in the third person (cf. v 17), and vv 21, 28, direct thanksgiving in the holy precincts (Crüsemann, *Studien zur Form-*

geschichte, 220–21). Vv 21, 28 serve as an introduction to the standard cultic thanksgiving (cf. 138:1), which culminated in the sacrifice of the thank offering, to which reference is implicitly made by mention of the altar (v 27); the procession has reached the court in which the altar of burnt offering stood (H. W. Wolff, "Ps 118" 254).

Who was the main speaker? He seems to act in some representative capacity, as leader of an associated group, in view of the changes from singular to plural in vv 19–20 and 26a, 26b. W. Robinson (*CQR* 144 [1947] 179–83) bizarrely urged that the psalm was a liturgy for the circumcision of a notable proselyte. Vv 5–19 have been understood as a communal thanksgiving in which "I" stands for the people (e.g. A. Cohen, *Psalms,* 389–93). Similarly J. Becker (*Israel deutet seine Psalmen,* 56–57) regarded the psalm as an eschatological thanksgiving, made up of different parts of a thanksgiving liturgy. S. B. Frost (*CJT* 7 [1961] 157–62) also found a process of re-interpretation at work, whereby vv 1–4, 29 adapted an original royal thanksgiving for communal use. Was the speaker of the main part a king then? Gunkel (*Die Psalmen,* 509), Wolff ("Psalm 118," 256), Crüsemann (*Studien zur Formgeschichte,* 217 note 4) and Kraus (*Psalmen,* 979) deny it, holding that vv 1–4 refer to proselytes and so are post-exilic. However, S. Mowinckel (*Psalmenstudien,* vol. 5, 43 note 2) and A. Weiser (*Psalms,* 725) combine an interpretation in terms of proselytes with a pre-exilic date. The Gunkel group interprets the reference to כל גוים "all nations," v 10, as use of a military metaphor to enhance the threat, which is certainly possible in the light of 59:6, 9 (cf. 27:3; 43:1), and vv 15–16 as a motif borrowed from an old song of victory and put to new use. This latter interpretation is by no means an obvious one: the text (cf. the echo of צדיקים "righteous" in v 20) more naturally suggests a celebration of victory over national enemies, in which case v 10 is to be understood thus, although כל is hyperbolical. Weiser (*Psalms,* 724–27) assigned the psalm to the autumn festival as an annual commemoration of earlier victories. A. R. Johnson (*Sacral Kingship,* 126) and J. H. Eaton (*Kingship,* 130), followed by A. A. Anderson (*Psalms,* 797, 800) place it in a dramatic ritual of the New Year festival in which the king participated in scenes of humiliation (v 18) and vindication. These reconstructions accord with a Talmudic tradition associating the psalm with the Feast of Tabernacles (*Sukk.* 45a, 45b), but they are not universally favored. Dahood (*Psalms III,* 155) relates the psalm to a literal military victory, and this straightforward understanding is probably correct. It may be that victories were commonly celebrated at the autumn festival after campaigns begun in the spring (cf. R. de Vaux, *Ancient Israel,* 251).

Structurally the stylistic elements of the psalm blend well with its formal ones. Vv 1–4 and 29 form an inclusive framework. The main part of the psalm is bound together by a sixfold use of יה in vv 5, 14 and climactically vv 17–19; significant too is לי "to me" in vv 6–7, 14, 19 (and 21). It divides into two strophes: vv 5–13 have the stem עזר "help" as their inclusive marker in vv 7, 13, while vv 14–19 have the stem צדק "righteous(ness)" in vv 15, 19, with עזי/עזרני acting as a strophic hinge in vv 13–14. It is noticeable that the triple use of עשה "do" concerning Yahweh's supremacy in vv 15–17 counters and confirms the human connotation in v 6. Toward the end of each strophe an infinitive absolute is used before an antithesis, in vv 13, 18; in both a threefold repetition occurs, at vv 10–12 and 15, 16. In the medley of voices in vv 20–28 the initial line caps v 19 with an affirmative echo, as a strophic hinge. It provides two key terms, the stem בוא "come," v 26, and זה "this," v 24 (cf. זאת, v 23). V 28 balances v 21 and yields two other key terms, אודה(ו) (cf. v 19) and the stem ישע "save" (cf. v 14). Other verbal threads used earlier are drawn together here (vv 5 and 21, 6, 15–17 and 21, 10–12 and 26, 14 and 21, 16 and 28).

For the messianic role of Ps 118 in the Jewish Hallel and the Midrash and in the ministry of Jesus see Str-B, vol. 1, 850; J. Jeremias, *Eucharistic Words*, 251–61. For a study of NT usage of the psalm in general see B. Lindars, *NT Apologetic*, 169–74, 179, 185.

Explanation

Like Ps 18, this psalm was evidently composed as a royal song of thanksgiving for military victory; but it is set in the context of a processional liturgy. In post-exilic times it was presumably used in periodic commemorations of Yahweh's past goodness to the Davidic dynasty and to Israel generally, as the climax of the Hallel psalms. It was a processional psalm begun outside the gates of the temple and continued inside (cf. 100:4).

A priest opens the proceedings with a call to praise. He challenges in turn two groups in the procession, to testify to Yahweh's abiding faithfulness, first the laity and then his fellow priests, and finally he seeks a resounding shout from one and all. In v 5 a new voice speaks, that of the central character of the psalm. The king bears witness before the congregation to Yahweh's liberating help in answer to prayer in time of crisis. He reflects upon lessons learned from the experience so that the congregation may take them to heart. He gives praise for Yahweh's powerful support and its corollary that natural human fears can give way to God-given triumph. Recourse to human allies and counselors comes a poor second to a practical faith in Yahweh (contrast 2 Kgs 16:5–7; Isa 7:1–13). He sets in rhetorical contrast the crisis and its sequel. On the one hand swarms of nations surrounded him and seemed likely to overwhelm him. On the other, prayerful trust in Yahweh's powerful name was the secret weapon that brought him victory and quelled the affray as quickly as it takes blazing thorns to burn away. Without Yahweh's aid all would have been lost.

He testifies in renewed tones of praise, using time-honored language of the song of victory (cf. Exod 15:2) to encapsulate his avowal of praise and report of deliverance. He echoes the army's songs celebrating Yahweh's saving vindication of his covenant people against their foes, in a tribute to his glorious enabling. He was brought face to face with death, but was spared. Now his renewed lease on life means opportunity to give this report of Yahweh's intervention on his behalf. He can even incorporate the crisis positively into his praise, as evidence of Yahweh's painful but loving discipline (cf. 89:31–34 [30–33]).

The king requests admission to the temple forecourt to sing his thanksgiving proper. The gatekeepers willingly accede to the request for him and (by implication) his entourage to enter: the victory is evidence enough of the covenant blessing that rests upon these men and makes them welcome to this place where conformity to the covenant is enshrined. Once inside the king bursts into thanksgiving to God for deliverance in answer to his prayer. The lay commoners join in the praise, reacting to the king's experience rather like the chorus in a Greek play. To aid their praise they cite a proverb which expresses the transition from humiliation to honor, and discern in it the supernatural work of Yahweh. They exhort each other to use to the full this opportunity for praise which Yahweh himself has provided (cf. 22:26 [25]).

This cultic occasion is opportunity too for receiving priestly blessing, which they crave in v 25. In response the priests pronounce blessings both upon the king who is present to give thanks to Yahweh and upon his company. Thrilled with the impartation of this blessing, the people affirm their faith in Yahweh as God indeed, and express their joy that he has made his face to shine upon them thus. Then instructions are given concerning the next stage in the cultic proceedings, which centers upon the altar. The king continues his thanksgiving, affirming his own commitment to Yahweh. The initial priestly voice rings out again at the end, urging praise for Yahweh's constant love, which has been evidenced afresh in the royal testimony and thanksgiving.

Like other royal psalms Ps 118 came to be imbued with messianic import and doubtless this is why it stands at the end of the Hallel psalms, Pss 113–118. It was claimed in the NT as Christological in connection with both the royal manifestation of the triumphal entry and the great twin themes of Christ's humiliation and glory. All four Evangelists use it in the Palm Sunday narrative (Matt 19:9; Mark 11:9–10; Luke 19:38; John 12:13), generally associating it with Zech 9:9. "Hosanna," the equivalent of "save" in 118:25, became used as a joyful shout of acclamation. According to Mark 12:10–11 (cf. 8:31; Matt 23:29; Luke 13:35), Jesus applied vv 22–23 to his coming passion and resurrection, and they ring out again on Peter's lips in Acts 4:11. V 22 of the psalm became an important element in the theological stone imagery of Eph 2:20–21; 1 Pet 2:4–8. Underlying the citation of v 6 in Heb 3:6 is doubtless a sense of the Christian community's oneness with the glorified Christ.

A Light to My Path (119:1–176)

Bibliography

Becker, J. *Gottesfurcht im AT.* AnBib 25. Rome: Pontifical Biblical Institute, 1965. Bergler, S. "Der längste Psalm—Anthologie oder Liturgie?" *VT* 29 (1979) 257–88. Deissler, A. *Psalm 119 (118) und seine Theologie. Eine Beitrag zur Erforschung der anthologischen Stilgattung im AT.* München: Karl Zink Verlag, 1955. Eaton, J. H. "Proposals in Psalms 99 and 119." *VT* 18 (1968) 555–58. Gordis, R. "The Asseverative Kaph in Ugaritic and Hebrew." *JAOS* 63 (1943) 176–78. Hermisson, H.-J. *Sprache und Ritus im altisraelitischen Kult. Zur "Spiritualisierung" der Kultbegriffe im AT.* WMANT 19. Neukirchen-Vluyn: Neukirchener Verlag, 1965. Holm-Neilsen, S. "The Importance of Late

Jewish Psalmody for the Understanding of OT Psalmodic Tradition." *ST* 14 (1960) 1–53. **Klopfenstein, M. A.** *Die Lüge nach dem AT.* Zürich: Gotthelf Verlag, 1964. **Kraus, H.-J.** "Freude an Gottes Gesetz." *EvT* 10 (1951) 337–51. ———. "Zum Gesetzesverständnis der nachprophetischen Zeit." *Biblisch-theologische Aufsätze.* Neukirchen-Vluyn: Neukirchener Verlag, 1972, 179–94. **Lipinski, E.** "Macarismes et psaumes de congratulation." *RB* 75 (1968) 321–67. **Müller, D. H.** "Strophenbau und Responsion." *Biblische Studien.* Wien: Holder, 1908. **Munch, P. A.** "Die alphabetische Akrostichie in der jüdischen Psalmendichtung." *ZDMG* 90 (1936) 703–10. ———. "Die jüdischen 'Weisheitpsalmen' und ihr Platz im Leben." *AcOr* 15 (1936) 112–40. **Noth, M.** "The Laws in the Pentateuch." *The Laws in the Pentateuch and Other Essays.* Tr. D. R. Ap-Thomas. Edinburgh: Oliver and Boyd, 1966, 1–107. **Perdue, L. G.** *Wisdom and Cult: A Critical Analysis of the Views of Cult in the Wisdom Literatures of Israel and the Ancient Near East.* SBLDS 30. Missoula, MT: Scholars Press, 1977. **Robert, A.** "Le Psaume 119 et les sapientaux." *RB* 48 (1939) 5–28. **Sawyer, J. F. A.** "Spaciousness." *ASTI* 6 (1967/68) 20–34.

Translation

1 (א) *How fortunate* [a] *are those whose way is blameless,*   (3+3)
    whose conduct is based on Yahweh's Torah!

2 *How fortunate are those who observe his terms,* [a]   (3+2)
    and seek him wholeheartedly,

3 *who, moreover, do not practice wrong*   (3+2)
    but base their conduct on his ways! [a]

4 *You yourself have commanded that your charges* [a]   (3+2)
    be carefully complied with.

5 *Would that my ways were firmly set*   (3+2)
    on complying with your laws! [a]

6 *Then I would not suffer humiliation,* [a]   (2+3)
    if I kept my eyes on your commands. [b]

7 *I give you thanks out of an honest heart,*   (3+3)
    as I learn your just rulings. [a]

8 *I will comply* [a] *with your laws:*   (2+3)
    do not completely abandon me.

9 (ב) *How can a young man*   (2+2+2)
    keep his path pure? [a]
    Indeed [b] *by complying with your word.* [c]

10 *I have sought you with my whole heart:*   (3+2)
    let me not stray [a] *from your commands.*

11 *I have hidden your sayings* [a] *in my heart*   (3+3)
    so as not to sin against you.

12 *You are blessed,* [a] *Yahweh:*   (3+2)
    teach me your laws.

13 *With my lips I repeat*   (2+3)
    all the rulings from your mouth.

14 *I find as much joy* [a] *in the way shown in your terms*   (3+2)
    as [b] *in all possible wealth.*

15 *I want to meditate on your charges*   (3+2)
    and keep my eyes on your paths.

16   I take delight in your laws,^a   (3+2)
      I do not forget your word.

17 (ג) Give your servant ^a the benefit of your aid ^b so that I may   (3+2)
      have life
      and comply with your word.
18   Uncover my eyes so that I may see   (3+2)
      wonders that emanate from your Torah.
19   As an alien do I lodge ^a in the world: (3+3)
      do not hide from me your commands.
20   I am overcome with intense longing   (3+2)
      for your rulings all the time.
21   You rebuke ^a the godless: (2+3)
      cursed ^b are those who stray from your commands.
22   Remove ^a from me   (2+2+2)
      insults and shame,
      because I have observed your terms.
23   Even though the authorities have plotted in session against me,   (3+3)
      your servant meditates on your laws.
24   Moreover, your terms are my delight,   (3+2)
      my counselors.

25 (ד) The dust ^a holds me prostrate: (3+2)
      give me the life promised in your word.
26   My ways I told you and you answered me: ^a   (3+2)
      teach me your laws.
27   Give me insight into the way taught in your charges   (3+3)
      so that I may meditate on your wonders.
28   I have collapsed ^a with intense sorrow: (3+2)
      make me stand upright as your word promises.
29   The way of faithlessness ^a   (2+2+2)
      take far away from me
      and dutifully ^b teach me your Torah.
30   The way of faithfulness have I chosen,   (3+2)
      your rulings have I taken to heart.^a
31   I hold fast to your terms, Yahweh: (3+2)
      do not let me be humiliated.
32   In the way shown in your commands do I run,   (3+2)
      since you enlarge my understanding.^a

33 (ה) Teach me, Yahweh,   (2+2+2)
      the way shown in your laws
      so that I may observe it as my reward.^a
34   Give me insight, and I will observe ^a your Torah   (3+2)
      and comply ^a with it wholeheartedly.
35   Make me tread the track of your commands,   (3+2)
      since that is what I want.
36   Turn my heart toward your terms   (3+2)
      rather than toward material gain.

37 *Avert my eyes*   (2+2+2)
    from looking at what is valueless, [a]
    give me life in your ways.

38 *Fulfill for your servant your sayings*   (3+2)
    given so as to prompt reverence. [a]

39 *Remove the dreaded insults*   (2+2+2)
    I am experiencing,
    since your rulings [a] *are so right.*

40 *Indeed I long for your charges:*   (3+2)
    give me life in your faithfulness. [a]

41 (ו) *And let your loyal love come* [a] *to me, Yahweh,*   (3+2)
    and your salvation promised in your sayings.

42 *Then will I have an answer for the one who insults me,* [a] (3+2)
    since I trust in your word.

43 *And do not withhold* [a] *from my mouth*   (2+2+2)
    a word of faithfulness, [b]
    since my hope is set on your rulings. [c]

44 *Then I will comply with your Torah continually,*   (3+2)
    for ever and ever.

45 *And let me walk in freedom,* [a]   (3+2)
    since I have applied myself to your charges.

46 *And I will declare your terms*   (2+2+2)
    in front of kings
    without embarrassment.

47 *And* [a] *I take delight in your commands,*   (3+2)
    which I love. [b]

48 *And I lift up my hands to you* [a]   (3+2)
    and meditate on your laws.

49 (ז) *Remember* [a] *the word given to your servant,*   (3+2)
    which you have made the basis of my hope.

50 *This has been my comfort in my suffering,*   (3+2)
    that your sayings can give me life.

51 *Godless men have cruelly derided* [a] *me:*   (3+2)
    I have not deviated from your Torah.

52 *I remember* [a] *your rulings* [b] *of old,* [c]   (3+2)
    Yahweh, and I take comfort.

53 *I am seized with passionate fury in reaction to the wicked* (3+2)
    who abandon your Torah.

54 *Your laws have been the theme of my songs* [a]   (3+2)
    in my place of lodging. [b]

55 *At night time I remember*   (2+2+2)
    your name, Yahweh,
    and I comply with [a] *your Torah.*

56 *This has been my practice,*   (2+3)
    that I have obeyed your charges.

⁵⁷ (ח) *Yahweh is my allotted portion:* ᵃ   (2+3)
    I promise to comply with your words.

⁵⁸   *I entreat* ᵃ *you with my whole heart:*   (3+2)
    treat me dutifully, ᵇ *as your sayings promise.*

⁵⁹   *I have given thought to my ways*   (2+3)
    and turned my steps toward your terms.

⁶⁰   *Without any delay I hasten*   (3+2)
    to comply with your commands.

⁶¹   *The snares* ᵃ *of wicked men are all around me—*   (3+2)
    I do not forget your Torah.

⁶²   *In the middle of the night*   (2+2+2)
    I rise to give you thanks
    for the justice of your rulings.

⁶³   *I am a friend*   (2+2+2)
    to all who revere you
    and comply with your charges.

⁶⁴   *Your loyal love,* ᵃ *Yahweh,*   (2+2+2)
    fills the world:
    teach me your laws.

⁶⁵ (ט) *You have treated your servant well,*   (3+3)
    Yahweh, as promised by your good ᵃ *word.*

⁶⁶   *Teach me discernment and knowledge,*   (3+2)
    since I rely on your laws.

⁶⁷   *Before I suffered, I used to stray,*   (4+3)
    but now I comply with your sayings.

⁶⁸   *You are good and you do good:*   (3+2)
    teach me your laws.

⁶⁹   *Godless people have smeared me with lies* ᵃ —   (4+4)
    I wholeheartedly observe your charges.

⁷⁰   *Their hearts are as gross as fat;*   (3+3)
    in my case, your Torah is my delight.

⁷¹   *It was good for me to be made to suffer:* ᵃ   (2+3)
    it has taught me your laws.

⁷²   *I reckon the Torah* ᵃ *from your mouth more precious*   (3+3)
    than thousands of gold and silver shekels. ᵇ

⁷³ (י) *Your hands made me and gave me my constitution:*   (3+3)
    give me insight to learn your commands.

⁷⁴   *May those who revere you see me and rejoice,*   (3+2)
    because your word is my basis of hope.

⁷⁵   *I know, Yahweh,*   (2+2+2)
    that your rulings ᵃ *are just*
    and that you have made me suffer out of faithfulness.

⁷⁶   *Please may your loyal love* ᵃ *be manifested to comfort me,*   (3+2)
    as your sayings promise your servant.

⁷⁷   *May your compassion come to me, so that I may have life,*   (3+2)
    since your Torah is my delight.

78   *Let the godless be put to shame for wronging me with lies.*[a]   (4+3)
     As for me, I meditate upon your charges.

79   *May those who revere you come back to me,*   (3+2)
     those who know [a] *your terms.*

80   *May my heart be wholly set upon your laws*   (3+2)
     so that I may not be put to shame.

81 (כ) *I feel exhausted, waiting for your salvation;*   (3+2)
     your word is the basis of my hope.

82   *My eyes are strained with waiting for your sayings:* [a]   (3+3)
     "When will you comfort me?" I ask.

83   *Though I am like a wineskin in the smoke,* [a]   (3+2)
     I have not forgotten your laws.

84   *How long must your servant endure?*   (2+2+2)
     When will you execute
     judgment on my persecutors?

85   *Godless folk have dug pits to trap me,* [a]   (3+2)
     people who do not conform to your Torah.

86   *All your commands are reliable;*   (3+3)
     but they persecute me with lies—help me!

87   *They have nearly brought my life on earth to an end,*   (3+3)
     But I have not abandoned your charges.

88   *Give me life in accord with your loyal love,* [a]   (2+3)
     and I will comply with the terms from your mouth.

89 (ל) *Forever, Yahweh,*   (2+3)
     your word [a] *stands firm in the heavens.*

90   *For generation after generation your faithfulness* [a] *endures:* (3+3)
     you have fixed the earth and there it stays.

91   *Today they* [a] *still stand ready for your rulings,*   (3+2)
     since all things are servants of yours.

92   *Had not your Torah been my delight,*   (3+2)
     I would have died of my suffering.

93   *Never will I forget your charges,*   (3+2)
     since through them you give me life.

94   *I am yours—save me,*   (3+2)
     since I apply myself to your charges.

95   *Wicked men are waiting to destroy me,*   (3+2)
     but I set my mind to your terms.

96   *Every aspiration I have seen fall short of realization:*   (4+3)
     your command is so wide in its scope. [a]

97 (מ) *How I love your Torah!*   (3+3)
     All day long it is my meditation.

98   *Your command* [a] *makes me wiser than my enemies,* [b]   (3+2)
     since it is always mine.

99   *I have greater understanding than all my teachers* [a]   (3+2)
     because your terms are my meditation.

100   *I have more insight than the aged*   (3+2)
     because I observe your charges.

101   *Away from every evil path have I kept my feet*   (4+3)
     in order to comply with your word.

102   *From your rulings I have not turned aside,*   (3+2)
     since you yourself have been my instructor.

103   *How palatable I find your sayings,*[a]   (3+2)
     more so than honey to my mouth!

104   *I gain insight from your charges,*   (2+2+2)
     and so I hate
     every faithless path.

105 (ℷ)   *Your word is a lamp for my foot,*   (3+2)
     a light along my track.

106   *I have bound myself with oath and pledge*[a]   (2+3)
     to comply with your just rulings.

107   *I am undergoing acute suffering:*   (2+3)
     Yahweh, give me the life promised by your word.

108   *Please accept the offerings of my mouth, Yahweh,*   (3+2)
     and teach me your rulings.

109   *I am always taking my life in my hand,*[a]   (3+2)
     but I do not forget your Torah.

110   *Wicked folk have set a trap for me,*[a]   (3+2)
     but I have not wandered from your charges.

111   *I have inherited your terms to possess forever,*[a]   (3+2)
     they are truly the joy of my heart.

112   *I incline my heart*   (2+2+2)
     to practice your laws:
     the reward[a] *is never ending.*

113 (ד)   *I hate people with divided loyalties,*   (2+2)
     but I love your Torah.

114   *You are my hiding place, my shield,*   (3+2)
     I put my hope in your word.

115   *Get away from me, you wrongdoers:*[a]   (3+3)
     I intend to observe my God's commands.

116   *Support me, as your word promises, so that I may have life,*   (3+3)
     and do not let me find disappointment resulting from[a] *my hope.*

117   *Uphold me so that I may be kept safe,*   (2+3)
     and I will always have regard[a] *for your laws.*

118   *You reject all who stray from your laws,*   (3+2)
     since their deceitfulness is a breach of the faith.[a]

119   *All the wicked people in the world you destroy as dross,*   (4+3)
     and so I love your terms.

120   *Dread of you makes my flesh creep*   (3+3)
     and I am afraid of your rulings.[a]

121 (ע) *I have done what is just and right:*   (3+2)
     do not leave me to my oppressors.

122   *Stand surety* ª *for your servant's welfare.*   (3+2)
     May godless folk stop oppressing me.

123   *My eyes are strained with looking for your salvation*   (3+2)
     and for your just sayings.

124   *Deal with your servant in accord with your loyal love*   (3+2)
     and teach me your laws.

125   *I am your servant: give me insight*   (3+2)
     so that I may understand your terms.

126   *It is time for Yahweh* ª *to act:*   (3+2)
     people have broken your Torah.

127   *Therefore* ª *I love your commands*   (3+2)
     more than gold, pure gold.

128   *Therefore all your charges I consider right,* ª   (3+3)
     I hate every faithless path.

129 (פ) *Your terms are wonderful,*   (2+3)
     that is why I observe them.

130   *The relevation* ª *of your words brings enlightenment,*   (3+2)
     it gives insight to the simple. ᵇ

131   *I pant open-mouthed*   (3+2)
     with longing for your commands.

132   *Turn to me, act dutifully* ª *toward me*   (3+3)
     in accord with the right of those who love your name.

133   *Direct my steps with your sayings,*   (3+3)
     do not let any evil master ª *me.*

134   *Release me from human oppression*   (3+2)
     and I will comply with your charges.

135   *Let your face shine* ª *on your servant,*   (3+2)
     teach me your laws.

136   *My eyes run with streams of water*   (3+3)
     because people do not comply with your Torah.

137 (צ) *You are just, Yahweh,*   (3+2)
     and your rulings are right. ª

138   *The terms you have imposed are marked by justice*   (3+2)
     and by complete faithfulness.

139   *My passion overwhelms me,*   (2+3)
     since my foes have forgotten your words.

140   *Your sayings pass all tests for purity,* ª   (3+2)
     your servant loves them.

141   *Insignificant and despised though I am,*   (3+2)
     I do not forget your charges.

142   *Your loyalty* ª *is always just,*   (3+2)
     your law is true.

143   *Trouble and distress have befallen me—*   (3+2)
     your commands are my delight.

144   *Your terms are ever just:*   (3+2)
       give me insight so that I may have life.

145 (ק) *I cry with my whole heart—*   (2+2+2)
       answer me, Yahweh:
       I will observe your laws.

146   *I cry to you, save me*   (2+2)
       and I will comply with your terms.

147   *Before morning twilight I rise to cry for help,*   (3+2)
       I set my hope on your word.

148   *Before the night watch(es)*[a] *my eyes are open*   (3+2)
       to meditate on your sayings.

149   *Hear my appeal in accord with your loyal love.*   (3+3)
       Yahweh, give me the life promised by your rulings.

150   *My persecutors* [a] *are coming close with malicious intent—*   (3+2)
       they are far from your Torah.

151   *You are close at hand, Yahweh,*   (3+3)
       and all your commands are true.

152   *Long ago I learned from your terms*   (3+2)
       that you founded them to last forever.

153 (ר) *Look at my suffering and deliver me,*   (3+2)
       because I have not forgotten your Torah.

154   *Take up my cause and champion me,*[a]   (3+2)
       give me the life promised in your sayings.

155   *Your salvation is far removed* [a] *from the wicked,*   (3+2)
       because they do not apply themselves to your laws.

156   *Your compassion is so multiplied, Yahweh:*   (3+2)
       give me the life promised in your rulings.

157   *My persecutors and foes are multiplied too—*   (3+2)
       I have not deviated from your terms.

158   *The sight of the faithless fills me with disgust,*   (3+3)
       because they do not comply with your rulings.

159   *See how I love your charges:*   (3+3)
       Yahweh, give me life in accord with your loyal love.

160   *The essence of your word is truth,*   (3+3)
       and every one of your just rulings lasts forever.

161 (ש) *The authorities persecute me without reason,*   (3+3)
       but it is your words that fill my heart with dread.

162   *I am gladdened* [a] *by your sayings*   (3+2)
       like someone who finds a lot of spoil.

163   *I hate and detest* [a] *faithlessness,*   (3+2)
       your Torah is what I love.

164   *Seven times a day* [a] *I praise you*   (3+2)
       for your just rulings.

165   *Those who love your Torah have ample security*   (3+4)
       and nothing can make them stumble.

¹⁶⁶   *I set my hope on your salvation, Yahweh,*   (3+2)
       and carry out your commands.
¹⁶⁷   *I comply with your terms*   (3+3)
       and love them dearly.
¹⁶⁸   *I comply with your charges and terms*   (3+3)
       because every way I take is open to your gaze. ^a

¹⁶⁹ (ת) *May my cry have access*   (2+2+2)
        to you, Yahweh,
        give me the insight promised by your word.
¹⁷⁰   *May my supplication be admitted to your presence,*   (3+2)
       deliver me, as your sayings promise.
¹⁷¹   *May* ^a *my lips pour out praise*   (3+2)
       because you teach me your laws.
¹⁷²   *May my tongue sing about your sayings*   (3+3)
       because all your rulings are just.
¹⁷³   *May your hand be ready to help me*   (3+2)
       because I have chosen your charges.
¹⁷⁴   *I yearn for your salvation, Yahweh,*   (3+2)
       and your Torah is my delight.
¹⁷⁵   *May I have life so that I may praise you*   (3+2)
       and may your rulings ^a *help me.*
¹⁷⁶   *I have strayed like a lost sheep:* ^a   (2+2+2)
       look for your servant,
       since I have not forgotten your commands.

Notes/Comments

1.a. See the comments on 106:3; 112:1.

2.a. Heb. עדות has the sense of "covenant stipulations": cf. 132:12 and see W. F. Albright, *Yahweh and the Gods of Canaan,* (London: Athlone Press, 1968) 92; M. Dahood, *Psalms III,* 173.

3.a. Heb. דרכים "ways" relate to Yahweh's moral demands upon men, which are themselves congruent with his own character.

4.a. Heb. פקודים are detailed rules for life associated with the covenant. The term occurs only in the Psalter (19:9; 103:18; 111:7). Cf. Aram. פקד "command." It functions here as the object of לשמר.

5.a. Heb. חקים are primarily covenant conditions (cf. 50:16; 105:10) written down and preserved for permanent observance.

6.a. Humiliation is personal misfortune compounded by being ostracized and taunted since it was recognized by victim and society as the corollary of disobeying Yahweh.

6.b. Heb. מצות is characteristic of Deuteronomy and expresses the insistent will of a personal God who is Israel's Lord.

7.a. Heb. משפטים, also characteristic of Deuteronomy, is primarily a forensic term, verdicts of the divine judge concerning moral issues. In vv 39, 75, etc. it has a future aspect and is the object of anticipation as the providential outworking of Yahweh's moral will in contemporary history.

8.a. A. Deissler (*Psalm 119,* 97) took as a profession of loyalty to the Torah, which the verbal form supports, but it would conflict with v 5. It is rather a promise of obedience (H. Gunkel, *Die Psalmen,* 517), which in Ps 119 is the characteristic development of the vow of praise associated with the individual complaint.

9.a. A question is typical of wisdom literature: cf. Prov 23:29, 30; Pss. 25:12; 34:13 (12).

9.b. R. Gordis (*JAOS* 63 [1943] 117) has taken the *kaph* as an emphatic particle. The ancient versions, except *Tg.*, ignore. The psalm uses שמר only in the sense of keeping the Torah.

9.c. Heb. דבר relates to the communication of Yahweh's covenant will to his people: it is used of the Decalogue in Exod 34:1, 28; Deut 4:13.

10.a. Heb. שגה refers to deliberate, not unconscious, sin.

11.a. Heb. אמרה is a variant of דבר; it often has the connotation of promise in the psalm.

12.a. For the divine ברוך-formula see W. S. Towner, " 'Blessed be Yahweh' and 'Blessed art Thou, Yahweh': The Modulation of a Biblical Formula." *CBQ* 30 (1968) 386–99: in this non-cultic setting "it stands as an expression of joy and praise within a meditation on God's righteous word" (393). It implicitly urges Yahweh to comply with the request of v 12b and expresses the psalmist's reason for it. Elsewhere a causal construction follows (cf. v 171; 28:6).

14.a. For the motif of joy in the psalm see H.-J. Kraus, *EvT* 10 (1951) 337–51.

14.b. *S* implies מעל "more than" (cf. vv 72, 127). But Deissler (*Psalm 119*, 104) has observed that in the OT it is never used in a comparative sense; for MT he compared 2 Chr 32:19.

15.a. The two verbs of the bicolon express a wish, as their cohortative form indicates (D. Michel, *Tempora*, 154).

16.a. Heb חקתיך is fem. plural only here in the psalm. For the variation cf. Deut 6:2, 17; Ezek 11:12, 20.

17.a. For a study of עבד in the psalm see C. Lindhagen, *The Servant Motif*, 262–70, 275, and cf. I. Riesener, *Der Stamm* עבד, 223–29.

17.b. Heb. גמל has the connotation of delivering from danger: cf. 13:6; 116:7 and K. Seybold, "גמל gāmal," *TDOT* 3 (1978) 30–32.

17.c. For the final sense of the cohortative see P. Joüon, *Grammaire* § 116i.

19.a. For the spiritualization of the concept of the גר see H.-J. Hermisson, *Sprache und Ritus*, 112–13. The resident alien had no territorial claim (cf. Gen 12:10). According to Lev 25:23 Israel comprised a group of גרים permitted to live on Yahweh's property and dependent completely upon him.

21.a. A. Caquot, ("גער gāʿar," *TDOT* 3 [1978] 52) relates to the divine shout of rage (cf. 104:7 and note) rather than to the sapiential meaning of reproof.

21.b. Probably ארורים is to be taken with v 21b, with LXX *S* Hier (Gunkel, *Die Psalmen*, 519, *BHS et al.*).

22.a. The ancient versions (and 11QPsª גול) imply גל "roll away" (cf. Josh 5:9). But MT may be kept with M. Dahood (*Psalms III*, 176) as the metaphor of a garment: cf. v 18 and Isa 47:7.

25.a. For the reference to Sheol see N. J. Tromp, *Primitive Conceptions*, 85–91. The psalmist's troubles are a deathlike experience. Deissler (*Psalm 119*, 118–19) and H. W. Wolff (*Anthropology*, 14) take נפש as "neck," as in 44:26 (25).

26.a. The psalmist appeals to an earlier complaint and divine answer in hope of another positive response.

28.a. For Heb. דלף "crumble" cf. Ugar. *dlp* (J. C. L. Gibson, *Canaanite Myths and Legends* [2nd ed.; Edinburgh: T. & T. Clark, 1978] 144; cf. Dahood, *Psalms III*, 177).

29.a. For Heb. שקר in the sense of betrayal of covenant values, contrasted with v 30, see M. A. Klopfenstein, *Die Lüge*, 55.

29.b. For the double object cf. Gen 33:5. The teaching of the Torah is regarded as an aspect of Yahweh's faithfulness to the covenant (cf. v 124): see K. W. Neubauer, *Der Stamm CH N N*, 86.

30.a. Probably sc. לב. G. R. Driver (*HTR* 29 [1936] 191) plausibly explained as an ellipse, comparing Heb. (לב) שים "put the mind (to), consider," and an Aramaism (שַׁוִּי לבא על). LXX οὐκ ἐπελαθόμην seems to be an attempt to render a difficult text, while *S*, which implies אויתי, betrays the influence of 132:13 at some stage (Deissler, *Psalm 119*, 125).

32.a. J. F. A. Sawyer (*ASTI* 6 [1967/68] 30) has related to the Solomonic traditions of wisdom of 1 Kgs 4:29, etc. and so to the intellectual grasp of a wide range of subjects. Wolff (*Anthropology*, 44) relates generally to liberation.

33.a. LXX *Tg.* translate עקב as "always," but cf. v 112 and 19:12. Conduct pleasing to Yahweh is itself conceived as a reward gratifying to the psalmist: cf. v 36 for the worthwhileness of the obedient life (A. Robert, *RB* 48 [1939] 19–20).

34.a. V 34b suggests that the verbs are not final but express a resolve (Michel, *Tempora*, 156).

37.a. Heb. שוא is part of the OT vocabulary for moral evil.

38.a. J. Becker (*Gottesfurcht im AT*, 274–75) has identified יראה with nomistic obedience, rather tortuously interpreting the text in terms of the word of promise contained in the law, which is given so that the law may be obeyed. The reference is probably more general: "given to prompt reverence." Some take יראתך in a concrete sense: "those who fear you" (A. A. Anderson, *Psalms*, 820; NEB).

39.a. Heb. משפטים here relates to divine intervention on the psalmist's behalf, executing a verdict of judgment in his favor (cf. 10:5; Isa 26:8, 9; Ezek 5:8).

40.a. Heb. צדקה refers to faithfulness to the covenant relationship: cf. the frequent כדברך "according to your word," and the like, and 103:17.

41.a. Singulars are to be read with LXX: ויבאני חסדך. Deissler (*Psalm 119*, 140) has observed that only here in the psalm would a plural of חסד occur and that S, which has a plural, is not a reliable guide, since it wrongly so renders in v 64. Probably MT's pointing of the verb was influenced by v 77.

42.a. The singular is probably collective.

43.a. Heb. תצל is probably defectively written for תאצל. MT "take away," from נצל, is contextually unsuitable (Deissler, *Psalm 119*, 143, following F. Perles).

43.b. MT adds עד-מאד "very much," which is generally deleted with S as contextually inappropriate and metrically difficult (e.g. Gunkel, *Die Psalmen*, 522; Kraus, *Psalmen*, 995; Anderson, *Psalms*, 821). Cf. LXX's addition in v 47: was the phrase a floating one attached to different places?

43.c. Heb. משפטיך probably does not relate to intervention, as in v 39. V 43b is an expression of trust in God's promise: note the external parallel in v 42b. For the concept of hope in Ps 119 see W. Zimmerli, *Man and His Hope in the OT* (SBT 2:20; London: SCM Press, 1968) 29–31.

45.a. Cf. Sawyer, *ASTI* 6 (1967/68) 29. The idea of spaciousness is spiritualized and here relates to life free from restrictions of distress and so free to develop its full potential.

47.a. The motivation of v 45b is here continued.

47.b. The deuteronomic concept of loving God is in Ps 119 applied to the Torah.

48.a. MT אל מצותיך אשר אהבתי looks suspiciously like a dittograph of v 47 for an original אליך, which would be metrically easier (Gunkel, *Die Psalmen*, 522; Kraus, *Psalmen*, 995). Worship of the Torah seems too extreme an attitude even for the psalmist.

49.a. Heb. זכר is commonly used as a plea in a complaint, for Yahweh to act in conformity with an existing commitment: cf. 25:6 (5) (B. S. Childs, *Memory and Tradition*, 34–36).

51.a. For LXX παρηνόμουν cf. παράνομος for נלוז "deride" in Prov 3:32.

52.a. For the role of human remembrance in psalms of individual complaint see Childs, *Memory and Tradition*, 60, 64.

52.b. Heb. משפטיך relate to God's judgments on Israel's enemies recorded in the biblical traditions: cf. 77:12–13 (11–12) (J. W. Rogerson and J. W. McKay, *Psalms 101–150*, 99).

52.c. Heb. מעולם "of old" apparently qualifies משפטיך (E. Jenni, "Das Wort ʿōlām im AT," *ZAW* 64 [1952] 225; Kraus, *Psalmen*, 1002). Some subordinate it to the verb (e.g. S. Bergler, *VT* 29 [1969] 265: "I have long . . ."), but v 55 suggests a present sense.

54.a. Dahood's rendering "my defenses" (*Psalms III*, 180) is philologically possible and fits the overall theme of comfort, but the motif of praise in v 55a supports the usual interpretation: cf. 92:2–3 (1–2).

55.a. A pointing וְאֶשְׁמְרָה "and during the watch" (Dahood, *Psalms III*, 180, following A. B. Ehrlich) would overcome the awkwardness of MT, but a plural is expected: cf. 63:7 (6).

57.a. An old levitical formula of dependence upon Yahweh for material support rather than upon tribal land (cf. Num 18:20) is used in complaints as an expression of trust: cf. 16:5; 142:6 (5) (Hermisson, *Sprache und Ritus*, 109–112). Deissler (*Psalm 119*, 156–57) and Dahood (*Psalms III*, 180) treat יהוה as vocative, but the stereotyped nature of the formula renders this expedient improbable.

58.a. Cf. Seybold, "Reverenz und Gebet. Erwägungen zu der Wendung ḥillā panîm," *ZAW* 88 (1976) 2–16, for a study of חלה פנים. He prefers the interpretation "make the face sweet" and relates it to prayer, here in a non-cultic spiritualized sense, as in 2 Chr 33:12.

58.b. Cf. Neubauer, *Der Stamm CH N N*, 84–85: חנני refers to Yahweh's faithful discharge of his relational commitment. Cf. v 132 and the comparable appeal to חסד in v 41.

61.a. For this complaint metaphor portraying enemies as hunters cf. 140:6(5).

64.a. Heb. חסד is here widened, as in 136:1–9; 145:8–9; Jonah 4:11, to Yahweh's care for all his creatures: cf. W. Eichrodt, *Theology of the OT*, vol. 1 (Tr. J. A. Baker; London: SCM Press, 1961) 239.

65.a. Dahood (*Psalms III*, 181) has plausibly suggested that the awkward טוב at the beginning of v 66 be taken with v 65 as טוב , which would provide inclusion for the line. The resulting 3+3 meter is matched in the context by vv 70, 72, 73.

69.a. Cf. Job 13:4. Here malevolent slander is in view (Klopfenstein, *Die Lüge*, 60).

71.a. Cf. Deut 8:16. 11QPsᵃ עניתני (cf. LXX) has probably been influenced by v 75.

72.a. Cf. Prov 3:14. Wisdom and Torah are identified (Deissler, *Psalm 119*, 173).

72.b. For this sapiential type of comparative saying cf. Prov 15:17, etc.

75.a. Cf. v 39. V 75a is a *Gerichtsdoxologie* (Kraus, *Psalmen*, 1003): cf. Josh 7:19.

76.a. Cf. K. H. Sakenfeld, *The Meaning of Hesed*, 230–31: חסד in the form of deliverance is asked for Yahweh's servant, as in 31:17(16); 69:17–18 (16–17); 143:12.

78.a. Cf. v 69. A contrast with v 75 is intended, although whether the enemies' slander is a consequence of the divine humbling or an aspect of it is not clear (Klopfenstein, *Die Lüge*, 64, 65).

79.a. Becker (*Gottesfurcht im AT*, 153 note 128) and Anderson (*Psalms*, 830) prefer K וידעו (=*Tg.*) "so that they may know," comparing v 125 for the construction. But most read Q וידעי with many Heb. mss. and LXX S Hier. For the synonymous parallelism cf. v. 63.

82.a. Here with reference to Yahweh's providential intervention like משפטיך in vv 39, etc.: cf. v 123.

83.a. Obviously the connotation is negative in the context. Bergler (*VT* 29 [1979] 274) interprets as swaying to and fro and so alluding to human inconstancy. But most take it as a figure for distress in general, regarding the wineskin as unused, shriveled and black.

85.a. Cf. v 61.

88.a. Cf. vv 124, 149, 159 and compare כדברך, vv 28, 65, etc.

89.a. Heb. דבר is here an expression of God's all-embracing purpose which is not only embodied in the Torah but reflected in the created universe (cf. v 91). It is here equated with divine wisdom (Robert, *RB* 48 [1939] 11).

90.a. Earlier scholarship tended to emend to אמרתך "your sayings" (Gunkel, *Die Psalmen*, 528, following D. H. Müller; also NEB, following G. R. Driver (*Textus* 4 [1964] 94), who explained the change as due to misread abbreviation). Certainly אמרה often follows דבר and occurs in the second line; but 36:6(5) and 89:3(2) confirm MT.

91.a. V 91b suggests that the heavens and earth are the subject.

96.a. Robert (*RB* 48 [1939] 10–11), observing a similar semantic range in Job 11:7, 9; 28:3, accordingly understood in terms of a contrast between limited human understanding and divine Torah-wisdom.

98.a. MT מצותך must be revocalized as a singular מצותך with one Heb. ms. and LXX in view of the preceding verb and following היא.

98.b. Vv 98a, 100 are an individual application of Deut 4:6 (Deissler, *Psalm 119*, 198).

99.a. Gunkel (*Die Psalmen*, 528) *et al.* have interpreted as a conflict with less Torah-oriented wisdom teachers. Deissler (*Psalm 119*, 199) has compared Jer 9:22, 23.

103.a. MT אמרתך needs to be vocalized as a plural אמרת(י)ך with a few Heb. mss. and LXX S Tg. in view of the plural verb.

106.a. Heb. קים (cf. v 28) is evidently used in the Jewish Aramaic sense of "swear, vow."

108.a. Heb. נדבות, lit. "freewill offerings," is here spiritualized as prayers of praise: cf. 19:15; 51:19(17); Heb 13:15 (cf. Hermisson, *Sprache und Ritus*, 57–58).

109.a. For this figure of danger cf. Judg 12:3, etc.: it means "the readiness to put one's life in danger of one's own accord" (Wolff, *Anthropology*, 20).

110.a. Cf. v 61.

111.a. The motif of the land (cf. Exod 32:13) is here transposed to a higher key.

112.a. Cf. v 33. LXX Hier so render. Anderson (*Psalms*, 836) compares Prov 22:4, but in the light of v 111b spiritual gratification is intended.

115.a. The imperative addressed to enemies is typical of the individual complaint: cf. 6:9(8).

116.a. For בוש מן "find disappointment from" see P. Haupt, "Critical Notes on Micah," *AJSL* 26 (1910) 228–31.

117.a. LXX S Tg. Hier all imply ואשתעשע "delight" for ואשעה, and it is adopted by Gunkel

(*Die Psalmen*, 530), Kraus (*Psalmen*, 995), *et al.* Deissler (*Psalm 119*, 215) has observed that alliteration with ואושעה favors MT.

118.a. MT is not tautologous: שקר relates to what is inconsistent with divine standards and תרמית to deceitful treatment (Klopfenstein, *Die Lüge*, 62–63). MT תרמיתם is often emended to תרעיתם "their purpose" (cf. Aram. תרעיתא) on the evidence of LXX (ἐνθύμημα) θ′ S Hier. But G. R. Driver (*HTR* 29 [1936] 191) took MT as an Aramaizing homonym, comparing Syr. *rm'* "intend." It is noteworthy that ἐνθύμημα also renders תרמית in α′ at Jer 8:5; 14:14, while LXX uses synonyms there and in Jer 23:26. Accordingly a different Heb. *Vorlage* is unlikely.

119.a. 11QPs ᵃ has חשבתי "I regard," which LXX too implies. Kraus (*Psalmen*, 995) so reads and in support Bergler (*VT* 29 [1979] 272) compares v 59, another עדות line. V 113 might be held to favor the change. But חשבת "you regard," read by some Heb. mss. and α′σ′ Hier is preferable: vv 118–19 appear to be a pair, like vv 116, 117, and לכן in v 119b implies a divine reference. Yet MT חשבת can stand as both reinforcing v 118 and preparing for the reaction of fear in v 120.

120.a. Becker (*Gottesfurcht im AT*, 41–42) has observed that the Torah partakes of the numinous fear of Yahweh, as in v 161. For the tension between love (v 119) and fear, which goes back to Deut 6:5, 13; 10:12 (cf. Ps 31:20, 24 [19, 23]), cf. Eichrodt, *Theology*, vol. 2, 298–99.

122.a. Heb. ערב means to take over responsibility for another, e.g. in respect of his debt: cf. Gen 43:9; Prov 11:15; Isa 38:14.

123.a. Cf. v 82.

126.a. V 126b suggests a vocative and so יהוה is sometimes read with one Heb. ms. and Hier. Dahood (*Psalms III*, 187) and NEB take the *lamed* as a vocative particle, as in Ugaritic. But for the change from third to second person cf. v 57.

127.a. Most follow B. Duhm (*Psalmen*, 268) in reading על כל "above all." But a deduction is not unfitting. The anticipated intervention of Yahweh is a double stimulus (vv 127–28), both to devotion to his revelation (cf. v 119) and to renouncing behavior alien to it.

128.a. MT פקודי כל "precepts concerning everything" is strange and violates the normal qualification of a Torah term with a divine suffix. LXX Hier seem to imply לכל פקודיך "according to all your charges (I go straight)." Dahood (Hebrew-Ugaritic Lexicography IV," *Bib* 47 [1966] 408) and J. H. Eaton (*VT* 18 [1968] 557–58) have proposed an emphatic *lamed*, כל פקודיך לישרתי, which has some merit in staying closer to MT.

130.a. 11QPs ᵃ S interpret as an imperative פְּתַח "open (. . . and bring)." σ′ Hier imply פֶּתַח "doorway": G. R. Driver, *HTR* 29 [1936] 191–92, observed that it hardly suits יאיר and that Acc. *pitū* "open" can also mean "reveal."

130.b. Cf. v 198. The use of פתיים "the simple," employed frequently in Proverbs, implies an identification of the Torah with wisdom (Deissler, *Psalm 119*, 228).

132.a. Cf. v 58.

133.a. *Pace* BHS LXX S do not imply ישלט "he will master" but wrongly construed און as feminine. For the sentiment cf. 19:14; Gen 4:7.

135.a. Cf. Num 6:25.

137.a. For the singular see GKC § 145r and cf. v 155.

140.a. Cf. 18:31 (30), but here אמרה is used of Yahweh's past revelation, not of his promise. Purity is a metaphor for truth (Deissler, *Psalm 119*, 237).

142.a. Cf. v 40.

148.a. The last watch from two to six o'clock is meant in the context. The plural indicates that the small hours were regularly used in this way.

150.a. MT רֹדְפֵי is generally repointed to רֹדְפַי with Heb. mss. and LXX σ′ Hier, since the psalmist's persecutors are intended; זמה is an adverbial accusative (cf. vv 84, 86, 157).

154.a. Cf. 43:1; 69:19 (18) for this vocabulary of the individual complaint.

155.a. Cf. v 137.

162.a. The paradoxical response of fear, v 161, and joy is paralleled in 86:4, 11. Anderson (*Psalms*, 844) derives it from the blessing and curse associated with the covenant.

163.a. The alternative pointing וָאֶתְעֵבָה "I detest" (cf. *BHS*) is preferable.

164.a. Contrast the three times of 55:18(17); Dan 6:11. Piety beyond the norm is indicated.

168.a. A sense of Yahweh's omniscience is one motive for obedience: cf. Job 31:4; Prov 5:20, 21 (Deissler, *Psalm 119*, 257). A. F. Kirkpatrick (*Psalms*, 731; cf. JB) understood as an appeal to confirm the truth of v 168a, but this is less obvious.

169.a. In the light of v 170a a cry for help is meant (N. E. Wagner, "רנה in the Psalter," *VT* 10 [1960] 439–40). It is poetically personified.

171.a. V 171a is probably a wish in view of the clear jussive form in the parallel v 172a.

175.a. Cf. v 39.

176.a. In the context of the psalm exposure to danger and being lost and lonely among foes are probably meant.

Form/Structure/Setting

Psalm 119 is an acrostic psalm like Pss 111, 112 and others. It is the most developed instance in the OT. The closest parallel is Lamentations 3, which contains twenty-two strophes of three lines. In this literary tour de force eight lines in each strophe begin with the same letter of the alphabet. This makes it by far the longest composition in the Psalter. The number of lines seems to have been determined by the use of eight synonyms for the focus of the psalmist's interest, the "Torah." Five of these occur too in Ps 19B, upon which this psalm may be dependent. Overall תורה occurs twenty-five times, דבר "word" twenty-four, משפטים "rulings" and עדות "(covenant) terms" twenty-three, מצוה or מצות "command(s)" twenty-two, חקים "statutes, laws" and פקודים "charges" twenty-one and אמרה or אמרות "saying(s)" nine-teen times. There is no regularity in their use. All eight occur once in four strophes, *ḥeth, yod, kaph* and *pe,* while the *waw* strophe uses one term twice, if MT is not emended in v 48. The other strophes exhibit seven or six of the synonyms, using them from seven to nine times in each case. The psalmist did not strive for symmetrical perfection: two synonyms appear per line in vv 16, 48 (in MT), 160, 168 and 172, and no synonyms in vv 3, 37, 90 and 122. There is a certain preference in the order of terms within a strophe, though no strophe attests it as a whole; the *nun* strophe comes closest and the *waw* one next. It is as follows, the brackets indicating substantially lower counts and reading from left to right: דבר, אמרה, (מצות), משפטים, תורה, (פקודים), עדות, חקים. The dominant word is תורה, as its highest total of occurrences and its use in v 1 indicate.

The complex acrostic structure set limits upon the logical development of the psalm. It has a randomness or more precisely a kaleidoscopic patterning of a certain number of motifs, which pervades even the *waw* strophe where the psalmist had complete control over his material. But rational ordering is not completely absent, and on closer inspection many strophes have their own distinctive emphases.

In form the psalm is most obviously a wisdom psalm. L. Perdue (*Wisdom and Cult,* 305) has enumerated its themes and vocabulary which are characteristic of wisdom literature (cf. J. K. Kuntz, "Canonical Wisdom Psalms," 204). The movement from motif to motif within an overall orbit is especially reminiscent of collections of proverbs. The poet's deliberate commitment to this style is demonstrable from the *waw* strophe, where he could control his material as he wished. To define the psalm more closely, it belongs to that branch of wisdom literature concerned with the Torah, which is also represented in the Psalter by Pss 1 and 19B (cf. R. B. Y. Scott, *The Way of Wisdom in the OT* [New York: Macmillan, 1971] 199, 200). A number of the elements of normal psalm literature feature, especially those of the individual complaint.

There is the description characteristic of the complaint, concerning the speaker, e.g. vv 25a, 143a, and concerning his enemies, e.g. vv 51a, 85, the confession of trust, e.g. vv 57a, 137a, and prayer for help, e.g. vv 94a, 149. Assertions of innocence as motivations for Yahweh to intervene appear in the form of devotion to the Torah, e.g. vv 30, 61, and obedience, e.g. vv 31a, 51b. The vow of praise associated with the complaint has become a vow of future obedience, e.g. vv 34, 44, 57b. The confession of trust is often Torah-centered, e.g. vv 20, 105. This orientation toward the Torah is also evident in the wisdom elements of the psalm, such as beatitudes, vv 1–3, and comparative sayings, vv 72, 127. The psalm's hymnic praise can often be included in the element of confession of trust, but often it is too strongly accentuated to be subordinated to the complaint in this way. Accordingly Ps 119 may best be described as a medley of praise, prayer and wisdom features.

There has been an emphasis in recent literature upon a cultic purpose for the psalm. E. Lipiński (*RB* 75 [1968] 348–49) has traced the character of the psalm to the priestly circle in Jerusalem concerned with the Torah. He describes its spirit as close to deuteronomistic circles of the sixth century B.C., comparing the view of K. Koch (cited below). He denies any specific wisdom element; the אשרי formula (vv 1–2) he ascribes to a cultic origin. Perdue has contested this particular point (*Wisdom and Cult*, 328 note 23), but he himself urges that the psalm was written by a sage as a prayer for cultic use (268, 312). S. Bergler (*VT* 29 [1979] 260, 286–87) completely rearranges the psalm into eight liturgical songs of twenty-two lines used at the Feast of Tabernacles, each song celebrating one of the terms for the Torah. In order to do this he revives the otherwise abandoned text-critical principle of D. H. Müller (*Biblische Studien*, 54–61), whereby perfect symmetry in the use of particular terms is "restored."

K. Koch (review of Deissler, *Psalm 119*, in *TLZ* 83 [1958] coll. 186–87) stressed the closeness of the psalm to Deuteronomy and absence of references to post-exilic literature. He assigned it to deuteronomistic circles of the exilic period. M. Weinfeld (*Deuteronomy and the Deuteronomic School* [Oxford: Clarendon Press, 1972] 280), in the course of claiming wisdom and nomistic elements in Deuteronomy, has criticized J. Becker (*Gottesfurcht im AT*, 87–88) for sharply distinguishing between the concept of "fear of Yahweh" in Deuteronomy and that in nomistic literature such as Ps 119. But he has drawn one distinction between the two standpoints: in the former work the nation is addressed, but in the latter the individual. He traces this difference to historical and social developments, such as loss of national independence, and speaks in terms of the post-exilic nomistic conception of the Torah as an object of more intense focus. M. Noth ("The Laws in the Pentateuch," 91) observed the quality of the Torah in Ps 119 as "a timeless entity," as in late wisdom literature generally. This element appears to put a certain distance between the two pieces of literature.

In implying a post-exilic dating for the psalm, Weinfeld sides with the majority opinion, most fully developed by A. Deissler, *Psalm 119*. Apart from dependence upon Deuteronomy, he not only stressed the wisdom elements of the psalm, an argument which in the light of Weinfeld's studies in Deutero-

nomy may not be so compelling as formerly, but also defined its style as anthological, echoing especially such OT books as Deuteronomy, Proverbs, Isaiah
and Jeremiah. Koch, ibid., attempted to counter this argument by insisting
that allusion to traditions rather than a literary use of texts is what the psalm
exhibits. But these so-called traditions appear so pronounced after Deissler's
researches that if Deuteronomy is claimed as a literary source, as Koch has,
it is hard to resist the claim that other literature is cited. The issue is rendered
all the more difficult by the lack of definition of Torah, etc. in the psalm. A
written form is strongly suggested by such verses as v 148, and a date after
Deuteronomy is necessitated. Commonly a date after Ezra, who was apparently
associated with the promulgation of the complete Pentateuch in Judah, has
been advocated (e.g. H. Schmidt, *Die Psalmen*, 220; Deissler, *Psalm 119*, 288;
Becker, *Gottesfurcht im AT*, 226). Deissler has reasonably defined the Torah
in Ps 119 as an anthology of sacred books including prophetic and sapiential
elements as well as the Pentateuch, and himself assigned it to the third century
B.C. This dating may be too late. In principle there appear to be insufficient
grounds for denying a post-exilic origin. In particular the presence of pronounced Aramaisms and terms characteristic of late or post-biblical Hebrew
(כעל, v 14, גרס, v 20, (ה)תאב, vv 20, 40, 174, קים, vv 28, 106, שוה, v 30,
טפש, v 70, שבר, vv 116, 166, יאב, v 131, שלט, v 133) is a weighty argument
for advocating it.

A cultic purpose is difficult to accept. The development of the elements
of the cultic complaint away from a cultic orientation toward expressions of
obedience and devotion to the Torah, cited earlier, implies a non-cultic setting.
For the phrase הלך בתורה "walk in the Torah" (v 1) S. Holm-Nielsen (*ST*
14 [1960] 25) compared the change of לכת לפני, "walk before," 1 Kgs 8:25,
to לכת בתורתי, 2 Chr 6:16. Significantly the former phrase is associated with
cultic psalmody (Pss 56:14 [13]; 116:9). It is not possible to give a precise
setting for the psalm beyond locating it in a background of Torah-oriented
wisdom teaching (cf. P. A. Munch, *ZDMG* 90 [1936] 703–10, for an attempted
definition of a precise setting). V 108 suggests primarily oral use for the
psalm. A pronounced feature of Ps 119 is the identification of the Torah,
etc. with wisdom (cf. Sir 24:23), especially in vv 72, 89, 98, as in the other
Torah psalms, and its didactic intent is clear. It has been suggested that it
was composed especially to close a collection of psalms as a counterpart
to Ps 1, in order to provide a framework for an earlier psalter, the implication then being that the psalms are part of God's word to be read
and studied (cf. Hos 14:9) (C. Westermann, *Theologia Viatorum* 8 [1961/62]
280–81).

Explanation

This elaborate acrostic is a literary monument raised in honor of Yahweh's
revelation of himself to Israel. Inspired by Deuteronomy and Proverbs especially, it glories in the תורה or divine pointing out of the way (cf. יהוה הורני
בדך, v 33). "Torah" seems to embrace not only the Pentateuch but also at
least Isaiah and Jeremiah and Proverbs as canonical scriptures in which God
has made known his character and purpose for his people. It is hailed as

Yahweh's communication of moral truth and demonstration of his grace and guidance. The psalm is an artistic pattern of recurring motifs used in conjunction with eight synonymous terms for the Torah. It is both a hymn in praise of the Torah and a prayer expressing man's continuous need of his Master's care. There is no hint of legalism in any of its twenty-two strophes. It breathes a spirit of devotion and celebrates the closest of relationships between the psalmist as "your servant" and Yahweh as "my God." Apart from vv 1–3 and 115, the whole psalm is addressed directly to Yahweh.

The *aleph* strophe contains appreciation and commendation of Israel's revelation-based ethics, using the forms of beatitudes and thanksgiving in vv 1–3, 7. It supplies two reasons for aiming at so high an objective, one of Yahweh's command, v 4, and, via a wish, a subjective one of a blessed life, vv 5–6. V 8 introduces a complaint petition, although v 6 has already broached a wish derived from the complaint. This is the first hint that the author-disciple is no dilettante composing poetry in an ivory tower but caught up in a situation of tension and distress, which he asks Yahweh to resolve with his helping presence.

In the *beth* strophe Yahweh is celebrated as the wisdom teacher par excellence (vv 9, 11, 12b; cf. Prov 7:1). He affirms the joy afforded by preoccupation with his moral teachings, and declares his desire to set his mind on, and to govern his life by, Yahweh's revealed standards. But he confesses that he cannot cope unaided and prays for God's personal help in his moral endeavor. The *gimel* strophe contains a strong element of complaint. Distressing circumstances, specifically persecution, v 23, prompt a double prayer characteristic of the whole psalm, for deliverance and for deeper insight into Yahweh's will for his life revealed in the Torah. A stranger in God's world, who has no natural right to belong there and depends entirely upon God's grace, he needs to learn God's ways (cf. 2 Kgs 17:26–27). He prays out of a strong sense of religious and moral values and a deep love of Yahweh's revelation, but is conscious of the gap between his faith and his spiritual ambition. His life is threatened and weakened, and he craves that fullness of life which is one of the psalm's heartbeats of desire.

The *daleth* strophe continues the complaint with a description of acute stress in vv 25a (cf. 44:26[25]), 28a and with a renewed double prayer. He pleads his loyalty as ground for Yahweh's help (cf. Ps 101 and explanation), but is conscious that only divine enabling can keep him going straight. Stronger ground is the promise of Yahweh's word itself, twice claimed, in vv 25b, 28b. The *he* strophe lends itself naturally to a series of prayers beginning with the causative *he* and so relating to divine working in the human life. Insight, moral guidance and deliverance from social disharmony are prayer themes, with particular emphasis upon a right sense of moral and material values.

There is an emphasis upon testimony among men to God's enabling in the *waw* strophe, in vv 42a, 43, 46. It is part of a double promise, the other part being that of obedience. It is a development of the old promise of praise associated with a complaint. The *zayin* strophe accentuates the comfort the poet has enjoyed in the midst of his suffering (vv 50, 52, cf. 54, 55a). He prefaces it with a prayer, v 49, which is backed with repeated avowals of trust and obedience. Memory too plays a dominant role, both God's and man's. Appreciation of Yahweh, on both an individual and universal level, and prayers (vv 57, 64) frame the *ḥeth* strophe, which is filled out by declarations of obedience and devoted praise.

The *ṭeth* strophe fosters appreciation of aspects of Yahweh's goodness (טוב). His past benefits, his revealed character, the positive value of suffering and the preciousness of the Torah are all themes of praise. The dynamic quality of the Torah is graphically expressed in v 72a: it enables the psalmist to hear the very voice of the living God speaking directly to him. The *yod* strophe begins with a striking prayer for Yahweh to complete his creative work in the individual life by developing his moral understanding of the Torah (v 73; cf. 139:13–16). A concern for the God-fearing community, vv 74, 79, takes the motif of v 63 further.

The complaint theme comes to the fore in the *kaph* strophe. It contains emotional depth expressed in the tearful yearning of vv 81, 82a, the outright questions of vv 82b, 84 and the exclamatory prayer of v 86. The persecuting enemies of vv 84, 86 appear all the blacker against the light of God's revealed character. By the same token his faithfulness shines out all the more, and mention of it serves to urge God to act now in conformity with it. The *lamed* strophe contrasts what stands with what perishes. The stable universe is a visible token of Yahweh's faithfulness. The results of the divine word in its creative and sustaining role are seen in the ordered world, whose order is homage to its Master. V 96 sums up the strophe. On the one hand the scope of God's revelation embraces the universe, for it is the expression of his will; on the other the feebleness of human potential (apart from God) is blatant. Devotion to God's Torah is the only means of sustenance: it is the divinely intended channel of true life. But in addition to its steady infusion of truth and grace, there may be need of direct and dramatic intervention in the believer's life. It is for this that the staccato prayer of v 94a craves.

The *mem* strophe is a quiet interlude without petition, meditating on the Torah as the source of true wisdom (cf. 1 Cor 1:18–25) and singing its praises. The secret of human understanding of it is practical obedience (cf. John 13:17). Yahweh is acclaimed as wisdom teacher via his Torah. V 102b makes clear that it is no do-it-yourself manual which God has handed over to man to use as best he can. It is the written part of a lifelong teach-in.

The *nun* strophe too contains much praise of the Torah, but it is interwoven now with complaint motifs. It is God's torch for a dark path, v 105. The psalmist resolves to observe it at whatever risk because he knows its value as a moral guide to life. The complaint motifs are introduced only to enhance this devotion: come wind, come weather, his determination is all the stronger. The Torah is a whole promised land of joy, and obedience to it brings its own reward. The *samek* strophe begins and (almost) ends with love, that love which is devoid of duplicity and expresses rather the wholehearted commitment of vv 2, 10. The psalmist gives vent to his devotion by means of contrasts: loyalty and treachery, hope of life and doom. His love for God and his revelation is balanced by a sense of the divine wrath. But it is God's power to which he can appeal, that protecting and sustaining power promised to those who ally themselves with God.

The key term of the *'ayin* strophe is עַבְדְּךָ "your servant,'" vv 122, 124, 125. It is used to claim Yahweh's patronage (חַסְד, v 125) in a strophe which is strongly marked by descriptions of a complaint situation. Divine action is implored, vv 124, 126, and the poet ventures to plead that he has done his part in the divine-human relationship, v 121. But help out of distress is not the only need: a petition for Yahweh to teach his Torah is sounded twice.

The *pe* strophe returns to the theme of appreciation of the Torah, vv 129–131, and its non-appreciation by others, v 136. It is the framework for the prayers of vv 132–135, lest the poet succumb to a double enemy, moral wrong and human oppression. Enthusiastic praise of Yahweh and his Torah marks the *ṣade* strophe, which is shot through with references to Yahweh's "righteousness." It prompts a prayer for deeper insight as the basis for a meaningful life. Uniquely life, elsewhere in the psalm contrasted with the stress of persecution, is associated with growth of understanding of the Torah.

The *qoph* strophe reflects strongly a complaint situation. Fervent prayers for assistance are accompanied by the assurance of Yahweh's closeness and the permanence of his revelation to which the psalmist has allied himself. Yahweh's Torah gives the promise of his living presence with the believer. It is doubtless for this reason that earnest early prayer is matched by an even earlier study of the written Torah. The element of complaint petition is intensified in the *resh* strophe, as the psalm draws to a close. Three times comes an appeal for life amidst an aura of death, vv 154, 156, 169. Yahweh's compassion and loyalty are the subject of poignant pleas. But, like the *qoph* strophe, this one concludes on the consoling note of the lasting nature of the Torah. Its permanence, which implicitly reflects Yahweh's own permanence, gives hope to the sufferer that his life will not be cut short.

The *s(h)in* strophe is mainly a prolonged avowal of piety whose function is to back up the appeals of the *resh* strophe. The psalmist realizes that a certain onus rests upon him to be faithful before he can lay claim to Yahweh's faithfulness, and he declares that he has discharged this as ably as he could. He has acted out of a consciousness of the watchful eye of God. The avowals are accompanied by an implicit petition for help. The poet pleads for שָׁלוֹם, the wholeness and peace promised to those who love God's Torah because it manifests God himself.

In the *taw* strophe the gamut of the psalm's concerns are reflected, a double prayer, an avowal of piety and a reference to the situation of complaint. V 175 notably acknowledges that praise is the purpose of life (cf. 115:18), while v 176 poignantly appeals to the Shepherd to rescue the suffering lost sheep. The double prayer of vv 169–70 and the appeal to Yahweh's "rulings" or judicial intervention illustrate the two poles of the psalm. At one end stands the revealed Torah, and it is for insight into this that the psalmist prays so that he may fulfill Yahweh's moral will in his life. At the other stands the hope of divine providential intervention, and for this too he prays out of his distress. The dual manifestation of God is itself bridged by the Torah's examples and promises of aid to the faithful. The psalmist is in the center, communing with God through the fellowship of prayer and looking this way with the eyes of faith and that way with the eyes of hope. From this double stance the same living God both manifests himself through the written revelation and can be expected to manifest himself through the providential overruling of adversity in the believer's life.

At first sight the natural heirs of Ps 119 are rabbinic Judaism and the more Judaistically oriented NT books of Matthew and James. But the formula "as it is written," which runs all through the NT, and especially the fruit of OT study evident in the writings of Paul illustrate the kinship of the solidly OT-based Christian writers with the spirit of Ps 119. There is the same concern with God's past written revelation and its moral and doctrinal standards. There is a similar hope fixed upon God in a context of opposition. Rightly understood, the psalm is a precursor of the finest flowering of both Judaism and the Christian faith.

The Irksomeness of Life   (120:1–7)

Bibliography

Brekelmans, C. H. W. "Some Translation Problems. Judges 5:29, Psalm 120:7, Jona 4:4, 9." *OTS* 15 (1969) 170–76. **Keet, C. C.** *A Study of the Psalms of Ascents. A Critical and Exegetical Commentary upon Psalms 120–134.* London: Mitre Press, 1969. **Seybold, K.** *Die Wallfahrtspsalmen. Studien zur Entstehungsgeschichte von Psalm 120–134.* Biblische-Theologische Studien 3. Neukirchen-Vluyn: Neukirchener Verlag, 1978. ———. "Die Redaktion der Wallfahrtspsalmen." *ZAW* 91 (1979) 247–68.

Translation

[1] One of the processional songs.[a]
To Yahweh in my distress [b]   (3+2)
I called—and he has answered me [c]—
[2] "Yahweh, rescue me   (3+2+2)
from lying lips,
from slanderous tongue." [a]
[3] What will you get from him   (3+2+2)
and what else will you get,[a]
slanderous tongue? [b]
[4] A warrior's sharpened arrows [a]   (3+2)
with brands of broom.[b]

[5] How wretched [a] I have been, lodging in Meshech,[b]   (3+3)
living among Kedar's tents.
[6] I have had enough of living [a]   (3+2)
among those who hate [b] peace.
[7] And for my part though I speak peaceably,[a]   (3+2)
they for their part [b] want war. [c]

Notes/Comments

1.a. Pss 120–134 form a collection of cultic songs of diverse origins, probably sung by pilgrims in festival processions: see the excursus after the commentary on Ps 134. Probably the psalm title was originally the title of the whole collection and was subsequently applied to the individual psalms (cf. GKC § 127e). The collective singular שִׁיר "song" (cf. 137:3) was then related to single psalms within the collection. The consequent awkward phrasing was improved in the heading to Ps 121.

1.b. For צָרָתָה "distress" see GKC § 90g. K. Seybold (*ZAW* 91 [1979] 259) relates the ending to the Aramaic emphatic state. The penultimate accentuation, well attested rhythmically in similar forms elsewhere, renders this explanation unlikely.

1.c. H. Gunkel (*Die Psalmen*, 538) *et al.* (cf. RSV) repoint to וְיַעֲנֵנִי and take the preceding verb as present in sense: "I call so that he may answer me." See *Form/Structure/Setting*.

2.a. MT employs an appositional construction here and in v 3 by pointing לָשׁוֹן "tongue"; cf. GKC § 131c. More usual would be a construct form לְשׁוֹן, attested by α' in v 3. It is possible that רְמִיָּה "slander" represents an adjective (Gunkel, *Psalmen*, 538): cf. post-biblical Heb. and Aram. רַמָּאִי. In that case לָךְ in v 3a would need to be pointed as a feminine לָךְ. Gunkel *et al.* delete the phrase here as a dittograph of v 3, while Seybold (*Wallfahrtspsalmen* 33) tentatively suggests that מִשְּׂפַת שֶׁקֶר "from lying lips" may be secondary. H.-J. Kraus (*Psalmen*, 1007) has defended the present length of text by observing that metrically the line matches v 3.

3.a. Underlying the question is the common formula of self-imprecation, particularly in the form found at 2 Sam 3:9 כֹּה יַעֲשֶׂה אֱלֹהִים לְאַבְנֵר וְכֹה יֹסִיף לוֹ "Thus will God do to Abner and thus will he add to him." Here מַה . . . וּמַה and the repeated preposition correspond to the doubled כֹּה and preposition. The first verb is varied to יִתֵּן "he will give" so as to prepare for the object nouns of v 4. The echoing of the formula which has a divine subject suggests that the verbs be so understood here. A repointing as passive forms (cf. *BHS*) is unnecessary. Gunkel (*Die Psalmen*, 538) who construed the verbs as indefinite active forms, claimed that a third person divine reference was unlikely after the direct address of v 2: see *Form/Structure/Setting*.

3.b. For the poetic address of the slanderous enemy or enemies cf. 52:6 (4).

4.a. The reference to weapons presupposes their metaphorical usage for slander, as in 52:4 (2); 57:5 (4); Jer 9:2, 7 (3, 8). Cf. especially 64:4, 8 (3, 7), where arrows of divine retribution are promised to arrowlike words.

4.b. The hard wood of the white broom, *Retama raetam*, was used for charcoal. Its lasting heat evidently made it a good incendiary weapon. For firebrands cf. 7:14; Isa 50:11.

5.a. Heb. אוֹיָה, elsewhere אוֹי, has been compared by Seybold (*ZAW* 91 [1979] 259 note 66) with Akk. *ūʾa*, *ūʾi*, *ayyi* "woe."

5.b. The juxtaposition of Meshech and Kedar is difficult. The nation of Meshech was located in the far north in the OT. Assyrian references place it northeast of Cilicia and east of Cappadocia, while according to Herodotus it was southeast of the Black Sea. Kedar in the OT is an eastern tribe of Arab nomadic herdsmen associated with the Syro-Arabian desert. Gunkel, following J. Halévy and H. Winckler, cut the geographical knot by emending מֶשֶׁךְ "Meshech" to מַשָּׂא "Massa," mentioned in Gen 25:14 as a son of Ishmael in association with Kedar (*Die Psalmen*, 539). Less drastically Seybold (*Wallfahrtspsalmen*, 36) has noted מֶשֶׁךְ in 1 Chr 1:17 as a counterpart to מַשׁ (Samaritan מֶשֶׁךְ) in Gen 10:23, as a son of Aram, while in Gen 25:13–14; 1 Chr 1:29–30 Kedar and מַשָּׂא are both sons of Ishmael. Accordingly he regards מֶשֶׁךְ here as one of a number of variant forms of name for an ethnic group in the same region as Kedar. However, מֶשֶׁךְ in 1 Chr 1:17 is more probably a textual error by assimilation to the name in 1:5 (W. Rudolph, *Chronikbücher* [HAT 21; Tübingen: J. C. B. Mohr (Paul Siebeck), 1955] 6). M. Dahood (*Psalms III*, 197) can accommodate deliberate geographical extremes by taking כִּי "that" as conditional: "Even were he to reside as far away as Meshech and Kedar, the psalmist would still feel too close to the hater of peace." But the standard OT usage of כִּי after אוֹי is to describe the deplored situation.

The most common interpretation is to judge the ethnic references to be simply metaphorical: the psalmist's enemies are no better than hostile barbarians (e.g. A. Weiser, *Psalms*, 743; A. A. Anderson, *Psalms*, 850). Then v 6 describes literally what v 5 describes picturesquely. In favor of this interpretation is the association with military power which both states have in the OT (Meshech, Ezek 32:26; 38:2–4; 39:1–3; Kedar, Isa 21:16, 17), which suits well the military metaphors of vv 4, 7.

6.a. Cf. Deut 1:6 רב לכם שבת "you have stayed long enough." Heb. רבת appears to be an Aramaism (GKC, 80f).

6.b. There is much textual support for reading a plural שׁוֹנֵאִי (cf. *BHS*): the singular in MT may well have resulted from scribal abbreviation (after עם-גחלי and עם-אהלי; cf. G. R. Driver, *Textus* 1 [1960] 114–16). Contextually vv 5, 7 seem to require a plural. But the singular could be collective in force. Dahood (*Psalms III*, 198) retains the singular as part of a characteristic shift to and from the plural in passionate complaints, and identifies with the singular of v 3.

7.a. Heb. אני שלום "I (am) peace" has probably been pushed forward in the clause for emphasis, and כי is to be regarded as concessive. C. H. W. Brekelmans (*OTS* 15 [1969] 174–75) and Dahood (*Psalms III*, 198) regard וכי as two emphatic elements. Gunkel (*Die Psalmen*, 539), following Halévy, H. Schmidt (*Die Psalmen*, 220), Kraus (*Psalmen*, 1007), *et al.* read וכן for וכי "(speak peace) and truth" (cf. Exod 10:29). Their metrical analysis of the line as 2+2+2 is a consequence of this emendation.

7.b. The note in *BHS* relating to המה "G δωρεάν = חנם" is doubly doubtful. In LXX המה is obviously represented by αὐτοῖς, as its order of words suggests. Gk. δωρεάν appears to have originated in an explanatory gloss attached to ἐπολέμουν με, prompted by 108 (109):3 καὶ ἐπολέμησάν με δωρεάν. The gloss was encouraged by the similarity of 119 (120): 3 γλῶσσαν δολίαν to 108 (109):2 γλῶσσα δολία. The dissimilarity of MT at both points locates the expansion firmly within the Greek tradition.

7.c. The force of the ל is to express the aim and object (cf. BDB 515a). Dahood (*Psalms III*, 198; cf. Brekelmans, *OTS* 15 [1969] 174–75) may be correct in regarding it as an emphatic *lamed*, repointing to לְמִלחמה and understanding a verb from v 7a: "but they (speak) only war."

Form/Structure/Setting

Determination of both the form and background of Ps 120 is hampered by difficulty in assessing its time perspective and degree of metaphor. If the psalm began at v 2 it could be simply classified as the complaint of an individual. A petition for divine aid against slanderous enemies (v 2) and a description of his distress together with an assertion of innocence (vv 5–7) are clear elements of a complaint. Gunkel (*Die Psalmen*, 538–39) observed that the exclamation of woe (אויה . . . כי, v 5: cf. Jer 10:19; Lam 5:16, etc.) and the expression רבת (v 6: cf. 123:4; 129:1, 2) belong to this form. Vv 3–4 may be regarded as an assertion of confident trust in Yahweh's vindication of the psalmist by punishing his foes.

But how may the first line be harmonized with the rest of the psalm? Gunkel did so by reconstruing its verbs (see *Notes/Comments*). A frequent expedient is to interpret it as an encouraging reference to answered prayer in the context of a previous situation of distress (e.g. C. C. Keet, *Psalms of Ascents*, 18; Dahood, *Psalms III*, 195, 196). As v 1aβ–b stands in MT it is characteristic of an individual thanksgiving. Most probably the whole psalm is to be classified thus (D. Michel, *Tempora*, 17). Kraus (*Psalmen*, 1008), Weiser (*Psalms*, 742), Anderson (*Psalms*, 848), Seybold (*Wallfahrtspsalmen*, 54) *et al.* regard vv 2–7 as a long quotation from a previous complaint, the answer to which the psalmist is now celebrating. However, if Yahweh is the subject of the verbs of v 3, as seems most likely, the change from the second person reads awkwardly after v 2, unless it reverts deliberately to the style of v 1. In that case vv 3–4 are to be understood as a thanksgiving element rather than a complaint one. The precise form of the psalm appears to be a thanksgiving for heard prayer rather than for a transformed situation. The situation remains the same, but the psalmist has received priestly assurance that Yahweh has heard his prayer, and for this he gives thanks. The circumstances are then those of 6:9–11 (8–10) after the complaint of 6:2–8 (1–7), where the psalmist bids his enemies leave him alone since Yahweh has heard his prayer, and confidently asserts their coming downfall. In similar vein the enemy or enemies are addressed in v 3 and their prospect of receiving their just deserts is proclaimed in vv 3–4. But the situation of distress materially, if not religiously and psychologically, remains unchanged. Thus vv 5–7 are an implicit appeal for Yahweh to act in accordance with his promise delivered from the sanctuary, reminding him of the dire circumstances of his personal environment. These verses are not simply a quotation from an earlier complaint but represent a plight which but for the implementation of the divine assurance still awaits him on return from the sanctuary.

The psalm has a disjointed ring on first reading. What is the formal connection between references to slander or false accusation—a standard motif of complaint—in vv 2–4, to foreigners in v 5 and to war and peace in vv 6–7? The harmony of the first and last motifs may easily be established. In Ps 35:20 speaking peace is contrasted with conceiving words of deceit, while in Ps 27:3 war is a metaphor for an extreme of slandering enmity (27:2). It is probable that v 5 is to be subordinated to this general background, especially as it is linked closely with v 6, so that it describes metaphorically the hostility of his neighbors, who behave like powerful foreign enemies, shooting verbal arrows (cf. Isa 21:17; Ezek 39:3) which are to be requited by a divine onslaught (v 4).

Seybold (*Wallfahrtspsalmen*, 54) tentatively recreates a precise background concerning a soldier accused of treason while fighting alongside Bedouin mercenaries. Taking אדבר "I speak" in v 7 as forensic, as in 127:5, he describes the cultic setting in terms of attendance at the temple for a divine verdict upon the charges, and associates the psalm with the entrance procedure at the temple gate. He clearly has the claim of innocence of v 7 in mind, but in fact for Seybold this belongs to the report of complaint contained in an overall thanksgiving, rather than specifically to the setting of the thanksgiving psalm as a whole. He appears to be straining to detect some relevance for the psalm in its position at the head of a series of pilgrim songs (cf. *Wallfahrtspsalmen*, 70).

The particular relevance for the psalm's eventual incorporation into a manual of processional songs for pilgrims seems to lie in a re-interpretation of v 5. It became a vehicle for the homesickness of devout expatriate Jews. Their place of residence in various parts of the Diaspora was no home away from home (גרתי "sojourned as an alien," v 5) and they knew from bitter experience the hostility of xenophobic neighbors. Before its inclusion in the collection its composition was probably already comparatively late in view of רבת in v 6 (and possibly רמיה, v 2: see *Notes/Comments*).

E. J. Kissane (*Psalms II*, 244) divided the psalm into an introductory first line and two strophes of three lines, vv 2–4 citing past prayer and vv 5–7 describing past distress. His exegetical interpretation of content was used as the main criterion of structure. There are, however, clear stylistic pointers to strophical structure. In vv 1, 5 לי (־ָה) and in vv 2, 6 נפשי are corresponding repetitions. The weapons of v 4 match "war" in v 7. These factors are signs of two strophes, vv 1–4 (four lines) and 5–7 (three lines). The first strophe is made up of two pairs of lines, united by the repeated "slanderous tongue." The prayer of v 2 is answered in v 1, and the question of v 3 in v 4. The two halves of the psalm are skillfully linked by the repetition of v 4's עם "with" and plural construct form in v 5 (and probably orginally in v 6). In the second strophe the presence of כי in vv 5, 7 provides inclusion. The second strophe is made up of a pair of lines and a single line. It is introduced by the exclamation of woe, explained in the rest of the strophe. Its intense "I—they" polarity is brought to a climax in v 7. An overall feature of the psalm is steplike repetition in vv 2–3 and 5–6 and 6–7.

Explanation

A worshiper has earlier poured out his complaint in the temple and been blessed with a priestly oracle assuring him that Yahweh has heard his prayer (cf. 6:9–10 [8–9]; 85:9 [8]). Eventually no doubt he would return to the sanctuary to render full thanksgiving for actual deliverance from the situation of distress which he left at home. But now his voice rings out in an interim thanksgiving for the assurance that God has heard his prayer and will solve his problem. For the encouragement of his fellow-worshipers he testifies to his personal experience of Yahweh as a God who listens to prayer.

His problem lay in the area of social relationships and concerned his acceptance in the community. He was the victim of lying and misrepresentation. He had suffered from slander, probably from one individual in particular. He had doubtless come to the sanctuary cowed and dispirited by these attacks. Now he is emboldened by God's promise of vindication. He trustingly accepts that promise and anticipates his rehabilitation in the community through the exercise of divine justice.

His persecutor had taken upon his lips the self-cursing formula of asseveration—and sworn a lie. He had staked his life upon his victim's culpability and fate with the terrible words of self-destruction: "God do so to me and more . . ." (cf. 1 Kgs 2:23). The tormentor must bear the destruction which he had called down upon himself, now that his victim has been liberated by the divine word of the sanctuary. Truth and justice are at stake. The God whom the persecutor had glibly invoked as guardian of these basic social virtues would act in favor of the suppliant. Arrows and firebrands of divine doom would be fitting reprisal for wounding words, the missiles of vindictive slander.

The psalmist has been speaking with the confidence of faith in God's recent promise to him. He turns in vv 5–7 to describe his life situation in an implicit prayer that the divine word will come true there. He has been treated like an enemy, like someone who does not belong to the community. It has been as if he lived among hostile foreigners equipped and ready to attack and wound. He pleads his own positive and peaceful overtures. A dove among hawks, he has had no success in restoring harmony, but only suffered unmitigated aggression. He has done what he could (cf. Rom 12:18). God alone can change the situation. Bolstered and armed with the divine word of support, he would go back hoping and trusting that the situation would be resolved to the glory of God.

The psalm hovers between divine promise and fulfilment, like so much of the Bible. Joy and sorrow are poignantly intermingled, equally valid and as yet unresolved. The virtues of truth and honor within God's community and the outworking of justice as God's will for his people are the ideals which this psalm celebrates. The divine pledge of support for the victimized, which characterizes so much of the law and prophets, shines out afresh over the life of an individual believer.

The original psalm received added meaning when it was selected to open a collection of pilgrim songs. Superficially it was transformed, but it brought its deeper significance intact through the transformation. For Jews of the Diaspora, who lived far from home and temple, it came to express their renewed conviction that the God of Israel was on their side and would give resources to cope with the hostility of foreign neighbors. They came as pilgrims, weary of life's struggles. Their coming to the sanctuary brought them renewal of hope and courage to live as God's people in an alien land. This broadening of the psalm's applicability prepared the way for the NT people of God to inherit it in turn (cf. 1 Pet 1:1–2; 2:11–12).

Able to Keep (121:1–8)

Bibliography

Eissfeldt, O. "Psalm 121." *Stat crux, dum volvitur orbis.* H. Lilje Festschrift, ed. G. Hoffmann and K. H. Rengstorf. Berlin: Lutherisches Verlagshaus, 1959. **Morgenstern, J.** "Psalm 121." *JBL* 58 (1939) 311–23. **Rasker, A. J.** "Psalm 121." *Herr, tue meine Lippen auf,* ed. G. Eicholz. vol. 5. 2nd ed. Wuppertal-Barmen: Emil Müller Verlag, 1961, 76–84. **Volz, P.** "Zur Auslegung von Ps. 23 und 121." *NKZ* 36 (1925) 576–85. **Weir, T. H.** "Psalm 121:1." *ExpTim* 27 (1915/16) 90–91.

Translation

[1] One of the processional songs: [a]
  I look up to the mountains [b]   (3+3)
    to see where my help is to come from.
[2] *The source of my help* [a] *is Yahweh,*   (3+3)
    maker of heaven and earth. [b]

[3] *He will not* [a] *let your foot stumble;* [b]   (3+2)
    your guardian will not slumber.
[4] *Of course,* [a] *no slumber,*   (2+2+2)
    no sleeping [b]
    marks Israel's guardian. [c]
[5] *Yahweh is your guardian,*   (2+2+2)
    Yahweh is your protection [a]
    at your right hand.

[6] *By day the sun will not strike you*   (3+2)
    nor the moon [a] *by night.*

⁷ *Yahweh will guard you*   (2+2+2)
   from all danger.
   he will guard your life.
⁸ *Yahweh will guard*   (2+2+2)
   your going and coming ᵃ
   henceforth for evermore.

Notes/Comments

1.a. See the note on 120:1. Heb. לְמַעֲלוֹת "processional," unique in the headings to Pss 120–34, probably serves to clarify the indeterminate nature of the construct form שִׁיר "a song": cf. GKC § 129c.

1.b. The exegetical value of הרים "mountains" has been variously assessed according to the interpretation of the psalm as a whole. Those who relate the mountains to a journey, implied in vv 3, 6, 8, often interpret negatively as a source of danger, referring to the mountainous terrain around Jerusalem (H.-J. Kraus, *Psalmen*, 1013) or on the journey from Jerusalem to the pilgrim's home (A. Weiser, *Psalms*, 746; A. A. Anderson, *Psalms*, 852) or on any desert journey (J. Morgenstern, *JBL* 58 [1939] 316). S. Mowinckel (*Psalmenstudien*, vol. 5, 48) and H. Gunkel (*Die Psalmen*, 540), following A. B. Ehrlich, understood in a negative cultic sense: הרים refers to mountain sanctuaries dedicated to different gods, in contrast to the true God of v 2.

Others give a positive value to the term, P. Volz (*NKZ* 36 [1925] 584) interpreted as heavenly heights, while O. Eissfeldt ("Psalm 121," 13) has related it more implicitly to heaven, where God is enthroned, above the mountains (cf. 123:1). M. Dahood (*Psalms III*, 200) finds a divine title of Yahweh analogous to צוּר "rock." C. A. and E. G. Briggs (*Psalms II*, 446) *et al.* have seen a positive cultic reference, to the mountains of Jerusalem (87:1; cf. perhaps 110:3). N. C. Habel (*JBL* 91 [1972] 328–29) has discovered contextual support for this interpretation in the cultic formulation closely associated with Jerusalem which appears in v 2b, so that vv 1–2 are consistent in their use of traditional Zion language. Then הרים refers to the cosmic mountain(s) on which Yahweh dwells: cf. 48:1–3; 87:1–3 and the reference to the sanctuary of Zion as the source of divine help in 20:3 (2).

A key factor in determining the meaning is the relation of the two cola of the line. The erroneous interpretation of מֵאַיִן "from where" as a relative (Jerome, Luther, KJV) encouraged a positive cultic interpretation of הרים. When it is construed as introducing a direct question, a contrast tends to be seen between the cola, which forces a negative connotation upon the term. But there is a third possibility, that v 1b represents an indirect question (T. H. Weir, *ExpTim* 27 [1915/16] 191; P. Joüon, *Grammaire* § 161g). Comparison with Gen 8:8; 27:21; Josh 2:4; Judg 13:6 demonstrates the feasibility of this suggestion; its congruence with Habel's terminological research serves to confirm it. Thus exegesis moves back to a point close to an earlier one which was grammatically unfounded but perhaps instinctively not distant from the truth.

2.a. The suffix presents difficulty. In the light of the confident vv 3–8, v 2 could well be regarded as initiating an answer to the question of v 1, given by another voice. Gunkel (*Die Psalmen*, 541), following K. Budde, and H. Schmidt (*Die Psalmen*, 221) emended to עֶזְרֶךָ "your help," as part of a conjectural reconstruction of dialogue in which vv 1 and 3, where רַגְלִי "my foot" and שֹׁמְרִי "my guardian" were read, were spoken by one voice and vv 2, 4, 5–8 by another. More simply Weiser (*Psalms*, 744) and Anderson (*Psalms*, 852) emend to a suffix-less עֵזֶר "help," not unreasonably explaining MT as assimilated to the form of v 1 and the original text as the expression of a general truth. The stance of Kraus (*Psalmen*, 1013) is attractive: keeping MT, he regards it as the personal testimony of a priest who speaks throughout vv 2–8. But since there are clear structural indications that a break occurs after v 2, not before, (see *Form/Structure/Setting*), the first person suffix is not only to be retained but must be equated with that of v 1, exegetically difficult though it may be.

2.b. For this epithet associated with the ancient cultic traditions of Jerusalem see Habel, *JBL* 91 (1972) 321–37.

3.a. G. R. Driver ("Isaiah I–XXXIX: Textual and Linguistic Problems," *JSS* 13 [1968] 37), followed by NEB, claimed that אל could be rendered "how?" Its usual lexical meaning as introducing a negative wish, upheld by Weiser (*Psalms*, 744), is possible in v 3a, but hardly so in v 3b in the light of v 4. Commentators generally appeal to GKC § 107p, 109e as evidence that it may introduce a negative statement as a subjective conviction or simply add emphasis (cf. Joüon, *Grammaire* § 114k; *HALAT*, 46b).

3.b. Lit. "give to stumbling." MT's article here and in 66:9 apparently safeguards a conviction that מוט functions as a noun. *BHS*'s counsel to read an infinitive לָמֹוט is rendered uncertain by the similar construction of וּלְמֹוט לא נתני in 118:18.

4.a. Heb. הנה "of course" calls attention to a fact upon which an asserted truth or conclusion is based (BDB, 243b, 244a).

4.b. Contrast the appeal to Yahweh to "awake" in complaints (7:7 [6]; 35:23; 44:24 [23]; 59:6 [5]) as a metaphor for inactivity.

4.c. Weiser (*Psalms*, 748) and Anderson (*Psalms*, 853) find reference to the Heilsgeschichte, the tradition of Yahweh's lordship over the nation's history. In that case C. Westermann's general statement is relevant, that "God's saving cannot be separated from his blessing; both are constantly interlocked and combined with each other" (*What does the OT Say about God?* [Atlanta: John Knox Press, 1979] 52). Kraus (*Psalmen*, 1014) notes the relevance of Yahweh's collective relationship with Israel for the individual and compares the individualization of the covenantal concept of the shepherd in Ps 23.

5.a. Heb. צל, literally "shade," is used as a metaphor for protection: cf. Num 14:9; Jer 48:45; Lam 4:20. It serves too as a transition to the theme of v 6.

5.b. Divine protection is signified: cf. 110:5.

6.a. The baleful effect of the moon was widely held in the ancient Near East: cf. Matt 4:24; 17:15 σεληνιάζεσθαι "be moon-struck."

8.a. The pair of verbs refers to daily work as primarily consisting of going out of the town to work in the fields and returning in the evening (cf. Deut 28:6; 31:2; Josh 14:11). Here there is possibly also a nuance of going back from worship to daily life and in due course returning to the sanctuary at the time of the next festival (cf. Deut 23:2–4 [1–3]).

Form/Structure/Setting

The elucidation of the form and setting of Ps 121 depends upon the interpretation of its personal pronouns and in particular the change from first to second person. Does the psalm represent a true dialogue—or is it simply a monologue enhanced by the literary trappings of a dialogue whereby an individual is really speaking to himself? The latter position has been held by a number of scholars, including Morgenstern (*JBL* 58 [1939] 323). Appeal is generally made to Pss 42/43 as a parallel, but it is difficult to substantiate a self-address without an explicit נפשי "my soul, self" in the text (for 27:14 see Kraus, *Psalmen*, 370, who explains as a priestly oracle, and also J. H. Eaton, *Psalms*, 87).

If the psalm contains a true dialogue, various options still remain. Volz (*NKZ* 36 [1925] 583–84) viewed the psalm as a father's blessing upon his son who is bound for Jerusalem as a pilgrim. But the text itself does not specify the nature or destination of the journey. K. Seybold (*Wallfahrtspsalmen*, 55, 69) follows Volz so as to give a coherent reason for the psalm's early positioning in a collection of pilgrim songs. More commonly the psalm is interpreted as a cultic dialogue between a pilgrim and a priest. Typical of this position is Kraus (*Psalmen*, 1012), who, inspired by Mowinckel (*Psalmenstudien*, vol. 5, 48–50) and Gunkel (*Die Psalmen*, 541), characterizes it as a farewell liturgy, with the major priestly contribution consisting formally of a blessing with overtones of an oracle of salvation (cf. Ps 91). Certainly the statements of vv 3–8 are in the nature of promises rather than in that of the wishes of a customary benediction, though the contents suit a benediction. Weiser (*Psalms*, 746) has pointed to the liturgical and solemn ring of the answer. Habel's discussion of the cultic nature of the language of vv 1–2 lends further support. A variant interpretation within this cultic designation is that of H. Schmidt, who judged the psalm to be rather an entrance liturgy (*Die Psalmen*,

222; cf. 118:26). J. W. Rogerson and J. W. McKay (*Psalms 101–150*, 115) leave open the issue whether a greeting or parting blessing features in the psalm. The content of the blessing, whether referring to a journey or to everyday life, appears to suit better a final blessing. The similarity of the first line of the concluding Aaronic blessing of Num 6:24–26 (ישמרך . . . "and keep you") to the psalm's theme of divine keeping confirms this judgment (cf. L. J. Liebreich, *JBL* 74 [1955] 35, who regarded the psalm as an exposition of ישמרך). Yet other refinements of a cultic interpretation are that of Eaton (*Psalms*, 280; *Kingship*, 83) and Dahood (*Psalms III*, 199), that a representative of Israel receives blessing on behalf of the people (cf. Mowinckel's view that vv 1–4 comprise a prayer of the community, in *Psalmenstudien*, vol. 5, 48–49), and that of Eissfeldt ("Psalm 121," 12–13), that a convert to Yahwism is encouraged by a priest to continue steadfast in his new faith. The psalm is often regarded as post-exilic in origin, but there are no internal indications of its date.

Structurally the psalm is marked by inclusive elements, the repetition of the stem בוא "come" in vv 1, 8 and the double appearance of the preposition מן "from" in both vv 1–2 and 7–8. The strophical divisions of the psalm appear to be vv 1–2, 3–5 and 6–8, an introductory strophe of two lines and then two of three lines each. The meter of the first (3+3) is differentiated from the double series of 3+2, 2+2+2, 2+2+2 in the second and third. V 7 is not to be scanned as 3+2 with Gunkel (*Die Psalmen*, 539) and Kraus (*Psalmen*, 1011): cf. Dahood, *Psalms III*, 202. The divine name occurs twice at the ends of the paired strophes, the second and third (vv 5, 7, 8. יהוה is not to be deleted in v 8 with 11QPsª *pace BHS*), and once near the end of the first (v 2). The triple participles of שמר "guardian" in the second (vv 3, 4, 5) are matched by its triple imperfect forms in the third (vv 6, 7, 8). In the first line of the third strophe the explicit reference to day and night probably corresponds to the implicit timing of the first line of the second (vv 3, 6). Five second person suffixes occur in the second strophe and a further five in the third. In the second, two negative lines precede a single positive line; the third, appropriately more affirmative by way of climax, has one negative line followed by two positive ones. Step-parallelism occurs in all three strophes, at vv 1, 2, 3, 4, 7, 8. Both the first and the third end with cultic formulations. In the light of the evidence of a finely structured network of strophes it is difficult to agree with Seybold that vv 4 and 7 be regarded as secondary (*Wallfahrtspsalmen*, 33, 61, 63, 88).

The particular role of the psalm within a subsequent collection of processional songs must remain uncertain. Antiphonal singing was probably maintained, perhaps in a choral setting. The psalm would fit the conclusion of a festival, but it was not necessarily so used. Its positioning near the beginning of the collection need have no special significance.

Explanation

In the first two verses of the psalm an individual believer speaks out of the devotion of his heart. His faith has been quickened and fed by participation in the festival worship of the temple. He knows both the helplessness of standing alone in life and the true, divine source of the help he needs in order to face life in the everyday world to which he will shortly be returning. The festival is nearly over, and it is only here in this sacred mountain place of revelation and worship that he may find the key to coping with workaday life. Here in Zion, where traditionally Yahweh was acclaimed as "maker of heaven and earth," he has rediscovered that the whole world lies in his hands. Responding with renewed faith to this God's claims upon himself, he has learned the corollary of God's care amid the concerns of daily life.

His insight is endorsed by a solemn voice speaking with religious authority in vv 3–8. The content of the confirmatory message is akin to the priestly blessing bestowed at the conclusion of worship (Num 6:24–26); but in form it is closer to a report of a divine oracle. It does not simply express powerful wishes evoking divine blessing, but carries the stronger tones of certain promise of such blessing. The individual worshiper has learned aright the relevance of his worship to the rest of life, but he is graciously given a powerful word to take home in confirmation of his personal faith.

In all the paths of life he is promised the ever-vigilant protection of God (cf. 91:11, 12). The covenant bonds between Yahweh and the community of Israel include within their scope the individual member of that community. Israel's experience of salvation throughout its existence may be mirrored in the Israelite's life. The constant presence of God, ever living, never sleeping, would ward off the threats which beset his daily course. The blazing sun and the sinister moon feature as polar examples of the many vicissitudes which fill the mind with fears both rational and irrational and stop life fulfilling its positive potential. Day and night Yahweh stands guard (vv 3, 6). Life is so full of dangers, but Yahweh's help is a match for them all. He is well able to keep his own safe in his loving care. As the believer walks in step with the rhythms which make up daily life and represent the providential ordering of human existence (cf. 104:23), he may do so with the assurance that God is with him in his daily toil and rest, ever helping and protecting.

So the pilgrim is bidden Godspeed and leaves with the repeated drumbeats of the message, "Yahweh guards," resounding in his ears. He leaves the sacred place of Yahweh's special presence, assured nevertheless that Yahweh goes with him. The potent promise, "I will be with you," avails not only for heroes of the faith such as a Moses or a Joshua, but passes in turn to ordinary believers from villages up and down the land and from abroad. As they are sent back into the world to live and work, they may have the assurance that the Lord of the world is their escort and they live out their post-festival lives under his care.

It is easy to cavil at such psalms as this and Ps 91. The particularity of biblical religion here especially comes to the fore with an appearance of scandalous presumption. In practical terms life cushioned from all unpleasantness was never the lot of the Israelite, any more than it has been that of the Christian. But believers in any age hear this message deep in their hearts and are encouraged thereby to bear the heat and burden of the day and to sleep with contentment. God's servants may entrust their lives to him as to a faithful Creator and derive strength from the knowledge that the peace of God keeps their hearts and minds (Phil 4:7; 2 Tim 4:18; 1 Pet 4:19).

Jerusalem the Golden   (122:1-9)

Bibliography

Jeremias, J. "Lade und Zion." *Probleme biblischer Theologie,* ed. H. W. Wolff. München: C. Kaiser, 1971. **Schreiner, J.** *Sion-Jerusalem Jahwes Königssitz.* SANT 7. München: Kösel-Verlag, 1963. **Wolff, H. W.** "Psalm 122." *Herr, tue meine Lippen auf,* ed. G. Eichholz. vol. 5. 2nd ed. Wuppertal-Barmen: Emil Müller Verlag, 1961.

Translation

[1] One of the processional songs.[a] Davidic.[b]

I was so pleased with [c] *those who said to me*	(3+2)
"We will go to the temple of Yahweh." [d]	
[2] *Our feet are standing* [a]	(3+2)
within your gates, [b] *Jerusalem—*	
[3] *Jerusalem, built* [a] *as a city should be,* [b]	(3+2)
closely compact, [c]	
[4] *where the tribes go up,*	(3+2)
the tribes of Yah(weh).	
It is stipulated that Israel should give thanks	(3+2)
to Yahweh's name.	
[5] *There* [a] *sits* [b]	(2+2+3)
the tribunal of justice,	
the tribunal of the Davidic court—	
[6] *Pray for Jerusalem's peace:* [a]	(3+2)
"May those who love you [b] *prosper securely.* [c]	
[7] *May peace lie within your ramparts,*	(3+2)
secure prosperity within your citadels."	
[8] *For my brothers' and neighbors' sakes* [a]	(3+2)
I say: "Peace be within you." [b]	
[9] *For the sake of the temple of Yahweh our God*	(3+2)
I will seek your good.	

Notes/Comments

1.a. See the note on 120:1.

1.b. Two Heb. mss, the oldest text of LXX and *Tg.* lack the royal annotation. That the psalm was composed by David is not to be deduced: it is spoken by a visitor to Jerusalem (vv 1–2) and presupposes the existence of the temple. V 5 probably inspired the annotation, which may then be taken as "concerning the Davidic king." J. H. Eaton (*Psalms,* 281) has suggested that the psalm was regarded as an indirect intercession for the dynasty.

1.c. H. Gunkel (*Die Psalmen,* 543) *et al.* read בְּאׇמְרׅם "when they said" (cf. EVV). MT refers to a source of joy (C. C. Keet, *Psalms of Ascents,* 31; cf. BDB, 970a).

1.d. For this standard invitation to pilgrimage cf. 1 Sam 11:14; Isa 2:3; Jer 31:6.

2.a. Either a past (cf. GKC § 116r) or present reference may be intended here, as in the cases of עלו "go up" and ישבו "sit" in vv 4–5. D. Michel (*Tempora*, 242) is probably correct in judging that a present significance is intended in all three instances. For the use of the perfect of the verb היה "to be" in direct speech in a stative sense to refer to a situation which arose in the past and persists into present time cf. G. S. Ogden, "Time and the Verb היה in OT Prose," *VT* 21 (1971] 453 and Gen 42:11, 31.

2.b. LXX "courts" need not presuppose a Heb. בחצרין *pace BHS*. In the book of Esther αὐλή is the standard rendering for שער "gate." LXX may have been influenced by Aram. תרע "gate, court" (cf. Dan 2:49 MT LXX θ').

3.a. Heb. בנויה is interpreted as "rebuilt" by some, including Keet (*Psalms of Ascents*, 32) and K. Seybold (*Wallfahrtspsalmen*, 39, 40, 88).

3.b. The force of the *kaph* is uncertain. It is best taken as a *kaph veritatis* (BDB, 454a; cf. R. Gordis, *JAOS* 63 [1943] 177).

3.c. LXX σ' Hier imply (ש)חֶבְרָה "sharing, participation," apparently referring to fellowship enjoyed by the pilgrims. A. Weiser (*Psalms* [1962] 750) adopts this reading, loosely rendering the phrase "where the assembly of the people meets." B. Duhm (*Psalmen*, 271) and H. W. Wolff ("Psalm 122," 108) also emend לה to לנו in accord with the first plural references of vv 1, 9. Probably MT is to be retained and interpreted of the solidly built and so impregnable character of the city (cf. H.-J. Kraus, *Psalmen*, 1018). See the discussion of J. Schreiner with this conclusion (*Sion-Jerusalem*, 284–85).

5.a. Heb. כי is probably emphatic. H. Gunkel (*Die Psalmen*, 542–43) and M. Dahood (*Psalms III*, 206, cf. 204) take as causal, understanding that Israelite duty to worship at Jerusalem was based upon its political role as capital; but such a grounding is hardly correct. Schreiner (*Sion-Jerusalem*, 287) more plausibly relates to the judicial function of the central sanctuary (cf. Deut 17:8–13), administered by the Davidic dynasty: that Jerusalem possesses this role is reason for Israelites to come there. But even so vv 4–5 are better coordinated.

5.b. The subject of the verb is used by metonymy for judges (BDB, 442b). The plural noun may refer to royal officials (cf. 2 Sam 15:3).

6.a. The language is reminiscent of the standard phrase of greeting שאל לשלום ל "ask for the peace of" (cf. Jer 15:5 where it is used of Jerusalem), probably deliberately so: Jerusalem is to be greeted with a prayer for its welfare.

6.b. MT אהביך "those who love you" is sometimes emended to אהליך "your tents (=houses)" with the support of one Heb. ms, e.g. by Gunkel (*Die Psalmen*, 544), BHS ("*prb 1*") and Seybold (*Wallfahrtspsalmen*, 88), to accord more closely with v 7. A. F. Kirkpatrick aptly contrasts "all who hate Zion" in 129:5 (*Psalms*, 741).

6.c. LXX καὶ εὐθηνία probably presupposes an understanding of ישליו as וְשַׁלֵּיו: cf. the apparent use of שֶׁלֶ(י)ו as a noun in Job 20:20 (LXX σωτηρία); then the following אהביך was accommodated by rendering as a dative. If ושלוה was read (*BHS*), it could have originated as a marginal note of a ms variant to שלוה in v 7 (cf. note 7 ᵃ in *BHS*), which was wrongly taken as a correction of ישליו in v 6.

8.a. The explanation that the psalmist speaks as representative of absent friends (Dahood, *Psalms III*, 207) provides a poor parallel with v 9. Reference is apparently made to Jerusalem's significance for the covenant community.

8.b. Or "I will utter, i.e. wish, peace upon you."

Form/Structure/Setting

The psalm is spoken by an individual (vv 1, 8, 9) who functions as a member of a larger group (vv 2, 9) and at one point addresses that group (v 6). These factors, together with the psalm's references to the temple and Jerusalem, identify the speaker as a pilgrim visitor to the holy city. Gunkel's formal analysis of the psalm (*Die Psalmen*, 542–43), adopted by Kraus (*Psalmen*, 1016) and Wolff ("Psalm 122," 107), was as follows: vv 1–2 comprise an introduction celebrating the joy of pilgrimage, in vv 3–5 Jerusalem is praised and in vv 6–9 prayerful good wishes are uttered upon the city in the framework of a summons (v 6a) and a vow (v 9). In form the psalm is closely related to the

Songs of Zion (Kraus, *Psalmen*, 1016). Most of these songs feature Zion's universal role in grandiose terms (Pss 46, 48, 76), but this one, like Ps 84, regards Jerusalem with a pilgrim's warmth of religious emotion rather than with depth of theological learning. But a knowledge of Zion theology and of the character of the more sophisticated Songs of Zion appears to be presupposed. J. Jeremias ("Lade und Zion," 190) has observed that the third and final part of a Song of Zion regularly contains imperatival clauses with variable content (46:9, 11 [8, 10]; 48:12–14 [11–13]; 76:12 [11]). Here too this pattern is followed, in vv 6–8. As Jeremias also noted, the second part of a Song of Zion may celebrate Yahweh's defense of Zion against the nations (48:5–7 [6–8]; 76:4–10 [3–9]) and contain a characteristic שם or שמה "there" (48:7 [6]; 76:4 [3]; cf. 87:4, 6; 132:17; 133:3). The latter phenomenon occurs in the second section of the psalm at vv 4–5, while the former may be reflected in the reference to the strongly built nature of the city in v 3 (compare vv 3, 7 with 48:4, 14 [3, 13]). The mention of Yahweh's שם "name," v 4, is paralleled in 48:11 (10); 76:2 (1), while "Israel" also features in 76:2 (1). The double reference to pilgrimage and the administration of justice in vv 4–5 has no parallel in a Song of Zion, but finds interesting confirmation in Isa 2:2–4 (=Mic 4:1–3), which is an eschatological adaptation of the Songs of Zion genre (cf. L. C. Allen, *The Books of Joel, Obadiah, Jonah and Micah* [NICOT; Grand Rapids: Eerdmans, 1976] 243–44, 323–26). This dual testimony suggests that the combination played a larger role in Zion theology than in the Songs of Zion extant in the Psalter, and serves to endorse Schreiner's understanding of v 5 (cf. Kraus, *Psalmen*, 1018–19; Wolff, "Psalm 122," 109) as Davidic mediation of divine justice associated with the sanctuary (cf. note 5.a. in *Notes/Comments* and ושפט "and he [=Yahweh] will judge," Isa 2:4).

The setting of the psalm is indicated in vv 1–2. A pilgrim has come to Jerusalem to worship at one of the festivals (cf. Exod 23: 14–17) and stands among the group of fellow-pilgrims with whom he has journeyed (cf. Luke 2:44). It has been disputed whether the psalm envisages the arrival of the pilgrim (Gunkel, *Die Psalmen*, 542; Kraus, *Psalmen*, 1016; A. A. Anderson, *Psalms*, 854; Wolff, "Psalm 122," 108) or his departure (Weiser, *Psalms*, 750; Schreiner, *Sion-Jerusalem*, 284): the verb of v 2 is ambivalent. Similarly vv 6–9 could be understood in terms of greeting or farewell. However, the association of the phraseology of v 6a with a formula of greeting and the psychological fittingness of an outburst of joy and praise at the time of a pilgrim's arrival are weighty factors in assessing the timing of the psalm. Its cultic setting was probably a procession to the temple (cf. Pss 24, 100) in which it functioned as a solo contribution to communal worship.

The dating of the psalm has also been a matter of dispute, especially in view of the ambivalent verbs of vv 4–5. It seems more natural to understand these verses as the psalmist's celebration of Jerusalem's contemporary glories, and so to assign the original psalm to a pre-exilic date (cf. Kraus, *Psalmen*, 1017). A post-Deuteronomic dating has been urged in view of the allusions to centralized worship in v 4 (e.g. Gunkel, *Die Psalmen*, 543). But Weiser (*Psalms*, 750) and Schreiner (*Sion-Jerusalem*, 283) have aptly pointed to 1 Kgs 12:27–28 as evidence to the contrary. On grounds of historical actuality

T. Ishida (*Royal Dynasties*, 147) has assigned the psalm to the period of Josiah's achievement of national reunification around Jerusalem as cult center. However, there may have been some degree of idealization of Jerusalem's role present in the text from the beginning. The relative particle ש in vv 3–4 may be a dialectal feature rather than a sign of lateness. G. Wanke (*Zionstheologie*, 106–17) has claimed that the Songs of Zion, in particular Pss 46, 48, 84, 87, are essentially post-exilic, but his position has not gone unchallenged (cf. H.-M. Lutz, *Jahwe, Jerusalem und die Völker zur Vorgeschichte von Sach. 12:1–8 und 14:1–5.* [WMANT 27; Neukirchen-Vluyn: Neukirchener Verlag, 1968] 171–77, 213–16; Kraus, *Psalmen*, 499).

The poetic structure of the psalm has been variously analyzed. At least three scholars have divided it into five pairs of bicola (J. A. Montgomery, *JBL* 64 [1945] 383; S. Mowinckel, *Real and Apparent Tricola in Hebrew Psalm Poetry* [Oslo: H. Aschehoug, 1957] 101; E. Beaucamp, *RSR* 56 [1968] 211). There is obvious support in the material for such pairing of lines, but can they be grouped more closely? Dahood (*Psalms III*, 203–4) favors a tripartite division, vv 1aβ–4a, 4b–5, 6–9. More appealing is an analysis into an introduction of two lines, vv 1aβ–2, and two strophes of four bicola, vv 3–5, 6–9 (J. Schildenberger, *Estudios Eclesiásticos* 34 [1960] 683). This division accords well with Gunkel's analysis of form, cited above. Both of the main strophes begin with references to Jerusalem. The introductory strophe and the final one are bound together inclusively not only by mention of the temple, בית יהוה in vv 1, 9 (Dahood, *Psalms III*, 207), which is echoed by בית דוד "house of David" in v 5, but also by the first plural suffixes of vv 2, 9 and by direct address of Jerusalem. The last strophe is marked by sixfold alliteration playing upon the name "Jerusalem" (שלום "peace" three times, שאלו "pray, ask," ישליו "prosper securely," שלוה "secure prosperity"). Apart from the foregoing, step-parallelism occurs in adjacent cola in vv 4–5. Seybold (*Wallfahrtspsalmen*, 24–25, 62–63, 88) has judged vv 4aβ–b, 5b and 9 to be secondary because of their generalizing or theological content, but these parts do not jar with the other material in a pilgrim's version of a Song of Zion (for the royal reference of v 5b cf. 84:10 [9]), and the inclusive nature of vv 1, 9 has an original ring.

Explanation

A pilgrim, come to worship in Jerusalem at one of the festivals, captures in song his joyful fascination with the scene and the occasion. With a full heart he glances back, around and forward. He traces his joy to the time when local leaders announced a communal pilgrimage to the temple. He had anticipated this visit so keenly, and now at last he and his fellow-pilgrims are here.

Echoing the more formal Songs of Zion, the psalmist admires the massive, fortresslike structure of the city, which evokes the theme of impregnability, celebrated in Zion theology. In praise of Jerusalem he cites its role as religious center of the federation of tribes, which were bound together in a common allegiance to Yahweh. It had taken over from earlier cultic centers the function of intertribal sanctuary. As such it was responsible too for the administration of justice (cf. Deut 17:8–13). This role had passed to the Davidic dynasty, to be guarantor under God of law and order in Israel (cf. 101:8; 2 Sam 8:15; 15:2–6; Jer 21:12; Mic 4:14 [5:1]).

It was customary to offer greetings of peace (שׁלום) on entering a home or community (cf. 1 Sam 25:6; Matt 10:12–13). Here it is especially appropriate: it echoes a popular play upon the name of Jerusalem (cf. Heb 7:2; contrast Luke 19:41–42). The psalmist urges his fellow-pilgrims to bring their prayers of greeting that the city may be enabled to live up to its name. The welfare and safety of Jerusalem were the key to the blessing of the whole community. The boon of peace and prosperity for the capital would radiate out over Yahweh's people, "those who love" Jerusalem. All members of the covenant community would benefit from the welfare of the holy city, the touchstone of blessing. At its heart lay the temple dedicated to the God of the covenant. If it was to be a worthy setting for this jewel, the city merited stable prosperity.

So the psalmist, in impassioned address to the beloved city, expresses his good will and devotion. As the first and last verses especially make clear, this devotion is God-centered. It is a reflection of the crucial importance of the theocratic institutions of temple and monarchy. They stood as material manifestation of the care and claim of the covenant God for and upon every member. Jerusalem was the focus of national unity, a unity which was grounded in worship and issued in the harmonious ordering of life. True brotherhood was realized at this center of the community, where God's revelation of both his grace and his moral will was enshrined (cf. Heb 12:22–13:16).

Grace to Help (123:1–4)

Bibliography

Goeke, H. "Gott, Mensch und Gemeinde in Ps. 123." *BibLeb* 13 (1972) 124–28. **Magne, J.** "Répétitions de mots et exégèse dans quelques Psaumes et le Pater." *Bib* 39 (1958) 177–97.

Translation

[1] One of the processional songs.[a]

I look up to you,	(3+2)
* enthroned* [b] *in heaven.*	
[2] *Just as the eyes of slaves*	(3+2)
* look to their master's hand,*[a]	
as the eyes of a slave girl	(2+2)
* look to her mistress's hand,*[b]	
so our eyes look to Yahweh our God	(3+2)
* till he gives us liege aid.*[c]	
[3] *Give us liege aid, Yahweh, give us liege aid,*	(3+3)
* because we have had more than our fill of contempt.*	

⁴ *More than our fill have we had*   (3+2+2)
  *of the mockery of the carefree,*ᵃ
  *the contempt of the arrogant.*ᵇ

Notes/Comments

1.a. See the note on 120:1.

1.b. For the appositional -*y* morpheme see GKC § 90m and D. A. Robertson, *Linguistic Evidence*, 69–76. The motif of Yahweh's heavenly kingship was one of the cultic traditions of Jerusalem (H.-J. Kraus, *Psalmen*, 1022, cf. 94–98).

2.a. The relationship between hand and eyes has been variously explained, in terms of looking for the hand to desist from punishment, to give the slightest gesture of the master's commands or to give food. This last interpretation is to be preferred (A. F. Kirkpatrick, *Psalms*, 743; H. Gunkel, *Die Psalmen*, 544; M. Dahood, *Psalms III*, 209; Kraus, *Psalmen*, 1022). The description of Yahweh in 104:27–28 as a father figure dispensing food to his household is to be compared; an even closer parallel appears in the adaptation of the passage in 145:15–16 (אֵלֶיךָ . . . עֵינֵי ‏יָד . . . "eyes . . . to you . . . your hand"). Total dependence for the supply of needs is the point of the similes, which suits well the prayer and situation of vv 2b–4.

2.b. Gunkel, (*Die Psalmen*, 544) observed that it was likely that there would be a number of male slaves in a household but only one woman slave (cf. Hagar in Gen 16).

2.c. For the significance of the stem חנן "be gracious" see K. W. Neubauer, *Der Stamm CH N N*, 101–2. He found the passage to be a key one for his thesis that the stem basically reflects a relationship of solidarity between master and servant, to which appeal may be made to conform in loyalty.

4.a. Gunkel (*Die Psalmen*, 545), Kraus (*Psalmen*, 1021) *et al.* read לִשְׁאֲנַנִּים with one Heb. ms. and LXX in view of the preceding definite article prefixed to the construct state in MT (cf. GKC § 127g). G. R. Driver (*HTR* 29 [1936] 192) suggested repointing הַלַּעַג as a hiph'il infinitive construct הַלְעֵג. However, there is evidence which suggests that the construction in MT was permissible (see Dahood, *Psalms III*, 210, and literature cited there), in which case the minority tradition is to be dismissed as an easier reading.

4.b. K לְגַאֲיוֹנִים (so Vrs) is generally preferred to Q לִגְאֵי יוֹנִים "proudest oppressors." For the adjectival וֹן- ending see 124:5 and P. Joüon, *Grammaire* § 88Me. Gunkel (*Die Psalmen*, 545) *et al.* (cf. *BHS*) delete the last two words as a variant to the previous pair, but an irregular tricolon is unexceptionable (cf. Kraus, *Psalmen*, 34) and vv 3–4 are marked by repetition.

Form/Structure/Setting

The psalm is a communal complaint. Vv 2–4 fall into this formal pattern clearly as a confession of trust, a petition and a description of the situation of complaint which functions as a motivating force to support the petition. C. Westermann (*Praise*, 55, 80) finds the confession of trust so dominant that he classifies the composition as a communal psalm of confidence. The singular reference of the first verse is most probably to be explained as the personal avowal of a precentor or representative of the congregation before speaking on their behalf (Kraus, *Psalmen*, 1021, *et al.*).

The background to the complaint appears to be a long period of adversity in the light of vv 2b, 4. Generally the psalm's date of origin is set either in the exilic period or in that of post-exilic Judah (cf. Neh 1:3; 2:19; 3:36 [4:4]). It was composed for recitation in corporate worship as a vehicle of encouragement (v 2) and prayer.

The structure of the psalm has been analysed by J. Magne (*Bib* 39 [1958] 190) into two strophes, the first of four lines, vv 1–2, and the second of two lines, vv 3–4. This analysis suits the formal elements well. The first strophe is marked by a chiastic order, A B B' A' (עיני. . .אל‎, אל-יד-. . .כעיני‎ twice, עיננו אל‎). It is linked to the second by two hinges, שׁיחננו/חננו‎ and יהוה‎. The second strophe is characterized by a threefold doubling of terms, חננו‎, בוז(ה)‎ and שׁבע רב(ת)‎. The last line serves to develop v 3b. From another viewpoint vv 2–4 exhibit step-parallelism. K. Seybold (*Wallfahrtspsalmen*, 33, 61–62, 89) considers vv 1, 3 secondary, added to give precision and directness to an otherwise inexplicit psalm. Since the effect of these deletions would be to rob it of its stylistic artistry, his dismembering is to be regarded as doubtful.

Explanation

The community has long been suffering in adversity. The cultic representative who brings their prayers to Yahweh begins by expressing his own dependence upon God: Yahweh is the heavenly king for whose power human opposition is no match (cf. 2:4; Isa 40:22–23). His personal avowal of trust sets the tone for the communal words which follow. He leads his fellow-worshipers into a declaration of their own reliance upon Yahweh by means of a double simile. A word picture is drawn of a household of master, mistress and slaves, these last depending completely upon the former two for material support. The community acknowledges, and pleads, that the covenant relationship ("our God") places them in the position of slaves before their divine master. They are utterly reliant upon him. The corollary of this relationship is that he has committed himself to support them as his protégés. For this help they have been waiting and will wait on expectantly, conscious that they have no other help save his.

The psalm moves forward in direct appeal to Yahweh, claiming his help in a repeated plea expressing urgency and agitation. The petition is backed by a piteous statement of their situation of distress, to move God to intervene. Their suffering has become too much for them. Their actual adversity is left undescribed, but is reflected obliquely in vv 3b–4. Insult has been added to injury. Their disaster has been aggravated by the brutal jeering of others whose own lives are untrammeled by affliction.

This short psalm gives powerful expression to a reaction to human stress in terms of religious trust and hope. The two final verses resound like a repeated S.O.S. signal sent off by desperate men. But balance is supplied by the introductory strophe which aims to give a new clarity to eyes dimmed by suffering, by pointing to heaven. The precentor bravely leads the way in formulating the answer to the woeful situation. His implicit call to faith opens up a way forward by appeal to the supernatural resources which the God of the covenant can and surely will supply.

The psalm is reminiscent of Ps 94 in that devout leadership redeems a situation of adversity by guiding into paths of hope and by reminding the community of the covenanted mercies of their God. It was doubtless the psalm's opening affirmations of trust that led to its selection for the collection of processional songs. "God is still on the throne" was its reassuring message to pilgrims who longed for the establishment of his kingdom (cf. Heb 4:16; 12:2).

The Broken Snare   (124:1-8)

Bibliography

Crüsemann, F. *Studien zur Formgeschichte.* Schreiner, J. " 'Wenn nicht der Herr fur uns wäre!' Auslegung von Psalm 124." *BibLeb* 10 (1969) 16–25.

Translation

¹ One of the processional songs.^a Davidic.^b
Were it not for ^c Yahweh   (2+2+2)
   who took our side,
   let Israel declare—
² Were it not for Yahweh,   (2+2+3)
   who took our side
   when men attacked us,
³ then ^a they would have swallowed us alive,^b   (3+3)
   so furious was their anger against us.
⁴ Then the waters would have overwhelmed us,^a   (3+3)
   the torrent ^b would have gone above our necks,^c
⁵ then it would have gone above our necks—   (3+3)
   those raging ^a waters.

⁶ Blessed ^a is Yahweh   (2+2+2)
   who did not let us be
   a prey to their teeth.
⁷ We have escaped with our lives like a bird   (3+2)
   out of the fowlers' trap.^a
The trap is broken   (2+2)
   and we have escaped.
⁸ Our help consisted in the name ^a of Yahweh,   (3+3)
   maker of heaven and earth.^b

Notes/Comments

1.a. See the note on 120:1.
1.b. A few Heb. mss. and the oldest text of LXX lack this latter annotation. Its intent is not clear. It "may have been suggested by phrases resembling those of Davidic psalms, but the language points to a late date, and it can hardly be regarded as even an adaptation of an ancient poem" (A. F. Kirkpatrick, *Psalms,* 744). Perhaps similarity especially to Ps 118 (cf. vv 2–4, 5, 6, 10–13) suggested the annotation.
1.c. Cf. post-biblical Heb. and Aram. אילולי ש/ד (BDB, 530b; M. Jastrow, *Dictionary,* 49a).
3.a. The form אזי occurs for אז only in vv 3–5 in the OT. It has been found in a Hebrew letter of A.D. 134 or 135 discovered at Murabbaʿât (DJD, vol. 2 [1961] 156 [text 42, line 5]) in a similar context, introducing the apodosis after a conditional clause introduced by אללי ש. It also appears in a seventh-century B.C. Aramaic inscription (*KAI,* 3rd ed. [1971] 283–84 [Nr. 233, line 6]).
3.b. Cf. Prov 1:12. The enemies are compared with a monster which implicitly stands for Sheol.

4.a. As in v 3, there are again associations with Sheol: a fatal threat is posed. For the identification of Sheol with the waters of chaos cf. N. J. Tromp, *Primitive Conceptions,* 59–66; O. Keel, *Symbolism,* 73. For allusion to Sheol under the images of both a monster and drowning waters in a single context see Jonah 2:3, 6 (2, 5).

4.b. For נחלה cf. GKC § 90f, P. Joüon, *Grammaire* § 93i. K. Seybold (*Wallfahrtspsalmen,* 40) plausibly finds here the influence of the Aram. emphatic state. The term evokes the Palestinian wadi, which winter rains turned into a raging torrent.

4.c. For this primary sense of Heb. נפש, referring to the organ of breathing see H. W. Wolff, *Anthropology,* 13 and cf. Jonah 2:6 (5).

5.a. Cf. Targumic Aram. זידנא (Jastrow, *Dictionary,* 391a).

6.a. For indirect cultic blessing of Yahweh see W. S. Towner, *CBQ* 30 (1968) 389–90.

7.a. Lit. "setters' trap." For discussion of the phrase see G. R. Driver, "Reflections on Recent Articles. 2. Hebr. *môqēš* 'Striker,' " *JBL* 73 (1954) 131–36; Keel, *Symbolism,* 89, 91.

8.a. Reference is made to the invocation of the all-powerful name "Yahweh" in the prayer of complaint (J. W. Wevers, *VT* 6 [1956] 86; cf. 118:10).

8.b. For this traditional formula associated with the Jerusalem temple see N. C. Habel, *JBL* 91 (1972) 321–37.

Form/Structure/Setting

At first sight Ps 124 has the form of a thanksgiving of the community. If so, it is a rare phenomenon indeed in OT literature. In fact, while individual thanksgivings abound, the presence of national thanksgivings in the Psalter is a matter of dispute. F. Crüsemann (*Studien zur Formgeschichte,* 160–68) has shown that the language of this psalm is characteristic of individual compositions and has little or no background of cultic usage in communal settings. For instance, the particle לולא "were it not" (vv 1–2), which belongs to colloquial usage, primarily in the context of an argument, is rare in cultic poetry: its closest parallel is in a passage of individual thanksgiving, 94:17 (cf. 119:92; Gen 31:42). Similarly the blessing formula of v 6 occurs in the Psalms generally in individual complaints and thanksgivings, though in 68:20 (19) it is used in a communal hymn. The expression in vv 1–2 concerning God's being on one's side belongs to an individual's statement of confidence (אלהים/יהוה לי 56:10 [9]; 118:6), although it is used once in a communal Song of Zion at 46:2 (לנו אלהים). The metaphorical description of distress in terms of hunting and drowning find close parallels only in individual compositions: it was the prophets who gave them a wider, national connotation (cf. Isa 8:8; 28:15; Jer 47:2; 50:24). Thus in the light of cultic usage elsewhere, the psalm exhibits individual language clothed in plural dress. If first singular references had been used throughout, the psalm would correspond well not only in terminology but in form to an individual thanksgiving. Its introductory summary of deliverance (v 2), retrospect to the situation of trouble (vv 3–5), report of Yahweh's deliverance (vv 6b–7) and expression of praise and testimony which passes into a generalization (vv 6a, 8) would comprise a model psalm of solo thanksgiving (cf. C. Westermann, *Praise,* 102–11).

The significance of the reference to Israel in v 1b requires discussion both in form-critical and in contextual terms. J. Schreiner, (*BibLeb* 10 [1969] 18–20) has compared this element with the summons found in the communal hymn of praise: the initial summons, the praise of vv 6–7 and the concluding statement of trust follow the pattern of the hymn (cf. Westermann, *Praise,* 123, 130), as the basis for a national song of thanksgiving. It is doubtful whether this comparison is warranted or justified, especially since the summons of v 1b recurs exactly in 118:2 in an individual thanksgiving as a liturgical formula inviting a refrain of praise from those assembled for the service of thanksgiving in which the individual took part with testimony, praise and sacrifice. It is worth asking whether v 1b remained true to its formal origin as a living element of thanksgiving. Crüsemann (*Studien zur Formgeschichte*, 167), followed by Seybold (*Wallfahrtspsalmen*, 27, 61, 89) regards v 1aβ-b as secondary in a literary sense: the psalm, probably used originally by a group engaged in thanksgiving (cf. Ps 107), has been re-interpreted nationally and put upon the lips of the community. It is possible, however, that such a group, while testifying to their own deliverance, call upon the religious community to share their praise and to acknowledge that deliverance of the few has a representative character and demonstrates Yahweh's care for the people as a whole. This would give the psalm a viable role in a context of pilgrimage: a pilgrim group (cf. Ps 122) would encapsulate its local experience of threat and deliverance in such a psalm and invite communal praise. But there are two objections to such a reconstruction. It is difficult to explain a call to praise in identical terms to the group's own praise. The positioning of the summons after v 1aβ (contrast 118:2–4) seems to imply that v 1aβ is to be repeated and that vv 2–8 are to be recited communally or by a choir representing the community. Accordingly the first line is best understood as an introductory, priestly call for the psalm to be sung. This explanation corresponds to the structural unity of vv 2–8 (see below): v 1aβ-b appears to fall outside the psalm proper.

As Crüsemann urged, a group's song of thanksgiving, which not unreasonably uses the forms and terminology of an individual thanksgiving, has evidently been adapted to general, communal use. Form-critically, then, the psalm has a long history. Individual traits have been re-used to express the experience of a group, and then in turn the whole song of the group has been taken over into a communal setting. Was it then used solely for communal thanksgiving for particular experiences of deliverance? The presence of the psalm in the collection of Pss 120–134 suggests rather that it had a wider use, to express paradigmatically the community's sense of redemption as object of the divine Heilsgeschichte. Then Schreiner's comparison of the hymn of praise, though not helpful form-critically, is relevant as illustrating the eventual use to which the psalm was put. The positioning of the psalm next to Ps 123 may have been intended to assure that Yahweh answers his people's prayers.

Structurally the psalm falls into two strophes with the break after v 5 (cf. S. Mowinckel, *Tricola*, 102). This poetic structure corresponds to its formal division into vv 1–5, 6–7, 8; v 8, as will be seen, belongs poetically with vv 6–7. Both strophes contain chiastic passages: vv 4–5 exhibit a chiastic order and so do the two lines of v 7. Moreover Heb. נפשנו occurs both in vv 4–5 ("our necks") and in v 7 ("our lives"). Seybold's deletion of v 5 as secondary (*Wallfahrtspsalmen*, 29, 61, 89) damages the parallelism of the psalm. V 6 clearly the counterpart of vv (1aβ,) 2, 3 with its repetition of the divine name, negative elements (לא, לולי) and description of danger in terms of attacking beasts. Vv 6–7, the material corresponding to vv 2–5, appear to have been squeezed into three lines, instead of the corresponding four, to make room for the last, climactic line of v 8. V 8 harks back to vv 1–2 as an inclusion, not only in its use of the divine name but also in its content which is both synonymous (cf. 94:17 לולי יהוה עזרתה לי "unless Yahweh was my help") and antithetic ("man"/"maker of heaven and earth"). The psalm appears to have been composed as a pair of four-line strophes (cf. E. J. Kissane, *Psalms II*, 254), to which subsequently v 1aβ-b has been added as a consequence of its re-interpretation.

The post-biblical Hebrew and Aramaic elements in the psalm (see the *Notes/Comments* on vv 1, 3, 5 and observe too the relative ש in v 6) suggest that the origin of the psalm is late.

Explanation

A post-exilic song of thanksgiving composed for a group delivered from a perilous situation has been deemed worthy of wider use by the community at large. Its general terms, vivid metaphors and striking expression of heartfelt praise made it an irresistible choice for this honor. A priestly precentor introduces the first half-line; he urges the congregation, or a choir representing it, to take up the strains of the psalm. The very repetition serves to emphasize that they have no help but Yahweh. In vv 2–5 the pitting of his gracious help against otherwise fatal consequences is a colloquial and catchy way of expressing the conventional summary of deliverance and narration of the crisis from which one is delivered. The first complete line impressively begins with Yahweh and ends with man, a contrast found also in 56:12 (11); 118:6; Isa 31:3. Dire as it was, the threat inevitably dwindled away—from a divine perspective:

> "Yahweh, what is man . . .?
> Man is like a breath,
> . . . a passing shadow" (144:3, 4).

It is the people's joy that Yahweh has allied himself to them. The indefinite statement of vehement attack and the metaphors which represent the attacked as enshrouded by the pallid aura of Sheol have a particular aim: they forcefully express the conviction of the community that they are a saved people. They are acutely conscious that but for the grace of God they have no existence. Surveying their history, his people acknowledge that they owe their corporate life to his preservation from death's ravening jaws (cf. Isa 5:14) and drowning waters (cf. 69:3, 16 [2, 15]: "Our helper he, amid the flood of mortal ills prevailing" (Luther).

The second strophe begins by reiterating vv 2–3, but now in positive tones of praising testimony. Yahweh's protective grace is the secret of the community's survival till now, in face of the dangers that have dragged them down throughout their checkered history. The reversal of doom-laden danger by means of incredible rescue is dramatically described in terms of a pitiable trapped bird that surprisingly regains its freedom. The praise is now less direct, but behind the passive verb of brokenness is implicit divine activity. Freedom is prized as the gift of God.

The closing verse bears witness to divine help, using a traditional formulation of temple worship (cf. 121:2). The cries of God's people, invoking the powerful name "Yahweh," did not go unheard. He graciously came to their aid. What are human enemies (v 2), when the divine creator is a friend (cf. Isa 51:12–13; 1 Pet 4:19)? The one who gives life and meaning to the world has kept death at bay and against all odds has preserved Israel as his people.

Here in one beautiful psalm of praise are brought together Yahweh's ever-repeated gifts of salvation and renewal. The people, never immune from suffering, celebrate the redeeming power of God and are encouraged and sustained thereby (cf. 1 Pet 1:3–9). An almighty savior is the savior still! This is the glad testimony of the psalm.

Immovable As the Mountains (125:1–5)

Bibliography

Hurvitz, A. "אימתי נטבע בעברית הצירוף 'שלום על ישראל'?" *Leš* 27/28 (1964) 297–302. **Wanke, G.** *Die Zionstheologie der Korachiten.* BZAW 97. Berlin: A. Töpelmann, 1966.

Translation

[1] One of the processional songs.[a]
    Those who trust in Yahweh   (2+2+3)
      are like Mount Zion,
        which is immovable,[b] abiding [c] forever.
[2] *Jerusalem has mountains around it—[a]*   (3+3+3)
    and Yahweh is around his people
    henceforth and for evermore.[b]

[3] *The scepter of wickedness*   (2+2+2)
    will surely not remain
    over the land allotted [a] to the righteous,[b]
  or else the righteous might turn   (3+2)
    their hands [c] to wrongdoing.

[4] *Do good, Yahweh, to the good,*   (3+2)
    to those upright in their hearts.

⁵ *But those who turn aside to their crooked ways* ᵃ   (3+2+2)
  may Yahweh remove ᵇ
  together with the evildoers.
Peace be upon Israel. ᶜ

Notes/Comments

1.a. See the note on 120:1.

1.b. Cf. 46:6 (5). In the Songs of Zion Yahweh's supremacy is described in terms of victory over nations massed against Zion. Their attack is related to the threat of chaotic forces subdued at the creation of the world: cf. 93:1; 96:10; 104:5; G. Wanke, *Zionstheologie*, 68–70; H.-J. Kraus, *Psalmen*, 499. The stability of the world and that of Zion are organically linked in Zion theology.

1.c. For the meaning of Heb. ישׁב "abide" cf. Mic 5:3 (4), unreasonably regarded by M. Dahood (*Psalms III*, 215) as "tenuous evidence."

2.a. "Zion is . . . a modest hill. Its top is not as high as the tops of surrounding mountains: it lies 66 meters below that of the Mount of Olives, 76 meters below that of Mount Scopus, 33 meters below that of the hill to its west . . . and 53 meters below that of *ras el-mekkaber*" (O. Keel, *Symbolism*, 114–15).

2.b. This phrase is often regarded as secondary, e.g. by H. Gunkel (*Die Psalmen*, 550); Kraus (*Psalmen*, 1028). But it is to be retained with A. Weiser (*Psalms*, 758): it provides a good external parallel to לעולם "forever" in v 1.

3.a. Heb. גורל "lot, tribal allotment" is here used of the whole land.

3.b. Heb. צדיקים refers to those in right relationship with Yahweh through the covenant, whose lives are lived in conformity with that relationship.

3.c. For the phrase שׁלח יד "send (a) hand" see P. Humbert, " 'Étendre le main' (note de lexicographie hébraïque)," *VT* 12 (1962) 383–95.

5.a. Lit. "bend their crookednesses." For the concept of the purging of impure elements within the religious community see Weiser, *Psalms*, 64, 75–79; K. Nielsen, *Yahweh as Prosecutor and Judge* (Sheffield: University of Sheffield, 1978) 46–48.

5.b. Or "lead away": cf. Job 12:17, 19 for הלך used of Yahweh's punishment of leaders. "Allow to get lost" (D. Michel, *Tempora*, 115; cf. K. Koch, "Gibt es ein Vergeltungsdogma im AT?" *ZTK* 52 [1955] 16–17) is hardly strong enough. Here it appears to refer to exile: cf. Deut 28:36; 2 Kgs 24:15; Hos 2:16 (14).

5.c. The clause stands outside the metrical structure of the psalm; probably it was spoken by a priest as the answer to the choral prayer (S. Mowinckel, *Tricola*, 89–90). Gunkel (*Die Psalmen*, 549), Kraus (*Psalmen*, 1028); *et al.* regard as secondary. A. Hurvitz (*Leš* 27/28 [1964] 297–302) has surveyed the usage of the phrase in Hebrew literature and inscriptions and concluded that the formulation is post-sixth-century B.C. in origin.

Form/Structure/Setting

The psalm as a whole is a brief communal complaint. Its double petition and wish, directed toward selves and enemies, vv 4–5, follow an extended confession of trust, vv 1–3 (cf. C. Westermann, *Praise*, 52–55). The large proportion allocated to the confession of trust has encouraged classification of the psalm as a communal psalm of confidence (e.g. by Gunkel, *Die Psalmen*, 548). The formal structure of Ps 123 is comparable, except that this psalm exhibits only two elements of the complaint and Ps 123 has three.

The background of the psalm appears to be enemy occupation of the land (v 3, cf. Isa 14:5, 29; "evildoers," v 5). This situation suggests the post-exilic period as its time of origin. Gunkel's linguistic criteria (*Die Psalmen*, 549) are hardly decisive in confirmation; K. Seybold's tentative suggestion that עולתה "wrongdoing," v 3, has been influenced by the Aramaic emphatic state (*Wallfahrtspsalmen*, 40 note 28) is possible but not compelling (cf. GKC, § 90g; Dahood, *Psalms III*, 216).

The stylistic structure of the psalm consists of three strophes, each of two lines (Gunkel, *Die Psalmen*, 549; E. J. Kissane, *Psalms II*, 256; Mowinckel, *Tricola*, 101). The word play ימוט "immovable," v 1, and המטים "those who turn aside," v 5, provides inclusion, and so does the doubled use of the divine name in the first and third strophes in the same positioning, the first colon in the first line and the middle colon in the second. The first strophe is marked by external parallelism (הרים/הר "mountain[s]," עולם "forever," Zion/Jerusalem and a double comparison). The second has a chiastic structure, in respect of צדיקים "righteous" and terms for wickedness, which befits its central position. The last strophe is antithetic and has double terms for the good and the wicked. Seybold (*Wallfahrtspsalmen*, 49, 61–62, 64, 90) regards vv 1 and 4 as secondary, the first verse on account of its reference to Zion, which he judges to be a redactional mark of the collection of Pss 120–134. Such deletion leaves completely out of account the artistic patterning of the psalm, as does his judgment that even with the recensional additions the psalm remains an incomplete torso.

Explanation

Post-exilic Judah is under the control of a foreign power. In the course of worship in the temple, Yahweh's people bring to him in prayer this situation (cf. Neh. 9:36–37), which is aggravated by the collaboration of certain Jews in flagrant breach of their ancestral faith. It is this faith that is foremost in the worshipers' prayer. Echoing the Songs of Zion (cf. Pss 46, 48, 76 and Isa 28:16), they affirm that their security is as permanent as the impregnable city. It is not self-confidence that prompts this assertion, but confidence in Yahweh. The second verse reinforces the significance of the opening phrase of the psalm and explains the divine basis of the people's security. Vivid reference is made to the ring of mountains surrounding Jerusalem. To the eye of faith they became a symbol of Yahweh's everlasting protection (cf. 34:8 [7]; Zech 2:9 [5]). The confidence of the covenant community depends upon their knowledge of Yahweh's continual care for them.

Armed with this twofold guarantee of Judah's salvation, the psalm dares to draw a conclusion for the contemporary situation. Foreign occupation is a travesty of Israel's traditional theology, which inextricably linked the covenant between Yahweh and the (obedient) people with the gift of the land (cf. Deut 11:22–25; Isa 57:13; 60:21). The people's sole tenancy is a divinely given privilege to which they may boldly lay claim before Yahweh in an implicit appeal for his intervention. He will surely not allow such profanation to continue lest his people grow weary in their faith and turn away from him in despair (cf. Mal 3:15; Matt 24:12), ceasing to maintain the moral outworking of the covenant in their lives.

The concluding strophe develops both of the preceding ones in turn, in a direct prayer. First, on the basis of his covenant care for the faithful, Yahweh is asked to intervene actively in the religio-political situation. There is no warrant for the human partners to the covenant to undergo the covenantal curses (cf. Deut 11:26–28; 28:63). On the contrary, their endeavors to conform in spirit and behavior with the standards of the covenant constitute an appeal to Yahweh to fulfill his own obligations (cf. Prov 2:21–22). The final verse takes up the concept of aversion to foreign (current) and Jewish (potential) wickedness in v 3. This concept is made a plea for Yahweh to deal with renegades who have broken the covenant and forfeited their share in the land, by expelling both them and their foreign patrons ("evildoers"). These apostates are sharply distinguished from the faithful of the previous verse: they have no part in the covenant. Their apostasy is not regarded as compromising the community at large before God.

The psalm closes with a priestly benediction in response to the prayer (cf. 1 Sam 1:17), calling down God's blessing of weal upon the troubled people. "Israel" stands for the faithful. Paul's apparent echo of the benediction in Gal 6:16 is true to the psalm's limiting of the true Israel to those who conform with God's will for their lives (cf. Rom 2:29).

Psalm 125 gives valuable insight into the faith of the post-exilic Judean community. It reveals a society struggling with the pressures upon it and represents the endeavors of its religious leaders to hearten it with encouragement and prayer. Zion theology and Deuteronomic and sapiential teaching are harnessed to the task of supporting the people's faith. Yahweh's protective power and faithfulness to his promises concerning the people and land are theological factors used to bring comfort and hope to the faithful and to encourage moral perseverance (cf. 1 Cor 10:13; 2 Tim 2:12, 19). The discrepancy between traditional faith and contemporary experience is channeled positively into ardent, polarized prayer.

God Can Do It Again (126:1–6)

Bibliography

Beyerlin, W. *"Wir sind wie Träumende."* Studien zur 126. Psalm. SBS 89. Stuttgart: Verlag Katholisches Bibelwerk, 1978. **Borger, R.** "Zu שבות/ית." *ZAW* 66 (1954) 315–16 **Dietrich, E. L.** שוב שבות. *Die endzeitliche Wiederstellung bei den Propheten.* BZAW 40. Giessen: A. Töpelmann, 1925. **Magne, J.** "Répétitions de mots et exégèse dans quelques Psaumes et le Pater." *Bib* 39 (1958) 177–97. **Morgenstern, J.** "Psalm 126." *Homenaje a Millás-Vallicrosa.* Vol. 2. Barcelona: Consejo Superior de Investigaciones Cientificas, 1956. **Strugnell, J.** "A Note on Ps. 126:1." *JTS* 7 (1956) 239–43.

Translation

[1] One of the processional songs.[a]
　When Yahweh restored　　　　　　　　　　　　　　　　　(2+2+2)
　　Zion's fortunes,[b]
　　we were[c] like dreamers.[d]
[2] Then were filled with laughter our mouths　　　　　　　(3+2[a])
　　and our tongues with happy shouts.

Then it was said among the nations:	(2+2+2)
"Yahweh has done a great work b	
in his dealings with them."	
3 Yahweh did do a great work	(2+2+2)
in his dealings with us;	
we were so glad.	

4 Yahweh, restore a our fortunes b	(3+2)
like river beds in the Negeb. c	
5 Those who sow with tears a	(2+2)
with happy shouts do reap. b	
6 The one who carries the bag a of seed	(3+3)
weeps as he goes along;	
but b the one who carries his sheaves c	(3+2)
comes home with a happy shout.	

Notes/Comments

1.a. See the note on 120:1.

1.b. For the phrase (cf. v 4a) and unique Heb. form שִׁיבַת "fortunes" see the eighth-century B.C. Seifîre inscription (3:24 = *KAI*, 3rd ed. [1971] Nr. 224, line 24) שיבת אלהן השבו "the gods brought about the restoration [of my father's house]." The common emendation to שבות (H.-J. Kraus, *Psalmen*, 1031; *BHS et al.*) is thus unnecessary (M. Dahood, *Psalms III*, 218). The noun evidently functions with the qal conjugation as an internal, cognate accusative with an objective genitive ("turn with a turning towards"): cf. E. L. Dietrich, *Wiederstellung*, 28–37.

1.c. The time perspective of vv 1–3 has been strongly disputed. The time of the initial בשוב "when (Yahweh) restored" is indeterminate of itself and dependent upon the main verb. In v 2 the verbs with אז "then" may relate either to the past or to the future. H. Gunkel (*Die Psalmen* 551) took the verbs of vv 1b, 3 as "prophetic" perfects (cf. GKC § 106n) in a divine oracle. B. Duhm (*Psalmen*, 274) and D. Michel (*Tempora*, 243) have also related the passage to the future (in view of v 4), but regarded it as a meditation upon a future event. In that case vv 1–3 might be rendered (cf. GKC § 106o) "When Yahweh has restored . . . , we shall have become . . . (v 2) Then will . . . (v 3) Yahweh will have done . . . ; we shall be glad." An objection to both these future interpretations is the extreme awkwardness of v 3 after the certainly past tense of the perfect (הגדיל לעשות) "did do a great (work)" in v 2b. W. Beyerlin (*Träumende*, 35–37) compares the construction of vv 1aβ, 2 (ב with the infinitive construct and a doubled אז "then" with imperfect verbs) with the future sentences of Job 33:15–16; Prov 1:27–28. He regards v 1b as parenthetical (cf. Gen 2:4b–7) and present (cf. 122:2): "When Yahweh restores— we are like dreamers—then will . . ." V 3a also relates to the future, while v 3b like v 1b refers to the present, anticipating the future (see further in *Form/Structure/Setting*). Here too the awkwardness of (הגדיל לעשות) in vv 2b, 3a referring to different times creates difficulty. Would not the psalmist more naturally have said (יגדיל לעשות) "will do a great (work)," conforming with the earlier future imperfects? Moreover, the change of time in the parenthetical v 1b makes the first line read most awkwardly. Beyerlin's claim that v 1b as well as v 2a, 2b would have to be expressed with אז and an imperfect verb, if like them it was the consequence of the initial temporal clause, is not compelling. The two lines of v 2 may function as main clauses independent of v 1aβ-b (cf. Isa 35:5–6; 58:8–9). For the construction of v 1aβ-b cf. 114:1–2.

1.d. J. Strugnell (*JTS* 7 [1956] 239–43) rendered "as hale men, as men who had been / were healed," comparing the parallelism of restoring fortunes and healing in Hos 6:11–7:1. He claimed the support of *Tg.* and LXX: (a) *Tg.* היך מרעיא דאיתסיין "like sick people who are cured," understood MT in terms of the other Heb. (and Aram.) stem חלם "be strong, healthy" (rather than presupposing כחלים "like sick people" [*BKH, BHS*]); (b) LXX rendered the verb as in Isa 38:16 (cf. *BHS; contra BHK* which retroverted as כנחמים). He also regarded S *'yk hnwn dḥdyn* "like those who rejoice" as a paraphrase of this second stem (in terms of v 3b), although this is not necessarily the case. Significantly 11QPs^a reads כחלומים or כחלימים according to S. Speier, "Sieben Stellen des Psalmentargums in Handschriften und Druckausgaben," *Bib* 48 (1967) 507 (already tentatively suggested as an alternative by J. A. Sanders, *Psalms Scroll*, 25). The first possibility could be an adjective "sound, healthy" like the second: cf. M. Jastrow, *Dictionary*, 468a, 471a. Heb. חלם, which Jastrow explained as a passive participle, is more probably a stative adjective: cf. GKC § 50f, 84 ᵃm. The strong exegetical tradition, adopted by NEB ("like men who had found new health") is possible, but in the light of the overall context Kraus (*Psalmen*, 1031) is doubtless right in regarding it as less probable. Beyerlin (*Träumende*, 19–31) has rightly urged caution in interpreting MT in terms of dreaming, lest an alien, anachronistic meaning be read into it. He himself understands the text as a dreamlike anticipation of Yahweh's future restoration of Zion: in OT thought dreams can reveal the divinely determined future, and so the speakers describe themselves as "like dreamers," in the sense that they look forward to it and were certain that it would come. He also regards כחלמים as an allusion to Joel 3:1 (see *Form/Structure/Setting*). More probably the reference to dreaming is to be compared with Isa 29:7–8 ("like a dream . . ."), where a hungry or thirsty man dreams that he is eating or drinking. It is true that there the dreamlike experience is characterized as unreal and doomed to frustration, but that is only because it is stressed that the dreamer awakes. In the dream itself the need is felt to be met and it is not till awaking that the dreamer realizes otherwise. Waking is here irrelevant to the simile, which describes the welcome reversal of a situation of need.

2.a. Gunkel (*Die Psalmen*, 550) scanned as 2+2+2, and J. Morgenstern ("Psalm 126," 111–12) and Beyerlin (*Träumende*, 33) as 4+2 (likewise vv 1, 3), but it is more probably 3+2 (Kraus, 1032): אז "then" is to be taken metrically with the next word, as in v 2b.

2.b. For הגדיל לעשות "do a great work" cf. Joel 2:21; cf. too הגדיל in 1 Sam 12:24 and עשה גדלות "do great things" of Yahweh in Deut 10:21; Pss 71:19; 106:21. The event is implicitly compared with the Heilsgeschichte.

4.a. Dahood (*Psalms III*, 220), who relates the whole psalm to the past, regards שובה as a *qatala* form "šābāh or the Phoenician form šōbāh," so that vv 1 and 4 both describe the same past event. Cf. the tentative proposal in *BHK* to read a standard שב.

4.b. For the semantically irrelevant variation of K שבות and Q שבית, see R. Borger, *ZAW* 66 (1954) 315–16.

4.c. In summer, in the arid south especially, the wadi beds were dry (cf. Joel 1:20) until the winter rains filled them. It is with this latter phenomenon that comparison is made. "Most of these floods swept into the Mediterranean and were useless in antiquity; however, along these river beds are located most of the springs and wells of the Negeb which were essential for permanent habitation" (Y. Aharoni, *The Land of the Bible* [Tr. A. F. Rainey; London: Burns and Oates, 1967] 24; cf. N. Glueck, *Rivers in the Desert* [London: Weidenfeld and Nicolson, 1959] 92–94).

5.a. Behind this apparent proverb lies mythological antecedents of the burial and revival of the fertility god, which may be illustrated from Egyptian and Ugaritic texts, but "the poet had long ago lost any memory that this antithesis was rooted in the ancient Canaanite cult drama" (F. F. Hvidberg, *Weeping and Laughing in the OT* [Leiden: E. J. Brill, 1962] 132; cf. A. Weiser, *Psalms*, 762).

5.b. The verse is hardly a continuation of the prayer of v 4 (RSV "May . . ."): v 6 amplifies v 5, and v 6a cannot be so construed.

6.a. See *HALAT*, 610b; Dahood, *Psalms III*, 221.

6.b. "The infinitive absolute is used to give emphasis to an antithesis" (GKC § 113p).

6.c. P. Joüon (*Grammaire*, § 90e) by analogy with שדים/שדות distinguished between אלמום "particular sheaves" (here and in Gen 37:7a) and אלמים "sheaves" in general (Gen 37:7b).

Form/Structure/Setting

As so often in the Psalms, assessment of the form depends upon judgment concerning the psalm's chronological perspective. The major problem of the psalm is the relation of vv 1, 4: both refer to a reversal of fortunes. Are they to be equated or differentiated? Dahood (*Psalms III*, 216) has equated them uniquely by interpreting the verb of v 4 as a (past) perfect. In fact he

construes all the verbs in the psalm as past, and so can regard it as a hymn
of thanksgiving composed for one of the festivals. But usually v 4 is taken
as a petition spoken in the name of the community. Equation of vv 1, 4
then is associated with regarding vv 1–3 either as a meditation upon the
future (Duhm, Michel: see *Notes/Comments*, note 1.c.; cf. Weiser, *Psalms*, 760)
or as a combination of present anticipations of the future and future statements
(Beyerlin, *Träumende*, 31; see *Notes/Comments*, note 1.c.) or as an oracular
pronouncement (Gunkel, *Die Psalmen*, 551) to which the people respond with
a prayer for its fulfilment.

The alternative is to differentiate between the events of vv 1 and 4. Reversal
of national fortunes need not be a single, isolated event: cf. H. W. Wolff's
rendering of Hos 6:11 as "whenever I restored the fortunes of my people"
and his reference to "an event which happened repeatedly in the course of
Israel's history" (*Hosea*, 106, 123). Then vv 1–3 constitute a historical retrospect to Yahweh's praiseworthy intervention in the past (Kraus, *Psalmen*, 1034;
A. A. Anderson, *Psalms*, 865; C. C. Keet, *Psalms of Ascents*, 49–50). Kraus
(*Psalmen*, 53) has compared their role with 44:2–4 (1–3). The advantage of
this orientation is that it overcomes the difficulties of verbal coordination
involved in those interpretations which relate vv 1–3 to the future (see note
1.c. in *Notes/Comments*).

There remains the function of vv 5–6. Those who relate vv 1–3 to the
past tend to regard the final verses as a prophetic promise, comparing the
structure of Ps 85 (Kraus, *Psalmen*, 1032; J. H. Eaton, *Psalms*, 285). Otherwise
they are usually taken as a declaration of confidence (Gunkel, *Die Psalmen*,
552; Weiser, *Psalms*, 762; Beyerlin, *Träumende*, 40; cf. Kraus, *Psalmen*, 53),
which is a characteristic element of the complaint form. The stylistic structure
of the psalm (see below) points to the latter explanation: a prophetic voice
in vv 5–6 would entail a break within the psalm after v 4, but there are
clear artistic signs of a major division after v 3. Accordingly the psalm as a
whole is to be judged a communal complaint, the central petition of which
is bordered by a reminder of Yahweh's past aid to motivate future intervention
and by a strong affirmation of coming blessing.

The cultic setting of the psalm can hardly be precisely defined. The references to natural phenomena in vv 4b–6 have been taken as indications that
the autumn festival was the cultic occasion of the psalm, which could have
constituted a prayer for fertility and blessing for the coming year (cf. Weiser,
Psalms, 760; Anderson, *Psalms*, 864; Eaton, *Psalms*, 285). Beyerlin has rightly
condemned such a precise setting, observing the metaphorical nature of the
fertility references, and concludes simply that the psalm was recited in the
communal cult (*Träumende*, 40).

The historical background has been diversely explained. Dahood (*Psalms
III*, 217–18) claims the psalm as pre-exilic on account of the eighth-century
Aramaic parallel to שׁיבת "fortunes" in v 1 and the "archaic forms" which
he discovers, and finds it impossible to interpret v 1 in terms of a specific
restoration. Weiser attempts no historical earthing of the psalm's language,
relating it simply to "the cult community's expectation of salvation in times
of adversity" (*Psalms*, 760). Beyerlin, on the other hand, specifically ties the
psalm to an exilic setting in Judah, interpreting the restoration of fortunes

as the (future) restoration of the Judean community, after its dissolution in 587 B.C. (*Träumende*, 49, 60). He urges that the psalm is closely based in its terminology upon the preaching of Joel, which with Kapelrud and Rudolph he dates in the late pre-exilic period. The soundness of this major plank in Beyerlin's total reconstruction of the psalm must be questioned: it is more likely that Joel belongs to the post-exilic period (see L. C. Allen, *The Books of Joel . . . and Micah*, 19–25). It is noteworthy that Morgenstern used parallels with Joel to justify a post-exilic dating for the psalm, in the third century B.C. ("Psalm 126," 115–16). Moreover, an assertion of dependence upon Joel must be weighed against Joel's oft observed propensity to echo and re-use earlier prophetic and cultic language (see note 3.d. in *Notes/Comments* of Ps. 110).

The repeated phrase שׁוב שׁבות/שׁיבת "restore fortune" is obviously a crucial one in the psalm. Although not exclusively prophetic (cf., e.g., Job 42:10), its associations are mainly prophetic or dependent upon prophecy. Scholars have queried the dating of a number of the prophetic passages in which the expression occurs in the books of pre-exilic prophets, yet it is clearly pre-exilic in origin (Hos 6:11) and was certainly used in exilic times (Lam 2:14; Ezek 39:25). The majority of its contexts presuppose, whether in historical fact or prospect, a situation of severe divine judgment, a great divide in the experience of the religious community, on the farther side of which lies restoration to favor which finds concrete expression in restoration to the land and national exaltation (see, e.g., Jer 29:14; Joel 4 [3]:1; Amos 9:14; Zeph 2:7; 3:20). Jerusalem sometimes plays an explicit role in the passages which use the phrase in question (Jer 33:6 [cf. 30:18]; 31:23; Joel 4 [3]:1). If vv 1–3 are interpreted with reference to the past, it is hardly possible to avoid relating them to the return from exile and the rebuilding of the temple and city of Jerusalem. Of particular interest for this psalm is Ps 14:7, where restoration of the people of God is linked with a wish that salvation may issue from Zion. Either the verse or the whole psalm is probably post-exilic (Kraus, *Psalmen*, 247; Anderson, *Psalms*, 131), and the verse accordingly provides a parallel to vv 1, 4. Isa 52:8 too may well be significant. In Second Isaiah "Zion" is used as a cipher for the restored religious community: at Isa 52:8 Yahweh's return (שׁוב) to Zion is the occasion for shouts of joy (רנן) and the revelation of his power before the nations (הגוים). The psalm may well in its first half celebrate such a restoration, but in the tones of Ps 14:7 go on to claim other prophetic promises of national prosperity (cf. H. Schmidt, *Die Psalmen*, 227; Kraus, *Psalmen*, 1034; J. W. Rogerson and J. W. McKay, *Psalms 101–150*, 124). Its post-exilic dating may well be confirmed by the Aramaic שׁיבת "fortunes" in v 1.

Structurally the psalm has been divided by J. Magne (*Bib* 39 [1958] 191) into vv 1–4 and 5–6. He found strophic inclusion in the repetition of שׁבות/שׁוב שׁיבת and a chiastic order, with vv 2b and 3a functioning as an inner pair. He urged that this structure favored the emendation שָׁב "restored" (*BHK*) in v 4. Magne significantly left out of his table of repeated terms the comparative particle of vv 1b, 4b. That and the repeated רנה "happy shout" in vv 2aβ, 5b seem to suggest that the lines vv 1aβ–2aβ and 4–5 are the initial, parallel two lines of separate strophes. This impression is reinforced by the chiastic order of words in both second lines, vv 2aα-β, 5. Accordingly v 3 is the final line of one four-line strophe and v 4 the first of a second. The stylistic variation of form between שׁיבת and שׁבות may have been intended as a pointer to a new beginning at v 4 and as a means of differentiating the changes of fortune as separate events. There is a climactic ring about v 3: it echoes elements taken from the three earlier lines: היינו "we were" (v 1b), the motif of joy (v. 2aα-β) and the praise of Yahweh's great deed (v 2b). The second strophe is structured differently. The last two lines, v 6, serve to amplify v 5, and exhibit external parallelism. This may well suggest that נשׂא "the one who carries" is repeated deliberately *contra* the frequently made suggestion (e.g. *BHS*) to delete the former as a vertical dittograph. The repetition may function as a designed counterpart of the repeated reference to Yahweh's great deed in the last two lines of the earlier strophe.

Explanation

The community of God's people meditate in tones of praise upon Yahweh's earlier activity on their behalf. They look back to a turning point in their fortunes, most probably to the re-establishment of the worship of the religious community in Jerusalem after the Babylonian exile. It was a dream come true; it marked a sharp reversal of the harsh reality of their former distress. In the court of the sanctuary they recall their reaction of joyful excitement and record the Gentiles' reactions of awe, whereby even they were forced to admit that Israel's God must be the author of such a transformation. The recipients add their own praise in confirmation. Their experience was of a piece with Yahweh's miraculous acts of salvation in their earlier history; it rightly called forth a response of glad testimony.

The self-reminder of earlier divine intervention has served as an encouragement to believe that Yahweh would again intervene so signally. He has the power to bless his people in their land. The retrospect has functioned too as a virtual inducement to their God, in whose presence they have met, to come once more to their aid. The psalm moves to an explicit appeal in v 4. The cycle of misfortune and deliverance celebrated in v 1 has half come round again. The community bring their prayer for restoration with the hope that Yahweh will repeat his saving activity (cf. 106:43–44; Judg 3:9, 15). That the Lord of history has such power is attested by his work as Lord of nature. Even the summer drought of the Negeb is succeeded by the welcome winter floods through the wadis. So Yahweh can intervene again in salvation, and to him is brought a plea that he may do so. Their parched lives need renewing. A time of great divine work has given way to a period of "small things" (cf. Zech 4:10); frustration and difficulty dog the steps of the post-exilic community. But with confident tones they affirm their faith that Yahweh will repeat his work of transformation. Reassurance is found in the fact that harvest follows seedtime in the divinely regulated calendar of the year (Gen 8:22). A proverb is used to express the people's plight and hope of renewed life. Traditionally, sowing had overtones of sorrow as a sign of death (cf. John 12:24; 1 Cor 15:36). But the toil and tears of frustration would eventually give way to a harvest of blessing for the community (cf. 30:6 [5]).

So God's people are sustained with the resource of prayer and with the assurances of both his past salvation and his inherent faithfulness. Present distress is no argument for the denial of Yahweh's power or grace (cf. 77:8–11 [7–10]). As he had reversed a calamitous past, he could be relied upon to reverse a painful present. He would, as it were, send his rain of blessing and crown their work of sowing with a welcome harvest. Hope lends wings to their prayer, and both are grounded in Yahweh's historical revelation of his character as faithful to his covenant people. In similar vein the early church was urged to look away from suffering to glory, with a conviction that the God who had begun a good work would faithfully bring it to completion (2 Cor 4:17, 18; Phil 1:6; 1 Thess 5:24).

The Secret of Human Achievement
(127:1–5)

Bibliography

Bussby, F. "A Note on שֶׁנָא in Ps. 127:2." *JTS* 35 (1934) 306–7. **Dahood, M.** "The *aleph* in Psalm 127:2." *Or* 44 (1975) 103–5. **Daiches, S.** "Psalm 127:2. A New Interpretation." *ExpTim* 45 (1933) 24–26. **Emerton, J. A.** "The Meaning of *šēnā'* in Psalm 127:2." *VT* 24 (1974) 15–31. **Hamp, V.** " 'Der Herr gibt es den Seinen im Schlaf.' Ps. 127:2d." *Wort, Lied und Gottesspruch*. Festschrift für J. Ziegler, ed. J. Schreiner. Würzburg, Stuttgart: Echter Verlag, 1972. **Hillers, D. R.** *Treaty-Curses and the OT Prophets*. BibOr 16. Rome: Pontifical Biblical Institute, 1964. **Kuntz, J. K.** "The Canonical Wisdom Psalms of Ancient Israel: Their Rhetorical, Thematic and Formal Dimensions." *Rhetorical Criticism. Essays in Honor of J. Muilenburg*, ed. J. J. Jackson and M. Kessler. Pittsburgh: Pickwick Press, 1974. **Lipiński E.** "Macarismes et psaumes de congratulation." *RB* 75 (1968) 321–67. **Perdue, L. G.** *Wisdom and Cult.* SBLDS 30. Missoula, MT: Scholars Press, 1977. **Rickenbacher, O.** "Anhang: Einige Beispiele stilistischer Analyse alttestamentlicher Texte." *Stilfiguren der Bibel*, ed, W. Buhlmann and K. Scherer. BibB 10. Fribourg: Verlag Schweizerisches Katholisches Bibelwerk, 1973. **Schmidt, H.** "Grüsse und Glückwünsche im Psalter." *TSK* 103 (1931) 141–50. **Thomas, D. W.** "A Note on זָרְמְתָּם שֵׁנָה יִהְיוּ in Psalm 90:5." *VT* 18 (1968) 267–68.

Translation

[1] One of the processional songs.[a] Solomonic.
> *If Yahweh does not build a house,*   (3+3)
> *in vain will its builders have toiled* [b] *over it.*
> *If Yahweh does not guard a city,*   (3+3)
> *in vain will the guard have stayed awake.* [b]

[2] *In vain do you act*   (2+2+2)
> *who rise early* [a]
> *and rest* [b] *late.* [c]
> *Some eat bread for which they have labored* [d]—   (3+3)
> *this is the way* [e] *he confers honor* [f] *on those* [g] *he loves.*

³ *Take notice,*ᵃ *sons are what Yahweh gives,*   (4+3)
  *fruit from the womb is a reward from him.*ᵇ
⁴ *Just like arrows handled by a warrior*   (3+3)
  are sons born in one's youth.
⁵ *How fortunate* ᵃ *is the man*   (2+2+2)
  whose quiver ᵇ
  he ᶜ *fills with them.* ᵈ
  Such ᵉ *do not suffer humiliation when they argue* ᶠ   (2+2)
  with adversaries at the gate.

Notes/Comments

1.a. See the note on 120:1.
1.b. The Hebrew perfects have future perfect force (P. Joüon, *Grammaire* § 112i).
2.a. LXX τοῦ ὀρθρίζειν does not necessarily represent a Hebrew infinitive (cf. *BHS*), but probably renders the appositional participle as a definition of what is in vain (cf. R. W. Funk, *A Beginning-Intermediate Grammar of Hellenistic Greek* [2nd ed.; Missoula, MT: Society of Biblical Literature, 1973] 658, with reference to Luke 17:1).
2.b. Heb. שבת "rest" probably signifies arriving home after the day's work: cf. 2 Sam 7:1 where it is contrasted with military activity. The pair קום/ישׁב "rise, sit" is used in place of the common בוא/יצא "go out, come in."
2.c. LXX μετά "after" probably represents not אחרי (*BHS*) but an interpretation of MT as מאחרי, which is rendered thus at Deut 29:21.
2.d. The accentuation in MT takes אכלי לחם העצבים "eaters of bread for which they have labored" with the preceding line, as a further participle qualifying לכם "you." However, metrically the phrase belongs with the next clause; it is worth asking whether the bicolon can be understood as a syntactical unit. D. N. Freedman *apud* M. Dahood, *Psalms III*, 223, has noted that the two lines of v 2 exhibit a chiastic word play שוא לכם "in vain do you act" and שנא לידידו "honor on those he loves." A chiastic pattern can be observed further in the participial phrases; the participle אכלי may function as *casus pendens* "as for those who eat . . ." (cf. GKC § 116w), taken up later in the line by לידיד(י)ו "on those he loves" (S. Daiches, *ExpTim* 45 [1933] 25). Heb. העצבים "labors" is to be taken in a positive sense: cf. Prov 14:23 "In all labor (עצב) there is profit" (cf. Prov 5:10; Ps 128:2).
2.e. I. e. by enabling them to eat the fruit of their labors (cf. Daiches, *ExpTim* 45 [1933] 25). This divine blessing (cf. 128:2) is implicitly contrasted with the futility curse of another's eating what one had sown (Job 31:8: see *Form/Structure/Setting* below). H.-J. Kraus (*Psalmen*, 1036) rightly refuses to alter MT to כי "for" with LXX (and two Heb. mss.) or to אכן "surely." MT can hardly be rendered "surely" *pace* J. A. Emerton, *VT* 24 (1974) 19.
2.f. Heb. שׁנא, evidently intended by the Massoretes as "sleep," with Aram. orthography for שׁנה (GKC § 80h), has defied exegetes' efforts to explain, whether taken as object of the verb or as an accusative of condition or time (GKC § 118i). Emerton has rightly queried whether the notion that God blesses man when the latter does nothing is congenial to the ethos of Israelite wisdom literature to which the psalm belongs (*VT* 24 [1974] 20). The need for diligence and warning against idle sleep are a regular theme in Proverbs (e.g. 6:6–11). The argument of V. Hamp that the phrase נתן שׁנה "give sleep" is attested by Ps 132:4; Prov 6:4 ("Ps. 127:2d," 76) founders upon the fact that its usage is quite different. D. Winton Thomas (*VT* 18 [1968] 268) agreed with F. Bussby (*JTS* 35 [1934] 306–7), that the significance is here "sexual intercourse" on the basis of Gk. ὕπνος "sleep" in this sense in Wis 4:6; 7:2, and he found the same meaning in Ps 90:5. Emerton's dismissal of this suggestion as a "very dubious speculation" (*VT* 24 [1974] 24) can hardly be gainsaid. L. G. Perdue (*Wisdom and Cult*, 298), taking ידיד "beloved" as a feminine reference, as in Jer 11:15, has explained MT as a rejection of a practice of overwork which leads a man to give only sleep to his beloved wife and not sexual intimacy; but he preferred to read שוא "vanity" with a similar result, rendering "for [presumably reading כי] such a one gives to his beloved nothing."
Dahood (*Or* 44 [1975] 103; cf. *Psalms III*, 223–24; "Hebrew-Ugaritic Lexicography XI," *Bib* 54 [1973] 361–62) renders "prosperity" by recourse to a homonymous stem שנא, which he

compares with *šnʾ* attested in Syr. *šaynâ* "prosperity" and Eth. *seneʾ* "peace." In fact the Syriac noun more probably derives from a stem *šʾn* (R. Payne Smith, *Thesaurus Syriacus*, vol. 2 [Oxford: Clarendon Press, 1901] col. 4012; cf. *šayyen* "pacify"; Heb. שׁאן), though Dahood does postulate metathetic roots *šʾn* and *šnʾ*. The rendering "prosperity" would fit the context well, but Syr. *šayna* means primarily "peace." "Peace" might provide a contrast to עצבים as "anxious toil," but Dahood himself takes the latter as "idols." The best suggestion yet offered is that put forward by Emerton, *VT* 24 [1974] 25–31. He has related שׁנא (=שֶׁנָה) to a cognate stem attested in Syr. *ǎanâʾ* "sublimity, great honor," Arab. *saniya* "shine, be high in rank" and probably Ugar. *šnt* (cf. Emerton, *VT* 24 [1974] 28–29; J. C. L. Gibson, *Canaanite Myths*, 102, with reference to *šntk* in Krt 6:57–58). This stem has already been plausibly discovered in Prov 5:9; 14:17; 24:21 (see W. McKane, *Proverbs*, 316, 405–6, 468, for discussion and bibliographical references). Comparison with Prov 5:9–10 is rewarding: there שׁנתך "your honor" (to be pointed שְׁנָתְךָ in parallelism with הודך "your wealth") is associated with עצביך "your labors, hard earnings" in a context related to the futility curse. Here the "honor" conferred by Yahweh is the success with which he crowns their efforts in that they are able to eat what they have labored to produce.

2.g. MT ידידו "those he loves" was probably earlier a defective writing (ו-) for ידידיו, read by two Heb. mss. LXX S Hier rendered as plural. The singular form may be linked with the reference to Solomon in the heading.

3.a. Heb. הנה "take notice" calls attention to what follows.

3.b. Heb. שׂכר "reward" shares the suffix of לידידו (Dahood, *Psalms III*, 224) or, more probably, it may be understood from the previous נחלת יהוה "what Yahweh gives."

5.a. See the note on 112:1.

5.b. LXX mistranslated as τὴν ἐπιθυμίαν αὐτοῦ "his desire." The translator either did not know the meaning of אשׁפה, "quiver," which occurs only here in the Psalter, or failed to recognize it in this context. Conceivably he related it to the stem שׁאף "pant, long for," although this equivalence does not occur in the Gk. OT. Kraus (*Psalmen*, 1038–39) plausibly finds a mental background for the comparison of v 4 in the figurative phrase for arrows בני אשׁפתו "sons of his bow" (Lam 3:13).

5.c. In the light of v 3 Yahweh is clearly the subject. The divine reference then parallels that of v 2b.

5.d. E. Lipiński (*RB* 75 [1968] 351) follows the accentuation of MT by taking מהם "with them" with יבשׁ(ו) ("be ashamed of them") and scanning v 5 as 2+3, 2+3. But a penultimate line 2+2+2 neatly matches the corresponding line in the first strophe, v 2aα-γ; Kraus, *Psalmen*, 1038–39, and evidently *BHS* scan both lines thus.

5.e. Heb. יבשׁו "suffer humiliation" has often been emended to a singular יבשׁ with LXXˢ (e.g. A. Weiser, *Psalms*, 763; Kraus, *Psalmen*, 1038–39; cf. *BHK*), and so, conjecturally, has the following verb ידברו "they argue." Dahood (*Psalms III*, 225) explains as a (surely confusing in this context) third singular ending in *-û*. The plurals do match those in the final line of the previous strophe, v 2aδ-b; the singular references earlier in v 5 may be regarded as collective.

5.f. Heb. דבר את has a forensic connotation. Lipiński, *RB* 75 [1968] 351 note 130; Dahood, *Psalms III*, 225; and *HALAT*, 201b relate to the other stem דבר: "repulse (enemies)." Dahood's argument concerning consistency of metaphor is hardly relevant: there is no metaphor in v 5b, and the military simile of v 5a can easily apply to the forensic defense of v 5b. A military reference would nicely match the urban defense of v 1b, but the use of the sign of the definite object before אויבים "adversaries" would be awkward.

Form/Structure/Setting

Psalm 127 is a wisdom poem. It consists of two extended wisdom sayings or proverbs (vv 1–2, 3–5). It does not conform closely to most other wisdom poems. Of the seven rhetorical criteria suggested by J. K. Kuntz for classifying such psalms he could find two, a simile (v 4) and the אשׁרי ("how fortunate") formula (v 5); it exhibits two of the four thematic criteria, one partially, the life of the righteous (a corresponding antithetical description of the wicked is lacking, except perhaps by implication in vv 1–2), while the other is counsel concerning everyday conduct, in vv 1–2; it contains only one term characteristic of sapiential vocabulary, אשרי ("Canonical Wisdom Psalms," 190, 208, 214–15). Accordingly R. E. Murphy ("Wisdom Psalms," 164) was prepared to see in the psalm merely wisdom influence, a reflection of preoccupations of the sages, vanity and the divine gift of sons, and he claimed that the psalm defies conventional classification. The composition appears to stand closer to standard wisdom literature than to the Psalter. For the first motif may be cited the Book of Ecclesiastes and, in the wider sense of divine (over-) ruling of human affairs, Prov 16:3, 9; 21:31 (cf. Jas 4:13–14); for the second the narrative of Job. Perdue (*Wisdom and Cult*, 297–98) has given a useful formal analysis of the psalm: two conditional proverbs (v 1, cf. Eccl 10:10–11), an admonition (the whole of v 2, according to his own exegesis), a synonymous proverb (v 3), a comparative proverb (v 4) and an אשרי saying (v 5). Vv 1–2 are related to the futility curse, for which see D. R. Hillers, *Treaty Curses*, 28–29.

Perdue is doubtless right in denying any cultic setting for the psalm: it contains no specifically cultic sayings nor does it exhibit parallels to any type of cultic poetry. A setting of the autumn festival has been urged by some scholars (J. H. Eaton, *Psalms*, 268; cf. A. A. Anderson, *Psalms*, 866). Dahood (*Psalms III*, 223) interprets the psalm as a wisdom poem composed for a king, mainly in view of his military interpretation of ידבדו "they argue" in v 5. Lipiński (*RB* 75 [1968] 352) has revived the suggestion of H. Schmidt (*TSK* 103 [1931] 145–48) concerning the life setting of the psalm: it is a song of congratulations sung at the birth of a son. Vv 3–5 are then the focus of the psalm, while vv 1–2 are preparatory, emphasizing that all comes from Yahweh: the phrase יבנה בית "build a house" in v 1 refers metaphorically to raising a family, as in Gen 16:2; 30:3; Exod 1:21; Ps 113:9. Kraus (*Psalmen*, 1037) also interprets v 1 thus, but is reluctant to allow vv 3–5 to determine the role of the whole composition so specifically: rather, the two sayings which make up the psalm are both concerned with establishing a family and refer to the suffering and joy in store for the father.

Overall it does seem best to regard the psalm as a specimen of popular, didactic religious wisdom poetry. Its incorporation into the collection of processional songs raises the question whether the references to "house" and "city" in v 1 would not naturally in such a context be interpreted as indicating the temple and Jerusalem, and function as a warning to be alert to Yahweh's personal will rather than trust in these mighty religious symbols (cf. 125:1). A similar interpretation, probably subsequent in view of its more specialized nature, underlies the reference to Solomon in the heading. Heb. לשלמה is probably to be taken as "concerning Solomon." It does not reflect merely the association of Solomon with wisdom literature: it appears to represent a homiletical application of certain elements of the psalm to the person and work of Solomon in building the temple. Its underlying methodology is strikingly akin to the later NT Christological application of psalm material. The focal points of this interpretation are clearly יבנה בית "build a house" in v 1 and לידידו "those he loves" in v 2 (cf. the name ידידיה "Jedidiah" in 2 Sam 12:25), probably שנא "sleep" as an allusion to the night vision at Gibeon (1 Kgs 3:3–15) and perhaps in v 1 the protection of the city, withdrawn in the reign of Solomon's successor (1 Kgs 14:25). This "meaningful contextualization" (J. Sawyer, *Semantics in Biblical Research* [SBT 2:24; London: SCM

Press, 1972] 13) illustrates the importance of Israel's sacred history to later generations and conveys an implicit hope that Yahweh would once again work mightily among and through his chosen people (cf. 126:4).

The date of the original composition can hardly be verified: A. Weiser has rightly stated that in view of its general terms "it belongs to the timeless world of the proverb" (*Psalms*, 764). Dahood (*Psalms III*, 223) regards it as pre-exilic in consequence of his military and royal view of v 5; similarly Lipiński (*RB* 75 [1968] 353) assigns it to the end of the monarchical period, seeing in v 5 a reflection of the invasions at the end of the Southern Kingdom. The incorporation of the psalm into the present collection was clearly a post-exilic phenomenon, while the re-interpretation in terms of the Solomonic era probably occurred later still.

The unity of the psalm is by no means assured. A sizeable number of scholars have regarded it as an amalgamation of two separate, unrelated sayings (e.g. H. Gunkel, *Die Psalmen*, 553–55; Weiser, *Psalms*, 764; G. Fohrer, *Introduction*, 292; C. C. Keet, *Psalms of Ascents*, 54–55; K. Seybold, *Wallfahrtspsalmen*, 30). Reference has already been made to the interpretation of יבנה בית in v 1 in terms of establishing a family. This expedient does create a good link with vv 3–5, but it is difficult to accept it as the original meaning: the juxtaposition with guarding a city suggests rather that it is intended as a literal task. The Sumerian hymn to the goddess Nisaba cited by Kraus (*Psalmen*, 1039; A. Falkenstein und W. von Soden. *Sumerische und akkadische Hymnen und Gebete* [Zürich: Artemis-Verlag, 1953] 65–67) provides a more weighty argument: it celebrates her as one without whom no house, city or palace is built and as one who gives children. This combination of motifs parallel with those of the psalm does suggest its unity (cf. Anderson, *Psalms*, 866).

Does the stylistic structure of the psalm provide compelling evidence of unity? Dahood (*Psalms III*, 222–23) has found inclusion in the correspondence between עיר "city," v 1, and שער "gate (of the city)," v 5, and in the alliteration of *b* sounds in the first and last lines and of *š* sounds in the second and penultimate lines. The poem clearly falls into two four-line strophes, vv 1–2 and 3–5, which obviously exhibit an initial word play בוניו "builders" and בנים "sons." There are further parallel features. More precisely the repetition בונים, יבנה in v 1 corresponds to בנים, בני in vv 3–4, while the divine name יהוה occurs twice in v 1 and once in v 3. Also כן "thus" appears in vv 2, 4 and the (doubled) negative of v 2 is inclusively repeated in the last line of the second strophe, in v 5 (see too the parallels given in *Notes/Comments*, notes 5.b., 5.c. and 5.d.).

There is also evidence of a chiastic relationship between the strophes. Both vv 2b and 3 feature divine gifts; in v 2aγ (כן) לחם תעצבים "the bread of labor (thus)" is paralleled in בני הנעורים (כן) "(thus) the sons of youth" in v 4b; and אשרי "fortunate" in v 5a corresponds to שוא "in vain" in v 2aα. Outside this tight nucleus lie the less rigidly coordinated vv 1, 5b, matched in their negatives and combinations of individual and communal concerns. V 1 paves the way for v 2 with examples of labor in vain, while v 5b reinforces v 5a with a concrete instance of defensive aid.

From another aspect the chiastic order in v 2 (שוא ל : ל שוא "vanity, honor") mentioned in *Notes/Comments* note 2.d., has a parallel in vv 3–4, בני : בנים "sons, sons of." The second strophe is itself tightly interlocked with overlapping terms or step-parallelism. Apart from בנים/בני, there is the גבור/הגבר ("warrior, the man") pair in vv 4, 5a and the doubled אח in vv 5a, b. The important role played by v 3 within the network of the psalm gives no support to Seybold's claim that it is a theologically motivated redactional addition (*Wallfahrtspsalmen*, 30 note 19, 62). Further stylistic features of the psalm have been noted by O. Rickenbacher in his appendix to *Stilfiguren der Bibel*, 100–2.

The careful structuring between the strophes points to the unity of the composition, disparate though it may appear to the modern reader. At its core lies the twin evidence of divine blessing, לחם העצבים "the bread of labor" and בני הנעורים "the sons of youth." Before and after are placed amplifying statements, negative in the first case and positive in the second.

Explanation

The wisdom ideology of ancient Israel traced to the mystery of divine providence the gap that so frequently yawns between human effort and achievement: man proposes, but God disposes. Earthly life was regarded as essentially the arena of divine salvation and judgment, blessing and curse. The will of God was ignored at man's peril, not only in the realms of military activity (2 Sam 2:1), national internal policy (Hos 8:4) and foreign policy (Isa 30:1), but also in the ordinary life of the individual believer. Futility curses in common use, which the prophets exploited to express divine judgment, dwelt upon the grim possibility of labor in vain. To build a house was no guarantee of prolonged habitation: another might live in it (Isa 65:22–23; Amos 5:11; cf. Deut 28:33). Such a futility curse is here angled in a Godward direction. Yahweh's smile of favor, or rather his active involvement in the undertaking, is essential. Both the prophets and the covenant sanctions of Deut 28 associated futility sayings with hostile invasion. Whether independently or not, the same aura of meaning lies implicitly over the first line, in view of the continuation in terms of a threat to communal security. The secret of such security—or its negation—rests with God (cf. Ezek 28:26; Amos 3:6), over and above the sentry on the lookout for enemy attack.

A constant motif of futility curses was derived from the area of agriculture or viniculture (Job 31:8; Hos 4:10; Amos 5:11; Mic 6:14). The damning of a man's efforts in the fields from dawn to dusk by attack (Lev 26:16) or drought (Lev 26:19–20) or pestilence (Deut 28:38) haunted the farmer. It was blessing indeed to eat the fruit of one's labors instead of laboring in vain. It was sure evidence of Yahweh's love for that man (cf. Ps 60:7 [5]) that such an honor was bestowed upon him.

The first strophe teaches the lesson of divine sovereignty over human enterprise by way of warning against self-sufficiency. It pursues a negative course until it reaches a rhetorical climax of direct address in v 2a. It ends on a positive note, which is developed in the second strophe in terms of praise of God and commendation. A further ambition in the field of human endeavor now comes to the fore, a family of sons, who in a male-dominated society were prized more than daughters. The series of statements in Jer 5:17 is interesting to compare with the sequence found in the psalm: bread, sons and cities are there all objects of divinely instigated disaster (cf. Isa 65:22–23; Hos 4:10). The psalm concentrates upon the particular value of sons born to a man not too late in life: they would be old enough to protect their father in his declining years. If he were wrongly accused in the law court just inside the city gate (cf. Amos 5:12), they would rally round, ensuring that he was treated justly and defending his interests in a way denied to loners in society, such as widows and orphans (cf. Isa 1:23). They were God's arrows against injustice within the local community.

The psalm is an unusual one. Unlike other wisdom psalms, ethical values do not stand in the forefront. Rather than describing directly the standards of the righteous and decrying wickedness, the psalm intends to inculcate trust in Yahweh. God's "beloved" are not explicitly identified with the righteous, though the psalmist may have done this implicitly. Yahweh is the focus of the psalm: he has established his order over man's life and is the agent of his success or failure. He is the immanent Lord of the house and the city, of the field and the family. From within its comparatively unsophisticated culture, the psalm seeks to relate to God the concerns and values of everyday life.

The modern reader of Ps 127 finds himself detached from its cultural setting and so perchance from its message. Living as he does in days of overpopulation and birth control, he needs to appreciate the rigors of ancient society in constant need of replenishment against the ravages of disease, war and famine. Living as he may in a more secure and just society, in which he enjoys peace, freedom and lawful order guaranteed by a fair police force and judiciary, where urban alert systems and friends at court are unnecessary, the psalm's immediate impact upon him will be lost. More positively he may well regret the apparent passing of times when high value was set upon the family as the basic unit of society and as a divinely intended source of comfort and strength and, conversely, sphere of responsibility (cf. 1 Tim 5:4, 8).

Speaking out of its own culture, the psalm offers implicit praise of God's power in human affairs, and issues an indirect call to the individual to trust in him. Neither the city's defenses nor its law court can be substituted for divine protection: each man must have recourse to God's support and care, and never take it for granted, as he moves from enterprise to enterprise (cf. Jas 4:13–15). Man's basic insecurity is mirrored nakedly in this psalm. No formula of success is offered. But man is urged to stretch out his hand in trust and submission and to ascribe to God the praise for the success he does enjoy, recognizing in it his mighty hand. God rules and God overrules—to him be the glory. Theologically the psalm anticipates a Pauline emphasis upon "good works" within a Christian context of faith over against mere "works" (Eph 2:9–10). Labor is to be a matter of collaboration with God (1 Cor 15:10, 58). Under the new covenant there is an even closer intertwining of the believer's fortunes with his Lord, as Jesus reaffirmed, "Apart from me you can do nothing" (John 15:5).

God Is No Man's Debtor (128:1-6)

Bibliography

Kuntz, J. K. "The Canonical Wisdom Psalms of Ancient Israel." *Rhetorical Criticism. Essays in Honor of J. Mullenburg*, ed. J. J. Jackson and M. Kessler. Pittsburgh: Pickwick Press, 1974. ———. "The Retribution Motif in Psalmic Wisdom." *ZAW* 89 (1977) 223–33. **Lipiński, E.** "Macarismes et psaumes de congratulation." *RB* 75 (1968) 321–67. **Schmidt, H.** "Grüsse und Glückwünsche im Psalter." *TSK* 103 (1931) 141–50.

Translation

1 One of the processional songs.[a]
How fortunate [b] is everyone who reveres Yahweh,   (3+2)
  who walks in his ways!
2 You will certainly [a] eat what your toiling hands produce.   (3+2)
  How fortunate you are! You will get on well.
3 Your wife will be like a fruitful vine   (3+2)
  inside your house.
Your sons will be like olive shoots   (3+2)
  around your table.[a]

4 Take note,[a] this is how a man is blessed [b]   (3+2 [c])
  who fears Yahweh.
5 May Yahweh bless you from Zion   (3 [a])
  so that you see [b] Jerusalem faring well   (3+2)
  all your life long,
6 so that you see your grandsons.   (3+2)
  May peace rest upon Israel.[a]

Notes/Comments

1.a. See the note on 120:1.

1.b. See the note on 112:1.

2.a. Heb. כי has an emphatic force.

3.a. J. K. Kuntz (*ZAW* 89 [1977] 228) has defined the perspective of the retribution motif of the psalm as traditional, as in Pss 1, 32, 37, in contrast with the realistic aspect of Pss 34, 112 and the futuristic one of Pss 49, 73.

4.a. See the note on 127:3. The following כי in MT is problematic. M. Dahood (*Psalms III*, 229) claims for it an exclamatory force "how." It may be a partial dittograph of כן "thus" (H.-J. Kraus, *Psalmen*, 1041): cf. the evidence for its absence noted in BHS. Did it originate in a marginal variant of כן in 127:2 (cf. note 2 [c] in BHS there), misplaced due to the proximity of כן and יהוה in both 127:2–3 and 128:4?

4.b. Blessing, here mediated through the sanctuary, is manifested in Israel's "physical existence, in food and clothing, in the social and economic maintenance of the society in which they live, and in the continuance of life from one generation to the next" (C. Westermann, *What Does the OT Say about God?*, 44).

4.c. Dahood (*Psalms III*, 229) scans as 3+3, repointing MT יְבֹרַךְ as יְבֹרָךְ. BHS regards as a tricolon, evidently 2+2+2.

5.a. A. A. Anderson (*Psalms*, 869) scans v 5 as a tricolon 3+3+2 (similarly J. Schildenberger, *Estudios Eclesiásticos* 34 [1960] 684), but structurally the two latter cola must rank as a bicolon as a match for v 6 (see *Form/Structure/Setting*). It is possible that a short line consisting of a single colon is intended (cf. G. Fohrer, "Über den Kurzvers," *ZAW* 66 [1954] 199–236). It is often supposed that a second colon has fallen out (e.g. *BHK*, Kraus, *Psalmen*, 1041; cf. *BHS*): attempts to restore it include מקום קדשו "his holy place" (K. Budde, *ZAW* 35 [1915] 174) and עשה שמים וארץ "maker of heaven and earth" (S. Mowinckel, *Tricola*, 85). K. Seybold (*Wallfahrts-psalmen*, 33) regards the four words מציון . . . ירושלם "from Zion . . . Jerusalem" as a redactional expansion, but deletion would wreck the careful ordering of the psalm as a whole. The cola of vv 5–6 are sometimes juggled so that v 5aα gains a parallel colon and v 6b lies outside the metrical scheme, as at 125:5b: e.g. E. J. Kissane (*Psalms II*, 262) adopted the sequence vv 5aα, 5b, 6a, 5aβ, 6b.

5.b. The combination of *waw* and imperative here expresses consequence (GKC § 110f, i).

6.a. For this formula see the note on 125:5. Here it apparently functions as an integral part of the poem (Anderson, *Psalms*, 871).

Form/Structure/Setting

Psalm 128 is generally classified as a wisdom psalm. Kuntz ("Canonical Wisdom Psalms," 190–215) has observed that it contains two rhetorical motifs out of a total of seven in wisdom psalmody (the אשרי "fortunate" formula and the simile), two specific wisdom words (אשרי and דרך "way"; cf. ירא "fearer" akin to יראה "fear") and two thematic elements out of a possible four (the fear of Yahweh and counsel concerning everyday conduct, here concerning a large family as recompense for devotion). He further notes the unique pattern of development, whereby the third person utterance commending the fear of Yahweh passes into a second person enumeration of the rewards accruing, and then reverts to a third person reinforcing comment (vv 1–4; "Canonical Wisdom Psalms," 217). Kuntz's observations all apply to the first four verses: the psalm takes a complex turn in vv 5–6, which have the form of a priestly benediction. Have the wisdom elements been taken over into a composition intended for cultic use or, on the contrary, has cultic language been re-used in a non-cultic context of wisdom teaching? The latter explanation is advocated by J. Becker (*Gottesfurcht im AT*, 275–76; cf. G. Fohrer. *Introduction*, 292), the former by C. Keller ("Les beatitudes de l'AT," in *Maqqél shâqédh* [Montpelier: Causse Graille Castelnau, 1960] 93–94; cf. R. E. Murphy, "Wisdom Psalms," 161, 167). J. H. Eaton (*Psalms*, 287, cf. Anderson, *Psalms*, 869) has noted that the fertility theme would suit the autumn festival.

H. Schmidt (*TSK* 103 [1931] 142) assigned the psalm to a precise secular setting, the welcome given to a host at the door of his house. On the other hand, E. Lipiński (*RB* 75 [1968] 347–48), helped by his view that the אשרי formula was originally cultic (but see L. G. Perdue, *Wisdom and Cult*, 328 note 23), has described the psalm's setting as totally cultic, though composite. Vv 1–3 are ritual felicitations welcoming the faithful on their arrival at the sanctuary, while vv 5–6 are a benediction introduced by a rubric (v 4; cf. Num 6:23). Since both parts were used at the same service, they were inscribed on a single sheet as an aide-memoire for the officiating priest.

Kraus, ibid., has raised the possibility that the priestly benediction of vv

5–6 involved a different speaker from vv 1–4. Seybold (*Wallfahrtspsalmen*, 55) leaves open the suggestion that the psalm was a priestly blessing upon departing pilgrims.

Structurally v 4 appears to belong with vv 5–6 (see below), while כן "thus" *pace* Lipiński refers back to the preceding verses. The pattern of ideal third person speech (v 4) followed by specific second person language (vv 5–6) accords with vv 1, 2–3. Vv 5–6 are not a standard priestly benediction, but after v 4 possess a hypothetical value with the implicit promise: "If you fulfil this condition, you will receive such a blessing" or, more likely, "May you fall into this category so that you are blessed." However, the references to Zion and Jerusalem, if part of the basic text *pace* Seybold, seem too specific to permit a totally desacralized interpretation. Accordingly, one should envisage a less formal use of the benediction in the course of a temple festival, in a setting of priestly instruction or even non-priestly instruction among pilgrims. Noteworthy is A. Weiser's description of the psalm (*Psalms*, 767) as a parenetic exegesis of some sort, developed out of the practice of pronouncing blessing and used in community worship. Was the psalm composed specifically for use as a processional song, rather than being used secondarily for this purpose, as most of the psalms in the collection were? The inclusion of v 6b within the poem, in contrast to 125:5, supports this hypothesis. It is significant that promise of blessing is contained in a processional context in Ps 24 (v 5).

A number of scholars divide the psalm after v 4 (e.g. Weiser, *Psalms*, 767; Eaton, *Psalms*, 287; Kraus, *Psalmen*, 1041–42; cf. Dahood, *Psalms III*, 229, who describes ירא יהוה "fearer of Yahweh" as forming an inclusion with v 1). Rather, the break must come after v 3, as its detailed stylistic patterning reveals. The phrase ירא יהוה heralds the beginning of separate strophes. The doubled beatitude (אשרי(ך) "(you are) fortunate" in vv 1–2 is matched by the doubled term of benediction יברך, יברכך "blessed" in vv 4–5, in both cases involving a change from third to second person. The pair of lines in v 3, exhibiting external parallelism (כ, כ "like"), corresponds to the pair vv 5aβ-b, 6, which both begin with וראה "and see" and are linked by chiastic order (the word play ירושלם "Jerusalem" and שלום "peace," שלום and טוב "good" [cf. 122:8–9] and religious center and community in vv 5aβ, 6a, and the second person references in v 5b, 6b); moreover, בניך "your sons" in v 3b is capped by בנים לבניך "your grandsons" in v 6. Other correspondences between the strophes are טוב "good" in vv 2, 5, כל "all" in vv 1, 5, and כי in vv 2, 4, if it is original in the latter case. Heb. ראה "see" in vv 5–6 gives an inclusive wordplay with ירא "fearer" at the head of both the psalm as a whole and the second strophe. Seybold's deletion of v 1 as a generalizing expression of vv 2, 3 (*Wallfahrtspsalmen*, 33, 62) and part of v 5 (see *Notes/Comments*, note 5.a.) as redactional additions leaves the psalm stylistically impoverished. The careful structuring of the present psalm has a ring of creative artistry about it. It is difficult to believe that it was the work of a redactor whose professed interests were theological in nature.

The psalm is generally regarded as post-exilic. The incorporation of the שלום formula of v 6b into the poem and probably the mixed form of the psalm support this view. In the collection it is a companion piece to Ps 127,

with its common interest in the family and hard-won harvest (cf. "Jerusalem,"
128:5, "the city," 127:1; אשרי, 127:1 and 128:1; הנה, 127:3 and 128:4), although this psalm is less profound in outlook than the previous one.

Explanation

Here is traditional wisdom teaching, presented evidently in the context
of a religious festival at Jerusalem. Before the pilgrims or a representative
member of their ranks is set the ideal of a life dedicated to God in reverent
obedience to his moral will. The beatitude form, which has a wide-eyed,
yearning quality (cf. 1 Kgs 10:8), is used to commend such a life style.

Like any good teacher and preacher, the psalmist moves quickly from the
general to the particular and individual: "This good fortune may be yours
in specific terms." The nature of the good fortune contingent upon a religiously motivated life is elaborated as achievement in the basics of life, which
are understood as good harvests and a large family of sons. Banished is the
futility which grimly pervaded the first half of Ps 127. Fertility, material and
physical, is promised as an incentive to obey. It is the dream of any primitive
society struggling for survival, close to the bread line and victim of barrenness
and bereavement.

The botanical similes fill out the promise with emotive content. The vine
and olive tree, sources of the staple products of Palestine along with cereal
crops, brought enrichment to daily life and made it worth living (cf. 104:15).
The pictures of joy and fertility conjured up by the grape-laden vine (cf.
Ezek 19:10) and the suckers springing up round the old olive tree served
to preach as powerful a message to the mind as any television commercial
communicates to the eye.

The divine origin of such fortune is now spelled out, in terms of blessing.
Blessing is the largesse of life in abundance from the generous hand of Yahweh
himself. He is no man's debtor: trusting obedience is not overlooked. Primarily
blessing is a cultic term: the sanctuary was the medium of its bestowal. At
the close of the festival the priest would send the pilgrims back to their
homes and labors with a benediction from Yahweh (cf. Num 6:23–27; Ps
121), but its fulfillment depended upon each pilgrim's attitude of heart and
life to his God. The hope is expressed in v 5 that the individual pilgrim
may be found fit to receive the general promise of blessing as a reality in
his own experience.

Dear to the pilgrim was the welfare of Jerusalem—in addition to his own
welfare (v 2)—since within its walls lay the temple (cf. 122:6–9). Season by
season the pilgrim would return to this earthly link with Yahweh, to worship
and to receive fresh benediction upon himself, his work and his home. Only
if the holy city survived and prospered, could he continue to experience
this blessing. He was conscious of an essential bond between his personal
life and this focal point of the religious community. From the private concerns
of the first half, the psalm has moved beyond what might have seemed a
"little boxes" mentality to an expression of communal solidarity relating to
the spiritual center of the nation.

V 6a manifests a further expansion of interest. It expresses not only a wish for long life, but a hope for the future of the family and so of the community at large, as the closing wish makes clear. For the community not only was the welfare of its religious capital necessary, but also an unbroken human chain, generation after generation. Only thus, from father to son to grandson, would "Israel" live on, the covenant nation committed to worship and obey its Lord, the chosen people privileged to enjoy his blessing.

The simple philosophy of the psalm, though presented in seemingly absolute terms, receives qualification even in the OT and certainly in the NT (cf. Job; Hab 3:17–18; Rom 8:35–39). But for many it must have proved a good working principle of life; such categorical promises of material endowment are not absent from the NT (Matt 6:33; 2 Cor 9:6–12; cf. Phil 4:19), despite a shift to a less earthly emphasis. It is of a piece with the essence of OT theology, which proclaimed the triangular relationship of Yahweh, Israel and the land, and stressed the sovereign beneficence of Yahweh in granting and maintaining his people's life in the land. Whatever qualifications this black and white representation required and received, upon those who did enjoy what they were taught to regard as Yahweh's ongoing care there ever remained the onus to bring their firstfruits to the sanctuary; here they were to redeem their firstborn in worshipful thanksgiving and with declaration of continued reliance upon Yahweh and conformity to his will (cf. Deut 26:1–15).

The Resilience of Faith   (129:1–8)

Bibliography

Crüsemann, F. *Studien zur Formgeschichte.* **Driver, G. R.** "Studies in the Vocabulary of the OT. 1." *JTS* 31 (1930) 275–84.

Translation

[1] One of the processional songs.[a]
Many a time [b] have they afflicted me since my youth,   (3+2)
    let Israel declare,
[2] Many a time have they afflicted me since my youth,   (3+2)
    yet they could not defeat me.
[3] On my back plowmen [a] plowed,[b]   (3+2)
    making long furrows. [c]
[4] Yahweh is loyal: [a]   (2+3 [b])
    he has cut off the yoke [c] of the wicked.

[5] All who hate Zion   (3+2)
    will [a] be put to shame and repulsed.
[6] They will be like grass on the roofs,   (3+3)
    which withers before [a] it can shoot up,[b]

7 *which cannot fill the reaper's palm*   (3+2)
  nor the sheafbinder's robefold,[a]
8 *and passers-by do not say,*   (3+3)
  "Yahweh's blessing rest upon you."[a]
  We bless you in Yahweh's name.[b]   (4)

Notes/Comments

1.a. See the note on 120:1.
1.b. For רבת "many times" see the note on 120:6.
3.a. LXX reflects הרשעים "the wicked" (cf. *BHS*). That the change of text already occurred at the Hebrew level is rendered probable by 11QPs[a] רשעים. The variant is not simply a corruption based on v 4, but doubtless an explanatory gloss in terms of v 4, which was subsequently taken as a correction of חרשים "plowmen" and displaced it. For this type of textual adaptation see the note on 102:18.
3.b. F. Crüsemann (*Studien zur Formgeschichte*, 170–71) has compared a Ugaritic text, *UT* 67. 6:11–22, in which harrowing one's body is a metaphor for wounding oneself as part of Canaanite mourning customs. Here he understands enemy oppression to be the cause of such a rite of self-humiliation (cf. Mic 4:14 [5:1]). The active nature of the Hebrew expression here renders so direct a meaning unlikely. Rather, the usual interpretation is to be preferred, that underlying the metaphor is the notion of scourging: cf. Isa 51:23.
3.c. For מעניות cf. Ugar. ᶜnt "furrows." Not knowing the term, LXX related it to עון "iniquity" and S to ענוה "submission," but neither necessarily represents a different *Vorlage*.
4.a. Heb. צדיק signifies conformity to a norm, here to the obligations of the covenant.
4.b. A 3+2 meter is less suited to the sense.
4.c. Lit. "rope," here with reference to the harness of the ox drawing the plow: cf. Job 39:10. Does the metaphor change, so that the speaker now represents the ox wearing the yoke (cf. 2:2) rather than the plowed field? It is quite feasible that the previous metaphor is continued: Yahweh prevents the wicked continuing their oppression by, as it were, breaking the harness (Crüsemann, *Studien zur Formgeschichte*, 171).
5.a. Many, such as D. Michel (*Tempora*, 162), A. Weiser (*Psalms*, 770) and M. Dahood (*Psalms III*, 230), and most modern versions construe the verbs in vv 5–6a as jussives, regarding the clauses as wishes: see *Form/Structure/Setting* below.
6.a. Heb. קָדְמַת, here functioning as a conjunction, is identical with the Aramaic preposition used in biblical and Targumic Aramaic (cf. Heb. קָדְמַת Gen 2:14, etc.). The construct form corresponds to the usage of the construct state before a short relative clause (cf. GKC § 130d).
6.b. The meaning required for שלף is "shoot up." BDB (1025b) tentatively suggested a development of the basic meaning of the verb, "draw out, off," as "draw out (the blade)." G. R. Driver (*JTS* 31 [1930] 277), judging this development very forced, regarded the verb as denominative, "produce a stalk," from a noun cognate with Acc. *šulpu* "stalk" and late Heb. שֶׁלֶף "stubble." The emendation שֶׁקָּדִים תְּשָׁדְף "which the east wind scorches" (H. Gunkel, *Die Psalmen*, 560; H.-J. Kraus, *Psalmen*, 1043; Weiser, *Psalms*, 770; *et al.*) and consequent deletion of יבש "withers" as an explanatory gloss are hardly necessary. Dahood (*Psalms III*, 233) has rightly drawn attention to the word play between יבוש "will be ashamed," v 5, and יבש here.
7.a. The reaper took hold of a handful of stalks in his left hand and cut them off below the ears (cf. Job 24:24); then the ears were collected and evidently carried inside the loose fold of the robe above the gathered waist.
8.a. For this blessing given to the reapers cf. Ruth 2:4. There is no need to conclude that the simile changes so that Zion's adversaries are now compared with the harvesters rather than with grass (e.g. J. W. Rogerson and J. W. McKay, *Psalms 101–150*, 131; cf. K. Seybold, *Wallfahrtspsalmen*, 28, who makes this interpretation a basis for regarding v 8a as a redactional addition facilitated by a misunderstanding of v 8b as part of the figure). "You" relates back to the reaper and sheafbinder. The negative reference to a harvest blessing grimly reinforces the idea that attack upon Zion is an ill-omened venture devoid of fulfilment.
8.b. To regard this final line as an emphatic repetition of v 8aβ (e.g. Dahood, *Psalms III*, 233) or as the workers' response (*Tg.*; cf. Ruth 2:4) gives a labored effect. It is rather to be viewed as a cultic benediction (Kraus, *Psalmen*, 1046; Weiser, *Psalms*, 770, 772; *et al.*): see *Form/*

Structure/Setting. The solemn pronouncement of Yahweh's name over his people evoked the power to fulfill their aspirations: cf. Num 6:24-27 (cf. J. W. Wevers, *VT* 6 [1956] 82-86; O. Grether, *Name und Wort,* 47).

Form/Structure/Setting

Psalm 129 is fraught with difficulty for the form critic. C. Westermann (*Praise,* 81) has explained it as a declarative psalm of praise of the people, in other words a communal thanksgiving. In support of this designation he has analyzed the psalm as an introductory summary (vv 1aβ, 2), a looking back to the time of need (v 3), praise (v 4a), a report of God's acts (v 4b) and wishes against God's foes (vv 5-8); the final element has been borrowed from the communal complaint (*Praise,* 84-86, 117). Kraus (*Psalmen,* 1044) has criticized the complexity of this position, which has to appeal to different genres.

Dahood (*Psalms III,* 230) has concentrated upon the latter half of the psalm in order to determine the genre: it is a communal complaint, consisting of a description of oppression and preservation (vv 1-3) and a prayer for the overthrow of God's present enemies. He could have justified the role of vv 1-3 in a complaint by citing the references within other communal complaints to Yahweh's past saving deeds (cf. Westermann, *Praise,* 55-56). On the other hand, Kraus, (*Psalmen,* 1044) G. Fohrer (*Introduction,* 292) and A. A. Anderson (*Psalms,* 871-72) have designated the psalm as a communal song of confidence. Kraus compared Pss 46 and 125 and understood vv 5-8a as statements concerning the future. Since this genre is a development of the complaint (cf. H. Gunkel and J. Begrich, *Einleitung,* 131), the retrospective element of vv 1-4 fits straightforwardly into the overall structure of the psalm (cf. 46:7 [6] and for the whole psalm cf. 44:2-4, 5-9 [1-3, 4-8]).

The correct understanding of vv 5-8 is obviously crucial. The comprehensiveness of v 5 (כל "all") suggests a general rather than a specific reference. It seems to correspond structurally to רבת "many times" in vv 1, 2: much affliction in the past is apparently compared with all hostility in the future. It is significant that the only reference in the Psalter to all enemies being put to shame occurs in 6:11 (10), which is a confident assertion. Comparable too is 97:7: "All worshipers of images are/will be put to shame." These comprehensive parallels suggest that vv 5-8a comprise statements of confidence rather than wishes.

It is difficult to accept a designation of vv 1-4 in terms of a national thanksgiving, on two scores. First, thanksgiving characteristically celebrates a single event, while here a whole history of deliverance is surveyed. Secondly, F. Crüsemann (*Studien zur Formgeschichte,* 160-74) has given good grounds for deleting such a designation from the list of form-critical genres, so that neither Ps 124 nor Ps 129 can be properly so labelled. He has demonstrated that the language of vv 1-4 is closer to individual psalms than to communal ones: Heb. נעורים "youth" is used in the Psalter of an individual's youth; the verb צרר "oppress" is comparable with the participial noun used often to refer to an individual's enemies and only in 74:4, 23 to national foes. Also, שנא

"hater" with a personal genitive characteristically relates to an individual's adversary in the Psalter, except in 106:10, 41. Crüsemann concluded with Weiser (*Psalms*, 771–72) that שנאי ציון "haters of Zion" in v 5 primarily referred to a political and religious group within the community who fail to receive the blessing of the covenant (v 8) and that the individualistic language of vv 2–4 has been put into the mouth of the community at large, as in Ps 124 under the influence of prophetic adaptation of such communal language (*Studien zur Formgeschichte*, 168–73).

For all Crüsemann's significant research, he did not manage to provide such a comprehensive analysis of the psalm as he did for Ps 124. It is common to compare the first singular references to Israel with Isa 12:1–2; 61:10; Jer 10:19–24 (Kraus, *Psalmen*, 1044–45). But it may be asked whether vv 2–4 did not primarily feature a personification of Zion. In that case others champion her cause in vv 5–8a, identifying the "wicked" of v 4 as "haters of Zion," and their confidence is confirmed by another, priestly, set of voices in v 8b. In the first part of this liturgical complex, vv 2–4, the first person address by a personified Zion is in line with a literary tradition attested elsewhere in the OT: cf. Isa 49:14; Jer 4:31; Lam 1:9, 11, 12–16, 18–22; 2:20–22 and, for a statement of confidence, Mic 7:8–10. All the individual-oriented references of vv 1–5 would be explicable, if Zion speaks in vv 2–4. Vv 2, 4 would be an allusion to Yahweh's victory over the nations in conflict with Zion, celebrated in the Songs of Zion, Pss 46, 48, 76. Kraus (*Psalmen*, 1045) himself finds reference to this tradition in v 5. The metaphor of plowing in v 3 may develop the prophetic saying of Mic 3:12: "Zion will be plowed into a field." Heb צרריך "your foes" in 74:4, 23 is used in the context of the destruction of Zion, while קצץ "cut" occurs in a Song of Zion, 46:10(9), with reference to divine victory. Subsequently the original liturgy, which was probably composed in the post-exilic period in view of the Aramaisms of vv 2, 6, 7, was supplied, like Ps 124, with a new initial line, which in this case put Zion's speech upon the lips of the religious community at large; probably vv 2–8a was confined to a single voice or vocal group.

The psalm falls obviously into two strophes, vv (1) 2–4 and 5–8. Dahood (*Psalms III*, 230–33) takes v 4 with the second, construing קצץ as a "precative perfect" and detecting an inclusion יהוה צדיק "Yahweh is loyal" and בשם יהוה "in Yahweh's name" in vv 4, 8. The latter phenomenon can as easily mark symmetrical conclusions of strophes. Apart from the divine name, vv 2, 8a, 8b, the only other interstrophic repetition is the negative לא in vv 2, 7, 8a, although כל "all," v 5, may phonetically recall יכלו "defeated," v 2, as well as being a semantic parallel to רבת "many times," v 2. The lines of the second strophe are tightly bound together by word echoes or step parallelism: יבשו "shamed" and יבש "wither," vv 5–6 (see *Notes/Comments*, note 6.b.), the relative ש, vv 6, 7, the negative לא, vv 7, 8a, the stem ברך "bless" and the second plural suffix, vv 8a, 8b. Both strophes are marked by extensive figurative language. They are hinged by רשעים "wicked," v 4, and שנאי ציון "haters of Zion," v 5. It is significant that v 5 nestles firmly into the psalm stylistically as well as exegetically: Seybold's deletion of it as redactional because of its generalizing nature and contextually irrelevant reference to Zion

(*Wallfahrtspsalmen*, 28) is not justified. He has made interesting comments concerning the alliteration and parallelism of vv 2–4 (*Wallfahrtspsalmen*, 48).

Explanation

The religious community is encouraged by a cultic precentor to take upon their own lips a testimony to Yahweh's repeated aid, which probably had originally been celebrated concerning Zion. The victory of Yahweh over enemies ranged against the holy city had long been a traditional theme of assurance and praise (cf. Pss 46, 48, 76). The resurgence of Jerusalem at the end of the exile likewise bore witness to his power demonstrated on the city's behalf. In the subsequent interpretation in terms of "Israel" this religious truth received even wider warrant: it could trace back to the Exodus (cf. Hos 11:1) the history of God's saving grace over against the oppressor's plowlike scourge (cf. Isa 1:5–7; 51:23).

Specific reference to Yahweh comes by way of climax at the end of the first strophe, in v 4. The mystery of the continual resilience of God's city and people is thereby explained. V 4 triumphantly amplifies v 2b, after v 3 has grimly developed v 2a. To use J. B. Phillips' paraphrase of 2 Cor 4:9, the capital and community were often knocked down, but never knocked out. They revived and survived as a testimony to a long history of God's pledged faithfulness.

In vv 5–8a the community originally broke in as advocates of their city's future. The verses came to function as a continuation of their speaking, in assurance of their security under God, assembled as they were in the holy city. As before, Zion, the place of God's special presence, is to be the touchstone of his purposes: its adversaries always find themselves the losers eventually. Their attacks would be doomed to failure (cf. 2:1, 6). For all their seeming potential, they would come to nothing, like grass with no depth of soil (cf. Isa 37:27; Mark 4:5–6). The simile is expanded, like the metaphor in the former strophe, and culminates in a somber negation of blessing. The well-omened harvest scene is evoked only to be denied.

By contrast the benediction of v 8b, issued by a priestly group, rings out all the more forcefully. Over the community and their advocacy of Zion is pronounced Yahweh's powerful name in blessing, so that he may endorse their testimony of confidence in him and crown their faith with experience.

Psalm 129 is no trite statement of an easy faith or a shallow optimism. It is not insignificant that the song of confidence is an outgrowth of the prayer of complaint in which distress is tearfully brought before Yahweh. God's people, as they sang this song, were doubtless painfully aware not only of past ordeals but of present threats. They had learned both from history and from experience that the light of salvation lies at the end of a dark tunnel of suffering. They sang this song in the night, as it were. By faith rather than sight they clung to God's past revelation of himself as champion of a particular city and people. With the courage that sprang from a real faith they dared to assert that their divine help in ages past was their hope for years to come.

The Riches of His Grace   (130:1-8)

Bibliography

Airoldi, N. "Note critiche ai salmi (Ps. 130:1; 38:5; 102:8)." *Augustinianum* 10 (1970) 174–80. _____. "Salmi 116 e 130." *Augustinianum* 13 (1973) 141–47. **Ceresco, A. R.** "The Chiastic Word Pattern in Hebrew." *CBQ* 38 (1976) 303–11. **Cornill, C. H.** "Psalm 130." *Karl Budde zum siebzigsten Geburtstag,* ed. K. Marti. BZAW 34. Giessen: A Töpelmann, 1920. **Johnson, A. R.** *The Cultic Prophet and Israel's Psalmody.* **McKeating, H.** "Divine Forgiveness in the Psalms." *SJT* 18 (1965) 69–83. **Porúbčan, S.** "Psalm 130:5–6." *VT* 9 (1959) 322–23. **Schmidt, W. H.** "Gott und Mensch in Ps. 130. Formgeschichtliche Erwägungen." *TZ* 22 (1966) 241–53. **Skehan, P. W.** *Studies in Israelite Poetry and Wisdom.* CBQMS 1. Washington, D.C.: Catholic Biblical Association of America, 1971. **Snaith, N. H.** *The Seven Psalms.* London: Epworth Press, 1964. **Volz, P.** "Zum Verständnis von Psalm 16 und Psalm 130." *Karl Marti zum siebzigsten Geburtstag.* BZAW 41. Giessen: A Töpelmann, 1925. **Westermann, C.** "Psalm 130." *Herr, tue meine Lippen auf,* vol. 5, ed. G. Eichholz. Wuppertal-Barmen: Emil Müller Verlag, 1961, 606–12.

Translation

[1] One of the processional songs.[a]
  Out of the depths [b] I invoke you, Yahweh: (3+3)
[2]   Lord, listen to my cry.
  May your ears be attentive   (3+2)
    to my imploring [a] cry.

[3] If you were to take iniquities into account,[a] Yah(weh),[b]   (3+2)
  Lord, who could stand? [c]
[4] But [a] with you there is forgiveness [b]   (3+2)
  so that you may be revered.[c]

[5] I wait for Yahweh,[a]   (2+2+2)
  I wait with longing [b]
  and in his word I put my hope.
[6] My longing is for the Lord,[a]   (2+2+2)
  more intent than that of watchmen for the morning,[b]
  watchmen for the morning.[c]

[7] Put your hope, Israel, in Yahweh,   (3+3+3)
  for with Yahweh there is loyal love [a]
  and redemption [b] with him in abundance,
[8] and he it is who will redeem Israel   (3+2)
  from all their iniquities.

Notes/Comments

1.a. See the note on 120:1.
1.b. The psalmist's troubles are described as deep waters of chaos which typify (the proximity of) Sheol and separation from Yahweh: cf. 69:3, 15 (2, 14) and N. J. Tromp, *Primitive Conceptions,*

57–58. It is not necessary to read מעמקי-ים "from the depths of the sea" with N. Airoldi, *Augustinianum* 10 (1970) 174–77.

2.a. For the servant-master relationship implicit in תחנוני see K. Neubauer, *Der Stamm CH N N*, 140 (cf. אדני "Lord," vv 2, 3, 6, and חסד "loyal love," v 7).

3.a. Lit. "keep" i.e. not overlook: cf. 1 Kgs 17:8; Job 7:20 and the metaphor of divine storage of sins in Deut 32:34; Hos 13:12, etc.

3.b. See the note on 118:5.

3.c. Cf. Ezra 9:15; Ps 76:8 (7); Nah 1:6. W. H. Schmidt (*TZ* 22 [1966] 245–46) has explained the question as an adaptation of the question of the entrance liturgy (מי יקום "who shall stand" 24:3; cf. 15:1), here generalized.

4.a. Lit. "for," introducing the reason for the negative implication of the condition of v 3a.

4.b. For divine forgiveness in the Psalms see H. McKeating, *SJT* 18 (1965) 69–83.

4.c. Or "so that you are revered," expressing consequence (P. Joüon, *Grammaire* § 169g). Forgiveness increases the sinner's reverent awe of and trust in Yahweh: cf. 1 Kgs 8:38–40. J. Becker (*Gottesfurcht im AT*, 170–71) has interpreted in a cultic sense of worshiping with reverence. Apart from here the niphal of ירא "fear" occurs in the OT only in the participle. It was probably for this reason that the ancient versions mistranslated. *Tg.* Vg derived from the stem ראה "see," while LXX θ'σ' rendered νόμου, interpreting תורא as תורה "law" (the suffix σου "your" in LXX θ' was probably an addition of the translators and hardly implies תורתך "your law" *pace BHK* and *BHS*). For the Gk. variant ὀνόματος "name" see the list of inner-Greek νόμος-ὄνομα variants in J. Ziegler, *Beiträge zur Jeremias-Septuaginta* [Göttingen: Vandenhoeck & Ruprecht, 1958] 85, to which 2 Chr 6:16 LXX should be added.

5.a. For the divine direct object see the examples cited in BDB, 875b; an emendation ליהוה is hardly necessary. Vv 5–6 have been the object of much text-critical study (e.g. by S. Porúbčan, *VT* 9 [1959] 322–23; cf. *BHK*), but MT is to be retained.

5.b. For נפש as the seat of desire here and in v 6 see H. W. Wolff, *Anthropology*, 15–17, 52.

6.a. Cf. Judg 5:9 לבי לחוקקי ישראל "my heart goes out to Israel's commanders."

6.b. LXX S Hier imply not מאשמרת הבקר, *contra BHK* and *BHS*, but משמרים לבקר (cf. Exod 12:42). LXX's addition "till night" is probably an exegetical addition (cf. perhaps עד-לילה Isa 38:12, 13).

6.c. S Hier took as an accusative of duration of time (cf. GKC § 118k), while LXX rendered in terms of the preceding phrase.

7.a. For the association of חסד "loyal love" with deliverance and forgiveness see K. D. Sakenfeld, *The Meaning of Hesed*, 224–27. For its further combination with the motif of hope cf. 33:18–22.

7.b. Heb. פדות here refers to deliverance (C. Westermann, "Psalm 130," 609) as the visible sign of divine forgiveness, rather than actually to forgiveness of sins (W. H. Schmidt, *TZ* 22 [1966] 252). "Here we must not unduly spiritualize . . . . Nowhere, in fact, is this word *padhah* used of redemption from sin alone; it always marks deliverance from some tangible and visible menace, which may or may not be regarded as a consequence of the suppliant's sin" (H. Wheeler Robinson, *Redemption and Revelation in the Actuality of History* [London: Nisbet, 1942] 223).

Form/Structure/Setting

It is by no means clear to which genre this psalm should be assigned. The difficulty stems from two causes, the ambivalent timing of the perfect verbs in vv 1b, 5 and the role of vv 7–8. If the verbs are interpreted as past ("I called, I waited . . ."), they belong to a thanksgiving: cf. 66:17; Jonah 2:3 (2) for the first verb and 40:2 (1) for the second, in such a context. P. Volz ("Psalm 16 und Psalm 130," 287–96) and A. Weiser (*Psalms*, 773) opted for this understanding of the psalm, while H.-J. Kraus (*Psalmen*, 1048) regards it as a possibility. Then v 1b introduces a previous complaint cited in vv 2–4, vv 5–6 are a testimony addressed to the religious community and vv 7–8 may be interpreted as an exhortation, associated with the thanksgiving form, to strengthen the community's faith. Volz deleted v 7a with LXX[s] and regarded vv 1b–4 and the rest of vv 5–8 as two parallel statements, the first directed to Yahweh and the second a statement of faith concerning him.

W. H. Schmidt (*TZ* 22 [1966] 244 note 4) has objected that there occurs in the psalm no narration of Yahweh's deliverance, such as is characteristic of the thanksgiving. The strength of his objection is debatable: the psalm does not represent any form completely. He himself classifies the psalm as an individual complaint which deviates from the basic form (*TZ* 22 [1966] 241). This is in fact the designation of most scholars, such as Kraus, *Psalmen*, 1048, who prefers it, C. Westermann ("Psalm 130," 606), C. H. Cornill ("Psalm 130," 38), O. Eissfeldt (*Introduction*, 115 note 44), G. Fohrer (*Introduction*, 292), M. Dahood (*Psalms III*, 235) and A. A. Anderson (*Psalms*, 874–75). Cornill ("Psalm 130," 38) noted the *qinah* meter within the psalm, which is so often characteristic of a complaint, although he unwisely sought to make every line conform to this model. The verbs of vv 1b, 5 can have a present significance (D. Michel, *Tempora*, 80). Vv 1b–2 are to be taken together, as the parallels in 17:6; 141:1 suggest; for the reference to present distress 86:7; 102:3 (2) are to be compared. They constitute the address and introductory petitions characteristic of a complaint. The psalm contains no standard description of distress—apart from the initial מעמקים "depths" in v 1b—nor plea for help. Their place is taken by an indirect confession of sin and implicit prayer for forgiveness in vv 3–4. Schmidt (*TZ* 22 [1966] 241) has observed that such a confession usually represents only one part of a total description of distress (cf. 38:19 [18]; 69:6 [5]). Westermann ("Psalm 130," 607) has suggested that a direct plea for help is missing precisely because of a sense of the gulf that lies between the psalmist and Yahweh because of his sin. Vv 3–4 are intended to urge Yahweh to bridge the gulf: to err is only human and to forgive divine. Vv 5–6 are a confession of confidence referring to Yahweh in the third person; for the verbs 25:5, 21; 38:16 (15) are to be compared.

Vv 7–8 have been variously interpreted. Kraus (*Psalmen*, 1048, 1050–51) has suggested that it is a priestly exhortation giving an assurance of salvation to the religious community among whom the psalmist is speaking. Westermann ("Psalm 130," 609) views only the praise of Yahweh's redeeming grace in v 7aβ-b as original and understands vv 7aα, 8 as a later application of the psalm to the community, adapting it to the present collection of Pss 120–134. He here follows S. Mowinckel (*Psalmenstudien*, vol. 3, 53 note 7), but understands it simply as a communal supplement to an individual psalm, like 3:9 (10), etc., rather than implying a communal re-interpretation of the psalm. Dahood (*Psalms III*, 235) regards vv 7–8 as an original part of the psalm, commending to the community the psalmist's own attitude (cf. P. W. Skehan, *Israelite Poetry*, 60; Becker, *Israel deutet seine Psalmen*, 68 note 96); they do not make the psalm into a communal complaint, but rather the speaker is distinguished from Israel. His argument assumes that the speaker of vv 7–8 is that of the whole psalm. Schmidt (*TZ* 22 [1966] 251) takes the whole of vv 7–8 as an addition to the basic psalm. Likewise C. B. Houk ("Syllables and Psalms. A Statistical Linguistic Analysis," *JSOT* 14 [1979] 58) has claimed that statistical analysis of vv 7–8 demonstrates their difference from vv 1–6 and so their redactional nature.

Anderson (*Psalms*, 877) has urged the primary nature of vv 7–8 on the ground of their close theological and other similarities with vv 1–6 (cf. J. W. Rogerson and J. W. McKay, *Psalms 101–150*, 133). In this respect it is relevant to cite the observation of A. R. Ceresco (*CBQ* 38 [1976] 308) that vv 5–7 exhibit a chiastic pattern (שמרים לבקר :: משמרים לבקר : הוחלתי יחל "I put my hope : watchmen for the morning :: watchmen for the morning : put hope"). Ceresco used this phenomenon as an argument against the deletion of שמרים לבקר as a dittograph (cf. *BHK*, *BHS*) and also noted the presence of chiastic repetition in v 7 (פדות :: יפדה : ישראל : ישראל "Israel : redemption :: redeem : Israel"). In fact, Ceresco's example from vv 5–7 may be seen as part of a larger pattern covering vv 3–8: repetition appears in vv 3, 8 (עונות "iniquities," עונתיו "his iniquities") and vv 4, 7 (כי-עמך "for with you," כי-עם-יהוה "for with Yahweh"). Apart from this overall chiastic structure, which commences after the introductory vv 1b, 2 and runs right through the psalm, there are the smaller chiastic grouping within v 7 and the local repetition within vv 5–6 (נפשי . . . נפשי "my soul . . . my soul," קויתי . . . קותה "I wait . . . waits") which expresses well yearning, continuing hope (Volz, "Psalm 16 und Psalm 130," 294).

There are thus structural grounds for regarding vv 7–8 as part of the original composition. It is worth asking whether they cannot be given an adequate role within the genre of the psalm. Does the psalm fall into the category of complaint which attests a favorable divine intervention and includes the psalmist's glad response (cf. Westermann, *Praise*, 80)? Examples may be given of the communal concern of 28:8–9 (cf. Kraus, *Psalmen*, 372, 375), the communal exhortation of 64:11 (10; cf. Kraus, *Psalmen*, 605–6) and especially that of 31:24–25 (23–24; cf. Kraus, *Psalmen*, 394) which concludes "Be strong, all you who wait for Yahweh." Then in this psalm a priestly oracle, the "word" awaited in v 5, is to be understood as delivered after v 6. As evidence of Yahweh's loyal love and forgiveness, it prompts the psalmist to encourage the community at large to continue in their larger hope, in view of his own positive experience.

The function of the psalm within the collection of Ps 120–134 remains to be considered. Psalm 129 exhibited an individually formulated passage (vv 2–4), probably originally referring to Zion (v 5), re-interpreted in terms of "Israel" (v 1). The juxtaposition of Ps 129 and 130 suggests that a similar re-interpretation was imposed upon the latter. It is probable that the psalm was divided into voices or groups of voices, the first singing vv 1b–6 in the name of the community and the second vv 7–8, encouraging the community to stand firm in their hope. The original hope of a priestly communication of a divine oracle of salvation (Kraus, *Psalmen*, 1050; A. R. Johnson, *The Cultic Prophet and Israel's Psalmody*, 314) was transformed into hope for the fulfillment of the divine promises concerning Israel's salvation.

A further point needs to be made about the structure of the psalm. Strophically it seems to consist of four pairs of closely related lines, vv 1b–2, 3–4, 5–6, 7–8 (cf. Mowinckel, *Tricola*, 101; E. Beaucamp, *RSR* 56 [1968] 211. N. B. the pair of divine names or titles in each pair of lines) rather than two units of four lines, vv 1b–4, 5–8 (J. Schildenberger, *Estudios Eclesiásticos* 34 [1960] 675; Dahood, *Psalms III*, 235), in favor of which Dahood urges the second person divine references in vv 1b–4 and the third person in vv 5–8. The overall chiastic pattern serves to differentiate the first pair of lines from the rest, while the role of the last pair, both in the original and in the secondary interpretations of the psalm, sets it apart from the preceding verses.

The psalm has been claimed as pre-exilic in date by Dahood (*Psalms III*, 235), who regards it as spoken by a king in view of terminological parallels with Ps 86, which he takes as royal (cf. too Johnson, *The Cultic Prophet and Israel's Psalmody*, 316). Usually the psalm is regarded as post-exilic, both on account of its comparatively degenerate form and, a stronger argument, its language, namely קשׁב "attentive" (v 2), which recurs in 1 Chr 6:40; 7:15, and סליחה "forgiveness" (v 4), also in Neh 9:17; Dan 9:9.

Did the original psalm ever have a cultic setting? Eissfeldt (*Introduction*, 120) regarded the psalm as non-cultic in view of its "personal terms" and "deeply religious content" (cf. Volz, "Psalm 16 und Psalm 130," 296), hardly compelling arguments. Fohrer too (*Introduction*, 292) defines the psalm as a "personal devotional song with no cultic associations." W. H. Schmidt (*TZ* 22 [1966] 242, 249) views the psalm as "separate from the cult"; the word of v 5 he takes not as a priestly oracle but a late hypostatizing because it is parallel with "Yahweh." There does not appear to be a compelling reason to deny a cultic setting for the basic psalm.

In Christian tradition the psalm became one of the seven penitential psalms, the others being Ps 6, 32, 38, 51, 102 and 143 (cf. N. H. Snaith, *The Seven Psalms*).

Explanation

This psalm illustrates well the manifold relevance of the Scriptures, since its presence in the Psalter already embraces within its scope two interpretations, one relating to the individual and the other to the community. Originally it appears to have been a complaint in which by faith a Judean brought his problems to Yahweh in the temple. For the modern reader "depths" suggests despair; in its cultural setting the term evokes the sea of troubles in which the speaker is engulfed, a deathlike situation of separation from the living God. The description of calamity in such general and brief terms made the psalm ideal for recitation whatever the precise trouble of the sufferer might have been.

The psalmist cries for a positive hearing. But he is acutely conscious that he has little claim upon God, despite a master-servant relationship within the covenant. In this relationship he has proved an unprofitable servant, and the onus of maintaining it can now lie only with the Lord. His present suffering, as so often in the OT, is assumed to be due to his personal wrongdoing. Yet he derives comfort from the known character of Yahweh as a God who forgives (cf. 86:15): this divine quality transcends man's sinfulness. The rhetorical question in v 3 concerning this sorry state expects a negative answer. If Yahweh kept a strict tally of human sin and acted upon it in speedy punishment, none could go uncondemned at that bar of divine justice which providentially controls man's life (cf. 75:8 [7]); none would survive (cf. Gen 6:5–8). Yet the psalmist dares to remind God that he desires not the death of a sinner but restoration to life (cf. Ezek 18:32; 33:11)—to his greater glory. The sinning believer's obligation is thereby increased, and greater obedience and trust are the result. Such is God's better way.

In vv 5–6 the psalmist reflects upon this prospect of forgiveness, as yet unexperienced in his particular situation. His attitude is one of intense yearning and confident hope that his trauma of trouble—persecution or ill-health or whatever—will be resolved. He awaits a divine ruling from the sanctuary, to be delivered by a priest. Around him lurks a dark night of trouble, sinister with threat and fearfulness. He longs for relief, as ardently as the city sentinels peering into the darkness from the watchtower long for daylight and danger's end.

The psalm presupposes that the awaited positive response from God did come, as in Ps 22. In reaction the psalmist addresses the congregation and draws out from his own experience a lesson for the community at large. Yahweh's covenant attribute of "loyal love" has been attested once more as lavishly true. He does deliver from trouble and so in him lies the community's own hope for total reversal of the problems that beset it, consequences though they are of the nation's departure from Yahweh's covenant standards. Blame is due, but with God it is the prelude not to condemnation but to "redemption"—for those who turn to him in trusting, prayerful hope.

The communal implications already contained in this fine individual psalm evidently encouraged its re-use in a completely communal setting. Vv 1–6 became the voice of the personified community pouring out before Yahweh their prayers, confessing their sins and imploring him to forgive and restore (cf. Dan 9:4–19). They lay claim to divine promises of a glorious future for the covenant nation and, encouraged by a now priestly voice in vv 7–8, look forward to a new redemption surpassing that of the Exodus (111:9) and the return from Babylonian exile (Isa 50:2). Convinced that God has much more salvation and blessing in store for them than they have yet enjoyed, they plead with him to surmount the barrier of their own sinfulness, as they know he can.

The NT with its revelation of Christ gave a new dimension to the longings and affirmations of Ps 130. On the individual level 1 John 1:8–2:2 is its counterpart, assuring the believer that his failure can via confession ever find its remedy in God's grace. For the Christian this grace is grounded not only in a heart of love but in its disclosure through the death of Jesus as the objective basis of divine deliverance. From this initial redemption (Rom 3:23–25; Eph 1:7) is traced an arc which is to culminate in an awaited sequel for the church (Rom 8:19–25).

Childlikeness *(131:1-3)*

Bibliography

de Boer, P. A. H. "Psalm 131:2." *VT* 16 (1966) 287–92. **Quell, G.** "Struktur und Sinn des Psalms 131." *Das ferne und nahe Wort. Festschrift L. Rost,* ed. F. Maass. BZAW

105. Berlin: A. Töpelmann, 1967. **Skehan, P. W.** *Studies in Israelite Poetry and Wisdom.* CBQMS 1. Washington, D.C.: Catholic Biblical Association of America, 1971.

Translation

> [1] One of the processional songs.[a] Davidic.
> *Yahweh, my heart is not haughty* [b]   (3+3)
>   *nor are my eyes supercilious,* [c]
> *nor have I got involved* [d] *in matters too big*   (3+2)
>   *or too difficult for me.*
>
> [2] *Indeed,*[a] *I have composed* [b]   (2+2)
>   *and quieted my soul.*
> *Like a weaned child* [c] *carried by* [d] *his mother,*   (3+3)
>   *like the weaned child I carry,*[e] *is my soul.*
>
> [3] *Put your hope, Israel, in Yahweh*   (3+3)
>   *from now on and for evermore.*

Notes/Comments

1.a. See the note on 120:1.

1.b. For a "high heart" cf. Prov 18:12.

1.c. For "raised eyes" cf. Prov 6:17; 30:13; Ps 18:28 (27).

1.d. Lit. "walk, move."

2.a. Heb. אם־לא "if not" serves to introduce an asseveration after an implied oath. G. R. Driver (*JTS* 44 [1943] 21) suggested an adversative sense "but" on the analogy of Aram. אֶלָּא (cf. *HALAT*, 59a).

2.b. Heb. שׁוה is used of leveling ground in Isa 28:25.

2.c. Weaning from breast feeding took place around the age of three: cf. 2 Macc 7:27; 1 Sam 1:23–24. H. W. Wolff (*Hosea*, 21) has cited an Egyptian text: "Her breast was in thy mouth for three years" (The Instruction of Ani, *ANET*, 420).

2.d. Lit. "upon." G. Quell ("Struktur," 178–79) suggested this interpretation, referring to a scene of Syrian prisoners depicted in the Eighteenth Dynasty Egyptian grave of Hor-em-heb, which includes a Semitic woman carrying a child on her shoulders and a baby in a sling behind its brother (*ANEP*, no. 49). For later Jewish evidence for the carrying of a child to a festival on his father's shoulders or by his mother see Babylonian Talmud, *Ḥag.* 5b–6a; Mishnah, *Ḥag.* 1:1.

2.e. Lit. "upon," here with a first person suffix in MT. It is often taken with נפשׁי "my soul" and rendered "within me" (cf. BDB, 753b), but Quell ("Struktur," 178–79) has rightly urged that the parallel עלי in the preceding clause points to an identical rendering here. This final clause is sometimes deleted as a scribal error, e.g. by K. Budde, "Das hebräische Klageleid," *ZAW* 2 (1882) 42; NEB. P. W. Skehan (*Israelite Poetry*, 61) deletes עלי נפשׁי. An emendation of נגמולי to תִּגְּמָל "(my soul) is weaned" i.e. "quieted," suggested by S. Mowinckel (*Psalmenstudien*, vol. 1, 165 note 3), has been adopted by H. Gunkel (*Die Psalmen*, 564), A. Weiser (*Psalms*, 776), H.-J. Kraus (*Psalmen*, 1052) *et al.* The emendation has been encouraged by the indicative verb (ἕως) ἀνταποδώσεις in LXX^S (-δόσεις LXX^A, cf. σ' οὕτως ἀνταποδοθείη), but *pace* BHK it is merely an inner-Greek corruption of (ὡς) ἀνταπόδοσις (A. Rahlfs, *Psalmi cum Odis*, 312): LXX interpreted as כַּגָּמוּל עָלָי. P. A. H. de Boer (*VT* 16 [1966] 291–92) has compared כַּגָּמוּל עַל in 2 Chr 32:25 and interpreted the repeated כ "as . . . so." The relation of his own translation to the Hebrew is not clear, but he appears to take it as "As one deals with his mother, so (have I) dealt with (= עָלָי) my soul" i.e. he has made himself content, whatever his lot may be. Quell's interpretation, adopted by K. Seybold (*Wallfahrtspsalmen*, 37), appears to do most justice to MT.

Form/Structure/Setting

This psalm has an enigmatic quality about it, due in part to its brevity. It is generally taken as a psalm of confidence or trust in Yahweh, like Pss 16, 23, 62 (e.g. Gunkel, *Die Psalmen,* 564; Kraus, *Psalmen,* 1052; Weiser, *Psalms,* 776; A. A. Anderson, *Psalms,* 878; M. Dahood, *Psalms III,* 238). D. Michel (*Tempora,* 119) regarded vv 1–2 as a spiritualized form of a *Beichtspiegel* or confessional list related to the entrance liturgy of Pss 15 and 24. Quell ("Struktur," 181–85) took over this designation for vv 1–2a, detecting too implicit thanksgiving; but he regarded v 2b as a separate piece sung by a woman. For the origin of the two passages he referred to Mowinckel's suggestion (*Psalmenstudien,* vol. 6, 65–68) that in certain cases poems were written and deposited in the sanctuary at the thank offering service; in this case they were found in the archives and re-used in the collection of Pss 120–134 by the addition of v 3. Seybold (*Wallfahrtspsalmen,* 34, 37–38, 54) has largely adopted Quell's viewpoint, except that he regards vv 1–2 and perhaps v 3 as a personal expression of piety made at the gates of the temple by a woman pilgrim carrying her child.

The Davidic reference in the heading deserves some attention. It is possible that it was displaced from the heading to Ps 132 where it might appear to be more relevant: LXX ᵐˢˢ *Tg.* omit here and cf. לדוד "to David" 132:17 in the sense of the Davidic king. Dahood (*Psalms III,* 238) has opined that the psalm may well be a royal one. The psalm is usually regarded as post-exilic, but there is no compelling linguistic evidence for this dating. If Ps 62 is a royal psalm (J. H. Eaton, *Kingship,* 49–50), the similarity of v 2aβ to 62:2, 6 (1, 5) might be taken as supporting evidence. Significant too are the references to pride in royal psalms: 18:28 (27, עינים רמות "haughty eyes"); 101:5 (גבה עינים ורחב לבב "arrogant eyes and big ideas"). At least the heading may intend to pose a homiletic contrast with the reprehensible behavior of two Davidic kings, Uzziah and Hezekiah (2 Chr 26:16; 32:25 גבה לבו "his arrogant heart"; cf. too כגמול עליו in the latter verse). It is conceivable too that the psalm was regarded as an illustration of David's attitude to God in 132:1, in which case an interpretation ענותו "his humility" is presupposed in common with LXX *S* (cf. Prov 18:12 where ענוה is contrasted with גבה לב).

The relation of v 3 to the preceding verses is problematic. In the light of the communal (re-)interpretations of Pss 129 and 130 it is possible that the compiler of the collection added v 3a from 130:7 and, supplying the liturgical formulation of v 3b (cf. 113:2; 115:18), thereby gave vv 1–2 a new communal significance (Mowinckel, *Psalmenstudien,* vol. 1, 164–65). Then the expressions of faith of vv 1–2 are associated with patient waiting, just as in 37:7; Lam 3:26 the stem דמם "be silent, still," used here in v 2, is linked with the verbs of hope, יחל, used in v 3, and התחולל (cf. 62:2, 6 [1, 5]).

Structurally vv 1–2 may be divided into two pairs of bicola, the first characterized by a triple negative and the second by the repetitions of נפשי "my soul" and (phonetic) אם, אמו "if, his mother." The addition of a final bicolon, v 3, supplied an inclusive element, the divine name יהוה (cf. v 1).

Explanation

Tantalizingly brief though this psalm is, it evidently originated in an individual's profession of an active trust in Yahweh. He has come to realize both the value of submitting to him and the folly of pretentious pride which tries to defy the divine will. Not for him a spirit of self-sufficiency: he understands his own limitations and does not, beyond these, "seek great things" (Jer 45:5) for himself.

This state of spirituality has been attained only by struggling with his headstrong self. Many an outburst of self-will has had to be quelled. Eventually he has learned the lesson of dependence upon God. His metaphor for such dependence, that of the parent carrying a child, is well attested in the OT to describe the supportive care that Yahweh had ever given his covenant people since the wilderness period (Deut 1:31; Isa 46:3–4; Hos 11:3, as generally emended). The psalmist individualizes this communal caring (cf. 23:1), whether glancing at the child he was even now carrying or merely thinking of the welcome burden that was at other times his own or his wife's. Such was his relationship to God, the mother and father of his soul (cf. 27:10), and he would not have it otherwise.

It may have been the communal associations of the metaphor that impelled the compiler of Pss 120–134 to put the psalm to new use. Now vv 1–2 seem to become the concerted voice of the religious community, expressing their humble submission to the will of their Father. Their quietness of soul is to be demonstrated in a steady waiting for Yahweh to reveal himself in climactic grace and power. To this constant hope the community is called by the priestly summons of v 3.

The OT is not alone in making a child the model of humble faith in God: Jesus himself added his memorable Amen (Matt 18:1–4).

The King's Heritage of Blessing (132:1–18)

Bibliography

Bee, R. E. "The Textual Analysis of Psalm 132: A Response to Cornelius B. Houk." *JSOT* 6 (1978) 49–53. ———. "The Use of Syllable Counts in Textual Analysis." *JSOT* 10 (1978) 68–70. **Campbell, A. F.** *The Ark Narrative.* SBLDS 16. Missoula, MT: Scholars Press, 1975. **Caquot, A.** "La prophetie de Nathan et ses échos lyriques." *Congress Volume Bonn 1962.* VTSup 9. Leiden: E. J. Brill, 1963. **Coppens, J.** *Le messianisme royal. Ses origines, son développement, son accomplissement.* LD 54. Paris: Les Editions du Cerf, 1968. **Cross, F. M.** *Canaanite Myth and Hebrew Epic.* Cambridge, MA: Harvard University Press, 1973. **Eaton, J. H.** *Kingship.* **Eissfeldt, O.** "Psalm 132." *WO* 2 (1959) 480–83. **de Fraine, J.** *L'aspect religieux de la royauté israélite.* AnBib 3. Rome: Pontificio Instituto Biblico, 1954. **Fretheim, T. E.** "Psalm 132: A Form-critical Study." *JBL* 86 (1967) 289–300. ———. "The Ark in Deuteronomy." *CBQ* 30 (1968) 1–14. **Gese, H.** "Der Davidsbund und die Zionserwählung." *ZTK* 61 (1964) 10–26. **Hanson,**

P. D. "The Song of Hesbon and David's *NIR.*" *HTR* 61 (1968) 297–320. **Haran, M.** "The Ark and the Cherubim: Their Symbolic Significance in Biblical Ritual." *IEJ* 9 (1959) 30–38, 89–94. **Hillers, D. R.** "Ritual Procession of the Ark and Psalm 132." *CBQ* 30 (1968) 48–55. **Houk, C. B.** "Psalm 132, Literary Integrity and Syllable-Word Structures." *JSOT* 6 (1978) 41–48. ———. "Psalm 132: Further Discussion." *JSOT* 6 (1978) 54–57. **Ishida, T.** *The Royal Dynasties in Ancient Israel.* BZAW 142. Berlin: Walter de Gruyter, 1977. **Johnson, A. R.** *Sacral Kingship in Ancient Israel.* 2nd ed. Cardiff: University of Wales Press, 1967. ———. *The Cultic Prophet and Israel's Psalmody.* **Kraus, H.-J.** *Die Königsherrschaft Gottes im AT.* BHT 13. Tübingen: J. C. B. Mohr (Paul Siebeck), 1951. **Lipiński, E.** *La royauté de Yahwé dans la poésie et la culte de l'ancien Israel.* Brussels: Verhandelingen van de Koninklije Vlaamse Academiae voor Wetenschappen, Letteren en Schone Kunsten van Belgie, 1965. ———. *La liturgie penitentielle dans la Bible.* LD 52. Paris: Les Editions du Cerf, 1967. **Mettinger, T. N. D.** *King and Messiah. The Civil and Sacral Legitimation of the Israelite Kings.* ConB OT Series 8. Lund: C. W. K. Gleerup, 1976. **Perlitt, L.** *Bundestheologie im AT.* WMANT 36. Neukirchen-Vluyn: Neukirchener Verlag, 1969. **Porter, J. R.** "The Interpretation of 2 Samuel 6 and Psalm 132." *JTS* 5 (1954) 161–73. **Poulssen, N.** *König und Tempel im Glaubenszeugnis des AT.* SBS 3. Stuttgart: Verlag Katholisches Bibelwerk, 1967. **Roberts, J. J.** "The Davidic Origin of the Zion Tradition." *JBL* 92 (1973) 329–44. **Robinson, A.** "Do Ephratah and Jaar Really Appear in Psalm 132:6?" *ZAW* 86 (1974) 220–22. **Schmidt, W. H.** "אביר יעקב als Ausdruck Jerusalemer Kultsprache." *ZAW* 75 (1963) 91–92. ———. "Kritik am Königtum." *Probleme biblischer Theologie. Festschrift G. von Rad,* ed. H. W. Wolff. München: C. Kaiser, 1971. **Schreiner, J.** *Sion-Jerusalem Jahwehs Königssitz. Theologie der heiligen Stadt im AT.* SANT 7. München: Kösel-Verlag, 1963. **Weinfeld, M.** "The Covenant of Grant in the OT and in the Ancient Near East." *JAOS* 90 (1970) 184–203.

Translation

[1] One of the processional songs.[a]
  Remember,[b] *Yahweh, in David's favor*   (3+2)
  all his painstaking effort,[c]
[2] *how he swore to Yahweh*   (3+3)
  in a vow to the mighty one of Jacob: [a]
[3] *"I will never enter my tent house,*   (3+3)
  never climb upon my bed couch,
[4] *never permit my eyes sleep,*[a]   (3+3)
  my eyelids [b] *slumber,*
[5] *till I find a place* [a] *for Yahweh,*   (3+3)
  a tabernacle [b] *for the mighty one of Jacob."*
[6] *"Lo, we heard of it* [a] *in Ephratah,*[b]   (3+3)
  we found it [a] *in the countryside of Jaar.*[c]
[7] *Let us go to his tabernacle,*   (3+3)
  let us prostrate ourselves at his footstool. [a]
[8] *Arise, Yahweh, to your home of rest,*[a]   (3+3)
  you and your powerful ark.[b]
[9] *May your priests be clothed with righteousness,*[a]   (3+2)
  may your loyal ministers [b] *shout for joy."*
[10] *For the sake of your servant* [a] *David*   (3+3)
  do not turn away the face of your anointed one.

¹¹ *Yahweh swore to David*   (3+3)
    a sure oath ^a *on which he will not renege:*
"Members ^b *of your own progeny*   (2+3)
    will I set upon your throne.
¹² *If your sons keep my covenant*   (3+3)
    and my terms ^a *which I teach them,*
their sons too forever   (3+3)
    will sit upon your throne."
¹³ *For Yahweh has chosen* ^a *Zion,*   (3+3)
    desiring ^b *it for his royal seat:* ^c
¹⁴ *"This is my home of rest forever,*   (3+3)
    here will I sit enthroned, for such is my desire.
¹⁵ *With food* ^a *will I bless her abundantly,*   (3+3)
    her poor ^b *will I fill with bread,*
¹⁶ *while her priests will I clothe with salvation*   (3+3)
    and her loyal ministers will shout aloud for joy."
¹⁷ *"There will I make to grow a horn* ^a *for David,*^b   (3+3)
    I have prepared a lamp ^c *for my anointed one.*
¹⁸ *His enemies I will clothe in humiliation,*   (3+3)
    but upon his head his crown will gleam."

Notes/Comments

1.a. See the note on 120:1.

1.b. B. S. Childs (*Memory and Tradition*, 31), following H. Boecker (*Redeformen des Rechtlebens im AT*. [2nd ed.; WMANT 14; Neukirchen-Vluyn: Neukirchener Verlag, 1970] 110), finds here an appeal basically to Yahweh as judge, comparing Neh 5:19: Yahweh is asked to credit to David's account all his efforts. However, W. Schottroff (*Gedenken*, 225) has urged a cultic rather than a forensic setting for the term, citing Aramaic epigraphical evidence in which the builder of a sanctuary calls upon others to ask his god to "remember" him in the sense of rewarding with blessing.

1.c. LXX and S understood as עֲנָוֹתוֹ "his humility," which is preferred by A. R. Johnson (*Sacral Kingship*, 20 note 1) and D. R. Hillers (*CBQ* 30 [1968] 53). MT connotes self-affliction (cf. Lev 23:27, 29): cf. 1 Chr 22:14 where David's preparations for the temple are associated with "affliction" (עני).

2.a. For this archaic title, here anticipating its older use in the quotation of v 5, cf. Gen 49:24; Isa 1:24. J. Schreiner (*Sion-Jerusalem*, 177 note 1), followed by T. E. Fretheim (*JBL* 86 [1967] 291), regards it as an epithet of the ark, observing that Gen 49:24 is set in a blessing of Joseph within whose tribal territory the ark remained for a long period after the occupation of the land. P. D. Miller ("El the Warrior," *HTR* 60 [1967] 421–22) considers that underlying אביר is a title of El as warrior (cf. Ugar. *ṯr* "bull") which was transferred to Yahweh in a metaphorical sense ("mighty one").

4.a. For the ending of שׁנָת see GKC § 80g.

4.b. For an alternative view that עפעפים is a synonym of "eyes" see KB, 723b; M. Dahood, *Psalms III*, 244.

5.a. There is a link with the ark narrative imbedded in 1, 2 Sam: A. F. Campbell (*The Ark Narrative*, 139) has noted its concern for a "place" for the ark (1 Sam 5:11; 6:2; 2 Sam 6:17).

5.b. Heb. משׁכנות, lit. "encampment" (F. M. Cross, *Canaanite Myth and Hebrew Epic*, 95, 244 note 107), probably refers to the tent set up by David in Jerusalem to house the ark (H. Gese, *ZTK* 61 [1964] 16, 17; Fretheim, *JBL* 86 [1967] 294–96; cf. 2 Sam 6:17). W. H. Schmidt (*ZAW* 75 [1963] 91–92) has urged that the temple is in view, as in 43:3; 84:2 (1) and that משׁכנות is a Canaanitism corresponding to Ugar. *mšknt* used of a divine dwelling. However, the intentional parallelism with David's אהל "tent," v 3, to which Fretheim (*JBL* 86 [1967] 294–96) has drawn attention, probably supports the former interpretation.

6.a. The third feminine singular suffixes are generally related to the ark (ארון is feminine in 1 Sam 4:17; 2 Chr 8:11), here anticipating its mention in v 8, but originally probably presupposing an earlier mention in the source from which vv 6–9 were taken (see *Form/Structure/Setting*). Johnson (*Sacral Kingship*, 20; cf. Dahood, *Psalms III*, 244) has related them to David's vow first "heard of" or "come across" (מצאנוה) as a piece of oral tradition in the district of Bethlehem. But most probably vv 6–9 originally did not presuppose the vow of vv (2) 3–5. A repointing of the suffixes as masculine with reference to Yahweh, as in v 7 (H. Gunkel, *Die Psalmen*, 569) has little to commend it and is hardly necessary.

6.b. Heb. אפרתה "Ephratah" is most commonly related to the district in which Bethlehem lay, as in Ruth 4:11; Mic 5:1 (2); cf. Gen 35:16, 19; 48:7: David and his men in the Bethlehem area heard news of the ark. A few scholars (e.g. J. Schreiner, *Sion-Jerusalem*, 48–49; A. Weiser, *Psalms*, 780) connect it with the use of אפרתי "Ephraimite," e.g. in 1 Sam 1:1, and see a reference to Shiloh, the former home of the ark; then v 6a means "we heard (that) it was in Ephraim." A third interpretation construes the syntax of v 6a similarly but identifies the place name with Kiriath-jearim by appeal to 1 Chr 2:19, 24, 50, and understands the cola of v 6 as synonymously parallel (O. Eissfeldt, *WO* 2 [1959] 482; Cross, *Canaanite Myth and Hebrew Epic*, 94). Fretheim (*JBL* 86 [1967] 296–97), who leaves open whether Bethlehem or Kiriath-jearim is in view, interprets the verse in terms of a military operation to regain control of the ark, in which case אפרתה could refer to the Philistine garrison at Bethlehem (cf. 2 Sam 23:14) which had to be defeated. He understands the second verb as "find and secure" (cf. 116:3; 2 Sam 20:6; Lam 1:3; Hos 12:9 [8] and, less plausibly, the first not merely as "hear" but to act on the basis of hearing. A. Robinson's removal of both place names from v 6 by emendation (*ZAW* 86 [1974] 220–22) ignores the text-critical dictum *Lectio difficilior praestat*.

6.c. The reference is to Kiriath-jearim (cf. 1 Sam 6:21–7:2). Johnson, ibid., has interpreted in terms of the Bethlehem area via an understanding of יער "Jaar" as עיר "Jair" and an equation of David with "Elhanan ben Jair" in 1 Chr 20:5 (Q; cf. 2 Sam 21:19).

7.a. V 7a appears to be parallel with v 8 in describing an ark procession to the Davidic tent sanctuary promised in v 5, in terms first of exhortation to the people and then of an appeal to Yahweh who is represented by the ark. However, the relation of v 7a to v 7b is then not clear. If the footstool is the ark, as it certainly is in 1 Chr 28:2, how can it be described as both goal and burden of the procession? Gunkel (*Die Psalmen*, 566) and Cross (*Canaanite Myth and Hebrew Epic*, 95) understood v 7 as referring to a visit to the old sanctuary of the ark at Kiriath-jearim, but in view of v 5 the ark's new home is a more natural interpretation of משכנות here. E. Lipiński (*La royauté de Yahwé*, 331–32) and M. Haran (*IEJ* ([1959] 91 note 13) have taken v 7a, b as synonymous parallels, understanding הדם רגליו "his footstool" as a reference to the temple, as in Lam 2:1; but a reference to the ark would accord well with the historical description in 2 Sam 6:2. Fretheim (*JBL* 86 [1967] 297) regards the obeisance of v 7b as accompanying the processing of v 7a, but the partially parallel expressions in Gen 22:5; Pss 95:6; 96:8b–9a suggest that worship lies at the end of the journey. Most probably such is the case here: obeisance before the ark would take place when the ark was put down at the end of the procession (Schreiner, *Sion-Jerusalem*, 178; Johnson, *Sacral Kingship*, 20; H.-J. Kraus, *Psalmen*, 1063; *et al.*).

8.a. D. R. Hillers (*CBQ* 30 [1968] 49–51) has argued that the preposition ל be rendered "from," like Ugar. *l:* ל nowhere else occurs after קום with reference to place toward nor in a pregnant sense "arise (and go) to"; moreover, קומה "arise" as a divine address elsewhere in the Psalter is not processional but a call for help, while the usual understanding does not accord with Num 10:35 where the present formula is associated with the departure of the ark rather than its resting. Johnson (*The Cultic Prophet and Israel's Psalmody* 70 note 7) has replied by assigning to the preposition a purposive force "with a view to occupying (your rest)," comparing Jer 49:14; Ps 76:10 (9). However, there can be little objection to a sense of motion: the preparatory clause נבואה למשכנותיו "let us go to his tabernacle" in v 7a facilitates and explains the unusual construction in v 8a. The parallelism of the psalm as a whole (see *Form/Structure/Setting*) strongly suggests that the מנוחה "rest" is that of v 14, i.e. the destination. Hiller's understanding of v 8 as a petition for help will be discussed in *Form/Structure/Setting;* if vv 6–9 are a quotation from a ritual text, the aberrant sense of קומה receives explanation. As to the relation to Num 10:35, perhaps Num 10:33 may be utilized: the ark set out explicitly in order to seek a מנוחה for the Israelites: as there, setting out and resting may be associated here. Cross (*Canaanite Myth and*

Hebrew Epic, 94 note 14, 95) has followed Hillers in his rendering of the preposition, but interprets quite differently, in terms of a pilgrimage to the old sanctuary: again, the repetition of the noun in v 14 suggests otherwise. He notes that 2 Chr 6:41 reads לנוחך in place of למנוחתך and suggests that MT is a *lectio facilior* under the influence of v 14. He emends to לנחתך, relating to Ugar. *nḫt* which is used for a divine throne (cf. W. H. Schmidt, *Königtum Gottes in Ugarit und Israel.* [BZAW 80; Berlin: A. Töpelmann, 1961] 58). However, the Chronicles reading may be due to the influence of בנחה in Num 10:36 (cf. W. Rudolph, *Chronikbücher*, 215). His emendation violates the symmetry of the psalm (see *Form/Structure/Setting*) and depends to some extent upon his understanding of vv 13–18 as a later addition to the original composition.

Schreiner (*Sion-Jerusalem*, 178–79), followed by Fretheim (*JBL* 86 [1967] 300), has related Yahweh's "rest" to the people's finding rest in the land as a climax of the conquest (cf. 95:11; 2 Sam 7:1); Fretheim (*JBL* 86 [1967] 300) has compared 1 Chr 23:25 and appealed to the Holy War motif of v 8 and to v 18a. It is questionable how far this thought may be deduced from the psalm: it appears to be part of the theology of the Chronicler (cf. G. von Rad, *The Problem of the Hexateuch*, 97–98), but it is less obvious in Ps 132.

8.b. The ark is only here explicitly mentioned in the Psalter, but for other likely references see G. Henton Davies, "The Ark in the Psalms," in *Promise and Fulfillment*, ed. F. F. Bruce (Edinburgh: T. T. Clark, 1963) 51–61. It here visibly represents Yahweh. The genitive עז "power" expresses the ancient role of the ark in Holy War: cf. 1 Sam 4:3–8; Ps 24:8.

9.a. Fretheim (*JBL* 86 [1967] 293) has distinguished between צדק "righteousness" and ישע "salvation" in v 16: if the priests have the right attitude and ritual (cf. 1 Chr 15:12, 14), Yahweh will give salvation. Schreiner (*Sion-Jerusalem*, 178) saw a possible reference to 2 Sam 6:6–7 (cf. J. H. Eaton, *Kingship*, 126). More probably the different terms function as stylistic variants within the wish and promise: cf. תשועה "salvation" in the parallel wish in 2 Chr 6:41. The prayer is that the priests may convey God's salvation to the people in oracles of salvation (Kraus, *Psalmen*, 1064) which provide an answer for the typical prayer for salvation in the complaint (cf. 3:8 [7]; 106:47, etc.). Cf. 24:5 where צדקה and ישע are associated with divine blessing.

9.b. Is the religious community in view, as in 149:1, 5, etc.? K. Sakenfeld (*The Meaning of Hesed*, 244), on the basis of Deut 33:8 according to LXX and 4QDtʰ, has urged a special use of חסיד "pious one" with reference to the priesthood (cf. Gese, *ZTK* 61 [1964] 16; E. Slomovic, "Toward an Understanding of the Formation of Historical Titles in the Book of Psalms," *ZAW* 91 [1979] 379 note 89).

10.a. For the use of this title for David in the Psalter see I. Riesener, *Der Stamm עבד*, 229–32 (and in the deuteronomic literature 191–96). She has compared the present phrase with בעבור אברהם עבדי "for the sake of Abraham my servant" Gen 26:24 (*Der Stamm עבד*, 164).

11.a. Heb. אמת "sure oath" probably functions as object of the verb. For v 11b cf. 89:36 (35); 110:4.

11.b. Heb. (מ) "from" is used partitively as object: cf. GKC § 119w note 2; BDB, 580b. A word is often supplied *metri causa*, whether אקים "I will raise up" (e.g. Gunkel, *Die Psalmen*, 569 and Cross, *Canaanite Myth and Hebrew Epic*, 233 note 59, the latter urging haplography by homoeoarcton before אשית) or בנים "sons" (e.g. Fretheim, *JBL* 86 [1967] 289) or מלך "king" (cf. Tg.; e.g. Weiser, *Psalms*, 779) or מלכים "kings" (cf. Kraus, *Psalmen*, 1055). Either of the latter two could have fallen out between ממנה and מפרי, but it would be methodologically unsound to introduce to the psalm such a significant term not elsewhere found in it. It is hardly necessary to supplement the text (cf. Dahood, *Psalms III*, 246; Schreiner, *Sion-Jerusalem*, 105 note 9).

12.a. See the note on 119:2 and also J. A. Thompson, "Expansions of the עד Root," *JSS* 10 (1965) 237–39. The form of the suffix is unusual, עדותי being expected (cf. GKC § 91n). For the term cf. העדות 2 Kgs 11:12 in a coronation setting (Johnson, *Sacral Kingship*, 23–24).

13a. For the election of Zion see H. Seebass, "בחר bāchar," *TDOT* 2 (1977) 79–82.

13.b. Schreiner (*Sion-Jerusalem*, 53) has compared the stem חמד "desire" used of Yahweh in 68:17 (16) and noted that אוה (here derived from the quotation in 14) elsewhere has נפש "soul" as subject: the election of Zion is thus related to an intensely personal attitude on Yahweh's part. Kraus (*Psalmen*, 1065) has compared Yahweh's love (אהב) of Zion in 78:68; 87:2 (1).

13.c. Especially after the stem ישב "dwell" in a royal sense in v 12 מושב "seat, dwelling" here and in v 14 has a similar connotation: cf. Cross, *Canaanite Myth and Hebrew Epic*, 97, 246; W. Schmidt, *Königtum Gottes*, 65 note 9.

15.a. The second colon might suggest a personal term: hence the corruption χήραν "widow" in LXXˢ ᵉᵗᶜ· of θήραν "prey" (cf. A. Rahlfs, *Psalmi cum Odis*, 314; *Septuaginta-Studien*, vol. 2 [Göt-

tingen: Vandenhoeck & Ruprecht, 1907] 121), which is also used to render צִיד in the Greek
Genesis. G. R. Driver's suggestion (*JTS* 44 [1943] 21) to read צְדֶיהָ or צְדָיֶיהָ "her destitute
ones," comparing the Judeo-Aramaic and Syriac stem *ṣdy*, was adopted by NEB.

15.b. The covenant community depend upon Yahweh for supply of food (cf. Kraus, *Psalmen*,
108–11).

17.a. See the note on 112:9.

17.b. Heb. דוד "David" probably means the contemporary Davidic king. Gunkel (*Die Psalmen*,
568) considered that both he and David himself are signified.

17.c. Cf. 2 Sam 21:17; 1 Kgs 11:36 (נר) "lamp"), etc. for this metaphor for the permanence
of the dynasty. Cross (*Canaanite Myth and Hebrew Epic*, 97) followed P. D. Hanson (*HTR* 61
[1978] 304–20) in relating to Aram., Syr., Arab. *nyr* and Accadian *nīrum* "yoke" and rendering
"mandate." M. Noth subsequently abandoned his proposal to translate ניר as "new break, new
beginning" (see T. Ishida, *Royal Dynasties*, 103 note 116).

Form/Structure/Setting

Psalm 132 is notoriously complex; it may be preferable to begin to seek
clues to its interpretation from a study of its structure. The psalm falls into
two halves, with systematic repetition of the terminology of the first half in
the second. It is in this respect a larger edition of the royal Ps 101. Its scheme
of parallels is as follows: vv 1, 11a the divine name יהוה and לדוד "to David,"
vv 2, 11a נשבע "swore," vv 3, 4, 12a אם "surely, if," vv 5, 12b (also 14) עד
"until, ever," vv 8, 14 מנוחה "resting place," vv 9, 16 four terms in common,
vv 10, 17 דוד and משיח "anointed one." Thus a caesura occurs in the psalm
after v 10, and the composition can be categorized as two strophes, each of
ten lines. Gese (*ZTK* 61 [1964] 16) noted the inclusive nature of the Davidic
references לדוד and בעבור דוד in vv 1, 10. The symmetrical bipartite pattern
of the psalm indicates that such is their role, rather than marking the beginnings of strophes, as Fretheim (*JBL* 86 [1967] 292) urged in support of a
division into vv 1–9, 10–16, 17–18. H. Schmidt's division into two songs,
vv 1–7, 8–18, is also unlikely. The verbs of vv 10b, 11aβ, אל-תשב "do not
turn" and לא ישוב "he will not turn," function as an interstrophic hinge,
significantly changing from petition to affirmation. The shift may well support
Gunkel's characterization of the psalm as prayer and divine response (*Die
Psalmen*, 567; also Wieser, *Psalms*, 779–80; Johnson, *Sacral Kingship*, 19; Anderson, *Psalms*, 880, 883; *et al.*)

On the other hand, the prayers of vv 1, (8–) 10 have been regarded as
dominating the whole psalm, the rest being a series of arguments motivating
Yahweh to answer the prayers (J. Coppens, *Le messianisme royal*, 51; Lipiński,
La liturgie penitentielle, 101; T. Mettinger, *King and Messiah*, 100 note 7; cf.
Schreiner, *Sion-Jerusalem*, 105, 175, who regards vv 1–16 as a series of prayers
and motivations). However, this interpretation is less likely, since it implies
a major break either after v 9 or v 8, with each part of the psalm consisting
of prayer and supporting argument.

At first sight vv 8–10 might be taken together as a passage of prayer.
But it is difficult to see continuity in vv 8 and 10. Hillers (*CBQ* 30 [1968]
54) has interpreted vv 8–10 as a general prayer for help, plausibly relating
קומה "arise" in v 8 to the pattern of appeal attested by its usage in other
passages throughout the Psalter (e.g. 3:8 [7]; cf. Lipiński, *La royauté de Yahwé*,
443), but his interpretation depends upon his questionable understanding

of the following preposition as "from" (see *Notes/Comments*). Weiser (*Psalms*, 781) regarded v 8 as a petition for the cultic revelation of Yahweh in a theophany, but the inclusion of the ark in the address to Yahweh renders his view unlikely (Fretheim, JBL 86 [1967] 293 note 21; Hillers, *CBQ* 30 [1968] 52 note 14). Most scholars relate vv 6–9 to an ark procession commemorating its installation in Jerusalem; so the seeming echo of Num 10:35 in v 8 strongly suggests. O. Eissfeldt, *WO* 2 [1959] 483, made the plausible suggestion that these verses are an extract from an older poem (cf. K. Seybold, *Wallfahrtspsalmen*, 43; and cf. C. B. Houk's isolation of vv 6–9 on the basis of statistical analysis in *JSOT* 6 [1978] 56). If already existing material associated with a traditional ark procession has been employed, an explanation is provided not only for the break of continuity between vv 5 and 6, noted by Kraus (*Psalmen*, 1056) and others, but also for the awkwardness of vv 8–10, where the seeming sequence of petitions is not in fact homogeneous, since the first two verses conclude a quotation.

Thus v 10 is linked closely with v 1 as a framework of prayer which surrounds the supporting material of vv 2–9 (Schreiner, *Sion-Jerusalem*, 175). Vv 2–9 illustrate David's efforts on Yahweh's behalf (v 1) in terms of a sworn vow (vv 2–5) and evidence of its fulfillment (vv 6–9). The role of vv 6–9 is revealed by a threefold repetition of the vocabulary of v 5 in the following verses: מצא "find" in v 6, משכנות "tent" in v 7 and the stem קום "arise" (cf. מקום "place," v 5) in v 8. There is a conscious unfolding of v 5 in the movement of vv 6–8. The vow of vv 2–5 is marked off as a self-contained unit by two marks of inclusion, the divine epithet לאביר יעקב "to/for the mighty one of Jacob" at the end of vv 2, 5 and, within the first person material, the seemingly conscious parallel between David's tent and Yahweh's (משכנות, אהל) in vv 3a, 5b. Seybold (*Wallfahrtspsalmen*, 43) has plausibly suggested that vv 3–5 represent part of a cultic text which has been incorporated into the psalm.

The second half of the psalm echoes the first, unit by unit. Vv 11–12 function as a divine oath cited in response to David's. If, as is probable, a cultic prophet originally spoke vv 11–18, vv 11–12 comprise not a spontaneous answer but the citation of an older oracle (cf. Lipiński, *La liturgie penitentielle*, 101): David himself, rather than the contemporary Davidic king, is addressed. David's concern for Yahweh, revealed by the double divine epithet לאביר יעקב at the end of vv 2 and 5, is matched by Yahweh's concern for David's throne, stylistically shown in the repeated לכסא-לך "upon your throne" at the end of vv 11 and 12 (cf. Fretheim, *JBL* 86 [1967] 291). David's own efforts, introduced by the oath particle אם (v 3), are to issue in the corresponding moral endeavors of his successors, which are also introduced by אם, now a conditional particle (v 12; Schreiner, *Sion-Jerusalem*, 105).

Vv 13–16 are the intended parallel to vv 6–9 (Fretheim, *JBL* 86 [1967] 292–93). Fretheim noted the correspondence of vv 6, 13 in that they contain the only place names in the psalm (בשדי יער "in the countryside of Jaar," באפרתה// "in Ephratah" //בציון "in Zion"). Other parallels which may be cited between the two verses are that both are statements relating to the past and both contain an introductory particle (כי "for," הנה "lo") and third feminine singular suffixes. Vv 14–16 comprise divine promises in answer to the prayers and wishes of vv 8–9. V 15 corresponds to v 7 as a promise of blessing for the cult community in response to their visit to the sanctuary to worship; v 8 is linked with v 14 by the key word מנוחה "resting place," while v 16 clearly takes up v 9 in an affirming promise. Both Lipiński (*La liturgie penitentielle*, 101) and Seybold (*Wallfahrtspsalmen*, 43) have claimed that vv 14–18 cite older material. Although vv 17–18 are to be distinguished (see below), this suggestion may well be valid for vv 14–16. They may have served as a cultic sequel to the earlier citation of vv 6–9. After citing a traditional divine oracle concerning the Davidic dynasty, the prophet continues with another quotation, which he supplies with an introduction, v 13, modeling it in some respects upon v 6. The promise of a dynasty is undergirded by Yahweh's choice of Zion for his own perpetual enthronement, which connotes his presence at the sanctuary in blessing.

At first sight vv 17–18 are a continuation of vv 14–16, but closer examination indicates that there is a break after v 16, as after v 9. The clue to this break is the different perspective of the reference to Zion, in v 14 פה "here" and in v 17 שם "there" (Fretheim, *JBL* 86 [1967] 299; cf. Houk, *JSOT* [1978] 44, who, however, explains the change differently). As Fretheim has seen, and Schreiner before him (*Sion-Jerusalem*, 175), vv 17–18 represent the specific answer to the prayers of vv 1, 10. In fact the prophet gives a multiple answer which matches the ramifications of the overall prayer of vv 1–10. The two motivations for the prayer to be answered, vv 2–5, 6–9, are matched by a double reassuring reference to Yahweh's dynastic promise and choice of Zion. Both the prayer and the response appeal to two antecedent factors, in the first case to David's oath and its execution and in the second to Yahweh's oath concerning the Davidic monarchy and to his own kingship. The request to "remember" in v 1 is answered mainly by a virtual reminder of the revelation of Yahweh's twofold purpose. But finally a contemporary oracle is given in vv 17–18, in answer to the present prayers of vv 1, 10. The first strophe falls into four parts, vv 1aβ-b, 2–5 (=2+3–5), 6–9 (=6+7–9), 10; the second falls into three parts, vv 11–12 (=11aβ+11aγ–12b), 13–16 (=13+14–16), 17–18. The two separated lines of prayer, vv 1aβ-b, 10, are paralleled by two final, consecutive lines, vv 17–18; the other units each consist of four lines.

The psalm is fundamentally a liturgy in which king and prophet take part. That the king, or a cultic official speaking as his representative, recited vv 1–10 is indicated by v 10b, where the verbal phrase signifies rejecting a request (cf. 1 Kgs 2:16, 17, 20) i.e. the request of v 1 offered by the contemporary Davidic king. Accordingly it can be classified as a royal psalm, along with Pss 101, 110, etc. In content it is concerned with the divine role of Zion: Schreiner (*Sion-Jerusalem*, 175–77) has argued that Zion, not David, is the central theme of the entire psalm. Thus it could be categorized as a Song of Zion, with Gunkel (*Die Psalmen*, 568). The use of שם "there," v 17 (cf. 48:7 [6]; 76:4 [3]) might lend support to this designation, except that it is connected in the Songs of Zion with Yahweh's past deliverance of Zion. It is perhaps better to describe the psalm as primarily royal, but containing motifs reminiscent of the Songs of Zion.

Was the psalm used on a particular cultic occasion? It is very often linked with a ceremony re-enacting David's bringing of the ark to Zion and the establishment of Yahweh's sanctuary there. For such a ceremony there is evidence in 24:7–10 (cf. 2 Chr 35:3, discussed by Fretheim, *CBQ* 30 [1968] 8–11). The denials of Weiser (Psalms, 781) and Hillers (*CBQ* 30 [1968] 52–54) that v 8 refers to such a procession do not carry conviction. But equally Fretheim's attempt to relate the whole psalm, step by step, to a complex ceremony, which is reminiscent of the attempts of earlier scholars to reconstruct the Davidic enthronement ceremony from Ps 110, is too hypothetical. Moreover, it is difficult to square the evidence of the psalm's unity which he presents with its supposed origin in separate stages within an intricate ritual (*JBL* 86 [1967] 299).

In 2 Chr 6:41–42 vv 8, 9, 10b (cf. v 1aβ) are apparently quoted, in connection with Solomon's dedication of the temple. Since vv 8–9 seem to belong to different strata of the psalm, it is probable that the Chronicler was quoting from Ps 132 in its present form. But it is hazardous to assume that the psalm necessarily belonged originally to a commemoration of the dedication of the temple (Weiser, *Psalms,* 779). The Chronicler may well have used the psalmody familiar to him and his readers to illustrate the kind of praise used at the ancient cultic occasion (cf. E. Slomovic's discovery of a midrashic process in the use of the psalm, in *ZAW* 91 [1979] 379–80). Whether the psalm was used at a royal Zion festival held on the first day of the Feast of Tabernacles (Kraus, *Psalmen,* 1059; cf. *Königsherrschaft,* 27–99) depends upon a reconstruction of the temple ritual, to examine which lies beyond the bounds of this commentary. The psalm does not demand any date in Jerusalem's cultic calendar: its prayer need not be so tied, and its reassurance would be welcome at any time. All it demands is a temple setting. It may, but not necessarily, have been associated with a threat to the monarchy: the reference to enemies in v 18 is a standard ingredient of Davidic theology.

The period of the psalm's origin is fraught with controversy. Gunkel (*Die Psalmen,* 568) asserted rightly that it presupposes the Davidic monarchy as a contemporary institution and there is no hint that Jerusalem has suffered the exile. Accordingly it is difficult to regard the psalm as post-exilic with French scholars such as R. Tournay (review of *Libro Dei Salmi,* by D. G. Castellino, *RB* 63 [1956] 431). The two relevant areas of discussion are the amount of archaic language used in the psalm and the presence or otherwise of deuteronomistic terminology and ideology. Cross has stressed the profusion of archaic elements (*Canaanite Myth and Hebrew Epic,* 97; cf. Dahood, *Psalms III,* 242) in response to Hillers, who could find only שׁנה "sleep," v 4. However, even if Cross is right, little is gained, since the psalm includes much quotation, and earlier material has clearly been re-used within a later composition. Significant is D. A. Robertson's reference to אשׁר, v 2, and the *-m* suffix ın אלמדם, v 12, as "standard" or non-early elements, over against an archaizing" זוֹ, v 12 (*Linguistic Evidence,* 63, 143), though Cross has claimed that an original אלמדומו underlies the subsequently modernized verbal form in v 12 (*Canaanite Myth and Hebrew Epic,* 233).

The nature of the "covenant" in v 12 is a major source of contention. It is part of a wider debate over the usage and development of the term in the OT generally. A deuteronomistic interpretation in terms of the Mosaic covenant is urged by A. Caquot ("La prophetie de Nathan," 222), N. Poulssen

(*König und Tempel,* 132), L. Perlitt (*Bundestheologie,* 51), W. H. Schmidt ("Kritik am Königtum," 447 note 18) and Mettinger (*King and Messiah,* 256). Mettinger has compared v 12 with Deut 17:18–19. On the other hand, Gese (*ZTK* 61 [1964] 14), who claimed that the vocabulary of the psalm was pre-deuteronomistic, held that a covenant between Yahweh and David was in view, comparing 2 Sam 23:5, as does T. Ishida (*Royal Dynasties,* 107–8). Other champions of a Davidic covenant are Lipiński (*La royauté de Yahwé,* 145), Cross (*Canaanite Myth and Hebrew Epic,* 233–34) and Kraus (*Psalmen,* 1064). For עדותי "terms" in v 12b, העדות in 2 Kgs 11:12 has been compared, e.g. by Johnson (*Sacral Kingship,* 24), who understands it as a document embodying the basic terms of covenant with the house of David.

A closely related issue is the conditionality of the promise in v 12, with which 2 Sam 7:14–15 and Ps 89:29–38 (28–37) may be contrasted. Coppens compared the similar limitation, linked with the Mosaic covenant, in 1 and 2 Kings (cf. A. Lauha, *Die Geschichtsmotive,* 119). Mettinger has detected tension between vv 11 and 12, and claimed that the latter was a later adaptation of an older tradition (*King and Messiah,* 257). However, Weinfeld (*JAOS* 90 [1970] 196) has suggested that a conception of a conditional promise concerning the Davidic dynasty, developed especially after the division of the kingdom, existed alongside that of an unconditional promise and was taken up by the deuteronomists and turned into the core of their ideology, being related closely to the Mosaic law rather than to the more general idea of obligation found here in v 12. Cross (*Canaanite Myth and Hebrew Epic,* 233) has even claimed that the conditionality reflects the earliest form of the conception of monarchy, characteristic of David's reign before it was superseded by the Solomonic Canaanizing, unconditional ideology of kingship.

W. H. Schmidt has hailed the election of Zion, v 13, as a deuteronomistic feature ("Kritik am Königtum," 446 note 17; similarly Mettinger, *King and Messiah,* 256). However, Roberts (*JBL* 92 [1973] 343) has urged on the basis of 1 Kgs 14:1–18 that the tradition is a much more ancient one and was already firmly fixed before Solomon's death (cf. R. E. Clements, *God and Temple* [*Oxford: Basil Blackwell,* 1965] 49). Mettinger (*King and Messiah,* 278), who judges it possible that the psalm dates from the late pre-exilic period, has pointed to what he regards as an accumulation of deuteronomistic features. He includes the description of David as עבד "servant" in v 10 (cf. too 89:4, 21 [3, 20]; Jer 33:21, 22, 26), the phrase פרי בטן "fruit of the womb" in v 11, although it occurs too outside deuteronom(ist)ic literature, and נר "lamp" in v 17, although he admits a pre-deuteronomistic use in 2 Sam 21:17. He has compared בעבור דוד "for David's sake" in v 10 with the similar deuteronomistic למען דוד "on account of David" and observed that the latter phrase occurs three times alongside נ(י)ר (1 Kgs 11:34–36; 15:4; 2 Kgs 8:19).

It is difficult to come to a definite conclusion concerning the relation of the psalm to deuteronomistic thinking and phraseology. It is by no means improbable that, as Weinfeld has suggested, the deuteronomists drew upon older traditions in the formulation of their ideology. Accordingly it is not necessary to demand a date after Josiah on the score of apparent parallels. A similar riposte may be given to Poulssen's reference to the stem צמח "sprout" in v 17 as "messianically colored" (*König und Tempel,* 133), comparing

Jer 23:5; 33:15; Ezek 29:21; Zech 3:8; 6:12, as a basis for a post-exilic dating of the psalm. The roots of the term are probably much older: cf. Schreiner's citation of 2 Sam 23:5 and Isa 11:1 (*Sion-Jerusalem*, 106).

A further issue is the question of the relation of the psalm to 2 Sam 7. In particular it is often urged that Ps 132 exhibits a later development of the basic promise of Nathan in 2 Sam 7 (e.g. J. de Fraine, *L'aspect religieux*, 162; Mettinger, *King and Messiah*, 257). Two instances of such development are cited, the conception of the promise as a divine oath in v 11 (cf. 89:4 [3]) and the extension of the promise of a successor to descendants in general in v 12 (cf. 89:31, 37 [30, 36]). Complex literary issues concerning 2 Sam 7 would require discussion for a complete evaluation of the relation of the psalm to that passage. It is possible that a later form of the tradition of Nathan's promise is echoed in vv 11–12. The precise traditio-historical and literary relationship of the psalm to 2 Sam 6–7 is too large a subject to be handled here, but mention may be made of H. G. M. Williamson's suggestion ("Review of T. N. D. Mettinger, *King and Messiah*," *VT* 28 [1978] 506) that some form of the oracle of Nathan was preserved with the ark narrative.

Psalm 132 is a royal and prophetic liturgy which did not necessarily originate later than the period of Josiah. It harks back to older traditions concerning David's bringing the ark to Jerusalem, concerning the Davidic dynasty and concerning the importance of Zion. The psalm probably makes use of material concerning an ark procession, but need not itself belong to this cultic milieu. The other ancient themes must have been of constant relevance to the Jerusalem cult and do not demand a special annual occasion for their celebration. The location of the psalm within the present collection reveals a new role in a post-exilic period. It differs from all the other psalms in length and in dominantly royal theme and so was obviously included for a special purpose. It serves to illustrate the national hope of 130:7; 131:3 (cf. Seybold, *Wallfahrtspsalmen*, 71–72) as a longing for the messianic promises and Yahweh's Zion-centered purpose to come to fruition in the experience of God's people.

Explanation

A Judean king offers his prayer at the temple, perhaps on the anniversary of David's founding of the sanctuary by bringing the ark to Jerusalem. By way of appeal to Yahweh for blessing upon his rule, he harks back to David's strenuous efforts on God's behalf. Underlying his appeal is the concept of the solidarity of blessing which accrues from father to family (cf. Exod 20:6). In vv 3–5 the king cites a tradition concerning David's sworn vow to forsake his "tent" till he has found one for Yahweh and to allow himself no rest till Yahweh can take his rest. There is implicit reference to the ark, symbol of God's powerful presence.

The prayer now takes up another tradition to show how the vow was realized. This tradition, in vv 6–9, was evidently derived from a processional rite commemorating the removal of the ark from Kiriath-jearim to Jerusalem. The significance of "Ephrath" in v 6a is controvertible; the verse probably gives a report of a journey from Bethlehem to Kiriath-jearim, recited by a choir representing David and his men (cf. 1 Chr 13:3). In its new setting the tradition reads as David's voice still reciting how he, together with his contemporaries, took steps to implement his vow. There follows an exhortation from the choir to begin the procession, which is to culminate in worship where the ark is finally set down. The most natural interpretation of v 8 suggests that the ark itself was carried in the procession featured in the tradition here cited. In an age-old cry (cf. Num 10:35) which evokes the ancient concept of Holy War, Yahweh is bidden proceed in triumph to the sanctuary (cf. 24:7–10). Originally the procession would have finished at the tent sanctuary erected by David; after the building of the temple, that would have become its destination. Prayers are offered for the sanctuary, specifically for the priests in their role of dispensing oracle and blessing, and for the sacred choirs that God may give warrant for their songs of praise.

Now the king, standing in the very place that marks the journey's end and having rehearsed before Yahweh the story of the first journey, returns to his initial plea. He craves a favorable hearing for the request he brings, "for David's sake." The traditional title "servant," betokening both privilege and responsibility, is used of David. The founder of the dynasty served his Lord well and in return blessing is sought for the contemporary king.

The royal prayer receives an affirmative answer, evidently delivered by a cultic prophet in the first instance. The reply is an artistic echo of the prayer. First, the king is reassuringly reminded that David's labors for his Lord did not go unrewarded. A tradition of the basic promise through Nathan (cf. 2 Sam 7; Ps 89) is taken up. Yahweh, too, had sworn an oath, promising dynastic succession to King David. David functions, however, not only as a mediator of blessing to his successors but also as a model of commitment. His vow and efforts were to be matched by his descendants' devotion to the Davidic covenant. The two-sidedness of the pact is stressed in a forceful manner: kerygma and paraenesis are intertwined in this version of the royal tradition.

Having in v 11aα-β introduced Yahweh's oath, the prophet provides a preface to another divine oracle, in v 13, before citing it in vv 14–16. This oracle may well have been closely associated originally with the tradition quoted in vv 6–9, since it echoes much of its contents: if so, an older liturgy has been incorporated into a new liturgical composition. The prophet gives his own emphasis to the quotation by selecting from it the emotional term "desire" and linking it with the election of Zion. Yahweh has committed himself with enthusiastic fervor to the city where David brought the ark long ago. There he reigns in its sanctuary, on the invisible throne above the ark which represents its footstool (v 7). David's installation of the ark had served to fulfil Yahweh's sovereign initiative. The specific point which the prophet is constrained to make is that from this divine throne the earthly throne of the Davidic dynasty derives its authority ("for," v 13). This revelation of his purpose provides a firm foundation for the dynasty.

The old oracle continues with promise of blessing for the community. The divine patron of the sanctuary would indeed bless the nation gathered for worship in Zion: their needs would be met. The ministers of the sanctuary would mediate not only this effective blessing and delivering grace to the people but also their resultant praise back to Yahweh.

If the patron had made such lavish promises of benefits for the people, would not the king too be the recipient of blessing? Yes indeed. The prophet adds to his citations an inspired word of assurance in vv 17–18, in precise reply to the prayers of vv 1, 10. Zion, the divine seat, is the source of Yahweh's saving grace preeminently for the royal representative of the people. The presence of God constitutes a promise of both strength and stability for the reigning Davidide. The latter would share in the triumph symbolized by the ark (v 8): victory and majesty would be his.

Psalm 132 has much in common with other royal psalms: the divine promise of victory and the linking of the dynasty with Zion occurs in Ps 2, and the divine oath in 89:36 (35); 110:4. This psalm is unique in its warm and intensely personal presentation of the key characters David and Yahweh. The effect is achieved both by the reciprocal first person references and by the impression of unflagging, resourceful service on David's part and of satisfied yearning and lavish generosity (N.B. the stressed verbs of vv 15a, 16b) on Yahweh's part. Above all, it elaborates the close relationship between the dynasty and the sanctuary: the latter, as the throne room of the heavenly king, provides a mainstay for the former. On either side of the Davidic throne stands the ancient, renewed dynastic promise and the cultic presence of its divine patron. But the present king inherits David's role as responsible servant, obliged to bow the knee in obedience as in prayer.

In the present collection the psalm took on a new, poignant character as an expression of the messianic hope and as a pointer to the cloud of glory yet to surround Mount Zion (cf. Ps 102). In the NT there is perhaps surprisingly little use of the psalm. Apart from the reference to v 5 in the anti-temple polemic of Stephen in Acts 7:46, there is a quotation of the divine oath of 132:11 in Peter's speech at Acts 2:30. The messianic interpretation already assigned to the psalm by the time it reached the Psalter is not only endorsed but focuses in fulfillment upon the risen Jesus as the "Christ" (cf. 132:17) who sits enthroned at God's right hand (110:1).

The Family of Faith   (133:1–3)

Bibliography

Braslavi, J. "כטל פרמון שיורד על הררי ציון." *Bet Miqra* 49 (1972) 143–45. **Keel, O.** "Kultische Brüderlichkeit—Psalm 133." *FZTP* 23 (1976) 68–80. **Kuntz, J. K.** "The Canonical Wisdom Psalms of Ancient Israel: Their Rhetorical, Thematic and Formal Dimensions." *Rhetorical Criticism*, ed. **J. J. Jackson** and **M. Kessler.** Pittsburgh: Pickwick Press, 1974. **Norin, S.** "Ps. 133. Zusammenhang und Datierung." *ASTI* 11 (1978) 90–95. **Power, E.** "Sion or Si'on in Psalm 133 (Vulg 132)?" *Bib* 3 (1922) 342–49. **Skehan, P. W.** *Studies in Israelite Poetry and Wisdom.* CBQMS 1. Washington, D.C.: Catholic Biblical Association of America, 1971.

Translation

[1] One of the processional songs.[a] Davidic.
  How good, to be sure, how fine it is   (3+3)
   for [b] *brothers to stay together!* [c]

² *It is like the sweet* ᵃ *oil upon the head*   (3+2)
  coming ᵇ *down upon the beard,*
  Aaron's beard ᶜ *which* ᵈ *came down*   (3+2)
  over his body. ᵉ
³ *It is like the dew of Hermon* ᵃ *which comes down*   (3+2)
  upon the mountains ᵇ *of Zion.* ᶜ
  That ᵈ *is where Yahweh*   (2+2+2)
  has ordered the blessing to be,
  life ᵉ *for evermore.*

Notes/Comments

1.a. See the note on 120:1.
1.b. P. W. Skehan (*Israelite Poetry*, 63), followed by O. Keel (*FZTP* 23 [1976] 68) rendered "where brothers live together," in view of שׁם "there" in v 3, but a phenomenon rather than its precise location seems to be in view here.
1.c. The phrase probably had its origin in the custom of the extended family, whereby brothers lived together with their father after marriage (Deut 25:5; cf. Gen 13:6; 36:7). A. Phillips (*Ancient Israel's Criminal Law* [Oxford: Basil Blackwell, 1970] 124 note 78) considers that brothers lived together thus until children were born, whereupon younger brothers would set up separate households. The psalm is frequently regarded as a commendation of this sociological practice e.g. by H.-J. Kraus (*Psalmen*, 1068) and A. Weiser (*Psalms*, 783–84). An older interpretation is of a cultic nature, in terms of the covenant nation of "brothers" worshiping together in Jerusalem (e.g. J. A. Alexander, *Psalms*, 527); it still finds support (e.g. A. A. Anderson, *Psalms*, 885; J. H. Eaton, *Psalms*, 294). Keel (*FZTP* 23 [1967] 68–80) has recently advocated this interpretation strongly. Then a secular expression relating to the family has been spiritualized here. For ישׁב "dwell" in the sense of temple worship see 27:4; 140:14 (13).
2.a. Heb. כַשֶּׁמֶן is sometimes emended to כְּבֹשֶׂם so that the following טוב may be regarded as a noun "perfume" (cf. *HALAT*, 356a).
2.b. For conformity with v 2a (and v 2b) an emendation of ירד "coming down" to שירד "which comes down," assuming haplography, is often advocated (H. Gunkel, Die Psalmen, 572; Kraus, *Psalmen*, 1067 *et al.*)
2.c. Gunkel, ibid. (cf. Weiser, *Psalms*, 783) emended זקן "beard" to כזקן "like the beard," thus obtaining three similes. For the proposed deletion of the line as secondary (cf. *BHS*) see *Form/Structure/Setting*. "Aaron" functions as a prototype of the high priest (Keel, *FZTP* 23 [1976] 76).
2.d. The antecedent appears to be the immediately preceding beard rather than the earlier oil: otherwise the line is hardly viable poetically. Keel (*FZTP* 23 [1976] 69) has noted that 11QPsᵃ so understood: it reads ירד (=יָרַד) "came down" here but יורד "coming down" before and after.
2.e. Keel (*FZTP* 23 [1976] 71–72, 74–75) has presented an impressive accumulation of arguments in favor of such an interpretation rather than the traditional "upon the collar of his robes." Heb. מדות means "measure, stature, size," here an intensive plural (cf. בית מדות Jer 22:14 and possibly אנשׁי מדות Num 13:32), while מד, מדים are used for clothes, though M. Dahood (*Psalms III*, 252) has pointed to one occurrence of Ugar. *mdt* "clothes" over against the usual plural. Mention of the collar would be strange since the beard as commonly worn would extend below the neck opening. In this context an especially long beard is probably in mind, as worn by dignitaries in the period of the Persian empire. Then על-פי, as elsewhere, signifies "according to."
3.a. The topographical difficulty of relating this northern mountain to Zion has been variously resolved (cf. note 3.c.). J. Braslavi (*Bet Miqra* 49 [1972] 143–45) has taken חרמון as an abstract noun (cf. בתרון, רעבון) "holiness" from the stem חרם. It is often surmised to be a proverbial figure for copious dew, e.g. by Weiser (*Psalms*, 784) and Anderson (*Psalms*, 886); cf. the quotation from G. A. Smith, *The Historical Geography of the Holy Land* (21st ed.; London: Hodder & Stoughton, 1931) 65, concerning excessive Syrian dews, cited by A. F. Kirkpatrick (*Psalms*, 771) and Dahood, (*Psalms III*, 252). Keel (*FZTP* 23 [1976] 76) has suggested a plausible explanation in terms of

religious polemic, comparing 48:3 (2), where Zaphon, the mountain of divine habitation, is used of Zion as the true divine dwelling place (cf. 89:13 [12]; he claims that the emphatic שׁם "there" in the final line supports his interpretation.

3.b. For the plural cf. 87:1; 121:1. S. Norin (*ASTI* 11 [1978] 92) has proposed a pointing as a singular with *ḥireq compaginis* הַרְרֵי (cf. 11QPsᵃ הר).

3.c. Following A. Jirku, Gunkel (*Die Psalmen*, 571) emended to עֵיֹון (misprinted in *BHS* as עֵיֹון) "Ijon" at the foot of Mount Hermon (cf. 1 Kgs 15:20; 2 Kgs 15:29). Other common proposals are ציה "dry place" (e.g. Kraus, *Psalmen*, 1067) and the synonymous ציֹון. E. Power (*Bib* 3 [1922] 346–47) proposed שׂיֹאן = שׂיֹון "Siʾon" (cf. Deut 4:48), understanding Siʾon as the mountain range of which Hermon was the name of the highest summit.

3.d. Heb. כי "for" is probably emphatic (Keel, *FZTP* 23 [1976] 76 and note 37) rather than causal, as it is generally taken.

3.e. MT חיים "life" is omitted by 11QPsᵃ. It is sometimes regarded as a gloss (cf. *BHK*). D. N. Freedman *apud* Dahood, *Psalms III*, 253, has defended its presence on the grounds of a word play אחים-חיים "brothers" in vv 1, 4 and suggested that the term was deleted in 11QPsᵃ on dogmatic grounds.

Form/Structure/Setting

The interpretation of the psalm and its form-critical clarification depend upon conclusions concerning the amount of secondary or recensional material within it and concerning its focal point. An investigation of the role of the psalm within the present collection, Pss 120–134, is an appropriate starting point for discussion. The overlapping of terminology with the previous and/ or next psalms leave little room for doubt. "Zion" clearly functions as a prominent motif, as in 132:13; 134:3, along with שׁם "there" (cf. 132:17); so, too, does the concept of blessing, as in 132:15; 134:3. Accordingly the weight of the psalm in its present context falls heavily upon v 3 and its cultic content. It is possible that the psalm has undergone re-interpretation and supplementation. "Zion" in v 3 has frequently been regarded as a corruption (see *Notes/Comments*) or as a redactional change (K. Seybold, *Wallfahrtspsalmen*, 26), and difficulty in the understanding of the present text makes conjectural emendation an attractive course. Seybold (*Wallfahrtspsalmen*, 26) has also regarded v 3aγ-b as a redactional addition, along with v 2cγ-b. The latter line is often deleted, as a complication of the first simile in comparison with the second (e.g. Kraus, *Psalmen*, 1067) or on the grounds that historical allusion to Aaron's consecration is out of place in a simile (H. Schmidt, *Die Psalmen*, 236). Anyway, its deletion serves to remove a cultically oriented element in the psalm, and together with the emendation of ציֹון "Zion" directs the interpretation away from a cultic interpretation. Then the way is open for regarding the psalm as a non-cultic wisdom poem, as most commentators have done since Gunkel (*Die Psalmen*, 570). Both R. B. Y. Scott (*The Way of Wisdom*, 133) and J. K. Kuntz ("*Canonical Wisdom Psalms*," 191, 199, 208, 210) have analyzed its form thus. Scott regarded the exclamation of v 1 as a counterpart to the אשׁרי ("how fortunate") formula. Kuntz has defined the psalm as an expanded proverb celebrating fraternal harmony and containing a rhetorical element and the similes of vv 2–3 but no wisdom vocabulary. The last line of the psalm is then generally understood as subordinate to the first, a commendation of brotherly unity as a prelude to divine blessing (e.g. Kraus, *Psalmen*, 1069). H. Schmidt (*Die Psalmen*, 237) ventured to suggest a setting for such a wisdom psalm: it was used as a greeting from a guest on entering a home where brothers lived together as an extended family.

R. E. Murphy ("Wisdom Psalms," 156–67) significantly did not include the psalm in his list of wisdom psalms. Keel (*FZTP* 23 [1976] 77–78) has drawn attention to its affinity with the Songs of Zion; in particular the less formal type represented by Pss 84 and 122 may be compared. He has plausibly aligned the first bicolon with the motif of aesthetic pleasure in reaction to the temple and Zion, to be found in the Songs of Zion, 48:3 (2); 84:2 (1); 122:1, and elsewhere in the Psalter, 27:4; 50:2, 55:15 (14) (*FZTP* 23 [1976] 80). Comparable too is the use of שם or שמה "there" with respect to Zion in 48:7 (6); 76:4 (3); 122:5, which may support Keel's view that in v 3 it refers both to Zion and to v 1 understood in terms of a cultic gathering (*FZTP* 23 [1976] 78–80; cf. Dahood, *Psalms III*, 252, whose exegesis of the psalm appears, however, to be inconsistent). In form, then, the psalm is probably to be regarded as a Song of Zion influenced by wisdom characteristics.

Like Ps 122, it was sung by pilgrims in the course of celebrating festivals at Jerusalem. Keel (*FZTP* 23 [1976] 79) has bolstered his Zion-centered understanding of the psalm by appeal to a stylistic feature, an apparent word play between ציון "Zion" and צוה "commanded" in v 3. The reference to Aaron's flowing beard in v 2 he has defended (*FZTP* 23 [1976] 70), together with Weiser (*Psalms*, 785), as a positive contribution to the psalm by stressing downward movement in anticipation of the cultic blessing from Yahweh in the final line; on the other hand, Gunkel (*Die Psalmen*, 571), H. Schmidt (*Die Psalmen*, 236) and Kraus (*Psalmen*, 1069) have interpreted the reiterated descent in terms of an older or richer brother helping a younger or poorer one. It is possible that the two key nouns of the last line take up the similes, divine "blessing" being associated with its priestly mediator and "life" with dew falling upon Zion. If "Zion" is the original reading in v 3, it probably confirms the presence of "Aaron" in v 2: both similes then have a cultic reference.

The northern provenance assigned to the psalm by Gunkel, ibid., and Seybold (*Wallfahrtspsalmen*, 38–39) depends largely upon acceptance of the emendation עיון "Ijon" in v 3, although Dahood (*Psalms III*, 250) also urges it, rather strangely in view of his retention of ציון "Zion." The psalm is generally regarded as post-exilic, particularly in view of the relative conjunction ש "which." Kirkpatrick's suggested historical interpretation in terms of encouraging settlement in Jerusalem in the period of Nehemiah (*Psalms*, 770) has found little support. Norin (*ASTI* 11 [1978] 90–95) has attempted to assign the psalm to another historical setting, the period of Hezekiah and the projected union of north (cf. "Hermon") and south under the aegis of common worship in Zion (cf. 2 Chr 30); his interpretation appears rather forced. The Davidic reference in the heading is difficult to explain. It is not unanimously attested (cf. *BHS*). It could be a misplacement from the heading to Ps 132, a more obvious candidate for the annotation.

Structurally the psalm appears to exhibit a concentric pattern. In the first and last lines אחים "brothers" and חיים "life" represent an inclusive word play (Freedman *apud* Dahood, *Psalms III*, 253). Moreover, each line ends with a superlative expression and contains a pair of positive terms, טוב "good" and נעים "pleasant," ברכה "blessing" and חיים. The alliterative pair ציון "Zion" and צוה "commanded" in the final pair of lines correspond to the repetition of טוב "good" in the first pair. The second and penultimate lines are linked by the repetition of כ "like." The three middle lines all include ירד על "coming down upon." The repetition of זקן "beard" in the second and third lines is perhaps balanced by the doubled שירד "which came/comes down" in the third and fourth, as distinct from the shorter ירד "coming down" in the second. The parallelism of the first and last lines serves to confirm Keel's understanding of them (*FZTP* 23 [1976] 78 note 41) as having equal weight and accordingly sharing a cultic reference.

Explanation

The opening verse of this Song of Zion may originally have been a wisdom saying commending the continuance of married brothers in the family homestead (cf. Deut 25:5). If so, it was evidently put to new use, to celebrate the gathering of Judean pilgrims in Jerusalem to worship at time of festival. The crowds in the holy city were a beautiful perspective of the nation, bound together as it was not only by race but by covenant relationship with God.

To convey his appreciation of this visible fellowship of faith the psalmist draws two word pictures. The first harks back to the consecration of Aaron as high priest (cf. Exod 29:7; Lev 8:12). The fragrant anointing oil (cf. Exod 30:23–25, 30), poured over his head, trickled right down his long beard. The sacramental anointing was a divine commissioning (cf. 1 Sam 9:1) of this majestic prototype, so that he might be Yahweh's mediator at the sanctuary. The family of God were gathered at the cultic place where fragrant grace flowed down.

The second illustration, concerning the dew, is a simile with positive overtones of divinely sent refreshment. It lends itself easily to spiritual application, as in Hos 14:5. The significance of "Hermon" is not clear. The reference may be to the amount of dew which befits a sacred mountain. Zion's claims to be such eclipsed those of Hermon (cf. 68:16–17 [15–16]; 87:2). It alone was the divine dwelling place; it inherited, as it were, the dew given liberally to Hermon. "Zion" is a key word which serves to explain and to resume v 1. It paves the way for the amplification of the final line, which gathers up all that goes before. Zion is the place of Yahweh's appointment, to which his people have rightly come to seek his means of grace. It is the source of blessing, mediated through the priesthood (cf. Num 6:23), and of abundant life (cf. 36:10 [9]) invoked thereby upon the labors of future days. The well-being of the community depended upon pilgrimage to this sacred place where divine grace came down.

Like Ps 122, this psalm indicates the high place assigned in OT theology to Zion as focus of the divine presence. It also provides a background for the later conception of a heavenly counterpart, "Mount Zion, city of the living God . . . , the assembly of the firstborn who are enrolled in heaven," to which a new pilgrim people are making their way and whose benefits they already enjoy in part (Heb 12:22–24; 13:14–16; cf. Gal 4:26; Rev 14:1).

The Circle of Blessing (134:1–3)

Bibliography

Albright, W. F. "Notes on Psalms 68 and 134." *Interpretationes ad Vetus Testamentum Sigmundo Mowinckel septuagenario missae.* Oslo: Forlaget Lang Og Kirke, 1955. **Crüsemann, F.** *Studien zur Formgeschichte.* **Habel, N. C.** "Yahweh, Maker of Heaven and Earth: A Study in Tradition Criticism." *JBL* 91 (1972) 321–37.

Translation

1 One of the processional songs.[a]
Come,[b]
bless Yahweh, all you servants [c] of Yahweh,   (4+4)
   who are standing [d] in Yahweh's house by night.[e]
2 Raise your hands [a] towards [b] the holy place   (3+2)
   and bless Yahweh.

3 May Yahweh bless you [a] from Zion,   (3+3)
   maker of heaven and earth.[b]

Notes/Comments

1.a. See the note on 120:1.

1.b. Heb. הנה "come" is here used uniquely with an imperative. H. Gunkel (*Die Psalmen,* 573) considered that it was wrongly inserted here from 133:1. Probably redactional adaptation rather than scribal error was responsible: the insertion served to stress the continuity of this psalm, as the final one in the present collection, with what precedes (cf. ציון "Zion" 133:3; 134:3). At any rate metrically it seems to stand in anacrusis: the meter is probably 4+4, as Gunkel urged (*Die Psalmen,* 572).

1.c. It is significant that עבדים "servants" nowhere else refers to priests and/or Levites (I. Riesener, *Der Stamm* עבד, 228), although the verb עבד "serve" and the noun עבדה "service" do. In 113:1; 135:1 it appears to mean the community at worship. Accordingly a reference to cultic personnel (e.g. S. Mowinckel, *Psalmenstudien,* vol. 5, 46; H. Gunkel und J. Begrich, *Einleitung,* 411; A. Weiser, *Psalms,* 786; J. H. Eaton, *Psalms,* 295; C. C. Keet, *Psalms of Ascents,* 107; M. Dahood, *Psalms III,* 254; cf. *Tg.* which inserts a vocative כהניא "priests" in v 2) is less likely (C. Lindhagen, *The Servant Motif,* 100–103; A. A. Anderson, *Psalms,* 887; J. W. Rogerson and J. W. McKay, *Psalms 101–150,* 141; H.-J. Kraus, *Psalmen,* 1070).

1.d. The attributive participle can describe either activity which is taking place in the present ("who are standing") or continuous and regular duty ("who stand"): cf. P. Joüon, *Grammaire,* § 121i. In the latter case it refers to ministers of the temple, and indeed עמד "stand" is often so used, as in Deut 10:8; 18:7; 1 Chr 23:30. In the former case it can refer to the worshiping community, in which case the congregational usage in Lev 9:5; Jer 7:10 is relevant.

1.e. Joüon (*Grammaire* § 136b) suggested that the plural לילות "nights" referred to "night hours" (cf. 16:7; 92:3); similarly Dahood (*Psalms III,* 254) renders "the watches of the night." Mowinckel, (*Psalmenstudien,* vol. 5, 46 note 5) regarded the plural as intensive (*"Tiefnacht"*).

2.a. The phrase describes a gesture associated with addressing Yahweh in prayer (28:2; cf. 77:3 [2]) or, as here, in praise (63:5 [4]). It is predicated in those places of ordinary members of the community, but could presumably also be used of the praise of cultic personnel.

2.b. NEB renders "in the sanctuary," but the accusative is much more likely to indicate direction toward (cf. GKC § 118f, g). Heb. קדש can signify the temple together with its precincts or the temple itself or its nave or its inner chamber (cf. BDB, 371b). Comparison with 5:8; 138:2 suggests that the main temple building is meant.

3.a. The singular pronominal suffix more probably refers here to the community than to an individual. It is a stereotyped element, as in Num 6:24. For the content of divine blessing see note 4.b. in *Notes/Comments* on Ps 128.

3.b. For this divine appositional phrase and its association with Zion see N. C. Habel, *JBL* 91 (1972) 321–37.

Form/Structure/Setting

In form and content this brief psalm falls into two unequal parts, a hymnic call to praise, vv 1–2, and a priestly benediction, v 3. The stylistic structure of the psalm supports this analysis: the repeated injunction ברכו את-יהוה "bless Yahweh" in the first colon of the initial line and in the second colon of the second forms an inclusion, which serves to mark off vv 1–2 from v 3 (cf. J. Schildenberger, *Estudios Eclesiásticos* 34 [1960] 684). However, v 3 is by no means unrelated. It echoes both the verb ברך "bless" and יהוה "Yahweh," but now in a reverse sense whereby the divine name is subject rather than object of the verb. It is probable then that different voices utter the two parts, so that the psalm is a short liturgy, as Gunkel (*Die Psalmen*, 572) designated it.

The interpretation of the psalm is hampered by the ambiguity of the reference to the addressees in v 1aγ, b. The usage of עבדי יהוה "Yahweh's servants" elsewhere in the OT is a weighty consideration; the verb עמד "stand" in v 1b need not refer technically to the ministry of cultic officials (see *Notes/Comments*). If the collection of Pss 120–134 comprises processional songs, it would be appropriate for worshipers to be called to praise in this final psalm. Moreover, if Ps 135 was intended to supplement the collection (cf. K. Seybold, *Wallfahrtspsalmen*, 74–75) and if the same phrase עבדי יהוה in 135:1 is rightly understood as a reference to the congregation, a similar understanding of 134:1 is presupposed.

The psalm gives the impression of breaking off at the end of v 2: the usual implementation of praise (cf. F. Crüsemann, *Studien zur Formgeschichte*, 78) or reason for praise is not supplied after the reiterated call to praise. It is possible that a gap is to be assumed during which the religious community sang in praise; in that case the psalm represents extracts from a larger liturgy. K. Seybold (*Wallfahrtspsalmen*, 59, 74) regards v 3a as redactional, so that v 3b originally represented Yahweh's praiseworthiness, the creation of the world. But in the light of Gen 14:19; Ps 115:15 the two cola of v 3 dovetail well together.

A cultic setting for the psalm is clear from the twofold reference to the temple and the mention of Zion. A precise reconstruction of that setting is hardly possible. H. Schmidt (*Die Psalmen*, 237) suggested that vv 1–2 may reflect the context of a psalm of thanksgiving sung by an individual who called the community to join in his own praise. Those who regard the psalm as an interchange between the congregation and priests often reconstruct the setting as the pilgrims' departure from Zion. At the end of the day or of the whole festival the people encourage the priests and/or Levites to continue in praise during the night (cf. 1 Chr 9:33) and in return receive a final priestly blessing (Weiser, *Psalms*, 786; Crüsemann, *Studien zur Formgeschichte*, 78; Seybold, *Wallfahrtspalmen*, 66, 69).

Not enough is known about cultic procedure in the OT period to clarify the reference to לילות "night(s)" at the end of v 1. Communal worship at night seems to be presupposed by Isa 30:29 (cf. O. Kaiser, *Isaiah 13–39* [Tr. R. A. Wilson; London: SCM Press, 1974] 308). Gunkel (*Die Psalmen*, 572) envisaged a gathering at the temple the night before one of the festivals. Later Jewish tradition associates nocturnal services with the Feast of Tabernacles, the ceremony of water libation during the nights of the festival (cf. Mishnah, *Sukk.* 5:4). Accordingly it may have been associated with the autumn festival. There are no indications in the psalm as to the date of its original composition.

Explanation

This psalm raises a number of problems, some of which are created by its brevity. But certain factors are clear. Its position at the end of the שיר המעלות "processional songs" collection must be taken seriously, whatever its antecedents. Moreover, the reader must listen to the loud message of the psalm as some kind of interchange of blessing.

In vv 1–2 the time and place—especially the place—are plainly indicated. The occasion is a cultic one, evidently a service held at night, not improbably at the Feast of Tabernacles. Is it a priestly voice we hear urging the gathered people to praise Yahweh (cf. 135:19a)? They stand in the temple courts ready to raise their hands toward the temple, hallowed as the earthly dwelling place of Yahweh. Concerted praise of voices and hands will acknowledge his power and their dependence upon and commitment to him through the covenant ("servants").

Commitment is a two-way relationship, and so is blessing. It is a lopsided duality. In Eph 1:3 the divine and major portion is represented as taking the initiative. In this cultic context the role of the priestly benediction at the close of a service determines the order. The worshipers will leave enriched and strengthened, with the invocation of divine blessing upon them ringing in their ears: "May that power which has been acknowledged in praise come flooding into your own lives!"

In the first part of the psalm the priestly voice has stressed the localization of the congregation in the temple precincts close to the divine presence ("holy place"). In the last verse another priestly voice seems to ring out, reinforcing the sacredness of the locality by the special term "Zion." Zion is Yahweh's powerhouse: through it is channeled his own almighty power. Thus the extended description of the religious community in terms of space and time can now be replaced by a description of Yahweh as one who by right of creation controls both heaven and earth. Zion is a doorway that opens out into the power behind the world. Blessing extends in a remarkable circle. Dynamic potential is given to those who give Yahweh sincere acknowledgment of his power. Essentially it is unsought and comes as a gracious byproduct of worship. In keeping with this attribute of power the divine object of blessing becomes an active subject. He generously shares with his devoted followers from his own resources of omnipotence so that abundant life may be theirs.

Excursus: The "Songs of Ascents"

Bibliography

Keet, C. C. *A Study of the Psalms of Ascents. A Critical and Exegetical Commentary upon Psalms 120–134.* London: Mitre Press, 1969. **Liebreich, L. J.** "The Songs of Ascents and the Priestly Blessing." *JBL* 74 (1955) 33–36. **Press, R.** "Die zeitgeschichtliche Hintergrund der Wallfahrtspsalmen." *TZ* 14 (1958) 401–15. **Seybold, K.** *Die Wallfahrtspsalmen. Studien zur Entstehungsgeschichte von Psalmen 120–134.* Biblische-Theologische Studien 3. Neukirchen-Vluyn: Neukirchener Verlag, 1978.

Psalms 120–134 comprise a separate, consecutive collection, while Pss 135–137 appear to be a supplement to the collection (K. Seybold, *Wallfahrtspsalmen*, 74–75). The title which stands at the head of each psalm, slightly varied in Ps 121, probably functioned originally as the name for the group as a whole (see *Notes/Comments* note 1.a. for Pss 120 and 121). The title has been variously explained. Two of the suggestions are of a literary nature. The first relates to a poetic feature found within the collection, steplike parallelism, whereby a term used in one line is echoed in the next. However, the phenomenon is not restricted to this particular group of psalms nor does it appear consistently in all the members. M. Dahood (*Psalms III*, 195) with the aid of a Qumran text has assigned to מעלות a new meaning "extolments," regarding it as a designation of the praising character of the psalms; he admits that it does not suit all the constituent psalms. A further suggestion is of a historical kind. Heb. מעלות is related to the use of the verb עלה "go up" in Ezra 2:1; 7:9; the collection may then be regarded as a series of songs sung by exiles or groups of exiles (N.B. the plural) returning to Judah. A refinement of this view has been put forward by R. Press (*TZ* 14 [1958] 401–15), who has dated the collection in the final years of Babylonian exile. He regards the language of Pss 123–133 as symbolic for the exile and return to rebuild the temple and the community. However, a number of these psalms appear to presuppose post-exilic conditions rather than mere aspirations.

The remaining suggestions are more or less cultic in nature. A Jewish tradition in the Mishnah relates the fifteen Songs of Ascents to the fifteen steps leading up from the court of the women to the court of Israel in the temple complex (*Mid.* 2:5; *Sukk.* 5:4). The steps "correspond to" the Songs and upon the steps "the Levites used to sing psalms" on the first day of the Feast of Tabernacles. It is not precisely stated that the Songs were sung there and then, but it may well be implied. A different relation to "steps" has been mooted by L. J. Liebreich (*JBL* 74 [1955] 33–36; for yet another, adduced by E. Lipiński, see below). Liebreich interpreted the collection as an elaboration of the key terms of the Aaronic benediction of Num 6:24–26, which according to Tosepta, *Soṭa* 7:7 was pronounced upon the steps of the temple porch. However, not all the psalms contain such key words: three, Pss 124, 126 and 131, lack them. Yet overall the relationship of the psalms to the priestly benediction is striking and in some cases may well illustrate the influence of the latter.

The most popular understanding of the title is to relate it to the established use of the verb עלה for pilgrimage (e.g. 24:3; Isa 2:3). In the most recent and detailed study of the Songs of Ascents, K. Seybold has defined the collection as a kind of *vade-mecum* for pilgrims, a series of prayers and songs or perhaps texts for meditation (*Wallfahrtspsalmen*, 73). More precisely מעלות has been interpreted as processional ascents to the temple, in view of the use of the verb to refer to this final stage of pilgrimage, a cultic procession (2 Sam 6:12, 15; 1 Kgs 13:33; 2 Kgs 23:2; H.-J. Kraus, *Psalmen*, 18; cf. S. Mowinckel, *The Psalms in Israel's Worship*, vol. 2, 208). For other allusions to cultic processions Pss 24; 42:5 (4); 100; Isa 26:2; 30:29 may be compared. The cultic language to be found within the collection and the apparent participation of priests in a number of its texts favors this final suggestion. Lipiński (*La royauté de Yahwé*, 448) has linked this view with the concrete sense of "steps" for מעלות: the "songs of the stairway" refer to the stairway of Neh 12:37 at the Fountain Gate, which was included in the processional route leading to the temple.

The most evident feature of the psalms which make up the collection is their diversity. Yet there are common features. One is their brevity, apart from Ps 132; another is their preoccupation with Zion. Seven of the fifteen psalms contain the term, viz. 125, 126, 128, 129, 132–134; Ps 122 has "Jerusalem." Three others contain formulations associated with Zion (121, 123, 124), while Pss 130 and 131 at least contain calls to the religious community of "Israel," evidently gathered in the temple precincts. In Ps 127 "house" and "city" were probably reinterpreted within the collection in terms of the temple and Jerusalem. Only the introductory psalm, 121, is missing from this tally.

The apparent dating of the original composition of the psalms varies: 122 and 132 seem to be pre-exilic, 123 exilic or post-exilic and 120, 124–126, 128–130, 133 post-exilic; while 121, 127, 131, 134 contain no clues for dating. A variety of form-critical genres have been assembled in the collection, including a wisdom poem, two Songs of Zion, a royal song, an individual thanksgiving psalm and communal complaints. A number of the texts appear to have been reinterpreted for use in the collection, which clearly came into being in the post-exilic period, as for instance the reference to (past) return from exile in 126:1 indicates.

The first three psalms are individual ones and were presumably sung as solos. Psalm 120 is a thanksgiving for heard prayer concerning persecution: it was reinterpreted as a song for Diaspora Jews from hostile environments. Psalm 121 is a liturgy associated with the end of a festival. Psalm 122 is a Song of Zion sung in procession to the temple: this psalm and Ps 133 may represent the nucleus of the processional collection to which psalms from other cultic settings were attached. The next group, Pss 123–126, are all communal in nature. Psalms 123, 125, 126 are complaints. Psalm 124 is an adaptation of a group's song of thanksgiving to a communal hymn of praise, perhaps inserted to assure that Yahweh does answer his people's prayers and certainly according with the statements of confidence present in the adjacent complaints. Psalms 127 and 128 are a pair, in respect of their didactic and domestic themes. The former is a wisdom poem which has been reinterpreted to refer to the temple and Jerusalem ("house," "city"), while the latter also aims to instruct and may have been composed specifically for the collection, to teach pilgrims to Zion. Psalm 129 is a Zion-centered liturgy, a communal psalm of confidence. The final five psalms have a certain coherence and sequence. Psalms 130 and 131 introduce the motif of the hope of the community. Psalm 130, originally an individual complaint and answer, has been re-used as a liturgical communal complaint, in view of its proximity to Ps 129. Psalm 131, an individual psalm of confidence, has also been re-interpreted in communal terms, with a final priestly summons. In Ps 132, a royal psalm, the hope of the previous pair of texts is defined in messianic and Zion-oriented terms. The last two psalms echo the motifs of blessing and Zion already present in Ps 132. Psalm 133 is a Song of Zion (with wisdom influence) for pilgrims; Ps 134 is a priestly liturgy calling the community to praise and bestowing benediction.

Thus it is possible to perceive some kind of grouping and sequence within the collection; but there is no total coherence apart from the nearly unbroken thread of Zion. Little more can be said about the origin and compilation of the fifteen psalms. Seybold has drawn attention to the similarities between texts, which may point to a common period and background. He has interestingly categorized all of them apart from Ps 132 as a series of basically lay poems originally brought to the temple as votive gifts at the thank offering service and subsequently taken from the temple archives and revised for a new use (*Wallfahrtspalmen*, 60–61). His suggestion for their origin depends upon an earlier one of Mowinckel concerning individual thanksgiving psalms, which G. Quell applied to Ps 131. Seybold's conclusions are achieved by way of many snips of the scissors, to cut away recensional addition of various kinds, representing the official theology of the temple. There are indeed some clear signs of recensional activity within the collection, as might reasonably be expected; but it is doubtful whether they are as widespread as Seybold has claimed and consequently whether it is possible to distinguish so sharply as he has done between lay and official strata within the collection.

Sovereign Grace (135:1–21)

Bibliography

Baumann, E. "Struktur-Untersuchungen im Psalter (2)." *ZAW* 62 (1949/50) 115–52. **Crüsemann, F.** *Studien zur Formgeschichte.* **Preuss, H. D.** *Der Verspottung fremder Religionen im AT.* BWANT 5:12. Stuttgart: W. Kohlhammer Verlag, 1971. **Pytel, R.** "Zur Exegese von Ps. 135:17." *Folia Orientalia* 11 (1969) 239–44. **Schildenberger, J.** "Bemerkungen zum Strophenbau der Psalmen." *Estudios Eclesiásticos* 34 (1960) 673–87.

Translation

1 Hallelujah.[a]
Praise Yahweh's name, (3+3)
   praise it, Yahweh's servants [b]
2 who are standing [a] in Yahweh's house, (3+3)
   in the courts of our God's house.
3 Praise Yah(weh) [a] because Yahweh [b] is so good, (3+3)
   celebrate his name with music because it [c] is so lovely,
4 because Jacob it was whom Yah(weh) chose [a] as his own, (3+3)
   Israel as his special possession.[b]

5 For I know myself that Yahweh is great, (4+3)
   that our God is greater than [a] all gods.
6 Anything Yahweh pleases (3+3+3)
   he does in heaven and on earth,
   in the seas and all the deeps.[a]
7 He is the one who gets the clouds to rise from the ends of the earth, (4+3+3)
   who makes [a] flashes of lightning [b] for the rain,
   who brings [c] the wind out of his storehouses.

⁸ *He is the one who struck down Egypt's firstborn*   (3+3)
  of man and ᵃ *beast alike;*
⁹ *He sent signs and portents*   (3+2+3)
  into the midst of Egypt ᵃ
  against Pharaoh and all his servants.
¹⁰ *He is the one who struck down many nations*   (3+3)
  and killed mighty kings—
¹¹ *King Sihon* ᵃ *of the Amorites*   (3+3+3)
  and King Og of Bashan
  and all Canaan's kingdoms ᵇ—
¹² *and gave their land as a heritage,*   (3+3)
  a heritage for his people Israel.
¹³ *Yahweh, your name will endure forever,*   (3+3)
  Yahweh, proclamation of you ᵃ *for generations,*
¹⁴ *because Yahweh vindicates* ᵃ *his people,*   (3+3)
  showing compassion for his servants. ᵇ

¹⁵ *The nations' idols are silver and gold,*   (4+3)
  products of human hands.
¹⁶ *They have mouths but cannot* ᵃ *speak,*   (4+4)
  eyes but cannot see.
¹⁷ *They have ears but cannot hear*   (4+4)
  nor is there ᵃ *any breath in their mouths.* ᵇ
¹⁸ *Their makers will* ᵃ *become like them,*   (3+3)
  so will anyone who trusts in them.

¹⁹ *House of Israel,* ᵃ *bless Yahweh,*   (3+3)
  house of Aaron, bless Yahweh,
²⁰ *house of Levites, bless Yahweh,*   (3+4)
  you who revere Yahweh, ᵃ *bless Yahweh.*
²¹ *Blessed be Yahweh from Zion,*   (3+2)
  he who resides in Jerusalem.

Hallelujah

Notes/Comments

1.a. See the note on 106:35 and cf. 113:1.

1.b. See the notes on 113:1; 134:1. Strangely H.-J. Kraus (*Psalmen*, 1073) emends the text here but not in 113:1.

2.a. See the note on 134:1.

3.a. See the note on 118:5.

3.b. The proposal to delete יהוה "Yahweh" with OL ᴳ, S (*BHK*; cf. *BHS*, NEB) yields neater parallelism within the bicolon (A. A. Anderson, *Psalms*, 890), but the sixfold repetition of the divine name (יהוה, יה) in vv 1–4 may well have been intended to match that in vv 19–21 (cf. *Form/Structure/Setting*)

3.c. The antecedent appears to be שמו "his name" rather than celebrating Yahweh (BDB, 653b) or Yahweh (RSV): H. Gunkel (*Die Psalmen*, 575) compared 54:8 (7).

4.a. For the election of Israel see especially B. E. Shafer (*ZAW* 89 [1977] 20–30), who has compared Ps 47; Deut 4:32–40, 7:6–8, 10:12–11:17 and drawn attention to a recurring semantic field, in this case סגלה "special possession," נחלה "heritage" (v 12) and the patriarchal motif יעקב "Jacob"; cf. also K. Koch, *ZAW* 67 (1955) 205–26.

4.b. For סגלה see M. Weinfeld, *Deuteronomy*, 226 note 2: in a Ugaritic text a vassal king is called the *sglt* of his overlord, while in an Akkadian text found at Alalaḫ a king is described as the *sikiltum* of his goddess. The term thus has both covenantal and religious overtones in its ancient Near Eastern setting.

5.a. M. Dahood (*Psalms III*, 260) has correctly explained the syntactical construction of מן "from" as comparative, in the light of Exod 18:11, upon which this line appears to be based.

6.a. The reference is to the subterranean waters: cf. Exod 20:4; Pss 24:2; 136:6.

7.a. For the perfect verb see P. Joüon, *Grammaire* § 112l.

7.b. Lightning often accompanies heavy rain in Palestine. A conjectural emendation of ברקים "lightning" to בדקים "rents," claiming the support of Ugar. *bdqt ʿrpt* "rents in the clouds" ([Anon.] *Bib* 34 [1953] 263–64; NEB; cf. Gen 7:11; 8:2, etc.) is hardly necessary: cf. Dahood, *Psalms III*, 261.

7.c. Heb. מוֹצֵא "he who brings," irregular for מוֹצִיא may be due to the retraction of the tone (GKC § 53o) or be intended to provide assonance with מאוצרותיו "out of his storehouses."

8.a. The prevailing meter of the psalm suggests that ועד be read for עד with many Heb. mss. (and *S*); otherwise the meter is 3+2.

9.a. See the note on 116:19. A second person address would be out of place here. Cf. Dahood (*Psalms III*, 151, 261) who explains ־כי as an emphatic particle in a construct chain. Kraus (*Psalmen*, 1073; cf. Gunkel, *Die Psalmen*, 575) suggests that the phrase originated as a variant of בכורי מצרים "first born of Egypt" in v 8, but this is unlikely. He claims that after v 8 a reference to the Reed Sea miracle follows in v 9 (likewise A. Lauha, *Die Geschichtsmotive*, 68), which would mean that the phrase is an intrusion. But it is noteworthy that שלח "send" lacks the conjunction and so does not necessarily imply chronological sequence. The reference is more probably to the plagues: cf. Deut 6:22; 11:3; 34:11; Neh 9:10. For the singling out and prior placement of a particular plague in v 8 cf. the note on 105:28. For a study of the phrase אתות ומפתים "signs and portents" in the OT see B. S. Childs, "Deuteronomic Formulae," 30–39.

11.a. The threefold prefixed *lamed* is the emphatic particle (Dahood, *Psalms III*, 262).

11.b. Heb. ממלכות need not mean "kings" here (Dahood, *Psalms III*, 262): the sequence may well be chiastic, with this term harking back to גוים "nations" in v 10a.

13.a. Heb. זכר "remembrance" refers to the utterance of the name of Yahweh in cultic praise, while שם "name" relates to the spoken name (Childs, *Memory and Tradition*, 71; W. Schottroff, *Gedenken*, 295).

14.a. Lit. "judges." Divine justice in the OT and especially in the Psalms often has the character of defending from oppression and so can here be linked with compassion: see C. S. Lewis, *Reflections on the Psalms* (London: Geoffrey Bles, 1958) 9–19. The verbs of v 14 have a present sense (D. Michel, *Tempora*, 115).

14.b. For עבדיו "his servants'" see I. Riesener (*Der Stamm* עבד, 226–28), who relates the term to the covenantal concepts expressed in v 4. C. Lindhagen (*The Servant Motif*, 153), comparing 69:37 (36); 102:29 (28); 136:22, has noted that in hymns it is associated with Yahweh's mighty protection and loving care of Israel.

16.a. For the modal sense of the verbs in vv 16–17 see the note on 115:5. For the attack on idolatry in vv 15–18 see the note on 115:4. G. von Rad (*Wisdom in Israel*, 178) has noted the rational treatment of the subject, based on a secularized understanding of the world, in contrast to an earlier prohibition simply on the basis of sacral law.

17.a. Deletion of the pleonastic יש "there is" is favored by *BHS* and advocated by Kraus (*Psalmen*, 1073). Recourse to Ugar. *bl it* (Dahood, *Psalms III*, 262, with reference to N. Sarna) provides a parallel to לא יש rather than to אין־יש. A pointing אֵין־יש, with interrogative Aram. אָן, "is there?" is attractive: cf. 1 Sam 21:9 (8) and G. R. Driver (*Notes on the Hebrew Text and Topography of the Books of Samuel* [Oxford: Clarendon Press, 1913] 176), who compared Aram. אית. R. Pytel (*Folia Orientalia* 11 [1969] 239–44) proposed a reading ואין יש i.e. "they have noses (אף), but there is no breath in their mouths." He claimed the support of *Tg.*, which, however, has probably suffered assimilation to 115:6.

17.b. An emendation to באפיהם "in their nostrils" (NEB; cf. Gunkel, *Die Psalmen*, 575, who, following Ehrlich, emended to באפיהם ["smell"] ריח) is not necessary. Gunkel regarded the double reference to "mouth" in vv 16–17 as inelegant, but the order in vv 15–18 appears to be chiastic: "the nation's idols" in v 15a corresponds to v 18b, their fabrication in v 15b to their fabricators in v 18a, using the stem עשה "make" twice, a mouth (singular) without speech in v 16a to one without breath in v 17b, and eyes (dual) without sight in v 16b to ears (dual) without hearing in v 17a (R. L. Alden, *JETS* 21 [1978] 208).

18.a. In 115:8, in the overall context of a complaint, the verb has a jussive force, but here, set in a hymn, it appears to express a confident statement.

19.a. See the note on 115:9.

20.a. See the note on 115:11.

Form/Structure/Setting

Psalm 135 is a hymn. The overall structure follows a standard pattern: an imperatival call to praise (vv 1–3), typically using the verb הללו "praise," introduces the reason for praise in the form of an introductory summary or series of summaries (vv 3–5). This summary is developed into the main declaration of Yahweh's praiseworthiness as Creator (vv 6–7) and as Lord of history (vv 8–12). Like Psalm 136, the hymn is rounded off with a repeated call to praise (vv 19–20). So runs C. Westermann's general analysis (*Praise*, 122–30); he also draws attention to v 14 as a typical closing statement in praise of God's grace.

F. Crüsemann (*Studien zur Formgeschichte*, 125, 127–29) has concentrated on form-critical details. He observes that vv 1–4 comprise a unit as an imperatival hymn. V 5 marks a new beginning: an individual makes a statement of faith which represents the body of the hymn. V 7, with its hymnic participles and theme of Yahweh's control of the natural world, is distinguished from vv 8–12, a series of clauses, in part relative, with perfect verbs and the theme of Yahweh's work in history. The latter verses, apart from the relatives of vv 8, 10, accord perfectly with the style of the imperatival hymn. V 13 addresses Yahweh, while v 14, with its third person divine reference, begins afresh. Vv 15–18 consist of polemic against idols; vv 19–20 echo the opening call to praise, and in v 21 an expression of indirect blessing of Yahweh (cf. W. S. Towner, *CBQ* 30 [1968] 390), including a participial formula, closes the psalm. Gunkel (*Die Psalmen*, 575) and E. Baumann (*ZAW* 62 [1949/50] 147) both deleted v 21 as an interpolation, but Crüsemann has urged that the diversity of the elements of the psalm makes this expedient difficult to substantiate.

The heterogeneity of the psalm manifests itself in a manner other than the form-critical. Much of the psalm has a suspiciously familiar ring: the attentive reader finds himself assailed by a conglomeration of snatches of other parts of the OT. V 1aβ-b looks like 113:1 in reverse, and v 2a like 134:1bα. V 4 is strongly reminiscent of Deut 7:6; 14:2, and v 5 even more so of Exod 18:11 adapted and recast into a poetic form. V 6a is very similar to 115:3, while v 7 appears to be a partial adaptation of Jer 10:13 (= 51:16). Vv 10–12 seem to be derived from 136:17–22, with phrases inserted at vv 10a and 11b. V 13 appears to echo Exod 3:15; Ps 102:13 (12). V 14 corresponds to Deut 32:36 verbatim. Vv 15–18 are 115:4–8 in briefer form. Vv 19–20 are comparable with 115:12–13. It is a moot point whether these correspondences are to be explained as due to a common cultic tradition or to literary borrowings. A. Weiser (*Psalms*, 788–89) characteristically maintains that stylized forms have been employed (cf. Anderson, *Psalms*, 889). This explanation may well be true in certain cases, such as vv 1, 2, 13. But in others it is difficult to dismiss an impression of specific quotation, so close, numerous and otherwise rare are the parallels: e.g. vv 5, 6, 7, 10–12, 14, and especially vv 15–18, where in v 17 אף "nose" (115:6) has seemingly been given a literary reinterpretation as the conjunction.

However, commentators have rightly praised the resultant composition. It "possesses real vigor of rhythm and spirit" (A. F. Kirkpatrick, *Psalms*, 773); "the author has created a coherent and impressive composition" (Anderson, *Psalms*, 889). Noteworthy is the re-use of the material in vv 15–18 to function no longer as a negative confession of trust with a final wish, but as implicit praise of Yahweh matching the explicit praise of vv 5–7 (see below). The new role given to v 14 as a general statement of Yahweh's care rather than a promise of future intervention, as in Deut 32:36, is also impressive.

The date of origin of the psalm is generally agreed to be quite late in the post-exilic period, apart from Weiser (*Psalms*, 788–89) who regards it as probably pre-exilic. The former impression is given not only by the "secondhandness" of its contents but by such linguistic and grammatical features as the relative ש "who" in vv 2, 8, 10 and the forms והרג "and killed" and ונתן "and gave" in vv 10, 12 (*pace* Dahood's repointing as infinitives absolute in *Psalms III*, 261–62, following J. Huesman).

The setting of the psalm was clearly cultic: the references to the religious community and temple personnel in vv 1–2, 19–20 indicate that it was used at a temple festival. Weiser (*Psalms*, 790) has urged that it was used at the Feast of Tabernacles in view of the weather phenomena cited in v 7. Others have suggested that it was composed for the Passover (cf. vv 8–9), especially since there is no reference to Sinai (Kraus, *Psalmen*, 1074; cf. Anderson, *Psalms*, 888) and it is widely held that the Feast of Tabernacles commemorated the Sinai covenant. However, the concept of covenant is strong in the psalm, and v 3 may evoke not only Deut 7:6 but Exod 19:5; accordingly usage at the autumn festival is not to be ruled out. In its present placing in the Psalter the psalm appears to function as part of a supplement to the Songs of Ascents (K. Seybold, *Wallfahrtspsalmen*, 74–75): there are echoes of Ps 134 in vv 2, 19–21, including a reference to Zion. But it is possible too that at an earlier stage both Pss 135 and 136 functioned as a continuation of 111–118 before the insertion of Pss 119 and 120–134 (Westermann, *Theologia Viatorum* 8 [1961/62] 282): the "Hallelujah" framework (cf. Pss 111, 113, 116) and the links with Ps 115 lend some support to this suggestion.

Structural analysis of the psalm yields some interesting discoveries. Baumann's attempt (*ZAW* 62 [1949/50] 145–48) has the air of a self-imposed scheme: eight strophes of pairs of bicola, achieved by the rejection of vv 11, 15–18, 21. E. J. Kissane's structure (*Psalms II*, 277)—six strophes of four and three lines alternately—works, but leaves a suspicion that more remains to be said. J. Schildenberger (*Estudios Eclesiásticos* 34 [1960] 686), who regularly built upon Kissane's work, analysed the psalms in terms of introductory and closing strophes (vv 1–3, 19–21), both of three bicola, and then the body of the psalm comprising first and third strophes (vv 4–7, 15–18) with matching four bicola and antithetical content, and a second strophe containing three

sub-units (vv 8–9, 10–12, 13–14), in which v 11 as a tricolon constitutes the
center of the psalm. This analysis, with which that of Kraus (*Psalmen*, 1076)
may be compared, requires only partial refinement. The matching of beginning and ending is clearly correct, but Kissane was wiser in postulating an
initial strophe of four lines, vv 1–4, which form-critical study (see above)
confirms. Then inclusive elements manifest themselves: the repetitions of
the divine name (sixfold) and of בית "house" in vv 2, 19, 20 and of ישראל
"Israel" in vv 4, 19, as well as the parallel verbs of praise. Vv 5–7, three
lines including two tricola and so eight cola, correspond to vv 15–18, again
eight cola but now in the form of four bicola: the double occurrence of the
stem עשה "do, make" in both is to be noted, and also the formal repetition
of רוח "wind, breath" at vv 7, 17; moreover the assonance in v 7b is matched
by that of v 17a. Schildenberger's analysis of the middle strophe is correct,
except that the focus is hardly upon v 11 but upon the middle sub-unit and
perhaps especially its climactic line, v 12: so its content suggests. In the
first and third sub-units עבדיו "his servants" are contrasted, those of Pharaoh
and those of Yahweh, while the third also resumptively echoes עמו "his people"
of the second. Crüsemann (*Studien zur Formgeschichte*, 129), followed by Kraus
(*Psalmen*, 1073), regarded v 14 as a new beginning, but despite the change
of person (cf. 22:26 [25]; for the alternation of divine person elsewhere in
hymns cf. Crüsemann, *Studien zur Formgeschichte*, 225–26) it seems rather to
round off v 13 by giving the reason for praise. The third person references
of v 14 may in fact be due to its nature as a quotation of Deut 32:36. The
structure may be summarized as concentric with five strophes, vv 1–4 corresponding to vv 19–21, vv 5–7 to vv 15–18 and the middle vv 8–14.

Attempts have been made to regard the psalm as an enlargement of a
shorter composition. As noted above, Bauman (*ZAW* 62 [1949/50] 148) took
vv 11, 15–18, 21 as redactional, and Seybold (*Wallfahrtspsalmen*, 74; cf. Gunkel,
Die Psalmen, 575) views vv 14–21 as secondary. Some support may be afforded
to suggestions of this kind by structural considerations. It is possible that
at an earlier stage the psalm consisted of vv 1–14. The recurrence of certain
elements could be explained thus. Heb. שם "name" would have had an inclusive role in vv 1, 3, 13, and also ישראל. "Israel" in vv 4, 12; moreover, the
note of praise in vv 13–14 would be resumptive of vv 1–3. Then the use of
Ps 115 in v 6 may have suggested the addition of other material from it or
inspired by it in vv 15–20 (cf. the contrasts with idolatry in the contexts of
Jer 10:13, echoed in v 7, and of Deut 32:36, used in v 14, which pave the
way for vv 15–18); but so skillfully was it done that the psalm was actually
improved in structure and impact. There can be no certainty about this suggestion of a two-stage composition for the psalm. H. D. Preuss (*Verspottung*, 252)
has contended that vv 15–18 breathe a different air from v 5: "idols" smack
of an addition to a psalm which can speak freely of "gods." Childs (*Exodus*,
328), on the other hand, has urged that Exod 18:11 (= v 5) should not be
taken too literally: "Surely when the Psalmist praises God with such words
as 'Yahweh is great . . . our Yahweh [sic] is above all gods' (135:5), there
is no vestige of polytheism left." Certainly in such a heterogeneous composition there is no conclusive obstacle to regarding vv 15–18 as an integral
part of a single compilation.

Explanation

A priestly summons to praise rings out over the temple courts to the post-exilic congregation, assembled perhaps for the Feast of Tabernacles. The description of Yahweh as "our God" in v 2 ushers in the covenant theme of the psalm. The ground for praise is first cited in general terms as the grace of Yahweh's self-revelation ("name") and then more sharply as that dynamic event of his election of Israel which inaugurated a special relationship with them.

The singer introduces the next part of the psalm as a personal confession of faith, which blends beautifully with the communal setting. He makes Jethro's testimony (Exod 18:11) his own. With a touch of pride he praises the power of "our Lord" as supreme in the sphere of godhead. The entire universe—heaven, earth and subterranean deeps—assigned by other nations to a pantheon of gods, is in fact at the sole service of his sovereign will. As in Jer 10:13, the rainy season upon which Israel was so dependent for survival is cited as faith's illustration of his providential control of the world of nature.

The psalmist moves into the heart of the psalm, vv 8–14. Yahweh's almighty power of vv 5–7 has been used specifically in history on Israel's behalf. Two events are selected for mention. The death of Egypt's firstborn is singled out as the climax of the divinely instigated plagues which resulted in that great nation's submission. The event serves as a preface to the highlight of Yahweh's demonstration of power for Israel in vv 10–12, which makes use of 136:17–22: his defeat of massive opposition and his consequent presentation of the land to his own people as pledge of the covenant. The psalmist is moved to address Yahweh directly in v 13. So tremendous is this act of grace that it surely deserves unending praise to echo back to him through the corridors of time. Deut 32:36 is adapted in v 14 to teach a permanent lesson from past proof of patronage: Yahweh has shown himself to be a God who saves and cares, whose character it is to come to the help of his oppressed people. Here indeed is fuel for praise ("for"). Because their God is so powerful in nature and in history, Israel is assured of his powerful aid.

Passing beyond the peak of his composition, in vv 15–18 the psalmist artistically uses 115:4–8 as a foil to his avowal of faith in vv 5–7. The satire on alien religions enhances the pre-eminence of Yahweh. These Jewish in-jokes about the powerlessness of cultic images serve to contrast the made with the Maker of vv 6–7. The logical conclusion concerning the doom of their devotees underlines the welfare of Yahweh's worshipers.

The psalm is rounded off with renewed calls to praise. Each sector of the religious community is urged to make its own contribution to the service of worship and thus to create a harmony of utmost praise (cf. Rom 15:6). Layman, Aaronite priest and his assisting Levite, in fact every worshiper gathered there in the temple, Yahweh's earthly home, is bidden bless his divine host.

In Ps 135 older materials are unashamedly recycled to create a new composition of praise. The harmony of concerted worship, for which it pleads in vv 19–20, itself finds artistic illustration in the blending of older voices to form a contemporary medley: for example, in v 5 Jethro's testimony comes alive again as a vehicle for the psalmist's own conviction. The psalm is a classic example of that triangular relationship which sums up OT theology, between Yahweh, Israel and the land. In Jerusalem, the sacred center with which each point of the triangle is vitally linked, the covenant community celebrate the lordship of their God (vv 5, 14), who has condescended to use his majesty as tool of his grace toward them, manifested especially in his love-gift of the land.

Ever Faithful, Ever Sure   *(136:1–26)*

Bibliography

Alonso-Schökel, L. "Psalmus 136 (135)." *VD* 45 (1967) 129–38. **Andrews, D. K.** "Yahweh the God of the Heavens." *The Seed of Wisdom. Essays in Honor of T. J. Meek,* ed. W. S. McCullough. Toronto: University of Toronto Press, 1964. **Auffret, P.**"Note sur la structure littéraire du Psaume 136." *VT* 27 (1977) 1–12. **Lauha, A.** *Die Geschichts-motive in den alttestamentlichen Psalmen.* Annales academiae scientarum, fennicae 16:1. Helsinki: Suomalainen Tiedakatemia, 1945. **Ludwig, T. M.** "The Traditions of Establishing the Earth in Deutero-Isaiah." *JBL* 92 (1973) 345–57.

Translation

> [1] *Give thanks to Yahweh, for he is so good—*   (3+3 [c])
>   *for* [a] *his loyal love is everlasting.* [b]
> [2] *Give thanks to the God of gods* [a]*—*   (3+3)
>   *for his loyal love is everlasting.*
> [3] *Give thanks to the Lord of lords—*   (3+3)
>   *for his loyal love is everlasting.*
>
> [4] *. . . To him who alone has performed great wonders* [a]*—*   (4+3)
>   *for his loyal love is everlasting,*
> [5] *to him who made the heavens* [a] *with wisdom* [b]*—*   (3+3)
>   *for his loyal love is everlasting,*
> [6] *to him who spread out the earth* [a] *over the waters—*   (3+3)
>   *for his loyal love is everlasting,*
> [7] *to him who made the great lights* [a]*—*   (3+3)
>   *for his loyal love is everlasting,*
> [8] *the sun to rule over the day—*   (3+3)
>   *for his loyal love is everlasting,*
> [9] *the moon [and stars]* [a] *to rule over the night—*   (3+3)
>   *for his loyal love is everlasting.*
>
> [10] *. . . To him who struck down the Egyptian's firstborn* [a]*—* (3+3)
>   *for his loyal love is everlasting,*
> [11] *and brought out Israel* [a] *from among them—*   (3+3)
>   *for his loyal love is everlasting,*

¹² *with strong hand and outstretched arm—* (4+3)
   for his loyal love is everlasting,
¹³ *to him who cut* ª *the Reed Sea apart—* (3+3)
   for his loyal love is everlasting,
¹⁴ *and let Israel pass through it—* (3+3)
   for his loyal love is everlasting,
¹⁵ *but shook off* ª *Pharaoh and his army into the Reed Sea—* (4+3)
   for his loyal love is everlasting,
¹⁶ *to him who led his people* ª *through the wilderness—* (3+3)
   for his loyal love is everlasting.

¹⁷ . . . *To him who struck down great kings—* (3+3)
   for his loyal love is everlasting,
¹⁸ *and slew famous kings—* (3+3)
   for his loyal love is everlasting,
¹⁹ *King Sihon* ª *of the Amorites—* (3+3)
   for his loyal love is everlasting,
²⁰ *and King Og of Bashan—* (3+3)
   for his loyal love is everlasting,
²¹ *and gave their land as a heritage—* (3+3)
   for his loyal love is everlasting,
²² *a heritage to his servant* ª *Israel—* (3+3)
   for his loyal love is everlasting.

²³ . . . *Who remembered* ª *us* ᵇ *when we were down—* (3+3)
   for his loyal love is everlasting,
²⁴ *and rescued us from our foes—* (3+3)
   for his loyal love is everlasting,
²⁵ *who gives food to all living creatures* ª— (3+3)
   for his loyal love is everlasting.
²⁶ *Give thanks to the God of heaven* ª— (3+3)
   for his loyal love is everlasting.

Notes/Comments

1.a. F. Crüsemann (*Studien zur Formgeschichte*, 32–35) takes כי "for" in a deictic sense in the responses of the second cola of the psalm; but it is difficult to differentiate its usage from that in v 1a, where it appears to be causal (cf. the second note on 106:1).
1.b. Heb. לעולם "everlasting" has an adjectival force (P. Joüon, *Grammaire* § 141a). For the liturgical formula of v 1 see the third note on 106:1.
1.c. Or 3+2, and so throughout. The solemnity of the constant refrain suggests that כי has its own beat.
2.a. For the divine titles of vv 2, 3 cf. Deut 10:17. They have a superlative force.
4.a. The colon has been regarded as metrically overloaded, and the deletion of either נפלאות "wonders" or גדלות "great" has been recommended (cf. *BHK;* 11QPs ª omits the latter); but H. Gunkel (*Die Psalmen*, 577) observed that the 4+3 meter in vv 12, 15 makes it unexceptionable here. M. Dahood (*Psalms III*, 265–66), impressed by the omission of the second term in 11QPs ª

(cf. the minor textual evidence cited in *BHS*) and the excessive syllable count of v 4a, regards the two terms as alternative readings. Heb. נפלאות can be used of Yahweh's works in both nature and history; the structure of the psalm indicates that here it refers to the former (cf. Alonso-Schökel, *VD* 45 [1967] 131, and *Form/Structure/Setting* below).

5.a. Part of a cultic formula is echoed here (N. C. Habel, *JBL* 91 [1972] 333); cf. 115:15; 134:3, etc.

5.b. The addition of בתבונה "with wisdom" links it with the wisdom tradition (cf. Prov 3:19; Jer 10:12), although R. N. Whybray (*Intellectual Tradition*, 139) has suggested that the term may here refer simply to creative skill such as that of an artificer. Hypostatization (Dahood, *Psalms III*, 266) is unlikely.

6.a. For this cultic formula see T. M. Ludwig, *JBL* 92 (1973) 347–49.

7.a. LXX adds μόνῳ "alone" (cf. v 4). The addition most probably originated in the Greek tradition: in both vv 4 and 7 μεγάλα precedes.

9.a. It is difficult to resist the impression that וכוכבים "and stars" is an interpolation incorporating a terse marginal note based on Gen 1:16. Metrical considerations carry little weight (cf. note 4.a.), but the omission of the object sign and article (contrast את-השמש, את-הירח) and the mandate given only to the moon in the psalmist's apparent source, Gen 1:16, represent serious objections to MT; most commentators recommend deletion. Then a singular לְמֶמְשֶׁלֶת "to rule," as in Gen 1:16, is to be read with some Heb. mss. and the ancient versions for MT's subsequently adapted and clumsy plural term.

10.a. The preposition *beth* seemingly specifies the object more closely: cf. its occasional usage to denote the direct object of הכה listed in BDB (645a, 646a) and the construction with two accusatives in 3:8 (7); Lam 3:30.

11.a. For an analysis of the deuteronomic and deuteronomistic formulae of vv 11a, 12a see B. S. Childs, "Deuteronomic Formulae," 30–39. He regards the restriction of the former one to the specific event of leaving Egypt prior to the crossing of the Reed Sea as based on the usage in the Tetrateuch and deuteronomic corpus and developed from its original general sense of redemption.

13.a. Heb. גזר "cut" is used only here with reference to the Reed Sea miracle (cf. בקע "cleave" in Exod 14:16, 21). Alonso-Schökel (*VD* 45 [1967] 132) finds here historicized use of myth, comparing the slaying and dismembering of Tiamat (cf. Gen 15:17); a Ugaritic text apparently using this stem concerning battle with the dragon, *UT* 52:58, has also been compared (H.-J. Kraus, *Psalmen*, 1080–81; cf. Dahood, *Psalms III*, 266). Cf. 106:9. While this nuance may well underlie the term, in the present context it has become a worn metaphor and appears to connote not hostility but simply divine power over nature.

15.a. Heb. נער "shake off" echoes Exod 14:27.

16.a. Alonso-Schökel (*VD* 45 [1967] 132) finds the change from ישראל "Israel" (vv 11, 14) significant as reflecting the constituting of the covenant people in the wilderness.

19.a. For the prefixed *lamed* here and in v 20a see the note on 135:11. The transjordanian kings Sihon and Og played a classic role in Israelite tradition as the first kings to be conquered (cf. Num 21).

22.a. I. Riesener (*Der Stamm* עבד, 227–28) compares the plural in 105:25; 135:14; cf. Isa 41:8, 9; 44:1, 2. Alonso-Schökel (*VD* 45 [1967] 132), comparing 135:1, sees a cultic use of the term, appropriate to Israel's occupation of the land.

23.a. Yahweh's faithfulness is here praised (Childs, *Memory and Tradition*, 41). W. Schottroff (*Gedenken*, 198–99) has drawn attention to the active nature of Yahweh's remembering: v 24a serves to define it. The time reference of vv 23a, 24a has been much disputed. Kraus (*Psalmen*, 1081) has suggested the Judges period. A. Lauha (*Die Geschichtsmotive*, 119–20) opted for the period of David and the defeat of the Philistines. Others, e.g. A. F. Kirkpatrick, (*Psalms*, 779), have preferred the Babylonian exile and return, while Alonso-Schökel (*VD* 45 [1967] 133; cf. Gunkel, *Die Psalmen*, 577) is among those who interpret of the whole range of history after the occupation of Canaan down to the psalm's present. The text is best understood as a recapitulation of the Exodus: מצרינו "from our foes" functions as a word play recalling מצרים "Egypt" in v 16 (P. Auffret, *VT* 27 [1977] 8; cf. 106:7, 11 and, for the interpretation, C. Lindhagen, *The Servant Motif*, 167): cf. Exod 4:23, 24. Schottroff (*Gedenken*, 199) has drawn attention to A. Weiser's misunderstanding of בשפלנו in terms of the inherent sinfulness of man over against God (*Psalms*, 793): rather it refers to enemy oppression, as v 24a makes clear.

23.b. Auffret (*VT* 27 [1977] 8) has noted the actualization of the history here.

25.a. Schottroff (*Gedenken*, 210), comparing 111:5, relates to the covenant people; but

כל־בשׂר "all flesh" has a universal connotation: cf. 104:27, 28; 145:15. Structurally (see *Form/ Structure/Setting* below) the psalm harks back to Yahweh's work in nature at this point.

26.a. For this post-exilic title see D. K. Andrews, "Yahweh," 145–57.

Form/Structure/Setting

Psalm 136 is an imperatival, antiphonal hymn in which the first colon of each line was presumably sung by a temple soloist or choir and the second by the congregation as a response. The liturgical formula of v 1, which properly belonged to the song of thanksgiving (cf. Jer 30:11; Pss 107:1; 118:1–4, 29) has here been applied to the hymn. Schottroff's definition of the psalm as a thanksgiving liturgy (*Gedenken*, 198, 280) is hardly correct in the strict sense. C. Westermann (*Praise*, 122–30, 140) has analysed its fairly typical formal structure as beginning with an imperatival call to praise and an introductory summary of the reason for praise (vv 1–3), elaborating with reference to creation (vv 5–9) and history in a lengthy narrative (vv 10–22) and an appended piece in praise of Yahweh's grace (vv 23–24) which includes preservation from hunger (cf. 33:19; 111:5; 145:14, 15), and concluding with an imperative, like Ps 135. In fact its overall pattern is very similar to that of the previous psalm. Crüsemann (*Studien zur Formgeschichte*, 74–76) has supplemented this analysis with a useful study of detail. Basically the titles and clauses of the first cola of vv 4–25 are a development of ליהוה "to Yahweh" in v 1, continuing its hymnic call and specifying to whom praise is due. After v 3 the imperative is to be understood throughout till v 26, as is indicated by comparison with Sir 51, which actually repeats the imperative throughout. The basic phrases introduced by *lamed* are often developed into clauses with finite verbs, which actually belong to the imperatival hymn as a ground of praise but here are anticipated in the summons. On the other hand, in vv 4–7, 10, 13, 16, 17 the hymnic participles have been set within the summons with prefixed *lamed.*

A cultic setting for the psalm is clear, but its precise role can hardly be determined. Kraus (*Psalmen*, 1079) has judged that the psalm's selection of historical material indicates its composition for the Passover; in favor may be claimed such a usage in Jewish tradition. On the other hand, H. Schmidt (*Die Psalmen*, 240) and Weiser (*Psalms*, 792–93) have discerned in v 25 a climactic allusion to the harvest festival celebrated in the autumn. The date of the psalm is evidently postexilic. The relative שׁ "who" (v 23), the forms וּנְעֵר "shake off" and וַנִּתֵּן "give" (vv 15, 21; *pace* Dahood, *Psalms III*, 267, in the latter case) and the Aramaic sense of פָּרַק "rescue" in v 24 point in this direction; moreover, its evident use of the varied literary traditions of the Pentateuch (Kraus, *Psalmen*, 1079) in addition to seemingly old, cultic material (e.g. in vv 6, 13) is consonant with this conclusion. For the role of the psalm in its present position in the Psalter the pertinent comments on Ps 135 (*Form/Structure/Setting*) may be compared.

The stylistic structure of the psalm has been subjected to extensive discussion, especially by L. Alonso-Schökel and P. Auffret. Crüsemann (*Studien zur Formgeschichte*, 75) categorically opposed even such analysis as introduction, body and conclusion; but definition of the artistic structure is not necessarily exhausted by his description of the psalm as a series of developments of ליהוה "to Yahweh" in v 1. Alonso-Schökel (*VD* 45 [1967] 130–32) denied that the contents of the psalm could be regarded simply as spokes of a wheel. He ventured to give just the analysis that Crüsemann deplored: introduction (vv 1–3) and conclusion (vv 23–26) clustering around a main section (vv 10–22). The introduction and conclusion contain the divine name and titles (vv 1–3, 26); the body of the psalm exhibits two series of dative participles and dependent finite verbs, the first four cosmic (vv 4–9) and the second four historical (vv 10–22). In vv 23–25 the syntactical form is changed to a relative clause and a nominative participle. In favor of a long central passage he pointed to the three references to Israel, at the beginning (v 11), the exact middle (עמו "his people," v 16) and the end (v 22). In fact it also occurs in v 14.

Pierre Auffret used this analysis as a stepping stone to his own (*VT* 27 [1977] 1–12). Vv 4–9, concerning creation, subdivide into vv 4–6 and 7–9, with the themes of heaven and earth, and day and night. The historical vv 10–22 subdivide into vv 10–15 (and then further into vv 10–12, 13–15), 16 and 17–22 (further into vv 17–20, 21–22), with the themes of Egypt (Exodus and Reed Sea), the wilderness and Canaan (kings and the land). Finally, vv 23–26 resume the earlier material in reverse, first history (vv 23–24), then nature (v 25): the earlier proportion of nature material to historical (three verses to six verses) is maintained (one to two), while the initial three lines of summons is whittled down to one. Auffret bases his analysis of vv 4–22 carefully upon the participial evidence: use of participles is seen as the pointer to fresh sections.

The French scholar has provided valuable insights into the psalm's development, but it may be asked whether they may not be incorporated into a more strictly strophic analysis. J. A. Montgomery divided the psalm into five strophes of irregular length, consisting of three, six, seven, six and four lines respectively (*JBL* 64 [1945] 383). One wishes that he had incorporated a discussion of his results. Independently the author has reached the same conclusion. After the introductory strophe with three similarly structured first cola (vv 1–3), the second (vv 4–9) consists of six lines which subdivide into one, two and three lines: the first (v 4) is a headline beginning with לעשה "to the doer" and the other two, explanatory units (vv 5–6, 7–9) begin likewise. Auffret (*VT* 27 [1977] 2, 9) attaches v 4 to vv 5–6 in view of the repetition of the adjective גדולים/ות "great" in vv 4, 7; but the repetition of לעשה is probably a more decisive factor. The third strophe (vv 10–16) has seven lines, which subdivide into three, three and one. In each of the first two units two lines cluster around a nucleus featuring Israel, as object of divine action, and "midst" (ישראל מתוכם "Israel from their midst," v 11; ישראל בתוכו "Israel in its midst," v 14; Auffret, *VT* 27 [1977] 3–4). They are tied inclusively by mention of "Egypt" and "Pharaoh" (vv 10, 15; cf. Auffret, *VT* 27 [1977] 3): two participles introduce the units. The final, supplementary line, also introduced with a participle, serves to put a seal upon Yahweh's redemptive work as truly complete; that too has a reference to Israel in the form עמו "his people." The fourth strophe (vv 17–22) comprises six lines which break up into four and two or even into three units of two lines. If the latter, each of the three is marked by repeated terms, of מלכים "kings" (vv 17, 18), of מלך "king" (vv 19, 20) and of נחלה "inheritance" (vv 21, 22). Like the third strophe the fourth begins with למכה "to him who struck" (v 17); it ends with the climactic ישראל "Israel" (v 22). The fifth strophe (vv 23–26) consists of four lines subdividing into two, one and one. The first unit (vv 23–24) is marked by a chiastic order and fourfold repetition of the first plural suffix. As Auffret has seen, there is a rapid, backtracking glance at earlier themes by way of inclusion. J. W. Rogerson and J. W. McKay (*Psalms 101–150*, 148) comment correctly on the relation of v 25 to what precedes that the psalm begins with the universality of God, concentrates in his particular revelation to Israel and then returns to a general statement about his universal providence. The close stylistic relationship of the third and fourth strophes, corresponding well to their common historical theme, has been noted. It remains to broach the links between the second and the fourth: both contain the adjective "great" (גדולים/ות, vv 4 [cf. 7], 17) in their initial lines and both mention ארץ, albeit in different senses ("earth," "land," vv 6, 21). Moreover, the use of *lamed* in the first cola as an alliterative counterpart to לעולם "everlasting" in the second, while running all through the psalm, is especially dominant in the second (fifteen times) and fourth (thirteen times). The effect of the links between the fourth strophe and the two earlier ones is to present its content as a crowning touch to Yahweh's work in the world at large and in his dealings with Israel. Perhaps by way of balance the final recapitulation singles out the Exodus as the instance of Yahweh's activity for Israel. The psalm exhibits an overall pattern ABCDcba.

Explanation

This post-exilic litany of praise challenges the congregation to an appreciation of Yahweh's grace. His beneficence, godhead and authority spotlight from different angles his active attribute of "loyal love" and serve to guarantee its permanence.

For Israel history began with the creation of the world and so with Yahweh, its one and only creator. The skies are a window to his wisdom; the earth, culturally described as poised remarkably but firmly over the primeval waters (cf. 24:2), is a cosmos won out of chaos. Not only space but time is God's gift, symbolized in its two great markers, the sun and moon. Both literary and cultic traditions are used as the quarries of the first main strophe, vv 4–9.

The same is true of the second, vv 10–16. In this selection of praiseworthy acts the psalm turns from the universal to the particular. For the secular historian history is a blend of chance and human personality, but for Israel it was God's stamping his own purpose and personality upon human experience. Here they are traced in the people's experience of the Exodus and its seal, the wilderness march. Liberation from Egypt was a demonstration of divine power. Likewise the Reed Sea crossing: the sea was slashed open and the arch-enemy was easily disposed of, army and all. This second main strophe has three (groups of) participants, Yahweh, Egypt and Israel. The third, vv 17–22, has the same threefold grouping, now with the kings of the land making up the threesome, as victims of Yahweh's power displayed in Israel's behalf. It brings to a climax this catalogue of themes of grace. Yahweh, creator and so owner of the earth (אֶרֶץ, v 6) generously bestowed part (אֶרֶץ) upon his people. His crusading energy on his vassals' behalf (v 22) brought Israel to its destined home.

The last strophe (vv 23–26) swiftly rewinds the poetic reel. The Exodus is reviewed, now as God's faithful deliverance not merely of a generation dead and gone but of "us" (cf. Amos 2:10). As contemporary members of the covenant nation, "we" were there in principle, participating in the divine salvation and certainly now living in the good of it. The creator God, too, worked not only in the past: his providential care extends yet to all his creatures in the steady supply of nourishment. So the psalm comes full circle to its starting point: the obligation of thanksgiving to Israel's great God, by now well proven, must—and surely will readily—be discharged by the worshiping community.

Paradoxically there is danger of overlooking the psalm's most dominant feature, the regular heartbeat of the congregational refrain. The first cola of the psalm serve to define the ramifications of divine love. Special revelation of God as savior sheds its warmth over the stark phenomena of nature and invests them with new meaning as evidence of his bountiful care which breathes in the air and shines in the light, as Robert Grant's hymn puts it. In turn, the saving events of the Exodus and its sequel are shown to be archetypal, not only by the resuming vv 23a, 24a but by the accompanying refrain. Like the crucifixion and resurrection in the NT, they pledge God's everlasting love for the people of the covenant. His continuing guardianship and guidance are hereby guaranteed. The closing strophe reinforces the relevance of the divine care; it also widens its range. Yahweh's blessing is confined neither to the past nor to the chosen people. His fatherly care (cf. 104:27) embraces all animate creatures, universal God as he is ("God of heaven"). By such means part of the way is paved for the universality of God's saving grace in the NT.

Living with the Pain of the Past (137:1-9)

Bibliography

Eitan, I. "An Identification of tiškah yĕmīnī, Ps. 137:5." *JBL* 47 (1928) 193–95. **Freedman, D. N.** "The Structure of Psalm 137." *Near Eastern Studies in Honor of W. F. Albright,* ed. H. Goedicke. Baltimore: Johns Hopkins Press, 1971. **Guillaume, A.** "The Meaning of *tôlēl* in Psalm 137:3." *JBL* 75 (1956) 143–44. **Kellermann, U.** "Psalm 137." *ZAW* 90 (1978) 43–58. **McKenzie, J. L.** "The Imprecations of the Psalter." *AER* 111 (1944) 81–96. **Steidle, B.** "Von Mut zum Ganzen Ps. 137 (136)." *Erbe und Auftrag* 50 (1974) 21–30. **Wilson, J. K.** "Hebrew and Akkadian Philological Notes 3." *JSS* 7 (1962) 173–83.

Translation

1 *Beside* [a] *Babylon's* [b] *rivers,* [c] *there we sat* [d] *and* [e] *wept* *when we remembered Zion.*	(2+2+2)
2 *On the poplars* [a] *in that region* *we hung our lyres.*	(2[b]+2)
3 *For* [a] *there our captors* *asked us for words of song,* *our mockers* [b] *for joyfulness:*	(2+2+2)
"Sing for us *one of the songs* [c] *of Zion."*	(2+2)
4 *How could we sing* *Yahweh's songs* *on foreign soil?* [a]	(2+2+2)
5 *If I forget you, Jerusalem,* *may my right hand wither.* [a]	(2+2)
6 *May my tongue stick to the roof of my mouth* *if I do not remember you,*	(3+2)
if I do not set Jerusalem *above my highest joy.* [a]	(3+2)
7 *Remember,* [a] *Yahweh,* *against the Edomites* [b] *Jerusalem's day* [c]—	(2+2+2)
those who said "Lay bare, lay bare *down to its foundations."* [d]	(3+2)
8 *Lady Babylon,* [a] *you devastator,* [b] *how fortunate* [c] *is the one who repays you* *with the treatment you gave us.* [d]	(2+2+3)
9 *How fortunate is the one who seizes and dashes* *your children against the rocks.* [a]	(3+2)

Notes/Comments

1.a. LXX provides a heading τῷ Δαυιδ "Davidic" to which the Lucianic text adds (διὰ) Ἰερεμίου "(through) Jeremiah." The latter reference was intended to compare the attacks on Edom and Babylon in Jer 49, 50; moreover, the piels שלם "pay" and נפץ "dash" of vv 8–9 recur in Jer 51:24 and 20–26, respectively (E. Slomovic, *ZAW* 91 [1979] 361–62).

1.b. M. Dahood (*Psalms III*, 269) and D. N. Freedman ("Structure," 191) read בבבל "in Babylon" with 11QPs [a] for MT בבל "Babylon," the former noting that a parallel colon of seven syllables would then occur at the beginning of vv 1 and 2, and the latter also explaining MT as due to haplography and urging that structurally parallel beginnings to vv 1–2 are required as a counterpart to אשרי "how fortunate is the one who" in vv 8–9. For the structural issue see *Form/Structure/Setting* below. U. Kellermann (*ZAW* 90 [1978] 45) has observed the scantiness of the evidence for the new reading.

1.c. Apart from the rivers Euphrates and Tigris and their tributaries there was also an intricate canal system intersecting the southern Babylonian plain.

1.d. D. Michel (*Tempora*, 83) has interpreted the verbs of vv 1–3 as present. This is possible, but it is bound up with the larger question of reconstructing the setting of the psalm as a whole (see *Form/Structure/Setting*).

1.e. Dahood (*Psalms III*, 269) and Freedman ("Structure," 191) render גם as an adverb "loudly," finding a cognate of Ugar. *g* "voice" and an adverbial *m*. C. J. Labuschagne ("The Emphasizing Particle גם and its Connotations," in *Studia biblica et semitica T. C. Vriezen dedicata* [Wageningen: H. Veenman, 1966] 194–99) has vigorously opposed this explanation, urging that the normal emphasizing particle introduces a climax in a series of verbs, as elsewhere but more often גם: cf. Gen 30:8; Job 21:7; Ps 118:11.

2.a. The *populus euphratica* is in view; it looks more like a willow than a true poplar (J. V. K. Wilson, *JSS* 7 [1962] 175–76, who equates it with Acc. *ṣarbatu*, as well as Arab. *ʿarabun*).

2.b. Vv 2, 5 are generally scanned as 3+2, but Freedman ("Structure," 204 note 24) plausibly takes as 2+2: cf. v. 3b.

3.a. Heb. כי "for" is more probably causal, supplying the reason for v 1, than emphatic.

3.b. Heb. ותוללינו is problematic. Word play with תלינו "we hung" in v 2 appears to support its consonantal integrity and thus to discourage emendations reconstructed from LXX *S* or *Tg.* (ומוליכינו; ושללינו. Cf. *BHS*), which may be simply guesses from the context. The form in MT suggests derivation from ילל "howl" (cf. תושב "settler"), which is perhaps used of cruel exultation in Isa 52:5 (BDB, 410a), but is generally associated with distress. Dahood (*Psalms III*, 271) has linked with the poʿel of הלל "mock," taking ת as a participial prefix by comparison with 139:21 and envisaging elision of ה (cf. σ´ "those who boast against us," cited in *BHS*). Less anomalous is Freedman's suggested relation to הָתֵל "mock, deceive," from a secondary stem תלל ("Structure," 192); then presumably ותוללינו is required. G. R. Driver ("Notes on the Psalms," *JTS* 36 [1935] 155–56) and A. Guillaume (*JBL* 75 [1956] 143–44) compared Arab. *talla*, rendering respectively "those who took us prisoners" (thus NEB "our captors") and "our slavedrivers."

3.c. Heb. שיר "song" is here collective (H. Gunkel, *Die Psalmen*, 581): cf. the note on 120:1. Freedman ("Structure," 191, 193) renders "songbook, hymnal."

4.a. Cultic sanctity and worship were confined to the land of Israel: cf. Y. Kaufmann, *The Religion of Israel*, 126–31; M. Haran, *Temples and Temple-Service in Ancient Israel* (Oxford: Clarendon Press, 1978) 41 note 47. The verse expresses well the sense of being "alienated from the place which gave identity and security, . . . from all the shapes and forms which gave power to faith and life" (W. Brueggemann, *The Land*, 8) as a result of the exile.

5.a. LXX Hier construed תשכח as passive "be forgotten." M. Scott (*Discoveries*, 162) ingeniously proposed restoration of כח lost by haplography after תשכח: "forget strength." An emendation תִּכְחַשׁ or תֶּחֱכָשׁ "grow lean" and so "wither," functioning as a word play, is often proposed (*BHK, BHS*; Kraus, *Psalmen*, 1082; cf. כחש in 109:24). I. Eitan (*JBL* 47 [1928] 194–95) noted that the parallelism requires a verb expressing loss of the faculty of motion. He mentioned a tradition known to Ibn Ezra that MT represents a hapax legomenon meaning תיבש "wither" (cf. 1 Kgs 13:4) and explained the text as a case of metathesis of כבש, for the sake of assonance; he compared Arab. *kasiḥa* "be crippled, weak-handed." Building on Eitan's comparison, KB (458b) and *HALAT* (478a) emend to תֶּכְשַׁח. Attempts have been made to relate שכח to Ugar. *ṯkḥ* (cf. the note on 102:5 and Dahood, *Psalms III*, 271). There is no certainty as to the meaning of this stem (cf. J. C. De Moor, "Ugaritic *ṯkḥ* and South Arabian *mṯkḥ*," *VT* 14 [1964] 371–72), but it is commonly rendered as "be hot, passionate" (cf. J. C. L. Gibson, *Canaanite Myths*, 160), whence a derived meaning "wither (from heat)" is plausible.

6.a. For ראש in the sense of "chief" cf. Ezek 27:22; Cant. 4:14. Dahood (*Psalms III*, 268, 272) rendered the unique phrase as "raise . . . upon my head in celebration." Freedman ("Structure," 193, 197–98), pointing the verb as qal אֶעֱלֶה, translates "I will ascend Jerusalem with joy upon my head," for the direct object comparing Num 13:17 and for the latter phrase Isa 35:10.

7.a. For זכר ל "remember to disadvantage" cf. "remember to someone's advantage," 132:1. H.-J. Boecker (*Redeformen*, 110) has found a basic forensic connotation: Yahweh is invoked as judge in an accusation (cf. B. S. Childs, *Memory and Tradition*, 32). But W. Schottroff (*Gedenken*, 233), comparing Jer 18:19–21, interprets less specifically of Yahweh's intervention in punishment.

7.b. At first sight mention of Edom looks intrusive; but, as Freedman ("Structure," 201) has shown, it is of a piece with other sixth-century B.C. literature. Kellermann (*ZAW* 90 [1978] 57–58) offers an interesting reconstruction of the historical situation: the Edomites broke off an alliance with Judah shortly before the fall of Jerusalem in 587 B.C. (cf. Jer 27:3) and sent to

Jerusalem a delegation offering surrender, who aimed to prove their allegiance to the Babylonians by the encouragement of v 7b and by the attitude of Obad 11. See, however, B. Oded, "Judah and the Exile," in *Israelite and Judaean History,* ed. J. H. Hayes and J. M. Miller (London: SCM Press, 1977) 470–71.

8.a. For the personification of cities and countries with בַּת "daughter," a phenomenon found especially in the prophetic literature see A. Fitzgerald, "*BTWLT* and *BT* as Titles for Capital Cities," *CBQ* 37 (1975) 167–83. Kellermann (*ZAW* 90 [1978] 48) emends to בַת־אֲדוֹם "Lady Edom" (cf. Lam 4:21–22) to produce continuity with v 7 and especially to give point to סֶלַע "rock" in v 9 as a word play on the Edomite city Sela. Understanding it literally rather than as a general expression or a formulation derived from Judean experience at the hands of the Babylonians, he considers it significant that there are no rocks in Babylonia, whereas the region of Edom was mountainous.

8.b. MT הַשְּׁדוּדָה is literally "devastated," possibly with a future connotation "doomed to be devastated," as θ' took it (cf. κJV). J. H. Eaton (*Psalms,* 299), Freedman ("Structure," 202–3) and Kellermann (*ZAW* 90 [1978] 45–46) are among those who retain MT as *lectio difficilior.* Freedman claims that elsewhere in the OT שׁדד is used only of action against Babylon, never by Babylon. An active form, attested by σ' S Tg. is favored by most scholars, viz. הַשֹּׁדְדָה or, conforming more closely to MT, הַשֹּׁדְדָה (cf. בְּגֹלְדָה, Jer 37:10). The context seems to require a ground of punishment, as a counterpart to . . . הָאֹמְרִים "those who said" in the second line of v 7.

8.c. For the beatitude formula see the note on 106:3. Here it has a rhetorical force in the context of an imprecation (E. Lipiński, *RB* 75 [1968] 354). See further in *Form/Structure/Setting* below.

8.d. The authenticity of v 8b has been widely questioned. Gunkel (*Die Psalmen,* 582) rejected it as a gloss on grounds of meter—hardly conclusive—and superfluity. A study of structure (cf. *Form/Structure/Setting*) yields opposing arguments. If the object sign were absent, its presence in vv 7, 9 would match the solemn occurrences in vv 1, 4. On the other hand, לָנוּ "to us" might be regarded as an echo of v 3b, and so too may the construction of verb and cognate noun. Freedman ("Structure," 202) retains v 8b without query. Kellermann (*ZAW* 90 [1978] 16) judges it an addition inspired by Jer 50:29, which calls for the punishment of Babylon, but then one would surely have expected a closer approximation of language; Jer 51:6 might have been a more plausible source to suggest.

9.a. This barbarous practice was a feature of ancient Near Eastern warfare: cf. the statement of Nah 3:10; the oracles of Isa 13:16 (against Babylon); Hos 14:1 (13:16) and Nah 3:10. It effected total destruction by making war upon the next generation. Though not uncommon, it aroused shock and horror (cf. 2 Kgs 8:2), and so the psalm here reaches an emotional climax. The note of retaliation obviously carries over from v 8: "The imprecation holds up a mirror to the Babylonian atrocities against Jerusalem and flashes the scene back onto the perpetrators as their coming recompense" (Eaton, *Psalms,* 299). For the difficulties raised for the Christian reader by such an attitude see the comments on Ps 109, including the references to J. L. McKenzie's article (*AER* 111 [1944] 81–96). Here McKenzie relates the note of good fortune to "the very limited sense of being unwitting instruments of divine justice. . . . Behind the figure [of v 9] is the true sense of the psalmist, which is a desire of divine vengeance for the crimes of the wicked. In committing all vengeance to God [cf. v 7], the psalmist excludes personal revenge." "The evil which the psalmist desires for the sinner is no more than the satisfaction of divine justice, and no more than God will inflict upon those who persevere in their sin" (*AER* 111 [1944] 93, 95–96). B. Steidle (*Erbe und Auftrag* 50 [1974] 24) has observed that the negative expression of an eminent positive love for Zion is displayed here: Edom-Babylon is the implacable counterpart to Zion and to Yahweh himself.

Form/Structure/Setting

Psalm 137 defies straightforward classification in form-critical terms. Gunkel (*Die Psalmen,* 580) commented that it begins as if it were a communal complaint, continues like a hymn and ends as a curse. Dahood (*Psalms III,* 269, cf. G. Fohrer, *Introduction,* 292) has characterized it as a complaint, and there is favorable evidence for this: besides the description of woe in vv

1–3, which refers both to the sufferers and to their foes, vv 5–6 can be understood as an implicit confession of trust, while v 7 is a petition for punishment.
These are elements of the complaint (cf. C. Westermann, *Praise*, 52–64; and
for זכר "remember" in v 7 cf. Schottroff, *Gedenken*, 35). The demand of v
3 is related to the mocking questions of complaints (79:10; 115:2; Kraus,
Psalmen, 1084). Schottroff (*Gedenken*, 145), followed by Kellermann (*ZAW* 90
[1978] 48–51), has endeavored to do justice to the psalm as a whole by
describing it as a modified Song of Zion. There are two types, a formal communal one, such as Pss 46, 48, 76, 87, and an informal, individual one, such
as Pss 84, 122. Schottroff has drawn attention to the dominance of Zion/
Jerusalem (vv 1, 3, 5, 6, 7). Over against the past impossibility of singing
any of the Songs of Zion in exile, is set the present relative joy of self-commit-
ting loyalty to Jerusalem, which necessarily under the circumstances must
replace the normal praise, as worship is offered at the site of the destroyed
temple. Kellermann has developed this categorization by noting that direct
address of Zion (vv 5–6aβ) is an element of the Song of Zion (87:3; 122:2,
6–9; cf. Jer 31:23). The circumstances of a destroyed city required mention
of its destruction in v 7 as a reversal of the normal reference to its firm
construction (46:4, 6–8, 12 [3, 5–7, 11]; 48:9, 13–15 [8, 12–14]; 87:5; 122:6–
7). The beatitude formula in vv 8–9 belongs to the Song of Zion (84:5, 6,
13 [4, 5, 12]): it is retained but changed to an imprecation of those involved
in Zion's destruction. The mingling of elements of the complaint and of
the Song of Zion reflect the nearest the psalmist can get to the latter in
straitened circumstances. Schottroff's form-critical description and Kellermann's amplification comprise an impressive insight into the psalm. Perhaps
reversal of a further characteristic element may be seen in vv 1–3: a narrative
describing with perfect verbs Yahweh's victory over foreign enemies at Jerusalem (48:5–7 [4–6]; 76:4–10 [3–9]; cf. 46:7, 9–10 [6, 8–9]; cf. J. Jeremias,
"Lade und Zion," 190), which typically uses the topographical adverb "there"
(שם 48:7 [6]; שמה 76:4 [3]) is here transformed into a bitter report involving
the loss of Jerusalem. A questionable part of Kellermann's analysis is his
treatment of the self-cursing formulae of vv 5–6 as a motif of innocence,
comparing Job 31:22; Ps 7:6 (5) at the end of a confession of innocence
(*ZAW* 90 [1978] 50): the psalmist affirms his innocence in failing to sing a
standard Song of Zion despite return from exile. The past verbs in the conditional clauses of Job 31:5–40; Ps 7:4–5 (3–4), over against the imperfect (present and future) verbs here, warn against drawing so close a parallel. As Kraus
(*Psalmen*, 1085) has seen, vv 5–6 represent a double vow. In this individual
part of the psalm their tone, though not their precise form, invites comparison
with the vow of praise characteristic of the individual complaint (cf. Westermann, *Praise*, 75–78). Since their intent is praise of Zion, even more relevant
is the expression of individual devotion in the informal type of the Songs
of Zion, 84:3 (2); 122:9 (cf. 43:4). The self-cursing form appears to have
been re-used for this purpose.
    Determination of the psalm's setting depends first upon the correct under-
standing of vv 1–3. If they describe a contemporary experience (cf. note
1.d. in *Notes/Comments*), the whole psalm is an exilic composition. Michel
(*Tempora*, 83) has argued from vv 5–9 that the exile was not yet over (cf. A.

Lauha, *Die Geschichtsmotive,* 123). However, Kellermann (*ZAW* 90 [1978] 49) has demonstrated the logical differences between vv 1–4 and their sequel: while in vv 3–4 the psalmist refuses to sing a Song of Zion, in v 6 he sets under a curse any failure to sing and play in Jerusalem's honor. Most scholars understand from the perfect verbs and repeated adverb םש "there" the psalmist's distance in time and space from exilic conditions. But what of the setting which is reported in vv 1–4? Kraus (*Psalmen,* 1084) has found reference to a service of formal complaint. On the other hand, Kellermann (*ZAW* 90 [1978] 53–57) has presented a good case for understanding the verses in terms of a non-cultic mourning lament, akin to the funeral lament. Mention of sitting and weeping (cf. Isa 47:1; Ezek 26:16; Job 2:8) and the non-use of the joyful lyre (cf. Gen 31:27; Job 30:31) are significant pointers in this direction.

Vv 1–4 lie in the past for the psalmist: in vv 5–6aγ he can address Jerusalem directly, as present there. The psalm "reveals the sufferings and sentiments of people who perhaps experienced at first hand the grievous days of the conquest and destruction of Jerusalem in the year 587 B.C., who shared the burden of the Babylonian captivity and after their return to their homeland now, at the sight of the city still lying in ruins, give vent with passionate intensity to the feelings lying dormant in their hearts" (Weiser, *Psalms,* 794). The early years of return from exile, either before the rebuilding of the temple (537–516/5 B.C.) or of the city walls (537–445 B.C.) were evidently the period in which the psalm was composed. It is not strictly necessary to presuppose that the psalmist was ever in Babylon (cf. J. W. Rogerson and J. W. McKay, *Psalms 101–150,* 150), but the passionate pathos of vv 1–4 may suggest that he spoke from experience. It is sometimes suggested that he was a levitical singer. *Pace* Fohrer (*Introduction,* 292) and Westermann (*Theologia Viatorum* 8 [1961/62] 283) the psalm probably had a cultic setting, in view of its content (cf. Kellermann, *ZAW* 90 [1978] 54–55). The role of the psalm in the Psalter, closing the supplement to the Songs of Ascents (cf. Seybold, *Wallfahrtspsalmen,* 74) may indicate that it was used as a processional song. In later Jewish tradition the psalm was employed on the ninth of Ab at the service commemorating the destruction of Jerusalem. It is possible that it was originally used at such a cultic setting (cf. Zech 7:3; 8:19).

Discussion of the poetic structure of the psalm has by no means been marked by unanimity. E. J. Kissane (*Psalms II,* 285), followed by J. Schildenberger (*Estudios Ecclesiásticos* 34 [1960] 675) and S. Mowinckel (*Tricola,* 102), advocated a regular division into three strophes of four lines, vv 1–3, 4–6, 7–9. J. Magne (*Bib* 39 [1958] 194–95) and Dahood (*Psalms III,* 269) have preferred a longer initial strophe, vv 1–4, followed by three shorter ones, vv 5–6, 7, 8–9. This grouping corresponds closely to the changes in aspect and number in the development of the psalm. Moreover, from the table of repeated terms plotted by Magne it is clear that the repetition of the object sign תא in vv 8–9, corresponding to that within vv 1–4 at vv 2, 4, afforded him justification for this division. Magne drew attention to the centrality and so importance of vv 5–6 in the poem. Dahood has noted the change of address in the three latter strophes, to Jerusalem, to the Edomites (on his understanding) and to Babylon.

Freedman ("Structure," 187–205) may have been inspired by Magne's explanation to develop his own structural analysis. The psalm has a concentric pattern. On the outside lie parallel units, vv 1–2, 8–9: the repeated preposition עַל "upon" followed by noun and *beth* "in" (see note 1.b. of *Notes/Comments*) in vv 1–2 are mirrored in the repeated אַשְׁרֵי שֶׁ "how fortunate . . . who" of vv 8–9; both vv 1, 8 are tricola and mention בָּבֶל "Babylon." Near the edge of the psalm vv 3, 7 match in featuring quotation of enemies with plural imperatives. Deeper into the psalm lie the two lines vv 4, 6aγ-b, each made up of conjunction and verb, object sign and object, and עַל "upon" with a genitival phrase. At the heart of the composition cluster vv 5–6aβ, with their precise chiastic order.

In his analysis Freedman has been able to tie together certain phenomena of the psalm most impressively. Two questions which need to be asked are whether he has done justice to sufficient phenomena and whether he has correctly interpreted the phenomena used in building up his own suggested structure. The inclusion בָּבֶל "Babylon" in vv 1, 8 need not of course have anything to do with divisions within the psalm. There are some seemingly key terms in the psalm which do not feature in the analysis, viz. זכר "remember" in vv 1, 6aγ, 7 and ירושלם/ציון "Zion/Jerusalem" in vv 1, 3, 5, 6aα, 7. The former term may point to a tripartite division, vv 1–3 (or 4), 4 (or 5)–6, 7–9, and the latter pair could support these demarcations. Freedman is surely right in highlighting the similarities between vv 4, 6aγ-b. However, their parallelism may be due to quite a different reason from concentricity. It is noteworthy that v 4 in a "we" sequence appears to cap the narrative of vv 1–3 with a differently structured sentence. Something similar occurs in the course of v 6: after the tightly bound ABB′A′ patterning of vv 5–6aβ, there is an extra line which breaks the pattern and changes to a third person reference to Jerusalem, while maintaining the first person singular subject and developing further the conditional clause of v 6a. The parallel structuring of vv 4, 6aγ, by which Freedman lays such store, appears to be continued in v 9. Its combination of conjunction and verb, object sign and object, and prepositional phrase invites comparison with the earlier matching lines. It is true that the genitival phrase at the end of vv 4, 6 is not reproduced, but nor is that at the center of v 4 in the other two cases, although the suffixed form in v 9 affords partial correspondence.

There are thus good grounds for reckoning with three strophes, vv 1–4, 5–6, 7–9, consisting of five, three and four lines respectively. The third clearly subdivides into two units, vv 7a-b, 8–9, united by their imprecatory tones and concerned with Edom and Babylon respectively, for which the related terms בְּנֵי "sons" and בַּת "daughter" are used, and both giving grounds for complaint using article and participle (see note 8.b. in *Notes/Comments*). Vv 8–9 are a pair of beatitudes. The repeated initial and (nearly) final Zion/Jerusalem references of vv 1, 3 and 5, 6 are in this strophe replaced by a word play ירושלם/ישלם "Jerusalem," "will repay" in vv 7, 8. The second strophe is dominated by chiasmus. The first strophe artistically paves the way for the next two by embracing the structures of both. First it falls into two units, vv 1–2 and the explanatory vv 3–4 which are linked closely by the fourfold repetition of שִׁיר "song(s), sing." The parallelism of the units is expressed by the repetition of שָׁם "there" in vv 1, 3. In the first unit the first two cola of v 1 are matched by the similarly structured second line. However, there are also signs of chiasmus in the first strophe: תְלִינוּ/תּוֹלָלֵינוּ "we hung," "our mockers" at the center are bordered by צִיּוֹן "Zion" and probably enveloped by the parallelism of עַל-נַהֲרוֹת בָּבֶל "beside the rivers of Babylon" and עַל אַדְמַת נֵכָר "on foreign soil." Double schemes within a poetic unit are not unattested in Hebrew psalmody (see the analysis of Ps 111). First one and then the other are taken up and developed in the succeeding strophes. The quotations of the first and third (vv 3, 7) echo the intrusion of the "I" speech throughout the central strophe, while the divine name at the end of the first strophe and the beginning of the third (vv 4, 7) artistically echoes the chiasmus of the second. Moreover, prepositional terms with third feminine suffixes בְּתוֹכָהּ "within her" and בָהּ "in her," occur in the second lines of the first and final strophes; the repeated לָנוּ "to us" occurs in their penultimate lines. The direct note of joy in the first two, refused in the first and embraced in the second, is indirectly taken up in the beatitudes of the third, which resolve the antithesis of the other two and affirm the second by expressing desire for the punishment of those who made their initial joy impossible.

Explanation

Psalm 137 is a modified version of a Song of Zion. The religious community of Judah in the immediate post-exilic period mingle their devotion to the holy city with tones of anguish. The typical narrative passage celebrating the impregnability of Zion and its divine protection has to give way to a report of mourning in a foreign land. The normal trilogy of Yahweh, Zion and defeated foe is replaced by a tragic threesome of the victorious enemy, Zion and the defeated nation, with Yahweh very conspicuous by his absence, except as a figure of past tradition (v 4). The misery of vv 1–3 is accentuated in the Hebrew by ninefold repetition of the ending -nû ("we," "our"), which carries a ring of pathos, as in Isa 53:4–6.

Their grief was much more than homesickness. As they sat in an attitude of mourning beside a tree-lined canal, they were haunted by memories of Zion. They were the bittersweet memories of festivals and fellowship with God and with believer, and the tortured memories of the ruins to which God's earthly home and the capital of his realm had been reduced. Their lyres, once used to accompany God's glad praises, rested up in the branches, idle, silent. Tautingly their enemies bid them sing one of the old Songs of Zion. That was neither the time nor the place, however. Age-old traditions of worship had been traumatically overthrown and their content seemingly nullified. By the location of the psalm immediately after two psalms which celebrate Yahweh's gift of the land to the covenant nation, the reversal here expressed is conveyed in even more poignant tones than when the psalm is read in isolation.

Thankfully that scene of absolute misery belongs to the past. However, the wound, though closed over by return, still aches with pain. The ruined city bears sad witness to the mystery of fact in conflict with faith. But faith triumphs. The psalmist doffs his role as voice of the community, in expression of his heightened emotion. He pledges his utter commitment to Jerusalem and echoes the note of joy associated with the individual Songs of Zion, such as Pss 84 and 122. His devotion takes the form of a solemn vow invoking upon himself the penalty of physical handicap (cf. Matt 5:28–30). May he never be able to play the lyre again or sing again, should he forget! Just as in the Songs of Zion praise of Zion represents praise of God, so here his expression of loyalty to Jerusalem is a measure of his loyalty to Yahweh, since the city symbolizes the divine presence.

However, the joy has sought him through pain, and it is pain that drives him to articulate the closing portion of the psalm, vv 7–9, in which the participants of vv 1–4 largely reappear, but now with new roles, as if rearranged in a shaken kaleidoscope. The implicit contrast between the sure foundation of the city of God normally celebrated in the Songs of Zion and its present ruined state, prompts a prayer for punishment. Yahweh will surely not stay in the background as hero of a dead tradition, but must come to the fore. His declared will in establishing Jerusalem as the legitimate channel of access to him encourages the psalmist to intercede on its behalf. The human memories of vv 1, 5 must surely have a divine counterpart—not leaving such an outrage in the limbo of unpunished sin but remembering and acting in retaliation upon the Edomite collaborators (cf. Obad 11–14). An even greater measure of guilt attaches itself to the Babylonian invaders. Borrowing the beatitude form from the Song of Zion, the psalmist uses it ironically in commendation of dire reprisal. In the light of v 8 Judah had evidently suffered the fate of v 9, and it is for this cultural expression of total warfare that demand is made. For the sake of divine justice their turn must come.

Perhaps the citizen of a European country who has experienced its invasion and destruction would be the best exegete of such a psalm. The passion that throbs in every line is the fruit of suffering. Is it ignoble? Certainly not if one takes seriously the religious framework of the psalmist. It is difficult to detach from the concepts of a chosen nation, a territory possessed by divine right and a holy city, such valid corollaries as holy war and a divine crusade against the violators of such concepts. The issues of national liability and forfeiture of the covenant gifts, which are stressed in prophetic and deuteronomic literature, do present a different perspective upon Judah's experience from the one espoused by the psalmist, evidently of cultic provenance. But Isaiah could hold together in tension the paradox of Assyria as agent of the divine will and yet culpable transgressor (Isa 10:5–15); and the psalm is in line with exilic and post-exilic prophecies which promise the heaviest of reprisals (cf. Isa 13:16; 14:22). Jeremiah's acceptance of Babylonian sovereignty (Jer 29:4–7) could never be God's final word to the OT believer (cf. Jer 50–51).

The Christian faith teaches a new way, the pursuit of forgiveness and a call to love. Both its intrinsic non-nationalism and its facility to fall back upon an eschatological final reckoning, the Last Judgment, aid such a course. Yet is there forgiveness for a Judas (cf. John 17:12) or for the Antichrist? Psalm 137:9 forms part of the OT backdrop to the new Babylon of Rev

17–18, and there, too, fierce, unsentimental joy is inculcated upon saint and angel (Rev 18:20). The psalmist's passion is not simply an expression of nationalism, even when it is appreciated that in the OT nationalism is itself a kind of religious virtue: it is a measure of his sense of an ultimate sin committed against God. The meaning of Jerusalem to him, its sacramental role in God's revealed purposes as reflection of the divine, could permit no lesser retribution. It is his love for God that makes him curse: his God is not mocked.

God's Hand in My Life (138:1–8)

Bibliography

Bardtke, H. "Die hebräische Präposition *naegaed* in den Psalmen." *Forschung zur Bibel* 2 (1972) 17–27. **Crüsemann, F.** *Studien zur Formgeschichte.* **Dahood, M.** "The Root GMR in the Psalms." *TS* 14 (1953) 595–97. **Emerton, J. A.** "A Consideration of Some Alleged Meanings of יד in Hebrew." *JSS* 15 (1970) 145–80. **Thomas, D. W.** "The Root יד in Hebrew. 2." *JTS* 36 (1935) 409–12.

Translation

¹ Davidic.
   I give thanks ᵃ *with all my heart,*ᵇ   (3+3)
      before the gods ᶜ *I celebrate you with music.*
² *I prostrate myself toward your holy temple*   (3+2+2)
      and give thanks to your name
      for your loyal love and your faithfulness,
   because you have made your name and promise   (2+2)
      *to surpass all else.*ᵃ
³ *At the time I called, you answered me*   (3+3)
      *and made me exultant,*ᵃ *putting strength within me.*

⁴ *Let all the kings in the world give you thanks*   (4+3)
      in reaction to hearing of the promises of your mouth,
⁵ *and let them sing of Yahweh's ways,*   (3+3)
      that Yahweh's glory is so great.
⁶ *For, high as Yahweh is, he looks upon the lowly,*   (4+3)
      but from afar he takes cognizance ᵃ *of the proud.*

⁷ *When I walk amid trouble,*   (3+3)
      you grant me life in face of my enemies' fury.
   *You stretch out your hand,*ᵃ   (2+2)
      your right hand helps me.
⁸ *Yahweh acts as avenger* ᵃ *on my behalf.*   (3+3+3)
      Yahweh, your loyal love is everlasting.
      Do not abandon the product ᵇ *of your hands.*

Notes/Comments

1.a. Heb. mss, including 11QPsᵃ, and the ancient versions add the divine name, which is expected as a vocative to which the second person may refer. But M. Dahood's stylistic objection that it upsets the precise chiasmus of the bicolon (*Psalms III*, 276) is noteworthy. MT's shorter text is to be preferred as the harder reading.

1.b. That is, with the conscious devotion of the will (H. W. Wolff, *Anthropology*, 53). Cf. 9:2 (1); 86:12; 111:1. LXX's addition (cf. *BHS*) "because you have heard the words of my mouth" has been hailed as part of the original Hebrew text by F. Crüsemann (*Studien zur Formgeschichte*, 249; JB) on the ground that it improves the metrical sequence of vv 1–2, allowing two bicola of 3+3 and two of 2+2. But it is suspiciously like v 4b, and A. A. Anderson (*Psalms*, 901) is more likely to be correct in deriving the addition from v 4b. Most probably it was originally a marginal correction of the Greek of v 4b, dispensing with the extra πάντα "all"; it was wrongly attached to v 1 because of the similarity of ἐξομολογήσομαι/σἀσθωσάν σοι in vv 1a, 4a, and the third plural verb and second person pronoun were adapted to suit the new context.

1.c. H. Gunkel (*Die Psalmen*, 583) compared בגוים "among the nations" and the like in 18:50 (49); 57:10 (9); 96:3. Here the thanksgiving is an implicit testimony to Yahweh's power not only to surrounding pagan nations but to their gods. Their apparent rivalry to Yahweh is dealt a blow by the manifestation of his might. LXX characteristically weakened to ἀγγέλων "angels"; also *S mlkʾ* "kings" is probably a corruption of *mlʾkʾ* "angels" under the influence of 119:46 and also of v 4 (A. Vogel, *Bib* 32 [1951] 53, 202). *Tg.* דייניא "judges" is an exegetical rendering in accordance with its understanding of Ps 82 (H.-J. Kraus, *Psalmen*, 1088). H. Bardtke (*Forschungen zur Bibel* 2 [1972] 22) has explained in general terms of a confrontation with the divine and the holy within the temple precincts.

2.a. MT reads rather clumsily "you have made your promise great above all your name," i.e., apparently by fulfilling his promise Yahweh has surpassed all earlier revelation of himself. Various attempts have been made to improve the text, none of which has a ring of certainty. The simplest is to read absolute כֹּל for construct -כָּל and to insert ו before the final noun (H. Schmidt, *Die Psalmen*, 243; RSV); similarly Dahood (*Psalms III*, 277) who, however, takes על-כל as "before all," corresponding to "before the gods" in v 1, and understands the copula ו. Kraus (*Psalmen*, 1087), followed by Crüsemann (*Studien zur Formgeschichte*, 249) inserts ו and also assumes loss by haplography of השמים "the heavens" before שמך "your name," urging that v 2b is otherwise too short: "you have made greater than all the heavens . . ." NEB "thou hast made thy promise wide as the heavens" reads שָׁמַ(י)ךָ for שמך (L. H. Brockington, *Hebrew Text*, 153). The text is sometimes shortened by plausible deletion of שמך as an intrusion from v 2aβ (e.g. *BHS*).

3.a. Cf. רָהַב "pride," Targum Aram. רהב "be proud, arrogant." LXX need not represent תרהבני: cf. post-biblical Heb. הרהיב "declare great"; רַהַב "pride, greatness" (M. Jastrow, *Dictionary*, 1453). MT is to be retained as *lectio difficilior* over against תַּרְבֶּה "make great," which is read by Kraus (*Psalmen*, 1087), RSV *et al.*, following S. The final two words of the line appear to function as a circumstantial clause. For the association of עז "strength" with the stem רהב cf. גאון עז "pride of strength," Ezek 24:21; 30:6, 18; 33:28. Cf. NEB "and make me bold and valiant hearted."

6.a. D. Winton Thomas (*JTS* 36 [1935] 409–10) proposed a pointing as piʿel יְיֵעַ "he humbles," linking with Arab. *waduʿa* "become still" and claiming that the verb of v 6a, which implies looking kindly, requires an antithetical reference to punishment. NEB has concurred, reading a pausal יֵעַ (Brockington, ibid.). J. A. Emerton (*JSS* 15 [1970] 171, 177) ably defends Thomas's derivation both in principle and in this instance. The applicability of the cognate treatment to cases of ידע in the OT need not be denied, but it may be queried whether the traditional "know" is here inappropriate. Grammatically the form in MT is generally taken as a variant of יֵדַע (GKC § 69b note 1, 69p). For the thought of v 6b cf. 73:11; Job 22:13, where presumed divine lack of knowledge is associated with the impunity of the wicked, and Job 11:11; 34:25, where divine knowledge has a sinister connotation. Dahood (*Psalms III*, 279–80), following Gunkel (*Die Psalmen*, 582), takes the cola as synonymous, גבה "the proud" continuing רם "great, high" in v 6a and ייֵדַע in a positive sense "care for": "and though the Lofty he heeds." Although this interpretation is syntactically possible, the usual understanding is supported by the parallelism of Isa 10:33b.

7.a. For the positive sense of the phrase cf. Prov 31:20.

8.a. A transitive force has traditionally been assigned to גמר "come to an end" here and in 57:3; in both cases the difficult ellipse of an object "what he has begun, his purpose" has then to be assumed. A meaning "wreak vengeance," which fits both contexts, is attested both by Ugar. *gmr* and by LXX ἀνταποδώσει "will requite," *Tg.* בישׁא ישׁלם "will repay evil" and in 57:3 Hier *ultorem* "avenger": cf. Dahood, *TS* 14 (1953) 596–97; J. C. L. Gibson, *Canaanite Myths*, 144; *HALAT*, 190a. For the semantic development Dahood has compared that of the stem שׁלם.

8.b. A singular מעשׂה "product," read by many mss. and implied by *S*, is required in the context (Kraus, *Psalmen*, 1087; *BHS*, et al.). Dahood (*Psalms III*, 282) construes as a plural of majesty. Gunkel (*Die Psalmen*, 585), comparing GKC § 93ss, took MT, which is supported by 11QPsᵃ, as a case of unusual orthography for מעשׂה.

Form/Structure/Setting

This individual thanksgiving uses a number of the elements of its genre (cf. H. Gunkel and J. Begrich, *Einleitung*, 265–84; Crüsemann, *Studien zur Formgeschichte*, 249–51). An introductory declaration of thanksgiving (vv 1–2), in this case expanded theologically, is followed by a summary account of Yahweh's answer to the psalmist's prayer and deliverance (v 3). Vv 4–6 are a hymn summoning kings to join in praising Yahweh's greatness: cf. the imperatival call for the world to praise in the processional hymn for the thank offering service, 100:1–2 and in 66:1–4, and the universal jussive calls of 22:28, 30 (27, 29; cf. Kraus, *Psalmen*, 322; NEB). Here there is rather unusual oscillation between address of Yahweh and third person reference. Oscillation in divine references is a standard feature of thanksgiving psalms (cf. Crüsemann, *Studien zur Formgeschichte*, 225), but in the call to praise third person references are expected, as in vv 5–6. The direct address of v 4 carries over from vv 1–3. Theoretically it is possible to take the verbs of vv 4a, 5a as imperfect and so future forms. Psalm 86:9 might be cited in support, but there the future hope is a direct and logical development of the statement regarding Yahweh's uniqueness in v 8 (cf. 102:16 [15] after v 13 [12]). A jussive summons here corresponds well to the psalm's genre. Vv 7–8a comprise a confession of confidence in which the psalmist speaks of Yahweh's aid to him in general terms. Such avowals are more characteristic of the individual complaint, but parallels in thanksgiving psalms may be found in 18:29–30 (28–29); 118:6–7, 14a. The passage is addressed to Yahweh apart from a third person reference in v 8aα, which takes the form of testimony. It issues into a theological affirmation (cf. 18:31 [30]), which is associated with the formula of praise used at the thanksgiving service (cf. Jer 33:11). The psalm closes with a prayer, which accords well with the form of direct address that the psalm has mainly used. It is not common in the thanksgiving song, but there are parallels at 40:12 (11); 118:25 (cf. 33:22).

C. Westermann (*Praise*, 111, 117, 122, 129) has drawn attention to a number of motifs. In v 2 occurs the term חסד "loyal love" which is characteristic of the thanksgiving psalm with reference to God's deliverance in time of need (cf. 18:51 [50]; 66:20; 92:2; 116:5; 118:1). The summarizing statement of praise in v 6 contrasting exaltation and humbling is the counterpart of the double wish in the complaint and has parallels in 18:28 (27); 107:39–41. V 8aβ illustrates a feature of this type of psalm, a statement about the totality of God's actions placed at the end (cf. 34:22; 92:15). The motif of preservation in v 8b, used to supplement the overall theme of deliverance, is rare, but 107:9 may be compared (cf. 33:22).

The setting of the psalm is clearly the forecourt of the temple, in view of v 2. Crüsemann (*Studien zur Formgeschichte*, 251), following Gunkel (*Die Psalmen*, 583; *Einleitung*, 277–79), regards the psalm not as sung to accompany a thank offering, which the psalm does not mention, but as a "spiritualized" form unaccompanied by sacrifice but sung still in the temple precincts. He has pointed to the degeneration in style whereby prayerful statements and testimony, properly distinct in the basic form, are jumbled together, and considers it evidence for loss of the original full setting.

The psalm has been interpreted as a royal song of thanksgiving, notably by S. Mowinckel (*The Psalms in Israel's Worship*, vol. 2, 29, 32), Dahood (*Psalms III*, 276) and J. H. Eaton (*Kingship*, 63). Parallels with other royal psalms, especially with Ps 18, and the reference to kings in v 4 are cited in support. Such an ascription would clearly suit the Davidic heading to the psalm, if it was originally sung by a Davidic king. Gunkel (*Die Psalmen*, 584), followed by Kraus (*Psalmen*, 1088), objected that a king would pray inside the temple (cf. 2 Sam 12:20; 2 Kgs 19:14) rather than in the forecourt (v 2). Eaton, ibid., has reasonably countered this objection by observing that thanksgivings would be likely to take place in the court by the great altar on which the accompanying sacrifices were offered. He prefers this setting to that of Dahood, who envisages the king absent from Jerusalem on a military campaign and directing his prayer in the direction of the temple (*Psalms III*, 277). Against A. Weiser's contention that v 6a implies that the speaker was a simple member of the religious community (*Psalms*, 798), it has been urged that humility before God was a royal ideal (Dahood, *Psalms III*, 279, comparing עבד "servant" in 89:40, 51 [39, 50]; Eaton, *Kingship*, 180). But v 6 does read more like a general statement relating to classes of people. Overall there does not seem to be evidence compelling enough to categorize the psalm as royal with any certainty. The royal associations of vv 4–5 may be adequately explained by the process whereby members of the community took over expressions properly and originally spoken by a king (Gunkel, *Die Psalmen*, 583; Kraus, *Psalmen*, 1089). Then the heading may attest the psalm's subsequent attachment to an existing Davidic collection or may have a homiletical purpose. In this connection it is of interest to note that the Lucianic text of LXX adds to the heading Ζαχαρίου "of Zechariah," an ascription related to vv 4–5: "The theme of universal recognition of God's grandeur and glory is an important part of Haggai's and Zechariah's prophecies" (E. Slomovic, *ZAW* 91 [1979] 362).

A. F. Kirkpatrick (*Psalms*, 783), Anderson (*Psalms*, 901) and others (cf. the list in Gunkel, *Die Psalmen*, 583) regard the psalm as a communal thanksgiving in which a solo voice represents the community in returning thanks for the Babylonian exile. Kirkpatrick found allusions to the exile and return in very many psalms where other scholars have failed to detect them. He pointed to parallels with Isa 40–66 and Ps 102:16–23 (15–22); in this instance Kraus (*Psalmen*, 1088) has concurred in the former case, if only to the extent of postulating a post-exilic dating for the psalm on their basis. Kirkpatrick compared v 5 with Isa 40:5; 60:1, and v 6 with Isa 57:15; 66:2. Kraus has seen the influence of Deutero-Isaiah in v 1b and traced a parallel with the concept of Israel's role as witness to the nations' gods concerning Yahweh's saving work in Isa 43:10; 44:8. However, the parallels adduced do not appear to be distinctive enough to carry conviction. Similarities may be adequately explained as due to common cultic traditions. Certainly they do not necessitate a communal interpretation for the psalm and the lone plural in MT at v 8 can hardly bear such weight. In any case Kirkpatrick's strongly eschatological interpretation of the psalm which underlies his references to Isa 40–66 and Ps 102 is unlikely on form-critical grounds. The date of the psalm may be left an open question (cf. J. W. Rogerson and J. W. McKay, *Psalms 101–150*, 153). Crüsemann's observations concerning form-critical breakdown may be relevant, but it is difficult to tie such changes to precise chronology.

The psalm clearly divides into three sections or (Dahood, *Psalms III*, 276) strophes, vv 1–3, 4–6, 7–8. The central strophe is bound together as a unit by the fourfold mention of the divine name and the threefold occurrence of כִּי "when, that; for." Around it cluster the other two, linked by the motif of deliverance from distress (vv 3, 7). Heb. חַסְדְּךָ "your loyal love" functions as an inclusive and parallel element (vv 2, 8), while the repetition of שְׁמֶ֑ךָ "your name" in v 2 corresponds to that of יָד(י)ךָ "your hand(s)" in vv 7, 8. The second strophe takes up a number of terms used in the first: כֹּל(ב) "all," vv 1, 2, 4; וְאוֹדֶה/אוֹדְךָ "I give thanks," vv 1–2, cf. יוֹדוּךָ, v 4; הִגְדַּלְתָּ "made great," v 2, cf. גָּדוֹל, v 5; אִמְרָתֶךָ "your saying," v 2, cf. אִמְרֵי פִיךָ "promises of your mouth," v 4.

Explanation

In the temple forecourt a worshiper utters his song of thanksgiving. His face is turned toward the main building, where Yahweh graciously presenced himself (cf. 1 Kgs 8:29). He sings with enthusiasm: his personal experience constitutes for him proof positive of the reality and power of Israel's God and so a defiant challenge to all rival claims. In tones of praise he theologizes from his experience. He has seen Yahweh's loving care at work in his life. It has been his privilege to witness the supreme validity of God's self-revelation and of his promises. Then in simpler vein the psalmist gives the reason for his thanksgiving, answered prayer and restored vitality and morale.

So overwhelming is his sense of wonder and indebtedness that he transfers his thanksgiving theme to a broader canvas. He is painfully aware of the inadequacy of his little contribution of praise to so great a God. Surely nothing but the concerted thanksgiving of the monarchs of earth could get anywhere near to matching the praiseworthiness of this unique God (cf. v 1) whose habit is both to promise and to perform, manifesting his transcendent power. The wonder of it is that his heavenly majesty is allied with grace. The psalmist's own experience enables him to deduce a general principle of divine magnanimity. It has illustrated afresh a polarity in God's dealings (cf. Luke 14:11; 18:14), a kindly concern for those who subordinate themselves to him (cf. 1 Pet 5:6) but ill-boding omniscience of the behavior of the self-willed (cf. vv 7, 8).

The singer is not content to allow his generalizing to stay on the level of theological truths concerning God's ways with humanity. He adapts it to express his intensely personal appreciation. Yahweh is praised as one whose wont it is to deliver him from affliction and to restore him to fullness of life. Yahweh's protection and vindication are a pattern that he has experienced time and time again. He is personally qualified to sing the motto of the thanksgiving service concerning the constancy of divine grace. Yet he dare not take it for granted: it must ever be balanced by constant submission. His final word must be a prayer that, just as he has known God's molding hand upon his life thus far, so he may continue to encounter his gracious presence (cf. Job 10:3, 8–12; Eph 2:10; 1 Pet 4:19).

Honest to God   (139:1–24)

Bibliography

Allen, L. C. "Faith on Trial: An Analysis of Psalm 139." *Vox Evangelica* 10 (1977) 5–23. **Baumann, E.** "Der 139. Psalm—ein Bekenntnis der Metanoia." *EvT* 11 (1951) 187–90. **Behler, G. M.** "Der nahe und schwer zu fassende Gott. Eine biblische Besinnung über Ps. 139 (138)." *BibLeb* 6 (1965) 135–52. **Bernhardt, K.-H.** "Zur Gottesvorstellung von Psalm 139." *Kirche—Theologie—Frömmigkeit. Festgabe fur G. Holz zum 65. Geburtstag.* Berlin: Evangelische Verlagsanstalt, 1965. **Bullard, J. M.** "Psalm 139: Prayer in Stillness." *SBL 1975 Seminar Papers*, vol. 1. Missoula, MT: Scholars Press, 1975, 141–50. **Danell, G. A.** *Psalm 139*, UUÅ 1951:1. Uppsala: A. B. Lundequistka Bokhandeln; Leipzig: Otto Harrassowitz, 1951. **Holman, J.** "Analysis of the Text of Ps. 139." *BZ* 14 (1970) 37–71, 198–227. ———. "The Structure of Psalm 139." *VT* 21 (1971) 298–310. **Hommel, H.** "Das religionsgeschichtliche Problem des 139. Psalms." *ZAW* 47 (1929) 110–24. **Koole, J. L.** "Quelques remarques sur Psaume 139." *Studia biblica et semitica T. C. Vriezen dedicata.* Wageningen: H. Veenman, 1966. **Krašovec, J.** "Die polare Ausdruckweise im Psalm 139." *BZ* 18 (1974) 224–48. **Lapointe, R.** " 'La nuit est ma lumiere' *wā'ōmar 'ak-ḥōšek yᵉsûpēnî wᵉlaylâ 'ôr ba'adēnî* (Ps 139:11)." *CBQ* 33 (1971) 397–402. **Mannati, M.** "Psaume 139:14–16." *ZAW* 83 (1971) 257–61. **Muller, H.-P.** "Die Gattung des 139. Psalms." *17. Deutscher Orientalistentag 1 vom 21. bis 27. Juli 1968 in Wurzburg.* Teil 1. ZDMG Supplementa 1. Wiesbaden: Franz Steiner Verlag, 1969, 345–55. **Pettazzoni, R.** *The All-Knowing God.* Tr. H. J. Rose. London: Methuen, 1956. **Pytel, R.** "Psalm 139:15. Versuch eine neue Deutung." *Folia Orientalia* 13 (1971) 257–66. **Schüngel-Straumann, H.** "Zur Gattung und Theologie des 139. Psalms." *BZ* 17 (1973) 39–51. **van Uchelen, N. A.** "אנשׁי דמים in the Psalms." *OTS* 15 (1969) 205–12. **Wagner, S.** "Zur Theologie des Psalms 139." *Congress Volume Göttingen 1977.* VTSup 29. Leiden: E. J. Brill, 1978. **Wolverton, W. I.** "The Psalmists' Belief in God's Presence." *CJT* 9 (1963) 82–94. **Wurthwein, E.** "Erwägungen zu Psalm 139." *VT* 7 (1957) 165–82. **Young, E. J.** *Psalm 139: A Study in the Omniscience of God.* London: Banner of Truth Trust, 1965.

Translation

[1] Director's collection.[a] Davidic. A Psalm.
Yahweh, you examine me [b]   (2+2)
  and you yourself [c] *know me,*
[2] *you know when I sit down and get up,* [a]   (3+3)
  you sense my thought from far away,

³ you analyse ª when I travel and when I rest; ᵇ   (3+3)
  in fact, with all my behavior you are familiar.

⁴ For example, a word does not need to be on my tongue   (3+3)
  for you to know all about it, Yahweh.

⁵ Back and front you enclose me,   (3+3)
  you put your hand upon me. ª

⁶ Such knowledge ª is wonderful and beyond me,   (3+3)
  it is so transcendent I cannot attain it.

⁷ Where could ª I go to avoid your spirit? ᵇ   (3+3)
  Where could I get away from your presence?

⁸ If I went up to heaven, you would be there.   (3+3)
  If I lay down in Sheol, ª there you would be.

⁹ Were I to use ª the wings of the dawn ᵇ   (3+3)
  and go and live at the farthest part of the sea,

¹⁰ your hand would be even there to guide ª me,   (3+3)
  your right hand would take hold of me.

¹¹ Or were I to ask ª the darkness ᵇ to cover ᶜ me,   (3+3)
  the light around me to turn into night,

¹² even darkness is not too dark for you,   (3+3+2)
  night is as light as the day,
  light and dark are just the same. ª

¹³ Indeed ª you yourself created ᵇ my kidneys, ᶜ   (3+3)
  you wove me together ᵈ in my mother's womb.

¹⁴ I give you thanks because   (2+2+2)
  you ª are awesomely ᵇ wonderful,
  so wonderful are the things you have made. ᶜ

  You have known ᵈ my being through and through;   (3+3)
¹⁵ my bone structure was not concealed from you
  when I was being made in secret,   (3+3)
  worked in motley fashion deep down in the earth. ª

¹⁶ Your eyes saw my embryo, ª   (3+3)
  and in your book ᵇ are all written down
  days that were planned ᶜ   (2+3)
  before any of them occurred. ᵈ

¹⁷ How difficult ª I find your thoughts of me, ᵇ God!   (4+3)
  How vast they are in their totality!

¹⁸ If I tried to count them, they would be more than grains of sand.   (3+3)
  If I came to the end, ª I would not have finished with you. ᵇ

¹⁹ I wish you would kill the wicked, ª God,   (3+4)
  and that bloodthirsty men ᵇ would leave me; ᶜ

²⁰ men who mention ª you maliciously,   (3+3)
  who talk ᵇ falsely, your foes. ᶜ

²¹ Do I not hate those who hate you, Yahweh? ª   (4+3)
  Don't I loathe those who attack ᵇ you?

²² I do hate them, hate them utterly,   (3+3)
  I regard them as enemies of mine.

23 *Examine me, God, and know my mind,*   (4+3)
   probe me and know how anxious I am,
24 *see if I have been behaving as an idolator* ª   (3+3)
   and guide me in the ancient ᵇ *path.*

Notes/Comments

1.a. For discussion see H.-J. Kraus, *Psalmen*, 25; A. A. Anderson, *Psalms*, 48. J. F. A. Sawyer ("An Analysis of the Context and Meaning of the Psalm-Headings," *Transactions of the Glasgow University Oriental Society* 22 [1967/68] 35–36), on the basis of instructions in Accadian ritual texts which specify the official appointed to utter them, has rendered "to be recited by the official in charge."

1.b. The perfect and imperfect consecutive verbs are best regarded as present in force (D. Michel, *Tempora*, 244), just as those in vv 2–5 always are. The reference is to Yahweh's general insight into the psalmist's life. The imperatives of v 23 imply willing submission on the latter's part. In a similar way תנחני "would guide me" at v 10 is taken up by the imperative נחני "guide me" in v 24. Kraus (*Psalmen*, 1094) has interpreted the verbs as past and relating to a previous judicial examination, which vv 19–24 anticipate as a quotation. J. L. Koole ("Psaume 139," 177) has drawn attention to his inconsistency in thus isolating the verbs of v 1 from the ones that follow. M. Dahood (*Psalms III*, 285–86) takes the first verb as a precative perfect and the second as jussive (ותדע) "and know"): "examine me and know me. . . .' " This achieves parity between vv 1 and 23; but the existence and frequency of usage of the precative perfect are still very much a matter of debate. J. Krašovec (*BZ* 18 [1974] 227 note 9) has observed that Dahood's treatment violates the development of the psalm as a whole, which rises to a crescendo, beginning in low narrative key and closing with a passionate appeal.

1.c. With Dahood (*Psalms III*, 286) the personal pronoun at the head of v 2 in MT is to be attached to the end of v 1: "both verses profit metrically." For the pronoun following the verb cf. GKC § 135a, b.

2.a. Krašovec (*BZ* 18 [1974] 232–33) has studied the polar expressions used in the psalm to express totality: in vv 2a, 3a, 5a they are used within single cola, while in vv 8, 9, 11 they extend to whole lines. In this connection J. Holman (*VT* 21 [1971] 301) has noted the contrast between the representations of man and of God in vv 1–12. On the one hand there is the multiplicity of the psalmist's activities and the agitation of various human possibilities; on the other is the majestic superiority of God's knowledge, expressed in sober, calm tones, comprehending everything by the mere fact of his presence.

3.a. Lit. "scatter, winnow, sift," here used metaphorically. The verb has also been explained as a denominative of זרת "span" and so meaning "measure off, determine" (cf. *HALAT*, 268b, 279a).

3.b. Heb. רבע has usually been explained as an Aramaism for the standard רבץ "lie down." Dahood (*Psalms III*, 287) has related to Ugar. shaphel of rbʿ "bring (?)" and so basically "come, arrive"; but the quite different meaning assigned by J. C. L. Gibson, *Canaanite Myths*, 107, 157, is to be noted.

5.a. The force of the expressions of v 5a, b is ambiguous. Heb. צור used in v 5a is often used in a hostile sense "besiege," but it can be employed of protection. Similarly Yahweh's כף "palm" or hand can refer to his loving care or punishment. Probably the verse is to be pressed to neither extreme but is simply a neutral statement of God's absolute control of the psalmist's movements (Dahood, *Psalms III*, 288).

6.a. MT דעת may be an error by haplography for הדעת "the knowledge" (*BHS*). For the anarthrous noun cf. אור "light" in v 11, where, however, G. R. Driver (*JTS* 44 [1943] 22) reads האור, also via haplography.

7.a. The verbs of v 7, like that of v 6, have a modal force (Michel, *Tempora*, 244). The psalmist did not want to escape Yahweh; "escape would be impossible if he wished it" (A. F. Kirkpatrick, *Psalms*, 787). E. J. Young (*Psalm 139*, 45), comparing v 24, considered that a consciousness of his own sin made him want to escape, but this misunderstands the whole psalm. Rather, the text is an implicit protestation of innocence: the psalmist rejoices in God's presence (cf. v 10; Anderson, *Psalms*, 907). Amos 9:2–4 treats the motif of human inescapability from

God in a way similar to that of vv 7–10, rhetorically instancing contrasted areas to build up an impression of the inevitability of punishment for sin. There the "Hound of heaven" pursues fugitives from justice. Here the perspective is different: the psalmist, wherever he went, would find himself confronted with a God who was already there. As a man he can be at only one place in the world at once, but God is everywhere.

7.b. The vital power of Yahweh's personal activity (רוּחַ "your spirit") and his "face" (פָּנֶיךָ) express the immediacy of the divine presence in the world: it takes the form of constant encounter rather than automatic immanence (D. Lys, *Rûach, le souffle dans l'AT. Enquête anthropologique à travers l'histoire théologique d'Israël.* [Paris: Presses Universitaires de France, 1962] 281). According to W. I. Wolverton (*CJT* 9 [1963] 92), there is no concept of universal immanence here, but simply Yahweh's personal presence with the individual believer, as in 23:6.

8.a. The accessibility of Sheol to Yahweh receives a dual treatment in the OT. It is often denied in a stress that fellowship with God and enjoyment of his blessing are confined to this life (85:6 [5]; Jonah 2:5 [4]). While it is not within Yahweh's sphere of blessing, it is within his sphere of sovereignty (Job 26:6; Amos 9:2). Cf. H. W. Wolff, *Anthropology,* 106–8; N. J. Tromp, *Primitive Conceptions,* 199–201.

9.a. The imperfect verb has a conditional force here and also in v 18 (GKC § 159c).

9.b. Underlying the imagery is a mythological concept (cf. F. Stolz, *Strukturen,* 210), but for the psalmist it has become a vivid metaphor. LXX *S* took the object as כְּנָפַי "my wings (to the dawn i.e. the east)." The attractiveness of this pointing, adopted by JB, NEB and GNB, is that it provides two parallel areas, as in v 8, but probably the contrast is here more subtle for stylistic variation.

10.a. The emendation of תַּנְחֵנִי "guide" to תִּקָּחֵנִי "take" (H. Gunkel, *Die Psalmen,* 591; Kraus, *Psalmen,* 1093; *et al.*) to improve the parallelism and avoid a positive sense of providential care is not warranted nor is Dahood's repointing to תַּנְחֵנִי "you would lower (your hand) upon me" (*Psalms III,* 290). *S,* claimed by Gunkel to support the former change, simply inverted the two verbs of v 10. The resumptive יַחֵנִי in v 24 (cf. note 1.b.) guarantees the present text.

11.a. For the imperfect consecutive see GKC §§ 11x, 159f. Kraus (*Psalmen,* 1098) and others have found reference to a magic spell here. However, K.-H. Bernhardt ("Gottesvorstellung," 23 and note 20) has observed that vv 8–11 cover a range of human impossibilities.

11.b. Despite 88:13 (12) an interpretation in terms of Sheol (G. A. Danell, *Psalm 139,* 16; Dahood, *Psalms III,* 291) is unlikely (Tromp, *Primitive Conceptions,* 95–96).

11.c. The semantic thought is fairly clear from the context, but the etymology of יְשׁוּפֵנִי is most uncertain. Generally the text is emended to יְשׁוּכֵנִי "cover me," with the presumed support of σ′ Hier (*BHS*). G. R. Driver ("Some Hebrew Verbs, Nouns and Pronouns," *JTS* 30 [1929] 375–77) suggested that שׁוּף be related to Arab. *šaffa,* used (in the fourth form) of a cloud approaching close to and skimming over the earth, and thus here "sweep close over"; he observed the close relationship between double *'ayin* and *'ayin waw* verbs. Dahood (*Psalms III,* 291), restructuring the clause, has related to Arab. *šāfa* "watch."

12.a. The last clause is commonly rejected as a gloss (cf. *BHS*). For a thorough presentation of the case for and against see Holman, *BZ* 14 (1970) 62–64. He finally accepts its authenticity, as a rhetorical climax (cf. J. Muilenburg, "A Study in Hebrew Rhetoric: Repetition and Style," in *Congress Volume Copenhagen 1953* [VT Sup 1; Leiden: E. J. Brill, 1953] 108). S. Wagner ("Theologie," 365–66) finds the clause theologically significant as the conclusion to vv 11–12a: the dualism of a contrast between light and darkness is transcended and neutralized by Yahweh, unlike the gods of surrounding nations.

13.a. Heb. כִּי "indeed" is probably the affirmative particle here (Dahood, *Psalms III,* 292) rather than causal.

13.b. For the stem קָנָה see Anderson, *Psalms,* 909; cf. 104:24.

13.c. These organs function here, as elsewhere in the OT, as the seat of the conscience (Wolff, *Anthropology,* 65–66, 96).

13.d. The homonymous stem סכך "cover" is less likely than the one meaning "weave together," a byform of שׂכך: cf. Job 10:11. The allusion to cloth woven with different colored threads in v 15 (רֻקַּמְתִּי "I was worked") lends support.

14.a. MT "I am wonderful" (". . . wonderfully made" in KJV and RV is a rather forced rendering) is a minority reading in the total witness to the ancient text: LXX* *S* Hier imply נִפְלֵית, which the parallel v 6 favors. 11QPsᵃ נוֹרָא אַתָּה "you are awesome" lends some support (for נפליתי it has נפלאות "wonders").

14.b. Heb. נוֹרָאוֹת "awesome" is adverbial (GKC § 118p).

14.c. V 14aβ has been regarded as a gloss (cf. *BHS*). Holman (*BZ* 14 [1970] 67) has compared the semantic field of Exod 34:10 with that of v 14a.

14.d. The need for a colon parallel to v 15aα suggests a fresh division of lines and that the consonants of ידעת "know" be pointed יָדַעְתְּ: cf. vv 1–6 (Gunkel, *Die Psalmen*, 591; *et al.*; see further *Form/Structure/Setting*). Holman (*BZ* 14 [1970] 68) has aptly compared 69:6 (5); the non-plene writing ידעת in 11QPsᵃ may lend support. A change of מאד "much, exceedingly" to מאז "from of old" (Gunkel, *Die Psalmen*, 591) is not necessary nor is Dahood's interpretation of MT as מֶאָד, a dialectal form of מאז (*Psalms III*, 293–94).

15.a. For this individual treatment of creation see Wolff, *Anthropology*, 96–97. The final phrase appears to be based upon a folk belief of man's creation within the earth (cf. Wolff, *Anthropology*, 96–97). Either the psalmist speaks of his origin in primeval terms of that of mankind (cf. Job 10:9), giving a quite different perspective to that of v 13 (Danell, *Psalm 139*, 18), or else he simply uses it as a metaphor for the earlier one (cf. JB "in the limbo of the womb"; W. Eichrodt, *Theology*, vol. 2, 141). R. Pytel (*Folia Orientalia* 13 [1971] 262–66), since the final phrase is elsewhere associated with death (63:10 [9]; cf. Ezek 26:20), has interpreted the verse as a survey of life from the womb (v 13aβ), reading עָשִׂיתוֹ "you made it" (cf. LXX), to the grave רְקַבְתּוֹ "(and) you allow it to rot."

16.a. Heb. גלם "embryo" is thus used in Talmudic Hebrew. V 16aα has a staccato ring (see note 16.b.): it is possible that it is to be taken with v 15aβ1-b as a tricolon (3+3+3), in which case the latter of the two explanations offered in note 15.b. is the correct one (T. H. Gaster, *Thespis: Ritual, Myth, and Drama in the Ancient Near East* [New York: Schuman, 1950] 349), and the rest of v 16 forms another tricolon (3+2+3). Yet v 15aα does seem to look forward to v 15aβ. Attempts have been made to tie the first two cola of v 16 more closely in sense, notably by Gunkel (*Die Psalmen*, 592) who read גְּמָלַי "my deeds" with the apparent support of S *pwrᶜny* "my recompense" (cf. *HALAT*, 186b) and by Dahood (*Psalms III*, 295), reading גֵּלֶי-ם "my life stages," with an enclitic *mem*. Either provides an antecedent for כלם "all of them," which otherwise has to be taken as anticipatory.

16.b. For God's "book" in the OT see W. Schottroff, *Gedenken*, 303.

16.c. The stem יצר "mold, devise" is used of the divine purpose in the qal elsewhere (BDB, 427b, 428a). For the determinism of this verse see G. von Rad, *Wisdom in Israel*, 263, 282). He commented that in the pre-apocalyptic concept the individual's freedom was scarcely affected; in this psalm v 4 seems to confirm his comment. Here determination of length of life is evidently in view: cf. Exod 32:32–33; Job 14:5; Ps 69:30 (29) (Gunkel, *Die Psalmen*, 588; A. Weiser, *Psalms*, 806).

16.d. V 16b is of uncertain meaning, not helped by the dual tradition in MT, לו "to him" (Q) and לא "not" (K). E. Würthwein (*VT* 7 [1957] 179 note 1) took as a gloss referring to the Sabbath "and to him [God] belongs one of them." M. Mannati (*ZAW* 83 [1971] 259) took אחד "one" as referring to man with LXX: "and no man was in them," i.e. before any man had taken part in the succession of days.

17.a. An Aramaic sense "be difficult" for Heb. יקר "be precious" (cf. Dan 2:11) is demanded by the structural parallelism with the stem פלא "be wonderful, difficult" in vv 6, 14 (cf. *Form/Structure/Setting*). Krašovec (*BZ* 18 [1974] 226) envisages a *double entendre*: God's thoughts are difficult where toleration of the wicked is concerned (v 19), but also precious to the psalmist who gladly takes God's side (vv 21–22). His exegesis is linked with his structural view of v 17 as beginning a strophe, vv 17–22 (see *Form/Structure/Setting*). It appears unduly complicated, especially since v 18 seems to interrupt the presumed development of thought.

17.b. Heb. לי "to/of me," put at the beginning for emphasis, is probably governed by רעיך "your thoughts": cf. חשב ל 40:18 (17); 41:8 and חשב אל 40:6 (5); Hos 7:15.

18.a. MT "I awoke" is problematic. A reference to a morning trial (cf. 17:15; cf. W. Beyerlin, *Die Rettung*, 144–46), though possible in the total context of the psalm, would be abrupt. H. Schmidt who explained similarly (*Das Gebet*, 26 note 2) later abandoned this interpretation (*Die Psalmen*, 244). The traditional Christian understanding in terms of resurrection (so σ' *Tg.*), revived by Dahood (*Psalms III*, 296), is both contextually inappropriate (J. G. S. S. Thompson, "Sleep: An Aspect of Jewish Anthropology," *VT* 5 [1955] 424), who noted that death has not previously been mentioned in the psalm) and probably theologically anachronistic. Revocalization as הֲקִצֹּתִי "come to an end" (cf. three mss. cited by *BHK* as reading הקצתי) would at least fit the context, though it requires the postulation of a second stem קצץ as a (hiphᶜil) denominative from קץ (KB, 849a): cf. Sir 18: 4–7; 43:27–30 (Gunkel, *Die Psalmen*, 589). Rashi so understood the verb (Danell, *Psalm 139*, 19). The perfect then has a conditional force (cf. GKC § 159h): cf. the imperfect consecutive at v 11. Michel's objection that v 18a states that no end would be possible (*Tempora*, 245) is prosaic: the progression of thought may be as in Hos 9:11–12, 16; Mic 6:14.

18.b. Lit. "I (would be) with you still."

19.a. E. Baumann (*EvT* 11 [1951] 187–90) observed that the psalmist desires not so much the destruction of persons but of their pernicious influence, while Kirkpatrick (*Psalms*, 790) commented that evil for him was no abstract idea, it was embodied in evil men.

19.b. N. A. van Uchelen has concluded from his study of the phrase in the Psalter that it has a figurative sense (*OTS* 15 [1969] 210–12).

19.c. Only here in the whole psalm is direct address to God abandoned. It is possible that emotion has caused the change, but the abruptness of the reversion to divine address in v 20 suggests that the third person imperfect form implied by S Tg. (יָסוּרוּ "they leave") is original (cf. *BHS*). MT may betray the influence of 6:9 (8; Gunkel, *Die Psalmen*, 592) and/or 119:115.

20.a. An emendation יְמָרְךָ "defy you" is often advocated on the evidence of ε', a Greek translation used by Origen (*BHS*). The rarity of a personal object with the verb אמר "say" (cf. BDB, 56a) might favor it. However, it is noteworthy that the phrase אַנְשֵׁי דָמִים "men of blood" in v 19b is closely associated in the Psalms with wrongful speech (cf. van Uchelen, *OTS* 15 [1969] 208–10).

20.b. Heb. נשא "lift up" is either an orthographical variant or a scribal slip for נָשְׂאוּ: cf. Jer 10:5 and 11QPs ª נשאו. In consequence of the former note it is probable that an ellipsis of קוֹל "voice" is to be assumed, as in Isa 3:7; 42:2, 11.

20.c. Heb. עָרֶיךָ ("your cities"?—thus H. Junker, *Bib* 30 [1949] 207) is generally emended, either to עָלֶיךָ "(rise) against you" (Gunkel, *Die Psalmen*, 593; *et al.*) or to שִׁמְךָ "(utter) your name" (cf. BDB, 670b). The latter, however, although it neatly echoes Exod 20:7, is too far from MT consonantally (Gunkel, *Die Psalmen*, 593). G. R. Driver, (*JTS* 44 [1943] 22) read עָדֶיךָ with several Heb. mss., taking it as עָדְיְךָ "(take in vain) your onset" and comparing Arab. *ᶜadwa* "onset." The older view that equated it with Aram. עָר "enemy" (Dan 4:16) is worth reviving: α'σ' Hier Tg. so interpreted. It is not necessarily the counterpart of Heb. צָר: it may be derived from the stem עוּר (L. Delekat, *Asylie und Schutzorakel am Zionheiligtum* [Leiden: E. J. Brill, 1967] 105 note 2, following Levy and Jastrow; cf. the comparison of Aram. עָרָד "objection" in BDB, 1108a). Then it is to be construed appositionally (cf. Danell, *Psalm 139*, 20).

21.a. Kraus (*Psalmen*, 1100) has drawn attention to the psalmist's concern for Yahweh's honor: his hatred is by no means simply egotistic. Weiser (*Psalms*, 807, cf. 77) regarded the petition of vv 19–22 as "a kind of renunciation or protestation of innocence," dissociating the psalmist from the wicked, and so they are "not to be understood as expressing merely human hatred and vindictiveness."

21.b. Heb. וּבְמִתְקוֹמְמֶיךָ is to be read with a few mss. (*BHK*; cf. 11QPs ª וממתי). Cf. especially 59:2(1): Holman (*BZ* 14 [1970] 219) has compared with vv 19–22 the semantic field of 59:2–3 (1–2).

24.a. The repeated דֶּרֶךְ "way" indicates a reference to the common biblical concept of the two ways, one wrong and the other right (Weiser, *Psalms*, 808; cf. 1:6; Prov 12:28; Matt 7:13–14). More precise identification of the ways is here less certain. Heb. עֹצֶב "pain" (cf. 1 Chr 4:9; Isa 14:3) is difficult to relate to the context of denial of faithlessness. Is it a "hurtful way" (BDB, 780b) and, if so, is it a way that brings pain to others or one that leads to the pain of punishment (Weiser, *Psalms*, 807)? Delekat (*Asylie*, 255 note 5) suggested reading עֶצֶב, with reference to literal sickness: no guilt has made the psalmist ill. All such ambiguity is obviated by recourse to the homonymous term meaning "idol" (Isa 48:5; cf. Hos 10:6). A Jewish tradition to this effect is represented in Tg. (טָעֵין "those who go astray," esp. idolators) and also in 11QPs ª עצב. The latter apparently reflects an understanding as עָצָב "idol" (R. Tournay, "Recension de *The Psalms Scroll of Qumran Cave II* par J. A. Sanders," *RB* 73 [1966] 261). KB 730a emended to עֹקֶב "insidiousness" on the basis of Hier "deceit" and S "lying" (cf. Gunkel, *Die Psalmen*, 593), but more probably both these translations and LXX "iniquity" reflect attempts to make עֹצֶב "pain" meaningful.

24.b. If the former phrase has been rightly understood, it is probable that עוֹלָם be rendered thus: cf. Jer 6:16; 18:15 (in a context of idolatry) and Tg. "the way of upright men of old."

Form/Structure/Setting

An obvious break occurs in the psalm between vv 18 and 19 in both form and tone. The passionate outburst of vv 19–22 and the appeals within vv 19–24 contrast strangely with the quieter statement of the preceding material. H. Schmidt (*Die Psalmen*, 246) considered that vv 19–24 were a subsequent addition by the same author. M. Buttenwieser (*The Psalms Chronologically Treated* [New York: KTAV, 1938] 535–36) judged that vv 19–22 were misplaced, vv 19–20 originally belonging after 140:12 and vv 21–22 after 141:4. Both these suggestions appear influenced by cultural considerations. It has been claimed that the psalm would be one of the most beautiful in the Psalter if it finished at v 18 (E. Reuss, cited by Würthwein, *VT* [1957] 170). In fact, an impression of integrity is given by the device of inclusion, evidenced especially in the stems ידע "know" and חקר "examine" in vv 1, 23. Holman (*VT* 21 [1970] 301, 308) has cited too דרך, דרכי "way(s)" in vv 3, 24, the divine name in vv 1 (4), 21 and the stem קום "rise" in vv 2, 21.

The two unequal parts into which the psalm falls have been subjected to thorough analysis by Holman. He finds in vv 1–8 a parabola or concentric structure (*VT* 21 [1970] 302–7). At the center stands v 10, and it is surrounded at equidistant points by mutually echoing material. The note of praise in v 6 is matched at v 14, both including the terms ידע "know" and פלא "be wonderful." Heb. (רעי(ך "thought(s)" occurs in vv 2, 17, though for Holman only homonymously. Vv 7, 13 introduce new material, while vv 4, 16 both contain כל "all" and the motif of divine knowledge.

Holman has traced a fascinating network. However, it must be asked whether the content of v 10 is as important as so crucial a structural role would suggest. Moreover, the hymnic asides of vv 6, 14 seem to be further matched in vv 17–18, which find no comparable role in the above scheme. Holman does not need to do so because his understanding of v 17 removes the motif of direct praise of God, but as usually understood the passage cries out for some alignment with vv 6, 14. He has rendered a valuable service in demonstrating the close interlocking of vv 1–18 and also the role of vv 19–24 as a climax, both radical and integral, to the foregoing.

A common way of dividing the psalm is to find four units or strophes, vv 1–6, 7–12, 13–18, 19–24 (e.g. J. A. Montgomery, *JBL* 64 [1945] 383; Würthwein, *VT* 7 [1957] 176–78; S. Wagner, "Theologie," 359). It is easier to substantiate this structuring in some parts than in others. Vv 1–6 are bound together by the key word ידע "know" with Yahweh as subject (a noun in v 6), no less than four times. V 6 forms a fitting devotional conclusion. V 7 takes a new turn, with its rhetorical questions as prelude to statements concerning the psalmist's inability to hide from the omnipresent God. A third strophe could begin at v 13 with the new theme of God's creation of the psalmist, developed in subsequent verses. The conclusion of devotional praise in vv 17–18 neatly matches the end of the first strophe. Its greater length marks the climax of three parallel strophes before a fourth, which is different from the others, like the fourth beast of Dan 7. However, a difficulty arises in the presumed third strophe: v 14 like vv 6, 17–18 contains the motif of direct praise. Holman's scheme made some allowance for this phenomenon, but the present analysis ignores it. M. Mannati (*ZAW* 83 [1971] 257–61) has attempted to deal with this anomaly. She observes that vv 15–16 continue the theme of v 13, while v 14 breaks the chain of thought, appears to possess no metrical rhythm and has the maladroit repetition of the stem פלא "be wonderful." Accordingly v 14 may be judged a secondary prose comment. Then all the strophes have the same pattern, size and proportion: an introductory line (in the first case a colon) prefaces a central unit of three lines with strong unity of theme and form, which is followed by two concluding lines which have a change of construction and theme (vv 1 + 2–4 + 5–6; 7 + 8–10 + 11–12; 13 + 15–16 + 17–18; 19 + 20–22 + 23). A similar concern for uniformity of size encouraged Würthwein (*VT* [1957] 179 note 1) to delete v 14a and the first three words of v 16 as glosses, so as to achieve strophes of six lines throughout. Mannati's scheme is attractive, apart perhaps from a flaw that v 20 seems closer to v 19 than to vv 21–22. Metrically v 14 can be treated as in the *Translation* and in *Notes/Comments* above. The doubled term can be explained as emotional exuberance (cf. כל "all" in vv 3–4). Heb. מעשיך "your works" in the sense of works of creation (cf. 104:24) fits the preceding context.

R. Lapointe (*CBQ* 33 [1971] 401 note 40) has made a significant attempt to do justice to v 14. He has briefly suggested that the second strophe ends at v 14a. Then the first three all conclude in similar fashion, with a wondering exclamation (v 6) or with hymnic phrasing (vv 14a, 17–18). The suggestion is worth developing. At first sight it cuts across the thematic divisions cited above. It may be, however, that they were defined too sharply. Thematic overlap appears in v 5, which heralds the motif of the divine presence celebrated in vv 7–10, before the praise of v 6 which closes the first strophe. Likewise it is feasible that before the praise of v 14, v 13 introduces a motif to be developed in the next strophe. A. D. Rittersprach ("Rhetorical Criticism and the Song of Hannah," in *Rhetorical Criticism,* ed. J. J. Jackson and M. Kessler [Pittsburgh: Pickwick Press, 1974] 73) has observed that a strophe may build on a closing note of the previous one. The merit of this scheme is that, like Holman's, it recognizes as strategic the parallelism of vv 6–14, including the occurrence of the term פלא. Repetition is frequently a key to structure (cf. J. Muilenburg, "Hebrew Rhetoric," 97–111).

The dimensions of the fourth strophe have been variously determined. Dahood (*Psalms III*, 285, 296) makes it run from v 17 to v 22 on stylistic grounds, לי "to me" in vv 17, 22 being regarded as an inclusion (cf. Krašovec, *BZ* 18 [1974] 226). The layout in *BHS* links vv 17–20. Dahood (*Psalms III*, 284–85) has taken vv 23–24 together with v 1 as the frame of the psalm in consequence of his own grammatical analysis of v 1 (see note 1.b.). Rather than forming a specific frame the verses are better taken as exhibiting overall inclusion (see above). In strophic analysis there is always a danger of confusing minor divisions with major ones (cf. Anderson, *Psalms,* 911, who has distinguished vv 19–22 from vv 23–24).

Holman has observed correctly that a deep caesura lies between vv 18 and 19. The preceding material belongs closely together, marked inclusively by the repetition of רע "thought" in vv 2, 17. It may be divided into three strophes, vv 1–6, 7–14a, 14b–18, each concluding on a note of direct praise in vv 6, 14, 17–18, with the last and longer passage functioning besides as a conclusion. In the first two strophes vv 5, 13 anticipate the next ones; this element is necessarily lacking in the third. In the first strophe the body of material in vv 1–4 is introduced in the first line (N.B. the divine name in vv 1, 4), and likewise in the second v 7 introduces vv 8–10 (cf. Würthwein, *VT* 7 [1957] 177), but there is a further development of thought in vv 11–12, which is what makes it a longer strophe. In the third strophe the initial colon serves as a preface to vv 15–16. This strophe has its own marks of inclusion: the stems עצם ("bone," "be many") in vv 15, 17 and ספר ("book," "count") in vv 16, 18. In the first and third strophes the main material consists of four lines; in the second there is an extra two.

In vv 1–18 there is evidence of a loose chiastic structure, which is akin to Holman's concentric scheme. The second strophe is longer. In its main part it looks back: distance (vv 8–10, cf. v 2) is no security against God. It also looks forward: God has unimpeded vision (v 12, cf. vv 15–16). In the first and third, of uniform length, כל "all" in vv 3–4, 16 and the negative clauses of v 4a, 16b both emphasize the completeness of Yahweh's knowledge. This parallelism supports taking ידעת "know" in v 14b with the third strophe (see note 14.d.). The key word of the first then reappears in the third, which has a resumptive and reinforcing role.

Holman (*VT* 21 [1970] 307) has finely analyzed vv 19–24 as consisting of two antithetically parallel sub-units, vv 19–20 and 23–24, separated by a synonymously parallel pair of verses, vv 21–22; each of the three sub-units employs a different divine term, יהוה, אלוה and אל. The third term significantly concludes not only this second major part of the psalm but also the first, at v 17, while לי "to me" is associated with the ends of both, at vv 17, 22 (*VT* 21 [1970] 308). It may be added that this section gathers up material from the earlier one. It recapitulates the key verbs of its three strophes and repeats them as imperatives: ידע "know" from the first strophe (also the third), נחה "guide" from the second (v 10) and ראה "see" from the third (v 16).

Structural analysis provides a strong argument against E. Baumann's interpretation of the psalm (*EvT* 11 [1951] 187–90, followed by Eichrodt, *Theology*, vol. 1, 491), developing a suggestion of Weiser's (*Psalms*, 805). He postulated a turning point at v 13. In vv 1–12 the psalmist relates his former resentment at God's patronizing, intolerable control of his life; he contemplated fleeing like Jonah but judged it impossible. It was only when he gained a new insight into God's creative care that he was converted to identify with God's purposes. However, there is no structural indication of a break at this point within the tightly knit vv 1–18. It is preferable to try to view the section in terms of an even development of an overall theme from various angles.

The issue of the form of Ps 139 has engendered considerable discussion. Basically it is an individual prayer, in that it is addressed to God throughout. From the standpoint of primary genres it exhibits a mixed form. Vv 19–24 read like an individual complaint. The negative appeal of v 19 echoes that which regularly occurs in the complaint (cf. 17:13–14; 74:22–23). The two-sided perspective of vv 19–20, 23–24 is reminiscent of the double wish or petition used in the complaint (cf. 5:11–12 [10–11]; 35:26–27). Vv 21–22 are a strong assertion of innocence (Gunkel, *Die Psalmen*, 589). The earlier and longer portion of the psalm is quite different. It takes the form of a hymn or at least a meditation employing hymnic features. It has hymnic forms, rhetorical questions in vv 7, 17 and a verb of praising with a causal clause in v 14; it has hymnic material, such as praise of Yahweh's wonderfulness and awesomeness in v 14, of his works and thoughts in vv 14, 17 and of creation in vv 13, 15–16 (Gunkel, *Die Psalmen*, 587; cf. too H.-P. Müller, "Gattung," 346–49). Striking features, however, are the unusual but not unparalleled lack of an introduction and a subjectivity of treatment which breaks out of the form of the genre (Gunkel, *Die Psalmen*, 587). Müller ("Gattung," 349–51) has also drawn attention to wisdom motifs, which are found elsewhere in hymns (cf. Gunkel and Begrich, *Einleitung*, 87): the phenomenological rather than historical treatment, divine knowledge and presence and the ethic of the two ways.

To establish the overall unity of the psalm, to which the dominant "I—you" perspective of both sections points, it is necessary to subordinate one of the two types to the other. Thus G. Fohrer (*Introduction*, 292) has briefly characterized it as a (cultic) individual complaint, while C. Westermann (*Praise*, 139) has with almost equal brevity taken it as a psalm of praise majoring in the motif of creation. In support of Westermann might be cited Ps 104, which he links with this psalm: it concludes in vv 31–35 with complaint elements which are re-used as vehicles of praise and so are integrated into the hymn. However, in this case the complaintlike ending functions as a demarcated climax, as the study of structure has shown. Psalm 90 is a more fruitful parallel (S. Mowinckel, *The Psalms in Israel's Worship*, vol. 1, 24, 91). It is a communal complaint addressed to Yahweh, which delays its appeal until vv 13–17; the earlier and larger part of the psalm serves as a basis for the concluding appeal. The earlier portion is dominated by the concept of God's eternity, which is applied by contrast to the people's plight as a motivation for him to intervene. In the light of this parallel, vv 19–24 may be regarded as the key to the earlier part (R. Pytel, *Folia Orientalia* 13 [1971] 259). The psalm can be viewed as an individual complaint in a developed form, prefaced by a long passage praising divine attributes which the sufferer finds relevant to his situation. Comparable is Kraus's definition as an individual song of thanksgiving, to which his own view of the relationship between vv 1 and 23 compels him (see note 1.b.).

More precisely Mowinckel (*Psalmenstudien*, vol. 5, 91 note 1) defined Ps 139 as a complaint expressing innocence. The literary type of protestations of innocence, in the course of which the psalmist strongly affirms his loyalty to God, has been identified elsewhere in the Psalter, notably in Pss 5, 7, 17 (Gunkel and Begrich, *Einleitung*, 238–39, 251). Mowinckel explained the references to divine omniscience as a motif of innocence: God knows that he has been faithful. The protestation of innocence is here enlarged to cover most of the psalm, vv 1–18, in an extended treatment of different aspects of omniscience. Kraus (*Psalmen*, 1095) has characterized the section as containing elements of "judgment doxology," in which God's judgment is praised as infallible. Koole ("Psaume 139," 177) has fairly objected that this form is associated with confession of sin; but at least it invites comparison with that form. Müller ("Gattung," 353) has claimed that vv 1–18 contain no references to guilt or innocence, punishment or sparing. If, however, it does feature motifs associated with a claim of innocence (see further *Explanation*), they constitute implicit references.

Can a setting for the psalm be established? H. Schmidt (*Das Gebet*, 26 note 2) briefly included the psalm in a group of "prayers of the accused," for which he envisaged a judicial trial in a religious setting (cf. Exod 22:7–8 [8–9]; Deut 17:8–13; 1 Kgs 8:31–32); later he explained the psalm otherwise (*Die Psalmen*, 244–46). L. Delekat (*Asylie*, 253–56) and W. Beyerlin (*Die Rettung*, 11) have revived his forensic thesis in different forms. The former has reconstructed a complex procedure of an accused man seeking asylum at the temple, undergoing an ordeal and devoting the rest of his life to temple service (cf. v 18b). The latter did not include Ps 139 in his study, on the ground that it refers not to direct enemies of the psalmist but to God's enemies who have become his own. He conceives of a religious court which handled special cases. In general he is much less speculative than Delekat; in particular he attacks his notion of asylum in the Psalter as a literalization of metaphor. He claims that the eleven psalms he places in this category are statements made by the accused at various stages in the court proceedings, such as at a preliminary investigation.

The most notable exponent of Schmidt's basic thesis with regard to Ps 139 has been Würthwein (*VT* 7 [1957] 165–82), who was anticipated in some respects by A. Bentzen and Danell (*Psalm 139*). His conclusions have been largely followed by Weiser (*Psalms*, 802), Kraus (*Psalmen*, 1093) and Dahood (*Psalms III*, 284). The psalmist, accused of idolatry, faces trial at a religious court and indirectly calls upon Yahweh to attest his innocence by appeal to his complete knowledge of him and his circumstances. Vv 1–18 are comparable to the self-cursing of Job 31. Holman (*VT* 21 [1970] 309–10) has specified the type of idolatry as sun worship. Developing a suggestion made by Danell (*Psalm 139*, 31–32) he has found solar aspects ascribed to Yahweh in vv 1–18 and the concept of the sun god as god of justice underlying the appeal in vv 19–24. All powers ascribed by others to the sun god are attributed to Yahweh in a dramatic affirmation of orthopraxis. However, Bernhardt ("Gottesvorstellung," 24–25), pointing to vv 11–12, has denied any intended relation to a pagan sun god in the psalm. J. M. Bullard ("Psalm 139," 147), while accepting the psalm's setting as a cultic trial, is reluctant to specify the charge.

Quite a different cultic setting was postulated by Danell (*Psalm 139*, 32–33), who characterizes it as the king's avowal after his enthronement, comparing 1 Kgs 3:5–15. More generally J. H. Eaton (*Kingship*, 83–84) suggested that it was composed for a king under attack from his enemies (cf. Dahood's reference [*Psalms III*, 284] to a religious leader).

Würthwein's conclusions have not gone unchallenged, perhaps because they have met with widespread appeal and endorsement. Gunkel's characteristic assessment of the psalm as a non-cultic, private psalm in which older, cultic forms have been re-used, dismissed by Würthwein as the superimposing of a Protestant ideal (*VT* 7 [1957] 167; cf. in general K. Koch, *The Growth of the Biblical Tradition: The Form-Critical Method* [Tr. S. M. Cupitt; London:

A. & C. Black, 1969] 177), has been developed in a sapiential direction. O. Eissfeldt defined the psalm as a wisdom poem, "a devotional reflection . . . perhaps occasioned by the suspicion . . . that [the worshiper] has associated with the impious" (*Introduction,* 125; cf. G. von Rad, *Wisdom in Israel,* 40, 48). Müller ("Gattung," 354) similarly associates it with the wisdom school as an example of wisdom piety intended for theological instruction (cf. Wagner, "Theologie," 374–76). Koole ("Psaume 139," 176–80), comparing the psalm's motifs and vocabulary with nature material in Job, interpreted it as a (non-cultic) defense of a wisdom teacher who as an exponent of international wisdom has fallen under suspicion of importing foreign religion. The psalm presents Israel's natural science and is the first evidence of a conflict between faith and science. H. Schüngel-Straumann (*BZ* 17 [1973] 46–51) has related the psalm even more closely to Job. Its setting is polemic within the wisdom schools and the issue is the right attitude to God. She lays weight on v 6, as an echo of Job 42:2–3. Using the individual complaint form, the psalmist describes God as essentially full of mystery and intensely personal in his relation to man. In vv 19–24 he is attacking those wisdom teachers who speak of God from a theorizing standpoint, like Job's friends. They are in fact God's enemies and teach what is alien to true faith and doctrine.

The basic issue of a cultic or sapiential setting is not easy to resolve. As in all cultures, primary forms were capable of straying to a new habitat. But the traffic need not be reckoned as one way. One can conceive of wisdom elements in psalms as well as pure wisdom psalms; in such cases there is no necessity to see a clear-cut demarcation between wisdom and cult. R. E. Murphy ("Wisdom Psalms," 156–67) has argued on these lines and expressly excluded Ps 139 from the wisdom category: rather, it has wisdom elements incorporated in it. Similarly J. K. Kuntz ("Canonical Wisdom Psalms," 206–8), finding nine wisdom terms used in the psalm, urges that "it lacks sufficient stylistic and ideological peculiarities to warrant inclusion in the wisdom psalms category." "Its strikingly personal utterances and sustained and personal address to the deity signal its ineptness as a wisdom psalm. The sage was not the only individual in ancient Israel who was given to thinking about the omniscience and omnipresence of the deity."

Apart from Job 10:11, the parallels which have been adduced between the psalm and Job do not compel dependence; most can be found too in non-wisdom literature. Similarity of dramatic situation—and how typical in this respect is the book of Job?—provides reason for some overlap. A common tradition may underlie Job 10:11. It is significant that in Job 10:8–11 quite different images are used in quick succession, behind which "perhaps several quite lengthy creation stories lie" (F. I. Andersen, *Job: An Introduction and Commentary* [London: Inter-Varsity Press, 1976] 154).

There are no anti-cultic features in the psalm. Bernhardt ("Gottesvorstellung," 25–31) has shown that there need be no conflict between divine omnipresence and the concept of a holy place (cf. 1 Kgs 8:27). It is noteworthy that even within a wisdom milieu scholars have found it necessary to account for the psalm's background of accusation. The setting of a cultic trial would provide a reasonable explanation for this and for the psalm's mixed form of complaint and innocence motifs: cf. E. Gerstenberger's judicious acceptance of a religio-forensic setting in general ("Psalms," 204–5). The psalm provides no evidence permitting a precise reconstruction of its role within forensic procedure. In fact it is doubtful whether so particular a cultic setting is necessary. Beyerlin's omission of Ps 139 from his own list of juridical psalms (see above) cannot lightly be dismissed. It is more likely that the psalm is simply an individual complaint, as the similarly structured Ps 90 is a communal complaint. More precisely it is a psalm of innocence. In the background lies false accusation of some kind, but its nature is left unrevealed. The negative reference to idolatry in v 24 is merely a general profession of loyalty. The speaker brings a complaint to the temple, seeking to obtain vindication via a divine oracle and to this end affirming his innocence and faithfulness to God.

Parallels between the psalm and non-Israelite religious literature have been observed with respect to an omniscient god of judgment. Strikingly close in sentiment is the Indian hymn to Varuna in Atharva-Veda 4:16. H. Hommel (ZAW 47 [1929] 110–24), who cited, too, a Hittite parallel and an El Amarna one concerning the divine Pharaoh, thought in terms of Hittite culture as a bridge between India and Israel. However, the parallels are better judged as independent, natural religious developments (R. Pettazzioni, The All-Knowing God, 107–8, in the course of a comparative religious study; Bernhardt, "Gottesvorstellung," 26–28).

The date of the psalm has been considered beyond determination, e.g. by Kraus, Psalmen, 1095. Those who stress wisdom features tend to put it in the post-exilic period, as do those who link it closely with Job, although Dahood (Psalms III, 285) observes that the book has been assigned to the seventh century B.C. The Aramaisms of the psalm have been variously evaluated. Although early use of מלה "word" in v 2 (cf. Dahood, Psalms III, 287) can be established, it is less easy to explain away רע "thought" (with lamed as object sign?) in vv 2, 17, רבע "lie" in v 3, סלק "go up" in v 8, יקר "be difficult" in v 17 and קטל "kill" in v 19 (cf. the late אורה "light" in v 12). These forms, pervasive as they are, may well suggest a post-exilic date. The Davidic ascription, easily explicable in a royal setting (see above), is otherwise less so. The psalm exhibits but one possible early feature, the two preterite verbs in vv 13, 16, which in the presence of later ones give an impression of archaizing (D. A. Robertson, Linguistic Evidence, 54, 143, cf. 148). It may be that the psalm was taken into the Psalter from an earlier, Davidic collection to which it had been added by way of supplement.

Explanation

The speaker of the psalm has come to the sanctuary to present his prayer, hoping for a divine oracle to vindicate him. He protests his innocence of certain charges evidently brought against him, before Yahweh who has insight into the whole of his life. Every detail of his daily routine, every unspoken thought, is known to him. God knows him inside and out. In the OT such terms as "know," "examine," "see" (vv 16, 24) and "probe" (v 23) are used with God as subject to refer to his providential role as judge—not necessarily in a formal sense but by way of metaphor—punishing the guilty and acquitting the innocent. These associations of the terms used in the psalm indicate that the psalmist is in some situation of attack. The psalm is comparable with Jeremiah's appeal for vindication: "You know me, Yahweh; you see me and probe my attitude toward you. Pull them out like sheep for the slaughter" (Jer 12:3; cf. 15:15). The psalmist is not engaged in quiet reverie on a divine attribute, but pleading for justice to be done. A polemical element is implicit from the outset.

Yahweh is far away, as the transcendent God who observes all from heaven (cf. 11:4–5; Jer 23:23). He is also close by, surrounding the psalmist and controlling his movements. The psalmist reacts to God's omniscience with wonder: it is beyond his ken and too sublime to comprehend. In the area of knowledge a gulf lies between Yahweh and himself. He is driven to avow his own sense of limitation and inadequacy (cf. Job 42:2, 3b).

God's closeness, broached in v 5, is developed in the second strophe. The rhetorical question of v 7 is amplified into a series of examples: hypothetical locations above and below the earth and movement from east to west as speedy as the light of dawn. The key to the intent of the passage is the related statement of man's accessibility to Yahweh at Jer 23:24, in a divine threat of judgment: "Can a man hide himself in secret places so that I cannot see him? . . . Do I not fill heaven and earth?" So said the God who was great enough to see through the subjective claims of rival prophets (Jer 23:25–32). In similar fashion the psalmist states his awareness of his own availability to the divine judge. He cannot escape God: "before him no creature is hidden" (Heb 4:13; cf. the kinship of 4:12 to Ps 139:2, 4). Vv 7–10 imaginatively amplify Yahweh's knowledge of all his ways (v 3) from a different perspective. The personal life of the psalmist is related spatially to divine universality. More commonly in a treatment of God's judicial knowledge it is Yahweh's eyes that survey the world (cf. 11:4–5; Jer 16:17), but Jer 23:24b provides a parallel. The psalmist can hide nothing from God, and it is by this principle that he has lived. He has not tried to "hide deep from Yahweh" his "counsel" (Isa 29:15). The divine presence means God's personal control: if vv 7–10 develop v 3, they also amplify v 5. He controls not only the psalmist but the whole world, so that nowhere in God's world could anyone evade him: "Sheol and Abaddon lie open before Yahweh, how much more the minds of men!" (Prov 15:11).

V 11 veers to a related motif belonging to the sphere of divine judgment, as in Job 34:22: "There is no gloom or deep darkness where evildoers may hide themselves." Divine vision is a common variation of Yahweh's judicial knowledge (cf. Job 22:13–14). The superhuman character of divine sight irrespective of light—contrast Job 22:11a—is being affirmed. The link between the implicit reference to God's seeing in v 12 and mention of the kidneys as the organ of the conscience in v 13 may be found in Jer 20:20, an appeal to Yahweh as "you who test the righteous, who see kidneys and heart." The sequence of thought is as follows: God sees the psalmist at all times, even in the dark, and he sees into the depths of his being, into his conscience— and that is no surprise since God was responsible for its creation. The thought moves from facet to facet of divine judgment. Again the speaker confesses himself overwhelmed by awe at the majestic conception of Yahweh's relationship to himself and to the rest of the world (cf. vv 8–9) by right of creation.

He returns in the third strophe to express his underlying theme, God's complete knowledge of himself, varied in parallelism by reference to non-hiding, as in 69:6 (5). Inability to hide from Yahweh, treated from spatial and temporal aspects in vv 9–12, is now applied to the making of the individual, thus developing the motif of v 13. It is a further facet of the manifold concept of the divine judicial scrutiny, which finds expression in Isa 29:16: "Shall the potter be regarded as the clay?" (cf. the semantic field of 29:15 with the earlier part of the psalm). The statement there that "he has no understanding" is a repudiation of divine insight and human culpability (cf. Ps 94:7 and also 33:15). With similar (but positive) reasoning applied personally, the psalmist regards himself as the object of God's creative workmanship before his birth. The explicit reference to seeing is a reminder of the overall judicial theme.

Divine insight is matched by foresight. The motif of God's book can have forensic overtones: cf. Dan 7:10. The exhortation in *Pirqe Aboth* 2:1, "Know what is above you: a seeing eye and a hearing ear and all your deeds written in a book," is a significant parallel, except that the book reference is not prospective. Yahweh knows all the psalmist's days, the period of his life (cf. Gen 25:7).

In vv 17–18 the speaker draws the strophe and the whole psalm thus far to an end with a final exclamation of praise. If his own thoughts are an open book to God (v 2), God's are incomprehensible. He is filled with a sense of the divine mystery as a result of Yahweh's intense concern for him. His little mind is baffled by confrontation with the comprehensive, infinite mind of God. This is his reaction to a variety of motifs associated with the overall theme of God as the judge who knows men's hearts and holds them responsible. There is little new in the psalm, viewed atomistically: traditional motifs clustering around this concept and involving a number of theological ideas for this single end, are taken up. The contribution of the psalm is their skillful amassing in continuous array. The psalmist is trying to clear his name and establish his integrity in the spirit of the disciple Peter: "Lord, you know everything; you know that I love you" (John 21:17).

All this material proves to be the prelude to a more direct protestation of innocence in vv 19–22. He can safely call upon Yahweh to "kill the wicked." His appeal reveals that he does not identify himself with such, those who are utterly opposed to God's moral purposes. He utterly repudiates their company and attitude. Differentiating himself from all such, he aligns himself with Yahweh as his ally in the cause of morality. If God hates the wicked (11:5; cf. 5:7 [6]; Jer 12:8; Hos 9:15), the psalmist enthusiastically pledges his likemindedness (cf. 26:5). So he appeals to Yahweh as his moral champion who will vindicate his integrity, evidently impugned in some way. Just as in 26:1 a direct appeal for such vindication ("Vindicate me, Yahweh, for I have behaved with integrity") is followed by surrender to the divine scrutiny in 26:2, so in similar vein the psalmist here welcomes with a good conscience God's investigation. As too in 26:1 unswerving loyalty is professed, likewise the poet refers to idolatry as conspicuous by its absence. His dominant desire is rather to stay within the sacred traditions of Yahwistic faith, and to this end he needs to pray that divine guidance of his life, enjoyed hitherto (cf. v 10), may continue unabated.

The motif of innocence may strike the Christian as evidence of a pretentious spirit. However, as in the book of Job, there is no claim to moral perfection. The psalmist pleads not guilty to some charge, and it is in this relative light that his protestations are to be understood. The apostle Paul in turn knew the heartbreak of false blame. In a polemical context he took refuge in the positive theme of God's fair judgment and protested his integrity: "We preach not to please men but to please God who tests our hearts" (1 Thess 2:4; cf. 2 Cor 11:11; Gal 1:20). This opening of the conscience toward God brought with it a humbling, the psalmist found (vv 6, 14, 17). It also prompted praise, such as Paul too discovered when under attack: "The God and Father of the Lord Jesus, he who is blessed forever, knows that I do not lie" (2 Cor 11:31).

The psalm is remarkable for its subjective understanding of divine activity or, more precisely, its appreciation of the role of the individual as its object. The theology of the psalm is applied theology, the meaning of God for the believer in a particular situation of stress. It is God-consciousness not neatly intellectualized but let loose in his life in a frighteningly (v 14) pragmatic way. Not omniscience but constant exposure to divine scrutiny (Heb 4:13), not so much omnipresence as confrontation with an unseen Person at every turn, not omnipotence but divine control of a creature's life—these are the heart-searching themes of the psalm. Above all there is a sense of the existential reality of God: the divine "you" is as significantly real as the human "I." The Christian who professes faith in Immanuel may discover that his faith means something more, but certainly it should not mean less.

The Power of Prayer (140:1–14)

Bibliography

Barth, C. *Die Errettung vom Tode.* **Dahood, M.** " 'A Sea of Troubles': Notes on Psalms 55:3–4 and 140:10–11." *CBQ* 41 (1979) 604–7. **Greenberg, M.** "Psalm 140." *Eretz Israel* 14 (1978) 88–99. **Labuschagne, C. J.** "Some Remarks on the Translation and Meaning of *'āmartî* in the Psalms." *Die Ou-Testamentiese Werkgemeenskap* 5 (1962) 27–33.

Translation

1 Director's collection.[a] A Psalm. Davidic.
2 *Rescue me, Yahweh, from evil people;*   (4+3)
   from men [a] *of violence preserve me,*
3 *those who put their minds to evil schemes,*   (4+3)
   forever warmongering. [a]
4 *They use their tongues as incisively as a snake;* [a]   (3+4)
   secreted under their lips is a viper's venom. SELAH [c]

⁵ *Protect me, Yahweh, from the clutches of the wicked;*   (3+3+3)
   from men of violence preserve me,
   those who scheme to trip up my feet.
⁶ *The arrogant hide traps for me*   (3+3+3)
   and the corrupt ᵃ *spread nets;* ᵇ
   along the path they set snares ᶜ *for me.* SELAH

⁷ *I declare* ᵃ *to Yahweh,* ᵇ *"You are my God."*   (4+3)
   Listen, Yahweh, to my imploring cry.
⁸ *Yahweh, Lord, my strong savior,*   (3+4)
   you have given my head cover in time of battle.

⁹ *Do not grant, Yahweh, the desires* ᵃ *of the wicked.*   (4+3)
   As for their plots, O God, wrench them away. ᵃ SELAH
¹⁰ *The heads of those who surround me* ᵃ—   (2+3)
   may the harm done by their lips overwhelm them.
¹¹ *May coals be dropped* ᵃ *upon them,*   (3+4)
   may ill plunge them ᵇ *into pits,* ᶜ *no more to rise.*
¹² *May the slanderers lose their homes in the land;* ᵃ   (3+4)
   as for the men of violence, may evil hunt them and push them down. ᵇ

¹³ *I* ᵃ *know that Yahweh will undertake*   (2+2+2)
   the cause of the afflicted, ᵇ
   securing justice for the needy.
¹⁴ *The righteous will surely give thanks to your name;*   (3+3)
   the upright will abide in your presence. ᵃ

Notes/Comments

1.a. See the note on 139:1.

2.a. The psalm oscillates between singular and plural references to the psalmist's enemies, singular here and in vv 5a, 9, 12, and plural in vv 3, 4, 5b, 6, 10, 11. They have been interpreted as leader and group respectively. More probably the singular forms have a collective force: the close links between vv 2 and 3, 5a and 5b, so suggest (cf. O. Keel, *Feinde*, 68–69).

3.a. MT יגורו from a stem גור "attack" is generally revocalized as יְגָרוּ "incite (wars)" from גרה: cf. Prov 15:18; 28:25; 29:22 and *HALAT*, 194a. The phrase is a metaphor for verbal attack: cf. 55:21 (22); 109:3; 120:7.

4.a. Cf. 58:5 (4) for this figure of sharp, biting speech. M. Dahood (*Psalms III*, 301) aptly refers to the hissing sounds of the three cases of *shin* in the third colon.

4.b. LXX ἀσπίς "asp." The parallelism indicates that some kind of snake is in view. KB (702b) claimed Arabic lexicographical evidence for identifying with the horned adder. Jewish tradition thought in terms of עכביש "spider" (11QPs ᵃ; *Tg.* עכוביתא).

4.c. For this rubric see H.-J. Kraus, *Psalmen*, 22–24; A. A. Anderson, *Psalms*, 48–49.

6.a. MT וחבלים "and cords" can hardly continue פח "trap" in view of the intervening לי "for me." The consonantal text is better pointed וְחֲבָלִים (H. Gunkel, *Die Psalmen*, 594; *et al.*). G. R. Driver (*HTR* 29 [1936] 192), followed by Dahood (*Psalms III*, 302) and NEB, preferred חֲבָלִים, a *qattāl* noun form (cf. GKC § 84 ᵇb) attested in Syriac. MT's vocalization was caused by confusion with the two terms for trap in the verse.

6.b. Sense and meter suggest that the caesura belongs here (*BHS*).

6.c. Heb. מקשים refers primarily to the striker in a trap, but can be used by extension for the whole trap (Driver, *JBL* 73 [1954] 136).

7.a. As in 31:15 (14); 142:6, אמרתי "I say" introduces a confession of contemporary faith.

Each time it is preceded by a description of complaint and followed by a petition for deliverance (C. J. Labuschagne, "Some Remarks," 28).

7.b. Dahood (*Psalms III*, 302) and NEB take the *lamed* as a vocative particle, "O Yahweh." Cf. 119:126 and note.

7.c. Heb. תחנוני "imploring" has the connotation of a claim made on the basis of a master-servant relationship (K. W. Neubauer, *Der Stamm CH N N*, 138). The occurrence of אדני "Lord" in v 8 is significant in this respect.

9.a. LXX need not presuppose מאותי (cf. *BHS*) but may simply have revocalized the consonantal text: cf. או "desire" in Prov 31:4 (K).

9.b. MT ירומו (אל-תפק) "(do not promote) they rise" is a textual crux, generally resolved by taking with v 10 in some way. Thus Gunkel (*Die Psalmen*, 595), followed by Kraus (*Psalmen*, 1103), *et al*, read סלי (with two mss.) יָרִימוּ (cf. LXX σ') אַל "may those who despise me not raise (their head)." RSV transposes סלה and the verb, for which ירימו is read: ". . . lift up their head." G. R. Driver (*JTS* 44 [1943] 22), assuming a rare corruption of *samek* to ʿ*ayin*, read אַל-יָרֹם עָלַי "let not (the head . . .) be lifted up against me." Some corruption must clearly be assumed. The simplest change is to read (or תְּפָרְקֵמוֹ) אֵל תְּפָרְקֵמוֹ "O God, tear them away," assuming transposition of *resh* and *qoph*. For the metaphor cf. Job 17:11 נתקו זמתי "my plans are broken off." Cf. vv 10b, 12b for the resumptive suffix. For the second person jussive cf. תנצרני "preserve me" in vv 2, 5. For אל cf. אלי "my God" in v 7 and the parallelism of אל with אלהים at 83:2 (1) in an Elohistic psalm (cf. Kraus, *Psalmen*, 740). The meter is then 4+3, as in vv 2, 3, 7. There is a chiastic order, as in vv 2, 5.

10.a. It is often assumed that a verb is missing in v 10a, but ראש "head" can function as *casus pendens* (cf. v 12). Dahood (*Psalms III*, 304) took ראש as "poison" in view of שפתימו "lips" and חמת "venom" (v 4), but he had to resort to doubtful syntax. There is an intended contrast with v 8 (see *Form/Structure/Setting*), as Dahood came to recognize (*CBQ* 41 [1979] 606). For the thought of v 10 cf. 7:17 (16).

11.a. Heb. גחלים "coals" is a play on חמת "heat, poison" (v 4).

11.b. Q ימושו is evidently presupposed by LXX πεσοῦνται "will fall" and S nḥtn "will descend." The niphʿal is not otherwise used in this sense, but it is not unreasonable in view of the hiphʿil "let fall" in 55:4 (3), if MT is correct there: cf. post-biblical hithpolel "sink" (M. Jastrow, *Dictionary*, 740b). An emendation יַמְטֵר "may he rain" (Gunkel, *Die Psalmen*, 595; Kraus, *Psalmen*, 740; *et al.*), comparing 11:6, is often adopted.

11.c. In MT the third singular form reads awkwardly (cf. *BHS*). Earlier באש (גחלים) "(coals) with fire" is often emended to אש (גחלי) "(coals of) fire" (Gunkel, *Die Psalmen*, 595; *et al.*) on the supposed evidence of LXX BS Hier. LXX A ἐν πυρί is preferred as the older text by A. Rahlfs, *Psalmi cum Odis* 325. Dahood (*CBQ* 41 [1979] 607 note 10) has attempted to explain the *beth* as *beth comitatus*, comparing Isa 61:8. Both difficulties would be resolved by taking באש as an Aramaism "evil" (cf. BDB, 1084a), so that vv 10b, 11b, 12b are strikingly parallel in sense. The meter is then 3+4, as in vv 8, 12. For the confusion in MT cf. LXX ἐν πυρί (= בָּאֵשׁ) for בָּאֵשׁ "stench" in Amos 4:10.

11.c. Heb. מהמרות refers to watery pits, as Ugaritic and Arabic cognates attest: see *HALAT*, 524a.

12.a. Lit. "not be established" (contrast v 14b). The caesura should come at this point.

12.b. For לדחפת cf. post-biblical Heb. and Aram. דחף "push, thrust, knock down" (Jastrow, *Dictionary*, 293a; cf. late biblical usage supplied in BDB, 191a). The preposition expresses result (cf. BDB, 515a), "with a view to pushes."

13.a. Q ידעתי is to be read: cf. v 7.

13.b. For עני see Kraus, *Psalmen*, 108–11.

14.a. For the association of this motif with deliverance cf. 41:13 (12); 56:14 (13); 116:9 (C. Barth, *Die Erretung vom Tode*, 150). Worship in the temple carried with it the privilege of dwelling in Yahweh's land: thus vv 12α and 14b are antithetic (cf. R. E. Clements, *Transactions of the Glasgow University Oriental Society* 19 [1961/62] 16–28).

Form/Structure/Setting

Psalm 140 has the pattern of an individual complaint (cf. C. Westermann, *Praise*, 64). An address and introductory call for help is followed by a description of the psalmist's enemies (vv 2–4); this pattern is repeated in vv 5–6. A confession of trust, employing an initial אמרתי "I say" as an alternative to the common *waw* adversative (Westermann, *Praise*, 74 note 23), precedes petitions for Yahweh to be favorable to the psalmist and to intervene in reprisal against his enemies (vv 7–9). The latter element develops into wishes in vv 10–12 for their punishment. The psalm ends with sentiments of confident assurance, incorporating a vow of praise (vv 13–14). These sentiments are a variant of the second element of a double wish. The switch from divine address to third person reference after v 12 is common in complaints (see F. Crüsemann, *Studien zur Formgeschichte*, 225).

The psalmist, falsely accused, evidently uttered this complaint in a cultic setting (W. Beyerlin, *Die Rettung*, 33). J. H. Eaton (*Kingship*, 63–64), following A. Bentzen, has considered the psalm royal in view of the references to warfare in vv 3, 8, a close relationship to Yahweh (v 7), a link in v 11a with 18:13–14 (12–13) and the Davidic heading. Viewed cumulatively the evidence is impressive. However, the individual arguments have not the same strength: for instance, the war motif more obviously matches the hunting one as a metaphor for persecution. The date of the psalm's composition is considered by Kraus (*Psalmen*, 1104) to be beyond determination. Earlier attempts to link the enemies with the religious parties of later Judaism and so to assign the psalm to the fourth or third centuries B.C. (e.g. W. O. E. Oesterley, *Psalms*, 558) have been abandoned (cf. Gunkel, *Die Psalmen*, 594; A. Weiser, *Psalms*, 809). Dahood (*Psalms III*, 301) considers the psalm early in view of a large number of hapax legomena and archaic forms. D. A. Robertson (*Linguistic Evidence*, 66–68, 144) is inclined to consider the threefold מו-suffix in vv 4, 10 (cf. כמו, v 4) as significant for an early date, unless the standard ם- forms in vv 4, 11 imply that they are archaistic; the use of the relative אשר "who" in vv 3, 5 is a pointer to the latter explanation. The otherwise late stem דחף "push, knock down" in v 12 (cf. באש in v 11, as explained above) may indicate a postexilic date. For the Davidic heading the discussion in the *Form/Structure/Setting* section of Ps 139 may be compared; in this case similarity to other individual complaints thus superscribed earlier in the Psalter may have encouraged the ascription as a homiletic device.

Psalms 140–143 comprise a collection with generic genre and Davidic headings in common, to which Pss 138 and 139 may have been subsequently prefixed (Westermann, *Theologia Viatorum* 8 [1961/62] 282–83). A. F. Kirkpatrick (*Psalms*, 792) has enumerated their secondary differences from the rest of the psalms in Books 4 and 5 of the Psalter: three headings employ מזמור "psalm," which is comparatively rare in these Books, and once משכיל "maskil," otherwise not found, while the rubric סלה "Selah" is attached three times to Ps 140 and once to Ps 143, but nowhere else.

The structure of the psalm is not uncommonly envisaged in terms of five strophes, vv 2–4, 5–6, 7–9, 10–12, 13–14 (Kirkpatrick, *Psalms*, 793; J. A. Montgomery, *JBL* 64 [1945] 383; Dahood, *Psalms III*, 301; M. Greenberg, *Eretz Israel* 14 [1978] 94–95). Others have divided into vv 2–6, 7–12, 13–14 (Gunkel, *Die Psalmen*, 595; Kraus, *Psalmen*, 740). The former analysis accords well with סלה, often apparently a division marker, at vv 4, 6, 9. Moreover, breaks after vv 4 and 6 suit the form-critical duplication of vv 2–4 in vv 5–6. However, the appearance of the divine name in the first colon of vv 2, 5, 7, 13 may suggest that one should appear at the head of the penultimate strophe, viz. v 9. In that case v 9 is to be taken with vv 10–12 and detached from vv 7–9, in which there is a fourfold cluster of the name, so that the initial name of v 7 is accompanied by only two others, in vv 7b, 8a.

There is clear evidence of a chiastic scheme running from v 2 to v 12: רע "evil" and איש חמס(ים) "man of violence," vv 2, 12; שפתימו "his lips," vv 4, 10; and רשע "wicked," vv 5, 9. The scheme appears to frame vv 7–8 at the center. There is another, similar scheme in vv 3–12, centered on v 8: there ביום נשק "in day of battle" surely resumes כל־יום . . . מלחמות "every day . . . wars" in v 3, while סכתה לראשי "you covered my head" in v 8 prepares the way for ראש . . . יכסימו "may . . . cover the head" in v 10. If the psalm consisted of vv 2–12, would it not cry out to be divided on these grounds into three, vv 2–6, 7–8, 9–12? This division would match content, the first and third parts being concerned with the enemies and the motifs of the first being echoed in the third (see *Explanation*), while the second celebrates the psalmist's close relation to Yahweh. Indeed, A. Szörényi (*Psalmen und Kult im AT. Zur Formgeschichte der Psalmen.* [Budapest: Sankt Stephans Gesellschaft, 1961] 555–56) and E. Beaucamp (*RSR* 56 [1968] 211) have suggested that vv 13–14 are secondary. However, in Beaucamp's case at least the suggestion appears to have been based solely on a desire for uniformity, to secure strophes six cola long.

When one turns to vv 13–14, they seem to function as a formal parallel to vv 7–8. Both are two line expressions of confidence introduced by first singular verbs. (It is significant that from this perspective v 9 again belongs with the verses that follow it.) Are we then to conceive of an ABA'B' sequence of strophes, with vv 2–6 (again) matched in vv 9–12, and vv 7–8 in vv 13–14? No, for the last strophe, vv 13–14, provides evidence of an initial one ending at v 4. There is parallelism at the beginning of the first two strophes and at the end of the last two: synonymous parallelism at vv 2–3a, 5 and antithetic at vv 12 and 14 (12a//14b, 12b//14a [note the *sade-daleth* sequence in יצודנו "hunt" and צדיקים "righteous" and *lamed* introducing the final words]). In addition, the phrase לדחות פעמי "to trip up my feet" in v 5 seems to be echoed in לדחפת "for pushes" in v 12. It is noteworthy that in post-biblical Hebrew דחף interchanges with דחה (Jastrow, *Dictionary*, 293a). The counsel *frt dl* in *BHS* concerning the latter case thus appears to be ill-advised. This matching of vv 2, 5 with vv 12, 14 makes vv 2–4, 13–14 a frame around vv 5–12. In the light of the organic relationship between vv 13–14 and vv 7–8, the evidence points to vv 7–8 as a central strophe.

It appears then that one must allow for more than one artistic scheme in the psalm. There is a sequence of word markers which advance from vv 2–5 and then backtrack in vv 9–12, and another set which highlight v 8. The effect of this double chiastic sequence is to demarcate vv 7–8 as the heart of the section vv 2–12. The other scheme serves to pinpoint the individual strophes, with the final one reminiscent of the central strophe, vv 7–8, and to this end v 5 speeding the hearer forward and v 12 back. The strophes are thus vv 2–4, 5–6, 7–8, 9–12, 13–14. For the dual schematization Pss 111 and 137 may be compared.

Explanation

Psalm 140 was composed for use as a complaint offered in the sanctuary against cruel persecution. The situation envisaged is one in which troublemakers have been waging against the sufferer a campaign of calculated provocation. They have viciously stung him with the venom of their slander. His only hope is to appeal to Yahweh for vindication.

In vv 5–6 the appeal is repeated, to underline the speaker's strong sense of need. As he continues the description of his enemies, he adds to the figures of war and snakebite used in the first strophe a further ʼone derived from trapping. The thought of planning is developed by this means. With the cold determination of the fowler his victimizers have callously been creating situations of torment and harassment.

At the heart of the piece, in vv 7–8, the psalmist speaks of his personal faith. He recalls the ties of devoted submission that link him with his Lord. He can praise him for saving help in the past, looking back to times of danger when he was protected (cf. Isa 59:17; Eph 6:17; 1 Thess 5:8). Now that men have waged virtual war against him (v 3), he is turning for aid to a warrior who has been his proven ally, Yahweh—all the onus is on him, as the reiteration of the name proclaims.

He pleads therefore that the malicious intent of his persecutors may be frustrated. The negative motifs employed in the description of the first two strophes are taken up one by one and matched in corresponding prayer and wish. He asks that their scheming plots may be annulled. There is a moral law at work in the world whereby evil wreaks its own nemesis. It is by no means separate from Yahweh's own activity: he works through it, grinding steadily away with his mills of providential judgment. By contrast with the psalmist's own head being covered (v 8), he asks that theirs may be—with disaster earned by their own slander. He has suffered the heat (or poison) of their attacks, so their just deserts are the heat of divine judgment (cf. 11:6). They have tried to get him to fall into traps they set for him, so they too should be plunged into pits of destruction. They have hunted him with their snares, and they should be hounded in their turn. These sentiments are congruent with living in a cruel world where divine intervention was expected there and then—rather than in an afterworld, belief in which can make suffering more tolerable for the Christian. The psalmist appeals in v 12 to a covenantal concept: life in the God-given land was conditional upon obedience to his moral claims and so liable to forfeiture (cf. Exod 20:12).

The psalm closes with a note of conviction akin to that of vv 7–8. Now the concept of divine aid is given a future orientation. With confidence in a God who rights wrongs, the speaker looks forward to a time that will surely come, a time when the righteous, so often synonymous with the afflicted, will have cause to thank their divine champion in glad testimony to his saving grace. Even on the horizontal plane he does not stand alone, although hitherto in the psalm a strong sense of isolation has been implicitly conveyed. He is bound in fellowship with other believers, and they with Yahweh. The right to worship at his sanctuary (cf. 23:6; 27:4) is theirs, as a pledge of the privilege of living on in his land (contrast v 11; cf. 25:13; 37:9). In the covenant promise of God's vindication of his people lies his own sure hope.

The NT puts the psalm to explicit use only at Rom 3:13, where v 4 is quoted from the LXX in a catalogue of OT statements about human sinfulness. However, its confession of faith in a God who has saved and will yet save is transposed into a chord that characterizes the message of the early church (cf. Rom 5:9–10; 2 Cor 1:10; 2 Tim 4:17–18).

Temptations Within and Without (141:1–10)

Bibliography

Burns, J. B. "An Interpretation of Ps. 141:7b." *VT* 22 (1972) 245–46. **Junker, H.** "Einige Rätsel im Urtext der Psalmen." *Bib* 30 (1949) 197–212. **Pautrel, R.** " 'Absorpti sunt juncti petrae judices eorum' (Ps. 141 [140]:6)." *RSR* 44 (1956) 219–28. **Tournay, R.** "Le Psaume 141." *VT* 9 (1959) 58–64.

Translation

[1] A psalm. Davidic.

Yahweh, I am calling [a] *you: come to me quickly,* [b]	(4+4)
listen to my cry [c] *when I call you.*	
[2] *May my prayer be accepted* [a] *as incense* [b] *before you,*	(4+4)
and uplifted hands as an evening sacrifice.	
[3] *Set a guard,* [a] *Yahweh, on my mouth,*	(4+3)
and watch [b] *over the door of my lips.*	
[4] *Do not incline my mind* [a] *to evil speaking,* [b]	(3+3+3)
to involvement in deeds of wickedness [c]	
with men [d] *who are evildoers.*	
And may I not eat of their fancy food—	(4+4)
may the righteous strike me in kindness [a] *and rebuke me.*	
May the finest [b] *oil not adorn* [c] *my head—*	(4+4)
surely my prayer is continually [d] *directed against their evil acts.*	
[6] *When* [a] *they fall into the hands of the Rock,* [b] *their judge,* [c]	(4+3)
they will hear my words appreciatively.	
[7] *As if by one who ploughs and makes furrows in the earth,* [a]	(4+4)
our [b] *bones are strewn at the mouth of Sheol.* [c]	
[8] *Truly to you, Yahweh, Lord, are my eyes directed.*	(4+4)
In you I seek [a] *refuge: do not expose me to death.* [b]	

⁹ *Guard me from the jaws* ᵃ *of the traps they have set for me*   (4+3)
   and the snares of evildoers.
¹⁰ *May the wicked fall one and all into their* ᵃ *own nets,*   (4+3)
   while ᵇ *I myself* ᶜ *escape.*

Notes/Comments

1.a. The perfect has a present force (D. Michel, *Tempora*, 80).

1.b. LXX εἰσάκουσόν με hardly stands for שמעני "hear me" (*BHS*). Elsewhere in the Psalter πρόσχες "attend" represents חושה "hasten" (cf. the meaning "consider" which the verb has in post-biblical Hebrew and Aramaic), except here and in 71 (70):12. Here the translator decided to use it for the second verb האזינה "listen," an equivalent he employed elsewhere, and so rendered the first verb with a loose synonym. In 71 (70):12 too the translation varies from the normal under the influence of the context.

1.c. LXX implies a longer reading קול תחנוני "my imploring cry" under the influence of 140:7 (*BHS*). This time the difference did affect the Hebrew *Vorlage:* the variant translation in 140:7 LXX rules out influence within the Greek tradition.

2.a. Not here "be arranged, present itself" (BDB, 466a), but "be established" (by God: cf. the use of the polel with a divine subject) and so "be accepted" and not rejected: cf. 102:29.

2.b. The precise meaning of קטרת and the parallel מנחה (as in Isa 1:13) is disputed. M. Haran ("The Uses of Incense in the Ancient Israelite Ritual," *VT* 10 [1960] 117) explains them from the fact that the meal offering (מנחה) included in its ingredients a rare spice, frankincense: generally לבנה is the term used (Lev 2:1, etc.). Heb. קטרת is usually interpreted either as the smoke of the burnt offering (cf. 66:15) or as burnt incense, while מנחה could refer either to the meal offering which accompanied the burnt offering or specifically to the evening sacrifice. As H.-J. Hermission (*Sprache und Ritus*, 55) has observed, the precise sense is not important; reference is made to regular sacrifice, perhaps to the evening sacrifice, and the complaint may have been used at the time when it was offered (cf. Ezra 9:5; Dan 9:21). It is often suggested, e.g. by A. Weiser (*Psalms*, 811) and H.-J. Kraus (*Psalmen*, 1109) that prayer is mentioned as a substitute for sacrifice. But prayer and sacrifice are not mentioned as mutually exclusive, as if the former were offered in place of the latter: acceptability is the point at issue. The concept of sacrifice is spiritualized, but there is no separation from the cult (Hermission, *Sprache und Ritus*, 55; cf. A. A. Anderson, *Psalms*, 919).

3.a. M. Dahood (*Psalms III*, 310 and references) has suggested that in this oral context שמרה (and משמר in Job 7:12) means "muzzle." The vocalization of the noun has been queried, and a form שָׁמְרָה preferred (H. Gunkel, *Die Psalmen*, 597, *et al.*); but cf. אָכְלָה "food," עָהֳרָה "purity" for the form.

3.b. MT points as emphatic imperative (cf. GKC § 48i), but both the parallelism and the following prepositional phrase—the verb is never so construed elsewhere—point to a noun, as LXX *Tg.* render, possibly a form נְצְרָה (Gunkel, *Die Psalmen*, 597, following F. Buhl, *et al.*).

4.a. This is a remarkable expression of divine control over the mind: cf. 1 Sam 16:14; 1 Kgs 22:21–23; Ps 119:36.

4.b. Rather than "deed" דבר signifies "word" (LXX; Kraus, *Psalmen*, 1107), as a continuation of v 3 and prelude to v 4aβ.

4.c. MT reads somewhat strangely. G. R. Driver (*HTR* 29 [1936] 192) suggested transposing MT עללות ברשע "deeds in wickedness" to בעללות רשע "in deeds of wickedness."

4.d. Failure to recognize that v 4a is a tricolon (R. Pautrel, *RSR* 44 [1956] 219) has led to attempts to make v 4aγ parallel with v 4b, of which the most moderate from a text-critical viewpoint was that of Driver (*JTS* 44 [1943] 22), followed by NEB: אֶתְאֲשֵּׁם מִפּ "I was appalled by . . . ," אשם being a byform of שמם. For other suggestions see *BHK*. A further advantage of taking v 4aγ metrically with what precedes is that v 4b may be taken with v 5aα and v 5aβ with v 5b as bicola: they are marked by external parallelism, v 4b matching v 5aβ in a festive situation (cf. 23:5) and v 5aα corresponding to v 5b as antithetic positive counterparts.

5.a. The text of vv 5–7 is befogged with uncertainties (*BHS*). Heb. חסד "kindness," seemingly an adverbial accusative, is often repointed חָסִ(י)ד "the pious" and taken with the next verb as a synonymous parallel of the preceding (Gunkel, *Die Psalmen,* 598; *et al.*). For the doubling of verbs, here chiastic, cf. v 7a.

5.b. Heb. ראש can mean "choicest" (BDB, 911a) and may well do so here (Dahood, *Psalms III,* 312, who observes that word play is a feature of complaints) in a counterpart to מנעמיהם "their delicacies." A widespread emendation on the authority of LXX *S* is to read רָשָׁע "(the oil of) the wicked." Driver (*JTS* 31 [1930] 278; *HTR* 29 [1936] 193), followed by NEB, judged that LXX *S* represented רָאשׁ "tyrant," claiming an Arabic cognate, here and in Prov 13:23; 28:3; but it is significant that W. McKane (*Proverbs,* 463, 629) found such a lexicographical expedient unnecessary in the Proverbs passages.

5.c. MT יני is evidently an orthographical variant of יניא from נוא "refuse." It is then difficult, however, to make sense of the passage. The feasibility of RSV "Let the righteous smite me, it shall be a kindness; and let him reprove me, it shall be as oil upon the head; let not my head refuse it" (cf. H. Junker, *Bib* 30 [1949] 204) depends upon the highly questionable understanding of שמן ראש in terms of a comparison. The reading יניא in many mss. is most probably to be regarded as a misinterpretation of נָני "adorn," apocopated pi'el from נאה (Gunkel, *Die Psalmen,* 598; *et al.*). With v 5a a saying of Ahiqar is often compared: "My son, let the wise man strike you with a rod, but let not the fool anoint you with sweet oil."

5.d. The *waw* is often omitted or regarded as a corruption of *yod:* עודי, with first singular suffix, as in 139:18 (Anderson, *Psalms,* 921, following D. W. Thomas). Dahood (*Psalms III,* 312) regards the phrase as a hendiadys: "always and my prayer" and so "my constant prayer." More probably the not uncommon phrase עוד מעט ו "yet a little and . . ." (cf. BDB, 729a) is to be compared (Gunkel, *Die Psalmen,* 598); cf. too such phrases as ערב וידעתם "at evening you will know" (Exod 16:6; cf. GKC § 112oo).

6.a. The first verb is to be subordinated to the second in a temporal sense (cf. GKC § 111d); for the perfect its use in temporal clauses in a future perfect sense (GKC § 160o) may be compared.

6.b. As elsewhere in the Psalter (cf. BDB, 701a), סלע "rock" is to be taken as a divine title (J. P. Peters, *The Psalms as Liturgies* [London: Hodder and Stoughton, 1922] 479; R. Tournay, *VT* 9 [1959] 60; Dahood, *Psalms III,* 313). The word is often moved into v 7 (*BHS*), but four beats in v 6a suit the dominant meter of the psalm.

6.c. Heb. שפטיהם "their judges" may be a plural of majesty (cf. Tournay, *VT* 9 [1959] 60) for which see P. Joüon, *Grammaire* § 136d, e. Tournay wrongly cites Kennicott ms. 43 as reading שפטם: it actually reads שפטהם according to B. Kennicott, *Vetus Testamentum hebraicum,* vol 2, 431.

7.a. The comparative relation between v 7a and v 7b is not clear. It is here taken as that of agent, who causes upheaval of the soil and consequent scattering of clods with the plough (cf. F. Baethgen, cited by Gunkel, *Die Psalmen,* 598). For פלח "cleave" in the sense of ploughing (BDB, 812a) its usage in post-biblical Hebrew and Aramaic (cf. σ' γεωργός "farmer") is to be compared. A reading פֶּלַח יָבְקַע (*S*) "a millstone shatters" (Tournay, *VT* 9 [1959] 60, comparing Isa 8:14–15) or פֶּלַח יְבָקַע (LXX, *BHK*) "a millstone is split" not only renders בארץ "in the earth" otiose, but removes the *waw* which suitably links two verbs of similar meaning.

7.b. Generally עצמינו "our bones" is emended to עצמיהם "their bones" on the basis of LXX mss *S*. It is difficult to see how so straightforward a reading would have become thus corrupted in MT. In LXX the original ἡμῶν was probably adapted to αὐτῶν under the influence of the pronoun in vv 4, 5, 6. The first plural reference, isolated in a series of first singular forms throughout the psalm, is by no means easy, but it appears to relate to a description of complaint. 11QPs a reads עצמי "my bones," which remarkably supports Gunkel's emendation (*Die Psalmen,* 599); but it smacks of assimilation to the other first singular suffixes in the psalm. Dahood (*Psalms III,* 204) considers that MT represents a first singular form with an affirmative -n.

7.c. J. B. Burns (*VT* 22 [1972] 245–46) has plausibly explained the origin of the imagery, here purely metaphorical, in terms of Mot, the Ugaritic god of death and the underworld, as a monster who devours, picks the bones clean and leaves them scattered near its mouth: cf. Isa 5:14.

8.a. The perfect has a present connotation (Michel, *Tempora,* 83).

8.b. Perhaps literally "empty my life" (BDB, 788b). H. W. Wolff (*Anthropology,* 19) considers that נפש "life" is here and in Isa 53:12 applied to the blood (cf. Deut 12:23) and so can be spoken of in terms of a liquid. But נפש may well refer to the throat or neck (cf. Wolff, *Anthropology,* 14–15), in which case the phrase means to lay bare and stretch the neck to have it cut by the sword.

9.a. Lit. "hands" and so "power": cf. Job 5:20.

9.b. Dahood (*Psalms III*, 314) points וּמִקְּשׁוֹת "and from the bows" on the ground that the plural of מוֹקֵשׁ is elsewhere מוֹקְשִׁים; however, Gunkel (*Die Psalmen*, 599) has noted a parallel form in Sir 35:20.

10.a. Dahood (*Psalms III*, 315) relates the singular suffix in v 10 to the divine סֶלַע of v 6, but characteristically the motif of v 10a employs a reflexive suffix or its equivalent: cf. 7:16–17 (15–16); 9:17b (16b); Prov 26:27. The suffix is evidently distributive (cf. GKC, 145m). Kraus (*Psalmen*, 1108) reads a plural בְּמִכְמְרֵיהֶם "their nets" with the apparent support of S. Tournay (*VT* 9 [1959] 61) has rightly judged MT *lectio difficilior* and urged that יַחַד "one and all," which is to be taken with v 10a (*BHS*), facilitates a distributive reference.

10.b. For עַד "while" see BDB, 725a; KB, 681a.

10.c. Heb. אָנֹכִי "I" is placed before the conjunction for emphasis (Tournay, *VT* 9 [1959] 62).

Form/Structure/Setting

Like Ps 140, this psalm is an individual complaint. Its contents reflect this form (cf. C. Westermann, *Praise*, 64). An address, introductory cries and a wish for a favorable hearing (vv 1–2) are the prelude to petitions (vv 3–4a) which are reinforced by wishes (vv 4b–5). Three brief elements follow: an optimistic expression of confidence relating to the future (v 6), a descriptive complaint (v 7) and a confession of trust in Yahweh (v 8a-bα). Further petitions appear in vv 8bβ–9, while v 10 is virtually a double wish, with the second member subordinated to the first. There are some unusual features: the petition against temptation to evil words in v 4aα and the reference to a group, rather than to an individual, in the description of v 7, if MT is correct. The latter phenomenon is hardly to be compared with the generalization of 140:13–14 (12–13), but it invites comparison with 102:15, 21 (14, 20): the individual complaint is set against a background of communal or at least collective suffering. The former element is a wisdom motif found elsewhere in the Psalter (34:14 [13]; 39:2 [1]; cf. 119:36), and so is that of v 5aα (cf. Prov 27:6 and the Ahiqar reference above) and also the deprecating of association with the wicked in vv 4b, 5aβ (cf. Prov 1:10–15; Pss 1:1; 50:18). Accordingly wisdom elements are present in the psalm. However, vv 8–10 reflect the situation of persecution characteristic of individual complaints, and thus it is within this standard orbit that the psalm as a whole belongs.

Kraus (*Psalmen*, 1109) has assigned the psalm to a sapiential milieu, that of Torah-piety, like Ps 119. However, the cultic reference of v 2 is not to be ignored nor interpreted as indicating that the cult has been superseded. In this connection it is interesting to note that G. Fohrer (*Introduction*, 292) has judged the psalm to be a personal non-cultic song by an author connected with the cult. There is no reason, however, to reject a cultic setting for this psalm composed under wisdom influence (cf. in general R. E. Murphy, "Wisdom Psalms," 167).

Most take the wisdom links to indicate a post-exilic date for the psalm, which may well be so. However, the argument that the psalm is later than the fifth or fourth centuries B.C. because the extant Aramaic Sayings of Ahiqar derive in written form from that period (Tournay, *VT* 9 [1959] 63; cf. Gunkel, *Die Psalmen*, 597) is hardly viable. The link with v 5 does not demand dependence and in any case, if there is dependence, the chronological origin of proverbial sayings is notoriously difficult to determine.

Dahood (*Psalms III*, 309) has ventured to reconstruct a precise setting for the psalm: an Israelite living in the Northern Israelite dispersion after the fall of Samaria in 721 B.C. is brought to trial accused of non-participation in pagan rites and banquets. The psalm was written possibly in Phoenicia. This provenance is based on Phoenician links, דל "door" in v 3, a hapax legomenon in Hebrew (otherwise דלת), the plural form אישים "men" in v 4 (also Prov 8:4; Isa 53:3) and מנעמים "delicacies" also in v 4, another hapax, which occurs four times in the eighth century B.C. Karatepe inscriptions; cf. too בל "not." However, Tournay, ibid., has pointed to links with Phoenician in the late book of Ecclesiastes. J. H. Eaton (*Kingship*, 84–85), pointing to the Davidic reference in the heading, has suggested that the psalmist may have been a king in a situation of war, who laments slaughter suffered by his people (v 7). He looks for the overthrow of the enemy rulers and for their parleying (v 6). The use of סלע "rock" may be a play on Sela in Edom and indicate a campaign away from Jerusalem (v 2).

It must be admitted that the force of the Phoenician parallels are difficult to evaluate chronologically and geographically. The relation of the hapaxes to forms and not to stems may indicate simply coincidence of survival, in extant literary pockets, of forms otherwise more widely used in Hebrew. D. A. Robertson (*Linguistic Evidence*, 109, 144–45) judges the psalm undatable: while an early date is theoretically possible, the one early form (כמו "like" in v 7) cannot be admitted as evidence, because a similar distribution is present in non-early poetry. The royal and military situation reconstructed by Eaton is by no means demanded by the text. Probably the psalm is to be judged post-exilic. For the Davidic heading the relevant comments on Ps 140 may be compared.

The structure of the psalm has been variously analyzed, largely on the basis of form-critical elements and motifs. A crucial factor generally ignored is a stylistic pattern of repetition running through the psalm, notably לפי "on/at (my) mouth" in vv 3, 7, the stem שמר "guard" in vv 3, 9, פעלי און "evildoers" in vv 4, 9, (רשע(ים "wicked" in vv 4, 10 and ע(ו)ד "still, while" in vv 5, 10. These parallels may indicate a break after v 5, especially if another pair concerning the stem נעם "fine foods, pleasant" in vv 4, 6 is taken into account, or, if that is otherwise explained, after v 6, in which case the pair מידי, בידי "in/from hands" in vv 6, 9 is relevant. A further factor which may be considered is the fresh appeal and address with the divine name in v 8, which perhaps corresponds to v 3. Then strophes of vv 1–5, 6–10, subdividing into units of vv 1–2, 3–5, and vv 6–7, 8–10, may be envisaged. This result accords with the fourfold division found by Anderson (*Psalms*, 918); similar are those of Kraus (*Psalmen*, 1108), vv 1–2, 3–5, 6–7, 8–9, 10 (cf. Gunkel, *Die Psalmen*, 596–97) and of Dahood (*Psalms III*, 309), vv 1, 2–5, 6–10. Dahood isolates v 1 as introductory on the basis of the inclusion of the stem קרא "call."

It is noteworthy that the process of repetition mainly begins at v 3. It is thus possible to envisage three strophes, an introductory one in vv 1–2 and then two parallel ones on vv 3–6, 7–10. Then the divine name of v 3 deliberately resumes that of v 1, but that in v 8 is a random repetition in the course of the next strophe. The repetition of תפלתי "my prayer" in vv 2, 5, hitherto unmentioned, and of עָ(וֹ)ד in vv 5, 10 marks the (near) ends of strophes; in the previous scheme the former instance would mark the ends of sub-units and the latter those of strophes. A factor which suggests that v 6 be taken with the preceding is that it features in a cluster of close repetitions, embracing virtually the whole of vv 3–6. It involves רע "evil" in vv 4, 5 and the stem נעם "fine foods pleasant" in vv 4, 5, in an ABA'B' sequence. Moreover, the doubled אל "not" in vv 4, 5 is taken up in the single occurrence at v 8; this phenomenon would also fit the earlier scheme. The repeated לפי "on/at (my) mouth" in vv 3, 7 denotes the beginning of the first and second strophes, while the kindred בידי, מידי "in/from my hands" in vv 6, 9 mark the ends of the second and third. References to the enemies' downfall close both major strophes: נשמטו "they fall" in v 6 and יפלו "they fall" in v 10. This analysis does much more justice to the intricate pattern of repetition. There is a further case, לי "to/for me" in vv 1, 9, which gives overall inclusion (L. J. Liebreich, *HUCA* 27 [1956] 183 note 7), while the stem שמר "guard" in vv 3, 9 and רשע(ים) "wicked" in vv 4, 10 afford inclusion in the main strophes.

The second scheme, stylistically superior though it is, strangely finds less echo in divisions hitherto made. It corresponds exactly to that of D. Kidner (*Psalms 73–150*, 470–72). It partially conforms to that of J. W. Rogerson and J. W. McKay (*Psalms 101–150*, 162–63), who speak of v 7 as the beginning of the final plea for help, and to that made by both E. J. Kissane (*Psalms II*, 302) and J. Schildenberger (*Estudios Eclesiásticos* 34 [1960] 680), who have divided the psalm neatly into three strophes of four bicola, vv 1–4aβ, 4aγ–6, 7–10, the latter pointing to a development of thought whereby prayers for keeping from sin and for protection from attack are separated by an avowal of honesty. In fact, the psalm is basically a triad of prayers and wishes, in vv 1–2, 3–5, 8b–10. In the second strophe an expression of confidence is appended in v 6, while in vv 7–8a descriptive complaint and a confession of trust are prefixed.

Explanation

The psalmist brings his plea to the temple. He has watched the sacrifices being offered and the incense fumes rise, and knows that Yahweh has deigned to accept these contributions from priestly hands. He asks that his urgent prayers may likewise find favor.

He is ruefully aware that "bad company ruins good morals" (1 Cor 15:33). As a result of his association with evil men, pernicious speech has evidently passed his lips. He prays that Yahweh may help him to guard his tongue henceforth and may not lead him into temptation to wrong word or deed. He has resolved to leave their circle with its lavish hospitality. By contrast he has now come to prize the well-intentioned reprimand of good folk. He seeks consistency between his regular prayers and his outward life by making this radical break with his former associates. The convictions which he is now expressing are quite alien to their standards, but he looks forward with confidence to moral vindication in the form of God's providential intervention against them. The eventual result, he hopes and trusts, will be that judgment results in repentance (cf. Deut 4:30; Hos 3:4–5; contrast Isa 9:12 [13]; Amos 4:6), so that they are actually converted to his standpoint.

A great gulf yawns between expectation and present experience. The psalmist seeks to win sympathy by mentioning his plight. With a collective reference whose precise meaning is now lost to us, he includes others in his suffering. A somber aura of death pervades his life. He looks to Yahweh for help and avows his trust in him. The initial placing of the pronouns reveals that Yahweh is his only hope. An urgent prayer discloses the grim alternative if God does not protect and preserve him. The prayer form is developed into a final plea for guarding, which recalls his earlier prayer in v 3. Evidently he now has the wrath of his erstwhile companions to contend with. In their persecution they are like hunters, and he is the object of their manhunt. His only weapon against them is prayerful expression of his desire for justice to be done, so that they fall victims to their own scheming and he miraculously manages to survive.

Nobody Cares *(142:1–8)*

Bibliography

Barth, C. *Die Erretung vom Tode.* **Beyerlin, W.** *Die Rettung der Bedrängten in den Feindpsalmen der Einzelnen auf institutionelle Zusammenhänge untersucht.* FRLANT 99. Göttingen: Vanderhoeck und Ruprecht, 1970. **Bruce, F. F.** "The Earliest OT Interpretation." *OTS* 17 (1972) 37–52. **Hermission, H.-J.** *Sprache und Ritus im altisraelitischen Kult. Zur "Spiritualisierung" der Kultbegriffe im AT.* WMANT 19. Neukirchen-Vluyn: Neukirchener Verlag, 1965.

Translation

[1] A Maskil.[a] Davidic (when he was in the cave). A prayer.[b]

[2] *Aloud* [a] *to Yahweh I cry,*	(3+3)
aloud to Yahweh I plead for aid. [b]	
[3] *I pour out before him my worries,* [a]	(3+3)
my troubles before him I relate.	
[4] *When my spirit faints within,*	(3+3)
you are one who knows my path.	
[5] *I glance to the right* [a] *and look,* [b]	(3+2)
but nobody takes any notice of me.	
Escape is impossible for me,	3+2)
nobody cares about me.	
[6] *I cry* [a] *to you, Yahweh,*	(3+3+3)
I say: [b] *You are my refuge,*	
my sustenance [c] *in the land of the living.*	

⁷ *Listen to my shouting,* [a]   (2+2)
  since I am brought very low.
  Save me from my persecutors,   (2+2)
  since they are too strong for me.
⁸ *Bring me out of prison,*   (3+2)
  so that I can give thanks to your name.
  Around me the righteous will crowd, [a]   (3+2)
  when you treat me with kindness.

Notes/Comments

1.a. See the note on 101:2. M. Gertner ("Terms of Scriptural Interpretation. A Study in Hebrew Semantics," *BSO(A)S* 25 [1962] 22–24), followed by M. Dahood (*Psalms I*, 194) has deduced from the use of the verb in Neh 8:8 the meaning "sense-giving harmony," i.e. instruction by recitation and performing the musical art of singing. In that case the term refers to the method of rendering the psalm; the art of the much later Jewish cantor could be compared.

1.b. Heb. תפלה appears to be the technical term for a communal or, as here, individual complaint (K. Heinen, *BZ* 17 [1973] 103–5).

2.a. Heb. קולי "my voice/cry" has been explained as an instance of syllepsis whereby the verb agrees with the suffix of the subject (GKC § 144l, m). Dahood (*Psalms II*, 225) takes as an accusative of means.

2.b. K. W. Neubauer (*Der Stammm CH N N*, 137), although considering generally that the stem relates to a master-servant relationship and appeal to consequent obligation, finds the immediate context too general to discern this meaning here. However, the parallel v 6 (see *Form/Structure/Setting*) refers to a close relationship, upon which the psalmist bases his present appeal: cf. 57:2 (1).

3.a. See the note on 102:1.

5.a. The right was the place where the witness for the defense stood (109:31); it was also associated generally with help (16:8; 110:5; 121:5).

5.b. MT וראה "and look (imperative)" took the preceding הביט "glance" (cf. GKC § 113bb) as an imperative (addressed to Yahweh?); but the ancient versions (cf. 11QPsᵃ אביטה . . . ואר7אה) were more probably correct in construing the verbs as infinitives absolute (רָאֹה . . .).

6.a. The perfect is declarative in the cases of this and the next verb (D. Michel, *Tempora*, 92).

6.b. For this introduction to a confession of faith see the note on 140:7 (6).

6.c. Heb. חלק "portion, share" is culturally grounded in the Levites' support from dues paid to the sanctuary rather than from tribal lands (Num 18:20). In 16:5–6; 73:26; 119:57; Lam 3:24 the privilege is spiritualized so that Yahweh is acknowledged as the ground of support inasmuch as he is the provider of life (H.-J. Hermission, (*Sprache und Ritus*, 107–10). The addition of בארץ החיים "in the land of the living" (cf. 27:13) is here especially appropriate for the figure which concerned apportionment in the land of Israel; here it becomes sustenance in the world of life.

7.a. For רנה "shout" in the Psalter see N. E. Wagner, *VT* 10 (1960) 435–41; here it refers to the prayer of complaint.

8.a. Heb. יכתרו in the hiphʿil evidently means "surround" here and in Hab 1:4 (*HALAT*, 482a), like the piʿel in Judg 20:43; Ps 22:13 (12). Here it is intransitive, unlike the other cases; the preposition *beth* may have the sense of accompaniment or proximity (cf. BDB, 89a, b). D. Michel (*Tempora*, 253) has rendered "wait" with LXX, like the piʿel in Job 36:2, taking the preposition (there *lamed*) as "on my account." The structural contrast with the isolation of v 5 (see *Form/Structure/Setting*) favors "surround."

Form/Structure/Setting

Psalm 142 is like the previous psalm in possessing an extensive pattern of repeated terms which are determinative for the structure. These are primarily the stem זעק "cry" and the divine name preceded by the preposition אל "to" in vv 2, 6; אתה "you" in vv 4, 6; עלי "(with)in me" in vv 4, 8; ממני "from me" in vv 5, 7; and נפשי "me" in vv 5, 8. This evidence bisects the psalm into vv 2–5, 6–8. This result agrees with the structural description as two such strophes given by E. J. Kissane (*Psalms II*, 307) and J. Schildenberger (*Estudios Eclesiásticos* 34 [1960] 675). In an ill-advised attempt to achieve symmetry of size, five lines for each strophe, they found tricola in vv 4–5, as well as in v 6. A. A. Anderson (*Psalms*, 923–24) and H.-J. Kraus (*Psalmen*, 1112) have also isolated vv 6–8. Comparable is H. Gunkel's fourfold division (*Die Psalmen*, 600) into vv 2–4aβ, 4aγ–5, 6–7aβ, 7aγ–8.

Vv 5aγ and 6aβ function as two leaves of an interstrophic hinge: the parallelism of 59:17 (16)aβ-b may be compared. A feature of the first strophe is short bursts of repeated terms: קולי אל יהוה "my voice to Yahweh" in v 1a, b; לפניו "before him" in v 3a, b; לי "to me" in vv 4b, 5a; and אין "not" in vv 5a, b. The external parallelism of the two bicola in v 5, the chiastic arrangement (ABB'A') of those in v 4 and the verbs of speaking throughout those of vv 2, 3 suggest that the strophe subdivides into these three units (cf. the isolation of vv 2–3 by Kraus [*Psalmen*, 1112] and Dahood [*Psalms III*, 317]). A noteworthy stylistic phenomenon is the ABCC'BA' arrangement of v 3 (Dahood, *Psalms III*, 317).

A dominant feature of the second strophe is the cluster of three hiphʿil imperatives at the head of the two bicola of v 7 and the first of v 8; in the second cola the two prior ones begin with כי "since" and the last with a hiphʿil form with a prepositional prefix. Accordingly the structure of the second strophe is quite different from that of the first. A block of three bicola are surrounded by initial and final lines, the former a tricolon. In fact the role of the three middle lines appears to be to develop the tricolon of v 6 in the motifs of their initial cola. "Shouting" takes up the "cry" of v 6aα, "my persecutors" supplies the need for "my refuge" in v 6aβ, while "prison" seems to contrast with the motif of v 6b as an allusion to a Sheol-like experience (cf. 56:13 [12]; Isa 38:10–11). The last parallel was noticed by Dahood (*Psalms III*, 318). This structural parallelism sheds light upon the significance of מסגר "prison" in v 8a (see below). It is probable too that in respect of motifs there is a deliberate relationship between the first and second strophes: the fainting spirit of v 4aα corresponds to the low state of v 7aα (cf. Dahood, *Psalms III*, 318), the hunters of v 4b to the persecutors of v 7aγ and the miserable isolation of v 5 to the happy gregariousness of v 8aγ.

The genre of the psalm is an individual complaint. C. Westermann (*Praise*, 66–67) has provided an analysis, as follows: an introductory cry for help (v 2), descriptive complaint concerning foes (v 4b) and self (v 5), confession of trust (vv 4aβ, 6aβ-b), petition in terms of hearing (v 7aα) and of saving (v 7aγ), motifs to encourage divine intervention (v 7aβ, b), a vow of thanksgiving (v 8aβ) and assurance of being heard (v 8aγ-b). Strictly v 2 is an announcement of prayer, matched in v 6aα: the change between third and second persons is not uncommon in complaints (cf. F. Crüsemann, *Studien zur Formgeschichte*, 225). It is remarkable that the psalmist has been able to combine the linear development of form with a bilateral stylistic pattern.

G. Fohrer (*Introduction*, 292) has described the psalm as a personal song in cultic style. W. Beyerlin (*Die Rettung*, 134) left open the issue of a cultic setting. There seems to be no compelling reason to deny it; לפניו "before him" in v 3 may well, though not necessarily, point to it. The background to the psalm is enemy persecution. More specifically H. Schmidt (*Das Gebet*, 9–10) set the psalm within investigative proceedings held at the sanctuary, to which the speaker has been brought from a literal prison (v 8). The avowal of v 4aβ is taken as an assertion of innocence. However, Beyerlin (*Die Rettung*, 35) has pointed to the absence of forensic terminology in the psalm. Kraus (*Psalmen*, 1114) is inclined to think in terms of literal imprisonment, comparing 107:10–16. A. Weiser (*Psalms*, 813) and Anderson (*Psalms*, 922) leave the issue open. C. Barth (*Die Erretung vom Tode*, 103, 126) has urged that while perhaps Ps 142 (and Ps 143) was eventually regarded as a prisoner's prayer, originally the reference to imprisonment was intended metaphorically (cf. Isa 61:1). Gunkel (*Die Psalmen*, 600) compared 88:9; Lam 3:7 for the metaphor, and J. H. Eaton (*Kingship*, 82, 85) has cited 116:16. Dahood (*Psalms III*, 318; cf. N. J. Tromp, *Primitive Conceptions*, 154–56) has rightly seen in v 8 an allusion to Sheol on the internal evidence of the psalm, which is confirmed by the structural study above. Dahood actually takes the figurativeness further, envisaging the psalmist's foes as Death and his emissaries, and so the psalm as the complaint of an Israelite on his deathbed (*Psalms III*, 316–17); but there seems to be no valid reason for taking the enemies as other than human, as in the Psalter generally. Dahood's interpretation is closely linked with his predilection for seeing in the Psalms references to a positive afterlife (cf. *Psalms III*, 320).

Kraus (*Psalmen*, 1112) and Fohrer (*Introduction*, 292) have found it impossible to ascertain the date of the psalm. D. A. Robertson (*Linguistic Evidence*, 144–45), noting one early element זו "which" (v 4), judges it inadmissible as proof of great antiquity, because other, non-early psalms also contain scanty, random early forms. Eaton (*Kingship*, 85) has characterized the psalm as royal and thus pre-exilic, comparing parallels in royal psalms, especially 18:18 (17).

The Davidic reference in the heading, for which the pertinent comments on Ps 140 may be compared, is here supplemented with a historical note, elsewhere a feature found only in the first two Books of the Psalter. The heading of Ps 57 has a comparable note. F. F. Bruce (*OTS* 17 [1972] 48), drawing attention to the stem חסה "(take) refuge" in 57:2 (1); 142:6 and comparing the description of the cave of Adullam as a מצודה "stronghold" in 1 Sam 22:4; 2 Sam 23:14, remarks that it is difficult to find anything more substantial than this slender link as ground for the reference. J. W. Rogerson and J. W. McKay (*Psalms 101–150*, 167) consider that the old Jewish interpretation of יכתרו in v 8 in terms of crowning (σ' *Tg.*) suggested David's triumph after suffering at Saul's hands. They take the cave in the heading as that of En-gedi (1 Sam 24:4 [3]), which in a context of Saul's enmity certainly provides a closer link with the hostility in the psalm (cf. the [erroneous] plural איביך "your enemies" in 1 Sam 24:5 K). Support for an En-gedi reference has been adduced by E. Slomovic (*ZAW* 91 [1979] 377), who has plausibly suggested that the historicization resulted from the linguistic affinities between v 8 of the psalm and Saul's words outside the cave there. Word plays of a

midrashic kind were seen in מסגר "prison" (cf. סגרני "he delivered me," 1
Sam 24:19 [18]), צדיקים "righteous" (cf. צדיק, 1 Sam 24:18 [17]) and תגמל
"treat kindly" (cf. this stem twice in the sense "repay," ibid.). For this process
of historicization, which served to re-interpret the past, the first two chapters
of Ecclesiastes may be compared, where the author assumes the *persona* of
Solomon. The heading provides valuable evidence for a particular exposition
of the psalm, which has "a proper place in the history of biblical interpretation" (Bruce, *OTS* 17 [1972] 52; cf. B. S. Childs, "Psalm Titles and Midrashic
Exegesis," *JSS* 16 [1971] 149–50).

Explanation

Psalm 142 was composed for use as an individual complaint. The psalmist
begins by announcing his intent to tell his troubles to Yahweh in the sanctuary.
He derives comfort from the certainty of God's concern: he already knows
and understands his plight (cf. Matt 6:32). However, the speaker does not
conclude that prayer is thereby rendered unnecessary. Yahweh works via the
fellowship engendered by recourse to him, which strengthens the bond of
trust. The psalmist is suffering at the hands of enemies (v 7). He is caught
in the trap of their accusation or slander (cf. 38:13 [12]; 140:1–5) and cannot
extricate himself; nor can he find anyone who will help him. On the horizontal
plane he stands alone.

He is encouraged to bring an appeal to Yahweh and to confess his dependence upon him as his only resource and sole means of support in life. Developing v 1, he appeals for a positive hearing and for deliverance; he appends
motifs describing his sorry state, intended to move God to intervene. This
Sheol-like prison of distress is the antithesis of that life which Yahweh sustains.
The psalmist promises that, once God has let him out of this prison or trap,
he will bring to the sanctuary his thank offering together with thanksgiving
addressing Yahweh with titles of honor (cf. 116:13–14, 17; 118:28–29). In
assurance he anticipates renewed fellowship with other believers when he
celebrates with them God's favorable answer at the thanksgiving service and
meal (cf. 22:26–27 [25–26]). At the moment he is estranged from their fellowship (v 5), with his name besmirched by his foes (cf. 88:9, 19 [8, 18]; Job
19:13–19). Divine vindication is needed to prove to his fellow believers his
integrity. To that end he looks forward to a manifestation of God's grace
(cf. 113:7 [6]; 116:7), which will prove yet again his praiseworthiness.

My Only Hope (143:1–12)

Bibliography

Beyerlin, W. *Die Rettung der Bedrängten in den Feindpsalmen der Einzelnen auf institutionelle
Zusammenhänge untersucht.* FRLANT 99. Göttingen: Vandenhoeck & Ruprecht, 1970.
McKay, J. W. "Psalms of Vigil." *ZAW* 91 (1979) 229–47. **Sakenfeld, K. D.** *The Meaning
of Hesed in the Hebrew Bible: A New Enquiry.* HSM 17. Missoula, MT: Scholars Press,
1978.

Translation

¹ A psalm. Davidic.

Yahweh, hear my prayer,	(3+3+3)
listen to my plea for aid,ᵃ	
in your faithfulness answer me, in your consistency ᵇ—	

² but do not enter into legal proceedings ᵃ with your servant,ᵇ   (3+3)
  since in your sight ᶜ no living person can ever be ᵈ in the right ᵉ—

³ for ᵃ the enemy ᵇ has persecuted me,   (3+3)
  he has crushed my life into the ground.

He has made me sit in darkness   (3+2)
  like those long dead.ᶜ

⁴ My spirit within has fainted,   (3+3)
  in my inner being my heart is shocked.

⁵ I remember times long ago,   (3+3+3)
  I muse on all your activity,
  on what your hands have done do I meditate.

⁶ I stretch ᵃ out my hands to you,   (3+4)
  I am like parched ground in my yearning ᵇ for you. SELAH ᶜ

⁷ Hurry, answer me, Yahweh,   (3+2)
  my spirit has failed.

Do not hide your face ᵃ from me   (3+3)
  or I shall become like ᵇ those who descend to the Pit.ᶜ

⁸ Let me hear in the morning news of your loyal love ᵃ   (3+2)
  because in you I trust.

Let me know the way I should go ᵇ   (3+3)
  because to you I direct my desire.ᶜ

⁹ Let me be freed from my enemies, Yahweh—   (3+2)
  to you I come for shelter.ᵃ

¹⁰ Teach me to do your will,   (3+2)
  because you are my God.

May your good spirit lead me ᵃ   (3+2)
  onto level ground.ᵇ

¹¹ For your name's sake,ᵃ Yahweh, give me life.   (4+4)
  In your consistency bring me out of trouble,

¹² and in your loyal love ᵃ destroy my enemies   (3+3+2)
  and annihilate all who attack my life,
  because I am your servant.

Notes/Comments

1.a. For the association of the stem חנן "be gracious" with the obligation of a master-servant relationship see K. W. Neubauer, *Der Stamm CH N N*, 95, who calls attention to the terms for relatedness in vv 1b, 2, 8, 12.

1.b. Strikingly the stem צדק "be righteous" occurs both here and in v 2. In this case (and in v 11), as the associated term אמונה "faithfulness" shows, it refers to Yahweh's doing what is right in the light of his covenantal commitments (see the note on 111:3).

2.a. That is, "treat as if he were on trial" (A. R. Johnson, *The Cultic Prophet and Israel's Psalmody*, 267): for the phrase cf. Job 9:32, 14:3; Eccl 11:9, 12:14.

2.b. This term is characteristic of the individual complaint as a self-designation which brings into focus the bond of commitment between Yahweh and the psalmist, as a basis for non-punitiveness here and for positive intervention in v 12 (C. Lindhagen, *The Servant Motif*, 262–67; cf. I. Riesener, *Der Stamm* עבד, 223–26).

2.c. For לפני "before, in front of" in the sense of estimation cf. Prov 14:12; Jer 33:24.

2.d. The imperfect has a modal force (D. Michel, *Tempora*, 149).

2.e. For this confession of general sinfulness cf. 130:3. These two psalms are rare in implying that the covenant relationship can be sustained only on the basis of continual divine forgiveness (cf. 51:7 [5]; H. McKeating, *SJT* 18 [1965] 76–77).

3.a. Reason for the request of v 1 is given.

3.b. In the light of the plural nouns in vv 9, 12 the singular here has a collective sense (A. A. Anderson, *Psalms*, 927): see the note on 140:2.

3.c. On metrical and prosodic grounds the final colon has been regarded as an interpolation from Lam 3:7 (H. Gunkel, *Die Psalmen*, 603; *et al.*), with which v 3b coincides, apart from the word order in v 3bα. But a 3+2 meter indubitably occurs later in the psalm. See further *Form/Structure/Setting*. For "darkness" as a metaphor for a Sheol-like state see N. J. Tromp, *Primitive Conceptions*, 95–97.

6.a. The verb is a declarative perfect with a present sense (Michel, *Tempora*, 93). For this gesture of earnest prayer cf. 77:3 (2); Isa 1:15; Lam 1:17.

6.b. Lit. "my נפש is towards you": cf. 123:2 for the construction. Heb. נפש "throat," here in parallelism with "hands," stands in its thirsty dryness for needy man (H. W. Wolff, *Anthropology*, 11–12, 232).

6.c. See the note on 140:4.

7.a. In the OT this expression is used in a variety of senses from neutral to sinister (cf. S. H. Blank, *Prophetic Faith in Isaiah* [London: Adam and Charles Black, 1958] 189–90). Here there is a play on two senses: failure to attend to prayer (cf. 102:3 [2]) can have fatal consequences (cf. 104:29).

7.b. Heb. משל "be like" implies equivalence here rather than similarity: a complete experience of Sheol is envisaged (cf. Isa 14:10).

7.c. Heb. בור "pit" is a synonym for Sheol: cf. 30:4 (3); 88:4–5 (3–4).

8.a. The reference is here to a divine oracle transmitted via a cultic official, promising deliverance (W. Beyerlin, *Die Rettung*, 36), which is what חסד "loyal love" here connotes in the context of a relationship that on the human side is described in terms of trust, as in 31:15, 17 (14, 16); 32:10 (K. D. Sakenfeld, *The Meaning of Hesed*, 218–23, 228).

8.b. The imperfect is modal (Michel, *Tempora*, 149).

8.c. See Wolff, *Anthropology*, 16.

9.a. The general meaning is clear: a declaration of trust is required by vv 8aβ, 8b, 10aβ. But the text cannot be precisely ascertained, MT "I covered" is unintelligible; elsewhere with a human subject it signifies failure to confess sin (40:11 [10]; Job 31:33) or to testify to Yahweh's help (32:5), neither of which is applicable. 11QPs ª is unfortunately not extant here; S omits, doubtless in despair. Kennicott ms. 180 reads נסתי "I have fled," which is possible in the light of מנוס "flight" in 59:17 (16). Kennicott ms. 224 reads חסתי "I have taken refuge," although it is not elsewhere construed with אל "to." This reading may well underlie LXX κατέφυγον (BDB, 492a; *pace BHK* and *BHS*): the verb occurs only here in the Greek Psalter, but its noun is used frequently for a whole range of terms of refuge including מחסה "refuge, shelter" (45 [46]:1; 103 [104]:18). H.-J. Kraus (*Psalmen*, 1116) has suggested a noun form כָּסָתִי "my covering, protection," comparing Gen 20:16; also worthy of mention is כִּסְלָתִי "my confidence" (Gunkel, *Die Psalmen*, 603, following F. Perles; *lamed* may have fallen out before למדני "teach me"). Perhaps the most feasible reading is a passive form כֻּסֵּיתִי (Hier: see *BHS*): cf. Aram. איתכסי "conceal oneself, withdraw" and Syr. 'eṭkassî "be sheltered, protected."

10.a. The syntax is not clear: the verb may alternatively be a second person jussive like the parallel verbs of vv 11 and 12aα, in which case רוחך טובה is either an accusative of means "your good spirit" (M. Dahood, *Psalms III*, 325) or a separate noun clause, "your spirit is good," as MT punctuates. Comparison with Neh 9:20 (cf. also להנחתם in Neh 9:19) suggests the above translation. For the anarthrous adjective see GKC § 126z.

10.b. MT בארץ is to be preferred as *lectio difficilior*. The reading בארחה "in the way" in some mss. has been influenced by 27:11, while S (cf. *BHS*) assimilates to אֹרַח חַיִּים "way of life" in 16:11.

11.a. Cf. 106:8; 109:21.

12.a. Heb. חֶסֶד is "conduct corresponding to the covenant by which God helps his faithful" (N. Glueck, *Ḥesed in the Bible* [Tr. A. Gottschalk; Cincinnati: Hebrew Union College Press, 1967] 90). There is hardly justification, contextually or semantically, for rendering "strength" (L. J. Kuyper, "The Meaning of חַסְדּוֹ in Isa. 40:6," *VT* 13 [1963] 490–91, following F. Perles). Glueck (*Ḥesed*, 91) compared the similar use of אֱמֶת "faithfulness" in 54:7 (5). Sakenfeld (*The Meaning of Hesed*, 220–21) has observed that the corollary of deliverance was shame or destruction for the other side; she compares the secular usage of חֶסֶד, which involves taking sides not only for but against (cf. 2 Sam 16:17).

Form/Structure/Setting

The psalm is in form an individual complaint (cf. C. Westermann, *Praise*, 64). In vv 1–2 an address precedes introductory petitions for a favorable hearing, which conclude with a negative petition for forgiveness. Vv 3–4 contain the descriptive complaint in terms of the psalmist's enemies, the precise form of whose attacks is left unspecified, and of himself. Vv 5–6 comprise first an expression of confidence in the relevance of Yahweh's past dealings (cf. W. Schottroff, *Gedenken*, 130) and then an avowal of trust in Yahweh to meet his needs. A series of urgent petitions are found in vv 7–9, three for a hearing (vv 7–8aα), one for guidance (v 8aγ) and one for deliverance (v 9). Those of vv 8aβ–9 are expanded in vv 10–12 into two petitions for guidance (v 10), two for deliverance (v 11) and two for corresponding destruction of the enemies (v 12). The correlation of vv 11–12 is reminiscent of the double wish characteristic of the complaint. Interspersed with the petitions of vv 7–12 are five confessions of trust designed to move Yahweh to intervene.

H. Schmidt (*Die Psalmen*, 249) envisaged as the background of the psalm a murder trial, prior to which he has been committed to prison (v 3; cf. Kraus, *Psalmen*, 1116). Beyerlin (*Die Rettung*, 36–37) has postulated a cultic setting in view of the request for an oracle in v 8, but dissociated the psalm from those connected with proceedings at a religious court. He notes that not only is the characteristic protestation of innocence lacking, but there is admission of failings (vv 2, cf. 8aγ, 10). The significance of בֹּקֶר "morning" in v 8 has been variously assessed. C. Barth ("בֹּקֶר bōqer," *TDOT* 2 [1977] 226–28) has questioned the hypothesis of J. Ziegler ("Die Helfe Gottes 'am Morgan,'" in *Atl Studien Friedrich Nötscher*, ed. H. Junker and J. Botterweck, [BBB 1; Bonn: Hanstein, 1950] 281–88) that it has in the Psalter metaphorical reference to future divine help. The term has been associated with incubation in the temple (Johnson, *Cultic Prophet and Israel's Psalmody*, 270; cf. L. Delekat, *Asylie*, 9). J. W. McKay (*ZAW* 91 [1979] 229–47) has categorized Ps 143 as belonging to a group of psalms of vigil. He envisages a vigil either all through the night or commenced shortly before dawn, perhaps after sleeping in the temple. Anderson (*Psalms*, 926) considers that the psalm was recited in the temple the evening before the expected divine decision of v 8.

The psalm has been regarded as royal (Dahood, *Psalms III*, 322; J. H. Eaton, *Kingship*, 64; Johnson, *Cultic Prophet and Israel's Psalmody*, 271, 273–75) on grounds of the Davidic heading, proximity to the royal Ps 144 and terminological links with other royal psalms, such as עֶבֶד "servant" in vv 2,

12. As in the case of Ps 142, Dahood (*Psalms III*, 322–26) regards the psalmist, at least in vv 7–12, as on the verge of death and his enemies as the infernal powers, against whom the psalmist prays for resurrection and immortality.

A late date has been assigned to the psalm on the score of the theological development of its contents. (G. Fohrer, *Introduction*, 292). W. Eichrodt (*Theology*, vol. 2, 309; cf. Anderson, *Psalms*, 926) has seen a pointer to the post-exilic period in the generality of human sinfulness in v 2. Persian influence has been detected in the reference to the spirit in v 10, but contested by Kraus (*Psalmen*, 1119). Gunkel (*Die Psalmen*, 603) regarded the psalm as relatively late on the ground of numerous contacts with other psalms. On the other hand, A. Weiser (*Psalms*, 818) has explained them as simply due to a common liturgical style. Kraus (*Psalmen*, 1116), who regards the psalm as a formulation composed for the use of worshipers, is probably correct in concluding that there are no substantial grounds for assigning a late date to the psalm. Nor, however, is there good reason for considering the psalm early. D. A. Robertson (*Linguistic Evidence*, 144–45), referring to the single early poetic form זו "which" in v 8, considers it insufficient evidence of antiquity. For the Davidic reference in the heading the relevant comments on Ps 140 may be compared. The psalm marks the close of a small collection, Pss 140–143. In Christian tradition it has been regarded as the last of a series of penitential psalms, the others being Pss 6, 32, 38, 51, 102 and 130. They represent seven rungs on the ladder of repentance, this last one being a prayer against the Last Judgment (143:2. See N. H. Snaith, *The Seven Psalms*, 9–10). Kraus (*Psalmen*, 1119) has observed that the traditional understanding of the psalm depends upon a channeling of v 2 through Rom 3:20 and that v 2 was not the only source, since the prayers for guidance and renewal in vv 8 and 10 also contributed. For the role of 143:2 in the Pauline doctrine of justification by faith (Rom 3:20; Gal 2:16) see B. Lindars, *NT Apologetic*, 224, 238–39; L. C. Allen, *Vox Evangelica* 3 (1964) 11–12.

The division of the psalm into three strophes of five lines, advocated by E. J. Kissane (*Psalms II*, 309) and J. Schildenberger (*Estudios Eclesiásticos* 34 [1960] 675), has little to commend it. Gunkel (*Die Psalmen*, 602–3) rightly viewed the psalm as consisting of two parts, vv 1–6 (cf. סלה "Selah," v 6), 7–12, the former subdividing into vv 1–2, 3–4, 5–6. He arrived at these units on form-critical and prosodic grounds, depending in the latter case on deletion of v 3bβ, so that a tricolon and a bicolon made up each unit. Gunkel was concerned at the difference in structure of vv 7–12, so much so that he suggested that two poems may have been combined. Dahood (*Psalms III*, 322), taking up his suggestion, has described the psalm as two separate compositions closely related in language and thought, and apparently from the same hand. However, it is significant that the psalm comprises a form-critical unit, reflecting the standard development of a complaint; moreover, the evidence of inclusion (see below) points to a single composition. Gunkel's concern over the disparate structure of the psalm's two strophes might have been allayed by comparison with Ps. 142.

The proportions of the units detected in vv 1–6 by Gunkel may be confirmed by stylistic criteria: both vv 1–2 and 5–6 are marked off from the middle section by repetition of terms, the stem צדק "be righteous" in vv 1, 2 and the dual of יד "hand" in vv 5–6. Weiser (*Psalms,* 818) has correctly divided the second half of the psalm into two parts, vv 7–9 and 10–12. He has noted the repeated sequence of thought. As to actual words, it is noticeable that חסדך "your loyal love" is repeated (vv 8, 12) and also איבי "my enemies" (vv 9, 12). The unit of vv 10–12 is marked by inclusion, the corresponding אתה אלוהי "you are my God" and אני עבדך "I am your servant."

There is parallelism in the psalm's expression of thought which supports a break after v 6. The elements of petition, descriptive complaint and avowal which feature as blocks of material in vv 1–6 are split up and scattered through vv 7–12. Petitions appear in the first colon of every line and also in the second at vv 11–12. Complaint motifs feature in the second cola of the two lines of v 7. Avowels are found in the second cola of the four lines of vv 8–10 and in the third colon of v 12. The death motifs of the first strophe (v 3aγ-b) are matched by one in the second (v 7b). The bipartite structure of the psalm is also supported by the bifurcating of its initial vocabulary so that it reappears at the beginning or end of the second strophe: ענני "answer me" (vv 1, 7), אל "not" (vv 2, 7), (ל)פניך "before you, your face" (vv 2, 7), בצדקתך "in your righteousness" (vv 1, 11), עבדך "your servant" (vv 2, 12). It is noticeable that two terms bounce through the psalm at significant points: ארץ "land" (vv 3, 6, 10) and נפשי "my soul" (vv 3, 6, 8, 11, 12).

Explanation

This is a prayer composed for recitation in the temple by a needy individual, either in the evening or before dawn, as he anticipated priestly delivery of a divine oracle in the morning (v 8; cf. 5:4 [3]; 90:14). The basis of the appeal for aid is made plain at the outset and reiterated throughout the psalm: it is Yahweh's commitment to the covenant. The psalmist is a member of God's covenant family, and his pleas issue from within that relationship. Yet he is nervously aware of the personal risk involved in attracting God's attention to him and thus exposing himself to scrutiny (cf. 1 Kgs 17:18). His reference to human waywardness is no shoulder-shrugging excuse. It expresses a heartfelt conviction of the reality and power of wrongdoing. The relativity of all human morality over against divine absolutes means that he can make no demands upon God. He must throw himself upon covenant grace.

The situation is explained in strong but general terms which rendered the psalm suitable for many a suppliant. The speaker, reflecting the cut-throat society to which he belongs, has been the victim of ruthless persecution. His varied allusions to death underline its devastating effect upon him. He finds himself in the shadow of death, and feels as devitalized as any of the long forgotten shades imprisoned in Sheol (cf. 88:4–7, 11–13 [3–6, 10–12]). It has left him in a state of psychological shock and humiliation. The one truth that comforts him in his mental search for relief is Yahweh's record as savior in the past history of the nation (cf. 22:5 [4]; 77:6, 12–21 [5, 11–20]). In that history he sees a once-and-for-all revelation of God's character as one who saves and helps. Such precedents of achievement wrought by divine hands encourage him to pray. His own hands are stretched empty in a yearning gesture of need and dependence, from a situation of personal resourcelessness toward one who is the fountain of life (cf. 36:10 [9]; 63:2 [1]).

In the second half of the psalm the tempo quickens with an urgent, breathless series of appeals. He badly needs help before it is too late and death actually lays total claim to him. He pleads with Yahweh not to refuse to give favorable consideration to his praying. The covenantal basis of his appeal rises to the surface again in the reference to loyal love in v 8 and later in v 12. After repeated petitions for a hearing, pleas for direction and deliverance are offered. The former are backed by references to the speaker's plight, and the latter by avowals of personal trust in Yahweh. In his dire need there is none other to whom he is able or willing to go for help.

In the expansion of the petitions found in vv 10–12, those for guidance are significantly put to the fore. He requires advice and instruction to be included in the oracular response. But that alone would not be enough: to know what to do, valuable though it is, needs supplementing with the power to turn knowledge into achievement. To this end he pleads for a manifestation of God in personal power as a guide for life's journey, just as he had done for Israel of old (cf. Neh 9:19–20), and to preserve him from the pitfalls and obstacles he is now encountering. But first he needs deliverance. Returning to this motif in v 11, he prays in the midst of his deathlike experience (cf. v 3) for a renewal of life in accord with its potential. The basis of the prayer is an appeal that Yahweh be true to his name, i.e. his self-revelation as God of the covenant; other covenant motifs follow. The psalmist represents himself as belonging to that divine-human fellowship of patronage and protection. Avowals to this effect encompass the last portion of the psalm with an eloquent border: "You are my God"—"I am your servant." It is on this ground that he enlists God's aid to fight his battle against those who, unlike himself, have not pledged their lives to Yahweh and stand outside the covenant circle. Like an attacked vassal appealing to his overlord, he seeks vindication at God's hands, which in turn will prove a vindication of God's own pledges and power. The psalmist speaks from an OT framework of faith which expected salvation in God's present world, and from a stark life-or-death situation which put to a crucial test the reality of Yahweh's contemporary sovereignty (cf. Rev 6:10).

It is not surprising that such a psalm with almost Pauline emphasis upon (covenant) grace and faith did not go unnoticed by the apostle. He echoed v 2 in both Gal 2:16 and Rom 3:20. In the latter case the reference is the climax to a demonstration of the universality of human sinfulness (cf. Rom 3:9). Man's only hope is to throw himself upon God's free promise of salvation. The saving righteousness to which Paul turned in Rom 3:21 (cf. 1:17) is the actualization of that covenant attribute of righteousness which features in Ps 143:1b. In Christian terms it means God's undertaking to set sinful man right with himself, which becomes personally relevant through faith in Christ. It bursts its original covenantal context in order to create a new, universal covenant and to guarantee that mankind's opportunity matches mankind's need (cf. Rom 3:28–30).

Great Expectations   (144:1–15)

Bibliography

Baumann, E. "Struktur-Untersuchungen im Psalter. 2." *ZAW* 62 (1949/50) 115–52.
Cross, F. M., and **Freedman, D. N.** "A Royal Song of Thanksgiving: 2 Samuel
22 = Psalm 18." *JBL* 72 (1953) 15–34. **Habel, N. C.** *Yahweh Versus Baal: A Conflict of
Religious Cultures.* New York: Bookman Associates, 1964. **Held, M.** "The Root ZBL/
SBL in Akkadian, Ugaritic and Biblical Hebrew." *JAOS* 88 (1968) 90–96. **Jeremias,
J.** *Theophanie. Die Geschichte einer alttestamentlichen Gattung.* WMANT 10. 2nd ed. Neukir-
chen-Vluyn: Neukirchener Verlag, 1977. **Sakenfeld, K. D.** *The Meaning of Hesed in
the Hebrew Bible: A New Enquiry.* HSM 17. Missoula, MT: Scholars Press, 1978. **Schmidt,
W. H.** "Kritik am Königtum." *Probleme biblischer Theologie. G. von Rad zum 70. Geburtstag,*
ed. H. W. Wolff. München: C. Kaiser, 1971, 440–61. **Ziegler, J.** "Ps. 144:14." *Wort
und Geschichte. Festschrift für K. Elliger,* ed. H. Junker and J. Botterweck. Neukirchen-
Vluyn: Neukirchener Verlag, 1973, 191–97.

Translation

1 Davidic.
  Blessed be Yahweh, my rock,   (3+3+3)
    who has trained my hands for war,
    my fingers for battle,
2 *my loyal help* [a] *and fortress,*   (3+3)
    my stronghold and deliverer for me, [b]
  my shield and the one with whom I find shelter,   (3+3)
    who subdues peoples [c] *beneath me.*
3 *Yahweh, what is man that you notice him,*   (3+3)
    a human being that you take thought for him?
4 *Man is like a movement of air,*   (3+3)
    his lifetime like a passing shadow.
5 *Yahweh, spread apart your heavens* [a] *and come down.*   (3+3)
    Touch the mountains so that they smoke.
6 *Flash lightning and scatter them,* [a]   (3+3)
    send your arrows and rout them.
7 *Stretch out your hand from on high,*   (3+3)
    rescue me and deliver me
  from deep water, [a]   (2+3)
    from the power of foreigners
8 *whose mouths speak lies*   (3+3)
    and whose right hands are perjured hands. [a]
9 *O God, I will sing a new song to you,*   (4+3)
    upon a ten-stringed lute will I play to you,
10 *who have given victory to kings,*   (3+3)
    who rescued your servant David. [a]
11 *From the baneful sword rescue me*   (3+3)
    and deliver me from the power of foreigners
  whose mouths speak lies   (3+3)
    and whose right hands are perjured hands.

12 When ^a *our sons are like plants* ^b　　　　　　　　　　　(3+3)
　　full grown, in their youth,
　　our daughters like corner pillars carved ^c　　　　　　　(3+2)
　　for the structure of a palace,
13 *our garners are full, providing*　　　　　　　　　　　　　(3+3)
　　food ^a *of every kind,*
　　our sheep produce thousands,　　　　　　　　　　　　　(3+3)
　　ten thousands in our fields,
14a *our cattle are in fine fettle* ^b—　　　　　　　　　　　(3+3+3)
　　there is no plague ^c *nor abortion* ^d
　　nor bellowing ^e *in our broad meadows* ^f—
15 *how fortunate are the people for whom this is so,*　　　　(4+4)
　　how fortunate the people whose God is Yahweh!

Notes/Comments

2.a. Heb. חסדי "my loyal help" has frequently been the object of emendation (cf. *BHK*), such as חָסְנִי "my strength" (H.-J. Kraus, *Psalmen*, 1121). In 18:3 (2) and 2 Sam 22:2 סלעי "my rock" is its counterpart. Following F. Perles, L. J. Kuyper (*VT* 13 [1963] 490) has urged that here and in 59:10–11, 17–18 (9–10, 16–17) it means "strength," in parallelism with "fortress." Similarly M. Dahood (*Psalms III*, 329) has argued for a meaning "rampart." On the other hand, N. Glueck (*Ḥesed*, 97) maintained that חסד could be taken in its normal sense, the parallelism being justified inasmuch as the notion of strength is contained in the overall concept of the term. K. D. Sakenfeld (*The Meaning of Hesed*, 222–23) has agreed that "strength" is not an extra, independent meaning, but "a particular emphasis within the larger framework of meaning." A. A. Anderson (*Psalms*, 932) has claimed a chiastic order in the line, whereby חסדי is the counterpart of מפלטי לי "my deliverer." It appears to be significant that in the three pairs of terms of v 2a an impersonal term is paired with a more personal one. For its role עוז "help" may be compared, which develops in meaning personally to "one who helps" and occurs in association with מגן "shield" (33:20; 115:9–11) and מפלט "deliverer" (70:6 [5]).
2.b. For the pleonastic לי "for me," used for emphasis here and in 2 Sam 22:2, see GKC § 135m note 3.
2.c. The violence of the verb suggests that "my people" is not intended (Kraus, *Psalmen*, 1121). A plural עמים "peoples" appears in the seemingly basic 18:48 (47) and 2 Sam 22:48, and has much textual support here (cf. *BHS*), including 11QPs ^a. G. R. Driver (*Textus* 1 [1960] 113) posited scribal abbreviation (עמי for עמים) here and in Isa 51:4. Dahood (*Psalms III*, 330), following D. N. Freedman, has interestingly interpreted as עַמִּי, a construct form before a preposition, "the peoples subject to me."
5.a. N. C. Habel (*CBQ* 34 [1972] 424–25, 430) has allied the phrase here and in 18:10 (9); 2 Sam 22:10 with its use as a description of creation: it describes *creatio continua* whereby Yahweh pitches his heavenly tent as preparation for self-manifestation. But J. Jeremias (*Theophanie*, 25 note 2) was probably right in dissociating from Yahweh's creative activity. F. M. Cross and D. N. Freedman (*JBL* 72 [1953] 24 note 23) pertinently compared קרעת "you tore open" in a similar context at Isa 63:19 (64:1) and concluded that the present verb signifies "spread apart, open (as curtains)." It may be significant that a hiph'il is used here in differentiation from the creation-oriented qal: Cross and Freedman (*JBL* 72 [1953] 24 note 24) revocalize as a hiph'il in Ps 18:10 (= 2 Sam 22:10).
6.a. The suffixes of v 6a, b probably refer by anticipation to the enemies of v 7 (Anderson, *Psalms*, 933). Dahood (*Psalms III*, 330) relating them to the preceding nouns, takes ברק "lightning" as a collective singular, while H. Gunkel (*Die Psalmen*, 606) emended to ברקים "lightning bolts" and Jeremias (*Theophanie*, 25 note 3), following B. Duhm, to ברקיך "your lightning bolts."
7.a. For this metaphor for the psalmist's plight, based on the cosmological motif of Yahweh's victory over the rebellious, chaotic waters, see Habel, *Yahweh Versus Baal*, 66; N. J. Tromp, *Primitive Conceptions*, 64.

8.a. A breach of political alliance earlier ratified by oath and accompanying gesture (cf. Deut 32:40) is in view (M. A. Klopfenstein, *Die Lüge*, 38–39).

10.a. C. Lindhagen (*The Servant Motif*, 282) *et al.* have taken דוד "David" as a reference to the contemporary Davidide. However, the use of עבד "servant" in combination with the name דוד in the Psalter suggests rather that the historical figure is in view (cf. I. Riesener, *Der Stamm* עבד, 228–32): cf. 18:50–51 (49–50); 2 Sam 22:50–51. The implicit thought is that Yahweh who has helped earlier kings, from David onward, is to receive thanksgiving for help given to David's contemporary successor (Gunkel, *Die Psalmen*, 607).

12.a. MT אשר "who, that" has been regarded with suspicion: an emendation אשרי (G. R. Driver, *JTS* 44 [1943] 23, followed by NEB, "Happy are we whose sons . . . ," *et al.*) or a repointing to an imperative אַשֵּׁר "bless" (e.g. Kraus, *Psalmen*, 1121) has been suggested. LXX Sᵂ, rendering the suffixed nouns of vv 12–14 with third person plural possessive pronouns, made the section a description of the enemies, whose good fortune is disdained for a higher blessing in v 15. As it stands, it may express a purpose "in order that (. . . may be)" (KJV; J. H. Eaton, *Kingship*, 127; cf. BDB, 83b) or, better, a condition "when" (RV; cf. BDB, 83b, and for the extended subordinate clause cf. Lev 4:22). See further *Form/Structure/Setting*.

12.b. For consistency with the parallel simile Driver (*JTS* 44 [1943] 23) favored an architectural term "tall towers" (= NEB) or "pavilions," comparing Sab. *nṯ't* "kiosk," the Greek rendering of נטע at Sir 40:19 and the use of the verb in Isa 51:16.

12.c. Heb. חטב is best explained as a dialectal form of חצב "hew, cut": cf. the parallelism of חצב and בנה "build" in Prov 9:1 (Dahood, *Psalms III*, 332–33).

13.a. Heb. זן "kind," elsewhere only 2 Chr 16:14 and common in Aramaic, is evidently a Persian loanword (*HALAT*, 263b). Driver (*HTR* 29 [1936] 193–94), followed by NEB, considered an understanding in terms of food forced and proposed זן "food (of every kind)," comparing Aram. זיונא "food."

14.a. The translation of v 14 is most uncertain and a variety of interpretations have been offered. For a survey see J. Ziegler, "Ps. 144:14," 191–97. A major issue is whether and how much of the content of the verse is concerned with farming. Ziegler ("Ps. 144:14," 197) has rendered אלופינו (seemingly an alternative form of אֲלָפֵינוּ) as "our districts" and pointed the next word as מְסֻבָּלִים "without burdens." More commonly a farming reference is envisaged in v 14α and a reference to society at large in v 14αβ-b (see below). However, this interpretation leaves v 14α out on a limb. The problem may not be solved by taking it with v 13, so that בחוצותינו is at the beginning of a colon of three beats (Anderson, *Psalms*, 935): there appears to be intentional external parallelism between בחוצותינו "in our fields" at the end of v 13 and ברחבתינו "in our broad meadows" at the end of v 14 (see note 14.f.).

14.b. Heb. מסבלים most probably has some such meaning: cf. LXX παχεῖς "stout," S *šynyn* "strong," Hier *pingues* "fat" and α´ σ´ σιτευτοί or σιτιστοί "fatted." Aram. סָבַל "sustain" and סבול "sustenance" have been compared (Driver, *HTR* 29 [1936] 194–95; M. Held, *JAOS* 88 [1968] 92 note 49). Ziegler ("Ps. 144:14," 196) has objected that cattle were not fattened, apart from calves, but in Ezek 39:18 Bashan bulls are called fatlings. Other suggestions have been "laden with young, pregnant" and "well-laden" with produce (BDB, 687b).

14.c. Heb. פרץ has been understood in urban terms as "breach" in the city walls (e.g. Anderson, *Psalms*, 935). KB (781a), comparing 2 Sam 6:8, interprets as "decease." Kraus (*Psalmen*, 1120; *et al.*) takes as "accident" (cf. RSV), in support of which later Heb. פִּרְצָה "calamity" might be adduced. Since the cognate verb is used of "plague" in 106:29, it is possible that פרץ "outbreak" has this implicit connotation here. Then a series of different calamities affecting cattle may be envisaged in the tricolon, disease, loss of young and drought.

14.d. Heb. יוצאת is evidently a case of a feminine participle used as an abstract noun (Driver, *HTR* 29 [1936] 194–95; cf. GKC § 122s). It probably means "abortion" (KB, 375a; cf. the verb in Exod 21:22). On the urban interpretation it means "surrender" or "exile" (BDB, 423b; Dahood, *Psalms III*, 333; Ziegler, "Ps. 144:14," 197): the collocation of the stems פרץ and יצא in Amos 4:3 is compared. Held (*JAOS* 88 [1968] 92) renders the two clauses "there is none that breaks out and none that stampedes," but Ziegler ("Ps. 144:14," 192) has rightly accused him of cultural anachronism.

14.e. In the light of notes 14.c., d., f. צוחה "cry" may be a reference to cattle suffering from drought: cf. Joel 1:18. The term is used of human reaction to drought in Jer 14:2 (cf. Isa 24:[7–] 11; in v 11 F. Delitzsch, *Isaiah*, vol. 1 [Tr. J. Kennedy; Edinburgh: T. & T. Clark, 1891] 398, rendered חוצות "fields").

14.f. Held (*JAOS* 88 [1968] 92) rendered "ranges." Cf. מרחב "broad meadow" in Hos 4:16. The parallelism of חוץ and רחוב in the sense of "street" and "square" is common (cf. BDB,

982a). It may well have encouraged a parallelism in rural senses, as perhaps in Nah 2:5 (4), where C. A. Keller (*Nahoum*. [CAT 11b; Neuchâtel: Delachaux et Niestlé, 1971] 12) has rendered "fields . . . expanses."

Form/Structure/Setting

Psalm 144 has a mixed form. Vv 1–11 obviously comprise a royal composition, specifically a royal complaint. The main petitions of vv 5–7 (8) are prefaced with two elements, hymnic praise of Yahweh in vv 1–2 and a prayerful meditation upon human weakness in vv 3–4. W. H. Schmidt ("Kritik am Königtum," 460–61) has observed that the latter element functions as an attempt to arouse divine sympathy and so intervention, like the similar appeal in the royal 89:48–49 (47–48). The former element uses an indirect benediction formula (cf. W. S. Towner, *CBQ* 30 [1968] 389–90), followed by the ground of praise expressed in nouns and participial predications (cf. v 10). These latter are characteristic of royal psalms and different in form and content from standard hymnic participles (see F. Crüsemann, *Studien zur Formgeschichte*, 123–24). For hymnic praise of God by way of introduction to a royal complaint 89:2–9 (1–8) may be compared (cf. C. Westermann, *Praise*, 57). While in form it belongs to the thanksgiving (cf. 18:47–49 [46–48]), here in function it adds support to the subsequent prayer of complaint as an acknowledgment of Yahweh's power. The beginning of the prayer section is expressed in terms of theophany, whose form-critical history originated in the hymn (vv 5–6; see Jeremias, *Theophanie*, 129). It ends with a description of the enemies, an element which usually occurs earlier in the complaint (cf. Westermann, *Praise*, 64). V 9 is at first sight ambivalent. Is it a further present ascription of praise (cf. 89:2 [1]; 101:1)? Mention of "a new song" suggests rather that it is a vow of thanksgiving. Yet v 10 appears not, as one might expect, to give reason for future thanksgiving, but to praise for past victory (see note 10.*a.*). Vv 10bβ–11 virtually repeat the petitions and description of vv 7–8. Gunkel (*Die Psalmen*, 605–6; *et al.*, including *BHS*), observing that a vow of thanksgiving characteristically concludes a complaint, regarded this section as a variant of the earlier one; he used it as a partial basis for reconstructing vv 7–8. Kraus (*Psalmen*, 1122) has left the issue fairly open but judges that a resumption of vv 7–8 in this portion is not impossible. In view of the high degree of variation encountered in individual complaints (cf. Westermann, *Praise*, 64), it is probably unwise to let form dictate to the text.

Much of vv 1–10 has a close relationship with Ps 18, which has clearly inspired it in a literary sense. E. Baumann (*ZAW* 62 [1949/50] 148–49) well described the relationship not as mechanical borrowing but a re-ordering, reshaping and amplifying of the material, changing the perspective from a royal thanksgiving to a royal complaint. There is interesting alignment with the 2 Sam 22 recension in places (the addition of לִי "for me," v 2, with 22:2; הרודד "the subduer," v 2, cf. המוריד "who brought down," 22:48; singular בּרק "lightning," v 6, with 22:15).

The second part of the psalm, vv 12–15 is puzzling both in itself and in relation to vv 1–11. Its dominant first plural suffixes look like evidence of a communal composition. Gunkel (*Die Psalmen*, 607) described it as a separate piece lacking its own introduction and possibly originally a hymn or a communal thanksgiving. The final verse is a beatitude (see the note on 106:3); its second half is almost identical with 33:12. The tone of the verse, which as a whole revels in Yahweh's blessing demonstrated in the phenomena of vv 12–14, is very close to that of the beatitude in Deut 33:29 (cf. Pss 65:5 [4]; 94:12). Vv 12–14 are clearly descriptive, but whether of contemporary or anticipated joys it is difficult to establish. In the present context of vv 1–11 an impression of an implicit wish is given.

The relationship between the two parts of the psalm is complicated by considerations of chronology and setting. There can be no objection to regarding vv 1–11 as a royal psalm, a creative adaptation of parts of Ps 18, which belongs to the late pre-exilic period in view of the Aramaic sense of the stem פצה "redeem" in vv 7, 11. As a royal psalm, the Davidic heading is quite explicable. In turn vv 12–15 could be regarded as spoken by the king: the relevance of the material can be illustrated from 72:3, 16 (A. Weiser, *Psalms*, 823; Eaton, *Kingship*, 127; cf. Kraus, *Psalmen*, 1123). H. Schmidt (*Die Psalmen*, 250) and Weiser have considered the psalm a unit as a cultic liturgy in the setting of a royal festival. It is questionable whether this view does justice to the urgency of the petitions in the first part, to which Gunkel's characterization of the psalm's background as the antecedent of a military expedition (*Die Psalmen*, 605) does better justice. Eaton (*Kingship*, 127–28) is able to overcome this objection by his setting of a royal ritual of humiliation, but at the cost of a postulate which by no means all scholars are able to accept.

The language used in vv 12–15 makes it difficult to accept a pre-exilic dating for it (זן "kind," v 13; the relative ש "who(se)," v 15). Accordingly the royal composition of vv 1–11 appears to have been re-employed in the post-exilic period, not in a messianic sense, as the other royal psalms evidently were, but in contemporary application to the community. There is a parallel in Isa 55:3–5, where the community is represented as heir to the Davidic covenant (cf. O. Eissfeldt, "Promises of Grace to David in Isaiah 55:1–5 [Ps 89]," in *Israel's Prophetic Heritage*, ed B. W. Anderson and W. Harrelson [New York: Harper, 1962] 196–207). Protection from hostile neighbors is claimed by way of appeal to David and his dynasty (v 10), and prosperity for the community is craved. A twin response is sought from Yahweh, a response both of salvation and blessing (cf. Westermann, *What Does the OT Say About God?*, 78).

The structure of the psalm can hardly be defined in terms of strophes. Baumann (*ZAW* 62 [1949/50] 150–51), who did so categorize vv 1–11, was able to do so only after replacement of vv 7–8 by vv 10bβ–11. Kraus (*Psalmen*, 1122) has correctly denied that the repeated material functions as a refrain. Vv 9–11 have a resumptive role: they echo the praise, prayer and descriptive complaint of vv 1–8. The two cases of article and participle in v 10 (cf. vv 1–2), as well as v 11, constitute repeated elements. Divine address in vv 1, 3, 5, 9 mark off the formal divisions of the first part. In the second part vv 12–14 fall into a pattern of two, one and two lines. In the first pair an initial בנינו/בנותינו "our sons/our daughters" is capped by the same sequence of letters in the second cola (בנעוריהם; תבנית "in their youth; structure"; Kraus's emendation בערגתם in v 12aβ [*Psalmen*, 1121], following Duhm and Gunkel, is thus rendered doubtful). In the middle line (מזוינו) "our garners" is likewise capped by (מזן) "from . . . kind," while in the last pair the suffixes on the first words are repeated on the last. The two divine terms of v 15 neatly take up the two used in vv 1 (3, 5), 9. It is possible that אלהים "God" in v 9, not so used outside the Elohistic psalms (cf. Ps 108), was changed from יהוה "Yahweh" to secure this poetic climax. In v 12 אשר "when" not only provides a phonetic link with אשרי "how fortunate" in v 15 but operates as a hinge between the two parts of the psalm: it has just been used in v 11. Poetic artistry is much more evident in the second part than in the first.

Explanation

The major portion of the psalm, vv 1–11, was originally spoken by a Judean king in a historical context of broken alliance and military attack (vv 7–8, 11). Material quarried from an old royal thanksgiving, Ps 18, has been creatively re-used as a means of imploring fresh cause for joy. The king praises Yahweh for providing him with basic skills and subsequent aid in defense of the theocratic realm and in extension of its frontiers, the better to represent in the world Yahweh's power and greatness (cf. 2:6–10). The monarch humbly expresses his amazement at the grace he has received (cf. 8:5 [4]). How can it be that he, a mere mortal (cf. Neh 1:11), should be so favored? Like his fellows, he is of himself so ephemeral and insignificant. He is what he is only by divine grace (cf. 1 Cor 15:10).

By such means the king indicates his need of Yahweh's help, and hints that he should be its recipient once more. Now in direct prayer he describes the prospect of divine aid in terms of a theophany, the breaking into time and space of a colossal energy with devastating effect. Powerful as his enemies may be—a veritable resurgence of the primeval sea monster which once rebelled against God—Yahweh is greater still, the ancient victor (cf. 89:10–11 [9–10]). With such implicit confidence he implores God to use that power once more on his behalf. Aware of Yahweh's moral standards, the king gives assurance that wrong rests on the other side, in the form of breach of treaty and false claims. The term "hand(s)" resounds throughout the piece as the marker of a three-cornered confrontation. The aggressive "hand" or power (v 7b) of the king's enemies is soon to meet the king's "hands" (v 1)—but the latter have been trained by Yahweh, and it is hoped that the divine "hands" (v 7a) will reach down in reprisal and rescue.

In vv 9–11, resuming the motifs of praise, prayer and plight already expressed, the king makes a vow to sing and play in the temple a song of thanksgiving, newly composed for the occasion, in commemoration of God's coming to his aid. Even now he can give praise for the victories of the kings of the Judean dynasty, from David onward. But unjust threat looms large, and in a reiterated appeal he gives the circumstances of the emergency again, this time with the poignant detail of the "baneful sword."

The royal psalm became part of the heritage of the post-exilic religious community. They evidently used it afresh, to convey to Yahweh their own sense of dependence upon him to relieve the pressure of foreign neighbors. A supplement was added, whether original or from another source, in order to give more comprehensive coverage of their needs. The nation's whole future lay in his care. Implicit blessing is implored upon human progeny, crops and animal progeny, echoing in its content and order such traditional formulations as Deut 28:4. A new generation is needed, made up of sturdy boys and strong, fine girls who can work together to build a better nation. They look to God to provide such increase. They also offer their wish for full barns, which though not devoid of danger (cf. Deut 8:12–14; Luke 12:16–21) are welcome tokens of his covenant grace if accepted in trust and used for good. As if putting into practice the axiom that God can do more than they ask or think (Eph 3:20), they exuberantly ask for increase of their flocks beyond measure. Protection is needed not only from military attack but from such natural foes of their herds as disease, abortion and drought. God can ward off such dangers. They do not yet enjoy such gifts of plenty, but these will surely come. They do have the giver as their covenant God, and in him they exult, for himself as much as for his potential giving.

Tell of His Might, Sing of His Grace! (145:1–21)

Bibliography

Crüsemann, F. *Studien zur Formgeschichte.* **Liebreich, L. J.** "Psalms 34 and 145 in the Light of Their Key Words." *HUCA* 27 (1956) 181–92. **Munch, P. A.** "Die alphabetische Akrostichie in der jüdischen Psalmendichtung." *ZDMG* 90 (1936) 703–10. **Schottroff, W.** *"Gedenken" im alten Orient und im AT. Die Wurzel zākar im semitischer Sprachkreis.* WMANT 15. 2nd ed. Neukirchen-Vluyn: Neukirchener Verlag, 1967.

Translation

1   Praise. Davidic.
   א *Let me extol you, my God, O king,*   (3+4)
      and bless your name for ever and ever.
2 ב *Every day I want to bless you*   (3+4)
      and praise your name for ever and ever.
3 ג *Yahweh is so great and utterly praiseworthy:*   (4+3)
      his greatness is limitless.

4 ד *Let [a] one generation laud your work to another,*   (4+3)
      and your mighty acts let them proclaim.
5 ה *The majestic glory of your splendor let them declare,[a]*   (4+3)
      while your wondrous acts I make my theme;
6 ו *and of the power of your awesome acts let them speak,[a]*   (3+3)
      while your great acts [b] I recount.[c]

7 ז   *The proclamation* ᵃ *of your abundant* ᵇ *goodness*   (3+3)
     let them utter
     and of your consistency let them sing.

8a ח   *Yahweh is dutiful* ᵇ *and compassionate,*   (3+4)
     patient and greatly ᶜ *loyal.* ᵈ

9 ט   *Yahweh is good to all,*   (3+3)
     and his compassion covers all his handiwork.

10 י   *Let all your handiwork give you thanks, Yahweh,*   (3+3)
     and the recipients of your loyal love ᵃ *bless you:*

11 כ   *the glory of your reign let them tell*   (3+3)
     and your might let them declare,

12 ל   *making known to mankind his mighty acts*   (4+3)
     and the glorious majesty of his reign.

13 מ   *Your reign is a reign that lasts for all time,* ᵃ   (3+3)
     your dominion endures for all generations.

    נ   *Yahweh is faithful in all his words*   (4+3)
     and loyal in all his work. ᵇ

14 ס   *Yahweh supports all who fall*   (4+3)
     and raises all whose backs are bent.

15 ע   *The eyes of all look* ᵃ *to you*   (3+4)
     and you give ᵇ *them their food in due time.*

16 פ   *You* ᵃ *open your hand*   (3+3)
     and satisfy the desire of every living being.

17 צ   *Yahweh is consistent in all his ways*   (4+3)
     and loyal in all his work.

18 ק   *Yahweh is near to all who call on him,* ᵃ   (4+4)
     to all who call on him sincerely.

19 ר   *He effects the desires of all who revere him;*   (3+3).
     their cries for help he hears and he saves them.

20 ש   *Yahweh protects all who love him,*   (4+3)
     but all the wicked will he destroy.

21 ת   *The praise of Yahweh let my mouth declare*   (3+4)
     and let all flesh bless his holy name.
    . . . for ever and ever ᵃ

Notes/Comments

4.a. The verbs of vv 4–7, 10–11 have been regarded as present in force or as a combination of present and future (cf. D. Michel, *Tempora*, 152; A. Weiser, *Psalms*, 825–26). Form-critical considerations (see *Form/Structure/Setting*) suggest rather that they are jussive (H. Gunkel, *Die Psalmen*, 610; H.-J. Kraus, *Psalmen*, 1126–27).

5.a. For MT ודברי "and words of," taken with v 5b, is better read יְדַבֵּרוּ "let them declare" with 11QPsᵃ (ידברו) LXX S. The external parallelism of vv 5–6, evident in MT in the initial compound object with second singular suffix and the closing combination of a suffixed object and a first singular verb (see note 6.b.), supports the emendation. 11QPsᵃ ונפ "and your wondrous acts" (= LXX S) may likewise be preferable on the assumption of haplography in MT (A. A. Anderson, *Psalms*, 937).

5.b. The third plural verbs of LXX S here and of LXX Tg. in v 6b (cf. *BHS*), preferred by Gunkel (*Die Psalmen*, 611) *et al.*, are easier and so secondary readings: cf. the oscillation of v 21.

6.a. It is most unlikely that נפלאותיך "your wondrous acts" of v 5b is the subject of יאמרו "let them speak" (H. W. Wolff, *Anthropology*, 229): the single and grouped nouns of vv 5–6 all appear to be related objects.

6.b. The parallelism, both internal (Gunkel, *Die Psalmen*, 611; *et al.*) and external, suggests that the plural of K is preferable. The singular in Q is a harmonization with MT's verbal suffix (see note 6.c.).

6.c. For the plural of LXX *Tg.* retroverted as יְסַפְּרוּן "let them recount" by Gunkel (*Die Psalmen*, 611, see note 5.a.). M. Dahood (*Psalms III*, 337), comparing 11QPs ᵃ אספר "I recount," has most plausibly suggested an energic form אֲסַפְּרֶנָּה, which would certainly suit the external parallelism. For the energic form cf. G. R. Driver, "Hebrew Notes on Prophets and Proverbs," *JTS* 41 (1940) 163–64.

7.a. For זכר "proclamation" as cultic pronouncement see the notes on 111:4; 135:13.

7.b. Most probably a noun -רֹב or רֹב is to be read for the adjectival form in MT. Assimilation to the phrase רַב־טוֹב in MT at Isa 63:7 may have occurred. Alternatively a marginal רֹב, referring to the phrase רב-חסד which is always found elsewhere for גדל-חסד, may have displaced -רֹב here.

7.c. See the note on 143:1.

8.a. See note 8.b. in *Notes/Comments* of Ps 103 for this cultic formula. The priority of חנון "dutiful" is probably due to the exigencies of the acrostic, as in 111:4.

8.b. See note 5.a. in *Notes/Comments* of Ps 116.

8.c. Heb. גדל replaces the standard רב to provide a link with the instances of the stem in vv 3, 6.

8.d. Heb. חסד and in v 13b חסיד "loyal" refer not to the covenant relationship between Yahweh and Israel, as in vv 10, 17, but to his universal care in the light of v 9: see the note on 119:64.

10.a. Heb. חסידיך "recipients of your loyal love" could be a synonymous parallel of the subject of v 10a in view of v 8. However, elsewhere the noun relates to the religious community of Israel (see K. D. Sakenfeld, *The Meaning of Hesed*, 243). Probably they are the subject of the verbs of v 11, who in v 12 are to communicate to the rest of the world the tradition of Yahweh's power and kingship, so that they in turn will give thanks (v 10a).

13.a. Heb. עולמים "ages" is an intensive form, signifying no longer a period than the singular (E. Jenni, "Das Wort *'olam* im Alten Testament," *ZAW* 64 [1952] 244).

13.b. Kennicott ms. 142 so adds (see *BHS*) and LXX S reflect. 11QPs ᵃ also has this *nun* colon, but with אלוהים "God" for יהוה "Yahweh." Dahood (*Psalms III*, 335) is inclined not to regard the colon as authentic in view of missing letter-lines in other acrostic psalms. In this case structural considerations affirm its genuineness (see *Form/Structure/Setting*).

15.a. For the connotation of hopeful waiting in the verb see W. Zimmerli, *Man and His Hope*, 36; Wolff, *Anthropology*, 150.

15.b. MT adds להם "to them" which is metrically difficult: cf. the same addition in 11QPs ᵃ at 104:27 (*BHS*). Was it originally a marginal note לחם "bread," intended to record the counterpart to אכלם "their food" at the similar 136:25 (cf. 146:8)?

16.a. The chiastic order of the cola in vv 15–16 suggests that אתה "you" be read (cf. LXX σύ), either for -את (sign of direct object; Gunkel, *Die Psalmen*, 611) or better before -את (Dahood, *Psalms III*, 338), having been lost by homoeoarcton.

18.a. Heb. קראיו "those who call upon him" is probably not here in relation to cultic prayer but is a general term for the religious community of Israel: cf. vv 19a, 20a and also v 10b (J. Becker, *Gottesfurcht im AT*, 148).

21.a. Metrically this phrase does not appear to be part of the psalm proper. It probably represents a liturgical refrain: cf. the addition of 115:18 in many mss. (Kraus, *Psalmen*, 1127; *BHS*) and the refrain ברוך יהוה וברוך שמו לעולם ועד "Blessed be Yahweh and blessed be his name for ever and ever" after each line of the psalm in 11QPs ᵃ.

Form/Structure/Setting

In form Ps 145 is an acrostic poem which begins each bicolon with a fresh letter of the alphabet. In terms of standard genres it is a hymn, like the acrostic of Ps 111. The heading תהלה "praise" so categorizes it (Kraus,

Psalmen, 20–21). More precisely the psalm is similar to the imperatival type of hymn which prefaces the motifs of Yahweh's majesty and grace with repeated calls to praise (C. Westermann, *Praise,* 130–32). This formal pattern clarifies the function of the ambiguous verbs of vv 4–7, 10–12 as jussive: they are indirect calls to praise or wishes for praise, though irregular in that the verbs do not stand at the head of their clauses except in v 10 (F. Crüsemann, *Studien zur Formgeschichte,* 186, 298). Crüsemann (*Studien zur Formgeschichte,* 269–70, 298) has also drawn attention to the variant of the thanksgiving formula (cf. 111:1) used in vv 1–2 and to the hymnic participles of vv 14, 16, 20, the second of which is combined with a second person reference in a singular fashion.

Gunkel (*Die Psalmen,* 610) recognized that the alternating of calls to praise and grounds for praise is the key to the psalm's structure: vv 1–2 + 3 (also Kraus, *Psalmen,* 1128; Anderson, *Psalms,* 936; cf. A. Weiser, *Psalms,* 827) make up the first unit and vv 4–7 + 8–9 (also Kraus, *Psalmen,* 1129; Anderson, *Psalms,* 936) the second. The third likewise appears to be vv 10–12 + 13a (cf. Weiser, *Psalms,* 827; D. Kidner, *Psalms 73–150,* 481), and the fourth, with inversion of ground and summons in order to provide an inclusion for the whole psalm, vv 13b–20 + 21. In each of the three places where the substance of praise is given briefly there is a deliberate repetition of vocabulary for emphasis: the stem גדל "great(ness)" in v 3, רחם "compassion(ate)" in vv 8–9 and the noun מלכות "reign" in v 13. Perhaps the counterpart in the longer section is חסיד "loyal" in vv 13b, 17 (see below).

There do not appear to be strophes in any meaningful sense. The psalm divides into two halves, vv 1–9, 10–20, which subdivide into quarters, as above, with an overall ABA′B′ content of divine greatness and grace. The last verse picks up the terminology of the first two by way of inclusion: the verb ברך "bless," שם "name" and the stem הלל "praise" (cf. Dahood, *Psalms III,* 339). The first term significantly occurs in v 10 also; moreover, vv 10–13 resume the royal motif of v 1, using the stem מלך "rule." The reasons for praise in vv 13b–20 are twofold: Yahweh's common grace in universal providence in vv 13b–16 and his special grace to the religious community in vv 17–20: both begin with similar predications, repeating the divine name, חסיד "loyal" (in different senses), the double בכל "in all" and מעשיו "his work." The last instance has a parallel in the initiatory מעשיך "your work" in vv 4, 10, while מעשיו in v 9 may mark an inclusion with v 4 (for the deliberate variation of suffix see below). In the units vv 13b–16 and 17–20 there is other evidence of symmetry. The divine name and the sequence בכל, לכל "in/to all" appear in both vv 13b, 14 and vv 17, 18; the enthusiastic כל "all" occurs six times in each unit. In each unit, moreover, an initial line is expanded into three further ones (vv 13b + 14–16, 17 + 18–20). Heb. רצון "desire" occurs in each amplification (vv 16, 19); participles occur at the end of each (vv 16, 20) and also at the beginning of the former one (v 14: cf. קרוב "near," v 18), while the middle line speaks of needs met (vv 15, 19). This analysis makes it clear that vv 13b and 17 do not stand at the beginning and end of a section, as Weiser (*Psalms,* 828) considered.

Dahood (*Psalms III,* 336) has pointed to the stylistic phenomenon of chiasmus in the bicola of vv 2, 10, 20, 21. A. R. Ceresco has traced it over wider ·

areas in vv 11–12 (*CBQ* 40 [1978] 5–6, כבוד מלכותך "glory of your reign" : וגבורתיך "your might" ∷ גבורתיו "his might" : מלכותו . . . כבוד "glorious . . . his reign" and vv 17–19 (*CBQ* 38 [1976] 305, יעשה "he effects" : יקראהו "call upon him" ∷ קראיו : מעשיו). There is a noticeable conglomeration of five words containing adjacent *shin* and *mem* in vv 19–20, which appears to be a play upon "name" in v 20 (cf. the similar phenomenon in the closing verses of Ps 103). Support for this inference comes from v 18, which, as Kraus (*Psalmen*, 1129) has observed, hints at the divine name which his people invoke.

It is clear that form and stylistics share in elucidating the psalm's structure. False trails have been followed by E. J. Kissane (*Psalms II*, 318) and J. Schildenberger (*Estudios Eclesiásticos* 34 [1960] 686–87), who both sought symmetrical strophic patterns, the first envisaging four strophes of five verses after the introductory two verses and the second three strophes of three bicola and three of four bicola and a final verse, and also by L. J. Liebreich, who stressed word repetition at the expense of form. The latter (*HUCA* 27 [1956] 181–92) isolated vv 1–2, 10, 21 as the progressive blessing (ברך) of Yahweh by the psalmist, by the select few and by the world. The prelude, vv 1–2 with the key word הלל "praise," is followed by two strophes, vv 3–6 with the threefold stem גדל "great" and vv 7–9 with the key term טוב "good" and also the motif of justice. After the interlude, v 10, come the third and fourth strophes, vv 11–13 with the key noun מלכות "kingdom" and vv 14–20 which elaborate the motifs of the second strophe; v 21 is the postlude. Liebreich made some useful observations, but his results fail to account for what according to his perspective should be significant repetitions in the psalm: הלל in v 3 and גדל in v 8.

The versatility of the psalmist is obvious. He took the acrostic pattern in his artistic stride and found it no obstacle to a coherent development of his message. In this respect the psalm invites comparison with Ps 111. In fact, W. Schottroff (*Gedenken*, 294) has observed close links between the two psalms, not only as acrostic hymns but as employing the same cultic formula (111:4). the same motifs of Yahweh's greatness (111:2) and majesty (111:3) and his compassionate grace to Israel (111:4–6), and both employ זכר "proclamation" and נפלאתיו "his wondrous acts" (111:4). One might also adduce תהלה "praise" at the end of both psalms and the initial thanksgiving formulation at the beginning, and also צדקה "righteousness" in the sense of staunch consistency (111:3). It may be that the same author composed both; at least one psalmist has shown himself an apt student of the other's method.

The question of the relationship of Ps 145 to other psalms must be raised. Some parallels consist of standard formulations, e.g. in vv 1aβ (cf. 30:1aα; 118:28b) and 3a (cf. 48:2 [1]a; 96:4a). But vv 15–16 bear a close relation to 104:27–28. The similarity is even more marked when one observes the alternation of second and third divine references. The oscillation, not unparalleled in hymns (cf. Crüsemann, *Studien zur Formgeschichte*, 225–26) and explained here by Dahood (*Psalms III*, 338) as court style, has a high degree of regularity. The substance of praise is marked by use of the third person, as is customary (cf. Gunkel and Begrich, *Einleitung*, 48), in vv 3, 7–8, 13b–20. These passages are differentiated from the jussive summonses, in which direct address is employed (vv 1–2, 4–7). Deviations from this pattern seldom occur: in vv 12–13a, where Gunkel (*Die Psalmen*, 611) and others have emended with some ancient support (LXX *S* in v 12 and Hier in v 13a), and in v 21. That in v 12 may be due to its content of testimony; that in v 21 to mechanical continuation of the third person style of the preceding verses. Vv 15–16 are the only other cases. They are probably due to quotation from 104:27–28 where the second person is employed. If so, v 13 may likewise be a direct citation either of a stylized formula or of a particular poem to which both it and the (third person) Aramaic Dan 3:33; 4:31 (4:3, 34) bear common witness. Possible literary links with Ps 103 are שם קדשו "his holy name" after the verb ברך "bless" in 103:1; 145:21, the formula of 103:8 varied in 145:8 for reasons stated in notes 8.a.,c. above, יראיו "those who fear him" in 103:17 and 145:19 (after v 17) and the *shin/mem* play already mentioned. It is not insignificant that there are clear parallels between Pss 103 and 111. Accordingly it is possible to envisage Pss 103, 111 and 145 as emanating from the same circle. In this connection it is noteworthy that Crüsemann (*Studien zur Formgeschichte*, 301–2) ascribed Ps 104 to the same milieu as Ps 103.

The setting of the psalm is in fact controversial. P. A. Munch (*ZDMG* 90 [1936] 703–10; cf. *AcOr* 15 [1936] 112–40) ascribed it and the other alphabetic psalms to a non-cultic, educational setting. Crüsemann (*Studien zur Formgeschichte*, 297–98) has concurred, observing that in such psalms older, cultic forms have been adapted and in the process show signs of degeneration; similarly J. Becker (*Israel deutet seine Psalmen*, 74–75), who posits a non-cultic devotional setting. On the other hand, Weiser especially (*Psalms*, 827; cf. H. Schmidt, *Die Psalmen*, 252) has firmly categorized it as a hymn of the cult community, probably recited at the autumn festival, in view of the references to salvation history (vv 5–6) and to the harvest (v 15). In this cultic assessment Anderson (*Psalms*, 936) and G. Fohrer (*Introduction*, 293), among others, have concurred. Certainly there seems to be little reason to deny that the psalm with its hymnic form had a cultic function, unless it is insisted that acrostic psalms be denied such a function on principle.

The psalm is generally regarded as post-exilic. The Aramaizing term מלכות "reign" in v 13 is used more in later Hebrew, and likewise זקף "raise" in v 14; its associate Pss 103 and 111 appear to come from that period. For the Davidic reference in the heading the observations on Pss 139 and 140 may be compared. Its purpose may be homiletic, possibly establishing a link with Ps 30, with which it has a fair amount of language in common. In the Psalter it has been fittingly prefixed to the final collection, the hymns of Pss 146–150; in content it is especially close to Ps 146.

Explanation

Psalm 145 is a solo hymn of exuberant praise intended to stimulate the congregation to appreciate Yahweh's kingship. To this end it uses both prayerful address and hortative testimony. It is marked by skillful artistry, especially discernible in its acrostic form, of which the poet was a master, weaving its elegance neatly into the development of his thought.

The psalmist exhorts himself to lifelong praise of the God he worships: nothing less is sufficient response. He broaches by the royal title the theme he intends to explore from Yahweh's general revelation of his being and activity. The first ground of his praise appears in v 3: the greatness of Yahweh (cf. 104:1). His own praise, however extended, is inadequate for its subject: rhetorically he calls upon each generation of God's people to transmit to the next the tradition of his work in creation and in redemptive history, a tradition which reveals his kingly power (cf. 74:12–17; 95:3–7). The poet willingly owns himself to be a link in this living chain of worship of the great King. In v 7 the way is paved for the second cause of praise, which is formally stated in the following two verses. Yahweh, the great and mighty king, is good to all. Like every monarch worthy of the name, he cares for the subjects in his realm. The credal statement cited in v 8 (cf. Exod 34:6), a favorite text of post-exilic Jews, is used to summarize his constant goodness. At the close it is given a unique twist to show that Yahweh's greatness is supremely evidenced in his love. From v 9 it is clear that a universalistic significance is given to Israel's prime article of faith. Israel is not the only recipient of the divine "loyal love": it is manifested also in Yahweh's common grace to all his creatures. This motif of the kindly, bountiful king of creation, upon which the book of Jonah may be regarded as a commentary, is to be developed later in the psalm.

Moving to the second half of his composition, the poet proceeds to draw a further concentric circle of praise, as in Ps 103. It is fitting that all the world should respond in thanksgiving to its generous maker. In particular "the Church with psalms must shout," as George Herbert's hymn puts it, perhaps in reminiscence of v 10. The chosen people are the bearers of the sacred traditions of Yahweh's kingliness. Theirs is the prior task of testifying to the rest of the world. Their message serves to introduce a motif for praise in v 13. The God whose realm knows no spatial frontiers has no temporal limits to his reign either (cf. Dan 3:33, 4:31 [4:3, 34]). All time, all history are subject to him. Thus the adoring wish of vv 10–13a is that the mighty king may be owned king indeed forever.

The last and longest section expands the motif of God's loyal love. His royal patronage functions on two levels: each level is now introduced by a synonymous propositional text, in vv 13b, 17. First, the whole creation is dependent on Yahweh for his providential work. He it is who relieves human distress and affliction, and supplies resources for the hungry throughout the world. This royal work (cf. 72:3–4, 12–14, 16) is deduced by the believing heart from the phenomena of the steady, rhythmic world of nature and society. Secondly, Yahweh's loving care is demonstrated especially to that group of people who are privileged to invoke his name in worship, the community of Israel. Their needs too are met. With word plays upon the "name" of Yahweh, the psalmist testifies to his saving response to prayer, to his protective care—and to his punitive destruction. The final point picks up a hint dropped in v 18b: flouting of the moral laws of Yahweh's kingdom of Israel (cf. 101:8) invites providential judgment, whereas to love him is to obey (cf. Exod 20:6; 1 John 5:2–3).

The psalmist concludes his poem by repeating his initial self-exhortation to praise (cf. Pss 103, 104), for which he has just given fresh grounds in vv 13b–20. Again he is acutely conscious of its inadequacy, sincere as it is. Only a congregation made up of all God's creatures could render really worthy praise of his transcendent power.

Trust in God, Not in Man   (146:1–10)

Bibliography

Crüsemann, F. *Studien zur Formgeschichte.* **Habel, N. C.** " 'Yahweh, Maker of Heaven and Earth': A Study in Tradition Criticism." *JBL* 91 (1972) 321–37. **Lipiński, E.** "Macarismes et psaumes de congratulation." *RB* 75 (1968) 321–67. **Malchow, B. V.** "God or King in Psalm 146." *TBT* 89 (1977) 1166–70.

Translation

1 Hallelujah.[a]
   Praise Yahweh, I tell myself.[b]   (3+3+3)
2 *I want to praise Yahweh throughout my life,*
   to celebrate my God with music as long as I exist.

3 *Do not trust in rulers,*[a]   (3+3)
   in an earthling [b] *who cannot save.*
4 *His breath* [a] *leaves him, he returns to his native earth:*   (4+4)
   on that day his policies have perished.[b]
5 *How fortunate is the one whose help* [a] *is Jacob's God,*[b]   (4+3)
   whose hope [c] *is set on Yahweh as his God,*
6 *who made heaven and earth,*[a]   (3+3)
   the sea and everything in them.[b]

   He is the one who keeps faith forever,[c]   (3+3+3)
7 *brings about justice for the oppressed,*[a]
   gives food to the hungry.
   Yahweh sets prisoners free,[b]   (3+3+3)
8 *Yahweh opens the eyes of the blind,*
   Yahweh raises those whose backs are bent.
   Yahweh loves the righteous,   (3+3)
9 *Yahweh looks after foreign settlers,*
   the orphan and widow he relieves,[a]   (3+3)
   but the wicked he diverts from their course.[b]

10 *Yahweh will reign forever,*   (3+3)
   your God, Zion, for generation after generation.
                    Hallelujah

Notes/Comments

1.a. LXX adds Αγγαιου καὶ Ζαχαριου "Of Haggai and Zechariah." E. Slomovic (*ZAW* 91 [1979] 363–64) has explained the heading in midrashic terms of thematic (vv 6–7 and Zech 4:6) and linguistic (v 6 and Hag 2:6; vv 7, 9 and Zech 10:9–10) connections.

1.b. Cf. 104:1 and comment.

3.a. B. V. Malchow (*TBT* 89 [1977] 1167) has observed the royal associations of נדיבים "rulers" in the OT. He considers that disappointment with the pre-exilic Judean monarchy is specifically reflected here (*TBT* 89 [1977] 1168). Gentile domination is probably under consideration (Gunkel, *Die Psalmen*, 612).

3.b. There is a somber word play between אדם "man" here and אדמה "earth" in v 4. Heb. בן־אדם "son, of man (= man)" functions as a closer definition of נדיבים "rulers" (J. Krašovec, *Der Merismus*, 54–55).

4.a. Cf. H. W. Wolff, *Anthropology*, 33 for רוח "breath, spirit." The reference to "thoughts" in v 4b may suggest a *double entendre:* רוח can also mean "mind" (cf. the parallelism of Isa 19:3 and BDB, 925b).

4.b. The perfect verb expresses a fine sense of finality: cf. D. Michel, *Tempora*, 141.

5.a. *Beth essentiae* (cf. GKC § 119i) is used idiomatically with עזר "help." It has been regarded as a dittograph. Its absence in LXX, to which *BHS* appeals, is not strong evidence: it is not rendered in the similar phrase at Exod 18:4 (Ps 35 [34]:2 is textually uncertain: cf. *BHS*).

5.b. The pertinent background to this phrase is to be sought not in the cultic tradition of the Bethel sanctuary (E. Lipiński, *RB* 75 [1968] 350; N. C. Habel, *JBL* 91 [1972] 330; H.-J. Kraus, *Psalmen*, 1132) nor in literary allusion to Gen 32:12 (Lipiński, *RB* 75 [1968] 350) but more probably in Zion theology: cf. אלהי יעקב "God of Jacob" in the Songs of Zion, 46:8, 12 (7, 11); 76:7 (6); 84:9 (8).

5.c. For the motif of hope in hymnic psalms see W. Zimmerli, *Man and His Hope*, 36.

6.a. For this formula and its links with the Jerusalem cult see Habel (*JBL* 91 [1972] 321–37), who has observed that the standard formula has here been interrupted by אלהיו "his God" at the end of v 5 and expanded by v 6aβ, as indeed the difference in style between v 6aα and v 6aβ confirms. He compares this expansion with the prose formulation in Neh 9:6. The motif of Yahweh's עזר "help," traditionally associated with the formula (cf. 121:2; 124:8), has appeared in v 5.

6.b. The sentence should conclude here (*BHS;* see *Form/Structure/Setting*).

6.c. To secure closer parallelism עולם "forever" has been revocalized עֲוֵלִים "the wronged" (M. Dahood, *Psalms III*, 342) and עַוָּלִים "wrongdoers" (NEB).

7.a. This motif is used of Yahweh in a Song of Zion at 76:10 (9); it is associated with his kingship in 99:4 (cf. too 9:17 [16] in the light of 9:8, 12 [7, 11]).

7.b. V 7aβ-b are reminiscent in content and order of Yahweh's activities praised in 107:5, 9, 10, 14.

9.a. Cf. 68:6 (5) for this protective work of Yahweh in association with the sanctuary, where the ideals of ancient Near Eastern kingship are implicitly applied to him (cf. Kraus, *Psalmen*, 633). Release of prisoners features too, in 68:7 (6). For a similar divine ideal cf. 82:3–4. Malchow (*TBT* 89 [1977] 1168–69) has compared the mandate of the Judean king in Jer 22:3, finding an intended contrast between Yahweh's kingship and the failure of Judean kingship to live up to its ideals.

9.b. 11QPs ᵃ adds fragmentary material after v 9: cf. Lipiński (*RB* 75 [1968] 350) for a reconstruction.

Form/Structure/Setting

Psalm 146 is an individual hymn which speaks of Yahweh in the third person (F. Crüsemann, *Studien zur Formgeschichte*, 298–301). The structure of the hymn is generally an imperatival call to praise and an introductory summary of praise which is then developed in terms of Yahweh's work in creation and history, including his grace (cf. C. Westermann, *Praise*, 122–28). The psalm basically follows this scheme of summons and twofold praise, but treats it freely, incorporating heterogeneous elements. It opens with a doubled self-call to praise, evidently dependent upon 104:1, 33, 35 (Lipiński, *RB* 75 [1968] 349). The first is an adaptation of the first plural imperative opening the hymn. The second belongs properly to the thanksgiving song, although B. S. Childs (*Exodus*, 250) has observed that it is so common in hymns that it can be regarded as a stylistic feature of the hymn. In vv 3–4 there follows sapiential advice in the form of a second person plural warning and its explanation. This element may well be present via the song of thanksgiving which characteristically contains a didactic element such as a warning (cf. Crüsemann, *Studien zur Formgeschichte*, 299). From a hymnic standpoint vv 3–4 function as a negative foil, enhancing the praise which follows (cf. 2 Sam 2:3; Ps 75:5–6 [4–5]). Praise is initiated in v 5 by the form of a beatitude, which has the roles of commendation and implicit exhortation (see the notes on 106:3; 112:1) and here of indirect praise. The beatitude formula, as very often elsewhere (cf. C. Keller, "Les beatitudes," 97), contains the motif of trusting. This type of beatitude has here been integrated in vv 5–6aα with a cultic formulation specifying the "help" of "Yahweh who made heaven and earth" (see note 6.a. in *Notes/Comments*). The second part of this formulation has been expanded in v 6aβ and supplemented with further material in v 6b–9 in such a way that it all functions as an explanatory development of the beatitude (cf. Lipiński, *RB* 75 [1968] 349). In its hymnic role it supplies ground for praising Yahweh as creator of the world and providential controller of men's lives, and specifically illustrates the "help" of v 5. In reinforcement of this role, it employs in vv 6–7a the form of participles, basically a different hymn style; it continues in vv 7b–9 with a series of short clauses which all have the same explicit subject. The psalm concludes with further ground for praise in a statement concerning Yahweh's rule, in which Zion is addressed and implicitly called to praise; it is very similar to the conclusion of the hymnic Song of Moses (Exod 15:18; cf. Ps 29:10). Crüsemann (*Studien zur Formgeschichte*, 229) has claimed strong wisdom influence upon the psalm, noting its didacticism and comparing the use of hymnic participles in wisdom literature, but this is hardly necessary: for wisdom influence upon cultic hymns cf. R. E. Murphy, "Wisdom Psalms," 167. Nor is Lipiński's conclusion compelling (*RB* 75 [1968] 349–50): he regards the piece as a collection of materials from different sources and so considers vv 5–9 as originally independent, part of a communal hymn. A connection has been seen between the number of cola and that of the letters of the Hebrew alphabet (Gunkel, *Die Psalmen*, 612; Kraus, *Psalmen*, 1131), but it may well be coincidental rather than calculated.

This individual hymn has many of the motifs of the type of hymn classified as the Song of Zion. Parallels have been given in notes 5.a. and 7.a., while other motifs associated with the Jerusalem sanctuary were observed in notes 6.a. and 9.a. In the individual version of the Song of Zion the beatitude form, with similar trusting content, is used at 84:13 (12), while address of Jerusalem occurs in 122:2 and in the related 137:5. The motif of kingship appears in 47:9 (8); 48:3 (2); 84:4 (3) (cf. Kraus, *Psalmen*, 94–98). It is clear that the psalm has considerable Zion-oriented content. It is difficult to avoid the conclusion that it was composed for a cultic setting (G. Fohrer, *Introduction*,

293; A. A. Anderson, *Psalms,* 940), in spite of the hesitations of Kraus (*Psalmen,* 1132). A. Weiser (*Psalms,* 830), following H. Schmidt (*Die Psalmen,* 253) has assigned it to the autumn festival.

The psalm is generally assigned to the post-exilic period on the grounds of its form-critical development, its apparent use of earlier material and the lateness of its language, viz. שׁ "who" (vv 3, 5), עשׁתנות "thoughts" (v 4), שׂבר "hope" (v 5) and זקף "raise" (v 8).

Despite its aberrant elements the psalm does exhibit evidence of formal unity in its overall progression. In terms of content Malchow (*TBT* 89 [1977] 1167–70) has helped to demonstrate its consistently royal character. Can a coherent poetic structure be detected? An initial obstacle is found at a lower level in the determination of line lengths. Gunkel (*Die Psalmen,* 613), followed by Kraus, was surely correct in regarding not only vv 1b–2 but also vv 6b–7a and 7b–8a as tricola (*contra* S. Mowinckel, *ST* 13 [1959] 160). The third is so characterized by the change of style at the end of v 7a and by the fact that (*pace* Gunkel, *Die Psalmen,* 613, *BHS et al.*) the pair of bicola vv 8b–9 exhibit chiasmus (ABB′A′), which is enhanced by the word order within the cola. The second tricolon is marked by the articular differentiation of the first participle and by the threefold pattern of *lamed* prefixed to the final words of the cola. Gunkel himself conceived of the beatitude of v 5 as the center of the psalm: what precedes is its contrast and what follows is its justification (*Die Psalmen,* 613). While this observation is not incorrect, it does serve to depreciate the hymnic character of the psalm by overstressing what is but one element of praise. There are stylistic features which point to a structure of two strophes of four lines each (vv 3–6a, 6b–9), with separate introduction and conclusion of single lines (vv 1b–2, 10). E. J. Kissane (*Psalms II,* 322) came to a similar conclusion, although he did not justify it with any details and demarcated the strophes as vv 3–6, 7–9. Both strophes are marked by chiasmus, the first in vv 3, 5 with alternating motifs of help (together with the relative שׁ) and trust, and the second in consecutive lines, vv 8b–9aα, 9aβ-b, with alternating motifs of the words of Yahweh and his antithetically expressed moral attitude. Thus in each strophe a pair of lines are set apart from the other two. In the first case the first and third are thus differentiated and in the second the third and fourth. In the first strophe the pattern corresponds to the role of the second and fourth lines as commentary upon the negative and positive exhortations of the first and third which begin with the antithetic elements אל "(do) not" and אשׁרי "how fortunate." In the second strophe the first two lines have their own careful parallelism. The article prefixed to the participle of v 6b indicates a fresh start to a strophe as well as to a line: Gunkel's deletion (*Die Psalmen,,* 613, cf. *BHS*) removes this structural marker. The verb עשׂה "made," "brings about" in vv 6a, 7a acts as an interstrophic hinge. The introduction and conclusion 'to the psalm exhibit inclusion: they share the doubled motif of perpetuity and have matching references to "God" in the final cola after earlier ones to "Yahweh."

The psalm marks the first of a final collection of psalms of praise, Pss 146–50, which are all characterized by a framework of Hallelujahs (cf. Westermann, *Theologia Viatorum* 8 [1961/62] 283).

Explanation

The psalmist sings before the congregation his hymn of praise. His self-encouragement is an implicit invitation to them in turn to lift up their hearts in worship. The third person references to Yahweh indicate the element of testimony which pervades the psalm. The speaker begins by affirming his determination to offer lifelong praise. It is a measure of his appreciation of Yahweh (cf. 145:1–3). His praise is based upon consciousness of a personal relationship to Yahweh as his own God.

The first strophe is a medley of motifs of help, trust and power. These motifs are explored twice, first negatively, then positively. By way of indirect praise of Yahweh, such qualities are shown to be inapplicable in the case of foreign rulers under whose control evidently Judah now languished. Their creatureliness spells the transience of their policies: in spite of their apparent power, from a long-term standpoint they are powerless. "Salvation" or real help is therefore no component of their rule. Accordingly trust in them is deprecated as unjustified. This negative section acts as a foil to its divine antithesis. Yahweh, by implication Israel's true king (cf. v 10), the God of Jacob acclaimed in Zion, provides the help that his earthly rivals lack. Trust in him, the first stage of praise, will never find disappointment. He has power, the power of the creator traditionally celebrated in Zion. His creative power guarantees that, whereas the creaturely rulers of earth plan and resolve, he performs and achieves.

The psalmist has broached a customary element in the hymn, the work of Yahweh as creator. He naturally continues with its associated element, the work of Yahweh in the history of his people. He uses it in the second strophe within the particular framework of his psalm, exploring one of the earlier motifs, the help which Yahweh supplies (v 5). This relationship between vv 6b–9 and v 5 implies that it is still the community of God's people who are in view. The references to them as victims of various afflictions are descriptions, in part metaporical, of their contemporary weakness in political, economic and other areas.

Encouragement is intended as a byproduct of praise. "None shall find his promise vain" was Isaac Watts' felicitous interpretation in his paraphrase of the psalm. Yahweh, whose nature is faithfulness, is ever the answer to his people's needs, declares the believing psalmist. Yahweh lives up to the highest ideals of kingship as the source of justice and vindication (cf. 99:4). Food and freedom are his gifts; wholeness is his blessing. The defenseless can find in him their royal champion (cf. 68:6 [5]; Jer 22:2–3). He, too, it is who upholds the moral values of his covenant and requites with frustration any who flout them. Such has been the experience of the community of Israel from generation to generation. To him they have brought such needs and from him they have received resources in return. To him must praise be given back (cf. 107:4–22).

The concluding line of the psalm brings to completion the cycle of motifs re-commenced in the second strophe. The secret of Yahweh's help, there expounded, is his power as everlasting king, unlike the ephemeral rulers of vv 3–4. Zion, here seemingly used as a synonym for the religious community, is called to exercise trust in, as well as praise to, its God (cf. v 5).

The psalm is a vigorous reaffirmation of traditions intimately connected with the temple. It proclaims old truths to a new generation of God's people who stand in need of them. In a period of low morale they are urged to rededicate themselves to the God who has been their help in ages past. Faith is refuelled so that praise may be rekindled. The power of God as king, the true controller of his people's destiny, is attested in loyal acclaim.

God of Stars and Broken Hearts (147:1–20)

Bibliography

Blau, J. "*Nāwā thillā* (Ps. 147:1): Lobpreisen." *VT* 4 (1954) 410–11. Crüsemann, F. *Studien zur Formgeschichte.* Derenbourg, J. "Aus Briefen J. Derenbourgs an den Herausgeber." *ZAW* 5 (1885) 163–64. Ginsberg, H. L. "A Strand in the Cord of Hebraic Psalmody." *Eretz Israel* 9 (1969) 45–50.

Translation

¹ Hallelujah.[a]
   It is indeed [b] *good to make melody* [c] *to our God,*   (3+3)
    it is indeed pleasing to engage in fitting praise. [d]
² *Yahweh is rebuilding* [a] *Jerusalem*   (3+3)
    and gathering [b] *Israel's outcasts.*
³ *He it is who heals the broken-hearted*   (3+3)
    and bandages their wounds,
⁴ *counts the number of the stars,*   (3+3)
    calling them all by their names.
⁵ *Our Lord is great and most powerful;*   (3+3)
    his wisdom defies enumeration. [a]
⁶ *Yahweh relieves the oppressed,*   (3+3)
    he brings the wicked low to the ground.

⁷ *Respond* [a] *with thanksgiving* [b] *to Yahweh,*   (3+3)
    make melody with the lyre to our God,
⁸ *who covers the sky with clouds,*   (3+3+3)
    who provides rain for the earth,
    who makes grass grow on the mountains, [a]
⁹ *gives to animals their food,*   (3+4)
    to young ravens when they call.
¹⁰ *Not in the horse's strength does he find joy,*   (3+3)
    not in man's legs does he take pleasure:
¹¹ *Yahweh's pleasure is in those who revere him,*   (3+3)
    in those who put their hope [a] *in his loyal love.* [b]

¹² *Laud Yahweh, Jerusalem,*   (3+3)
  praise your God, Zion,
¹³ *because he has braced the bars of your gates*   (3+3)
  and blessed your sons within you.
¹⁴ *He it is who makes your territory prosperous and secure,* [a]   (3+3)
  fills you with the finest of the wheat,
¹⁵ *who sends his command to the earth—*   (3+3)
  his word [a] *runs fast* [b]*—*
¹⁶ *who gives snow like wool,* [a]   (3+3)
  scatters frost like ashes, [b]
¹⁷ *throws his hail like morsels of bread,* [a]   (3+3)
  water standing frozen [b] *before his cold.*
¹⁸ *He sends his word and it melts them;*   (3+4)
  he blows his breath, [a] *the water flows.*
¹⁹ *He declares his word* [a] *to Jacob,*   (3+3)
  his laws and rulings to Israel.
²⁰ *He has not done this for any of the nations,*   (3+3)
  he has not made such rulings known to them. [a]
                              Hallelujah

Notes/Comments

1.a. This rubric is used as a framework in Pss 146–150.

1.b. Heb. כי is evidently an emphatic particle (A. A. Anderson, *Psalms*, 944; cf. "ja," H.-J. Kraus, *Psalmen*, 1134). M. Dahood (*Psalm III*, 344) has considered it exclamatory, "how" (thus NEB). H. Gunkel (*Die Psalmen*, 615), judging that a hymn cannot begin with כי, regarded it as dependent upon the initial הללו-יה: "Praise Yah(weh), for . . . , for . . . ,"; likewise Kraus in his commentary (*Psalmen*, 1136), though inconsistently not in his translation. Anderson (*Psalms*, 944) has rightly observed that this expedient is inadmissible since הללו-יה stands outside the psalm proper: as in Pss 146, 148–150, it appears to be the initial part of a recensional frame. F. Crüsemann (*Studien zur Formgeschichte*, 131), noting that LXX attests a double הללו-יה, took the second as integral to the psalm, construing like Gunkel, but for זמרה "make melody" reading an imperative זמרו with one Heb. ms and deleting נאוה תהלה "fitting praise" as a gloss on נעים "pleasing," which used a phrase from 33:1 to explain that praise rather than "God" is the intended subject. The resultant sentence produces a conventional beginning and corresponds in form to 135:3. It has the advantage of paralleling the divine name with "God," as in the corresponding vv 7, 12. What makes the reconstruction implausible is the probability that LXX's extra הללו-יה is simply its missing one in 146:10. For the form of v 1, 92:2 (1) may be usefully compared.

1.c. For the pi'el infinitive with feminine ending see GKC § 52p.

1.d. LXX omits נאוה, doubtless regarding it as otiose. J. Blau (*VT* 4 [1954] 410–11) has reasonably explained it as an infinitive of the same type as זמרה. The semantic parallelism is thus ABCA'B'.

2.a. MT בונה "rebuilder of" is unexpected. Probably a verbal בונה "is, has been rebuilding" should be read. MT reflects a later standpoint, from which Yahweh was celebrated as (past) rebuilder.

2.b. The participle is continued with an imperfect in vv 2, 4, 14, 15, 16 (17). D. Michel (*Tempora*, 187–88) considers that the second verb in each case has a consecutive force.

5.a. For the stem ספר "count" in conjunction with divine wisdom cf. 139:18. Here מספר "number" is deliberately put in place of חקר "limit" in the basic Isa 40:28 (cf. *Form/Structure/ Setting*; emendation is not required *pace* Gunkel, *Die Psalmen*, 616), to suggest a contrast with v 5: Yahweh's numeracy cannot be matched (A. F. Kirkpatrick, *Psalms*, 822).

7.a. Or "sing," if there is another stem ענה with this meaning: see the discussion of F. I. Andersen ("A Lexicographical Note on Exodus 32:18," *VT* 16 [1966] 108–12).

7.b. Heb. תודה "thanksgiving" is here used generally for the praise of the whole community (H.-J. Hermisson, *Sprache und Ritus*, 38): cf. the use of the verb in this sense in 136:1–3, 26.

8.a. LXX mss add a colon derived from 104 (103 in LXX): 14aβ, completing the bicolon. There is widespread support in modern scholarship for regarding it as a reflection of authentic ועשב לעבודת אדם "and plants for man to cultivate" (e.g. Gunkel, *Die Psalmen*, 616; A. Weiser, *Psalms*, 833; Kraus, *Psalmen*, 1135). However, it is significant that A. Rahlfs (*Septuaginta-Studien*, Heft 2, 161, 224) did not assign it to the earliest text of LXX (contrast "G*" in *BHS*). There are two serious objections to the addition. It violates the parallelism of the three cola, in which is traced the divine treatment of comparable created masses (שמים "sky," ארץ "earth," הרים "mountains"); and it destroys the careful development of the psalm, whereby God's work in nature on man's behalf is reserved till v 14 (cf. *Form/Structure/Setting*). The initial participles with article prefixed in the three cola of v 8 structurally correspond to those in the bicola of vv 14–16. For similar secondary augmentation in LXX cf. 148:5.

11.a. For the motif of hope in hymnic psalms see W. Zimmerli, *Man and His Hope*, 36; H. W. Wolff, *Anthropology*, 152–53.

11.b. Dahood (*Psalm III*, 347) renders חסד "strength," taking up the interpretation of F. Perles elsewhere: see the comments on 143:12; 144:2. For the linking of חסד "loyal love" with terms of trust in the Psalter see K. D. Sakenfeld, *The Meaning of Hesed*, 228–29.

14.a. Heb. שלום has both these senses.

15.a. Yahweh's דבר "word" here and in v 18 controls natural phenomena. For the creative role of the divine word in the OT and in the ancient Near East see Kraus, *Psalmen*, 411–13. The notion of "sending" it, in v 18 and virtually here, has a cultic parallel in 107:20 and a prophetic one in Isa 9:7 (8). There human messengers bring it, but here it functions independently of a messenger and is itself a kind of messenger. The concept is a sophisticated version of the verbal דבר "speak" (33:9, cf. v 6) and אמר "say, command" (Gen 1:3, etc.; Job 37:6). In later times hypostatization was to develop from such beginnings as these verses contain (cf. W. H. Schmidt, "דבר dābhar," *TDOT* 3 [1978] 121). The דבר of v 19, reference to which J. W. Rogerson and J. W. McKay (*Psalms 101–150*, 182) find included here (cf. G. J. Blidstein, *Judaism* 13 [1964] 35), is quite distinct: the more intimate verb מגיד "declare" there so suggests (cf. Crüsemann, *Studien zur Formgeschichte*, 133).

15.b. For the use of עד in an adverbial expression cf. עד לשמחה "joyfully" in 2 Chr 29:30. The basic sense seems to be "to a fast/joyful degree."

16.a. The white (cf. Isa 1:18), fluffy nature of wool appears to be the point of the comparison (Gunkel, *Die Psalmen*, 616).

16.b. Here the whiteness of ashes is in view.

17.a. The size of hailstones is exuberantly extolled with some hyperbole.

17.b. MT has מי יעמד "who can stand?" A widespread emendation מים יעמדו "water standing (frozen)", suggested by J. Derenbourg (*ZAW* 5 [1885] 163), has a ring of certainty. In v 18 the twofold reversal of the processes of vv 16–17 appears to allude first to the melting of the snow, frost and hail, and then to the unfreezing of the water. The pattern of pairing participial clause and statement with imperfect verb throughout the psalm lends support to the emendation. For the non-divine subject cf. v 15b. MT is easily explained as the victim of scribal abbreviation (G. R. Driver, *Textus* 4 [1964] 79), a not uncommon cause for error in the ancient versions (cf. L. C. Allen, "The Greek Chronicles," 81–89). NEB has retained the letters of MT by daringly postulating a singular מי (L. H. Brockington, *Hebrew Text*, 156). The mention of water freezing in Job 37:10, with which chapter the psalm appears to have an organic relation (see *Form/Structure/Setting*), gives added support.

18.a. Heb. רוח here appears to mean primarily not "wind" but "breath": cf. Job 37:10 (נשמה "breath"); Isa 40:7 (with נשב "blow," as here) (D. Lys, *Rûach*, 280). A reference to the warm wind is not excluded.

19.a. Gunkel (*Die Psalmen*, 616) and Dahood (*Psalm III*, 349) prefer Q דבריו "his word," but the singular of K gives better structural alignment with vv 15, 18. Q has harmonized with the plurals of v 19b. It may be asked whether the *yod* in Q has to do with a missing divine name, by way of abbreviation (cf. Driver, *Textus* 1 [1960] 119–20): the parallel vv 6, 11 both contain יהוה "Yahweh." But it would create a four-beat colon in v 19a, unique in this psalm.

20.a. MT "they knew them" employs a resumptive suffix. A better vocalization, retaining the divine subject of the earlier colon, has been preserved via LXX S Tg., יְדָעָם "he makes known to them" (see *BHS*), of which 11QPsᵃ הודיעם "he made known to them" is an adaptation.

Form/Structure/Setting

Psalm 147 is a hymn. Crüsemann (*Studien zur Formgeschichte*, 131–34) has analyzed the composition in detail from a form-critical standpoint and demonstrated its amalgamation of the imperatival hymn form with that of hymnic participles. Calls to praise occur directly in vv 7, 12 and implicitly in v 1; the form of the call addressed to Jerusalem in v 12 Crüsemann has traced back to an original promise of salvation associated with the fertility cult, with verbs of praising replacing verbs of rejoicing (*Studien zur Formgeschichte*, 133). A standard continuation with כי "because" is found only in v 13, although Crüsemann wishes to restore it in v 1 (see note 1.b.). In its place hymnic participles, sometimes continued with an imperfect (cf. note 2.b.), occur in vv 3–4, 8–9, 14–17, the first or more in each set being preceded by the definite article. The form of the hymnic participle is adapted in vv 2, 6, 11 into noun clauses with participial predicates and a divine subject. Probably this is also intended in v 19, with subject understood. It falls outside the groupings of the regular hymnic participles; the psalmist would have prefixed the definite article to introduce the change of style, as in vv 3, 8, 14. The non-traditional content of the participial statement, as in vv 2, 11 (cf. Crüsemann, *Studien zur Formgeschichte*, 133), supplies a reason for adaptation of the basic participial style. Verbal clauses appear with imperfect verbs in vv 10, 18 and with an initial perfect in v 20.

C. Westermann (*Praise*, 122, 127–29) has helped to align the double content, in terms of creative greatness and covenant aid, with that of other hymns. Yahweh is praised as creator in v 4 and as controller of the natural order in vv 8–9, (14b) 15–18. Allusions to his historical work on his people's behalf are made in vv 2, 13, 19; they develop into more general statements of his grace in vv 3, 6, 13–14.

An important issue for this psalm is the question of its unity. Since the composition falls into three roughly parallel parts, vv 1–6, 7–11, 12–20, it has sometimes been suggested that it is a compilation of originally separate pieces. More recently Dahood (*Psalm III*, 344) has supported its division into two hymns, vv 1–11, 12–20, appealing to the fact that LXX starts a separate psalm at v 12 and to a stylistic conglomeration of word play and alliteration in vv 12–20. The psalm is usually divided into three strophes corresponding to its formal structure. Division into seven strophes of three verses, suggested by E. J. Kissane (*Psalms II*, 325) and S. Mowinckel (*Tricola*, 102) not only ignores the form-critical factor but cuts across the natural threesome of vv 14–16. There do appear to be patterns running through the psalm which point to its unity. Inclusion is provided by the references to Israel in vv 2, 19. The two verbal stems for praise in v 1 are taken up in the subsequent strophes, זמרה in זמרו "make melody," v 7, and תהלה "praise" in הללי "praise," v 12. Mention of Jerusalem, vv 2, 12, begins the first and third strophes, while each of the three commence with a suffixed אלהים "God" (vv 1, 7, 12). A particular word play characterizes the strophes: בונה "rebuilds,"

v 2, and (בֵנֵי(ךָ "(your) sons" in vv 9, 13. All the strophes end with antithetical
statements, in vv 6, 10–11, 19–20. Repetition of vocabulary in adjacent lines
marks each strophe, being climactically intensified in the third (vv 4–5, 10–
11, 18–19, 19–20). A group of three participles prefixed with the article appears in both the second and third strophes (vv 8, 14–16), and so does the
particular participle נֹתֵן "giving" (vv 9, 16).

There is a remarkable selective parallelism evident in the strophes. The
first consists of four elements after the implicit call to praise: references to
Yahweh's work in nature and to his strength (vv 4, 5) are set within a framework
of his activity on Israel's behalf (vv 2–3, 6) in a ABCA' pattern. In the second
strophe the pattern is BCA (vv 8–9, 10, 11): the initial element of the first
strophe does not appear in a corresponding position, and the third element
takes the form of a rejection of human strength. In the third strophe the
pattern is again varied, to ABA' (vv 12–14, 15–18, 19–20), with omission of
the C element. Thus the second and third strophes each drop a different
element of the full range of the first. The motifs of Yahweh's relation to
nature develop progressively: creation of the celestial stars (v 4), control of
celestial and earthly phenomena so as to provide vegetation and food for
animals and birds (vv 8–9), and control of earthly phenomena so as to provide
crops for his people (vv 14b–18). In the second and third cases there is a
chiastic order of divine seasonal activity: the straightforward sequence from
winter to summer is followed by a reversal. All this evidence, viewed cumulatively, is an impressive pointer to the unity of the psalm. An interesting feature
of the third strophe, apart from the three word plays of vv 16–18 and alliteration to which Dahood (*Psalm III*, 349) has referred, is a play which occurs
in most lines. The phonetic linking of יְרוּשָׁלַם "Jerusalem," v 12, with שָׁלוֹם
"peace," v 14, is echoed in each line of vv 15–18 by a *shin-lamed* sequence
(הַשֹּׁלֵחַ "who sends," שֶׁלֶג "show," מַשְׁלִיךְ "throws," יִשְׁלַח "he sends"), which
can hardly be coincidental.

The psalm appears to include literary references to Isa 40–66, Pss 33 and
104, Job 37–39 and to Deut 4. These borrowings have been skillfully woven
together with traditional psalm language into a new composition of praise.
In v 2 נִדְחֵי יִשְׂרָאֵל "Israel's outcasts" is derived from Isa 56:8 (cf. 11:12),
with a different verb for "gather" being employed. The phrase לַחֲבֹשׁ נִשְׁבְּרֵי לֵב
"to bind the broken-hearted" of Isa 61:1 underlies v 3. Vv 4, 5b are inspired
in a literary sense by Isa 40:26, 28. V 8b comes from Ps 104:14, the element
בְּהֵמָה "cattle, animals" being reserved for v 9a. The reference to ravens in
v 9b probably comes from Job 38:41, the common mention of lions and
birds in 104:17, 21 and in Job 38:39–41 having suggested the link. The contrast
of vv 10–11 is derived from Ps 33:17–18, a passage which probably was brought
to the psalmist's mind by the affinity of כֹּחַ . . . רֹב in Isa 40:26 with רַב־כֹּחַ
"abundance of power" in Ps 33:16, and by the conceptual similarity of קוֹי יהוה
"those who wait for Yahweh" in Isa 40:31 with Ps 33:18b, and also by a
reference in Job 39:19 to the war horse's גְבוּרָה "strength," which recalled
the linking of the war horse with the גִבּוֹר "strong man" in Ps 33:16–17. In
vv 15, 18 Yahweh's creative דָבָר "word" of Ps 33:6a supplies literary source
for the term's use in relation to the control of nature, while Job 37:6–10
(cf. 38:28–30) provide the sequence, vocabulary and motifs of most of vv

16–18. The collocation appears to be influenced by Isa 55:10–11, which compares the fertilizing force of rain and snow with the prophetic דבר (H. L. Ginsberg, *Eretz Israel* 9 [1969] 50). Vv 19–20 are apparently based on Deut 4:8, probably with a reference to the revealed, Mosaic דבר in Deut 4:2. The psalm seems to be the product of an interweaving of passage with passage in almost midrashic fashion.

In view of these literary references the psalm is clearly post-exilic, as indeed the content of v 2 indicates. A. Weiser (*Psalms*, 834–35) sees in v 2a simply a reference to Yahweh as the builder or founder of the sanctuary, and in v 2b possibly an allusion to a post-721 B.C. cultic assembly in which citizens of the Northern Kingdom took part. The implications of the two cola being set together in parallelism can hardly be overlooked in this way. It is difficult not to see a reference to return from Babylonian exile and probably to Nehemiah's reconstruction of Jerusalem. In this connection it is of interest to note that LXX, which divided the psalm into two, headed both with reference to Haggai and Zechariah, like Ps 146. It took its cue from the content of the psalm(s), vv 2, 13, which contain topics uppermost in the mind of Zechariah (E. Slomovic, *ZAW* 91 [1979] 364, who also compared v 10 with Hag 2:22).

The setting of the psalm was clearly cultic, as is generally acknowledged (e.g. G. Fohrer, *Introduction*, 293). Anderson (*Psalms*, 944) has suggested the Feast of Tabernacles as a likely specific setting, as a time when divine providence was considered; references to the gift of the law add some weight to this suggestion (cf. Deut 31:10–11). However, Kraus (*Psalmen*, 1136) may well be wiser in refusing to envisage a particular cultic situation.

Explanation

This post-exilic hymn is a medley of two interwoven themes, Yahweh's power in the sphere of nature, both as creator and as controller, and his patronage of the covenant people, demonstrated in recent history specifically and in the general attitude of grace which may be deduced therefrom. The psalm divides into three strophes, each with its own short exhortation to praise and a development in terms of this double content.

The return from exile is chosen as the basis for a worshiping meditation on Yahweh's character and purposes. The rebuilding of Jerusalem and the restoration of the old covenant community ("Israel") bear contemporary witness to his strong and tender care. The heartbreak of exile (cf. 137:1–4) has been replaced by the healing comfort (cf. Hos 6:1; 7:1) of being home again. The transcendent power which controls the stars—innumerable to all but Yahweh (Gen 15:5; Jer 33:22)—has been exerted on their behalf in the overthrow of Babylon and the rehabilitation of his people. Yahweh's traditional work of moral vindication for the sake of the oppressed has been manifested once more (cf. 75:3–11 [2–10]).

The second strophe amplifies the twin motifs already broached, Yahweh's relations to nature and to the elect nation. As in v 1, the covenantal tie between him and the people ("our God") is celebrated. The tie turns awe at nature's impressive cycle of cloud, rain and greenery into proud praise. The dramatic contrast of the Palestinian seasons and scenery is traced to

him. The rain after months of drought and the green mantle laid over the
bare earth, are his work. By such powerful means Yahweh demonstrates his
beneficence to the creatures of earth, even animals and birds. The people's
response must be an overwhelming sense of his strong power (cf. v 5). The
strength of war horse and infantry is a pale substitute, alien to the divine
will from which God's people must take their cue. Temptation to achieving
power by such ways and fawning envy of those who possess such power
(cf. 146:3) are false trails to success. The trust and worship of the religious
community and patient waiting upon Yahweh for his covenant aid are qualities
to be prized instead of a carnal rush to arms or military alliance—that way
lies madness (cf. Isa 30:15–16; 31:1).

Rather, stresses the third strophe, Yahweh is to be praised as the provider
of Jerusalem's security and as the one who has been building the new generation of the community who have now met within its walls for worship. The
happy word שלום (peace) provides a bridge between security and prosperity.
The wheat crop, which illustrates prosperity, is the outworking of Yahweh's
power and care. The winter processes by which animal and bird are, under
God, eventually fed are also the means whereby his people's need for food
is met. The psalmist glories in Yahweh's word of power. He issues his command and it is executed; he speaks and, presto, it is done. This word is the
instrument of the will of the transcendent God. The psalmist uses it as a
frame (vv 15, 18a) for his account of winter weather and combines it with a
more personal and even anthropomorphic conception of divine control in
vv 16–17, 18b. Like a child delighting in the snow, he revels in an excited
description of severe winter conditions such as were comparatively rare in
Palestine. Snowflakes, frost and hailstones are tossed down to earth like so
much confetti. The warm wind is the breath of God huffed at the ice to
make it melt. Yahweh is present and active in such phenomena. Yet his immanence is carefully bracketed with his transcendence, to avoid misunderstanding
of this picturesque quasi-identification of deity and nature: it is held in tension
with Yahweh's sending from afar his word to do the work.

As in the first strophe reference to nature served to highlight the bordering
motifs of Yahweh's dealings with his covenant people (cf. Isa 40:26–31), so
here in the third strophe the psalmist reverts to a motif congruent with,
and explanatory of, vv 13–14. He stays with the concept of the word, able
to use it interchangeably for natural and special revelation. It has a spiritual
counterpart in Yahweh's communication of covenant law. The psalmist exclaims in wondering surprise: what a unique privilege is Israel's! Yet the
very content of the exclusive privilege spells responsibility, the onus of obedience to the declared will of God.

The psalm is the fruit of deep meditation upon sacred literature, as the
section on *Form/Structure/Setting* indicated. Arranging and reworking what
he read into his own artistic composition, the psalmist produced a new song
of praise. He exults in a God at work in nature and in recent history, a
God whose spoken word is heard by the ear of faith both in the winter storms
and in the recited law. Yahweh's power is harnessed to his grace. Yet this
divine generosity lays obligations upon his chosen people, not only to praise
but ever to trust with hope and to obey.

A Universal Choir (148:1–14)

Bibliography

Alfrink, B. "L'expression šamaim ou šemei haš-šamaim dans l'AT." *Mélanges E. Tisserant*, vol. 1. Gitta del Vaticano: Biblioteca Apostolica Vaticanna, 1964. **Hillers, D. R.** "A Study of Psalm 148." *CBQ* 40 (1978) 323–34. **MacKenzie, R. A. F.** "Ps. 148:14bc: Conclusion or Title?" *Bib* 51 (1970) 221–24. **Neiman, D.** "The Supercaelian Sea." *JNES* 28 (1969) 243–49. **von Rad, G.** "Job 38 and Egyptian Wisdom." *The Problem of the Hexateuch and Other Essays*, Tr. E. W. T. Dicken. Edinburgh: Oliver & Boyd, 1965.

Translation

1 Hallelujah.[a]
  Praise Yahweh from the heavens,[b]   (3+3)
  praise him in the heights.
2 *Praise him, all his angels,*   (3+3)
  praise him, all his hosts.[a]
3 *Praise him, sun and moon,*   (3+3)
  praise him, all shining stars.[a]
4 *Praise him, heaven of heavens*   (3+4)
  and water above the heavens.[a]
5 *Let them praise Yahweh's name,*   (3+3)
  because[a] at his command they were created[b]
6 *and he set them in position for ever[a] and ever,*   (3+3)
  making a rule that will never lapse.[b]

7 *Praise Yahweh from the earth,*   (3+3)
  sea monsters[a] and all the deeps,
8 *fire[a] and hail, snow and mist,[b]*   (4+4)
  storm wind that acts upon his word,[c]
9 *mountains and all hills,*   (3+3)
  fruit trees and all cedars,[a]
10 *wild animals and all of the domestic kind,*   (3+3)
  reptiles and winged birds,
11 *kings of the earth and all peoples,[a]*   (3+3)
  rulers and all judges[b] of the earth,
12 *young men and maidens too,*   (3+3)
  old men and youngsters alike.
13 *Let them praise Yahweh's name,*   (3+3+3)
  because his name alone is supreme,
  his majesty is over[a] earth and heavens,
14 *and he has raised a horn for[a] his people,*   (3+3+3)
  even renown[b] for all the recipients of his loyal love,[c]
  for the Israelites, the people close to him.[d]

Notes/Comments

1.a. See the note on 147:1. LXX, as in the previous psalms, adds a heading concerning Haggai and Zechariah. E. Slomovic (*ZAW* 91 [1979] 364) has suggested that it derives from a linking of v 11 with Zech 8:21.

1.b. M. Dahood (*Psalms III*, 352) has cautioned against accepting the shorter text of 11QPs ᵃ (cf. *BHS*).

2.a. The plural in 103:21 (cf. 103:20aα) supports Q. The minority reading of K (cf. *BHS*) follows the singular of 1 Kgs 22:19, etc. The other use of the term (in the singular) to denote sun, moon and stars (Deut 4:19, etc.) prompted the subsequent mention of them in v 3.

3.a. LXX (cf. *BHS*) reflects basically a י/ו error (D. R. Hillers, *CBQ* 40 [1978] 325).

4.a. For the ancient Near Eastern cultural conception of the celestial fresh water sea reflected here, as in Gen 1:7; 7:11; Ps 29:10, cf. the note on 104:3 and see Neiman, *JNES* 28 [1969] 243–49. B. Alfrink ("L'expression *šamaim*," 6) equates השמים "heavens" in v 4b with the firmament of Gen 1:6–8, where it is so identified, and interprets the superlative phrase of v 4a as the space in which the reservoirs of water are located; then v 4 exhibits synonymous parallelism like vv 1, 2.

5.a. LXX S amplify the reference to 33:9b by prefixing 33:9a. The extra material is usually regarded as secondary and due to parallel assimilation. Hillers (*CBQ* 40 [1978] 325), on slender grounds regards it as authentic. See the discussion in *Form/Structure/Setting* below.

5.b. Heb. ויעמד "and it stood" in 33:9b, changed here to נבראו "were created," was taken up in v 6 as a causative verb. For the stem ברא "create" see the note on 102:19 and references.

6.a. Hillers (*CBQ* 40 [1978] 325–26), observing that לעד לעולם "forever and ever" occurs only here and in 111:8, interprets עד as "ordinance," parallel to חק "ruling." While this rendering is theoretically not impossible, the fact that in Ps 111 the phrase of v 8 is broken into its constituent elements at vv 3, 5, 9, 10 with a clearly synonymous sense (see *Form/Structure/Setting* of Ps 111) renders Hillers' claim unlikely here.

6.b. The conjectural emendation to a plural, urged by H. Gunkel (*Die Psalmen*, 619), H.-J. Kraus (*Psalmen*, 1140) *et al.*, conforms well to OT usage (cf. Job 14:5; Ps 104:9; Jer 5:22), but is unnecessary. The singular of MT may be retained: for the use of the verb cf. Esth 1:19; 9:27 and the related Aram. די-לא תעדא, Dan 6:9, 13 (Hillers, *CBQ* 40 [1978] 326).

7.a. Cf. Gen 1:21 and the note on Ps 104:26.

8.a. I.e. presumably lightning.

8.b. Heb. קיטור normally means "smoke." Here it appears to mean "mist" in this catalogue of wintry weather conditions. Gunkel (*Die Psalmen*, 619) compared Jewish Aram. קטרא "smoke, mist." Hillers (*CBQ* 40 [1978] 326), finding a reference to theophany here, equates it with עשן "smoke," so used in 18:9 (8); Joel 2:30; cf. Ps 104:32. Then presumably the order is to be taken as chiastic (cf. Dahood, *Psalms III*, 354). LXX S Hier rendered "ice": cf. LXX's translation πάχνη "frost" at 119 (LXX 118): 83. Thus it is not necessary to presuppose a *Vorlage* קרח "frost, ice," as is generally assumed: an exegetical tradition underlies the rendering.

8.c. For דבר "word" see 147:15 and note.

9.a. The pair of terms are used by way of merismus to refer to all trees, cultivated and uncultivated (J. Krašovec, *Der Merismus*, 131).

11.a. Hillers, *CBQ* 40 [1978] 327, has noted J. Barr's convincing refutation of attempts made by G. R. Driver and J. Gray to render לאמים "rulers" by recourse to Accadian and Ugaritic evidence (*Comparative Philology and the Text of the OT* [Oxford: Clarendon Press, 1968] 133, 172, 254–55, 329).

11.b. Hillers (*CBQ* 40 [1978] 327) has raised a substantial objection to Dahood's proposal (*Psalms III*, 354), following D. N. Freedman, to achieve ABA'B' parallelism by treating שפטי "judges" as an orthographical variant of שבטי "tribes."

13.a. I.e. is demonstrated over their extent (cf. כסה הודו "his majesty covered" as a parallel to מלאה "filled" in Hab 3:3), rather than transcends them: cf. Isa 6:3; 33:5.

14.a. I.e. given a high horn to them. For the imagery cf. 75:11 (10); 89:18 (17). LXX S took the verb as future, viz. וירם "and he will raise" (rather than ירם, *BHS*). Hillers (*CBQ* 40 [1978] 327) reads a jussive ירם "may he raise up," observing that a wish or petition typically concludes a hymn.

14.b. The clue to the understanding of the controverted second colon lies in the recognition of external parallelism between vv 13aβ and 14aα and between vv 13b and 14aβ. Yahweh's supremacy and majesty is reflected in the exaltation and renown bestowed by him upon his people. For the parallelism of נשגב "supreme" and the stem רום "be exalted, raise" Isa 2:11; 26:5; 33:5 may be compared, and for that of תהלה "praise, renown" and הודו "his majesty," Hab 3:3. Heb. תהלה is characteristically used of Israel's standing in the world vis-à-vis other nations, as in Deut 26:19; Jer 13:11; 33:9 (cf. BDB, 240a, b). Syntactically it stands in loose apposition to קרן "horn"; the preposition *lamed* which occurs twice in the final two cola continues the sense of the first in v 14aα. The addition in 11QPs ᵃ at 149:9 לבני ישראל עם קודשו "to the children of Israel, his holy people" appears to be a misplaced variant reading for the last colon, inspired by Deut 26:19, where reference to Israel as תהלה, the object of praise of all nations, is followed by עם קדש "a holy people." Accordingly already in this old explanatory reading an understanding of תהלה as Israel's "renown" is envisaged. The sense of the verse seems to be that Yahweh's historical intervention on his people's behalf has raised their stock in the world. The psalm's juxtaposition to Ps 147 appears to suggest a redactional interpretation in terms of the restoration of the Judean community after the Babylonian exile (cf. A. F. Kirkpatrick, *Psalms*, 825, 828, *et al.*). This interpretation was apparently the one intended by the psalmist himself: comparison with Jer 33:7, 9 lends considerable support. The final pair of cola has been detached from the psalm proper and viewed as an *Unterschrift* (Gunkel, *Die Psalmen*, 618; Kraus, *Psalmen*, 1141). Developing this interpretation, R. A. F. MacKenzie (*Bib* 51 [1970] 221–24) has regarded it as a title to Ps 149, already present before the redactional framework of Hallelujahs was added. He observed that six of its seven words are found in that psalm and only one in Ps 148. Hillers (*CBQ* 40 [1978] 328) finds MacKenzie's proposal unconvincing: "His argument from vocabulary is without much force since we are dealing with very short compositions in Pss 148, 149, and he is unable to cite any other parallel for such a bicolon as the title of a biblical psalm." In fact, these various attempts to sever the line from the body of the psalm is a counsel of despair, to be avoided if the line can be integrated feasibly.

14.c. See the note on 145:10.

14.d. The proposal to read a plural קרביו "(the people of) those close to him" (Gunkel, *Die Psalmen*, 619, *et al.*; cf. *BHS*) accords better with the adjacent plural references; but MT can stand as a stylistic expansion of עמו "his people" earlier.

Form/Structure/Setting

Psalm 148, basically an imperatival hymn in form, is marked by development of the call to praise in the naming of those summoned (F. Crüsemann, *Studien zur Formgeschichte*, 72). The substance of praise (vv 5b–6, 13aβ–14bα), introduced by the conventional כי "because," has in proportion a minor role. In this respect the psalm is the reverse of Ps 147. Yahweh's work in creation and control of the heavenly order is the subject of the first ground; that of the second is a combination of his majesty as creator of earth and heaven and his historical intervention for his people's sake (C. Westermann, *Praise*, 131). The psalm has a bipartite structure, signalled by the initial, parallel summarizing calls of v 1aβ and v 7a. Dahood (*Psalms III*, 352) has divided the psalm into three parts, a call to the celestial sphere in vv 1–6, to the nether world in v 7 and to the terrestrial in vv 8–13a, with a conclusion reflecting on the relationship between the Lord of history and his people in vv 13b–14. Hillers (*CBQ* 40 [1978] 328) is surely correct in dubbing this division "very unbalanced" and its author "misled by a desire to translate ארץ as 'underworld.' While this sense is well-known in other biblical passages, it is not especially appropriate here, where ארץ "earth" is a title balancing שמים "heavens." We must not demand perfect logic of the psalmist's cosmology; we must permit him to list dragons and deeps, fire and storm-wind under the rubric 'earth.' " He himself observes that שמים and ארץ "are a traditional pair, linked often in both poetry and prose, and are here used to make parallel

sections of the psalm. Near the close of each section (vv 5, 13) stands a
jussive יהללו 'let them praise.' The difference between A and B is marked
by contrasting syntax, in A imperatives prevail; in B, vocatives" (*CBQ* 40
[1978] 327–28). A. Weiser (*Psalms*, 837–38) also divided the psalm into three,
with sections beginning at vv 1, 7, 11. Hillers (*CBQ* 40 [1978] 328) has characterized this structuring as "grammatically dubious" and resulting in "very
uneven divisions." J. Schildenberger (*Estudios Eclesiásticos* 34 [1960] 680), noting the demarcation of vv 5–6, 13–14, has regarded them as final sub-units
of their respective strophes; he divides the first strophe into three such units
of two bicola and the second into three of two bicola and a last one of three
bicola. These divisions are compatible with S. Mowinckel's breakdown of
the psalm into a series of strophes of two bicola (*Tricola*, 102). In fact, *pace*
Mowinckel (*Tricola*, 86), who posited the loss of two cola between v 13 and
v 14, vv 13–14 appear to consist of two tricola, as Hillers (*CBQ* 40 [1978]
324) prints them in his translation. This analysis is supported by the parallelism mentioned in the note 14.b. above: the tricola have an ABCB′C′D parallel
structure.

The second strophe is longer than the first in two respects. The series
of calls to praise consists of three pairs of bicola, whereas the first strophe
contains two. Secondly the statements of praise comprise two tricola instead
of two bicola. Formally each gives a double reason. The parallelism between
ויעמדם "he set them in position" at the head of v 6 and וירם "and he raised"
beginning v 14 has strangely been generally overlooked, together with the
consequent correspondence of vv 6, 14 as second motivations for praise after
vv 5b, 13aβ-b. The proportionate size of those first reasons (1/2 cola) and
the second ones (2/3 cola) corresponds to the lengthening of the imperatival
calls to praise by an extra unit of two bicola in the second strophe. The
extra doubling of כל "all" in v 11 in comparison with vv 2, 9 is also significant.
In each case an extra part is added in the composition of the second strophe.
This consistent phenomenon suggests that Hillers is incorrect in regarding
the addition of LXX *S* in v 5 as part of the original Hebrew text (see note
5.a. above). In fact the number of clauses (2+3) in vv 5b–6 has become the
number of cola in vv 13b–14. The shorter dimensions of the first strophe
is associated with the fewer number of addressees and the consequent multipli-
cation of imperatives required to make up a reasonably sized strophe. However, the psalmist has chosen so to do: he has deliberately placed in the
second strophe what might be regarded as celestial phenomena (v 8; cf. 104:4).
Accordingly his aim in lengthening the constituent elements of the second
strophe appears to have been to create a climactic effect.

There is evidence of various chiastic arrangements. The first bicolon in
the first strophe naming those called to praise (v 2) corresponds to the last
pair of bicola in the second (vv 11, 12) in addressing rational beings, unlike
the following calls in the first strophe and the preceding ones in the second.
In fact, apart from the "improper" v 8, there is an almost perfect reversal
of elements within vv 2–4 and vv 7b–12 in the order of articulate beings,
individual inanimate objects and large tracts, the upper heavens and heavenly
waters being chiastically parallel to the deeps and the land of hills and moun-

tains. Another chiastic arrangement is the summarizing reference to ארץ ושמים "earth and heavens" in v 13 after dealing in separate strophes first with the latter and then with the former (Hillers, *CBQ* 40 [1978] 328). Yet another is the attachment of divine suffixes to groups mentioned at the beginning and end of the psalm (vv 2, 14). These stylistic reversals are used, along with differences of length and syntax, to vary the basic evidence of parallelism between the two strophes, mentioned earlier. To the latter may be added the double mention of the primary terms שמים "heavens" and ארץ "earth" in the final unit of the respective imperatival summonses (vv 4, 11) and the sole uses of the preposition *lamed* in vv 6, 13–14. Overall inclusion for the psalm is provided by the stem הלל "praise" in vv 1, 14.

Kraus defined the psalm in terms borrowed from H. Richter as a "mixed form between the hymn and nature wisdom" (*Psalmen*, 1141). He has referred to the Egyptian tradition of compiling lists of the component parts of the world, the Onomastica. In this respect he has followed the comparative work of G. von Rad (*Problem of the Hexateuch*, 281–91). The latter cited the Rameses Onomasticon and the Onomasticon of Amenope which lists all that Ptah god of Memphis has created. However, Hillers (*CBQ* 40 [1978] 329–31) has raised objections against finding such literary antecedents to the psalm. First, there is a great difference in scale between the brief psalm and the long, elaborate Egyptian lists. Secondly the resemblance between the psalm and the lists and other compositions cited by von Rad lies not in overall order but only in selected parts; even there it is not remarkable and the overlap between Amenope's enormous list of items and the psalm need not be more than coincidental. Hillers describes the psalm as typically hymnic: it brings together items which appear singly or in smaller groups elsewhere in the Psalter and echoes such listing of created entities as are to be found in Pss 8, 29, 104. "One could conclude that Ps 148 grows out of the common practice of addressing imperatives to God's creation, an old theme which is then elaborated by drawing elements typical of the body of the hymn back into the introduction" (*CBQ* 40 [1978] 331). There are other factors besides, claims Hillers: a tradition is echoed in which "elements of the creation are deified; the god is first praised by the other gods" (*CBQ* 40 [1978] 331). Such a hymnic tradition is attested in Mesopotamian and Egyptian hymns (cf. the traces in Pss 19; 29; 89:6, 13 [5, 12]; 103:20–22), which Hillers proceeds to cite (*CBQ* 40 [1978] 332–34). Accordingly he finds the psalm's literary antecedents in an ancient Near Eastern hymnic tradition rather than one of encyclopedic learning. He appears to be making a valid point in finding hymnic parallels to the psalm. However, the listing of vv 7b–12 is so pronounced and unrelieved by verbs that it may be wiser to acknowledge, too, the general influence of such a tradition as that preserved in the Onomastica as a factor in the prehistory of the form of the psalm.

Gunkel (*Die Psalmen*, 618–19) found expressions from Gen 1:1–2:4 used in the psalm: from 1:11 in v 9, from 1:24–25 in v 10 and from 2:4 (in order) in v 13. J. W. Rogerson and J. W. McKay (*Psalms 101–150*, 184–85) have gone further in regarding the psalm as a version of Gen 1:1–2:4 suitable for use as a hymn. Their supporting claim that vv 1–6 correspond to Gen

1:1–19 and vv 7–14 to 1:20–2:4 must be judged an overstatement. The evidence points rather to the partial influence of the Genesis account of creation upon the psalmist.

A cultic setting is generally ascribed to the hymn, without further specification of usage being possible. A reflection of the esteem in which it was held in ancient times may be seen in the imitation of it in the apocryphal Song of the Three Young Men (Dan 3:52–90) and in Sir 43. The date of the psalm is usually regarded as post-exilic. If the exegesis of v 14 given above is correct, the psalm itself says as much. Hillers (*CBQ* 40 [1978] 328–29) has noted the mainly late associations of the psalm's terminology, especially of עשה דבר "perform [someone's] word" in v 8 and of עבר in the sense of an enactment passing away. He argues that since the Chronicler in the fourth century knew at 1 Chr 16:36 of a division into books and a fivefold division of the Psalter seems to be essential to the redactional scheme, the fifth book was then in existence. Accordingly he finds the early fourth century B.C. a plausible date for the psalm. This is in fact an argument for a *terminus ad quem*, and the psalm could well be somewhat earlier.

Explanation

This hymn which features rhetorical calls to creation to praise its God is an expression of the praiseworthiness of Yahweh. God's people need helpers, as it were, in their own praise. Their loudest and longest praise cannot match his work and status. Only with the concerted voices of all his creatures can a significant attempt be made to reflect his majesty back to him. The exuberant word כל "all" rings out in a striving for totality of praise. The enumeration of elements is also a poetic means of manifesting indebtedness to him for the range of his creation, and itemizing his glory that fills the earth (Isa 6:3). The calls to praise thus serve also to express praise.

In the first of the two strophes the heavens and their denizens are urged to make their contribution to a universal chorale. Their articulate members, the angelic retinue in Yahweh's celestial palace and temple, comprise a choir singing to their lord and king. Their inanimate components are metaphorically personified into agents of his praise: the radiant lights and the heavenly ocean. Together they are challenged to praise Yahweh for their creation and everlasting preservation, for their endowment with particular roles by the great creator. They can each tell of the glory of God and proclaim his handiwork (19:2 [1]). Just as a fine piece of craftsmanship brings glory to its craftsman, so the destiny of the created world is to glorify Yahweh by reflecting his power. By fulfilling their divinely allotted functions, the works of the celestial creation exist as eloquent witnesses to his self-revelation through them.

The terrestial world too must yield its complement of praise, urges the second strophe. The ocean deeps with their giant whales are further evidence of his power. Nature with its wild forces, untameable by man, is the instrument of his mighty will, and communicates his transcendence. The rugged land masses, the trees and the lower orders of animate creation attest landscaping artistry and keen attention to detail on the part of their divine architect.

In coming to man, the climax of creation, the psalmist has come full circle to the articulate praise of v 2. He calls upon all, from the large sectors of humanity with their leaders to society's smaller groupings by sex and age, to bring their distinctive, conscious praise. In v 12 he probably eyes the religious community gathered in Jerusalem for worship (cf. Joel 2:16–17): Judah serves to represent mankind in their praise (cf. 96:1–3). Reason enough for praising lies in Yahweh's unique sovereignty and in the revelation of his majesty throughout the terrestial and celestial spheres. Whatever power each of their elements possesses is delegated from him. A more intimate source for praise is found in his bestowal of exaltation upon his covenant people, so that they enjoy renown. The re-establishment of the community of Judah after the exile most probably underlies the reference to Yahweh's historical activity on their behalf (cf. 126:2–3). Interpreted as his signal intervention, it has enabled them to share in some measure his attribute of majestic splendor, so that they are praised as he is praised (cf. Dan 2:46–48). By covenant grace his people have come, as it were, to sit in a high place with him, in the terms of Eph 2:6. As is theologically proper for his representatives on earth (cf. Deut 26:19; Ps 89:28 [27]), they reflect something of his grandeur in the privilege and potential which are theirs. The old religious community ("Israel") has been wonderfully restored (cf. Ezra 3:1; 6:21), and they can celebrate their nearness to him, set apart as they are to engage in his service and to enjoy his blessing (cf. Exod 19:6; Lev 10:3; Ps 65:5 [4]; Isa 61:6).

Firstfruits of Victory   *(149:1–9)*

Bibliography

Coppens, J. "La royauté de Yahvé dans le Psautier." *ETL* 54 (1978) 1–59. **Schreiner, J.** *Sion-Jerusalem Jahwes Königssitz.* SANT 7. München: Kösel-Verlag, 1963.

Translation

1 Hallelujah.[a]
    Sing to Yahweh a new song,   (4+3)
      his praise in the congregation of recipients of loyal love.[b]

2 *Let Israel rejoice in their maker,*[a]   (3+3)
      let Zion's sons exult in their king.[b]

3 *Let them praise his name with dancing,*[a]   (3+3)
      let them celebrate him with music of timbrel and lyre

4 *because Yahweh takes delight in his people,*   (3+3)
      glorifying the oppressed[a] *with saving victory.*

5 *Let the recipients of loyal love jubilate in the triumph,*[a] (3+3)
      let them shout for joy where they lie prostrate.[b]

6 *Let high praises be in their throats*   (3+3)
      and two-edged swords in their hands,[a]

⁷ for ᵃ punishment ᵇ to be executed ᶜ upon the nations,   (3+3)
    chastisement upon the peoples, ᵈ
⁸ for their kings ᵃ to be manacled with chains   (3+3)
    and their nobles with iron fetters,
⁹ for judgment to be executed upon them, as decreed: ᵃ   (4+3)
    that will mean honor for all recipients of his loyal love.
                              Hallelujah

Notes/Comments

1.a. See the note on 147:1.

1.b. For this designation of the religious community see the note on 145:10.

2.a. Yahweh brought the covenant nation into existence: cf. Deut 32:6; Pss 95:6; 100:3. This old cultic title was taken up in Isa 44:2; 51:13. The form עשׁיו "his makers" may be a plural of majesty. P. Joüon Grammaire, (§ 136e) judged this the probable explanation, although GKC (§ 124k) preferred to regard this and similar forms as singulars with retention of the original yod of a lamed he stem.

2.b. The kingship of Yahweh was especially celebrated in the Jerusalem sanctuary: cf. H.-J. Kraus, Psalmen, 94–98.

3.a. Dancing was one feature of religious rejoicing: cf. 30:12 (11); 87:7; 150:4.

4.a. For this designation for the people and its connotation of helplessness apart from Yahweh's help see Kraus, Psalmen, 108–11. Cf. 18:28 (27); 147:6.

5.a. Heb. כבוד "glory" belongs to the same semantic field as the stem פאר "glory" used in v 4b; here it alludes back to that glorifying activity of Yahweh.

5.b. Heb. על-משׁכבותם is difficult to comprehend. It can hardly be taken as "upon their beds" and referred to individuals' private praising at night (M. Dahood, Psalms III, 357): the cultic associations of the verbs of v 5 (for the second see N. E. Wagner, VT 10 [1960] 435–41) and the obvious resumption of the call to praise of vv 1–3 appear to rule out this interpretation. Beds or couches were associated with the fertility cult (cf. Hos 5:14), but such a reference would hardly be appropriate here. The only way to do justice to the cultic context appears to be to render "upon their places of lying," taking lying as a reference to prostration (cf. A. A. Anderson, Psalms, 953). This explanation labors under the difficulty that nowhere else is the stem שׁכב so used. But the semantically related stem נפל "fall" is used with reference to religious prostration (e.g. Job 1:20) and by extension it is not impossible that the otherwise associated term שׁכב (cf. Judg 5:27) was so employed. Some scholars have rejected what appears to be an involved rationalization in favor of emendation: e.g. על-מערכותם "according to their battle ranks" (H. Gunkel, Die Psalmen, 621) or על-משׁפחותם "according to their families" (Kraus, Psalmen, 1145, et al.; cf. Num 1:18). The assonance משׁכבותם . . . בכבוד, repeated in v 8 ונכבדיהם בכבלי "and their nobles with fetters [of iron]), is a warning against emendation.

6.a. The cultic sense of the first colon and thus the correspondence of vv 5–6 to vv 1–3 point to the conclusion that either a sword dance (Dahood, Psalms III, 358; cf. v 3) or a dramatic portrayal of fighting with swords or at least a brandishing of swords (Kraus, Psalmen, 1147) is in view. See Form/Structure/Setting.

7.a. Vv 7–9 are loosely related to what precedes by three cases of the preposition lamed, which present a series of future aims represented by infinitives.

7.b. For נקמה "avenging" see G. E. Mendenhall, The Tenth Generation (Baltimore: Johns Hopkins University Press, 1973) 69–104.

7.c. It is left unclear whether the subject of the infinitives in vv 7–9 is the community or Yahweh or both. Arguments for the second alternative are the other uses of the phrase עשׂה נקמה "execute judgment" in Judg 11:36; Ezek 25:17 and the divine suffix in v 9b, which implies that Yahweh has been implicitly in view.

7.d. For the division in MT see 108:4 and note.

8.a. J. Coppens (ETL 54 [1978] 47–48) has suggested that the delegated punitive mission is limited to the overthrow of kings and nobles, so that their nations are liberated, but it is difficult to interpret v 8 as a restriction of v 7. The sequence of thought is like that of Deut 7:23–24: the capture of kings signifies the totality of the nations' defeat.

9.a. It is not possible to define precisely the meaning of כתוב "written." It may be a reference to the Holy War traditions fixed in writing, such as those which enjoined the destruction of the nations of Canaan (e.g. Deut 7:1–2; A. Weiser, *Psalms,* 840) and/or to prophetic passages which promised eschatological victory (e.g. Isa 24:21–22; 45:14; Joel 4 (3):9–16, 19–21); or it may refer to decrees written in God's heavenly records concerning future judgment for past offenses against his people (cf. Dan 7:10; Anderson, *Psalms,* 954). J. Schreiner has suggested a reference to an old victory psalm (*Sion-Jerusalem,* 208). See further *Form/Structure/Setting.*

Form/Structure/Setting

In form Ps 149 is an imperatival hymn, but contains an unparalleled departure from this basic form in vv 7–9, where future aims are stated (F. Crüsemann, *Studien zur Formgeschichte,* 79 note 3). The first three verses are an extended summons to the religious community to praise Yahweh, leading up in the usual way to the ground for praise in v 4. Dahood (*Psalms III,* 356) ignores the form-critical background to v 4 by taking v 4a as a causal clause subordinate to the chronologically future v 4b. Vv 5–6 renew the call to praise, although in unusual terms in v 6b.

More precisely the psalm appears to be a hymnic song of victory (cf. C. Westermann, *Praise,* 90–92). It might be inferred that it was written to celebrate a particular recent victory (v 4; Schreiner, *Sion-Jerusalem,* 207), which was taken as a foretaste of more victory to come (vv 7–9). The participle of v 4 describes the victory as a manifestation of the general activity of Yahweh on his people's behalf; the following imperfect must have the same connotation (cf. GKC § 116x). Dahood (*Psalms III,* 356) has designated the psalm as a hymn sung in the religious assembly on the eve of a battle against the nations. This interpretation leans heavily upon vv 7–9; his attempt to support it from v 4 does not commend itself on either form-critical or syntactical grounds. In similar vein Kraus (*Psalmen,* 1146) has suggested the use of cultic traditions of the attack of the nations used in the Songs of Zion (e.g. Pss 46, 48), by way of the community's preparation for foreign attack. Another approach has been to place the psalm against a purely cultic background, envisaging it as part of a celebration idealizing Yahweh's kingship (A. Weiser, *Psalms,* 839) and a dramatic representation of salvation history in which "the conventionalized representation of the past also had a present and future significance" (Anderson, *Psalms,* 952; cf. J. H. Eaton, *Psalms,* 314).

It is most probable that the psalm is an eschatological hymn which looks forward to a future victory wrought by Yahweh on the people's behalf (e.g. Gunkel, *Die Psalmen,* 620; D. Kidner, *Psalms 73–150,* 489; cf. Westermann, *Praise,* 142–51, for this category). In support may be cited the relationship of the psalm to Pss 96–98, which are eschatological in tone (cf. Kraus, *Psalmen,* 833–49). The "new song" of v 1 accords with 96:1; 98:1, which praise the coming dynamic intervention of Yahweh into history in a new, unprecedented and final manner. As in those psalms, the kingship of Yahweh is invoked (v 2). Another common factor is the dependence of both those psalms of the divine king and this one upon Isa 40–66. Isaiah 61 has six points of contact with the psalm: ענוים "oppressed," 61:1, as in 149:4; רצון "will" and נקם "avenging," 61:2, cf. 149:4, 7; the stem פאר "glory" twice in 61:3, as in 149:4; ציון "Zion," 61:3, as in 149:2; משפט "judgment," 61:8, as in 149:9.

Isaiah 60 provides another host of parallels: כבוד "glory," 60:1, 2, as in 149:5; the sequence of גוים "nations" and מלכים "kings," 60:3, 11, as in 149:7–8; the pi'el פאר, 60:9, as in 149:4. Also significant is the prospect of the nations' submission or, failing that, destruction in Isa 60:12, 14: in 60:12 the stem חרב "destroy" may be echoed in its homonym "sword" in 149:6. Mention too may be made of the destructive passage in Isa 66:15–16, the stem שפט "judge" and חרב in v 16 according with 149:6, 9, which is significantly followed by a positive attitude to the nations in 66:18–21; of Isa 45:14 in which enchained (בזקים, as in 149:8) foreigners submit to Israel; and of Isa 46:13 where תשועה "salvation" and the stem פאר occur together, as in 149:4b (ישועה "saving victory"). It is difficult to avoid the conclusion that like Pss 96–98 this psalm is building upon the motifs of the future victory of Yahweh over the nations and of the exaltation of Israel. The psalm appears to have emanated from a similar tradition to that of Pss 96–98 and to develop its themes.

The setting of the psalm is clearly cultic, as the content of vv 1–3 makes plain. It is often assigned to the Feast of Tabernacles in view of the references to Yahweh's kingship in v 2 (cf. Anderson, *Psalms*, 952). The dating of the psalm has been a matter of dispute. Weiser (*Psalms*, 839) and Dahood (*Psalms III*, 357) have considered it preexilic. Linguistic links with Isa 40–66, especially the verb פאר "glory" of v 4, a hapax legomenon in the Psalms, have been regarded as cultic borrowings in the prophetic material. But its similarity of tone to Pss 96–98 point to a common dependence upon Isa 40–66. Kraus (*Psalmen*, 1146; cf. A. F. Kirkpatrick, *Psalms*, 829) has envisaged the period of Nehemiah as suitable for what he regards as a cultic representation of the ancient tradition of the attack of the nations upon Jerusalem in anticipation of an actual attack. A Maccabean dating, once prevalent, is now generally abandoned.

The structure of the psalm has been disputed. There are two main schemes. The first is a threefold division into vv 1–3, 4–6, 7–9. It provides symmetrical strophes and does justice to the obvious triad, vv 7–9. Among its advocates are S. Mowinckel (*Tricola*, 102), J. Schildenberger (*Estudios Eclesiásticos* 34 [1960] 679), Weiser (*Psalms*, 840) and E. Beaucamp (*RSR* 56 [1968] 211). The other division, a twofold one into vv 1–4, 5–9, is favored by Gunkel (*Die Psalmen*, 621), Kraus (*Psalmen*, 1145) and Eaton (*Psalms*, 314–15). It relies upon form-critical considerations, the concluding element of v 4 and the fresh call to praise in v 5. A stylistic phenomenon provides help in determining which structural suggestion is correct: the preposition *beth* has a striking role throughout the psalm. Its occurrence in the nine lines (1/2/2/2/1/2/2/2/ 1) follows a definite pattern, which does not favor a symmetrical threefold arrangement. The pattern could point to a concentric structure with v 5 at the heart; but there are not lacking pointers to a strophic division. In v 5 כבוד "glory" and in v 9 its associated term הדר "honor" appear to provide inclusion for the strophe, while the former noun and the associated verb יפאר "glorify" in v 4 function as the two parts of an interstrophic hinge. Heb. חסידים "recipients of loyal love," v 1, is echoed at the beginning of the second strophe, v 5, and by way of inclusion in חסידיו "recipients of his loyal love," v 9. There are signs too of another poetic scheme, a concentric one, apart from the last example and the pattern formed by the preposition *beth:* the first three lines, with the repeated stem הלל "praise" in the first and third and מלכם "their king" in the second, find correspondence in the last three, with the repeated לעשות "to execute" and the related נקמה "avenging" and משפט "judgment" (cf. 2 Sam 24:13, 16 [12, 15]) in vv 7, 9 and מלכיהם "their kings" in v 8. There are parallels elsewhere in the Psalter for dual or multiple schemes.

There is little warrant for regarding the psalm as a development of the last line of Ps 148 (Kidner, *Psalms 73–150*, 489 cf. J. W. Rogerson and J. W. McKay, *Psalms 101–150*, 187). The sharing of six out of seven words of the last line with this psalm is at first sight impressive. But תהלה "praise" (149:1) appears to mean "renown" there, so that לכל חסידיו "to all recipients of his loyal love" is the only significant parallel. However, the similarity provides apt reason for the present juxtaposition of the two psalms.

Explanation

Yahweh's praises are sung in prospective faith. The religious community meeting in Zion's temple are bidden look forward to the time when he will intervene in a new, dynamic way in their experience and so give cause for a new song of praise (cf. Isa 42:10). It is the destiny to which the covenant points, a covenant marked by the loyal love of Yahweh for his people. To him they owe their existence and so their allegiance; thus they await an event that will spell the culmination of their role in the world, the manifestation of his kingship and their royal service (cf. 98:3–6). To this God praise is due for what he is going to accomplish. The praise of dedicated lips is not sufficient: it must be augmented by worshipful body movement and by melody of percussion and strings. This totality of praise is necessary as a response to Yahweh's traits of favor to, and vindication of, his own people, which eventually they hope to see demonstrated in a climactic manner.

The call rings out again, to rejoice in anticipation of glory (cf. Rom 8:18–25), which is the destined target of covenant grace (cf. Rom 5:2). Victory granted to the oppressed (v 4) requires warfare, a war to end all wars: evidently representatives of the community brandish, or dance with, swords to symbolize the future martial justice of their God (cf. 96:13; 98:9). The victory will be his, won by his power (v 4; cf. 98:1b-2, 3b). The liability that accrues to the nations for oppression of Israel will be punished by the divine judge. He will ensure that eventually justice is done. The effectiveness of the retribution will be sealed by the capture of their rulers and ruling classes. By such means the prophetic promises of Isa 40–66 will be fulfilled so that, for instance, every knee will be made to bow to him and every tongue swear allegiance, as Yahweh had sworn in solemn promise (Isa 45:23). Then God's people, as representatives of this king of kings, would come into their own and be recognized before the world (cf. Rom 8:19).

Psalm 149 summarizes aspects of the covenant relationship and the hopes that grew therefrom. Its nationalism is but the corollary of the particularism of the old covenant. The psalm emanates from the "day of small things" when servitude to foreign powers seemed a bitter reversal of the theological implications of worship of the one true God (cf. Zech 4:10; Neh 9:6, 36–37). His people sensed the enormous disparity between faith and sight. In such a psalm as this, however, they are encouraged to eschew despair and to look for the dawn of a new day when justice would be seen to be done (cf. 2 Thess 1:4–12). Sustained by the prophetic word, they are to wait expectantly, with praise already in their mouths, their music and their dance movement. At a later date Zechariah the priest would gather up such OT hopes as this psalm represents, and re-orient them in celebration of the inauguration of a new, transcendent fulfilment, in the hymn of the Benedictus (Luke 1:67–79).

A Crescendo of Praise   (150:1-6)

Bibliography

Crüsemann, F. *Studien zur Formgeschichte.*

Translation

¹ Hallelujah.^a

Praise God in his sanctuary,^b	(3+3)
praise him in his strong firmament,^c	
² praise him for his mighty acts,	(3+3)
praise him in accord with his immense greatness.	
³ Praise him with blast of horn,^a	(3+3)
praise him with harp and lyre,	
⁴ praise him with timbrel and dance,	(3+3)
praise him with strings and flute,	
⁵ praise him with sounding cymbals,	(3+3)
praise him with clashing cymbals.	
⁶ Let everything that breathes ^a praise Yah(weh).^b	(3 ^c)

Notes/Comments

1.a. See the note on 147:1.

1.b. Both the location and the syntactical role of קדשו "his holiness" have been queried. If the earthly temple is meant, the bicolon of v 1 may urge praise from both earth and heaven (H. Gunkel, *Die Psalmen*, 622; H.-J. Kraus, *Psalmen*, 1149, *et al.*). On the other hand, M. Dahood (*Psalms III*, 359) has noted that the employment of synonymous parallelism in the rest of the psalm suggests the same here, so that the first colon refers to the heavenly sanctuary. J. H. Eaton (*Psalms*, 316) has interpreted קדשו as referring to both sanctuaries; certainly the earthly temple is closely associated in the OT with its heavenly counterpart (cf. R. E. Clements, *God and Temple*, 68–69). A. A. Anderson (*Psalms*, 955) has defined the two qualifications in v 1 as descriptions of where Yahweh dwells and observed that vv 3–5 imply that human worshipers are here addressed. All these different interpretations are theoretically possible. Against Anderson's may be cited the parallel 148:1, 7 (Gunkel, *Die Psalmen*, 623). The human address of vv 3–5 need not rule out a rhetorical call to others earlier in the psalm. The use of אל "God" may well be significant: it not infrequently has celestial associations in the Psalter (19:2 [1]; 29:3; 82:1; 89:8 [7]; cf. 90:2; 95:3).

1.c. The firmament reflects divine power (19:2 [1]). Here a call to the heavenly host is probably intended or at least included: cf. 148:1–4. Dahood (*Psalms III, 360*) takes עז as "fortress" (cf. 8:3 [2] and BDB, 739a).

3.a. For the musical instruments of vv 3–5 see E. Werner, "Musical Instruments," *IDB* 3 (1962) 469–76. Here the blast of the horn may refer to an initiatory note: cf. 81:4 (3); Judg 6:5. A summons to three groups in vv 3–5 has been suggested: to the priests in v 3a, to the Levites in v 3b (and 5?) and to the people playing secular instruments in vv 4, 5 (A. F. Kirkpatrick, *Psalms*, 832; Gunkel, *Die Psalmen*, 622; cf. 135:19–20).

6.a. The whole animate creation is summoned to praise.

6.b. See the note on 118:5.

6.c. The psalm ends with a single colon (Gunkel, *Die Psalmen*, 622; Kraus, *Psalmen*, 1148; cf. Fohrer, *ZAW* 66 [1954] 199–236).

Form/Structure/Setting

Psalm 150 is a series of calls to praise, normally a constituent part of the hymn, but here, as in Ps 134, used independently: in v 2 what would otherwise be grounds for praise have been incorporated into the summons (cf. F. Crüsemann, *Studien zur Formgeschichte*, 28, 79). Crüsemann has attempted to explain the character of the psalm by reference to vv 3–5: music is invited as the response to and implementation of the call to praise, so that verbal implementation was necessarily excluded from the psalm. However, this explanation ignores v 6.

The psalm is the last of the collection of psalms with a "Hallelujah" framework (Pss 146–150). It is usually regarded as a closing doxology to the last book of the Psalter (e.g. C. Westermann, *Theologia Viatorum* 8 [1961/62] 283–84; cf. 106:48 and note), although it may not be concluded that it was composed for this purpose: its content suggests that it was written for a cultic setting. Gunkel (*Die Psalmen*, 623) argued that the absence of the instruments of v 4b from Chronicles implies a date of origin later than the composition of Chronicles. The difficulty in determining the degree of rhetoric in the psalm takes cogency from his argument.

S. Mowinckel (*Tricola*, 86–87) divided the psalm into three strophes, vv 1–2, 3–4, 5–6, but it is difficult to justify this or any strophic structure. Yet the psalm does clearly divide into three parts. V 6 with its change of verbal construction and climactic content forms a conclusion. Vv 3–5 represent a unit introduced by an introductory colon, v 3a, concluded by the parallel cola, vv 5a, b and having at its heart three parallel cola, vv 3b–4b. Vv 1–2 have an introductory role as basic calls to praise and implicit grounds for praise: the parallel structuring of vv 1b, 2b (הללוהו "praise him" + construct noun with prepositional prefix + genitive noun with third masculine singular suffix) confirms the pairing of vv 1, 2. The divine names אל (v 1) and יה (v 6) provide inclusion for the psalm. Vv 1–5 of the psalm are tied together by the ninefold—semantically varied—use of the preposition *beth*, twice in each line except for v 2, as well as the tenfold summons to praise. The psalm begins to move toward a climax at v 4 by the doubling of pairs of musical instruments, compared with v 3. In v 5 the repetition of צלצלי "cymbals," literally and onomatopoeically the loudest instruments, takes it further, while

the comprehensiveness of v 6 completes it. The repetition of the pair of
letters *shin* and *mem* in vv 5, 6 (נשמה "breath," שמע "sounding") may be
intended to prepare the way stylistically for the final יה "Yah(weh)," by suggesting the divine שם "name."

Explanation

This final psalm not only concludes the special group of praising psalms
(146–150), but appears also to represent a doxology to the fifth book and
indeed to the whole Psalter. It is an extended call to praise which combines
exuberant, sincere rhetoric with the realities of temple worship. It grapples
with a recurring problem of worshiping hearts, to which the Psalter so often
bears witness, the problem of how to render to God adequate praise. A fervent
call is issued to powers above to engage in worship. The very call gives an
enhanced sense of Yahweh's awesome majesty (cf. 103:20–21; 148:1–2) as
God of the heavenly sanctuary. Incorporated in the next summons to worship
is the traditional substance of praise, Yahweh's "mighty acts," his creative
and continuing work in the natural realm and his work on Israel's behalf in
human history. It all reflects his superlative greatness—and praise must ever
strain to match such sublime material with its own superlatives.

Vv 3–6 serve to develop the explicit theme of v 2b. The role of music in
temple worship was to aid the efforts of praising voices. Here every type of
instrument—wind, string and percussion—is called to perform its distinctive
part, so that their players' skill may promote and amplify the praise of voice
and heart. Together with the visual and mobile art of the sacred dance, they
create a loud symphony of praise, as a response to the glory of God, and
rise to a crescendo in the "clashing cymbals."

If heavenly creation is to praise (v 1), no less are the creatures of earth
so obliged. Every animate being is to fulfill its highest function by praising
the creator. Only such a total terrestial choir can come anywhere near to
reflecting the greatness of Yahweh. The recensional framework of the psalm
echoes the call with its own Hallelujahs. And, widening out from the psalm
as center, it is intended that each generation in turn should add its own
ripple of Amens. The onesidedness of this hymn of praise, as a series of
summonses without the corresponding grounds for praise, gives a fascinating
open-ended effect to the psalm. If all who hear and all who read it are drawn
to fill their hearts with a conviction of God's praiseworthiness and to answer
these strenuous calls to worship with equally fervent praise, this psalm will
have accomplished its noble aim.

Index of Authors Cited

Index of Principal Subjects

Acrostic psalms 89, 95, 139, 294
Ark 37, 203, 209

Blessing 110, 154, 174, 176, 182, 185, 210, 218, 292

Covenant 22, 37, 42, 55, 92, 110, 161, 168, 210, 227, 309, 317, 321
Creation 10, 16, 26, 28, 31, 34, 233, 261, 303, 310, 313, 316

David 86, 209, 278, 291
Deliverance 65, 115, 124, 137, 142, 165, 190, 268, 281, 285

Edom 69, 236, 242
Egyptian plagues 39, 41, 43
Election 37, 54, 210, 222, 227
Exile 53, 64, 174, 241, 309
Exodus 43, 48, 54, 92, 105, 233

Faith 110, 115, 124, 168, 199, 227, 268, 275, 285
Fear of Yahweh 10, 22, 89, 93, 108, 120, 136, 140, 143, 185, 192, 222, 261
Forgiveness 18–19, 22, 195, 242, 281

Glory 15, 48, 69, 101, 110, 316
Guidance 142, 154, 285

History of Israel 40, 92, 165, 190, 227, 233, 303
Hope 14, 54, 144, 169, 196, 269, 306

Idolatry 49, 107–8, 110, 227, 253, 262
Innocence 6, 256, 261

Jerusalem 10, 15, 86–87, 159, 168, 174, 178, 185, 190, 210–11, 215, 242, 309

Kingship, Davidic 6, 86–87, 124, 159, 210, 291
Kingship, divine 15, 23, 86, 92, 101, 161, 210, 297–98, 303, 318

Land 3, 42–44, 55, 69, 92, 104, 137, 168, 186, 228, 234, 236, 268
Law 44, 93, 97, 140–41, 310
Loyal love 2, 18, 20, 22, 53–55, 69, 118, 125, 137, 192, 196, 234, 247, 281–82, 287, 294, 298, 321

Messianic psalms 5, 87, 124–25

Name of Yahweh 10, 15, 22–23, 48, 101, 124, 157, 163, 188, 285, 324

Omniscience 138, 247, 261
Oracle 59, 149, 154, 194, 260, 281

Peace 144, 159, 310
Penitential psalms 14, 16, 195, 283
Persecution 14, 76, 149, 268, 284
Pilgrimage 150, 152, 154, 158, 215, 219

Reed Sea 45, 103, 233

Sheol 18, 22, 59, 108, 115–16, 162, 191, 261, 271, 279, 284
Solomon 178, 207, 279

Thank offering 59, 113, 115–16, 279
Theophany 26, 28, 33–34, 104–5, 289, 291

Wilderness 39, 43, 48, 54, 92, 106, 233

Index of Biblical Texts

A. The Old Testament

D. New Testament